A PLUME BOOK

A WORLD OF CURIOSITIES

DR. JOHN OLDALE is a scientist by training, a lawyer by profession and an explorer by passion. He is a Fellow of the Royal Geographical Society, speaks five languages and has traveled some half a million miles, visiting over 90 countries. He has outrun knife-wielding brigands (twice), been rescued from a sub-Antarctic beach, faced down a charging buffalo and breakfasted on 37 sorts of mushrooms in a Korean monastery. He lives with his family in a former village pub in Hampshire.

Praise for *A World of Curiosities*

"Turn to any page in this compendium of countries and you'll be surprised and amazed by its vast array of far-flung facts from around the world. Sure to satisfy the appetite of any lover of trivia."

—Don Voorhees, author *The Book of Totally Useless Information*

"An absolute winner! A fascinating and entertaining spin around the world, its oddities and its secrets."

—Noel Botham, author of *The Book of Useless Information*

"Jam-packed with facts of every description from the horrific to the hilarious. My life has been richer since I read that, in order to cram more showings into the day, one cinema in South Korea made *The Sound of Music* shorter by cutting out the songs."

—Caroline Taggart, author of *I Used to Know That*

A World of Curiosities

Surprising, Interesting, and Downright Unbelievable
Facts from Every Nation on the Planet

JOHN OLDALE

A PLUME BOOK

PLUME
Published by the Penguin Group
Penguin Group (USA) Inc., 375 Hudson Street, New York, New York 10014, U.S.A.
Penguin Group (Canada), 90 Eglinton Avenue East, Suite 700, Toronto, Ontario, Canada
M4P 2Y3 (a division of Pearson Penguin Canada Inc.)
Penguin Books Ltd., 80 Strand, London WC2R 0RL, England
Penguin Ireland, 25 St. Stephen's Green, Dublin 2, Ireland
(a division of Penguin Books Ltd.)
Penguin Group (Australia), 250 Camberwell Road, Camberwell, Victoria 3124, Australia
(a division of Pearson Australia Group Pty. Ltd.)
Penguin Books India Pvt. Ltd., 11 Community Centre, Panchsheel Park,
New Delhi – 110 017, India
Penguin Group (NZ), 67 Apollo Drive, Rosedale, Auckland 0632, New Zealand
(a division of Pearson New Zealand Ltd.)
Penguin Books (South Africa) (Pty.) Ltd., 24 Sturdee Avenue, Rosebank,
Johannesburg 2196, South Africa

Penguin Books Ltd., Registered Offices: 80 Strand, London WC2R 0RL, England

Published by Plume, a member of Penguin Group (USA) Inc.
Originally published in Great Britain by Particular Books, an imprint of
Penguin Books Ltd., as *Who, or Why, or Which, or What?*

First American Printing, May 2012
1   3   5   7   9   10   8   6   4   2

Ⓟ REGISTERED TRADEMARK—MARCA REGISTRADA

ISBN 978-0-452-29783-8
CIP data available

Printed in the United States of America
Design by John Oldale

To Alison, my partner in life's adventure,
ἧς ἄτερ οὐκ ἂν ἔγωγ' ἔγραφον οὐδ' ὁτιοῦν.

屋根より高い鯉幟
大きい真鯉はお父さん
小さい緋鯉は子供たち
面白そうに泳いでる

'Higher than the rooftops are the koinobori
The large carp is the father
The smaller carp are the children
They seem to be having fun swimming.'

—The Japanese *koinobori* song (sung by families),
with thoughts of Ben and Sam

CONTENTS

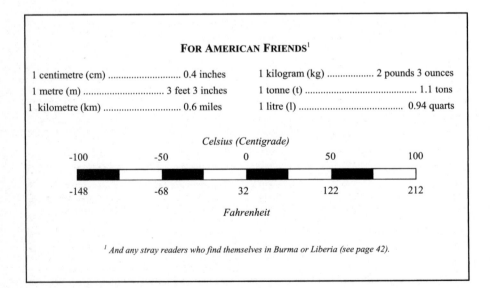

FOR AMERICAN FRIENDS[1]

1 centimetre (cm) .... 0.4 inches

1 metre (m) .... 3 feet 3 inches

1 kilometre (km) .... 0.6 miles

1 kilogram (kg) .... 2 pounds 3 ounces

1 tonne (t) .... 1.1 tons

1 litre (l) .... 0.94 quarts

Celsius (Centigrade)

-100	-50	0	50	100
-148	-68	32	122	212

Fahrenheit

[1] *And any stray readers who find themselves in Burma or Liberia (see page 42).*

———————— PREFACE ————————

'A journey of a thousand miles begins with an airport bus.'

—Contemporary observation (with apologies to Lao-tzu)

A selection of codpieces—the height of 16th-century fashion

This is an unfashionable book because I am an unfashionable person. In the era of the specialist, when it's possible to write a 288-page book entitled *The Changing World of Inflammatory Bowel Disease*, it's my misfortune to have wanted to write a book of approximately the same length covering the whole of the globe.[1] The root of my trouble is that I'm fascinated by every aspect of our planet, and, due to this, am completely unable to think of anything that I could happily leave out. The problem is a serious one. While it has become the 21st-century way to know a lot about a little, I've been left behind, chugging along in the 19th, knowing—I like to think—a little about a lot.

My approach to interrogating the world is very hands-on. I have always believed that, faced with a puzzle, there's nothing like actually going and giving it a prod. In a sense, my addiction to this sort of in-person exploration can be said to have been a true road-to-Damascus conversion, given that my first and decisive experience of it came quite literally on the road to that ancient city when, aged 18, a school-friend and I drove a tiny and ancient Fiat from London to Damascus and back. However, the desire, if not the ability, to see the world goes back much further, as far as I can remember—but coming on especially powerfully during interminable Latin lessons when my mind would slip free from parsing the 1st conjugation, and roam quizzically across the wall map of the Roman Empire above the teacher's head. Who exactly were the Scythians?[2] And why was Morocco marked as Mauretania?[3] Far more intriguing, I felt, than *amo, amas, amat*.

In the 30 years since that first long trip to Syria, I've been lucky enough to have poked my way around roughly half the world's countries—many repeatedly, and almost all with great joy. Although I didn't know it at the time, those three decades of journeys were in a very real sense spent researching this book. So, with that in mind, I have included the map on the following page, giving some of my personal highs and lows from the road.

JOHN OLDALE; LONDON, JULY 2011

[1] *The closest* A World of Curiosities *gets to the pressingly important topic of inflamed intestines is its discussion of diarrhoea (under Bangladesh).* [2] *This was a better question than I knew since, despite disparaging references in the Bible ('the ultimate barbarians'), Shakespeare's* King Lear *('child-eaters') and the works of Herodotus ('bloodthirsty savages who scalped their enemies for napkin cloths'), few people in ancient history have remained as elusive as these shadowy warriors from the Steppes who, more than a millennium before the Mongol Hordes, roamed from Mongolia to the Danube.* [3] *It was Mauretania first and Morocco later (see under Morocco for more on the origins of the name). Modern Mauritania, lying far to the south of the Roman province, belongs to the fine tradition of African countries named for historical regions that were somewhere else entirely—along with Ghana and Benin.*

Thank you ~ Kiitos ~ शुक्रिया *~ Diolch ~ Mahalo ~ Takk ~ Спасибо ~ Merci ~ Juspajaraña ~* شكرا ~

Gracias ~ Go raibh maith agat ~ Asante ·

My sincere thanks go to the fabulous team at Penguin who have helped in the creation of this book. First mention must go to my patient and insightful editors, Georgina Laycock, Simon Winder, Marina Kemp and, in the US, Becky Cole; and to Emma Horton, my indefatigable copy-editor. No less valued have been the contributions of Maria Garbutt-Lucero, Rebecca Lee, Rita Matos, Alistair Richardson and, no doubt, others whose names I do not know (not forgetting also special pirate correspondent, Bernard   Horton). They all know what they've done. Separate thanks go to Oli Munson, my unflappable agent, and Susan Grossman for encouraging the spark of an idea. Away from the world of publishing, among the many who have given practical help and encouragement in various and wonderful ways are my wife (everything), parents (scrutiny, succour and childcare), mother-in-law (more childcare), Efi Alston, Alice Chapman, Jess Dawe, Rebecca Dowman, Maureen Freeborn, Lisa Good, Diana Hopkins, Toni Kirby, Reinout Koopmans, Hollie McCallum, Mike Potter and Professor William Berg of Gearhart, Oregon (profound classical erudition).

· Obrigado ~ Nagode ~ Terima kasih ~

~ ありがとう ~ Misaotra ~ Tenki ya ~ ขอบคุณคุณ *~ Danke ~ Köszönöm ~ Grazie ~* 谢谢 *~ Qujanaq*

INCIDENTS AND OBSERVATIONS IN THE GENESIS OF *A WORLD OF CURIOSITIES*
A SELECTION OF PERSONAL HIGHS AND LOWS FROM THE AUTHOR'S TIME ON THE ROAD

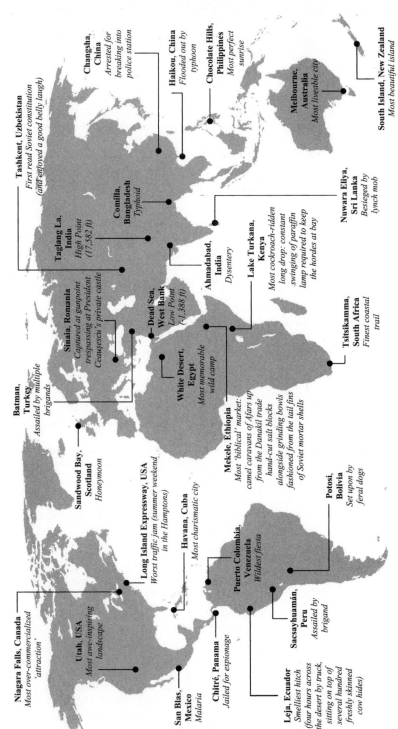

Changsha, China
Arrested for breaking into police station

Haikou, China
Flooded out by typhoon

Chocolate Hills, Philippines
Most perfect sunrise

Melbourne, Australia
Most liveable city

South Island, New Zealand
Most beautiful island

Tashkent, Uzbekistan
First read Soviet constitution (and enjoyed a good belly laugh)

Comilla, Bangladesh
Typhoid

Nuwara Eliya, Sri Lanka
Besieged by lynch mob

Taglang La, India
High Point (17,582 ft)

Ahmadabad, India
Dysentery

Lake Turkana, Kenya
Most cockroach-ridden long drop: constant swinging of paraffin lamp required to keep the hordes at bay

Sinaia, Romania
Captured at gunpoint trespassing at President Ceaușescu's private castle

Dead Sea, West Bank
Low Point (-1,388 ft)

Tsitsikamma, South Africa
Finest coastal trail

Batman, Turkey
Assailed by multiple brigands

White Desert, Egypt
Most memorable wild camp

Mekele, Ethiopia
Most 'biblical' market: camel caravans of Afars up from the Danakil trade hand-cut salt blocks alongside grinding bowls fashioned from the tail fins of Soviet mortar shells

Sandwood Bay, Scotland
Honeymoon

Long Island Expressway, USA
Worst traffic jam (summer weekend in the Hamptons)

Havana, Cuba
Most charismatic city

Potosí, Bolivia
Set upon by feral dogs

Niagara Falls, Canada
Most over-commercialized 'attraction'

Utah, USA
Most awe-inspiring landscape

Puerto Colombia, Venezuela
Wildest fiesta

San Blas, Mexico
Malaria

Chitré, Panama
Jailed for espionage

Sacsayhuamán, Peru
Assailed by brigand

Leja, Ecuador
Smelliest hitch (four hours across the desert by truck, sitting on top of several hundred freshly skinned cow hides)

A World of Curiosities

—————————— INTRODUCTION ——————————

'Pick a flower on Earth and you move the farthest star.'

—Paul Dirac (1902–1984), on universal interconnectedness. Dirac was a British theoretical physicist who, among other achievements, furnished the first cogent link between the twin pillars of modern physics, relativity and quantum theory, and was first to predict the existence of antimatter.

A World of Curiosities is a collection of some of the more unusual facts concerning every nation on Earth—from the largest (China, population 1,337 million) to the most miniscule (Vatican, population 500). It has been written, above all, to be dipped into during idle moments or, more pertinently, perused on the loo. If this is where you find yourself as you read these words, then all well and good; you may wish to skip straight to the practical information contained at the end of this introduction under How to Use This Book, or simply plunge right in.

If, though, you have a little more time, it may be of assistance to know that when selecting material for inclusion in this book, my guiding principle—beyond the overarching criterion of intrinsic interest—was a wish to illustrate something of the character of each country, and, especially, how even the most seemingly obscure and inconsequential of nations have contributed to the diversity of our collective cultural heritage and played at least a walk-on role in the flow of events and ideas that shape the everyday experience of everyone. That diversity is breathtaking: in my research, it quickly became apparent that if something can be imagined, it probably has happened somewhere and sometime. Nevertheless, underlying everything, we are all human and, ultimately, we share the same roots. With the passage of time, those interconnections have often become deeply buried, and are now only noticed, if at all, through muffled echoes and tantalizing hints. However, such deep linkages are, for the author, possibly the most intriguing aspect of how the world works and, where appropriate, I have sought to draw them out.

To give a concrete example, when handed a map, we today take it for granted that north will be at the top.[1] But why should this be? It would seem that the Greco-Egyptian geographer Ptolemy, living in the second century CE, was the first person to have drawn maps with north shown this way. His choice was, in a sense, obvious, since north is the direction in which the Pole Star—the fixed point about which the heavens seem to rotate—always appears to lie,[2] giving north prime importance in the eyes of travellers since the dawn of humanity. (Knowing the direction of north, all the other cardinal directions can readily be found.) While logical, Ptolemy's choice of north is far from necessary. Islamic cartographers traditionally placed south at the top of their maps since, if one faces the sunrise, south lies to the right (with north to the left), and, betraying humanity's general bias for the right hand over the left, this led them to favour the south. Ancient Chinese map-makers also chose south for the top of their charts. However, in this case, it was on the pragmatic grounds that Chinese compass needles pointed south.[3] For its part, Europe mostly abandoned the old Ptolemaic convention for much of the Middle Ages, and orientated maps with east at

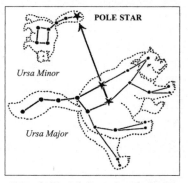

POLE STAR

Ursa Minor

Ursa Major

How to find the Pole Star in the night sky: the constellations of Ursa Major and Ursa Minor

[1] *Ardent Antipodeans excepted.* [2] *When seen by observers in the northern hemisphere. The Pole Star (also known as Polaris) lies below the horizon in much of the southern hemisphere.* [3] *Magnetic compasses necessarily point in two directions: north and south, each being at the opposite end of the compass needle. Neither is innately dominant, and the choice between the two for use as the description for the direction in which a compass is said to 'point' is purely a matter of convention. While Europeans chose north, the Chinese happened to choose south.*

S E

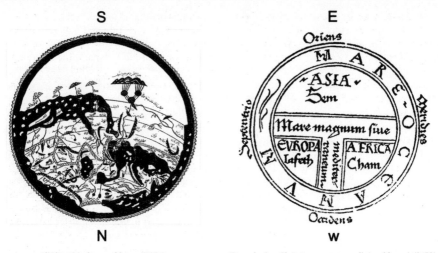

N W

Al-Idrisi Muslim world map (1154)   Etymologiae *Christian* mappa mundi *(world map) (1472)*

the top.[1,2] The easterly orientation[3] only yielded once more to Ptolemy's use of north with the advent of the Age of Discoveries, when practical men of the sea became the principal consumers and producers of cartography in place of dilettante noblemen and spiritually minded clerics—and it is their professional usage that finally entrenched today's north-at-the-top convention worldwide.[4]

But while it turns out that the presence of north at the top of the map is far from a universal and self-evident truth, with different cultures at different times having explored multiple map orientations, what goes unchallenged by all is that the 'top' of the map should merit special and more important treatment. Why not the bottom, or left or right sides? The pre-eminence of the top seems an altogether more fundamental property shared by almost all—if not all—cultures on Earth. To give further examples, virtually all writing systems start at the top of each page and work down,[5] while the earliest supreme god of the Indo-European peoples was Dyeus, god of the daytime sky above our heads.[6] Indeed, this preference for 'top' runs so deep that not even an echo of the reason for its adoption apparently now remains. (One can, of course, still speculate that the ultimate explanation lies with biology since, in a standing posture, the head is at the top of the body, and the head is where the field of vision, and hence seat of personal consciousness, is perceived to be.)

Given an effective remit of any place, any time, *A World of Curiosities* covers an unusually broad sweep of territory and, as a result, contains in excess of 15,000 individual references (which are accessible for those who are interested through the link at the back of the book). However, special mention must be made of the Wikipedia website (www.wikipedia.com) which, despite only having been launched in 2001, now has 24,452,000 English-language pages covering every topic under the sun—and many considerably further away. Such an assemblage of information dwarfs all previous gatherings of

[1] *Strictly speaking, the maps were produced with Jerusalem at the centre and Paradise, deemed to be to the east of Jerusalem, at the top. But, since Jerusalem, let alone Paradise, lay to the east of anywhere in Western and Central Europe, in practice this amounted to an east-at-the-top orientation.* [2] *There were exceptions: the 11th-century St. Pierre Sallust map of Ghent, Belgium, has west at the top.* [3] *The word 'orientation' itself comes from 'orient' and means literally 'aligning with the east'.* [4] *One modern exception to the north-at the-top rule is the category of polar maps, which are oriented with the relevant pole at the centre instead.* [5] *The chief exception is the Hanunó'o script of the Mangyan people, which is written in columns radiating out from the writer's body—see under the Philippines for more.* [6] *The remembrance of Dyeus comes down to us through many early Indian and European gods such as Zeus, Jupiter (from 'Dyeu-pater' meaning 'Father Dyeus') and the Nordic Týr, as well as more indirectly the expression 'adieu' and the word 'deity' itself. Dyeus is discussed further under Kazakhstan.*

public knowledge by orders of magnitude—in comparison, the latest edition of *Encyclopaedia Britannica* runs to just 32,640 pages. The power this brings to any desktop, anywhere from uptown Manhattan to the Congolese rainforest, is world-changing, and, in writing this book, I have made full use of it. Given its peer-edited structure, the reliability of Wikipedia's content has naturally often been closely questioned. A 2005 study in the respected scientific journal *Nature* found an accuracy level approaching that found in traditional expert-written encyclopaedias.[1] But, nevertheless, I have used Wikipedia primarily as a gateway—at which it excels—and, in the vast majority of cases, have gone on to more specialist publications or primary sources to verify and expand upon the original information. Like the scientists in *Nature*, I have found Wikipedia to be largely reliable (especially in more technical areas of knowledge), but it is far from infallible. Sometimes errors seem to have arisen as genuine misunderstandings, but in other, often more entertaining, cases the Wikipedia 'fact' can be exposed as a deliberate plant. My favourite is the 'fact' that the high priests of ancient Sumer used to put Sumerian kings across their knees once a year and soundly smack them to make sure they didn't forget their lowly position in the eyes of the gods. This titbit seemed to be too good to be true, and sadly, after extensive checking, so it proved. The priestly spanking had been dreamt up as an erudite April Fool's hoax some years ago, and has subsequently entered general circulation unshackled from the giveaway clue of its publication date.

Of course, despite my best efforts, errors will still have crept into *A World of Curiosities*, and for those, as well as the inevitable smattering of over-simplifications, misinterpretations and uninformative explanations on my part, I apologize.

[1] *Giles, J., Nature 438, 900–901 (15 December 2005).*

HOW TO USE THIS BOOK

● **CONTINENT SYMBOLS** indicate the continent—or, in the case of transcontinental countries, continents—in which a country is situated.[1] The country can then be more precisely located using the relevant map found at the end of the book. The continent symbols are as follows:

Africa	♥
Americas	♦
Antarctica	★
Asia	♣
Europe	♠
Oceania	●

[1] *Armenia and Cyprus are wholly located within Asia. However, by convention, they are treated as primarily European countries. Here they are listed as both.*

● **GREETINGS**. Typical greetings are given in the dominant local language of each country, or, if two local languages are substantively dominant (such as Dari and Pashto for Afghanistan *below),* in both languages. Where several local languages are in widespread use, greetings in the local lingua franca—often the former colonial language—are shown. The expression given at bottom left translates as 'hello'; that at bottom right is 'goodbye'. If the greetings are enclosed by square brackets, they are properly written in a non-Latin script, but have been transliterated here for convenience.

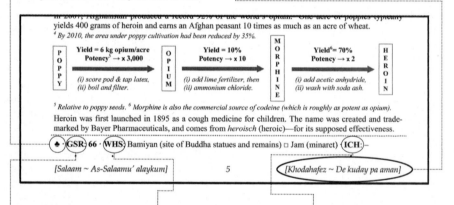

in 2007, Afghanistan produced a record 92% of the world's opium. One acre of poppies typically yields 400 grams of heroin and earns an Afghan peasant 10 times as much as an acre of wheat.
[4] *By 2010, the area under poppy cultivation had been reduced by 35%.*

| POPPY | Yield = 6 kg opium/acre Potency[5] → x 3,000 *(i) score pod & tap latex, (ii) boil and filter.* | OPIUM | Yield = 10% Potency → x 10 *(i) add lime fertilizer, then (ii) ammonium chloride.* | MORPHINE | Yield[6] = 70% Potency → x 2 *(i) add acetic anhydride, (ii) wash with soda ash.* | HEROIN |

[5] *Relative to poppy seeds.* [6] *Morphine is also the commercial source of codeine (which is roughly as potent as opium).*
Heroin was first launched in 1895 as a cough medicine for children. The name was created and trademarked by Bayer Pharmaceuticals, and comes from *heroisch* (heroic)—for its supposed effectiveness.

♣ GSR: 66 · WHS Bamiyan (site of Buddha statues and remains) □ Jam (minaret) ICH:–

[*Salaam ~ As-Salaamu' alaykum*]   5   [*Khodahafez ~ De kuday pa aman*]

● **GLOBAL SIGNIFICANCE RANKING**

Also standing for 'Google Search Rank', GSR gauges each country's contemporary prominence in the eyes of the world using its internet footprint as a proxy measure. More specifically, it ranks each nation according to the number of results returned by a Google search of its name.[2] A full table of GSR rankings is given at the end of the book.

[2] *Results for the common name in English and the chief local language combined, with websites listing all countries stripped out.*

● **WORLD HERITAGE SITES**

All World Heritage Sites within a country are listed here with a brief description (unless obvious). Administered by UNESCO and established in 1972, the World Heritage Site system provides recognition, and sometimes conservation funding, for the best of the best cultural and natural treasures worldwide. While selections can be subject to politics and national zeal or sloth, the list is considered the global gold standard for international heritage.

● **INTANGIBLE CULTURAL HERITAGE**

All cultural practices within a country that have been proclaimed 'elements of Intangible Cultural Heritage' by UNESCO are listed with a brief description. Intangible cultural heritage is the term that has been adopted for aspects of a culture that can be recorded (such as singing, music or dance) but not physically touched. If the initials 'ICH' are absent, UNESCO has not yet listed any cultural elements relating to that state.

———— AFGHANISTAN ● فغانستان ————

'Easy to march into, hard to march out of.'

—Alexander the Great (a comment made after his invasion of Afghanistan, 329 BCE)

ROCK VS HARD PLACE. When it came to the big power rivalries of the 19th century, none was played out on a grander scale than the 'Great Game' between Britain and Russia—with Afghanistan as the unenviable cockpit of confrontation where the competing claims threatened to come face to face.[1] One echo of that century-old clash of empires is the curious tentacle that sprouts from the 'top' of the modern country, stretching east for 200 miles to China. Known as the Wakhan corridor *(shown below)*, the sliver of desolate Himalayan plateau was, in 1892, affixed to Afghanistan by the British and Russians jointly purely to avoid the discomfort of a common frontier.

RUSSIAN EMPIRE [2]

AFGH.

CHINA

BRITISH RAJ [3]

[1] *It was largely to avoid Russia's imperial tsar outranking Britain's 'mere' queen in the eyes of the area's rulers that Disraeli forced through the 1871 Royal Titles Act, against prevailing republican sentiment, so promoting Victoria to Empress of India.* [2] *Now Tajikistan.* [3] *Now Pakistan.*

ROOTS. Afghanistan is the original home of the carrot and remains its centre of diversity in the wild. Although cultivated for millennia, for most of this time just the leaves were eaten—chopped as a herb like its relative, parsley. Only in the Middle Ages did people start to eat the root. Care should be exercised, however, as overindulgence causes one's nose to turn orange[7] (a condition known as carotenoderma).

[7] *And, less visibly, one's palms and soles, and the backs of one's knees (all being areas of high sweat gland density). Further really extreme carrot consumption gives the entire body surface a distinctive yellow hue.*

CHEM-INT. Viagra forms a potent part of the CIA's armoury in the battle for the hearts and minds of Afghan tribal elders. Operatives have found a discreet gift of little blue pills does wonders for intelligence cooperation and, conferring, as it does, a very private pleasure, doesn't compromise a source's future value in the same way as, say, a shiny Rolex or wad of bills.

'Pork, pig, pig oil, anything made from human hair, satellite dishes, cinematography and equipment that produces the joy of music, pool tables, chess, masks, alcohol, tapes, computers, VCRs, television, anything that propagates sex and is full of music, wine, lobster, nail polish, firecrackers, statues, sewing catalogues, pictures, Christmas cards.'

—Partial list of 'unclean' (and hence banned) items maintained by the Taliban Ministry of Virtue and Prevention of Vice

CHASING THE DRAGON—FROM POPPY TO HEROIN

In 2007, Afghanistan produced a record 92% of the world's opium.[4] One acre of poppies typically yields 400 grams of heroin and earns an Afghan peasant 10 times as much as an acre of wheat.

[4] *By 2010, the area under poppy cultivation had been reduced by 35%.*

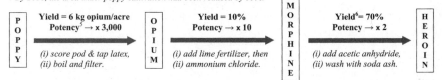

| POPPY | Yield = 6 kg opium/acre
Potency[5] → x 3,000

(i) score pod & tap latex,
(ii) boil and filter. | OPIUM | Yield = 10%
Potency → x 10

(i) add lime fertilizer, then
(ii) ammonium chloride. | MORPHINE | Yield[6]= 70%
Potency → x 2

(i) add acetic anhydride,
(ii) wash with soda ash. | HEROIN |

[5] *Relative to poppy seeds.* [6] *Morphine is also the commercial source of codeine (which is roughly as potent as opium).*

Heroin was first launched in 1895 as a cough medicine for children. The name was created and trademarked by Bayer Pharmaceuticals, and comes from *heroisch* (heroic)—for its supposed effectiveness.

♣ · **GSR**: 66 · **WHS**: Bamiyan (site of Buddha statues and remains) □ Jam (minaret)

———— ALBANIA • SHQIPËRIA ————

'With Pickaxe in One Hand and Rifle in the Other.'

—Cold War signature tune of Albania's Radio Tirana

THE WORKS OF HOXHA. Enver Hoxha, Albania's dictator-for-life from 1945 to 1985, was a true Stalinist's Stalinist. He wrote 79 volumes of memoirs (*Albania Is Forging Ahead Confidently and Unafraid,* etc., etc.), killed off his prime minister and first Central Committee, built 700,000 concrete bunkers—the prototype tested by live tank fire with its designer inside—and ground his country into absolute poverty and isolation. In between, he found time for plenty of banning, including jeans, miniskirts, lipstick, pre-marital sex, boxing, bananas, Westerners, Yugoslavs, Russians, Chinese and God. He declared beards—symbolic to his Muslim and Orthodox Christian citizens alike—illegal and sent those caught baptizing children to prison for life.

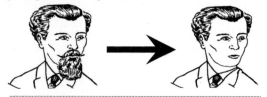

NORMAN CONQUEST (I). When, in 1081, the Normans lined up against the Byzantine Empire at Dyrrachium on the Albanian coast, the battle went badly until they reprised an experimental new tactic first tried out at the Battle of Hastings—the fixed lance charge. In its aftermath, the Normans overran much of the southern Balkans before they had to hurry back to Italy to rescue the pope (who had been besieged by the Holy Roman Emperor).

'The wolf sleeps, the enemy doesn't.' —Gheg[1] proverb	*'Can you live with the heart of a rabbit?'* —Tosk[1] proverb

[1] *The two kindred of Albanians. They live in the north and south of Albania respectively, but are as one when it comes to the love of a good quarrel.*

GET-POOR-QUICK SCHEME. Up to 90% of Albanians lost their life savings in 1997, when multiple pyramid investment companies collapsed. Since such pyramid schemes need an exponential rise in members to keep going, the sticky end was inevitable: the mathematics they follow is the same as for a nuclear chain reaction—making them, in effect, investment atom bombs.

Investors Needed

Time from Start

THE HOUSE OF ZOG

- **FATHER**: King Zog I (ruled 1928–39), survived 55 assassination attempts. Fearing poisoners, Zog installed his mother as Head of the Royal Kitchens; he was also the only modern leader to return fire during an assassination attempt (wounding one of three assailants at the Vienna Opera House). In exile, Zog rented a floor of London's Ritz Hotel, paying his bill in gold bullion bars.

- **SON**: Crown Prince Leka I, former Second Lieutenant in the British Army and arms-trader. Leka bought Ronald Reagan an elephant from Harrods, escaped arrest in Gabon brandishing a bazooka from the door of his jet and in 1993 entered Albania using a self-issued Royal passport which, under 'profession', stated 'king'.

- **GRANDSON**: Born in Johannesburg, Albania,[2] Prince Leka II is a civil servant who helps out with good causes in his spare time; hobbies include music and volleyball.

[2] *The South African government declared the hospital room where his mother, Queen Susan, gave birth to him Albanian territory for one hour.*

NORMAN CONQUEST (II). During the Hoxha era, Norman Wisdom's comedies were the only western films that could be shown. His slapstick antics constituted a 'communist parable on the class war' (apparently).

♠ · **GSR**: 116 · **WHS**: Berat & Gjirokastra (museum towns) ▢ Butrint (classical ruins) · **ICH**: Iso-polyphony (singing style)

————— ALGERIA ● الجزائر —————

'There is but one truly serious philosophical problem, and that is suicide.
Judging whether or not life is worth living amounts to answering
the fundamental question of philosophy.'

—Albert Camus

SUFFER THE LITTLE CHILDREN. Original sin was given its central place in Christian thought through the teachings of St. Augustine of Hippo, a Romanized Algerian living in the 5th century. One consequence of the doctrine, from which Augustine did not shy, was that unbaptized infants automatically went to hell. Even by the standards of the Middle Ages this seemed harsh, so, to soften the blow, medieval theologians developed the idea of limbo—a place of mildest punishment or even, perhaps, limited joy. In its latest thinking, the Church has now gone further, offering the hope—without certainty—of heavenly ascent.

Uruç Barbarossa (1474–1518)

WHITE SLAVE TRADE. The Barbary Corsairs (privateers in Arab history books) captured an estimated one million Western Europeans and sold them into slavery. The first and most feared corsairs were the three Barbarossa brothers, based in Algiers.

HELL & ENVIRONS—A DESTINATION GUIDE	
Limbo	for those personally sin-free, but not baptized
Purgatory	pit stop for modest sinners outside Pearly Gates
Hell (Perdition)	abode of the damned, not at all nice

FIGURATIVELY SPEAKING. Algeria gave Europe its numbers via Leo Fibonacci, who grew up watching Arab merchants perform apparently effortless calculations using their exotic counting system. (Fibonacci didn't know it, but the Arabic way of counting had itself earlier been copied from an Indian original and then improved.) Twenty years later, Fibonacci wrote his *Liber Abaci*, which, apart from quantifying just what a good long-term investment a pair of rabbits should be, introduced Arabic numerals to the West. Although one squiggle is basically as good as another when it comes to representing a number, the clever innovation in the Arabic system (not present in the Indian version) was its positional basis. This is the rule that, in a number such as '111', each digit is multiplied by a factor of 10 compared to the digit to its right.[1] Suddenly, any number, however big, could be written in a consistent framework[2] and, with this, the door to modern mathematics was opened wide.

[1] *As in Arabic, Western numbers are still written right to left (i.e. with the initial units digit at the right), even though Western words are all written left to right.* [2] *The insertion of ad hoc symbols (e.g. L (50), C (100), D (500), etc.) in earlier number systems, such as the Roman, made basic arithmetic hard and more sophisticated mathematics impossible.*

Arabic Numeral Family

Indian (Brahmi)	−	=	≡	+	ᚺ	φ	?	ς	?	*Use:* India. (The Brahmi numerals have evolved into the contemporary Devanagri form.)
Eastern Arabic	٠	١	٢	٣	٤	٥	٦	٧	٨	٩	*Use:* Middle East (including Egypt), Sudan, Pakistan and Afghanistan.
Western Arabic	0	1	2	3	4	5	6	7	8	9	*Use:* The rest of world (including North Africa apart from Egypt).

♥ · **GSR**: 114 · **WHS**: Algiers (kasbah) □ Beni Hammad (ruined city) □ Djémila (Roman ruins) □ M'Zab (desert villages) □ Tassili n'Ajjer (mountains, rock art) □ Timgad (Roman ruins) □ Tipasa (Phoenician ruins) · **ICH**: Ahellil of Gourara (chanting with music and dance)

————— ANDORRA —————

'The great Charlemagne, my Father, unbound me from the Arabs,
Of Charlemagne's empire, I am the only surviving daughter.'

—Andorran national anthem

THREE ACTORS ASTRIDE THE ANDORRAN STAGE

CHARLEMAGNE defeated Andorra's Moorish occupiers in 806 and Andorrans have been thanking him ever since. His son Louis I granted a charter of liberties, but then the pace of reform slackened somewhat until Andorra ditched feudalism in 1993.

KAISER WILHELM may not have been able to find Andorra on a map, but it entered WWI against him anyway.[1] Awkwardly, when the conflict was formally concluded with the 1919 Treaty of Versailles, nobody remembered; so Andorra remained at war until 1939, when a separate peace treaty was signed—by which time the rest of Europe was 24 days into WWII.

BORIS I OF ANDORRA. A Russian émigré who arrived in Andorra in 1934, Boris took the country over and ruled for 14 days. Fatally, he declared war on the local bishop, who had him arrested by the Spanish police and sent on his way.

SENIOR CITIZENS. When it comes to life expectancy, Andorra is the most senior country on Earth—the average citizen reaching 82.5 years. The reason isn't entirely obvious, but presumably has more to do with mountain air and vigorous skiing than with the 1,000 shops flogging low-tax alcohol or the home-rolled Andorran cigars. Alternatively, it could be a lack of stress: Andorrans know neither unemployment nor income tax.

OLDEST OF THE OLD—EXTREME LIFESPANS

1,550 yrs	Animal[2] (*Antarctic sponge*)
405 yrs	Clam (*ocean quahog*)
226 yrs	Vertebrate (*scarlet koi*)
210 yrs	Mammal (*bowhead whale*)
122 yrs	Human (*Jeanne Calment, 1875–1997*)
77 yrs	Bird (*cockatoo*)
38 yrs	Cat (*domestic*)
28 yrs	Dog (*beagle*)

[2] The Turritopsis nutricula *jellyfish (see Caribbean Islands) appears, in principle, immortal; but checking the age of individuals is impossible.*

FREEPOST. Andorrans only need stamps if writing abroad—all domestic mail is delivered free of charge.

BOTTOM-FEEDING. When the devil wants to impart his infernal power to an Andorran witch (*bruixa*), he does so by biting her on the behind. Since it's said his mark never fades, this makes a witch simple to spot. However, for further proof, holy water can be applied, after which the devil's mark will stay put (but not, one presumes, a common or garden mole). It might be easier just to look a suspected hag in the eyes. If she's got four pupils, it's apparently a giveaway.

PRESIDENTIAL PERKS. The office-holder of the French presidency can expect royal treatment: not just because of his day job, but because he automatically becomes 'His Majesty Co-Prince of Andorra' as well.

▪ As Co-Prince, the French president receives a biennial tribute of 4 hams, 40 loaves and an unspecified volume of wine.

[1] *Not that the Kaiser would have been unduly worried. Andorra's army had 10 part-time officers (and no other ranks), with weapons and uniforms handed down through several generations. Nobody was so rash as actually to fight.*

♠ · **GSR**: 125 · **WHS**: Madriu-Perafita-Claror Valley (mountain landscape and traditional settlements)

ANGOLA

'In the end, the ballot must decide, not bullets.'

—Jonas Savimbi, UNITA leader (1975). Angola's 27-year civil war ended in 2002, after Savimbi was ambushed and killed in a storm of machine gun fire. (The country, however, still awaits its first free and fair elections.)

A typical home in Luanda. Two-thirds of Angolans live on less than $2 a day.

DES RES? Move over London, Paris and Tokyo, the Angolan capital, Luanda, is the most expensive city in the world.[1] A small flat costs $2m to buy (or $8,000 per month to rent), car hire is $600 per day and a takeaway burger $16.

[1] *Source: ECA International, Global Survey (2009).*

AMNESTY INTERNATIONAL was founded in 1961, when lawyer Peter Benenson took up the case of Agostinho Neto and seven others in the *Observer*. Following an avalanche of publicity, Neto was released; fourteen years later, he became Angola's first president.

MONKEY BITE. In 2005, northern Angola endured the world's worst outbreak of green monkey disease (also known as Marburg Hemorrhagic Fever), with over 300 people succumbing to gruesome deaths.[2] Even with treatment, the mortality rate reached 90% and as a result, frightened locals came to shun the emergency hospitals set up for them and, on one occasion, stoned health workers—accusing them of deliberately killing every patient they took.[3]

[2] *The deadly nature of the disease had previously attracted the interest of Soviet scientists, who had weaponized it in 1990 for delivery on ballistic missiles. The strain they used—'Variant U'—was taken from the body of the lead scientist, Dr. Ustinov, where it had mutated after he slipped and fatally injected himself while infecting guinea pigs.* [3] *By a strange quirk, those that do survive the disease often have no recollection of ever having been ill.*

TRIANGULATION—GETTING A FIX ON THE ATLANTIC SLAVE TRADE

AMERICAS

DESTINATION OF SLAVES
(Ranked)

1 .... Brazil (40%)
2 ... British West Indies (19%)
3 ..... Spanish Colonies (18%)
4 .. French West Indies (14%)
5 .... USA (6%)

Tobacco, Sugar, Rum

SLAVE NUMBERS BY CENTURY

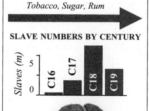

EUROPE

SLAVING NATIONS
(Ranked)

1 .... Portugal
2 .... United Kingdom
3 .... France
4 .... Spain
5 .... Netherlands

SEASONING

On reaching the Americas, most slaves were held in 'seasoning camps' for a year, where they were 'broken'. One in three died at this stage, but those that survived could be sold for a 50% premium over 'new Negroes'.

■ Europeans mainly relied on African trading partners to supply them with slaves. One of the most feared groups were Angola's Imbangala people. Unusually, they killed their own children at birth, relying instead on captured adolescents to replenish their population.

'Middle Passage' — *Slaves*
Guns, Beads, — *Cloth*

AFRICA

Angola had the largest slave 'factories' in Africa, supplying 40% of all those shipped across the Atlantic. In 1800, 88% of the Portuguese colony's revenue came from exporting slaves.

SLAVE BEADS

While often dismissed as 'trinkets', beads were widely used as currency by Africans, who had been importing agate 'monsoon' beads from India for 1,000 years before the Europeans arrived. Brought over by the ton, glass millefiori ('thousand flowers') beads from Murano, Venice, came to be the most prized.

■ Slave traffic wasn't (quite) one-way. After the BaKongo defeated a Portuguese army at the 1670 Battle of Kitombo, the Africans offered to sell the survivors to the Dutch as slaves.

♥ · **GSR:** 124 · **Exclave:** Cabinda · **WHS:** none

———————— ANTARCTICA ————————

'Great God, this is an awful place!'

—Captain Robert Scott, on reaching the South Pole (1912)

EGG-REGIOUS. Upon cooking, the yolks of penguin eggs become vivid orange-red, while the 'whites' turn to a greyish blue jelly—together making the boiled or fried varieties a challenging breakfast. Antarctic cooks have long got round this difficulty by focusing on a variety of disguised uses—cakes being common.

90° SOUTH. American personnel arriving fresh from home at the newly expanded US South Pole research base are prepared for it to be cold;

Office complex at the South Pole

but other more unexpected pitfalls include jetlag (the South Pole runs on New Zealand time), altitude sickness (at 9,300 ft the base is higher than most ski resorts) and sunburn (during the summer, the amount of sunshine per day is more than at the Equator). Blizzards are less of a concern—New York gets fifteen times as much snow as the South Pole. Once on site, facilities include two South Poles (the real one, which gets moved each New Year's Day and is marked by a stick, and a 'ceremonial' one marked by a glitzy barber's pole and lots of flags). Upon leaving, they can choose the 'South Pole International Airport' or the new 900-mile highway to the coast.

COLD WARRIOR. The South Pole should not be confused with the even bleaker Southern Pole of Inaccessibility—the point on the Antarctic continent furthest from any coast. Very few people ever venture there, but the spot is nonetheless easy to find as it's marked by Lenin's head staring resolutely towards Moscow from out of the featureless snow.[1]

[1] *The rooftop bust is all that is left visible of a derelict Soviet Antarctic base now buried by the snow.*

CHAMPION OF THE WORLD

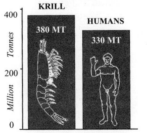

Measured by weight, the Antarctic krill is probably the most successful animal species on the planet.

STIR CRAZY. Despite rigorous selection, 5% of those overwintering at the South Pole and other Antarctic bases each year succumb to psychiatric disorders severe enough to warrant clinical intervention.

TRUE GRIT[2]

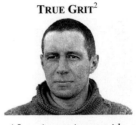

' I am just going outside and may be some time.'

—Lawrence Oates (16 March 1912). Due to a bullet wound sustained in the Boer War, one of Oates's legs was an inch shorter than the other. As a result, Oates actually limped the 860-mile route taken by Scott's party to the Pole and most of the way back, before, gravely ill, going to his death.

'Among ourselves we are unendingly cheerful, but what each man feels in his heart I can only guess.'

—Captain R. Scott, diary entry (March 1912). Shortly after writing this, Scott authorized the distribution of 30 opium tablets—a lethal dose—to each remaining man. None took the pills. Scott died last, on 29 March. It was 44 years before the next person reached the South Pole—by plane.

MEN WANTED FOR HAZARDOUS JOURNEY.

SMALL WAGES, BITTER COLD, LONG MONTHS OF COMPLETE DARKNESS, CONSTANT DANGER, SAFE RETURN DOUBTFUL.

HONOUR AND RECOGNITION IN CASE OF SUCCESS.

—Classified advertisement placed by Sir Ernest Shackleton (possibly apocryphal). In 1909, Shackleton got to within 112 miles of the South Pole before being forced to turn back.

[2] *Although arguably not in the same league as the explorers of Antarctica's 'heroic age', due recognition should also be given to 'Marathon' Don Kern—the first man to stand naked at both Poles.*

★ · **GSR:** 180 · **WHS:** none

——————— ARGENTINA ———————

*'An Argentine is an Italian who speaks Spanish, thinks he's French,
but would like to be English.'*

—Argentine saying

Evita

R.I.P.? Two years after her death from cancer in 1952, Argentina's military stole the embalmed body of world-conquering social activist and adored First Lady Eva Perón. Sixteen years later, the corpse turned up in a Milan crypt under the name 'Maria Maggi'. In 1971, it was exhumed and reinterred in Spain; then, three years later, the remains were transferred to the Presidential Palace in Buenos Aires. In 1976, they were exhumed a fourth time and moved to Recoleta Cemetery—where they now lie.

*'I am a gaucho,
the snake does not bite me
nor the sun burn my brow.'*

—José Hernández, *Martín Fierro* (1872)

PUKKA CHUKKAS. Buenos Aires hosts the world's most prestigious polo tournament: the Argentine Open. But Argentina's own national sport is *pato*—played on horseback to similar rules as polo, though minus the mallets. Today *pato* is played with a six-handled ball, but originally a live (initially) duck was deployed, sewn into a leather basket.

DIVINE. Other footballers have their fans, but Argentine hero and FIFA Player of the Century Diego Maradona is unique in having his own religion— the 40,000-strong Maradonian Church, set up to venerate his personage (but especially his left foot).

'A little with the head of Maradona and a little with the hand of God.'

—Diego Maradona

GLOBAL COWBOYS

Gaucho ('comrade') .... Argentina[1]
Buckaroo ('cowhand') .. California
Cowpunch ('cow-prodder') ..Texas
Gardian ('guard') .... Camargue
Gulyás[2] ('herdsman') ..... Hungary
Huaso ('orphan', rootless) .. Chile
Llanero ('plainsman') .. Venezuela
Paniolo ('Spaniard') .... Hawaii
Stockman[3,4] .... Australia
Vaquero ('cowman') ...... Mexico[5]

[1] Also Uruguay and S. Brazil. [2] Hence 'goulash', the stew first eaten by Hungarian cowboys. [3] As in 'livestock'. [4] A trainee is a jackaroo ('wandering white man') or jillaroo. [5] Also Cuba.

CHOW DOWN. Argentines are the world's champion carnivores. Each person chomps through 57 kg of beef annually—the weight of a typical teenager. However, this seems almost vegetarian beside the 180 kg consumed each year during the 19th century.

ARGENTINE STEAK CUTS

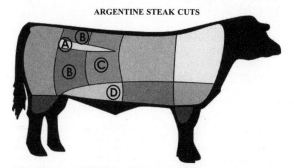

A *Bife de Lomo* > **B** *Bife de Chorizo* > **C** *Bife de Costilla* > **D** *Vacio*

← **Price & Tenderness**

'The natives feed on beef in such quantities that they throw themselves naked into cold water that they may retain the natural heat within their entrails. Their gluttony fills them so with worms[6] that they seldom live till 50 years old.'

—Capt. W. Rogers (1708)

[6] The beef tapeworm typically grows to 3 to 5 metres in the human gut (but the maximum length is 20 metres). Meat must reach a core temperature of 56°C to eliminate the risk of infection.

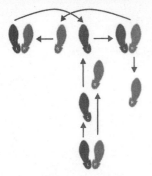

'Tango—a sad thought that is danced.'

—E. S. Discépolo

VERTICAL SEX. Tango is to Buenos Aires what the waltz is to Vienna. When the dance first reached Europe on the eve of WWI, its licensed eroticism took the continent by storm (even after suitable dilution). In London, the Waldorf Hotel's five shilling Tango Teas became *the* social meeting place, while Selfridges' Grand Tango Ball was declared the event of the 1913 season. Earls Court offered tango on roller skates; and orange, the colour of tango, was everywhere. More recently, clinical studies have found that the dance benefits the treatment of Parkinson's and Alzheimer's Diseases, as well as depression and anxiety disorders (most notably social phobias). To this end, the first International Tango-therapy Congress was organized in 2008, while Buenos Aires' main psychiatric hospital began fortnightly tango classes the following year.

NEAPOLITAN SOURCE. Buenos Aires Spanish is spoken with such a strong Italian accent that studies find it sounds closer to Neapolitan than any other dialect of Spanish. The accent comes from massive pre-war immigration from Naples, which, at the time, led the city's leaders to fear Spanish would be supplanted entirely.

'Argentina ... a country in which the sky is so huge men plant islands of eucalyptus over their houses to be covered from the blue.'

—A. MacLeish

INFLATION. Argentina has the world's highest rate of breast enlargement. Big bosoms have been objects of desire for almost all recorded history; but until the 19th century, women could only turn to corsets and ingenious bodices to make the most of their assets. When surgery was brought to bear, implants of ivory, glass beads, ox cartilage, polythene chips, wool and epoxy resin were all pioneered, but found wanting (and often perilous). Modern implants are almost all silicone shells filled with either saline solution or silicone gel, but even these have a 10-year rupture rate of 10%.

> **'Express Kidnapping'**
> A kidnapping in which the victim is held for just a few hours until the family pays a small, affordable ransom. The crime exploded in Argentina in 2001 after the economy nosedived.

CSI B.A. The first crime to be solved by fingerprinting was committed in Buenos Aires. In June 1892, Francisca Rojas murdered her two children, then cut a gash across her own throat and tried to pin the blame on a neighbour. When he denied any involvement, a search of the crime scene was undertaken and bloody fingerprints were discovered on a door post. The prints were unlike those of the suspect, but proved to be a perfect match to Rojas's own. When confronted with this evidence, Rojas confessed all and was later sentenced to life imprisonment.

LETTER FROM AN ARGENTINE REVOLUTIONARY

To my children:

Your father has been a man who acted according to his beliefs. Grow up as good revolutionaries. Above all, try always to feel deeply any injustice committed against anyone, anywhere in the world.

Until always, little children, a great big kiss and hug from Papa.

—Ernesto Che Guevera (1965, to be opened only in the event of his death)

♦ · **GSR**: 21 · **WHS**: Córdoba Jesuit Block (historic buildings) □ Cueva de las Manos (cave art) Iguazú (waterfall) □ Ischigualasto/Talampaya (fossils) □ Jesuit Missions of the Guaranis (ruins) □ Los Glaciares (glaciers) □ Quebrada de Humahuaca (ruins) □ Valdés Peninsula (wildlife) · **ICH**: Tango

——— ARMENIA ● Հայաստան ———

'Comrades! Respect the power of Armenian brandy. It's easier to climb to heaven than leave your chair when you've taken too much on board.'

—Maxim Gorky

WHEEL OF FORTUNE

WINNERS AND LOSERS IN THE GREAT SOVIET DISUNION

Relative Economic Performance of USSR Successor States (1991–2008) [1]

ARM	LAT	KAZ	EST	LIT	AZE	TUR	BEL	RUS	UKR	GEO	MOL	TAJ	KYR	UZB
							-6%	-9%	-31%	-34%	-36%	-55%	-56%	-59%
+66%	+55%	+52%	+51%	+34%	+17%	+12%								

[1] *Deviation from collective mean % growth in GDP per capita.*

Key: ARM Armenia, AZE Azerbaijan, BEL Belarus, EST Estonia, GEO Georgia, KAZ Kazakhstan, KYR Kyrgyzstan, LAT Latvia, LIT Lithuania, MOL Moldova, RUS Russia, TAJ Tajikistan, TUR Turkmenistan, UKR Ukraine, UZB Uzbekistan.

BOAT PEOPLE. The Armenian nation claims descent from Noah via his great-great-grandson Hayk (a builder who, in his youth, lent a hand with the Tower of Babel). In the many ages since, the Armenians haven't gone far. The snowy cone of Mt. Ararat, where the Bible says Noah's Ark[2] ran aground, lies within sight of Armenia's capital of Yerevan, and serves as the country's national symbol.[3]

[2] *Sunday school pictures of a yacht-sized vessel should be put aside. The dimensions given in the Bible suggest a displacement of 22,000 tons.* [3] *See the Armenian SSR seal (*above right*).*

ARMED AND EXTREMELY FRUITY. As home of the apricot,[4] Armenia could pose a unique problem for the US if it ever had cause to invade. US tank crews are highly superstitious about the fruit and won't even let their machines close to one.

[4] *The apricot's botanical name is prunus armeniaca ('Armenian plum').*

RADIO YEREVAN

Q. *Why doesn't the Politburo send cosmonauts to the moon?*

A. *They're worried they'll defect.*

During the Soviet era, Radio Yerevan's turgid Q&A format news magazine was the butt of jokes from Vladivostok to East Berlin.

CHURCH ELDER. Armenia was the first nation in the world to adopt Christianity, converting in 301 CE (36 years before the Roman Empire). By this time, an Armenian community had already been established in Jerusalem for 200 years, and, uniquely, Armenian Christians have clung doggedly on to their own corner of the Holy City ever since. Today, 2,500 live there, complete with Armenian Cathedral and monastery. The Armenians once had sole control of Bethlehem's Church of the Nativity too, and it's an Armenian inscription that you read on the door leading to the church's interior. One further oddity is San Lazzaro degli Armeni, a former leper colony in the middle of Venice lagoon. Taken over by Armenian scholar-monks in 1715, it still retains a global reputation as a font of Armenian culture and learning. In its library, the island monastery holds 150,000 books (many priceless) and an Egyptian mummy.

THE FOUR QUARTERS OF OLD JERUSALEM

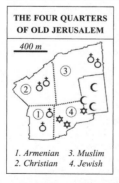

400 m

1. Armenian   3. Muslim
2. Christian   4. Jewish

NOAH'S ARK CHECKLIST: According to St. Hippolytus (170–236), the Ark contained: Noah and family ▪ Birds (14 of each species) ▪ 'Clean' animals (14 of each species) ▪ 'Unclean' animals (2 of each species) ▪ Adam's bones ▪ Supplies of gold, frankincense and myrrh ▪ Palisades of sharp anti-fornication spikes between males and females (all species).

♠♣ · **GSR**: 126 · **WHS**: Echmiatsin (church) ◻ Geghard (monastery) ◻ Haghpat and Sanahin (monasteries) · **ICH**: Duduk (Armenian apricot oboe) ◻ Khachkars (stone crosses)

—————————— AUSTRALIA ——————————

*'The man from Snowy River let the pony have his head,
And raced him down the mountain like a torrent in its bed.'*

—Banjo Paterson, *The Man from Snowy River* (1890). The full text of Paterson's
104-line poem is printed on the face of every Australian $10 banknote.

*'My initial thought was: it's
a lunatic ninja coming
through the window.'*

—Beat Ettlin (2009), on the moment
when a six-foot kangaroo invaded
his Canberra home, beat up his
family and trashed his house

K-POW! Boxing kangaroos became a staple of Australian country fairs following a celebrated five-round bout between 'Jack' and his trainer 'Professor Lindermann' in Melbourne in 1891. The pugilistic stance comes naturally to the animal, but in nature its purpose is to allow the kangaroo to clinch an opponent with its 'arms' while delivering a potentially disembowelling jump-kick with its clawed hind legs.

AUSSIE ICONS. When Australians were asked what swelled their breasts with pride and affection for their motherland, the Barrier Reef and Sydney Harbour Bridge might have been foreseen—but possibly not meat pies. However, when it came to fine dining, the 'dog's eye' (or, to the uninitiated, Aussie meat pie) romped home in the category of best-loved food. What, precisely, goes into a 'meat' pie can sometimes be a little vague, but, according to the FSANZ rules, buffalo, camel, cow, deer, goat, hare, pig, poultry, rabbit, sheep and kangaroo are all fine, as are ears, tendons, tongues, blood vessels and snouts (other organs are also fine, if labelled). Often eaten as a snack with just a slurp of 'dead horse' (tomato ketchup), pies stretch into a meal when served in a bowl of pea soup, with ketchup, vinegar and mint sauce—the classic 'pie floater'.

BIG IN THE WEST ... The world's largest monolith (single lump of rock) is Mount Augustus in Western Australia (*above*). Thrusting 2,820 ft above the surrounding plains, its scale dwarfs that of the much better-known Uluru/Ayer's Rock (*in grey*) near Alice Springs.

... BIGGER IN THE SOUTH The world's largest farm is South Australia's Anna Creek Station. Bigger than Israel, it has just eight full-time hands (supported by aircraft) and 3,000 cattle.

POLES APART. Although they sound very similar, the names 'Australia' and 'Austria' point in radically different directions: Australia comes from 'Southern Land' (the Latin *Terra Australis*), whilst Austria is 'Eastern Realm' (*Österreich* in German).

FEEL LIKE A STUNNED MULLET? SHE'LL BE APPLES—AN A TO Z OF STRINE[1]

Aussie salute ... hand action to brush flies off face		*Not the full quid* .... intellectually challenged
Bottle shop .... off licence		*Oldies* .... parents
Cactus……...............................……..... kaput		*Pommy shower* .... deodorant (Brits don't wash)
Dry as a dead dingo's donger .... not moist		*Quid* .... money
Eating with the flies .... eating alone		*Ridgy-didge* .... Real McCoy
Fair suck of the sav! .... you're kidding		*Seppo* .... American (septic tank = yank)
Grundies .... underpants		*True blue* .... genuine Australian
Hotel .... pub (with or without accommodation)		*Underground mutton* .... rabbit
Icy pole .... ice lolly, ice pop		*Vejjo* .... vegetarian
Just down the road ... can be reached within a day		*Willy willy* .... dust devil, also tropical cyclone
Kangaroos in the top paddock .... eccentric, odd		*XXXX* .... beer brand (from Queensland)
Liquid laugh .... vomit		*You bastard* .... term of endearment (usually)
Manchester .... bed linen		*Zack* .... sixpence (pre-decimalization)

[1] *Translation: 'At a loss? It'll be OK—an A to Z of colloquial Australian.'*

THE FOSSIL CONTINENT:
HOW LIFE BUBBLED UP DOWN UNDER

4,540 MA[1]
Earth forms

0 MA
(2011 CE)

4,400 MA

50 MA

BURIED TREASURE. Nowhere is the history of the planet written more clearly than in the rock of Australia. The continent holds both the oldest minerals and earliest fossils left to us today. These relics have survived for billions of years because, lacking volcanism or glaciation, and with the lowest rates of erosion anywhere, the island continent's landscapes are the most ancient on Earth. This enduring stability, coupled with longstanding isolation, has also preserved for Australia the most divergent ecosystems of any major landmass—exemplified, of course, by its marsupial mammals.

■ OLDEST MINERAL: Zircon crystals Ⓐ are all but indestructible and those found in the Jack Hills of Western Australia go 97% of the way back to the Earth's creation. Analysis shows they formed with water around, suggesting there were oceans, and so the chance of life, even then.

FIRST MARSUPIAL: Australia's marsupials are ■ a Chinese import, having arrived the long way, via Antarctica, following a 75-million-year journey. It's thought just one species made the full trip, a small dormouse-like creature related to the Chilean Monito del Monte Ⓒ.

first dinosaurs—230 MA

■ EARLIEST FOSSIL: A time-traveller landing on Earth would in all probability find the dominant form of life to be microbial slime. For 85% of life's existence—until something called the Cambrian Substrate Revolution, pretty much all there was to see was thousands of square miles of snot-like crust made from bacteria and indistinguishable archaea. Australia provides the earliest record of those glorious times (for a single-celled organism), through 3.5bn-year-old stromatolite fossils Ⓑ at Pilbara. By a quirk of fate, one of the few places where stromatolites still grow is nearby Shark Bay.

Cambrian Substrate Revolution—540 MA

THE TREE OF LIFE

All organisms on Earth share a common ancestor. The point at which this primordial blob crossed the hazy threshold between inanimate and animate matter is still uncertain. But whenever and wherever it happened, it marked the origin of life. From here, the relationship between every living thing that has ever existed can be shown by a family-tree-style diagram known in biology as a cladogram. Life's origin is conventionally shown at the centre (not, for reasons of space, the top) and the passage of time is shown by increasing distance from the centre, such that living species are around the rim. Homo Sapiens is marked thus: ●

3,500 MA

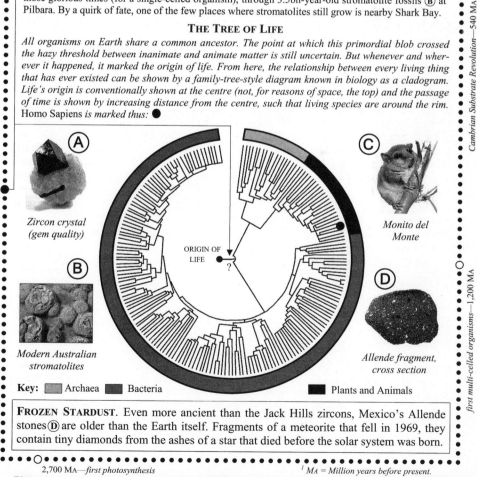

Ⓐ

Ⓒ

*Zircon crystal
(gem quality)*

*Monito del
Monte*

Ⓑ

ORIGIN OF
LIFE
?

Ⓓ

*Modern Australian
stromatolites*

*Allende fragment,
cross section*

Key: ▨ Archaea ▨ Bacteria   ▨ Plants and Animals

first multi-celled organisms—1,200 MA

FROZEN STARDUST. Even more ancient than the Jack Hills zircons, Mexico's Allende stones Ⓓ are older than the Earth itself. Fragments of a meteorite that fell in 1969, they contain tiny diamonds from the ashes of a star that died before the solar system was born.

2,700 MA—*first photosynthesis*

[1] *MA = Million years before present.*

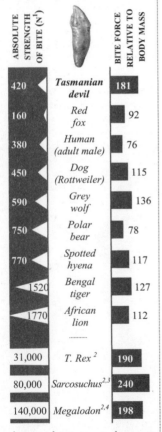

NO POODLE. Proportional to its bodyweight, the Tasmanian devil has the most powerful bite of any mammal alive. Though only as big as a mid-sized dog, pound for pound, it leaves lions and tigers in the shade, with a bite similar to a *Tyrannosaurus Rex* or *Megalodon*, the monstrous 50-tonne prehistoric shark.

ABSOLUTE STRENGTH OF BITE (N[1])		BITE FORCE RELATIVE TO BODY MASS
420	Tasmanian devil	181
160	Red fox	92
380	Human (adult male)	76
450	Dog (Rottweiler)	115
590	Grey wolf	136
750	Polar bear	78
770	Spotted hyena	117
1520	Bengal tiger	127
1770	African lion	112
....		
31,000	T. Rex [2]	190
80,000	Sarcosuchus [2,3]	240
140,000	Megalodon [2,4]	198

[1] Newtons. [2] Extinct species. [3] Bus-sized crocodile (see Niger). [4] See Malta.

HIPPY SKIPPIES. With around 50,000 acres of poppy fields, Tasmania supplies 50% of the world's legal opium. For obvious reasons, security is tight. However, that hasn't stopped crop circles mysteriously appearing. Pranksters, aliens and freak weather have all been considered but, in 2009, Tasmania's Attorney General announced the culprits had been fingered. Apparently, wallabies were going into the fields, eating the poppies and getting 'high as kites'. In this happy state, they would hop round in circles before wandering off to crash.

MEN WITH NO NAME

For when an identity is unknown, unimportant or undisclosable ...

Australia .... Fred Nerk		*Israel* .... Israel Israeli
Bosnia .... Marko Markovic		*Netherlands* .... Jan Jansen
Canada .... G. Raymond[5]		*New Zealand* .... Joe Blow
China .... Wuming Shi[6]		*Russia* .. Ivanov Ivan Ivanovich
Germany .. Max Mustermann		*UK* .... Joe Bloggs
Ireland .... Seán Citizen		*USA* .... John Doe

[5] *Since this name could be English or French.* [6] *Literally 'Mr. No-Name'.*

FAIR DINKUM. Australians tie with New Zealanders as the most charitable people in world[7] (except, perhaps, when it comes to the neighbours across the Tasman Sea).

[7] *Source: World Giving Index (2010).*

AUSSIES ON KIWIS[8]

'New Zealand is a country of thirty thousand million sheep, three million of whom think they are human.'

—Barry Humphries

[8] *For Kiwis on Aussies, see New Zealand.*

BEER WEATHER. Roughly every other morning from September to November, dense ropes of cloud form over Australia's tropical Gulf of Carpentaria; a mile or so across, each can be over 500 miles long. Travelling alone or in packs of up to eight, the clouds—known as Morning Glories—skim just a couple of hundred feet above the gum trees at close to 40 mph. Their imminent arrival is heralded by vicious squalls, but as they pass overhead the wind slackens to calm and there is an eerie silence. While scientists believe Morning Glories are linked to the local geography, they still can't fully explain or predict them despite 40 years of study. Locals have their own system, however: when the tabletops at the Burketown Pub curl at the corners, you can be sure a Morning Glory is on its way (or so they'll tell you).

OF MARSUPIALS AND MONOTREMES:
TWO AUSTRALIAN ANIMALS

KOALA. In 1929, the seminal work on the cerebral anatomy of animals dismissed the brain of the koala as 'ridiculously small'. It appears that eons spent on a toxic diet of eucalyptus leaves have shrunk the organ to the extent that the inside of a koala's head is now nearly half watery fluid, in which the two brain hemispheres—described as like a pair of 'shrivelled walnut halves'—slosh around tethered only by the spinal cord. In contrast, koala digits are highly evolved, as the marsupial is one of the very few non-primates to have fingerprints (the purpose of which is to improve grip). Indeed, koala prints are so like human ones that, even under a microscope, experts have failed to tell them apart.

ECHIDNA. While marsupials raise their young in a pouch, monotremes are mammals that lay eggs; and four of the five species are echidnas (the fifth is the platypus). The echidna's sex life is also distinctly odd. When looking for a mate, up to ten males will form an orderly nose-to-tail 'train' behind a female and follow her every footstep for weeks on end. When she finally signals she's ready, they then run round and round her in a circle, gouging out a groove in the ground, until she picks the one she wants.

SHAME ABOUT THE SHEILA. The title of the world's most prolific serial offender goes to Tommy Johns of Brisbane, who, by the time of his death in 1988, had clocked up 'nearly 3,000' arrests for being drunk and disorderly—a rate of twice a week over 30 years. Like many of his peers, Johns' drinking was shaped by licensing laws that, until the 1960s, forced pubs in much of Australia to close at 6 p.m. The purpose was, in part, to persuade men to spend more time with their wives, but the result was a nightly stampede to inebriation dubbed the 'six o'clock swill'.

DIRTY LAUNDRY. Forget Crocodile Dundee and the empty vastness of the outback; for 100 years Australia has been the most suburban nation on Earth—currently, 85% of its people squeeze on to just 1% of its land. It's fitting, therefore, that the Australian government has officially described the 'Australian way of life' to be synonymous with the Hills Hoist rotary clothes line (in 2007, voted the second greatest Australian invention of all time, after the ubiquitous ute[1]).

[1] Short for 'coupé utility vehicle'—a coupé car body with open truck bed.

FLESH AND BLOOD

Indecent

SYDNEY. In order to protect public decency, it was illegal to bathe in the sea in Sydney—or anywhere else in Australia—during the 19th century in daylight hours. However, in 1902, the ban was publicly flouted by William Gocher, who went for a dip at the city's Manly Beach at midday. Although he was immediately arrested, he was later released, and the law was soon repealed.

Inaugural

墨尔本

MELBOURNE. The Western world's first Chinatown was established in Melbourne during the 1850s. Booming during the Victorian gold rush, the state's Chinese population peaked at almost 10% of the total, triggering quotas, discriminatory entry fees and race riots.

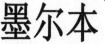

In a plain brown envelope

CANBERRA. Capital of Australia's sex trade, Canberra claims 16 licensed brothels, 15 sex shops and pornographic film-making as its second largest export (after pine). According to the local trade association, Canberra's brothels enjoyed their best trading ever during the 1994 Conference of the World Council of Churches—when business surged by 250%.

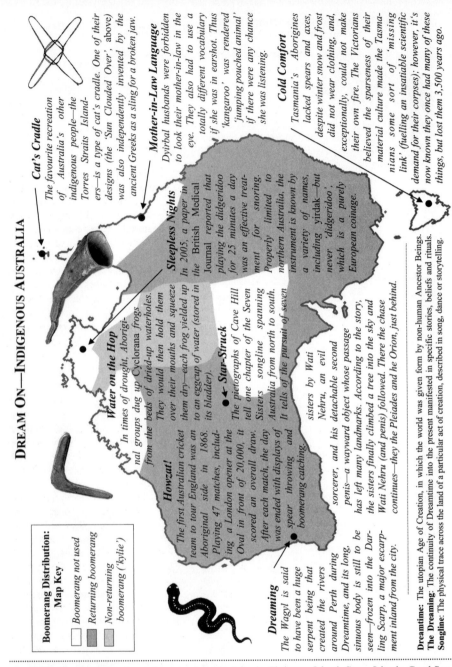

DREAM ON—INDIGENOUS AUSTRALIA

Cat's Cradle

The favourite recreation of Australia's other indigenous people—the Torres Straits Islanders—is a type of cat's cradle. One of their designs (the 'Sun Clouded Over', above) was also independently invented by the ancient Greeks as a sling for a broken jaw.

Mother-in-Law Language

Dyirbal husbands were forbidden to look their mother-in-law in the eye. They also had to use a totally different vocabulary if she was in earshot. Thus 'kangaroo' was rendered 'jumping pouched animal' if there were any chance she was listening.

Cold Comfort

Tasmania's Aborigines lacked spears and axes, despite winter snow and frost did not wear clothing, and, exceptionally, could not make their own fire. The Victorians believed the sparseness of their material culture made the Tasmanians some sort of 'missing link' (fuelling an insatiable scientific demand for their corpses); however, it's now known they once had many of these things, but lost them 3,500 years ago.

Sleepless Nights

In 2005, a paper in the British Medical Journal reported that playing the didgeridoo for 25 minutes a day was an effective treatment for snoring. Properly limited to northern Australia, the instrument is known by a variety of names, including yirdak—but never 'didgeridoo', which is a purely European coinage.

Water on the Hop

In times of drought, Aboriginal groups dug up Cyclorana frogs from the beds of dried-up waterholes. They would then hold them over their mouths and squeeze them dry—each frog yielded up to an eggcup of water (stored in its bladder).

Howzat!

The first Australian cricket team to tour England was an Aboriginal side in 1868. Playing 47 matches, including a London opener at the Oval in front of 20,000, it scored an overall draw. After each match, the day was ended with displays of spear throwing and boomerang catching.

Star-Struck

The pictographs of Cave Hill tell one chapter of the Seven Sisters songline spanning Australia from north to south. It tells of the pursuit of seven sisters by Wati Nehru, an evil sorcerer, and his detachable second penis—a wayward object whose passage has left many landmarks. According to the story, the sisters finally climbed a tree into the sky and Wati Nehru (and penis) followed. There the chase continues—they the Pleiades and he Orion, just behind.

Dreaming

The Wagyl is said to have been a huge serpent being that created the rivers around Perth during Dreamtime, and its long, sinuous body is still to be seen—frozen into the Darling Scarp, a major escarpment inland from the city.

Boomerang Distribution: Map Key

☐	*Boomerang not used*
▨	*Returning boomerang*
▨	*Non-returning boomerang ('kylie')*

Dreamtime: The utopian Age of Creation, in which the world was given form by non-human Ancestor Beings. **The Dreaming:** The continuity of Dreamtime into the present manifested in specific stories, beliefs and rituals. **Songline:** The physical trace across the land of a particular act of creation, described in song, dance or storytelling.

● · **GSR**: 13 · **Dependencies**: Ashmore and Cartier Islands, Christmas Island, Cocos Islands, Coral Sea Islands, Heard Island, Lord Howe Island, Norfolk Island · **WHS**: Australian Convict Sites ☐ Blue Mountains (eucalypts) ☐ Fraser Island (sand island) ☐ Gondwana Rainforests ☐ Great Barrier Reef Kakadu (tropical landscapes, ethnography, rock art) ☐ Ningaloo Coast ☐ Purnululu (karst landscape) ☐ Queensland Wet Tropics (rainforest) ☐ Riversleigh (fossils) ☐ Royal Exhibition Building (hall) ☐ Shark Bay (coast and stromatolites) ☐ Sydney Opera House (concert hall) ☐ Tasmanian Wilderness ☐ Uluru (Ayer's Rock monolith) ☐ Willandra Lakes (archaeology and fossils) ■ Heard Island (volcanoes, glaciers) ☐ Lord Howe Island (landscape) ☐ Macquerie Island (geology)

AUSTRIA ● ÖSTERREICH

'East of Vienna, the Orient begins.'

—Prince von Metternich

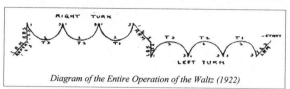

Diagram of the Entire Operation of the Waltz (1922)

BULLDOZED BY BISMARCK. But for an Emperor's hesitation, Germany could have been governed today from Vienna, not Berlin. From 1438 to 1806, Austria's Hapsburg dynasty ruled the Holy Roman Empire. Afterwards, they dominated the German Confederacy that replaced it. In 1848, the Frankfurt Parliament even invited Austria's Ferdinand I to become Germany's first emperor. But he equivocated, as it meant abandoning his eastern domains, and that was enough for Prussia to step in. Later, Bismarck, Prussia's Chancellor, gave the *coup de grace* by engineering the 1866 Austro-Prussian War, which left the Austrians totally defeated.

BOYS IN BLUE. Interpol was founded in Vienna in 1923 on the initiative of the city's Chief of Police. 'Interpol' is properly just the telegraphic address, but as the body's official title is 46 letters long, it is universally used.

POLICE IN SLANG WORLDWIDE
Asphalt Cowboy (Turkey) • Jack (Australia) • Bull (Germany) Khaki Kutta ('brown dog', India) • Eye (Singapore) • Rat (Portugal) • Jake (New York) Smurf (Portugal) • Snut ('dog's nose', Norway) • Musor ('trash', Russia) • Puerco ('pig', Mexico)

ROCK AND ROLL. In the 1780s, polite Viennese society was rocked by the introduction of a scandalous new peasant dance called the 'waltz' (from the old German 'to roll'). Previously, the balls that littered the imperial capital's social calendar had featured courtly dances like the minuet, but not only was the waltz danced by couples face to face, shockingly it required a gentleman to grasp his partner by the waist. Despite the raised eyebrows, the new craze caught on, and by the mid 19th century it had conquered the whole of Europe. In Austria, the most famous version, Johann Strauss's *On the Beautiful Blue Danube*, is traditionally played at midnight on each New Year's Eve.

'The hunt is like a dance for men, for the women the dance is the hunt.'

—Austrian proverb

DEATH TO REASON. To give birth in a 19th-century hospital was literally to dice with death. In 1847, at Vienna General Hospital you ran an 18% chance of dying if assisted by a doctor. But if it was a midwife, the risk was 2%. When Dr. Ignaz Semmelweis investigated, he found that, as was the practice across Europe, doctors filled their time waiting out labour by doing post mortems on the women who had just died. They also never washed their hands. When Semmelweis insisted they scrub up with bleach before going up to the wards, the death rate dropped to 3%. Despite the startling result, European obstetricians derided Semmelweis's findings.[1] Semmelweis then spent the rest of his life in ever more outspoken efforts to improve hospital hygiene. By 1865 his behaviour had become so embarrassing, his colleagues secretly sectioned him. A leading Viennese doctor then lured him into a lunatic asylum under the pretext of an inspection visit. Once inside, Semmelweis realized he had been tricked and tried to escape, but he was bludgeoned to the ground by guards and forced into a straitjacket. Two weeks later, he died from gangrene and the internal injuries received in the beating.

[1] *The rejection of awkward new ideas without consideration has since come to be called the 'Semmelweis reflex'.*

EXPRESS DELIVERY. The world's first consignment of rocket mail was delivered to the village of St. Rade-  gund in southern Austria in February 1931. Despite success (the letters were slowed by parachute), the man responsible, Friedrich Schmiedl, could not interest the Austrian Post Office further and the project fizzled. A more audacious attempt took place in 1959, when the US Post Office converted a cruise missile by replacing its nuclear warhead with two mail sacks, then fired it from a Navy submarine at Florida. Despite another success (the letters were retrieved, taken to the local post office, and sent on to their final destination by conventional means), the military soon buried the idea.

MORE DEAD THAN ALIVE. With 2.5 million plots in its Central Cemetery, Vienna is a city where the dead outnumber the living.

'If a composer could say what he had to say in words, he would not bother trying to say it in music.'
—Gustav Mahler

 CURSE OF THE NINTH. Musical lore holds that a composer who writes nine symphonies will die before finishing his tenth. This belief was first advanced by Mahler, who realized that fellow Austrian compos- ers Bruckner, Schubert and Beethoven[1] had all died at this stage. To avoid the same fate, Mahler didn't number the symphony following his eighth (giving it a name instead), so that his 'ninth', which came after, was already his tenth. Unfortunately, the ruse backfired since he died, aged 50, while still working on symphony number eleven—which he had named his 'tenth'. Not only that, but for those who believe in such things, Mahler seems to have been doubly cursed. After writing his *Kinderto- tenlieder* ('Songs on the Death of Chil- dren'), in the face of his wife's concerns that the title tempted providence, his eldest daughter contracted scarlet fever and died.

[1] *Although German by birth, Beethoven settled in Vienna as a young man and worked there for the rest of his life.*

WANTED

DEAD OR ALIVE
(OR MAYBE NEITHER)

CAT FLAP. In 1935, Austrian physicist Erwin Schrödinger posed the question: 'Is a cat locked in a box alive or dead?' The answer remains one of the biggest conun- drums in science. Schrödinger's question, of course, contained a couple of caveats: along with the cat, there was some poison gas released at random, and he was inter- ested in what happened to the cat before anyone opened the box to see. In the preceding decade, quantum mechanics had revolutionized physics by providing a coherent explanation for events at a micro- scopic scale. However, disturbingly, it seemed to suggest reality was a collection of different possibilities all smeared together. By talking about cats instead of sub-atomic particles, Schrödinger wanted to point up how counter-intuitive (and hard to square with perception) this new science seemed to be. Competing explanations have been put forward, but which (if any) is right is anybody's guess.

- **Copenhagen Response:**[2] the cat is truly both dead and alive until the box opens.

- **Many-worlds Response**: every event spawns two separate universes, so there is one universe in which the cat is dead and a parallel one in which it isn't.[3]

- **Ensemble Response**: quantum mechan- ics only applies to statistical averages, so the question is meaningless.

- **Relational Response**: reality is in the eye of the beholder based on the information available, but all points of view are equally valid.

[2] *The orthodoxy in Schrödinger's day and still the 'classic' view.* [3] *To be more accurate, there is a very large number of parallel universes, since the cat could have died at many different times and each possible time counts as a separate 'event'.*

'The only normal people are the ones you don't know very well.'

—Alfred Adler

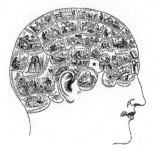

SEXUAL FRUSTRATION AMONG FISHES. As an ambitious student, Sigmund Freud dissected 400 eels in a fruitless search for hidden male genitalia, before eventually conceding defeat. Disappointed, he published his first scientific paper, 'Observations on the Testes of the Eel' (or maybe lack thereof), and cast around, deeply frustrated, for a new field of research. Ichthyology's loss was psychology's gain, and in due course Freud and his 'talking cure', the forerunner of psychoanalysis, became one of the most influential, if controversial, forces in 20th-century psychiatry.

'THE ROYAL ROAD TO THE UNCONSCIOUS'—A FREUDIAN ANALYSIS OF DREAMING

1. *Sensory inputs during sleep*
2. *Residues from previous day*
3. *Instinctive drives of the id (deep unconscious)*

combine
to create

DREAMS

Manifest Content: the dream as it is recalled.

Super-ego veils unconscious content

Latent Content: the dream's hidden meaning, being a part-gratification of repressed wishes.

IN YOUR DREAMS—THE TWELVE UNIVERSAL NIGHTMARES

Freud was interested in dreams as a way to gain access to the unconscious (or so he thought). However, more recent researchers have paid greater attention to the dream narratives themselves—described by Freud, somewhat dismissively, as the 'manifest content'. Some of the most memorable dreams are nightmares, and psychological studies have found almost all revolve round 12 core themes, recurring in all cultures and age groups.

Dream Theme	Commentary
1. Chases and physical attacks	*The primeval fear of being hunted and eaten by predators*
2. Injury, illness or death	*Teeth crumbling v. common (Freud thought it fear of castration)*
3. Falling (or drowning)	*Relic of evolutionary past linked to danger of falling out of trees*
4. Out of control car/plane, etc.	*Dreamers may feel powerless over events in their waking life*
5. Loss of (or damage to) home	*May have ancient roots in a biological drive to defend territory*
6. Failing (or being late for) test	*Triggered by need to achieve; some think also sexual anxiety*
7. Wrongly dressed in public	*Linked to feelings of vulnerability, also fear of loss of status*
8. Missing a boat/bus/train, etc.	*Associated with frustrations in waking life (rather than anxieties)*
9. Malfunctioning machine	*Esp. telephone; mostly female dreams = relationship anxieties*
10. Disasters: volcano, war, etc.	*Life spiralling out of control: can be overwhelmingly terrifying*
11. Trapped: burial alive, etc.	*Reflects the paralysis of most muscles during REM sleep*
12. Menaced by dead/spirits	*Rare but powerful dream: may arise from guilt or anxiety*

Source: Dr. P. Garfield, Universal Dream Key *(2001).*

EDELWEISS. The *Sound of Music* is the most successful musical film of all time[1] and third biggest-grossing movie.[2] Except for minor adaptations to period,[3] characters[4] and narrative,[5] it faithfully retells the true story of the von Trapp family of Salzburg. After the von Trapps fled, Heinrich Himmler moved into their home and later invited Hitler over to visit.

[1] *Especially in South Korea, where to reduce running time in order to allow more screenings per day, at least one Seoul cinema edited out all the songs.* [2] *Inflation-adjusted, after* Gone with the Wind *and* Star Wars. [3] *Maria came to the von Trapp family in the 1920s and had married Georg by 1927 (not 1938).* [4] *There were ten von Trapp children (not seven), and the eldest was a boy (not girl).* [5] *The family set off from Austria openly by train to Italy (not covertly on foot to Switzerland)—although, since they had just turned down an official request to sing at Hitler's birthday party, whatever the precise arrangements, it was probably a wise move.*

♠ · **GSR**: 25 · **WHS**: Graz (cityscape) □ Neusiedlersee (pastoral landscape) □ Pile Dwellings □ Salzburg (cityscape) □ Salzkammergut (lake and mountain landscape) □ Schönbrunn (palace and gardens) Semmering Railway □ Wachau (Danube Valley landscape) □ Vienna (historic city)

——— AZERBAIJAN ● AZƏRBAYCAN ———

'Neere unto Baku is a strange thing to behold
for there issueth out of the ground a marveilous quantitie of oile.'

—Geffrey Ducket (1574)

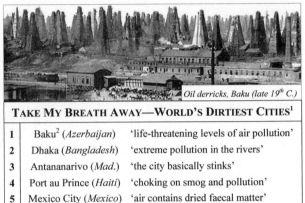

Oil derricks, Baku (late 19th C.)

TAKE MY BREATH AWAY—WORLD'S DIRTIEST CITIES[1]

1	Baku[2] (*Azerbaijan*)	'life-threatening levels of air pollution'
2	Dhaka (*Bangladesh*)	'extreme pollution in the rivers'
3	Antananarivo (*Mad.*)	'the city basically stinks'
4	Port au Prince (*Haiti*)	'choking on smog and pollution'
5	Mexico City (*Mexico*)	'air contains dried faecal matter'

[1] *Rankings: Mercer H&S Index (2007).* [2] *Baku may be bad (10% of residents have lung disease), but its satellite town of Sumqayit is worse, ranked with Chernobyl as one of the Earth's ten worst pollution blackspots. In Soviet times, Sumqayit's factories belched 100,000 tonnes of toxic smoke yearly, which has given the town cancer rates 50% above the national average and super-high rates of birth defects and stillbirths. Its main 'sight' is the cemetery set aside exclusively for babies.*

IS IT THE GAS MAN? IS IT A FILLING STATION?

No, it's Azerbaijan's national emblem. This Caspian Sea state is so soaked in hydrocarbons that oil oozes from the ground and venting gas feeds natural jets of flame. When Alexander the Great's army passed by, local tribesmen harried it by hurling pots of flaming oil that ignited its tents. More recently, Azerbaijan has given the world its first oil well, oil tanker and oil pipeline; and by the 1870s was pumping half the world's supply.

FIRST LADIES.

Azerbaijan was the first Muslim country to extend suffrage to women. They were first allowed to vote in 1917—before their suffragette sisters in the UK or US.

ENDGAME.

Born and brought up in Baku, Garry Kasparov is the highest-rated chess-player that has ever lived. Despite this, history is likely to remember him as the first World Champion to lose to a machine ('Deep Blue' in 1997).

CHESSBOARD POSITIONS

After ...	Number of Possibilities
1 move	400
2 moves	72,000
3 moves	9,000,000
4 moves	318,000,000,000
10 moves	169,518,829,100,544,000,000,000,000,000

HIC FUIT MAXIMUS.

Azerbaijan's Caspian Sea coast marks the furthest east that imperial Rome ever penetrated.[3] The sea was already known to the ancient Greeks, but where it led was hotly debated—most geographers thought it part of the Arctic Ocean.

[3] *A slab of Latin graffiti found at the seaside near Baku loosely translates as: 'The boys from the Twelfth Legion were here.'*

'THE SEVEN SEAS'
(AS SAILED BY THE ANCIENTS)

Sea	Chief Port[4]
1. Adriatic	Venice
2. Aegean	Athens[5]
3. Black	Odessa
4. Caspian	Baku
5. Mediterranean	Marseille
6. Persian Gulf	Dubai[6]
7. Red	Jeddah

[4] *In modern era.* [5] *Piraeus.* [6] *Jebel Ali.*

PIER GROUP.

Thirty miles offshore, in the open waters of the Caspian Sea, Oil Rocks is a fully-fledged town of 6,000 people, with 120 miles of streets, school, park, shops and apartment blocks all supported on a labyrinth of rusting trestles. Now about 30% submerged through lack of maintenance, the settlement nonetheless still produces 50% of Azerbaijan's oil.

♠♣ · **GSR**: 119 · **Exclave**: Nakhchivan · **Occupied**: Nagorno-Karabakh · **WHS**: Baku (walled city) Gobustan (rock art) · **ICH**: Ashiq (storytelling) □ Carpets □ Mugham (music) □ Novruz (New Year)

BAHAMAS

'I don't think I'd ever seen any place so pure and beautiful.
You can feel your pulse rate drop 20 beats.'

—Johnny Depp, on his Bahamian island

GLOBALIZATION. The 1492 arrival of Christopher Columbus on the Bahamian island of San Salvador, and thus the Americas, triggered the biggest economic interchange in history:

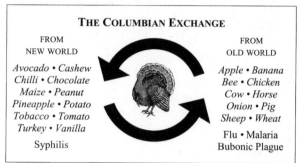

THE COLUMBIAN EXCHANGE

FROM NEW WORLD	FROM OLD WORLD
Avocado • Cashew	*Apple • Banana*
Chilli • Chocolate	*Bee • Chicken*
Maize • Peanut	*Cow • Horse*
Pineapple • Potato	*Onion • Pig*
Tobacco • Tomato	*Sheep • Wheat*
Turkey • Vanilla	
Syphilis	Flu • Malaria
	Bubonic Plague

THIRSTY WORK. Just 50 miles off Miami, Bahamian Bimini island was a favourite smugglers' den during Prohibition. Rum-runners pitted machine guns and yachts powered by aircraft engines against lumbering Navy cutters. Villains to a man, the bootleggers routinely watered their booze, save for a sole exception—a certain Captain Bill McCoy, who rapidly built an unmatched reputation for delivering the real ...

WHERE THERE'S MUCK ... Weighing up to 400 kg a lump, stale whale excrement is an unlikely luxury must-have. However, buffed up and rebranded as ambergris it adds a certain *je ne sais quoi* to the world's most exclusive perfumes; and outside of a sperm whale's gut, Bahamian beaches are the best places on Earth to find some.

'We are entering white water, nothing seems right. We don't know where we are, the water is green—no, white.'

—Flight 19's last message, as related by A. W. Eckert, *American Legion* (1962)

TRIANGLE THEORIES

- *Magnetic anomalies*
- *Methane eruptions[1]*
- *Rogue waves*
- *Secret weapons*
- *Legacy of Atlantis*
- *UFO activity*

However, both the US Coastguard and Lloyd's of London insurers estimate the incidence of unresolved losses within the Bermuda Triangle to be no higher than comparable areas elsewhere.

[1] *There are known to be deposits of methane ice beneath the seabed in the region. If suddenly disturbed, this could release methane gas, which would bubble to the surface. Rising as a froth, it would be unable to support the weight of a ship, which would instantly sink.*

Bahamas

HOODOO SEA. The Bahamas are the only major islands within the 'Bermuda Triangle' (*left*), a zone famous for its unresolved disappearances. Triangle stories took off after 'Flight 19'—five US Navy bombers on a 1945 training exercise—disappeared over the Bahamas, seemingly into thin air. Hours later, a search plane sent up to hunt for them vanished too, along with its crew of thirteen. No wreckage from either incident was ever found. The likeliest explanation is a tragic coincidence: the planes of Flight 19 probably got lost, and, believing they were over the Gulf of Mexico (to the west of Florida), flew east until they ran out of fuel; while the search aircraft was so notorious for fuel leaks aircrew were specifically ordered not to smoke—an instruction that was routinely ignored once in the air. Nevertheless, there's no getting in the way of a good tale.

♦ · **GSR**: 112 · **WHS**: none

───── BAHRAIN ● البحرين ─────

'That famous Iland Baharem, where they fish for the best Pearles.'

—Joseph Salbancke (1609)

ARABIAN GULF. The only island nation in the Middle East, Bahrain is slightly larger than Singapore, or, put another way, 15% smaller than Saudi Arabia's nearby King Fahd Airport, across the causeway at Dammam.

CULTURED (MARINE)

WILD

PEARLS IN X-RAY CROSS-SECTION

WISDOM OF PEARLS. Until the 20th century, Bahrain was the world's premier pearling port and, because divers had to lift one ton of oysters by hand to discover just one pearl, they were the most precious jewels on Earth. Then Englishman William Saville-Kent found a way to culture them using seed beads, and prices collapsed. While cultured pearls can be distinguished from wild ones by X-ray (*above*), chemically, both are just fancy bits of chalk mixed with horn.

HEAVEN SENT. Many scholars believe Bahrain is Dilmun, the setting for the Sumerian creation myth. If so, that may also make the island the Garden of Eden, since the description in Genesis stems from the same root.

SORE LOSER. The Qarmatians were a Bahrain-based fanatical religious sect whose name translates as 'They Who Write in Small Letters'.[4] Otherwise obscure, they earned lasting infamy in 930 CE, when they stole Islam's most sacred relic—the Black Stone—from Makkah and took it back to Bahrain. (Apparently, this was some sort of misconceived attempt to boost local tourism: the Qarmatians reasoned that Muslims would, as a result, be forced to go on pilgrimage to Bahrain instead of Makkah.) In any event, after 23 years, they returned the Stone in return for a huge ransom, hurling it over a mosque wall and so smashing it to pieces. According to Muslim tradition, the Stone's abductor, Abu Tahir, later died a horrible death, being afflicted by gangrenous sores and then eaten alive by maggots.

[4] *They also operated under the pseudonym 'The Greengrocers', referring to their strict vegetarianism.*

LEORNUNG AEFTER IEÐNESSE.[1] Bahrainis are the Arab World's most voracious readers, with 28 times as many books published per capita as across the region as a whole.[2] One difficulty faced by those writing in Arabic is that, by tradition, literature is written in Classical Arabic,[3] the language of the Qur'an. Since this is about as far removed from modern forms as Anglo-Saxon is from txting, very many otherwise literate Arab readers can't understand a word (the subject has to be taught formally at school—in effect, as a foreign language). Of course, writers could simply switch to their national vernacular; but then they would only have a local audience, instead of being able to broadcast their thoughts to the intelligentsia of 25 countries with a combined population of 350 million.

ONCE UPON A TIME—HOW STORIES START ACROSS THE WORLD

Classical Arabic ……..………. *There was, oh, what there was in the oldest of days and ages and times ...*

Afrikaans ……..……. *One day, a long time ago ...*
Armenian ……..……. *There was, there was not ...*
Catalan ………………..…….... *Time was time ...*
Chinese …………... *A very, very long time ago ...*
Dutch …………………..……..… *Once there was ...*
English ………..……………... *Once upon a time ...*
French ……………..……….... *There was a time ...*
Greek ……………..……. *Once, in another time ...*

Gujurati …………………………. *This is an old story ...*
Hindi ……………………......…………. *In one time ...*
Irish ……..…. *A, long, long, long time ago it was ...*
Macedonian …..………..…... *Once upon the time ...*
Maragoli (Kenya) ………..…….... *In olden days ...*
Persian ……...…………………. *One day, one time ...*
Scots ……..……. *In the days of auld lang syne ...*
Slovak …..………. *Where it was, there it was ...*

[1] *Anglo-Saxon: 'Reading for Pleasure.'* [2] *190 books per million people compared to 7 books per million regionally.*
[3] *Or, to be more precise, Modern Standard Arabic—but most Arabs make little or no distinction between the two forms.*

....

♣ · **GSR:** 93 · **WHS:** Qal'at al-Bahrain (archaeological site)

───── BANGLADESH ● বাংলাদেশ ─────

'I made a list of people who needed just a little bit of money. When the list was complete, there were 42 names. The total amount they needed was $27. I was shocked.'

—Prof. Muhammad Yunus (1974). In 1976, Yunus founded the Grameen Bank to provide microcredit to the poorest sectors of Bangladeshi society, excluded from normal bank lending. Still very much in business, Grameen has to date loaned $10bn to 8.4 million borrowers (97% of whom have been women) and inspired similar banks in 40 other nations. Grameen loans are distinguished by a number of unusual conditions seldom found in consumer credit agreements in the West: examples include promises to use pit latrines, boil drinking water and neither to demand nor give dowry payments.

THE ALPHA, BETA, GAMMA OF DELTAS

ARCUATE	BIRD'S FOOT	CUSPATE
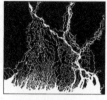		
Ganges Delta	*Ural Delta*	*Tiber Delta*

MUDDY WATERS. The Ganges Delta is the largest delta on Earth—220 miles across, home to 140 million people and mostly in Bangladesh (the remainder being Indian). All deltas, including the Ganges, rely on a complicated balance between river-borne sedimentation and marine erosion for their stability; but, depending on the local interplay of wave action, currents and seabed relief, most develop into one of three shapes (*see above*). In regions where the tidal range is large, however, rivers will flow into the sea as estuaries instead.

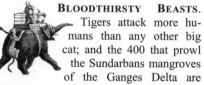

BLOODTHIRSTY BEASTS. Tigers attack more humans than any other big cat; and the 400 that prowl the Sundarbans mangroves of the Ganges Delta are notoriously the biggest man-eaters of all. Uniquely, even healthy animals seem partial to human prey, and collectively the Sundarbans tigers claim 30 or more human victims annually (down from 100 in earlier decades). One theory for the tigers' heightened aggression is that, drinking only brackish swamp water, they can never fully quench their thirst, leaving them irritable and, hence, unusually vexatious.

SOLID SUCCESS. Bangladesh's National Liberation War of 1971 was the occasion of the biggest medical breakthrough of the late 20th century. With 350,000 people in squalid refugee camps and stocks of the approved anti-diarrhoeal treatment all but exhausted, doctors began giving patients a simple salt and sugar solution instead. At a stroke, the death rate dropped from 30% to 4%. Since then, oral rehydration therapy has saved an estimated 50m lives worldwide, with a further 2m (mainly child) deaths being prevented each year.

Rotavirus Diarrhoea from an infected infant can contain up to 10,000,000,000,000 particles/gram: just 10 are needed to infect the next child.

FRUIT AND VEG—SWEETNESS

The mango is the national tree of Bangladesh.

Sugar content %

14

7

0

POT TOM CAR ORA PIN APP BAN MAN

Key: APP Apple, BAN Banana, CAR Carrot, MAN Mango, ORA Orange, PIN Pineapple, POT Potato, TOM Tomato.

> **EXITING AT A TROT.** *Adults in the West endure an average of one bout of diarrhoea a year, generally with only passing discomfort. Occasionally, however, the consequences are more severe. Historical celebrity deaths from diarrhoea and dysentery (diarrhoea with blood in the stool) include:*
>
> *Prince Albert · Sir Francis Drake · Thomas Jefferson · King John · Pyotr Tchaikovsky*

♣ · **GSR**: 81 · **WHS**: Bagerhat (Islamic architecture) □ Paharpur (Buddhist ruins) □ Sundarbans (mangroves) · **ICH**: Baul Songs (mystical folk songs of wandering minstrels)

—————— BARBADOS ——————

*'In the cool of the evening we rode in the country and were perfectly enraptured
with the fields of cane, corn and fruit trees in a delightful green.'*

—George Washington (1751). The only time the president ever set foot abroad
was six weeks spent on Barbados with his half-brother at the age of nineteen.

BARBADOS WATER * DEMON WATER
NELSON'S BLOOD * KILL-DEVIL
NAVY NEATES * TOM THUMB

RUM BUSINESS. Before he became president and got put on banknotes, George Washington scandalized moralists by doling out free rum at election time to anyone willing to put a cross against his name.[1] Unabashed, he went on to insist on a hogshead of Barbadian rum for his presidential inauguration party. Traditionally invented on Barbados, rum was consumed in prodigious quantities in the 18th century[2] and, since slavers could barter cargoes of the spirit for new ships, even helped fuel the slave trade. Mixed with lime juice, watered rum was also the basis of the Royal Navy's 'grog', issued daily to all sailors until 1970. Pirates, however, preferred 'bumboo', a stronger rum punch concoction with nutmeg and sugar, so superior in taste that press-ganged Navy sailors considered it sufficient incentive to swap sides.

[1] *During his 1757 campaign to be elected to the Virginia House of Burgesses, Washington bought over three pints of rum and other alcohol for every eligible elector in his district.* [2] *In pre-Revolutionary America, each adult male drank an estimated 20 gallons of rum annually, while Barbadians consumed three times this quantity.*

> *'Prince Philip and I send our warm good wishes to all of you.*
>
> *Splice the mainbrace.*
>
> *Elizabeth R'*

—The most recent 'splice the mainbrace' order, given
by Queen Elizabeth II at the Canadian Navy's
Centennial International Fleet Review (29 June 2010)

'SPLICE THE MAINBRACE' is the order in Commonwealth navies granting all eligible sailors a ration of rum (underage crew and teetotallers get fobbed off with lemonade). Today, it can only be issued by royalty and the navy's most senior command, who, if so minded, may add 'Mend and make clothes'—a half day's holiday.

LIGHT CAVALRY. Until recently, hiring a Mini Moke was an emblematic part of any holiday in the sun on Barbados. In its original role, however, it was intended to be a parachutable battlefield utility transport and the 1950s British answer to the Jeep. Unfortunately, the Moke's tiny wheels clogged in the slightest clag and, despite a game sales pitch suggesting four beefy soldiers would not have any difficulty carrying it over the muddy bits, by 1963 the vehicle had failed to sell a single unit. As a result, it was subsequently repitched first at farmers, and finally, in desperation, at anyone who could figure out a way to use it.[3]

[3] *One other such was as Pitcairn Island's sole motor transport, where a lone operational Moke was the world's most remote vehicle for over a decade until 1988.*

Discovered in 2008, the Barbadian thread snake is the world's smallest. Half the length of an earthworm and as thin as a strand of spaghetti, it's thought to be pushing the evolutionary limits of how tiny a snake can get—any smaller, and the hatchlings wouldn't be able to kill the insect grubs they feed on.

STATUTORY HOMICIDE. The Barbados Slave Code of 1661 put slavery on a formal legal footing for the first time in the English Caribbean. Purporting to protect the rights of both slaves and masters, it guaranteed slaves one new set of clothes a year, but neither the right to life[4] nor freedom from mutilation. The Barbadian text later became the model for similar codes introduced on other Caribbean islands and in England's North American colonies.

[4] *Even burning slaves alive was acceptable—although the master could face a $15 fine if the act was shown to be 'intentional'.*

♦ · **GSR**: 125 · **WHS**: Bridgetown (townscape)

Belarus ● Беларусь

> *'Belarus is an insane country. My advice is to get in and get out asap*
> *before the KGB take you to some dark hole and eat you.'*
>
> —Fengis (aid worker, 2004)

Minsk, Hero City of the Soviet Union—A Guide for Fraternal Visitors

KGB Headquarters. *The longest frontage along Minsk's main thoroughfare belongs to the Belarusian KGB, which, uniquely for an ex-Soviet state, remains in unreconstructed operation. Visitors may like to admire the building's fine Stalinist neo-classical detailing—but perhaps not too closely.*

Minsk Tractor Works. *A place of pilgrimage for aficionados of heavy agricultural automotive engineering, the Minsk Works was a bastion of the Soviet planned economy—and it still displays its 20-ft-high Order of Lenin to prove it. Still the mother of all tractor factories, the plant shipped its three-millionth tractor in 1995.*

National Library. *Opened in 2006 (but looking 30 years older), the library is the brainchild of Belarus's comb-over president, Alexander Lukashenko. Its $220m cost was met by 'spontaneous' donations from the nation's schoolchildren and a gift from Saddam Hussein (to say 'thanks' for sanctions busting).*

LIVING DOLLS. Almost all Belarusian children have had their appendix removed (whether required or not) because the operation is set routinely as a practical exercise for the nation's medical students.

I SPY. In 2006, Belarus erected a 10-ton statue of Felix Dzerzhinsky, the Belarusian founder of the Soviet secret police; prior to this, Belarus's highest hill had already been renamed in the secret policeman's honour.

MUSTN'T MUMBLE. The Pripyat Marshes of southern Belarus are thought to be the ancestral home of the world's 350m Slavs. The group's sudden appearance some time before the 6th century CE is somewhat mysterious, but it's thought the name 'Slav'[1] comes from the Slavonic word *slovo* meaning 'word' (i.e. someone who can be understood). This stands in contrast to the word *Němci* (or variations thereof) that is used in all of the Slavonic languages to refer to the neighbouring Germans to the west—which literally means 'mumbler' or 'mute'.

[1] *'Slav' is, in turn, the root of the English word 'slave' since, during the 10th century, vast numbers of Slavs were taken captive and sold into servitude after rebelling against the Holy Roman Emperor, Otto the Great.*

TOTALLY TUBER. Belarusian cuisine probably boasts the world's most exhaustive range of potato recipes, with over 300 to choose from, running the gamut from the celebrated national dish of *draniki* (potato pancakes) right through to potato jam. When still part of the USSR, Belarusians were, admittedly, nicknamed *bulbashi* ('potato-heads'), but this was only because the other Republics were jealous.

Josef Kaminski sculpture at Khatyn National War Memorial. Kaminski was the sole survivor when the villagers of Khatyn were massacred by Nazi troops in 1943. Overall, 25% of Belarusians were killed in WWII—the greatest proportionate loss of any country.

WESTERN SLAVS	EASTERN SLAVS	SOUTHERN SLAVS
Czechs	Belarusians	Bulgarians
Poles	Russians	Macedonians
Silesians	Ukrainians	Serbs/Croats
Slovaks		Slovenes

♠ · **GSR**: 32 · **WHS**: Belovezhskaya Pushcha (forest and bison) □ Mir (castle) □ Nesvizh (castle and church) □ Struve Arc (survey line) · **ICH**: Christmas Tsars (pageant)

─── BELGIUM • BELGIË • BELGIQUE ───

'It's no use waiting for your ship to come in
unless you've sent one out.'
—Belgian saying

BELGIAN MUSEUMS:
FIVE OF THE BEST

'Europe's most eccentric country' might be thought an unusual tagline. Nevertheless, it's one of Belgium's proudest boasts—and they've got the museums to prove it.

1 .... Chicory Museum
  A vegetable's untold story
2 .... Nest Museum
  Offers hands-on nest building
3...Washing-Machine Museum
  1,000 years of doing the laundry
4 .... Underpants Museum
  All exhibits are certified worn
5 .... Sewer Museum
  The bowels of Brussels laid bare

BLISTERING BARNACLES! To date, *Tintin* has sold over 200 million copies of his eponymous adventures. Belgians are wildly fond of the boy with the quiff, infeasible good fortune and his own butter lamp (awarded in person by the Dalai Lama

THE NINE ARTS

Since Georg Hegel, most of Europe has adopted a fivefold division of artistic endeavour. Arts six to eight were included later by common consent. But Belgium goes further and adds its beloved comics as ninth.

1 .... *Architecture*
2 .... *Sculpture*
3 .... *Painting*
4 .... *Music*
5 .... *Poetry[2]*
6 .... *Dance*
7 .... *Cinema*
8 .... *Television*
9 .... *Comic Strip*
[2] *Includes drama and literature.*

for services to Tibetan freedom), and proud of their country's outsize contribution to the comic strip generally—Brussels alone has 42 comic shops, three institutes and a museum.

GOD'S GIFT. Beer connoisseurs consistently rate Trappist *Westvleteren 12* the world's best beer. Customers are rationed to one case a month and must go to the monks to get it.

CHIP OFF THE OLD BLOCK. The humble chip was invented in Belgium around 1680, when, so the story goes, hungry villagers resorted to frying sticks of potato in place of their usual fish, after the local river froze over. Double-fried and smothered in mayonnaise, Belgian *frites* (*frieten* in Flanders) remain the best in the world.

'Belgium!'
—The rudest word in the Universe
(Hitchhiker's Guide to the Galaxy)

SPECTACLE. Once a year, 1,000 male residents of the town of Binche put on clogs, bells and identical 'Gilles' masks, and walk the streets throwing oranges at passers-by. Despite looking like a startled bank clerk, Gilles is supposedly a Peruvian Inca.[1]

[1] *The Binchois say the first Gilles represented Inca prisoners in a victory parade. (Belgium was Spanish at the time the Inca Empire was conquered.)*

SON OF AN ARCHITECT! Larger than St. Peter's Basilica in Rome, Brussels' grossly bombastic *Palais de Justice* (Court House) was reputedly Hitler's favourite building. When it was constructed in the middle of the 19th century, a whole city quarter had to be levelled to make way. This led to so much public anger that, for decades afterwards, 'Architect!' was one of the city's most offensive insults.

LOW COUNTRY. Belgium's highest point[3] is a car park in the middle of a bog.

[3] *As the Signal de Botrange is only 694m, the Belgians have added a concrete staircase to the magic 700m.*

FAMOUS BELGIAN CHECKLIST

Leo Baekeland (inventor—'Mr. Bakelite') • Plastic Bertrand (singer) • Jacques Brel (smoker) • Diane von Fürstenberg (fashionista) • Justine Henin (tennis player) • Audrey Hepburn (beauty) • John Houblon (first Governor of the Bank of England) • Georges Lemaître (astronomer who thought up the Big Bang) René Magritte (man with bowler hat) • Gerardus Mercator (cartographer) • Eddy Merckx (cyclist) Hercule Poirot (smug meddler) • Adolphe Sax (saxophone inventor) • Georges Simenon (writer) • Tintin (boy wonder) • Walter Arfeuille (world's strongest jaws)

TALK TALK. Home to NATO and the EU, Brussels hosts the world's largest press and diplomatic corps (1,000 and 56,000 members respectively). It's also said to hold one of the world's highest density of spies—no figures, obviously.

SMOKE WITHOUT FIRE. In 2008, the EU agreed a law to ban inflammable cigarettes. After implementation (expected in 2012), all cigarettes—to be known as RIP (Reduced Ignition Propensity) cigarettes—will have to self-extinguish.

WHAT PRICE AN MEP?
CONTRIBUTION TO EU BUDGET PER NATIONAL MEP—BY NATION (2007)

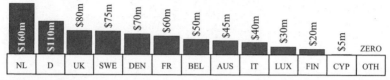

NL	D	UK	SWE	DEN	FR	BEL	AUS	IT	LUX	FIN	CYP	OTH
$160m	$110m	$80m	$75m	$70m	$60m	$50m	$45m	$40m	$30m	$20m	$5m	ZERO

Key: AUS Austria, BEL Belgium, CYP Cyprus, D Germany, DEN Denmark, FIN Finland, FR France, IT Italy, LUX Luxembourg, NL Netherlands, SWE Sweden, UK United Kingdom, OTH Others (15 countries pay negative net contributions).

GAS, GAS, GAS! In April 1915, the Ypres salient in Belgium witnessed the first poison gas attack of WWI, when the German Army discharged 168 tons of chlorine into the air. To protect themselves, Allied soldiers were told to breathe through wads of cloth soaked in urine (which neutralized the gas) and, although crude, this DIY measure worked well enough to hold the line until more formal measures could be designed. By the end of WWI, 125,000 tons of chemicals had been deployed, killing around 88,000 soldiers and injuring 1,250,000 more—many debilitated for life. One casualty was Corporal Adolf Hitler, who was so severely traumatized when temporarily blinded by a British gas shell in the final fighting at Ypres that he forbade German use of battlefield gas throughout WWII.

GERMAN POISON GAS CODES OF WORLD WAR I				
Shell Marking	*Attacks*	*Example*	*Odour*	*Notes*
White Cross	eyes	Xylyl Br.	pungent	tear gas—non-lethal, ineffective, little-used
Blue Cross	mouth	Clark I	none	vomiting agent—to force removal of gas masks
Yellow Cross	skin	mustard gas	horseradish	blister agent—incapacitating with 3% mortality
Green Cross	lungs	chlorine	pineapple	poison—lethal, but blocked well by gas masks
		phosgene	hay	poison—very lethal, caused 85% of gas deaths

IN PERPETUUM. Since 11 November 1929, local volunteer buglers have sounded the *Last Post* at Ypres' Menin Gate every evening[1] at 8 p.m. sharp, in memory of the 54,896 Commonwealth soldiers who fell in fighting around the town and whose remains have never been found. Although now reserved for honouring the dead, the *Last Post* was traditionally used in the British Army to signal the end of labours at the end of each day.

[1] *The ceremony was banned during the German WWII occupation. It was resumed on the evening Ypres was liberated by Free Polish forces whilst heavy fighting was still under way.*

BELGIAN BRASSICA. Brussels sprouts are biologically the same species as cabbage (and cauliflower, broccoli, kale and kohlrabi)—and, yes, they were first grown around Brussels. Their pungent odour, when overcooked, comes from hydrogen sulphide—the gas in sewers.

♠ · **GSR**: 36 · **WHS**: Belgian Belfries □ Bruges (townscape) □ Brussels (x2) (square/art nouveau buildings) □ Canal du Centre (boat-lifts) □ Flemish Béguinages (religious communities) □ Plantin-Moretus Museum (publishing house) □ Spiennes (flint mines) □ Stoclet House (art nouveau building) □ Tournai Cathedral **ICH**: Aalst Carnival □ Binche Carnival (festival) □ Bruges Holy Blood Procession (pageant) Falconry Geraardsbergen (feast) □ Giants and Dragons (effigies) □ Houten Jaarmarkt (winter fair)

————————— BELIZE —————————

'If the world had any ends, British Honduras would certainly be one of them.'

—Aldous Huxley (1934). Belize was formerly known as British Honduras.

LAND OF LOST SOULS. Disease-ridden, insect-infested, reef-rimmed and, crucially, lacking in gold: the Belizean coast was one piece of Central American real estate the conquistadores were happy to ignore. This left a blank on the map for less picky souls, beginning with the motley 'Baymen'—English and Scottish pirates who built harbours at the river mouths, then later turned to logging in return for a semi-truce with Spain. In the 19th century, a wave of Confederate desperados, escaping defeat in the American Civil War,[1] joined them, establishing Belize's sugar plantations (now the mainstay of the economy). Somewhat later, freedom-seeking Mayan refugees crossed the border when the last independent Mayan state slowly crumbled (*see right*). Then, after a brief pause, 3,000 buggy-driving Mennonite Germans appeared, keen to avoid burdensome lawmakers in Canada (and adding a dairy industry). And the influx still goes on; the country has recently absorbed two more groups—rich tax exiles (welcomed) and drug-runners (not).

[1] *During and after the American Civil War, more Confederate Americans fled to Belize than any other country.*

VANISHING TRICK. Much of Belize's interior now lies empty; but one thousand years ago, just before the collapse of Mayan civilization, it was filled with towns and villages. The nature of the catastrophe that overtook the Maya is—despite a huge research effort—still unknown.

POPULATION OF BELIZE

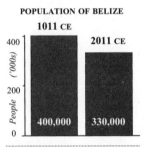

SOMETHING TO CHEW ON. From 1847 to 1901, Mayan rebels in Mexico ran an independent state called Chan Santa Cruz on Belize's northern border; their army was financed by smuggling *chicle* (used for chewing gum) through Belize City to Wrigley's.

Beak—with Belize's national bird attached

PARROT POOP. Belize's barrier reef is the world's second longest after Australia's, and its 450 islands (*cayes*) are a major tourist draw. All, however, are made of fish pooh: annually, parrotfish each excrete some 90 kg of chewed-up coral (i.e. sand), which then piles up into islands.

The Mayan idea of beauty amounted to looking as much as possible like a cob of corn.[2] Accomplishing this called for serious commitment and an early start. Parents gave their babies long tapering heads by compressing the cranium between two boards for the first few days after birth. When children grew older, they might also break their noses to make the bridge look bigger and slope continuously up to the forehead (adults accentuated their profile by wearing nasal inserts). Finally, parents would also dangle a small ball of thread just in front of their infants' faces in the hope of sending them cross-eyed.[3]

[2] *This was to emulate the corn god, emblem of youth.* [3] *It's not obvious how this relates to corn, but the look was considered attractive nonetheless.*

GEEK BEAK. The toucan's outsize bill is primarily a giant radiator to help it dissipate excess body heat.[4] But it may also be useful to bully other birds, since they allow toucans to plunder their nests without resistance. Along the edges are tooth-like serrations, while inside is a frilly tongue.

[4] *Unlike mammals, birds have not evolved the ability to sweat.*

◆ · **GSR**: 142 · **WHS**: Belize Barrier Reef · **ICH**: Garifuna Culture

BENIN • BÉNIN

'The White is concerned with commerce, and the Black must trade with the White. Let the Blacks do no harm to the Whites, and likewise, the Whites must do no harm to the Blacks.'

—Béhanzin, last king of Dahomey, one of the final African kingdoms to fall to European colonialists (in 1894). As early as 1770, the rulers of Dahomey were earning $400,000 a year selling other Africans to European slavers based at Ouidah.

Dahomeyan Flag

ROYAL SURGERY. Known to the Victorians as the 'Black Sparta' and greatly feared by all its neighbours, Dahomey was the most militaristic state in pre-colonial Africa. The king ruled as an absolute despot. But once a year, at a festival known as the 'Custom', anyone could—and did—petition their ruler without fear of retribution. Before responding, the king would consult with his ministers, but also with his ancestors. The method for achieving this was to whisper the enquiry into the ear of a 'messenger', who would then have his throat slit. A short time later, the answer would be received by the king's *vodun* priests by casting cowrie shells or other suitable means of divination. As many questions would be asked, it was usual at each Custom to dispatch hundreds of messengers, and on at least one occasion, following the death of a king, 4,000 were killed. Sending a frisson of gothic horror through Victorian parlours, muttered tales of human sacrifice were ultimately used by the French to justify their occupation and annexation of Dahomey (renamed Benin in 1975).

STRAW AND ORDER. Best pictured as ambulatory haystacks, *zangbetos* were once Benin's only police force, and they still prowl its villages searching for witches and thieves. Also called 'Nightwatchmen', the *zangbetos* are

animated by *vodun* initiates who move in a trance and, when they find a mark, erupt in an explosion of shaking and spinning—possessed, it is said, by spirits of the night.

LADYKILLERS. During the 19th century, up to one-third of Dahomey's army was female, including the Royal Guard. Known to fascinated Europeans as the Dahomey Amazons, and to their own people as *mino* ('our mothers'), the warriors themselves

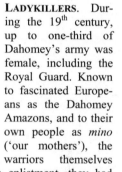

considered that, on enlistment, they had swapped sex—and indeed, according to the explorer Richard Burton, a 'corps of prostitutes' was provided for their exclusive use.

CHOOSE YOUR POISON. Like much of tropical Africa, Benin is heavily dependent on cassava as its core calorific staple (in the local Ewe language, the tuber is known simply as *agbeli*—'there is life'). However, if prepared wrongly, cassava has the potential to be deadly, since a single kilogram of root produces up to a gram of cyanide—enough to kill four adults. Normally, this doesn't pose much of a problem, as cooks long ago learnt how to process the root safely. (In Benin, this is often by fermenting it in water for three days, grating and frying.) But during civil unrest or famine, shortcuts get taken, with the result that in some parts of Africa up to 3% of people suffer from irreversible cyanide-induced paralysis. Paradoxically, there are non-toxic varieties of cassava available, but, without the cyanide, these are more susceptible to grazing by stray cattle or pilfering by thieves. So most farmers refuse to plant them, preferring to play Russian Roulette with their dinner over any risk of losing their crop.

♥ · **GSR**: 127 · **WHS**: Abomey (palace) · **ICH**: Gelede (animistic ceremony)

BHUTAN ● འབྲུག

'Be the same, while being distinctly different.'

—Planning Commission of Bhutan, *2020 National Mission Statement*

The Bhutanese **Druk***. Bhutanese call their nation Druk Yul—'Land of the Thunder Dragon'.*

LOST SHANGRI-LA. Timeless, reclusive and dedicated to the pursuit of harmony, Bhutan is invariably sold as the 'last Shangri-La'. But while there's probably nowhere else on Earth closer to it in spirit, the model for James Hilton's fictional utopia was more likely Muli, another Buddhist Himalayan kingdom now lost after being overrun by Chinese communists in the 1950s. Muli was visited in the 1920s by the explorer Joseph Rock (an old-school type who always travelled with a rubber bathtub). Afterwards, Rock wrote up his trip in the *National Geographic* magazine, and it is believed that this is where Hilton got the idea for the mountain paradise described in his wildly popular 1933 novel *Lost Horizon*.

THE GATELESS GATE. The fact that the yeti (known in Bhutan as the *migoi* or 'strongman') is almost certainly imaginary hasn't stopped the Bhutanese government from setting aside 250 square miles of unexplored territory in the east of the country as a reserve for its preservation. Opened in 2003, the Sankteng Sanctuary has yet to record any sightings, but this might be explained by the local belief that yetis walk backwards to foil trackers and, in any case, become invisible at will.

81

PERILS OF OLD AGE. Eighty-one is a risky age for a Bhutanese person, and not just for the obvious reason. While 80 and 82 are fine, to die at 81 is considered a major taboo,[1] and if you really can't wait, the only remedy for your family is to hang your body upside down inside the house until your corpse would have turned 82 and then burn it. Anything else will bring bad luck on the family and quite possibly the whole village too.

[1] *The taboo has come about because, in Bhutanese Buddhist teaching, there are 81 sorts of evil deed.*

HIGH STAKES. Bhutan's national sport, archery, is very much of the no-holds-barred variety. At inter-village level, both sides hire wizards (*tsips*) for each contest to cast spells at their adversaries and block incoming hexes. Meanwhile, as each arrow is fired off, women from the rival village flick scarves at it in flight to try to knock it off-course. The worst job, though, has to be that of the men assigned to stand beside each target to unnerve the opposing archers by jeering and darting in front of the bull's eye without warning.

SMILE—YOU'RE IN BHUTAN. In place of conventional GDP, Bhutan uses Gross National Happiness (GNH) as its measure of national progress. The idea may have something going for it, since academic studies find income is only one of numerous life circumstances that contribute to that state which most crave above all else. On the other hand, studies on identical twins indicate that 50% of our propensity to be happy is genetically pre-determined, with 40% a mix

DETERMINANTS OF HUMAN HAPPINESS

Life 10%
Genes 50%
Effort 40%

of conscious effort—taking exercise is one of the most effective short-term strategies—and more obscure factors. That leaves just 10% down to the sort of life circumstances (health, wealth, status, etc.) that might be amenable to outside intervention. If true, this would suggest Bhutan could be heading for disappointment, since it would seem true happiness may be beyond the capability of any government, however well-meaning, to deliver.

♣ · **GSR:** 176 · **WHS:** none · **ICH:** Drametse Mask Dance

——— BOLIVIA • BULIVYA • WULIWYA ———

'It is better to be thought a fool than to open your mouth and remove all doubt.'
—Traditionally spoken by Quechua mothers to their children

SHIPPING OUT. In 1879, Bolivia went to war with Chile over guano and saltpetre.[1] The stakes were very high: when Bolivia lost, it forfeited its entire coastline (and the disputed bird droppings). However, despite a now notable lack of briny, 130 years on Bolivia keeps a 5,000-man navy. The largest of any landlocked nation, it's still useful for checking Lake Titicaca hasn't vanished and marching round in circles on Bolivia's yearly 'Day of the Sea'.

Ensign of the Bolivian navy

[1] *Seabird excrement and naturally occurring sodium nitrate respectively, both used as fertilizer and formerly important in the production of gunpowder.*

UP THE CREEK WITH A PADDLE—GLOBAL BROWNWATER NAVIES

1. **Bolivia** .... 5,000 men inc. marines and special forces, 173 vessels
2. *Paraguay* .... 2,800 men inc. marines, 33 craft and presidential yacht
3. *Laos* ..... 30-35 rusting patrol boats mainly fail to sail on the Mekong
4. *Serbia* .... command ship and 15 smaller boats patrol the Danube
5. *Switzerland* .... 10 patrol boats on Lakes Constance and Geneva

SILVERMINE BLUES. In the 16th century, sky-high Potosi was the biggest city in the Americas, while the bleak Cerro Rico above it was the largest industrial complex in the world. Around 45,000 tons of silver were extracted at a cost of hundreds of thousands of lives. Although not much of a silver lining, the miners' two-year life expectancy meant most didn't have time to turn blue (a harmless but disconcerting result of long-term exposure to silver known as argyria).

Bolivia is the only South American country with an Amerindian majority. The Quechua and Aymara predominate, respectively making up 30% and 25% of the overall population.

BOWLED OVER. The Aymara and Quechua women of Bolivia and Peru are the last great wearers of the bowler hat. Created by the Bowler brothers in 1849 to protect the heads of Norfolk gamekeepers from low-hanging branches, it was adopted by the Victorian working classes and migrated to Bolivia with the British and Irish navvies who built its railways, and has thrived there ever since.

BACK TO THE FUTURE Almost all languages have their speakers travel forward through time with their backs to the past (as is implied by the English phrase 'our future lies before us'). Not so Aymara. Its speakers make the same journey facing backwards. So when Aymara speakers refer to the future, they gesture over their shoulders—which makes sense given one can 'see' one's past but never one's future.

PRECISELY. 'We' might seem a straightforward word, but Quechua demands more detail. Is it 'we, but not you' (*-iku*)? Or is it 'we, with you included' (*-chik*)? And once that's established, it's still necessary to specify how certain you are of every bit of information. Options are: *-m* (I saw it with my own eyes), *-chá* (I didn't see it, but I think it's likely) and *-si* (xyz says).

QUECHUA FROM THE BOTTOM UP. One of the most important words in Quechua culture is *siki* ('backside'). From this humble kernel, a whole rich vocabulary has been spun ...

Iskay siki .... two backsides (a son who spends as much time in his parents' house as with his wife)
Muyoq siki .... backside that goes round in circles (an enthusiastic but technically deficient dancer)
Ruiro siki .... round backside (a perpetual fidget; someone who can't sit still)
Rupaq siki .... hot backside (a promiscuous woman, one who is itching to jump into bed with a man)
Q'oyo siki ...... bruised backside (someone who moans about being cold—as cold turns the skin purple)
Siki sapa .... big backside (an obese person—the sense being that their bottom is too heavy to move)
Yuraq siki .... white backside (a white person; gringo)

♦ · **GSR**: 83 · **WHS**: Chiquitos (missions) ▢ El Fuerte (ruins) ▢ N.K. Mercado NP (flora) ▢ Potosí (mines) Sucre (cityscape) ▢ Tiwanaku (ruins) · **ICH**: Aymara Culture ▢ Kallawaya (rituals) ▢ Oruro (carnival)

———————— BOSNIA • BOSNA ————————

'I'm not afraid of humans, but what is inhuman in them.'

—Ivo Andric (Bosnian winner, Nobel Prize for Literature 1961)

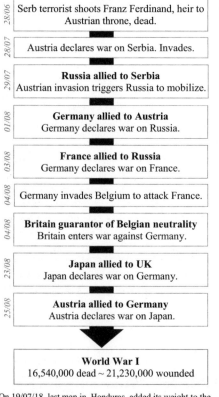

Black Hand sigil

Assassin no. 3

THE THIRD MAN. It was third time unlucky for world history when three Serbian-backed Black Hand assassins struck separately at Austria's Archduke Franz Ferdinand while he toured Bosnia's capital, Sarajevo, in an open car. Assassin no. 1 simply flunked it. (Reportedly, he later claimed a policeman was standing right behind him.) Assassin no. 2 did throw his grenade, but Ferdinand deflected it with his arm. Remarkably, the archduke then opted to continue the visit, albeit on a new route. No one told the driver, however, who took a wrong turn and got stuck—just outside the deli where assassin no. 3, who had given up for the day and knocked off, was getting a sandwich. Seizing the moment (while reputedly wetting his pants), no. 3 immediately squeezed off two rounds, killing the archduke and his wife and setting Europe[1] ablaze for the next four years.

[1] *Europe's loss was wildlife's gain. Archduke Ferdinand had been one of the world's most obsessive game hunters, and had accumulated over 300,000 trophies (which he meticulously diarized) before he himself was bagged.*

THE GREAT WAR MACHINE
COUNTDOWN TO WORLD WAR I (1914)

28/06
Serb terrorist shoots Franz Ferdinand, heir to Austrian throne, dead.

28/07
Austria declares war on Serbia. Invades.

29/07
Russia allied to Serbia
Austrian invasion triggers Russia to mobilize.

01/08
Germany allied to Austria
Germany declares war on Russia.

03/08
France allied to Russia
Germany declares war on France.

04/08
Germany invades Belgium to attack France.

04/08
Britain guarantor of Belgian neutrality
Britain enters war against Germany.

23/08
Japan allied to UK
Japan declares war on Germany.

25/08
Austria allied to Germany
Austria declares war on Japan.

World War I
16,540,000 dead ~ 21,230,000 wounded

On 19/07/18, last man in, Honduras, added its weight to the Allied effort; Central Powers capitulated 115 days later.

HO-HUM. Except that it's too long for anyone much to bother with, Bosnia is more properly known as Bosnia & Herzegovina. (The Herzegovina bit is somewhere down south, although its limits have always been rather hard to pin down.) However, Herzegovinians might perhaps have got more of a look-in if they'd stuck to their former name—the Land of Hum.

CHILD INCENTIVE SCHEME. During Ottoman rule, Bosnians were free to remain Christian on condition they gave one of their sons to the Empire. This requirement was later dropped due to over-subscription.

'Shell them until they can't sleep—don't stop until they are on the edge of madness.'

—Ratko Mladić[2] (directing the siege of Sarajevo)

[2] *Mladić was indicted for genocide and war crimes in 1995, but remained at large until eventual capture in May 2011.*

HANGING ON. The 1,425-day Serbian siege of Sarajevo, from 1992 to 1996, was the lengthiest in modern warfare. Some 469,000 inbound shells pulverized 35,000 buildings and killed 10,000 people—nearly all of them civilians, including 1,800 children.

The Sarajevo Tunnel: the only way in or out of the besieged city ran for 750 yards from an anonymous garage, under the airport runway, to the relative safety of the UN-held terminal.

♠ · **GSR**: 115 · **WHS**: Mostar (bridge) □ Višegrad (bridge)

BOTSWANA

'The highest form of war is dialogue.'

—Setswana saying. (Botswana has enjoyed unbroken democracy since independence from Britain in 1966.)

Botswana's Coat of Arms
'Pula' means 'rain'—of central importance in this desert country.

NATIONAL ANIMALS
(ON COATS OF ARMS)

Botswana .... Zebra
Jamaica .... Crocodile
Mauritius .... Dodo
New Zealand .... Sheep
PNG .... Bird of Paradise
Solomon Islands .... Shark
United Kingdom .... Unicorn

By far the most popular national animals, however, are lions (37 countries), followed by eagles (28 countries), then horses and bulls (10 countries each).

Botswana .... *The Country*
Batswana .... *Its People*
Motswana .... *One Person*
Setswana ..... *The Language*

BLACK OR WHITE? It's a centuries-old question, and for a long time the answer was thought to be white with black stripes. But examination of zebra embryos has shown the animals are, in fact, black, and it is the stripes that are white. Furthermore, the number of stripes depends on when, during gestation, the stripes start to appear. Different types of zebra can have anything from 26 to 80 stripes and theories suggest the later the stripes appear, the more are formed. Researchers are still unsure, however, what they are for. The classic explanation that they're camouflage is widely accepted, but in a recent twist, it's been argued the species the zebra is hiding from is not the lion but blood-sucking tsetse flies—which use blocks of solid colour as homing beacons when hunting for meals.

GULP. Spoken by 4,000 people in Botswana, !Xóõ is considered the world's most challenging language. Not only does it have more distinct sounds than any other (112 compared to 45 in English—and 45 is already high), but 70% of words start with one of 83 sorts of click. This isn't quite as bad as it sounds, since these are all variations on five core types, most already familiar to English speakers.

THE FIVE CORE CLICKS		
Symbol	**Name**	**Sound**
⊙	*Bilabial*	Air-kiss without pursing the lips
|	*Dental*	Sucking front teeth (as in 'tsk!')
!	*Alveolar*	The 'pop' of a bottle being uncorked
ǂ	*Palatoalveolar*	A bottle pop, but softer
ǁ	*Alveolar lateral*	Sucking on molars (as in 'tchk!')

ANTHILL MOB. Even more productive than tropical rainforest, swamps are the most fertile places on Earth—and in the Okavango Swamp, Botswana has one of the world's classic examples. As big as East Anglia, it's the place where the 800-mile Okavango River runs, quite literally, into the sand, forming the world's biggest inland delta. Within the delta are myriad small plant-built islands seeded from termite mounds, and each dry season 200,000 animals migrate from thousands of square miles around to gather on these until the next rains start, so creating one of the most exotic wildlife spectacles on the planet.

THE EARTH'S RICH HARVEST—FERTILITY[1] OF LANDSCAPES COMPARED

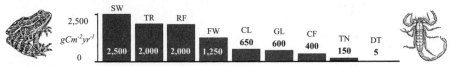

	SW	TR	RF	FW	CL	GL	CF	TN	DT
$gCm^{-2}yr^{-1}$	2,500	2,000	2,000	1,250	650	600	400	150	5

Key: CF *Conifer Forest*, CL *Cropland*, DT *Desert*, FW *Freshwater*, GL *Grassland*, RF *Reef*, SW *Swamps*, TR *Tropical Rainforest*, TN *Tundra*. [1] *Measured as the mass of inorganic carbon converted to living matter per unit area per year.*

♥ · **GSR**: 157 · **WHS**: Tsodilo (rock art)

BRAZIL • BRASIL

'Let the happiness begin.'

—King Momo, words spoken to start the Rio Carnival

2011

2010

2005

2000

1995

*'Enthusiasm is everything.
It must be taut like a guitar string.'*

—Edison Arantes do Nascimento (Pelé)

WORLD RANKINGS (FIFA)
■ ....Brazil
☐ ....Also-rans[1]
[1] *A field of 207 to choose from.*

DYING TO PARTY. Costing $80 million a year to stage, the world's largest transvestite gathering (aka Rio Carnival) is serious business. As the city's samba schools compete

for prestigious prizes and the six-figure sponsorships that follow, it seems anything goes. Before the 2007 carnival, AK-47-wielding hitmen killed the heads of two schools, while carnival judges received death threats if a certain other school didn't win. (It did.)

DOUBLE BIND. Brazil was the greatest slave-owning nation in the Americas with over 3,000,000 Africans transported across the Atlantic to work its sugar plantations.[2] Slavery became so prevalent that Brazil's slaves sometimes even owned slaves of their own.[3]

[2] *In comparison, the US imported 650,000 slaves.*
[3] *Negros de ganho were slaves who had to pay their owners a fixed sum each day, but could keep any surplus. Some used this to buy slaves of their own in order to generate the income to buy liberty outright.*

MEAT THE NEW NEIGHBOURS. Formerly prolific headhunters, the Wuy jugu of central Amazonia still use the word 'prey' (*pariwat*) to refer to strangers and food animals equally. When anthropologists first asked them to explain why they had practised headhunting, the Wuy jugu replied that it had been to collect heads. For logic, their answer can't be faulted.

DO YOUR OWN THING. Candomblé is the religion of African origin followed by two million Brazilians. Meaning 'dance in praise of the gods', it doesn't believe in good or evil, exhorting its faithful rather to embrace destiny fully—whatever it may be.

CATHOLIC CHURCH—BIG FIVE

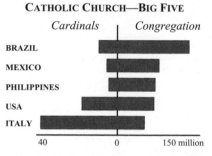

Cardinals | Congregation

BRAZIL, MEXICO, PHILIPPINES, USA, ITALY

40   0   150 million

CHRISTMAS CRACKERS. Since Brazil nut trees resist cultivation,[4] a small army of gatherers sets off into the jungle each rainy season to wait under the forest giants until their nuts drop off. Aside from keeping dentists busy over Christmas, the 40,000-tonne annual harvest gives a name to the 'Brazil Nut Problem'—the counterintuitive process by which the biggest nuts always rise to the top of a muesli box.[5] It's a mystery that still foxes scientists after decades of study, but part of the answer appears to lie in how muesli circulates as the box is moved around. It seems that as the muesli touching the sides gets shaken downwards, it forces the pieces in the middle up to make way. Although even large nuts can ride the central flow upward, they are too bulky to slide down again at the edges and so remain trapped on top.

[4] *The Brazil nut tree needs a special type of bee to effect pollination and the nuts then take 14 months to mature.*
[5] *The effect is also important in more significant but less familiar contexts, including drug manufacture, earthquake damage modelling and asteroid formation.*

CAIPIRINHA. Cut half a lime into wedges and put into a lowball glass with two teaspoons of sugar. Muddle, fill with ice, and add two measures (50 ml) of cachaça.

How Green Is That Cow?—Carbon Footprints Compared[1]

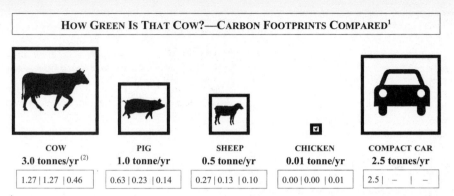

COW	PIG	SHEEP	CHICKEN	COMPACT CAR
3.0 tonnes/yr[2]	**1.0 tonne/yr**	**0.5 tonne/yr**	**0.01 tonne/yr**	**2.5 tonnes/yr**
1.27 | 1.27 | 0.46	0.63 | 0.23 | 0.14	0.27 | 0.13 | 0.10	0.00 | 0.00 | 0.01	2.5 | – | –

[1] *Area of each boxed image represents relative size of greenhouse gas emissions; boxed figures show the split between carbon dioxide, methane and nitrous oxide.* [2] *Emissions per year in carbon dioxide equivalent tonnes per head/vehicle.*

BAD BREATH AND TOILET TROUBLES. Brazil's 200 million head of cattle make up the world's biggest herd. They also dump the equivalent of over half a billion tonnes of carbon dioxide into the atmosphere each year. At a global level, farm animals contribute 18% of all greenhouse gas emissions—more than cars, planes and all other modes of transport combined. Not all of this is in the form of carbon dioxide: belching by livestock (cows are by far the worst culprits) accounts for one-third of the world's methane production, while manure releases two-thirds of its nitrous oxide. These two gases are, respectively, 23 and 300 times more potent planet-warmers than the much better-known carbon dioxide.

AVERAGE DISCHARGE OF SELECTED RIVERS

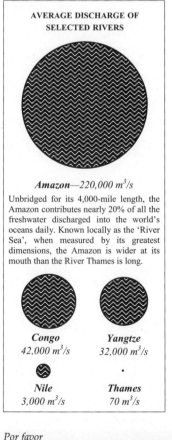

Amazon—220,000 m³/s

Unbridged for its 4,000-mile length, the Amazon contributes nearly 20% of all the freshwater discharged into the world's oceans daily. Known locally as the 'River Sea', when measured by its greatest dimensions, the Amazon is wider at its mouth than the River Thames is long.

Congo
42,000 m³/s

Yangtze
32,000 m³/s

Nile
3,000 m³/s

Thames
70 m³/s

HIP-FLOPS. Havaianas, the Brazilian brand icon that turned flip-flops into fashion, means 'Hawaiians' in Portuguese. Local names elsewhere include:

'Go-aheads' (S. Pacific) ▪ *'Thongs'* (Australia, Canada) ▪ *'Slip-slops'* (South Africa) *'Japanese ladies'* (Poland)

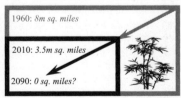

FLASHER. Amazonian Blue Morpho butterflies have one of the largest wingspans of any insect today— they can sometimes even be seen from low-flying aircraft, appearing as flashes of blue iridescence against the green rainforest canopy. However, at 20 cm, the Morpho's wingspan is puny beside that of a 300 million year-old dragonfly, *Meganeuropsis permiana*. Preying on frogs and other amphibians, this insect grew wings getting on for a metre across.

AXED. In 2004, the Amazon Rainforest was being cleared at the rate of six football pitches per minute, and shrank by an area the size of Israel in a single year. Since then, the pace of loss has slowed somewhat. But Brazil's status as the country where you're most likely to die by falling out of a tree continues to be under threat.

IT'S NOT A JUNGLE OUT THERE: THE WORLD'S SHRINKING RAINFORESTS

1960: *8m sq. miles*

2010: *3.5m sq. miles*

2090: *0 sq. miles?*

MAN-EATING FRUIT. In the Middle Ages, 'pineapples' grew on pine trees and were eaten by squirrels. Then Columbus came back from the Americas with an exotic new fruit[1] which some sourpuss likened to the home-grown squirrel-fodder. The joke had legs, and, after two centuries of culinary confusion, the original meaning made  way, becoming 'pine cone' instead. Though pineapples are now grown across the tropics, Brazil is the plant's home, and, today, the biggest producer. Apart from the fruit, it harvests the stumps for bromelain, a natural protein-digesting enzyme. Sold as a meat tenderizer, bromelain is so potent that if pineapple cannery workers didn't wear gloves, the flesh on their hands would quickly dissolve.

[1] *More precisely, 'fruits', as each pineapple is over 100 individual fruitlets.*

INDEX OF INDOLENCE. In the 19th century, Brazil's plantation owners grew the nails of their index fingers to inordinate lengths as a social signal that they never had to engage in manual labour.

FOR RICHER, FOR POORER. Residents of São Paulo enjoy a per capita income ten times that of their compatriots in Amazonas state—the equivalent of Austrians and Angolans living side by side in the same country.

A TALE OF THREE CITIES

RIO. Overlooking the city from the top of Corcovado mountain, Christ the Redeemer is the world's most iconic mega-statue. But it ranks only 54th in height. Ahead comes a mixed bunch, including two Marys, three Shivas, twelve Buddhas, three Soviet War Memorials and a Genghis Khan.

BRASILIA. Brazil's purpose-built capital is the global pin-up for the utopian planned city movement. Naturally, it doesn't work. Because its 1950s planners forgot to add housing for low-wage workers, the gilded core has long since sprouted a necklace of third-world satellite shanties.

SÃO PAULO. 'Like Reading, only further away,' so said a pre-war British traveller. 'Like Gotham' might now be an apter description. Gridlocked and decidedly dicey, the Southern Hemisphere's largest metropolis has sprouted the world's biggest helicopter fleet (503 aircraft and rising), putting it ahead of both New York and Tokyo.

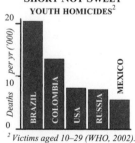

ROAD TO NOWHERE. There are 150 million street children in the world, with up to 8 million in Brazil. Three street children a day are murdered in Rio, mostly by drugs dealers and vigilante death squads; the majority expect to die before the age of 18.

SHORT NOT SWEET

YOUTH HOMICIDES[2]

Deaths per yr ('000)

BRAZIL · COLOMBIA · USA · RUSSIA · MEXICO

[2] *Victims aged 10–29 (WHO, 2002).*

STREET CHILDREN IN SLANG

Balados (wanderers) .... Congo
Bui Đòi (dust of life) .... Vietnam
Chinches (bedbugs) .... Colombia[3]
Marginais (marginals) .... Rio
Moustique (mosquitoes)..... Cameroon
Pajaros fruteros (fruit birds) ...... Peru
Polillas (moths) .... Bolivia
Resistoleros (little rebels) ... Honduras
Saligoman (dirty brats) .... Rwanda
Scugnizzi (spinning tops) .... Naples

[3] *Also desechables (disposables).*

♦ · **GSR**: 17 · **WHS**: Atlantic Forest (ecosystem) □ Bom Jesus do Congonhas (church) □ Brasilia (cityscape) □ Central Amazon (ecosystem) □ Cerrado (ecosystem) □ Diamantina (historic village) Discovery Coast (ecosystem) □ Fernando de Noronha (islands) □ Goiás (museum town) □ Iguaçu (waterfall) □ Jesuit Missions of the Guaranis (ruins) □ Olinda (museum city) □ Ouro Preto (museum city) □ Pantanal (ecosystem) □ Salvador (cityscape) □ São Cristóvão (square) □ São Luis (museum town) □ Serra da Capivara (cave art) · **ICH**: Samba de Roda (festival) □ Wajapi Expression (body art)

———————— BRUNEI ————————

'The Shelfare State'

—Local nickname, inspired by the dominant role of Shell Oil

BREAD AND CIRCUSES. Living in one of only six absolute monarchies left on the globe,[1] Bruneians have struck a Faustian bargain with their ruler, trading political freedom for a generous welfare state, zero income tax and the world's fifth highest per capita GDP. Free education and health-care, and subsidized housing and fuel, are all ultimately bankrolled by Shell, which has been pumping oil and gas from the Borneo Sultanate since 1929, and accounts for 90% of GDP. The largesse goes beyond essentials. Further perks include cut-price beef from Brunei's own Australian cattle ranch—at 2,262 square miles, larger than Brunei itself—and more roller-coasters per head than any other nation.

[1] *The world's other absolute monarchies are: Oman, Qatar, Saudi Arabia, Swaziland and the Vatican.*

NATURALLY POLITE. Melodramatically labelled 'the wild men of Borneo' by previous generations, the Penan are the island's last hunter-gatherers (although only about 200 now keep to a fully nomadic lifestyle in the rainforest). Based in Sarawak and Brunei's remote interior, the Penan are an exceptionally gentle and egalitarian people: traditionally they had no words for 'thank you' or 'thief', as sharing was assumed. Hunting pigs, deer and pythons with blow-pipes, the Penan are themselves preyed upon by sun bears, which curl up into balls and roll down hills to ambush them.

ONE-MAN TRAFFIC JAM. Wanting never to be short of a ride, Sultan Bolkiah of Brunei keeps a fleet of 1,932 luxury cars in five aircraft hangers attached to his palace. For slumming it, he has 531 Mercedes at his disposal, but for a quick burn into BSB (the capital) his 20 Lamborghinis are faster.

FLYING WITHOUT THE FEATHERS. Thanks to Brunei's oil wealth, 70% of the country remains primary rainforest, providing a sanctuary for probably the greatest diversity of specialist 'flying' animals found any-where.[3] Aside from the ubiquitous bats and birds, Brunei's forest is home to colugos (the closest living relatives to primates), able to glide for over 100 m, and the paradise tree snake—which 'swims' through the air from tree to tree with a sinuous wriggling motion.

[3] *The prevalence of evenly spaced tall trees and scarcity of lianas in Borneo's forests relative to Africa and Amazonia are thought to have favoured the evolution of gliding.*

NOT JUST FOR THE BIRDS: NATURE'S EXOTIC GLIDERS		
Animal Group	*Range*	*'Wing'*
Colugos	135 m	arm-to-leg skin flaps
Flying fishes	350 m	pectoral fins
Flying frogs	limited	webbed digits
Flying geckos	?	'wing-suit' bodies
Flying snakes	100 m	ribs distend to aerofoil
Flying squid	20 m	jet propulsion
Flying squirrels	50 m	arm-to-leg skin flaps

KING PONG. Borneo is the original home of the durian, described by aficionados as the 'king of fruits'. It certainly has a most commanding odour; writers battle to outdo each other in their descriptions: 'pig-shit, turpentine and onions garnished with gym sock,' according to Richard Sterling, while chef Anthony Bourdain comments, 'Your breath will smell as if you've been French-kissing your dead grandmother.'[2]

[2] *This hasn't deterred entrepreneurs from launching durian-flavour toothpaste and even durian-flavour condoms—150,000 were sold in a week (the fruit is supposedly an aphrodisiac).*

TRIPLE NATIONALITY. Borneo is the only island divided between three countries: Brunei, Indonesia and Malaysia. Of the three, Brunei (which shares the same etymological root as 'Borneo') is the only one that is exclusively based on the island, albeit sliced in two since 1890 by a stray piece of Malaysia.

♣ · **GSR**: 150 · **WHS**: none

———— BULGARIA ● БЪЛГАРИЯ ————

'Who is the best plant-breeder among the followers of Comrade Michurin?'
'Todor Zhivkov's mother—She crossed a pumpkin with a loud speaker
and got a viable hybrid.'

—Boris Chinkov. In the 1960s, Chinkov, an engineer, was imprisoned for telling this joke; he was eventually released
only after a personal plea from de Gaulle. ('Pumpkin' was the nickname for Zhivkov, Bulgaria's Cold War leader.)

TSARPOWER. Tsars had ruled Bulgaria for over 500 years before the first Russian (Ivan the Great) took a fancy to the term around 1480. A direct Slavic borrowing of 'Caesar', the title was intended to reflect a status equal to a Roman emperor, and, as such, could only be conferred by another emperor or a supreme religious leader. In the case of Bulgaria's first tsar, Simeon I[1], the coronation was carried out in 913 by the Patriarch of Constantinople (with a Bulgarian army camped at his gates).

[1]*Separated from his namesake Simeon I by 1,000 years, Simeon II is the world's only living tsar. Appointed ruler of Bulgaria in 1943 aged six, he was deposed by the communists in 1946 and bundled off to exile in Franco's Spain. However, in 2001 he pulled off a remarkable comeback when elected Bulgaria's prime minister (until 2005).*

WHERE 'YES' IS 'NO' (MAYBE)
BULGARIAN HEADSHAKING DECODED

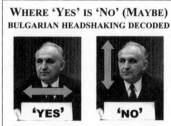

'YES' **'NO'**

Ⓐ *Classic Bulgarian head signals (common throughout Bulgaria).*

'NO' **'YES'**

Ⓑ *New-style Bulgarian head signals (common throughout Bulgaria).*

БОРИС ‖ ƧIЯOƐ

Pronounced 'bahREES' by the Slavs, the name 'Boris' is another Bulgarian innovation taken by the Russians and then broadcast to the world. Theories on its meaning differ sharply, with the main choices coming down to 'wolf' or 'godlike' depending on perspective—and perhaps, on occasion, political affiliation.

OH BULGAR! 'Bugger' is derived from 'Bulgarian' and first meant 'heretic'. Specifically, it was applied to the Bogomils, who originated in 10th-century Bulgaria and then spread across Europe (becoming better known in France as the Cathars). The connotation of sodomy was added in the 16th century, when it was supposed that any sect that interpreted the Gospels 'unnaturally' would set about sex in the same manner—a presumption given added vim by the pious celibacy of the Bogomil elders,[2] which stood in contrast to the more elastic mores of the era's mainstream clergy.

[2] *Dismissed by opponents as mere cover for an aversion to women.*

ONE FOOT IN THE GRAVE

WORLD'S GRUMPIEST NATION ▬ ? ▬▶ **AND FASTEST-SHRINKING POPULATION**

Generally speaking, a nation's satisfaction with life is closely linked to its income—with one exception: Bulgaria. Statisticians are at a loss as to any insight why, beyond Bulgarians just being born plain grouchy.

Sources: Economist *(L); CIA (R).*

After touching 9m in 1986, Bulgaria's population has now dropped to 7.5m and is set to fall to 5m by 2050. But since its pensioners already outnumber its workers, whether the country can continue to function that long is open to doubt.

♠ · **GSR**: 37 · **WHS**: Ivanovo (rock-cut churches) ▢ Kazanlak (tomb) ▢ Madara (cliff carving) Nessebar (ruined city) ▢ Pirin (mountains) ▢ Rila (monastery) ▢ Sofia (church) ▢ Srebarna (waterfowl) Sveshtari (tomb) · **ICH**: Bistritsa Babi (dancing grandmothers) ▢ Nestinarstvo (fire-dancing)

———————— BURKINA FASO ————————

'While revolutionaries can be murdered, you can't kill ideas.'

—President Thomas Sankara, one week before his assassination in 1987

BLACK BEAUTY. Numbering 27 million spread along the southern margins of the Sahara, the Fula are the world's most populous nomadic people. As a distinctive mark of beauty, Fula girls tattoo their bottom lip and gum black; then, once married, they tattoo their top lip as well.

ON BENDED KNEE. The Mossi of central Burkina practise some of Africa's most elaborate greetings. How the session (which can last half an hour) goes depends on perceptions of status. Essentially, the lesser-ranked person tries to position himself lowest. Thus, when two commoners meet, they shake hands; then, while exchanging pleasantries, each surreptitiously crouches down further, until, at the end of the greeting, they are both squatting on their heels—still shaking hands. If a commoner encounters a chief, however, the situation is more clear cut. The commoner lies down and throws handfuls of dirt over his head, symbolically burying himself.

Like Bobo Dioulasso's mosque (right), most traditional Burkinabe structures are built from the West African sun-dried mud brick known as banco, *reinforced with a framework of timber poles. Before drying, the mud is fermented with rice husks for strength, but new* banco *must still be reapplied yearly in an annual* crepissage.

BREATHTAKING. For a few weeks each winter, Burkina is struck by the *harmattan* roaring out of the Sahara. One of the world's more unpleasant winds, it blasts all the moisture out of the atmosphere, triggering nose bleeds, migraines, meningitis and even heart attacks, while at night, it drops temperatures to as low as 3 °C. When blowing strongly, the *harmattan* also brings a choking pall of sand in its wake, which grounds air traffic and sends everyone seeking shelter, bringing commercial and social activity to a halt for days on end. Rival theories for the origin of the name suggest either it has an Arabic root meaning 'the forbidden thing' (so making it a twin of *harem*—'the forbidden place') or it comes from the Ghanaian Twi language, and means 'tears your breath apart'. Either way, despite the bad press, it does do some good—but in South America, where the annual dusting of Saharan soil helps keep the Amazon rainforest fertile.

AXED. Burkina's best-known Fula was former president Thomas Sankara (often called 'Africa's Che Guevara'—both rode motorbikes, strummed guitars, oozed firebrand youthful charisma and got themselves killed). Coming to office in 1983, Sankara was proud to be the world's poorest president, drawing a monthly salary of $450 and remaining resolutely incorrupt.[1] His programme centred on fighting corruption, averting famine and promoting women's rights and reforestation. But, fatally, he was in too much of a hurry and, four years in, he was shot, torched and dismembered by his number two, and his body dumped in a pauper's grave. Sankara's political reforms were soon reversed, but his most lasting memorial is Burkina Faso itself—the new name he chose for the country (formerly Upper Volta). It means 'Land of the Upstanding People' in the two chief local languages.[2]

[1] *Upon his death, Sankara's assets were listed as: one car (Renault 5), four motorbikes, three guitars, one fridge and one freezer (broken).* [2] *Inspiration may have been drawn from Burkina's superbly named capital, Ouagadougou. Historically—arguably even more impressive—Wogodogo, it translates as 'place where people get respect'.*

♥ · **GSR**: 158 · **WHS**: Loropéni (fortress ruins)

BURMA ● မြန်မာ

'A most insidious form of fear is that which masquerades as common sense, condemning as foolish, insignificant or futile the small, daily acts of courage which preserve self-respect and inherent human dignity.'

—Aung San Suu Kyi (1991), democracy campaigner and 1991 Nobel Peace Prize laureate. Between 1989 and 2010, Aung San Suu Kyi spent 15 years under house arrest.

Still common in Burma, traditional snake charming works by dressing up the natural reactions of snakes— typically cobras—as a piece of theatre. So, when a charmer removes the cover from a snake's basket, it responds by rising up because this is its normal defence reaction. Then, once upright, it will follow the swaying of the charmer's flute not because it's hypnotized by the music (it can't hear it as snakes are essentially deaf), but because it needs to keep itself in position to strike back if the flute were suddenly to attack.

I Don't Give a Gram. Burma is one of only three countries not using the metric system. (The other two are Liberia and USA.)

Biting Baby. Fifteen times more venomous than a cobra, the krait is one of Burma's most feared snakes. Its poison works by blocking nerve signals, leading to paralysis and death by suffocation. Dr. Joseph Slowenski, the world expert on Burmese snakes, knew all of this when he was bitten by a 10-inch baby krait several days' walk from any hospital, so he instructed his assistants to give him mouth-to-mouth resuscitation while others went for help. Soon unable to breathe, Slowaski could nonetheless still write notes at first, and then, after that, continued to signal by twitching a toe for a further 15 hours. Sadly, the help never came; but, working in relays, his Burmese helpers kept him alive for 26 hours until his heart finally stopped.

Faith in Numbers. The Burmese have more serving monks per head of population than any other country in the world.

Reputed to combine the strength of a lion with the intelligence of a human, manussiha *guard nearly every pagoda in Burma.*

Croc Shock. The biggest loss of human life to wild animals came after the 1945 Battle of Ramree Island, when 900 Japanese retreated from the British through 10 miles of dense mangrove swamps: up to 400 soldiers were eaten by crocodiles in a single night.

	Entity	Function
	JUST BECAUSE YOU'RE PARANOID DOESN'T MEAN THEY AREN'T OUT TO GET YOU ... MOST SINISTER GOVERNMENT AGENCY TITLES—GLOBAL TOP FIVE	
1	**SLORC: State Law and Order Restoration Council** *(Burma)*	Military junta that ran Burma from 1988. Following a PR makeover, it was renamed as the State Peace and Development Council in 1997, until nominally abolished in 2011.
2	**Committee for the Promotion of Virtue and Prevention of Vice** *(Saudi Arabia)*	Employs 3,500 'religious police' to enforce dress codes, separation of the sexes, observance of prayer times and similar Wahhabist religious diktats.
3	**Antisocialist Conscience Investigation Team** *(North Korea)*	Many of these are deployed throughout North Korea to stamp on any hint of private enterprise (such as market trading); offenders are 're-educated' through hard labour.
4	**S-21 Chewing Unit** *(Cambodia, Khmer Rouge)*	Tasked with carrying out the harshest 'chewing' grade of prisoner torture. (The lesser grades were 'soft' and 'cruel'.)
5	**Imperial Thought Police** *(Japan, Early Showa Period)*	Pre-empting George Orwell's *1984* by 57 years, the Thought Police investigated perceived ideological threats up to 1945. By the start of WWII, its agents had made 59,000 arrests.

♣ · **GSR**: 149 · **WHS**: none

————————— BURUNDI —————————

'Our Burundi, may your name ring out through the Universe.'

—Burundian national anthem

'May you have herds of cattle.'

—Traditional greeting

	BEYOND THE BREAD LINE: WORLD'S POOREST [1]	
	Country	GDP/Cap.
1	Burundi	$100
2	Congo (DR)	$210
3=	Liberia	$320
3=	Guinea-B.	$320
3=	Zimbabwe	$320

[1] *2009 (Nominal),* CIA Factbook *and* IMF World Economic Outlook Database.

PIPED WATER. The Nile's ultimate source was discovered by explorer Burckhard Waldecker in 1934. It lies below Mt. Gikizi in southern Burundi, where the river trickles out of the ground through a length of PVC drainpipe (presumably a post-Waldecker addition). Modern travellers have an easier time locating the spot as the hill's top is crowned by Burundi's pyramid. Although, being just 3m high and made of crazy paving, it's neither as big nor, one suspects, as durable as its more illustrious peers 2,500 miles to the north.

THE RUZIZI RIPPER. Burundi's most famous resident is a 60-year-old serial killer named Gustave, who weighs over a tonne, is up to 6 m long, and, according to troops who've fired at him, swallows bullets with a smile. Based in the Ruzizi river and believed to be Africa's biggest crocodile, Gustave is credited with having eaten 300 people— including, it is said, a Russian ambassador's wife.

○ *IN CASE OF EMERGENCY*: Face to face with a hungry crocodile, one's options are admittedly limited. Nevertheless, some 'experts' suggest attempting to seize the fleshy glottis at the back of the animal's throat. This may just cause the beast to back off; however, a severed arm is perhaps a rather more foreseeable outcome.

EQUAL PARTNERS. Beside doing the childcare and chores, Burundi's women are expected to plant the crops—the idea being their fertility passes into the seeds. Men assist by observing and drinking banana beer through straws.

FLASH, BANG, WALLOP! Lightning is the most potent terrestrial example of plasma—the fourth state of matter, and the stuff that stars are made from. Across the world, lightning flashes around 40 times a second, but the epicentre of activity is Central Africa's Great Lake Basin, including Burundi, where annual flash rates reach 158 per square kilometre. At peak strength, each strike discharges enough power to supply half the world's electricity needs, while its core sizzles five times hotter than the surface of the sun. And if one's headed your way, you won't have time even to *think* about running—the tip streaks groundwards at 130,000 mph.

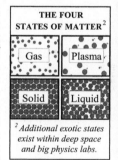

THE FOUR STATES OF MATTER [2]	
Gas	Plasma
Solid	Liquid

[2] *Additional exotic states exist within deep space and big physics labs.*

Average bolt length is 10 km

'If a girl says no to marriage, just wait until her breasts sag.'

—Kirundi proverb

Bolt width is 1 cm

♥ · **GSR**: 169 · **WHS**: none

CAMBODIA • កម្ពុជា

'To keep you is no benefit. To destroy you is no loss.'

—Khmer Rouge government slogan, frequently broadcast on Cambodian national radio while it held power (1975–79)

Angkor—Ta Prohm

Tempted? Skuon Market.

HOLIDAY IN CAMBODIA. The medieval Khmer capital of Angkor is thought to have been the world's biggest pre-industrial city, covering 400 square miles. More than one thousand temples are still visible, but Angkor Wat is the centrepiece, remaining the largest religious structure ever built—and sufficiently compelling for Jackie Kennedy to have insisted on touring, even at the height of the Vietnam War.

SUFFER THE LITTLE CHILDREN. Of the multiple perplexingly evil aspects of Pol Pot's Khmer Rouge, perhaps one of the most odious was its policy toward 'dictatorial instruments of the party' (otherwise known as children). Seen as pliable blank canvases, children were deliberately taken and twisted into some of the regime's most zealous executioners and torturers. Together with their adult associates, these mini comrades went on to murder around a million of their countrymen (roughly as many as died of starvation and disease after both money and medicines were abolished, and the de facto currency unit had collapsed to a scoop of rice).

LEXICON OF LUNACY—KHMER ROUGE NEWSPEAK

Brother Number One ... Pol Pot (his actual name was a secret)
Memory Sickness .... nostalgia (a capital offence)
New People .... urban Cambodians (wholly expendable)
Old People .... rural peasants (the only approved class)
The Organization .... Khmer Rouge (actual name was a secret)

CAMBODIAN CRUNCH. Fried with garlic until the legs go stiff, then lightly tossed in sugar, salt and monosodium glutamate, tarantulas are the favourite street food of the people of Skuon (also known as 'Spiderville' by other Cambodians). The foodie fad probably only began in the 1990s, but the arthropods are now bred on an industrial scale in holes in the ground to the north of town. The white head meat is said to be the best, tasting of 'chicken-cod'.

A TO Y ... AND SOME. Khmer has the world's longest alphabet with 68 letters in use (but no 'z').

KILLING FIELDS. As one Khmer Rouge general put it: 'A land mine is the perfect soldier—ever courageous, never sleeps, never misses.' Their legacy has given Cambodia the world's highest percentage of amputees (0.3%), of which a disproportionate number are children maimed while herding animals or playing in the fields.

HIGH

Danger

EXTREME

WHAT TO DO IF YOU STEP INTO A MINEFIELD ...

1. **Stand and wait**: shout a warning and call for rescue. ('Two days in a minefield is better than a lifetime as an amputee.') **If, and only if, this is totally impossible** ...

2. **Retrace footsteps**: only feasible if footprints are visible right to exit. Step exactly in footprint, do not tiptoe (but some mines trigger on second pass). Or ...

3. **Prod a path**: lie flat and prod at a shallow angle to soil using a stout implement to sweep out a horizontal fan, inch forward and repeat. Mark and avoid mines.

▶ *A land mine costs $3 to make but $1,000 to remove. Land mines left over from past conflicts kill 800 people monthly worldwide.*

♣ · **GSR**: 131 · **WHS**: Angkor (Khmer temples and ruined cities) □ Preah Vihear (Hindu temple)
ICH: Khmer Classical Dance □ Khmer Shadow Theatre

───── CAMEROON • CAMEROUN ─────

'The Big Shrimp.'

—Cameroon was named after the Portuguese word for 'shrimp' (*camarão*) by the first European to reach its coast, Portuguese explorer Fernando Pó. (Pó's arrival happened to coincide with one of the vast swarms of Cameroon ghost shrimp that gather in the river estuaries once every five years for just 10 days or so.)

THE EXPLODING LAKES OF CAMEROON

In the 1980s, two of Cameroon's lakes blew up without warning. The first, Lake Monoun, was a relatively minor affair. However, when Lake Nyos erupted in 1986, it left 1,700 dead and killed everything within 15 miles. The scientists were flummoxed; but they later worked out that the lake had become supersaturated with volcanic carbon dioxide, and, when disturbed, had vented 1.6m tonnes of the asphyxiating gas in a matter of minutes. In essence, it was exactly what would happen if you shook up a trillion Coke bottles in one go.

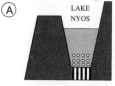

A. *CO_2 bubbles up from magma beneath lakebed and dissolves in lower layers of lake until the water is supersaturated.*

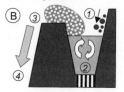

B. *Landslide (1) triggers mixing of lake water (2) that releases CO_2 in 80-ft-high water and gas tsunami (3), causing suffocating CO_2 cloud to flow downhill (4).*

JE GO ME WACH.[1] Propelled by home-grown urban music genres like Bend-skin, Camfranglais—a three-way fusion of French, English and Cameroonian creole—is rapidly becoming the lingua franca of Cameroon's big cities.

CONVERSE IN CAMFRANGLAIS

Bèley	pregnant (from 'belly')
Big rémé	grandmother
Bobis	breasts
Comot	leave (from 'come out')
Flop	a lot of
Johnny	walk ('Johnny Walker')
Létch	village (a contraction)
Lourd ...	have cash (means 'heavy')
Kojak	shaven-headed
Mental	spirit or conscience
Moeuf (also *chick, go*)	girl
Mouf	Get lost! (from 'move')

[1] *I'm about to take a shower.*

Masks of Africa—Bamum
This crest mask from Western Cameroon has been designed to project power to an awesome degree. The head is crowned by a 'prestige cap' worn by high-status leaders, the horns around the neck capture the strength of a wild animal, while the eyes are filled with silk taken from the nests of tarantulas, empowering the wearer with direct sight of the spirit world (as spiders are mediators of divination).

CRUSHING BLOW. One unhappy consequence of Cameroon's rising affluence has been an explosive upsurge in breast-ironing. Around 25% of Cameroonian girls—some as young as eight—are now thought to have their breasts crushed with hot stones or pummelled with pestles, coconuts or bananas. The mothers who do this are responding to the earlier onset of puberty caused by improved nutrition and believe that, by disguising its visible signs, they can protect their daughters from early teen pregnancy or even rape. But the price paid by the girls themselves is permanent pain and deformity, a high risk of infection and difficulties later in breast-feeding.

A NATION OF ANIMAL LOVERS. The poaching of wildlife for dinner is now considered a greater threat to Cameroon's natural heritage than deforestation: across Central Africa as a whole, it's estimated 2.5 million tons of wild bushmeat go into the pot every year. Nevertheless, for those still undeterred, sample cookery tips with tasting notes follow below.

Elephant ...... feet and trunk are best, rest is 'coarse-grained' and bland
Giraffe .... choice cut by far is the long, succulent tongue ('delectable')
Hippo ..... pot-roasted back with herbs is a delicacy; otherwise 'greasy'
Lion .... marinate steaks in vinegar and fry—'as good as venison'
Monkey ..... looks disturbingly like roast baby, but 'perfectly delicious'

♥ · **GSR**: 151 · **WHS**: Dja Reserve (rainforest)

———————— CANADA ————————

'For some reason a glaze passes over people's faces when you say "Canada".
Maybe we should invade South Dakota or something.'

—Sondra Gotlieb (while wife to Canada's US ambassador)

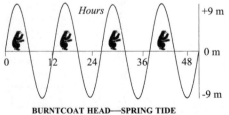

FOUR THINGS YOU DIDN'T WANT TO KNOW ABOUT POLAR BEARS

1. They are twice the size of tigers, and the world's largest carnivores.

2. Standing 4m high on hind legs, full-grown males are able to look an elephant in the eye.

3. In an all-out charge, polar bears are able to reach 25 mph, faster than almost any human.

4. *They are the only land animal to habitually consider humans a prey species.*

○ *WORST-CASE SCENARIO* ... 'Play dead' is the official advice if mauled by a black or brown bear. But these are usually not out to eat you. Polar bears are—and they're not fussy: rotting whale blubber is another favourite snack. If you can break free, you could try to outrun one (they overheat quickly). Otherwise, lacking a gun, you can always pray for divine intervention.

ROCK AROUND THE CLOCK. Burntcoat Head on the Bay of Fundy has the world's biggest ocean tides, with a spring range of 18 m. Fundy's tides are magnified by the funnel-like shape of the local coastline, but even far from any sea, the rock underfoot—and everything on it—flexes up and down by 20 cm twice each day, a so-called 'ground tide' due to the pull of the moon and sun.

BLAME CANADA. The US Army first tried to invade Canada in 1775. After initial progress, it was firmly repulsed. America tried twice more in 1812—with even less success. When a fourth invasion effort was mustered, the rank-and-file troops decided they'd had enough and baulked at crossing the Canadian border. The following year, the American army resumed invading with fresh enthusiasm, even briefly capturing Toronto. However, the rest of the year's invasions went nowhere. When America began invading yet again in 1814, the Canadians—by now really rather irritated—asked the British Navy to retaliate. The British seized Washington DC, raised the Union Jack, torched the White House and left. Rattled, the US Congress debated moving the capital to Cincinnati.

COUNTRY LANDOWNER. For much of the 19th century, the Hudson's Bay Company owned an area larger than any country today except Russia—about 10% of the world's land surface. The territory was put to use harvesting beavers, whose pelts were turned into top hats. Around 1850, however, silk stormed into fashion,[1] beaver looked old hat, and the market collapsed. In 1870, the company gave its land up and now runs a department store chain instead.

[1] *Due to the invention of umbrellas with steel (instead of bone) ribs. This led to a sharp price cut and, so, a rise in umbrella use—ending the need for waterproof top hats.*

EXCHANGE RATE[2] FOR ONE 'MADE' BEAVER

Tobacco	2 lbs	*Brandy*	1 gallon
Shoes	1 pair	*Shirts*	2
Pistol	1/4	*Knives*	8

[2] *Rate in 1733. Beavers were used as currency in northern Canada; a 'made' beaver was a pelt that had been worn.*

Hours

+9 m
0 m
-9 m

0   12   24   36   48

BURNTCOAT HEAD—SPRING TIDE

'The beaver, which has come to represent Canada as the eagle does the United States,
is a flat-tailed, slow-witted, toothy rodent known to bite off its own testicles
or to stand under its own falling trees.'

—June Callwood (Canadian journalist)

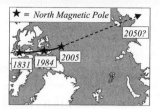

PERIPATETIC POLE.

After being settled in northern Canada since its 1831 discovery, in 1984 the North Magnetic Pole[1] abruptly started to sprint across the Arctic Ocean towards Russia. At the current rate, it should make landfall in Siberia about 2050.

[1] *This is the North Pole that compass needles point to, not to be confused with the Terrestrial North Pole about which the earth spins (which also moves, if far more feebly).*

DRIVE-THRU STEAK.

Not just good to look at, moose are powerful too. Each year Canadian moose attack more people than wolves and bears together, and their kicks can kill. But it's their dead bodies that are most dangerous, usually when coming through a car's windscreen.[2] In Newfoundland, there are around 700 moose collisions annually and the local radio stations flash regular 'moose sighting' traffic alerts.

[2] *Standing two metres at the shoulder on tall, spindly legs, moose fly straight over car bonnets, to impact the windscreen area directly—where their half-ton bodyweight flattens the roof struts and crushes the occupants. Seat belts and air bags are useless.*

WUNDERBAR.

Rated the fifth greatest Canadian invention of all time (just ahead of the pacemaker) and conceived as an answer to wartime elastic rationing, the Wonderbra was for decades sold to the women of Canada on its comfort and practicality. Then Eva 'Hello Boys' Herzigová added a little exposure, and the Wonderbra exploded worldwide as the sexiest undergarment under the sun. In 2008, British women even paid the Wonderbra the ultimate compliment—voting it the greatest fashion innovation in history.

NORTHERN MANITOBA TRAPPER'S FESTIVAL 2009

PROGRAMME

POLE CLIMBING ~ TEA BOILING ~ SLED PULL ~ LEG WRESTLING ~ AXE THROWING ~ GOOSE CALLING ~ LOG SAWING ~ TRAP SETTING ~ SNOWSHOE RACE ~ LOG THROWING ~ NAIL DRIVING

CANADIAN ... OR CANADIEN?

HOME LANGUAGE

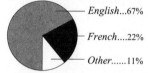

English...67%

French....22%

Other......11%

Anglophones who speak French: 9%
Francophones who speak English: 41%

> *'I'm a Canadian.
> It's like an American,
> but without the gun.'*
> —Kids in the Hall

STICK THAT.

Contrary to missionary reports of the time, totem poles have never served as idols. The grandest stood as ostentatious statements of wealth, while others (known as 'shame poles') were put up to embarrass defaulting debtors and sacred oath-breakers.[4]

[4] *In 2007, Eyak native villagers in Alaska commissioned an Exxon Valdez shame pole that depicted the CEO of Exxon at the time with a Pinocchio-like nose.*

MR. NICE GUYS.

Canadians are the world's best-liked people,[3] ahead of Australians and Italians. Their warmth, knowledge, approachability and allegedly lightning wit are all singled out for particular praise. [3] *Source: Anholt-GfK Roper Nation Brands Index (2009)—People Brand Ranking.*

TICK TOCK. A lake in Manitoba is the source of virtually all the world's caesium—one of only three metallic elements that melt like chocolate to the touch.[1] In 1967, caesium replaced the moon[2] as the fundamental basis of all human time measurement and the best caesium clocks are now accurate to one second in 60 million years.

[1] The others are francium and gallium. [2] The moon now officially orbits once per 21,700,079,489,987,337.6 periods of the radiation linked to the hyperfine level transition of a ground state Cs 133 atom—approximately.

WORLD'S LARGEST ...

LAKE (FRESHWATER)

L. Michigan-Huron[3]

Canada & US 46,000 sq. miles

LAKE ON AN ISLAND

Lake Nettilling

Baffin Island, Canada 2,000 sq. miles

ISLAND IN A LAKE

Manitoulin Island

Lake Huron, Canada 1,000 sq. miles

LAKE ON ISLAND IN LAKE

Lake Manitou

Manitoulin Island, Canada 40 sq. miles

[3] Huron and Michigan form one lake linked by narrows five miles wide.

TAR VERY MUCH. There's more oil under the ground in Canada than contained in the total proven reserves of the rest of the world combined. The catch is that it's not liquid, but a gunky, tarry sand. Not all is recoverable with current technology; nevertheless, Canada already exports more oil to the US than Saudi Arabia and Iraq jointly, and is fully self-sufficient at home—no bad thing, since it uses more energy per capita than any other major economy.

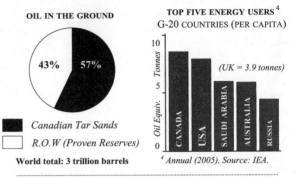

OIL IN THE GROUND

43% 57%

■ *Canadian Tar Sands*
□ *R.O.W (Proven Reserves)*

World total: 3 trillion barrels

TOP FIVE ENERGY USERS[4]
G-20 COUNTRIES (PER CAPITA)

(UK = 3.9 tonnes)

Oil Equiv. Tonnes

CANADA · USA · SAUDI ARABIA · AUSTRALIA · RUSSIA

[4] *Annual (2005). Source: IEA.*

CODENAME HABAKKUK. In WWII, the Allies launched a top-secret project in Canada to build unsinkable aircraft carriers out of artificial icebergs. Their scale was to be immense—around 2 million tonnes (four times the size of the largest oil tankers even today) and, as first conceived, nearly a mile long. To construct the vessels, British scientists invented a way of reinforcing ice with wood pulp to make it as strong as concrete, and Lord Mountbatten took a block to Quebec in 1943 to persuade the Americans to join in. Keen to prove its strength, he fired his pistol into it, whereupon the bullet reportedly ricocheted through the trousers of the Commander-in-Chief of the US Navy. The project was axed soon after, but not before a 1,000-ton prototype was built and sailed round a lake in the Rockies.

BLEEDING OBVIOUS. 'The most effective way to contain the rise of the undead is to hit hard and often.' So said a government-funded research paper from the University of Ottawa in 2009. Studying zombie-plague dynamics, academics discovered that, if unopposed, zombies would overrun a Manchester-sized city in three to four days. Attempts to capture and quarantine them might hold the line for six. Unsurprisingly, however, the only anti-zombie strategy with any hope of success was found to be relentless, unremitting attack. What the paper didn't reveal, though, is how you actually set about killing one.

♦ · **GSR**: 6 · **WHS**: Canadian Rockies (mountains, fossils) □ Dinosaur Provincial Park (fossils) □ Gros Morne (landscape) □ Head-Smashed-In Buffalo Jump (Native American history) □ Joggins (fossils) □ Kluane (mountains, icefield) □ L'Anse aux Meadows (Viking ruins) □ Lunenberg (museum town) Miguasha (fossils) □ Nahanni (wilderness) □ Quebec City (cityscape) □ Rideau (canal) □ SGang Gwaay (Native American culture) □ Waterton Lakes (landscape) □ Wood Buffalo NP (bison)

—————— CAPE VERDE ● CABO VERDE ——————

'If you write me a letter, I'll write you one back,
If you forget about me, I'll forget about you—
Until the day you come back.'

—Sung by Cesaria Evora (*Sodade*). Evora has achieved international success as a singer of *morna*, Cape Verde's most celebrated musical genre. Likened to Portuguese *fado* and African-American blues, *morna*'s lyrics speak of emigration, separation, love and loss—traditional themes all within the direct experience of very many Cape Verdeans.

EXIT QUEUE. Historically, Cape Verde has been a nation of emigrants going back almost to the time that the uninhabited Atlantic island chain was first settled (after which, for more than three centuries, the principal export was slaves), and, although new airports and the advent of mass tourism are beginning to turn the tide, it's still the case that as many people identifying themselves as of Cape Verdean origin live in the USA as in Cape Verde itself.

COLONY—MARK ONE. Founded by the Portuguese in 1462, Ribeira Grande (since renamed Cidade Velha) was the first European settlement to be constructed in the tropics and, with cathedral, fortress, walls and central slave market, served as the basic model for the hundreds of subsequent outposts that were built by the main European powers right across the globe.

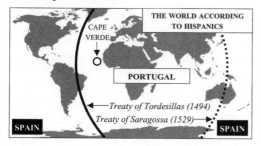

SOUTH EUROPE. Since 2005, Cape Verde has been pursuing EU membership as a long-term policy goal. While acknowledging its location off West Africa, the island country prefers to emphasize its shared history with Portugal and the fact that EU member Cyprus is in Asia.

SLICING THE PIE. Two years after Columbus reached the Americas in 1492, Spain and Portugal modestly agreed to split the globe between them. The resulting treaty, signed at Tordesillas, defined the dividing line not in terms of longitude but as lying 370 leagues west of the Cape Verde islands (neglecting to specify which).[1] Not surprisingly, even after the treaty was blessed by the pope, Europe's other countries reacted badly to what amounted to the biggest land grab in history—and, in practice, wherever the two Hispanic nations didn't have boots on the ground, the document was ignored. The division remains a live political issue since the primary claim to the Falklands advanced by Argentina is, in effect, that the group lies more than 370 leagues west of Cape Verde, and it has inherited Spain's sovereign rights. Chile meanwhile asserts the same argument to claim a slice of Antarctica as far as the South Pole.

[1] *In 1529, an equally arrogant treaty, signed in Saragossa (modern Zaragoza), purported to delineate where exactly in the Orient the two Hispanic claims met.*

Hurricane Ivan (2004): a classic Cape Verde-type hurricane. All five of the fiercest hurricanes that have hit North America or the Caribbean have been spawned in the waters around Cape Verde. The islands' far-easterly location gives nascent storms plenty of opportunity to suck energy from the Atlantic's warm surface waters as they cross the full width of the ocean, allowing them to unleash exceptional violence when they finally hit land.

♥ · **GSR**: 152 · **WHS**: Cidade Velha (historic town)

—— CARIBBEAN ISLANDS—LESSER ANTILLES ——

'No rain, no rainbow.'

—Caribbean proverb

SHIP AHOY! The waters of the Caribbean are best known for two things: buccaneers and cruise ships. Because of a recent upsurge in piracy,[1] the two have now collided. In order to repel boarders, modern cruise liners, such as the *Queen Mary 2*, have been fitted with Long Range Acoustic Devices (LRADs), first deployed by the US Navy on its warships. LRADs blast a beam of intense siren-like noise as loud as 155 decibels.[2] At 90 m, such a sound registers as physical pain, while closer in, it also induces nausea, permanent deafness and disturbed vision.[3] Although LRADs are deemed non-lethal weapons, sound can kill. Tests indicate that at 184 decibels laboratory mice start to shake apart.

[1] *The worst hotspot is the Indian Ocean, but incidents take place worldwide, including the Caribbean.* [2] *More than three times as deafening as a jet engine.* [3] *The eyeball starts to vibrate, which prevents the eye muscles from focusing.*

WHITE SLAVE TRADE. Britain's West Indian colonies were first developed on Irish slave labour. African slaves did not arrive in large volume until the latter part of the 17th century. By then, 60,000 Irish had already been forcibly transported to the Caribbean, where they were openly bought and sold. Treatment was harsh as Irishmen only fetched $8, against $30–$80 for the rarer Africans.

'We are looking at a worldwide silent invasion.'

—Dr. M. Miglietta, Smithsonian Tropical Marine Institute

JELLY BABIES. A 5-mm-long Caribbean jellyfish appears to have mastered the secret of immortality. *Turritopsis nutricula* (*above*) achieves the unique trick by being able to turn itself back into a sexually immature juvenile once it has become an adult. In principle, the animal can then flip-flop between youth and adulthood ad infinitum. Having conquered death, the jellyfish is now busy taking over the world. Hitching a lift in the ballast tanks of shipping, it is creating new colonies worldwide, and, wherever it gets started, numbers explode thanks, in part, to the ability of each new individual to keep on reproducing endlessly.

SPICE ISLAND. Grenada's nickname comes from the nutmeg grown there. At high doses, the spice gives a cannabis-like high—but the headaches and nausea that go with it make it a drug of last resort, such as in prison.

FATAL ATTRACTION. Each year, 1,500 tons of suntan lotion washes off the bodies of tourists into the Caribbean Sea. Even in trace amounts, the lotion triggers a viral illness which makes coral explode, leaving just a bleached skeleton. With rising visitor numbers, ever more damage is being done; so, as matters stand, the Caribbean's reefs face being literally loved to death.

DESERT ISLES—CARIBBEAN ISLANDS WITHOUT PEOPLE

Inhabited Islands } **2%**

Uninhabited Islands } **98%**

FOODIE. The word 'cannibal' came from '*Karibna*', the name the Caribs used for themselves, after Christopher Columbus fist observed the practice in the West Indies.[5] Carib cannibalism was for ritual rather than dietary reasons. For example, men would chew on a mouthful of flesh from a brave warrior killed in battle so as to absorb his fighting prowess.

[5] *An explorer who learned the hard way was de Verrazzano, discoverer of New York harbour, who was eaten in 1528.*

THOUGHTFUL. St. Lucia has the world's highest number of Nobel Prize-winners per capita.

Includes: Antigua & Barbuda, Dominica, Grenada, St. Kitts & Nevis, St. Lucia and St. Vincent & the Grenadines. *See separate entries for Barbados and Trinidad & Tobago.*

DISTRESS SIGNAL. The first recorded use of the skull and cross-bones motif was by French pirates in 1687. Their flag had a red background and may have been ironically nicknamed the '*joli rouge*' ('pretty red'). In any event, it is widely assumed that, mangled by the mouths of English pirates, the phrase later mutated into the familiar Jolly Roger. Since WWII, British submarines have been permitted to fly a Jolly Roger on their successful return to port after a kill.

THE PIRATE CODE. The Jolly Roger was the generic term for any pirate flag (not just the classic skull and cross-bones). Most pirates had a personal design, but they normally sailed under false colours or none. Only when prey was in range would a black Jolly Roger be hoisted. This was the signal to surrender: if the quarry failed to cooperate, the Roger would then be lowered and the red 'bloody' flag hoisted in its place; its meaning was explicit—henceforth expect no quarter.

THE REAL PIRATES OF THE CARIBBEAN AND THEIR PERSONAL FLAGS

LONG BEN (HENRY EVERY). One of the few to escape the noose, Every was also a slaver—with a twist: after he bought his slaves he enslaved their sellers too.

EMMANUEL WYNNE. A French pirate who preyed on English and Spanish merchantmen across the Caribbean. The hourglass on his flag warned time for surrender was short.

BLACKBEARD (EDWARD TEACH). The pirate archetype: in battle, Teach turned himself into a diabolical figure by plaiting burning cannon fuses into his huge beard.

BLACK BART (JOHN ROBERTS). Earning a bit part in *Treasure Island*, the tea-drinking Black Bart was the most successful pirate of all time capturing over 470 vessels.

CALICO JACK (JOHN RACKHAM). Captain and lover of the piratess Anne Bonny. After Jack was hanged, his tarred body was left in a cage on a sand bar off Port Royal.

CAPTAIN THOMAS (STEDE BONNET). A rich landowner, Bonnet reputedly only took up piracy to escape his wife. His start may have been odd, but not his end. Hanged.

♦ · **GSR**: n/a · **WHS**: Dominica: Morne Trois Pitons (rainforest and boiling lake) □ St. Kitts & Nevis: Brimstone Hill (fortress) □ St. Lucia: Pitons (tropical forest)

— CENTRAL AFRICAN REPUBLIC ● KÖDÖRÖSÊSE TÎ BÊAFRÎKA —

'Of all the African leaders, I was the greatest. Why?
Because I was the emperor. One step below me was the
King of Morocco. Then came all the others, simple presidents.'

—'Emperor' Bokassa, ruler of the Central African 'Empire' proclaimed from 1976–79

Quiz Time: Which of these five African colonies was the Central African Republic ('CAR') known as before independence:

A Bechuanaland; B Dahomey; C Rio de Oro; D Ubangi-Shari; E Upper Volta?

Bonus marks for correctly identifying all five modern states (*answers below*).

EMPEROR'S NEW CLOTHES. After Colonel Bokassa seized power in 1966, he inaugurated two orchestras and decreed that anyone aged between 18 and 55 would face imprisonment unless they could prove they had a job. This, however, was only a foretaste of the poisonous mix of madness, venality and squander that was to follow. Crowning himself emperor in 1977, Bokassa blew 30% of the nation's budget on a two-day coronation to which not a single foreign leader could be induced to come. But the final straw came in 1979, during national protests after he passed a law forcing all schoolchildren to buy new school shirts.[2] Seeing his Rolls Royce passing by, some children started throwing stones and Bokassa had his imperial guard round up any they could catch. By the next day, 100 children were dead—including, it later transpired, five that Bokassa had personally beaten to death with his ebony walking stick. Even without the unproven allegations that he had also eaten several, it was enough to repulse the world. Five months later, French paratroopers flew in overnight and Bokassa was gone.

[2] *The shirts in question bore Bokassa's portrait, were exclusively made at a factory owned by one of his wives and cost $150 each.*

TOP FIVE COUNTDOWN: MEGALOMANIAC MONIKERS

Ruler	Official Title
5. **Mobutu Sese Seko** (Congo DR)	*The All-Powerful Warrior Who, Because of His Endurance and Inflexible Will to Win, Will Go from Conquest to Conquest Leaving Fire in His Wake.*
4. **Idi Amin Dada** (Uganda)	*His Excellency President for Life, Field Marshal Al Hadji Doctor Idi Amin Dada, VC, DSO, MC, Lord of All the Beasts of the Earth and Fishes of the Sea, and Conqueror of the British Empire in Africa in General and Uganda in Particular.*
3. **Jean-Bédél Bokassa** (CAR)	*His Imperial Majesty Bokassa I, Emperor of Central Africa by the will of the Central African people, held dear in the bosom of the national political party, the Movement for the Social Evolution of Black Africa.*
2. **Haile Selassie** (Ethiopia)	*His Imperial Majesty Haile Selassie I, King of Kings, Lord of Lords, Conquering Lion of the Tribe of Judah, and Elect of God.*
1. **Kim Il Sung** (N. Korea)	*Eternal President.* (The clear, death-defying winner since Kim expired four years before he took the title.)

JAIL SPELL. Forty per cent of all criminal prosecutions in the CAR are for sorcery or witchcraft. Judges acknowledge there is usually little evidence in such cases, but defendants often plead guilty to avoid the lynch mob outside the door. For those who choose to tough it out, one seasoned defence lawyer advises two things: try not to look shifty, and don't cast any spells while in court.

HEART OF DARKNESS. The CAR has the world's lowest level of light pollution—helped, in part, by the Dzanga-Sangha rainforest, sprawling over the borders with Congo-Brazzaville and Cameroon, which is thought to hold some of the last significant tracts of land that remain to be explored.[1]

[1] *Others areas include isolated parts of Antarctica, Greenland, Amazonia, New Guinea and Western Siberia.*

Answers: A Botswana; B Benin; C Western Sahara (occupied by Morocco); D CAR; E Burkina Faso.

♥ · **GSR:** 159 · **WHS:** Manovo-Gounda St. Floris (wildlife) · **ICH:** Aka Polyphonic Singing

CHAD • TCHAD

'The Dead Heart of Africa.'

—Nickname for Chad, punning on both its landlocked location in the centre of the continent and the desolation of the Sahara that takes up most of its territory. Sadly, a third prong can be added, as the country has seen permanent war and unrest since independence from France in 1960.

TOYOTA WAR (1986–87). Not many motor manufacturers get a war named after them, but Toyota earned this accolade after its pick-up trucks played a decisive role in enabling the rag-tag Chadians to rout the Libyan Army and bring to an end its 15-year occupation of northern Chad. The breakthrough came after the Chadians found they could drive the Toyotas straight through the Libyan minefields without setting off the mines—so long as they kept moving fast enough. (Don't try this at home, but 60 mph should work.)

ENVIRONMENTAL HEADACHE. The dustiest place on earth is almost certainly central Chad's Bodélé depression. Trapped in a natural wind tunnel formed by flanking mountain ranges, it's blasted by dust storms on 100 days each year, *Aspergillus* sucking 700,000 tonnes of dust daily into the atmosphere. Lofted as far as the eastern USA, the Bodélé dust is far from innocuous. The region is a dried-out lakebed, and the grains come loaded with spores of the Aspergillus fungus. Fully viable after their airborne journey, these can grow into fungal balls inside the lungs of those who breathe them in, occasionally going on to invade the brain, where they form abscesses that are almost always fatal.

FLAG OF INCONVENIENCE. In the admittedly unlikely event that Chad and Romania were ever to hold a summit, protocol could be dicey since both states share a single flag. But while Chad's proud blue, yellow and red has flown over N'Djamena since independence, Romania only adopted its own identical tricolour in 1989. Strangely, nobody in Chad seemed to notice—even when the Romanians registered the worldwide copyright in 1997. So while Chad has history on its side, Romania can rely on the law.

FAMOUS FOR 15 MINUTES

Chad's greatest moment in history came in the 2000 US presidential election, when chad-counting briefly became a global obsession. Sadly, it transpires the little bits of paper punched from Florida ballot slips have nothing to do with the African nation,[1] but may derive from a name for 'riverbed gravel' in Scottish dialect. In any event, in case of future ballot duty, the four degrees of chad are as follows:

Pregnant .... *indentions only*
Tri-chad ...... *attached 3 corners*
Swinging ..... *attached 2 corners*
Hanging .... *attached 1 corner*

[1] *Chad takes its name from Lake Chad, which in turn comes from the Arabic* tsad *meaning 'lake' (making Lake Chad 'Lake Lake').*

ON THE CAMELOPARD.[2] Chad marks the northern limit of the giraffe. It's known, of course, for its extraordinary neck, but getting this evolutionary adaptation to work hasn't been easy. In order to lift blood 20 feet into the air, the giraffe has grown a 10-kg heart operating at double the blood pressure of other mammals and pumping 20 gallons a minute. But, as a result, it has also had to evolve built-in compression stockings to stop its legs from bursting and a special pressure regulator (known as a rete mirabile) to prevent the veins in its head from exploding when it stoops to drink. There is, however, one fringe benefit from the extreme height: when baby giraffes are born, they drop 6 feet on to their heads—a shock that reliably kick-starts the newborns into breathing.

[2] *The commonest name for a giraffe until the 19th century, coming from the fancied resemblance to the head of a camel and spots of a leopard.*

♥ · **GSR:** 177 · **WHS:** none

———————— CHILE ————————

'You can cut all the flowers, but you can't keep spring from coming.'

—Pablo Neruda, Nobel Prize Laureate for Literature and Chilean presidential candidate on behalf of the
Communist Party, who died 12 days after the 1973 coup that brought General Pinochet to power

CHILE[1] — THE LONG AND THIN OF IT

LORD OF THE WINGS. Boasting the biggest wing area of any bird, the Andean condor can soar majestically for 30 minutes between wingbeats. Less majestic is its habit of dribbling urine on to its legs to cool itself down with the evaporating liquid. (Fridges work in the same way, but without the urine.)

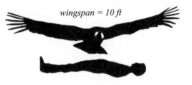

wingspan = 10 ft

DODO DOODLES. The early Easter Islanders invented their own unique script. Known as Rongorongo, it became extinct after Peruvian slave-raiders abducted the last person who could read it. At present, Rongorongo is undecipherable; but it is known that alternate lines were written upside down and back to front.

Rongorongo makes (right) you turn the page round after you finish every line.

SANTIAGO: *'I'm not a dictator. It's just that I have a grumpy face.'*

—Augusto Pinochet. During his rule from 1973 to 1990, 2,279 Chileans were killed by the state
for political reasons, including 17 primary schoolchildren and 48 secondary schoolchildren.

ONLY ME. Isla Robinson Crusoe is the island on which Alexander Selkirk was marooned in 1704 after falling out with his captain. Selkirk's life there alone, until his rescue four years later, inspired Daniel Defoe's 1719 novel—whence, since 1966, the island's name.

MOBY. Known as 'Mocha Dick' after Mocha Island, the real Moby Dick was a giant albino sperm whale that killed up to 30 whalers during the 1830s.

PYRO POWDER. Home of El Teniente, the world's largest mine with 1,500 miles of tunnels, Chile is the main global source of copper. Most of the metal becomes wiring and piping, but its most valuable application is to put the blue into the flash of fireworks. Adding other metals gives a rainbow of colour:

PYROTECHNIC PALETTE

Green	Barium	Silver	Aluminium
Orange	Sodium	White	Magnesium
Red	Strontium	Glitter	Antimony

HOT POTATO. There's perhaps no more heated dispute in greengrocering,[2] but the latest DNA study suggests 99% of the world's cultivated potato varieties originate from Chiloé Island, where artisan tubers, such as the blue, remain highly sought after.

[2] *Peru presses a forceful claim for a source north of Lake Titicaca, while Bolivia also claims the potato as its own.*

ROUNDING THE OVEN. Cape Horn is named after the Dutch port of Hoorn. Not a problem in English, but in the local Spanish it literally means 'Cape of Ovens'.

FROZEN OUT. Chile's sub-polar Magellan Forest is made up of refugee Antarctic tree species displaced after the ice sheets took over. As recently as three million years ago, a similar forest grew to within 400 miles of the South Pole.

[1] *By a linguistic fluke, 'Chile' may actually mean 'chilly': Chilean schoolchildren are taught that the name of their country comes either from the trilling call of a local blackbird or from the Aymara Indian word tchili—meaning 'snow'.*

2,500 miles

◆◆ **GSR**: 33 · **WHS**: Chiloé (churches) □ Humberstone and Sta. Laura Saltpeter Works (ghost towns)
Rapa Nui (Easter Island) □ Sewell (mining town) □ Valparaíso (cityscape)· **IHC**: Aymara (culture)

————— CHINA ● 中国 —————

'It is the empty space that makes the bowl useful.'

—Lao-tzu, *Tao Te Ching* (c. 400 BCE)

STRENGTH
Over the last 40 years, China's economy has grown 1,500% faster than that of the US.

WEAKNESS
Up to 760,000 Chinese die from environmental pollution every year.

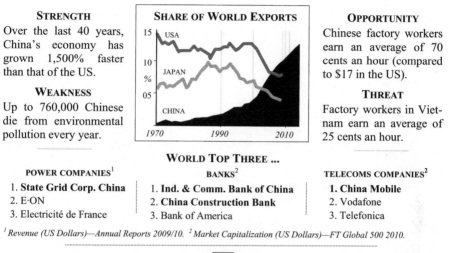

SHARE OF WORLD EXPORTS

OPPORTUNITY
Chinese factory workers earn an average of 70 cents an hour (compared to $17 in the US).

THREAT
Factory workers in Vietnam earn an average of 25 cents an hour.

WORLD TOP THREE ...

POWER COMPANIES[1]
1. **State Grid Corp. China**
2. E·ON
3. Electricité de France

BANKS[2]
1. **Ind. & Comm. Bank of China**
2. **China Construction Bank**
3. Bank of America

TELECOMS COMPANIES[2]
1. **China Mobile**
2. Vodafone
3. Telefonica

[1] *Revenue (US Dollars)—Annual Reports 2009/10.* [2] *Market Capitalization (US Dollars)—FT Global 500 2010.*

Beijing—Tiananmen Square: *Enlarged by Mao Zedong specifically to make it the largest city square in the world, and then again in 1976 for his mausoleum, it can hold 600,000 people. East and west sides are flanked by China's National Museum and the Great Hall of the People (Parliament) respectively, while on its northern edge stands the 8,707-room Forbidden Palace (home to China's emperors from the Ming dynasty onwards), entered through the monumental Gate of Heavenly Peace. Fixed to the gate, and visible throughout the square, is Mao's iconic 15-ft-high portrait—marking the spot where, on 1 October 1949, he proclaimed the People's Republic of China into existence.*

PIN-UP. From 1966 to 1969, China produced 5bn Mao badges in 50,000 different designs (but all with him looking left). Worn by 90% of Chinese, zealots pinned theirs through their skin as a sign of extra loyalty. Since badges were sold at a 50% loss, they grew to be a real strain on the economy. Finally, Mao himself called a halt, but for more material considerations: the aluminium consumed could have made 37,000 MiG fighters.

MING THE MERCILESS. The founder of the Ming dynasty, Emperor Hongwu, is remembered as China's most brutal and paranoid tyrant. If summoned by the emperor, civil servants got into the habit of going home to say their goodbyes to their families first. When Minister Qian Tang counselled the emperor against a book-burning edict, he took his own coffin to the audience, and, when he had finished, climbed in—saying it would be an honour to die for Confucius.

SKIN FLIX. Blue movies are unknown in China—the term is 'yellow films'. (But all pornography has been banned since 2008, with film studios ordered to 'correct wrong deeds'.)

RED LIGHT. Doctors' fees during the Zhou dynasty (c. 1000 BCE) were set by their personal cure rates over the previous year and their clinics had to put up a red lantern for every patient that died.

DIG IT. The world's biggest online game is *Happy Farm*. Each day, 23m Chinese log on to their own virtual allotments—though the biggest buzz is said to be stealing next-door's vegetables.

SHENG XIAO	**生肖**

SIGNOLOGY. The Chinese 12-year cycle of the Sheng Xiao (literally 'birth year resemblance') has been used for divination for longer than records have been kept. As in the Western horoscope, the sign—or animal—under which you are born is supposed to shape your character. However, the yearly cycle is only a starting point; also important are the monthly and two-hourly cycles—giving the 'inner' and 'secret' animals respectively—and the 10 'Heavenly Stems', allowing a total of 8,640 possible personality types altogether.

RAT: *'I rule'*

Tenacious · Shrewd
Envious · Scheming
1936–48–60–72–84–
1996–2008–2020

HORSE: *'I control'*

Cheerful · Astute
Fickle · Rude
1930–42–54–66–78–
1990–2002–2014

OX: *'I persevere'*

Reliable · Methodical
Stubborn · Blinkered
1937–49–61–73–85–
1997–2009–2021

GOAT: *'I depend'*

Righteous · Peaceful
Gloomy · Weak
1931–43–55–67–79–
1991–2003–2015

TIGER: *'I win'*

Powerful · Generous
Reckless · Moody
1938–50–62–74–86–
1998–2010–2022

MONKEY: *'I jest'*

Inventive · Artistic
Suspicious · Vain
1932–44–56–68–80–
1992–2004–2016

RABBIT: *'I retreat'*

Cautious · Lucky
Superficial · Aloof
1939–51–63–75–87–
1999–2011–2023

ROOSTER: *'I know'*

Practical · Alert
Puritanical · Critical
1933–45–57–69–81–
1993–2005–2017

DRAGON: *'I reign'*

Proud · Decisive
Arrogant · Brash
1928–40–52–64–76–
1988–2000–2012

DOG: *'I worry'*

Sociable · Loyal
Quarrelsome · Lazy
1934–46–58–70–82–
1994–2006–2018

SNAKE: *'I think'*

Wise · Sensual
Possessive · Cold
1929–41–53–65–77–
1989–2001–2013

PIG: *'I preserve'*

Sincere · Patient
Self-indulgent · Naive
1935–47–59–71–83–
1995–2007–2019

DEATH WISH. The man behind the Terracotta Army and Great Wall of China, Emperor Qin Shi Huang Di, could have almost anything that he wanted. As the first ruler to unify China[1], he enjoyed everything the 3rd century BCE could offer—ancient historians say a 28-mile covered walkway linked his palace to the summit of a sacred mountain, while its doors were guarded by magnetic metal detectors. However, it was the one thing he couldn't have that killed him. As he grew old, the Emperor sent out hundreds of people to search for the elixir of life, but to no avail, and so instead he turned to mercury pills prescribed by his doctors for immortality—which, needless to say, soon poisoned him.

[1] *Shi Huang Di's regnal name, Qin (pronounced 'Chin'), is the probable origin of the word 'China'.*

PUNISHMENT—WORLD'S MOST CAPITALIST STATES[2]

CHINA[3] (1,700)
R.O.W (79)
USA (32)
IRAN (388)
S. ARABIA (69)
IRAQ (120)

[2] *Executions (2009, except China—2008 (estd.)).* [3]*China has 68 capital offences including fossil-smuggling, dyke-breaching, pimping and credit card fraud. Time from sentencing to death can be as low as 14 minutes.*

RETREAD. As the new workshop of the world, what can be made in China seems limited only by the imagination—which may be inventive indeed. Retailing for as little as $30, the 'Jade Lady Membrane Man-Made Hymen' is made from elastic and comes pre-loaded with fake blood. Inserted 30 minutes before intercourse, the device will, according to the instructions, create a seamless illusion of virginity 'when accompanied by moans of pain'.

LAUGH AND A QUARTER OF THE WORLD LAUGHS WITH YOU—A CHINESE JOKE TASTER

A father wrote out a character and taught it to his small son. The next day, when the father was mopping the floor, he traced out the character with the mop and asked his son to read it. The child couldn't. 'But this is the character I taught you yesterday,' the father remonstrated. 'It's grown much bigger overnight,' answered the son, astonished.

TABLE CHINA

'Give a dog a tasty name and eat him.'

CARDINAL POINTS OF THE CHINESE KITCHEN:

THE FOUR CLASSIC CUISINES

Shandong (N)......pungent and earthy
Garlic, vinegar, soy, shark's fin; fry, braise

Guangdong (S)......fresh and balanced
Oyster sauce, seafood, snake; stir-fry, steam

Jiangsu (E)........tender and seasonal
Ginger, bamboo, carp; soups, sweet and sour

Sichuan (W)..........spicy and exotic
Chilli, bean paste, bear paw; flash-fry, pickle

'Enough food and a pipe full of tobacco makes you equal to the Immortals.'

Snapshot. *Instead of 'Cheese!', it's 'Aubergine!' all round when posing for photos in China. The name of the vegetable is* qiézi *in Chinese—pronounced 'chee-eh-dze'.*

Cat Food. *After a restaurant in Hailin was raided by police in 2005 for serving stir-fried tiger, the owner admitted that the dish was in fact strips of donkey meat soused in tiger urine from the nearby zoo—which gave its 'special' flavour.*

BEIJING ●

SHANGHAI

GUANGZHOU (CANTON)

Fujian's **Iron Goddess of Mercy Tea** *sells for $3,200 per kilo, making it the world's dearest cuppa.*

The Great Wall of China *was built with sauerkraut—the dish was invented 2,200 years ago to provide cheap and long-lived food for the vast army of labourers; it was probably exported to Europe 1,400 years later in the rations of Genghis Khan's army.*

Stretching It Out. *After turning 60, the Chinese traditionally eat a bowl of noodles for breakfast on each birthday. It's bad luck to cut the noodles, as long noodles symbolize a long life.*

Sachong *(sandworm) is a dish unique to Beihai. When deep-fried, the 6-inch worms are said to taste like fried onion rings with a chewy middle.*

Hungry Ghosts

From 108 BCE *to 1911* CE, *there were 1,828 famines somewhere in the Chinese Empire—almost one per year. The world's most deadly famine struck China from 1958 to 1961. Known officially as the 'Three Years of Natural Disaster' and to the rest of world as the 'Great Chinese Famine', it killed 36 million, largely due to Mao's collectivization of agriculture in his 'Great Leap Forward'.*

'Govern a family as you would cook a small fish.' (Very gently.)

'If you would be happy for a week, take a wife; if you would be happy for a month, kill a pig; but if you would be happy all your life, plant a garden.'

THE FORCE BE WITH YOU

At its plainest, the *yin-yang* symbol (Taijitu or 'Diagram of Ultimate Power') indicates how equal and opposite polarities come together to make up the whole (shown by the circle). The two teardrop segments symbolize flux, while the inner dots preview how one polarity transforms into the other. In Taoism, to which the Taijitu is most linked, the 'whole' is the all-pervading Tao, while the black (*yin*) and white (*yang*) halves represent the primordial feminine and masculine energies.

CONFUCIUS SAY

人之初 .... *People at birth*
性本善 .... *Are naturally good.*
性相近 ... *Their natures are alike,*
習相遠 .... *But their habits vary.*

From the 13th century until the Cultural Revolution, Chinese children were brought up with the *Three Character Classic* as their first proper book. Written in easy-to-remember character triplets, it taught Chinese vocabulary and grammar. But it also gave a first grounding in Confucianist thought, with the very first four triplets (*above*) stating the basic premise of Confucianism with admirable succinctness.

WHAT HAVE THE CHINESE EVER DONE FOR US?

TOOTHBRUSHES

While people have been chewing twigs for millennia, the first properly recognizable toothbrush—made from horse-tail hairs set in an ox-bone handle—was recorded from China in 1223. At the time, Europeans were using rags dipped in salt and soot.

GWEILO GAFFES. When Coca-Cola was first imported into China in 1928, it was sold locally as 'Ko-Ka-Ko-La', which, in at least one region, meant 'Bite the wax tadpole'. Within months, however, the corporation's marketing department imposed the current 'Ko-Kou-Ko-Le', translated as 'Joy to the mouth'. Pepsi (rendered as 'Hundred ways to luck') had troubles of its own when the slogan 'Come alive with the Pepsi Generation!' was reputedly taken to claim 'Brings ancestors back from the dead!'

CHINESE CHESTNUTS. *Play a harp before a cow · He who does not regularly put on clean socks will never get used to circus life · He who can predict winning numbers should not set off fire crackers.*

TOILET PAPER

A sneering reference from a visiting Muslim shows the Chinese were using toilet paper (instead of water) by 851 CE. In Europe, people grabbed whatever came to hand—Rabelais once suggested the ultimate in performance was the neck of a goose.

BURSTING POINT. In the peak Spring Festival holiday season, Chinese trains can get so crowded travellers stand like sardines even in the toilets. Given that journeys may last 24 hours or more, this presents a problem solved by many with steely stamina but by others through lateral thinking, unmasked by a 50% surge in sales of adult nappies.

MILK OF HUMAN KINDNESS. Shih-tzu 'lion dogs' used to be reserved for royalty, and were so prized each would be given a human wet nurse.

EXAMINATIONS

China's imperial examinations for civil service entry began in 605 CE and were set for the next 1,300 years. Only in 1806 did a Western civil service (Britain's) follow China's lead, after which exams were soon adopted in education generally.

MANDARIN DUCK. Entering the Chinese imperial examinations was a serious business. Individual exams could last 72 hours, spent closeted in a spartan exam cell, while in the Tang dynasty, the pass rate was only 2%. But for those that succeeded, the badge of one of the nine ranks of mandarin (*below*) awaited, and with it, a life of affluence and prestige.

Rank 1 (Highest) .... Crane
Rank 2 .... Golden Pheasant
Rank 3 ....…..... Peacock
Rank .... Wild Goose
Rank 5 ....Silver Pheasant
Rank 6 .... Egret
Rank 7 .... Mandarin Duck
Rank 8 ....…............... Quail
Rank 9 ..... Paradise Flycatcher

What Might Have Been—Or the Shape of Things to Come?

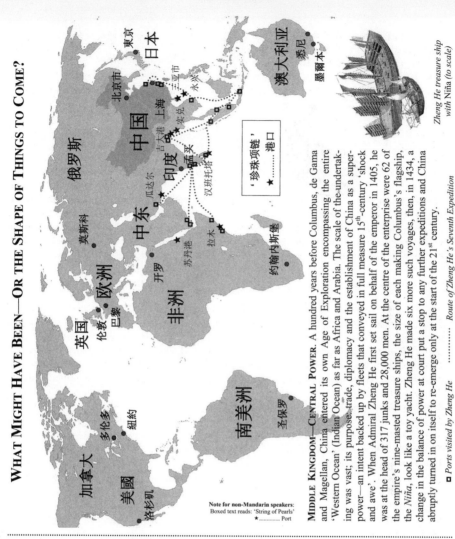

東京　日本

北京市　上海

中国　印度　孟买

俄罗斯

澳大利亚　悉尼　墨爾本

莫斯科　中东

欧洲　开罗　非洲　约翰内斯堡

英國　伦敦　巴黎

加拿大　多伦多　紐約　美國　洛杉矶　南美洲　圣保罗

瓜达尔　实兑　吉大港　汉班托塔　苏丹港　拉木

'珍珠项链'……港口

Zheng He treasure ship
with Niña (to scale)

Note for non-Mandarin speakers:
Boxed text reads: 'String of Pearls'
★ .... Port

□ *Ports visited by Zheng He*
········· *Route of Zheng He's Seventh Expedition*

MIDDLE KINGDOM—CENTRAL POWER. A hundred years before Columbus, de Gama and Magellan, China entered its own Age of Exploration encompassing the entire 'Western Ocean' (Indian Ocean) as far as Africa and Arabia. The scale of the undertaking was vast; its purpose trade, diplomacy and the establishment of China as a super-power—an intent backed up by fleets that conveyed in full measure 15th-century 'shock and awe.' When Admiral Zheng He first set sail on behalf of the emperor in 1405, he was at the head of 317 junks and 28,000 men. At the centre of the enterprise were 62 of the empire's nine-masted treasure ships, the size of each making Columbus's flagship, the *Niña*, look like a toy yacht. Zheng He made six more such voyages, then, in 1434, a change in the balance of power at court put a stop to any further expeditions and China abruptly turned in on itself to re-emerge only at the start of the 21st century.

♣ · **GSR**: 2 · **WHS**: Beijing (x3) (palaces/gardens/temple) □ Chengde (palaces) □ China Danxia (valleys) □ Datong (grottoes) □ Dazu (cliff art) □ Dengfeng (temples) □ Fujian (roundhouses) □ Great Wall of China □ Hangzhou (landscape) □ Huanglong (landscape) □ Huanren (Koguryo tombs) Huangshan (mountain) □ Jiuzhaigou Valley (landscape) □ Kaiping (towers) □ Leshan (Giant Buddha) Lhasa (palace) □ Lijiang (townscape) □ Longmen (grottoes) □ Lushan (sacred mountain) □ Ming and Qing Tombs □ Mogao (cave art) □ Mt. Qingcheng (temples) □ Mt. Wutai (monasteries) □ Mt. Wuyi (gorges and temples) □ Ping Yao (museum city) □ Qufu (temple) □ Sanqingshan (rock pillars) Sichuan Panda Sanctuaries □ South China Karst □ Suzhou (gardens) □ Taishan (sacred mountain) Wudang (architecture) □ Wulingyuan (sandstone pillars) □ Xian (Terracotta Army) □ Xidi and Hongcun (vernacular villages) □ Yin Xu (Bronze Age site) □ Yunnan (gorges and mountains) □ Zhoukoudian (human fossils) · **ICH**: Acupuncture □ Chinese Block Printing □ Chinese Calligraphy □ Chinese Junks Chinese Paper Cutting □ Chinese Seal Engraving □ Chinese Sericulture □ Chinese Timber Buildings Dragon Boat Festival □ Farmer's Dance (Korean) □ Gesar Epic (storytelling) □ Grand Song of the Dong □ Guqin (music) □ Hua'er (songs) □ Khoomei (Mongolian singing) □ Kun Qu Opera □ Li Textiles □ Longquan Celadonware □ Manas (Kirghiz singing) □ Mazu (ceremonies) □ Meshrep (Uyghur gathering) □ Movable-Type Printing □ Nanjing Yunjin Brocade □ Nanyin (music) □ Peking Opera Qiang New Year □ Regong (Buddhist art) □ Tibetan Opera □ Urtiin Duu (Mongolian singing) □ Uyghur Muqam (dance) □ Wooden Bridges □ Xi'an Wind and Percussion □ Xuan Paper □ Yueju Opera

—— HONG KONG ● 香港 * MACAU ● 澳门 ——
CHINESE SPECIAL ADMINISTRATIVE REGIONS
'One country; two systems.'

—Deng Xiaoping (speaking to Margaret Thatcher, 1982)

Hong Kong Island skyline with some of the city's 7,682 high-rise buildings.

I'M QUICKEST. An IQ averaging 118[1] makes Hong Kongers, collectively, the smartest people on the planet.

[1] *Culturally neutral tests, normalized to IQ = 100 for US.*

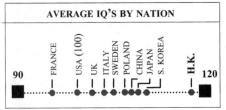

AVERAGE IQ'S BY NATION

90 · FRANCE · USA (100) · UK · ITALY · SWEDEN · POLAND · CHINA · JAPAN · S. KOREA · H.K. · 120

BATTERY FARMS. Ap Lei Chau is the planet's most densely populated island. Its 87,000 people squeeze into half a square mile. But this pales in comparison with the Kowloon Walled City (bulldozed in 1993), whose 33,000 people somehow existed in six acres—a 2ft by 3ft floor-level footprint each. Before it was pulled down, a fully equipped caving team went in to check through its empty passages and shafts.

SPACE PER PERSON COMPARED TO STANDARD TENNIS COURT

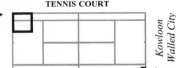

Ap Lei Island

Kowloon Walled City

UPWARDLY MOBILE. Home to more skyscrapers than New York and Chicago combined, Hong Kong is the most vertical city on Earth. Its tallest building, the ICC, reaches up to floor 118. But that's not to say it has 118 storeys. Like in much of East Asia, many buildings skip all floors ending in '4'. Due to its close links to the West, buildings in Hong Kong tend to skip '13' as well. So the ICC's floor 118 is actually its 106th storey. It's not just architecture that's affected by the curse of four. Consumer giants, including Nokia and Canon, often choose to move straight from '3' to '5' when numbering their global brands. The reason for all this excitement lies in phonics: in pinyin Chinese, 'four' (四, 'sì') sounds just like 'death' ('sǐ').

SPOTLIGHT ON MACAU

■ ROADHOG. Macau has the world's densest road network—12% of its total land area has been buried under tarmac.

■ CHIPPING IN. The Macau Venetian is the world's largest casino—it's half as big again as the Pentagon, and has 800 tables. Macau takes more money in bets than the entire Las Vegas strip.

SPIKY. Triads—Hong Kong's organized crime syndicates—are named for their triangle symbols. Current estimates suggest they have 100,000 members, down from 300,000 in their 1950s heyday.

ANATOMY OF A TRIAD

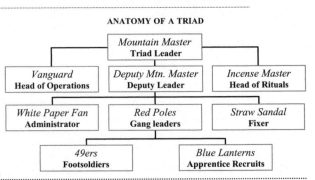

Mountain Master
Triad Leader

Vanguard
Head of Operations

Deputy Mtn. Master
Deputy Leader

Incense Master
Head of Rituals

White Paper Fan
Administrator

Red Poles
Gang leaders

Straw Sandal
Fixer

49ers
Footsoldiers

Blue Lanterns
Apprentice Recruits

♣ · **GSR**: 14 (Hong Kong) · **WHS**: Macau (cityscape)

COLOMBIA

'There is always something left to love.'

—Gabriel García Márquez (*One Hundred Years of Solitude*)

Muisca votive offering (gold)

GOLDEN HELLO. In Colombia, those seeking El Dorado have an easy time—Bogotá's international airport goes by the name. However, adventurers searching for the city of legend are, like explorers over the past 400 years, much less likely to be satisfied. Historically, El Dorado (literally 'the Golden One') was a person, not a place at all. To be specific, the king of the pre-Colombian Muisca people periodically became 'El Dorado' when he was coated from head to toe in gold dust and then rafted into the middle of Lake Guatavita to drop precious offerings into the water. However, when garbled reports reached the ears of the avaricious conquistadores, it was enough to convince them that, somewhere deep in the South American interior, there had to be a city of gold—thereby setting off quests that continue sporadically today. But while dreamers scoured the jungles in vain, within 50 years of the Spanish conquest more practical men began attempts to drain the Muisca's sacred lake. Their various efforts have not been total failures (among other things, an emerald as big as a hen's egg has been recovered), but each has been in some way thwarted, and most of whatever is on the lakebed still lies there today.

Living high in the Colombian Andes, the northern pudu is thought to be the world's smallest deer: full-grown adults can be as little as 13 inches tall and may weigh just 7 lbs.

GREEN WITH ENVY. Eighty per cent of the world's top-grade 'true'[1] emeralds are mined from three small areas in Colombia.

[1] *In the 1960s, American gem dealers relabelled vanadium beryl from Brazil as 'emerald' (so increasing the value of their holdings by 1,000%). However, British and European dealers have declined to recognize this change.*

ANATOMY OF A NARCO-STATE[2]

- Colombia's murder rate in 2002 was 32,000 deaths per year (or 88 murders every day).
- Colombia's kidnapping rate in 2000 was 3,700 abductions per year (or 10 kidnaps every day).

- At their peak, in the 1980s and 1990s, Colombia's drug cartels earned $110m every day.
- Three-quarters of the world's cocaine is still processed in Colombia.

Ocean-going narco-submarines are an increasingly important means of smuggling cocaine from Colombia into the USA, with around 60 setting out per year. Despite costing $1.5m each, they are scuttled on arrival—an affordable practice as a typical 10-ton cargo has a street value of $400m.

When the head of the Medellin Cartel, Pablo Escobar, decided to go into politics in 1986, his unusual opening gambit was to offer to personally pay off Colombia's national debt of $11 billion.[3] Despite this, Escobar was barred.

[3] *In 1989, he was listed by Forbes as the world's 7th richest man (worth $29bn).*

During the 1990s, the Cali Cartel kept 5,000 taxi drivers on its payroll, and also bugged all phone calls in and out of the US embassy. In Marsella, they killed so many people that the local authority was bankrupted by the cost of autopsies.

In 1985, M-19 guerrillas took the Supreme Court hostage and demanded it try Colombia's president. In an ensuing fire-fight, 11 out of the 25 top judges were killed.

Colombia's most powerful current drugs syndicate is thought to be the Norte del Valle Cartel. Past bosses have included 'Overall Man', 'Soap' and 'Lollipop'; the present one may be 'The Iguana', '06', 'Shirt Man' or 'Crazy Legs'.

[2] *Colombia may now have turned the corner: murders are down 50%, the guerrillas weakened and many cartels busted.*

♦ · **GSR**: 42 · **WHS**: Cartagena (historic city) □ Coffee Landscape □ Los Katíos (wildlife) □ Malpelo (marine life) □ San Agustín (statues) □ Santa Cruz de Mompox (townscape) □ Tierradentro (burial chambers) · **ICH**: Barranquilla Carnival □ Marimba Music □ Palenque de San Basilio (walled village) Popayán Processions □ Negros y Blancos Carnival □ Wayuu Pütchipü'üi (traditional judges)

————— COMOROS • KOMORI —————

'The Islands of the Moon.'

—Original Arabic name (Juzur al-Qamr)

PECULIAR PONGS. The Comoros supplies 80% of the world's ylang-ylang, an essential oil harvested from the flowers of a tropical tree. Described as having 'notes of rubber and custard', ylang-ylang oil is a key ingredient in Chanel No. 5, and an example of the exotic and unexpected ingredients sought out by top *parfumeurs* when composing some of the world's most exclusive perfumes.

WHIFFS OF THE WORLD—THE SECRET SMELLS BEHIND FAMOUS SCENTS			
Ingredient	*Source*	*Aroma*	*Notes*
Ylang-ylang	tropical flowers	rich, deep	70,000 flowers needed for 1 litre of top-grade oil
Aloeswood	rotten wood	dignified, ethereal	a mould infection—best are centuries old
Ambergris	whale faeces	sweet, earthy	must mature for months/years like fine wine
Hyraceum	hyrax urine	animal, fermented	harvested in petrified form, aka 'Africa Stone'
Tonka	tropical beans	vanilla, grassy	high doses lethal, derivatives used in rat poison

CLOUD-COUP-COUP-LAND. The Comoros have had an interesting history since independence in 1975. On top of the foreign interventions, civil conflicts, air disasters and the chief island's misfortune to be one of the world's largest active volcanoes sitting slap in the cyclone belt, they are best known as the kings of the modern coup—clocking up 21[1] in 35 years. Along the way, they have also seen a president reportedly blown up in his bed by an anti-tank missile, a Maoist revolution, al-Qaeda terrorists, gun-runners, sanction-busters and spies. Things got so bad that in 1997 the second largest island applied to France to be recolonized. (The request was denied.)

[1] *Four of these were by the same exceptionally persistent Frenchman, Bob Denard, who gave up his career as a washing-machine demonstrator to become France's leading mercenary. Rumoured to have had tacit government backing, he took part in over 20 coups and wars across Africa and the Middle East from 1961 to 1995. It wasn't all glamour though—in 1968, he launched an invasion of Congo with 100 men on bicycles.*

BUMPY JOURNEY—POST-INDEPENDENCE ROAD MAP

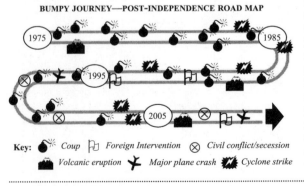

Key: ● *Coup* ⌂ *Foreign Intervention* ⊗ *Civil conflict/secession* ▲ *Volcanic eruption* ✈ *Major plane crash* ※ *Cyclone strike*

HIGHLY SPRUNG. In a welcome break with tradition, when Ahmed Abdallah Sambi took power in 2006, it was after a free and fair election. Mr. President still lives above his shop, The House of Mattresses, and fits running the islands around his commitments managing the mattress factory.

LOST AND FOUND. With its fins mounted on the end of fleshy stalks, the man-sized coelacanth was long thought the 'missing link' between fishes and four-legged animals. Known only as a fossil, it was believed to have become extinct 65 million years ago—until the first live specimen was found in 1938. Far from using its fins to 'walk', it turns out the coelacanth swims around while standing on its head.

♥ · **GSR**: 181 · **WHS**: none

CONGO-BRAZZAVILLE

'A memory unstained by human blood.'

—Inscription on the original tomb in Algiers of Franco-Italian explorer
Pierre de Brazza. (He was reburied as a national hero in Brazzaville in 2006.)

*Congo-Brazzaville or 'Little Congo' (officially the Republic of Congo) should
not be confused with Congo-Kinshasa (the Democratic Republic of Congo)—
its neighbour across the river and the giant of Central Africa (with almost 20
times as many people as its junior brother). The two Congos came about
through a race between the rival explorers Pierre de Brazza, for France, and
Henry Morgan Stanley, on behalf of the King of the Belgians—with de Brazza
taking the Congo's north bank and Stanley the south. Almost uniquely among*

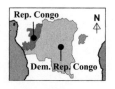

*those scrambling for Africa, de Brazza was a benevolent humanist who genuinely cared about the
Africans he encountered (and, for his pains, was eventually sacked as first governor of French Congo).
In contrast, Stanley's name has become a byword for Victorian cruelty and colonial oppression.*

MODEL MEN. The Aka Pygmies of northern Congo are
thought to be the world's most diligent fathers, undertaking 47% of childcare. Men typically cuddle their children
five times as often as in other societies; and, when an
infant is hungry, will give it a nipple to suckle until its
mother is present to feed it—an unusually arduous task as
Pygmy babies are proportionately the biggest in the world
(weighing, at birth, up to 10% as much as their mothers).

'There's a Free French garrison over at Brazzaville. [1,2]
I could be induced to arrange a passage.'

—Claude Rains to Humphrey Bogart, closing scene of *Casablanca* (1942)

[1] *In WWII, the city served as HQ for the Free French forces in Africa, led by
Félix Éboué—France's most senior black official.* [2] *'Brazzaville' was to have
been the title of a planned* Casablanca *sequel (later abandoned).*

*During the early 20th century, Pygmies
were in great demand as zoo exhibits
in both Europe and the US, with
explorers sent up the Congo to capture
'specimens'. As late as 2007, Pygmies
performing at a Brazzaville festival
were housed in the zoo, while other
musicians were put up in hotels.*

DECAPITATION. It's thought the River Congo was once the upper reaches of the ancient
Amazon, until the Atlantic opened up 120 million years ago—cutting the monster in two.
One clue is the Congo's wild final 200 miles as it surges to the sea. After flowing placidly
through the heart of Africa, the river suddenly drops 900 ft in a series of the most immense
rapids on Earth[3]—to a geographer, this abrupt increase in gradient is evidence that in the
past the river's path to the ocean was far longer. Despite losing the Congo, the truncated
Amazon continued to flow west into the Pacific until 15 million years ago, when the Andes
rose up—forcing the water to reverse direction and empty backwards into the Atlantic.

[3] *Known collectively as the Livingstone Falls. In places, the Congo's current reaches 30 mph, while the channel con-
stricts to a width of just 300 yards and the river deepens to as much as 640 ft (the deepest point on any river worldwide).*

OCEANS APART—HOW THE AMAZON–CONGO SNAPPED IN TWO

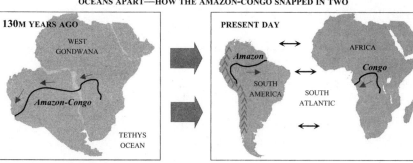

♥ · **GSR**: 122= · **WHS**: none

———————— CONGO-KINSHASA ————————

*'Nowhere did we stop long enough to get a particularized impression, but the
general sense of vague and oppressive wonder grew upon me. It was like
a weary pilgrimage amongst hints for nightmares.'*

—Joseph Conrad (*Heart of Darkness*, 1899), describing the passage of the novel's narrator up the Congo by riverboat

Masks of Africa—Kuba

*Original caption: 'People gathered in the forest for the passage of the steamer
"Roi des Belges" (1888).' The year after this photograph was taken, Joseph
Conrad captained the same riverboat on a voyage up the Congo, inspiring his
novel* Heart of Darkness. *In 1971, the Congo was renamed the Zaire (meaning
'the river that swallows all rivers'), but it reverted to 'Congo' in 1997 upon
the fall of President Mobutu, when the country also collapsed into an apocalyptic bout of rape and killing that has to date claimed over five million lives.*

*Representing a subversive hydro-
cephalic pygmy, the Bwoom is the first
mask seen by Kuban adolescent boys
during their initiation rites. After one
night, the boys are allowed to go into
their village wearing such masks to
scare the women and small children.*

CONGO—TAKE 1. From 1885
to 1908, Belgium's King Leopold II ran the Congo as his
private property. Greedy for
profit, Leopold set unrealistic
rubber quotas for each village
to harvest on pain of death—
resulting in mass slaughter so
appalling,[1] he was eventually
forced to cede the territory.

[1]*As proof of death, all the victims' hands
were severed and, since soldiers got a
bonus for each one they produced, hands
began to circulate as a parallel currency.*

CONGO—TAKE 2. From the
late 1980s to early 1990s,
President Mobutu Sese Seko
leased a Concorde jet for his
personal use and built an
airport at his hometown of
Gbadolite to accommodate it
(next to the only nuclear
bunker in Central Africa—
which he also constructed).

Left: *King Leopold II to Uncle Sam—
(1908 caption): 'Let me give you enough
rubber to make an elastic conscience.'*

SICK SECT. The Ebola virus is one of the nastiest diseases known to mankind. Highly
contagious, and with a mortality rate of up to 90%, it essentially turns its victims' innards
to pulp. The disease first emerged out of the Congo's rainforests in 1976, and epidemics
have erupted every few years since—typically prompting an emergency response from
teams of barrier-suited First World medics and epidemiologists. But in 1992 one such team
was not what it seemed. Following the death of a Japanese tourist from Ebola after going
gorilla trekking, the Aum Shinrikyo cult sent a team of 16 medical staff purportedly to
give aid, but in reality to harvest the virus in preparation for a planned terrorist attack back
in Japan. Thankfully, they did not succeed. (Three years later, however, they attacked the
Tokyo subway system with Sarin nerve gas instead, killing 12 and injuring 3,800.)

♥ · **GSR**: 122= · **WHS**: Garamba (rhinoceroses—probably now extinct) □ Kahuzi-Biega (gorillas)
Okapi Reserve (forest and okapi) □ Salonga (rainforest) □ Virunga (forests, volcanoes and gorillas)

———————— Costa Rica ————————

'Costa Rica is a country that's accustomed to elections every four years.
Clean, crystalline, transparent elections.'

—Oscar Arias, former president and Nobel Peace Prize-winner (2006)

Three Costa Rican Creatures

OPOSSUM. The males of this cat-sized marsupial possess a forked penis, which led early Spanish naturalists to believe that they mated with the female's twin nostrils.

SLOTH. Costa Rica's sloths are the size of badgers, but their prehistoric ancestors weighed more than elephants. Though extremely slow, when it's a matter of life or death, sloths can accelerate to speeds approaching 0.2 mph (in short bursts). For the rest of the time, they rely on camouflage, growing gardens of algae in their fur to turn it green.

GREEN TURTLE. The soup turtle of Victorian kitchens. Mock turtle soup substituted calf brains and feet to simulate the flaccid give of boiled turtle pulp at just a fraction of the price.

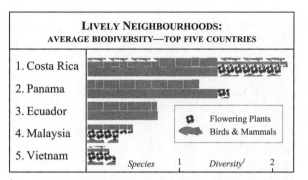

LIVELY NEIGHBOURHOODS:
AVERAGE BIODIVERSITY—TOP FIVE COUNTRIES

1. Costa Rica
2. Panama
3. Ecuador
4. Malaysia
5. Vietnam

Flowering Plants
Birds & Mammals

Species   1   *Diversity[1]*   2

[1] *Number of species divided by total land area (x 100 for plants; x 1,000 for birds and mammals). Source data: J. R. Paine, FAO Working Paper Series 4.*

DISARMING. In 1949, Costa Rica became the first country to abolish its army. The move was made by Figueres Ferrer, an associate of Fidel Castro, who seized control in the 1948 Costa Rican Civil War. In opting to outlaw all military forces (including his own), Ferrer consciously decided to follow the pacifist futurology of H. G. Wells over orthodox Marxist dogma. Further confounding expectations, he voluntarily stood down 18 months later. Since then, Costa Rica has known nothing but orderly democracy—in stark contrast to every one of its tooled-up neighbours.

HOME RUN. A single factory in the small Costa Rican town of Turrialba makes every baseball used in the American major league sport. Each ball takes 15 minutes to hand-stitch, and the factory turns out 2 million a year.

WISH YOU WERE HERE?
HAPPY PLANET RANKINGS[2]

1. Costa Rica....................76%
2. Dominican Rep. 72%
3. Jamaica........................70%
143 (*last*). Zimbabwe......17%

[2] *Life satisfaction and sustainability, New Economics Foundation (2009).*

DEAD FAMOUS. Several times a day, Costa Rican TV stations break into programming to announce the latest obituaries. As funerals are held within 24 hours of death, these death flashes help alert mourners.

ODDBALLS. South-west Costa Rica is littered with scores of stone spheres weighing up to 16 tonnes. The balls are around 1,000 years old; but, beyond this, they remain complete enigmas.

♦ · **GSR**: 45 · **WHS**: Guanacaste (dry forest) □ Talamanca (mountains, tropical rainforest) ■ Cocos Island (marine life, tropical rainforest) · **IHC**: Oxcarts

—————— CÔTE D'IVOIRE ——————

'Is there any serious man on Earth not depositing
part of his wealth in Switzerland?'

—Félix Houphouët-Boigny, President of Côte d'Ivoire (1960–93). Pursuing moderate policies at home and remaining firmly loyal to France abroad, Houphouët-Boigny earned economic success for his country and the sobriquet of 'the Grand Old Man of Africa' for himself, while pocketing around $8 bn.

HEAVEN'S GATE. Sandwiched between oil palms and scrubland fringing the upcountry town of Yamoussoukro, the Our Lady of Peace Basilica is the world's largest church. Built by President Houphouët-Boigny in 1988–90, its features include a corps of imported Polish priests and a large stained-glass window showing the president making a gift to an infant Jesus. Optimistically, the $300m complex[1] also includes a 40-room mansion with private swimming pool reserved exclusively for the pope (unused since consecration).

[1] *When outsiders wondered aloud whether this wasn't a mite extravagant for a small African country that is more Muslim than Christian, the president countered that he was paying for the church personally—a comment which many felt left the original question unanswered.*

Masks of Africa—Dan
The Dan of western Côte d'Ivoire believe strongly in the power of masks for protection. Ceremonial masks such as that above are worn by Dan to channel spirits. Away from home, Dan men will carry a small replica known as a 'passport mask', which serves both to establish ownership of their main mask and as proof of their identity.

FOOD OF THE GODS.[3] Côte d'Ivoire is the world's biggest producer of cocoa, accounting for 40% of the global harvest.

[3] *The botanical name for the cacao tree is Theobroma cacao—Theobroma meaning 'food of the Gods' in Greek.*

RIGHT ROYAL PALAVER. After Michael Jackson died in 2009, the villagers of Krindjabo in south-east Côte d'Ivoire made a formal request for repatriation of his remains. Their claim was based on his 1992 coronation, when, in a traditional ceremony under the village's palaver[2] tree, Jackson had been crowned 'king-in-waiting' of the Sanwi kingdom. As the request went on to explain, Sanwi royal protocol requires the bodies of all royal family members dying outside the kingdom to be returned for appropriate burial. While the Jackson estate's response isn't reported, it must be presumed it was negative as his body lies in Los Angeles.

[2] *Coming from the Portuguese* palavra *('talk'), the word 'palaver' entered English usage from West Africa as 18th-century trader slang for a negotiation with a local chief, usually under a shade tree set aside for this purpose.*

MONDAY'S CHILD ... Côte d'Ivoire's largest ethnic group, the Akan, name children according to the day of the week on which they are born. However, this can be overridden if special circumstances surround a birth—leaving some children to bear lifelong names that can be painfully frank ...

Afúom .... 'on the farm' *(born in a field)*
Ɔkwán .... 'on the road' *(born while the mother was travelling)*
Bekǒe .... 'war time' *(born during a war)*
Nyamékyɛ .... 'a gift from God' *(born after a long period without a child)*
Nyaméama .... 'what God has given' *(a premature or sickly child)*
Antó .... 'it didn't meet him' *(born after the death of the father)*
Yɛmpɛw .... 'we don't want you' *(born to a father who rejects the child)*

♥ · **GSR**: 134 · **WHS**: Comoé (rainforest and savannah) □ Mt. Nimba (mountain forest) □ Taï (rainforest) · **ICH**: Gbofe of Afounkaha (horn music, song and dance)

CROATIA • HRVATSKA

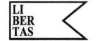

'Liberty is not sold for any type of gold.'

—Flag and motto of the Ragusan Republic

SNAP! Like the jaws of a hungry crocodile, Croatia wraps around Bosnia along Europe's oddest frontier.

From Vukovar (*V*), it's 190 miles to Dubrovnik (*D*) as the crow flies, but 600 miles by road via capital Zagreb (*Z*). The border dates from 1698, when Croatia wrenched herself free from the Ottoman Turks—at the price of leaving her former province of Bosnia in thrall for two centuries more.

TO GENERAL SECRETARY STALIN:

'Stop sending people to kill me. We've already captured five of them ... If you don't stop sending killers, I'll send one to Moscow, and I won't have to send a second.'

—Josip Tito (Croat-born leader of Yugoslavia). This message was found amongst Stalin's personal effects.

ROYAL PREROGATIVE. Packing shouldn't pose a problem for up to 1,000,000 visitors to Croatia each summer. Estimates suggest as many as 15% of holidaymakers are naturists, keen to enjoy the Med's most relaxed attitude to public nudity. The former King Edward VIII and Mrs. Simpson were unlikely trailblazers. In August 1936, they obtained formal permission to go skinny-dipping on the island of Rab.

ORATORY BY OTHER MEANS. Debate took a radical turn on 20 June 1928, when, in a stormy session of the first Yugoslavia's Parliament, a Serb deputy pulled a revolver and shot dead three Croat members, including the opposition leader. Shortly after, the king declared a royal dictatorship 'to save the people from parliamentary troubles'.

WARRIOR CHIC. The forerunner of the modern tie was first worn by 17th-century Croat soldiers, who knotted colourful scarves around their necks. After mercenaries from Croatia arrived in France, their exotic neckwear stirred Parisian society and dressing '*à la Croate*' fast became a must-do fashion. Soon afterwards, the new garment was christened the 'cravat'[1].

[1] *Versions of this form the word for any tie in most languages. The English 'tie' grew from the social importance that came to be attached to the way someone knotted their cravat. (For the record, there are 85 mathematically possible tie knots, the best-known being four-in-hand, Pratt and full- and half-Windsors.)*

NAME-CHANGE CITIES	
THEN	NOW
Ragusa	*Dubrovnik*
Batavia	*Jakarta*
Canton	*Guangzhou*
Christiana	*Oslo*
Constantinople	*Istanbul*
Edo	*Tokyo*
Leningrad	*St. Petersburg*
Leopoldville	*Kinshasa*
Reval	*Tallinn*
Saigon	*Ho Chi Minh City*
Salisbury	*Harare*

SPOT. Hailing from Croatia's coastal Dalmatia province, Dalmatians were once used as guard dogs by troops patrolling the frontier for Turkish raiders. The puppies are born pure white and the characteristic black or liver markings only appear after a couple of weeks.

DIRTY BUSINESS. The term 'ethnic cleansing' is thought to have first seen widespread use in documents produced by Croatia's pro-Nazi Ustaše government, referring to its policy of harassment and summary execution of Serbs (as well as Jews and Roma) during WWII.

♠ · **GSR**: 76 · **WHS:** Dubrovnik (museum city) ☐ Hvar (historic landscape) ☐ Plitvice (lakes) ☐ Poreč (basilica complex) ☐ Šibenik (Cathedral) ☐ Split (Roman palace) ☐ Trogir (museum town) · **ICH**: Croat Lace-Making (craft) ☐ Dubrovnik (St. Blaise festival) ☐ Gingerbread-making (craft) ☐ Gorjani (folk procession) ☐ Hrvatsko Zagorje (toy-making) ☐ Hvar (Easter procession) ☐ Istria (singing) Kastav (bell-ringing pageant) ☐ Ojkanje (singing) ☐ Sijnska Alka (knightly tournamant)

—————— CUBA ——————

'¡Venceremos!'

—'We will prevail!', slogan of the 1956–59 Cuban Revolution

LA-LA-LA-KICK. Cuban dances mostly offer a surfeit of style and grace. One exception, however, is the conga— first danced by African slaves while still locked in chain gangs. (The name is an adaptation of 'Congo'.) Since conga dancers often got highly excitable, a law was passed in the 1940s forcing those wanting to do the conga in Havana to get a police permit before forming a line. Its shuffling simplicity has since sent the dance worldwide.

CUBA LIBRE![1] Pour 50 ml white rum and 100 ml cola into a highball glass filled with ice. Optionally, add a dash of lime juice. Mix and garnish with lime wedge.

[1] *The cocktail was first mixed in Havana around 1900. Its name— 'Free Cuba!' in Spanish—was a toast taken from the battle cry of Cuban patriots during the country's struggle for independence, culminating in the 1898 Spanish-American War.*

'Ugly American' (c. 1950), taken by Constantino Arias, house photographer at the Hotel Nacional in Havana

LATIN LAS VEGAS. Under Fulgencio Batista, Castro's predecessor as Cuba's strongman, Havana became America's sin city in the sun. Teaming up with underworld heavyweights Meyer Lansky and 'Lucky' Luciano, Batista opened control of the city's casinos and racetracks to the US mob—and its members came in droves; while in December 1946, almost the whole of America's Mafia leadership met at the Hotel Nacional for their first nationwide underworld summit since Prohibition. (Cover was provided by Frank Sinatra, who was flown in for a concert.) More 'legitimate' US interests flourished too: ITT Corporation presented Batista with a gold-plated telephone as 'an expression of gratitude' for the 'excessive telephone rate increase' he imposed following US urging. Castro's revolutionaries ran Batista out of town on New Year's Day 1959, but never quite caught up with him—Batista died of a heart attack in exile in Marbella in 1973 two days before a Cuban hit squad was due to assassinate him.

'My good friend Roosevelt,   *May 6 1940*

I am very happy that you will be President. I am twelve years old. If you like, give me a ten dollar bill green American, because never I have not seen a ten dollar bill green American and I would like to have one of them.

Thank you very much. Good by. Your friend.

Fidel Castro.'

—Handwritten letter (in English)

'GUANTANAMERA'

Cuba's unofficial anthem features the patriotic lyrics of José Martí set to a song by Joseíto Fernández. The chorus, though, keeps the original words by Fernández—and laments a stolen sandwich.

NUCLEAR MELTDOWN. Even at the time, the 1962 Cuban Missile Crisis was recognized as the nearest the world had come to atomic annihilation. But it was only in 2002 that the West learnt just what a close-run thing it had been. At the height of the crisis, the US Navy trapped a Soviet submarine, the B-59, off Cuba and started dropping depth charges to force it to surface. Convinced WWIII had just broken out, its incandescent captain gave the order to prepare the sub's nuclear torpedoes for firing. Fortunately, his first officer, Vasili Arkhipov, disagreed, but it was only after heated argument that he ultimately convinced his hot-headed superior to cool down.

As a direct result of the Cuban Missile Crisis, a telegraph hotline was installed between the White House and the Kremlin in 1963. A telephone was not added until 1971 for fear of mistranslation.

Small Panatela · *Corona* · *Panatela* · *Churchill* · *Gran Corona* · *Toro*

For aficionados, choosing the appropriate size and shape of each cigar can add significantly to their enjoyment of smoking. Cigars contain three types of tobacco leaf: wrappers, which form the 'skin' and dominate the overall flavour; fillers, which form the cigar's body and are usually blended to add signature flavour nuances; and binders, used to hold the filler together. Making cigars fatter gives greater scope for the more complex flavours of the blended filler to be expressed (as well as giving more body to the smoke); but, particularly above a ring gauge of 50 (50/64ths of an inch), cigars burn more coolly as they get fatter, potentially muting the full spectrum of flavour. Cigar shape is less directly determinant of flavour. Nevertheless, figurados *(any shape other than the standard cylindrical* parejo*) are normally rolled by hand, and likely to be of higher quality. Also, to some, the belief—however fanciful—that their cigar has been rolled on the thigh of a dusky Cuban maiden adds materially to the overall pleasure.*

I'M ALL RIGHT, JACK. For many Americans, the most painful part of the 1962 imposition of trade sanctions against Cuba was the prohibition of Cuban cigars. But not for all. The evening before President Kennedy was to pass the ban, he sent his press secretary, Pierre Salinger, to scour Washington to replenish his personal stash. Only when Salinger had handed over 1,200 H. Upmann Petit Coronas did Kennedy sign the order into law.

CIGAR FLAVOUR PALETTE
Chewy · fruity · green · nutty oaky · spicy · sweet · woodsy
... And one that isn't mentioned: pyridine. The principal pong in 'cigar breath', pyridine was first isolated from bone oil. When pure, it has the smell of rancid fish.

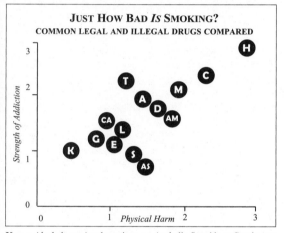

JUST HOW BAD *IS* SMOKING?
COMMON LEGAL AND ILLEGAL DRUGS COMPARED

Strength of Addiction (vertical axis, 0 to 3)
Physical Harm (horizontal axis, 0 to 3)

Key: A Alcohol, AM Amphetamines, AS Anabolic Steroids, C Cocaine, CA Cannabis, D Diazepam, E Ecstasy, G GBH, H Heroin, L LSD, K Khat, M Methadone, S Solvents, T **Tobacco**. *Source: D. Nutt et al., Lancet (2007).*

Melisuga helenae
Bee hummingbird

BIRD BUZZ. Hummingbirds are the only birds that can fly backwards. The smallest (and the smallest bird in the world) is the bee hummingbird. Restricted to Cuba, it weighs 1.8 g—half a teaspoon of sugar, or two bumble bee queens.

CLOSE, BUT NO CIGAR—HIGHLIGHTS FROM THE 638[1] ATTEMPTS TO KILL CASTRO

Who?	Plan	What happened?
CIA (1960)	Mafia hit (via John Rosselli)	attempts continued without success until 1962
CIA (1960)	poison pills (slipped by ex-lover)	pills melted before they could be used
CIA (1960)	cigars poisoned with botulinum	cigars were delivered, but evidently not smoked
CIA (1960)	explosive cigar	aborted (this alleged plot may be disinformation)
CIA (1963)	wetsuit dosed with fungal spores	suits were switched, Castro received a clean one
CIA (1963)	exploding seabed conch shell	dismissed as impractical after shells were bought

[1] *According to Fabian Escalante, former head of Fidel Castro's personal security. The CIA also considered lacing a TV studio with LSD to make Castro seem deranged and putting thallium salts in his shoes to make his beard fall out.*

♦ · **GSR:** 70 · **WHS:** Alejandro de Humboldt NP (tropical flora and fauna) □ Camagüey (townscape) □ Cienfuegos (townscape) □ Desembarco del Granma NP (cliffs and terraces) □ Havana (historic city) Santiago de Cuba (fortress) □ South-East Cuba (historic coffee plantations) □ Trinidad (museum town) □ Viñales (mountain valley) · **ICH:** Tumba Francesca (drumming and dance)

Parejo · *Torpedo* · *Pyramid* · *Perfecto* · *Presidente*

Classic cigar shapes.

Cigars drawn at 1/6ᵗʰ scale.

───── CYPRUS ● Κύπρος ● KIBRIS ─────

'Realizing they would never be a world power, the Cypriots have settled for being a world nuisance.'[1]

—George Mikes

LOOKING DIVINE—THE PERFECT FIGURE OF ALL TIMES

Willendorf Venus *c.* 22,000 BCE Hip/Height = 0.52	**Venus de' Medici[2]** *c.* 50 BCE Hip/Height = 0.21	**Erotic etching** *c.* 1530 CE Hip/Height = 0.30	**Supermodel** 2008 CE Hip/Height = 0.17

ANCIENT METALS AND RULING PLANETS

COPPER (*Venus*)

GOLD (*Sun*)

SILVER (*Moon*)

MERCURY (*Merc.*)

IRON (*Mars*)

TIN (*Jupiter*)

LEAD (*Saturn*)

CHIP OFF THE OLD BLOCK. Venus to the Romans, Aphrodite in Greece, the goddess of beauty and desire was—unusually enough—born motherless to her dad, Uranus, at Paphos on Cyprus. (As Hesiod has it, her revolting brother, Cronus, hacked off Uranus' testicles and cast them out to sea. There, they foamed into a lather that, on subsiding, revealed a fully formed and very adult goddess.)

**APHRODISIACS
FOR THE TRULY DESPERATE**

*Garlic • Slime eel • Tiger penis
Lizard snout • Rhino horn • Sea cucumber
Snails • Cobra blood • Asparagus
Rocket • Carrots • Lettuce*

 COPY CAT. The world's earliest pet cat has been found buried in a grave on Cyprus beside its presumed owner. Although the burial took place 9,500 years ago, dog's status as man's best—or, at least, oldest—friend isn't remotely threatened: a 12,000-year-old grave in Israel contains an elderly human cradling a puppy.

MEN ARE FROM MARS ... Because Cypriot mines produced almost all the Roman Empire's supply of the metal, Cyprus was known in classical times as the 'Island of Copper'.[3] Going further, since it was also the birthplace of the goddess of beauty (*see left*), ancient astrologers and alchemists decided that copper must therefore be the most feminine of metals, and so paired it off with Venus when associating each ancient metal with a 'ruling' planet (*see right*). It was all nonsense, of course; though (one assumes) by coincidence, it's now known that women's blood serum[4] contains 20% more copper than men's, which, in turn, contains 30% more iron—the metal deemed most masculine—than women's.

[3] The word copper is derived from Cyprus via the Latin cuprum—*meaning simply 'Cyprus metal'. [4] The blood fluid.*

CUT UP. Since the 1989 fall of the Berlin Wall, Nicosia has been the world's only divided capital, bisected by the UN-patrolled Green Line[2] separating the ethnically Greek Republic of Cyprus and the Turkish Republic of North Cyprus (recognized only by Turkey). The island's third state is Britain, which is sovereign over 98 square miles (3% of the island).

. [1] UN peacekeepers have been stationed on Cyprus since 1964—the UN's longest deployment. [2] Arms cropped for clarity

♠ · **GSR**: 103 · *De Facto* **Seceded Territory**: Turkish Republic of Northern Cyprus · **WHS**: Choirokoitia (Stone Age site) □ Paphos (mosaics) □ Troodos (churches) · **ICH**: Lefkara (lace-making)

—— CZECH REPUBLIC[1] • ČESKO ——————

'Optimism is the opium of the people.'

—Milan Kundera, *The Joke* (1967)

[1] *The Czech Republic is in the select company of the Dominican and Central African Republics as one of only three countries without an accepted short-form name in English. The problem stems, of course, from the sundering of the old Czechoslovakia, leaving the Slovaks with the handy 'Slovakia' and the Czechs with a problem. The Czech Foreign Ministry's official recommendation for the English language is 'Czechia'. But, needless to say, this has sunk like a stone. A more mellifluous option might be to revert to the area's traditional name—Bohemia.*

Left margin (vertical): Czech beers (selected): Budweiser Budvar • Medved • Urquell (ideally *tankovna*) • Staropramen • Troobacz • Velkopopovický Kozel

NO WAGE SLAVE. The word 'robot' is taken from the Czech *robotnik* ('slave'), and entered the English language via Karel Čapek's futuristic 1920 play *Rossum's Universal Robots* (in which a robot rebellion leads to the extinction of the human race). In retrospect, Čapek acknowledged the parallel with the legendary 16th-century Golem of Prague: a powerful clay automaton, animated by the city's chief rabbi to serve the Jewish community, that runs violently amok until eventually stopped.

Golem of Prague

The world's second largest cockroach is the rhinoceros cockroach of Queensland, Australia, which can grow as big as the palm of an adult human's hand. This, however, is still puny compared to the largest: Franz Kafka's Gregor Samsa—the benighted travelling salesman from Prague who awoke in 1912 to find he had transformed into a monstrous insect.

THE DEFENESTRATION OF PRAGUE

In 1618, a group of Protestant nobles threw two eminent Catholics and their secretary, Philip Fabricus, out of a Prague Castle window. Perhaps miraculously, all three survived the 70-ft drop: Catholic sources cited the wings of angels, while Lutheran witnesses averred to the steaming mound of equine excrement directly beneath. In any event, the defenestration ignited the Thirty Years War—arguably the most destructive European conflict since the barbarian invasions, while Fabricus was later ennobled as Baron Longdrop.

EMOTIONAL VOID. Apart from writing works such as *The Metamorphosis* (*see above*), Czech author Franz Kafka harboured a long-term self-destructive fantasy of suicide by autodefenestration; and to sharpen the painful pleasure, he regularly slept beside an open window. Nonetheless, although he did die early (of tuberculosis), he held off the siren call.

SUPPLY AND DEMAND: Not only do the Czechs boast some of the most celebrated beers around,[2] they are also the world's biggest beer drinkers—downing a staggering (pun intended) 276 pints for every man, woman and child yearly; while at Chodová Planá you can even bathe in the stuff,[3] followed up with something described as a 'drinking cure' (and they've actually managed to corral a physician into saying it's therapeutic).

[2] *The towns of Pilsen (now Plzeň) and Budweis (now České Budějovice) gave their names to Pilsner and Budweiser for starters.* [3] *This may admittedly be somewhat sticky—during the Communist era, Czech girls dipped their curlers in beer before application, due to the oversight in successive Five Year Plans of the production of anything better suited.*

Right margin (vertical): International beer styles (selected): ale (old, pale, etc.) • bitter • bock • lager • lambic • pilsner • porter • Rauchbier • stout • Weissbier

♠ · **GSR**: 39 · **WHS**: Brno (modernist house) □ Český Krumlov (medieval townscape) □ Holašovice (baroque village) □ Kroměříž (gardens) □ Kutná Hora (cathedral) □ Lednice-Valtice (pastoral landscape) □ Litomyšl (castle) □ Olomouc (monument) □ Prague (historic city) □ Telč (medieval townscape) □ Třebíč (Jewish quarter) □ Zelená Hora (church) · **ICH**: Falconry □ Hlinecko (Shrovetide processions) □ Slovácko Verbuňk (male dance)

———— DENMARK • DANMARK ————

*'People understand me so poorly that they don't even understand
my complaint about them not understanding me.'*

—Søren Kierkegaard, Danish philosopher and founder of existentialism

WHEELS OF INDUSTRY. An output of 306 million tyres per year makes Lego—a contraction of the Danish phrase 'play well'—the world's biggest tyre manufacturer. Like every other piece, the tyres have to be made to tolerances of 10 μm (microns) to ensure just the right degree of 'stickability'.

CONFUSED?

World's highest taxes ☑
+
World's most expensive electricity ☑
+
200% tax on new cars[3] ☑
⇩
Happiest country in world[4]

[3]*Not if electric (but see above).*
[4]*Source: US Nat. Science Found.*

NO FAIRY TALE. Despite spending his whole life looking for love (male or female) and multiple failed proposals, Hans Christian Andersen never found happiness. After death, a letter from his youthful first crush was found worn in a pouch against his chest.

DANISH MERMICIDE

Perched petitely on her rock in Copenhagen harbour, Hans Christian Andersen's Little Mermaid would seem a study in inoffensiveness. However, for reasons that have usually never been revealed, she has, over the years, been subject to an extraordinary degree of violence.

PEOPLE POWER. Denmark has some of the shiniest green credentials in the world,[1] but one area in which the Danes have been particularly innovative is in the recycling of themselves. Since 2006, Denmark's 31 crematoria have sold 1.6 tonnes of hip and knee replacements for recycling each year. However, in 2010, Aalborg Crematorium went a step further by connecting its chimney to the district heating system. More crematoria are now set to follow, and a purpose-built crematorium on Zealand will heat 100 homes full-time when it comes on-stream. While perhaps unusual, this may be no more than redressing the balance since, ordinarily, cremating a body releases greenhouse gases equivalent to driving coast to coast across the USA.

[1]*For example, 150,000 Danes own or part-own their own wind turbine.*

1964 ……….......……	*Decapitated*
1984 ….....…	*Right arm amputated*
1990 …..……	*Partially decapitated*
1998 …....…....……	*Decapitated*
2003 ……	*Blown up with dynamite*

The police take each attack very seriously and after both decapitations put a murder squad on the investigation (without results).

Great Dane

BAND OF BROTHERS. According to Saxo the Learned's *Deeds of the Danes*,[2] Denmark was founded by brothers Dan and Angul. After some time, however, Angul left and Dan began to rule as king alone—at which point both the people and the country adopted his name. Angul, meanwhile, migrated south to form his own tribe, the 'Angles', who likewise took the name of their founder. Later, the Angles successfully invaded southern Britain and renamed the conquered territory 'England' in their own honour. And thus, if Saxo is to be believed, England and Denmark are unique among countries in bearing fraternal names.

[2] The Gesta Danorum, *written in Latin in the early 13th century as the first full history of Denmark.*

PRINCE OF DENMARK. *Deeds of the Danes* (*above*) is also notable for the story of Amleth, the inspiration for Shakespeare's *Hamlet*. As *Deeds* tells it, Amleth was a Viking princeling who, after feigning madness, killed his uncle to avenge his father's murder. In the Danish version, however, Amleth also travelled to Britain, married the Queen of Scotland and was later slain in a full-scale battle with the King of Denmark.

QUIZ TIME: WHICH OF SHAKESPEARE'S PLAYS FEATURE THE FOLLOWING COUNTRIES?

*1. Albania, 2. Austria, 3. Cyprus, 4. Czech Republic, 5. Denmark, 6. Egypt, 7. France,
8. Greece, 9. Italy, 10. Lebanon, 11. Libya, 12. Spain, 13. Syria, 14. Turkey.*

Answers on next page.

EVERY DAY OF THE WEEK—OUR HEATHEN HEIRLOOM

The days of the week in English ultimately reflect the seven 'planets' of ancient Ptolemaic astronomy, but the names themselves are rooted in the 6th-century influx of Angles, Saxons and Jutes from Denmark and Frisia. Originally conceived in the fog of Sumerian proto-history, the convention of linking each day to a planet was later adopted by the Romans, who renamed them after their own planetary deities (Mars, Mercury, Venus, etc.). This is what persists in Latin Europe (e.g. the Spanish *martes*, *miércoles*, *viernes*, etc.), but under something known as the *interpretatio germanica*, northern Europe's tribes—including Angles and friends—ditched the Imperial pantheon for the home-grown version, which is why modern English honours not Jove but the old pagan German-Nordic gods.

Sunday: the sun's day. *Sunna* was the sister of the moon; she is fated to be eaten by a huge wolf (Sköll) at the end of our epoch.

Saturday: Saturn's day. The odd day out, in English it has kept its Roman name. In Danish, however, it's *lørdag*—'bath-day'—the day when Vikings took their weekly bath.

Monday: the moon's day. Like his sister the sun, *Máni* is destined eventually to be caught and consumed by a ravening wolf (in this case, Hati) that even now pursues him across the sky.

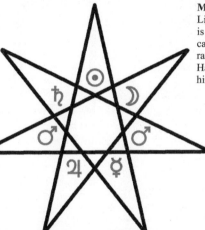

Friday: the day of *Frigg* (or *Freyja*), the shape-shifting (and wanton) wife of Wodan and goddess of love. No known lupine linkages.

Tuesday: the day of *Týr*, the one-handed god of battle glory. (Týr's other hand was swallowed by Fenrir, the father of all monstrous wolves.)

Thursday: the day of *Thor*, the hammer-wielding thunder god. Thor tried twice to forge a chain able to bind Fenrir (*see right*) before dwarves did the job for him.

Wednesday: the day of *Wodan* (*Odin*), god of wisdom and shepherd to the newly dead. Wodan is scheduled to be gobbled by Fenrir wolf, once it breaks free (*see left*).

TGI FRIDAY—BUT WHY? The order followed by the days of the week isn't random but is dictated, with a twist, by the distance from the Earth of each day's 'planet' in Ptolemaic astronomy. The twist is that individual hours, as well as days, are ruled by the 'planets', and it is the hourly sequence—which repeats weekly—that matches the Ptolemaic distances directly. The planet ruling the first hour of each day then gives that day its name.

1. Twelfth Night (*Illyria*). 2. Measure for Measure (*Vienna*). 3. Othello. 4. Winter's Tale (*Bohemia*). 5. Hamlet (*Elsinore*). 6. Antony & Cleopatra (*Alexandria*). 7. Henry V (*Agincourt*, *Harflour*, *Paris*, *Picardy*); Pt I Henry VI (*Angers*, *Anjou*, *Auvergne*, *Bordeaux*, *Gascony*, *Orleans*, *Rouen*); All's Well That Ends Well (*Marseille*, *Paris*, *Roussillon*); King John (*Angiers*). 8. Midsummer's Night Dream (*Athens*); Timon of Athens; Two Noble Kinsmen (*Athens*); Julius Caesar (*Philippi*). 9. All's Well That Ends Well (*Florence*); Antony & Cleopatra (*Actium*, *Messina*, *Misenum*, *Rome*); Cymbeline (*Rome*); Coriolanus (*Antium*, *Corioli*, *Rome*); Julius Caesar (*Rome*); Merchant of Venice (*Belmont*, *Venice*); Much Ado About Nothing (*Messina*); Othello (*Venice*); Romeo & Juliet (*Mantua*, *Verona*); Taming of the Shrew (*Padua*); Titus Andronicus (*Rome*); Two Gentlemen of Verona (*Mantua*, *Milan*, *Verona*); Winter's Tale (*Sicily*). 10. Pericles (*Tyre*). 11. Pericles (*Pentapolis*). 12. Love's Labour's Lost (*Navarre*). 13. Antony & Cleopatra. 14. Comedy of Errors (*Ephesus*); Julius Caesar (*Sardis*); Pericles (*Antioch*, *Ephesus*, *Mytilene*, *Tarsus*); Troilus & Cressida (*Troy*).

♠ · **GSR**: 53 · **WHS**: Jelling (burial mounds) □ Roskilde (cathedral) □ Kronburg (castle)

DJIBOUTI

'This has always been our home, so we have always been here to greet whatever foreigner landed on our shores. Arabs, Persians, Greeks, French—there have been so many, and all have found it too hot to stay.'

—Hassan Ali Muhammad, Djiboutian folklorist

Afar nomad (1950s)

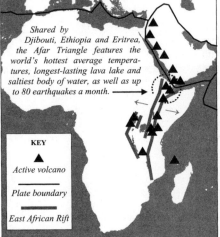

Shared by Djibouti, Ethiopia and Eritrea, the Afar Triangle features the world's hottest average temperatures, longest-lasting lava lake and saltiest body of water, as well as up to 80 earthquakes a month. →

KEY

▲

Active volcano

▬▬▬

Plate boundary

▬▬▬

East African Rift

'It was impossible to exaggerate the importance that the Afar attached to castrating their victims, rating as they did a man's prowess by the number of his kills.'

—Wilfred Thesiger (1935). Due to their implacable hostility towards outsiders, the Afars of the Danakil Desert were formerly the most feared of all African peoples. Into the 1980s, intruders caught in their territory were routinely killed, following which their genitals would invariably be cut out, dried and used as a trophy, heaping additional dishonour on the corpse.

ROAD TO NOWHERE. A $20 billion dollar road link connecting Arabia's poorest and least stable country (Yemen) with the tiny and scarcely populated scrap of African desert that is Djibouti might not sound a sure-fire investment winner. Add in that the plan requires the world's longest suspension bridge supported by pylons twice as high as France's Millau Viaduct, crosses an intense seismic zone peppered with active volcanoes and is to be built by one of Osama bin-Laden's brothers and the financial risk would seem daunting. Nevertheless, this is what was officially unveiled by the two countries' governments in 2008—although it should be added that ground has yet to be broken.

SPLITTING UP. Djibouti sits squarely on the Afar Triangle, where the East African Rift—a gargantuan tear that's unzipping the continent of Africa—meets the Red Sea. While it's thought it will take a million years for a new sea to open, the process is already visibly underway: in 2005, a 35-mile-long crack spread across the desert in just three weeks.

DOGMEAT. One of Africa's most endangered top predators, the African wild dog, still finds a refuge in Djibouti's Goda Mountains. Although far less well known than Africa's photogenic big cats, the wild dog, when working as a pack, can be considered the continent's ultimate killing machine.

KILL RATE PER HUNT—AFRICAN CARNIVORES

African wild dog ... 80%		Cheetah 50%	
Leopard 70%		Spotted hyena 40%	
Chimpanzee 52%		Lion 30%	

♥ · **GSR**: 163 · **WHS**: none

— DOMINICAN REPUBLIC ● REPÚBLICA DOMINICANA —

*'The one part of the West Indies where you meet no beggars is that country
so very suspect in democratic circles, the Dominican Republic.
And if this doesn't make begging a respectable profession, what will?'*

—Dane Chandos (1945)

BIGGER THAN GOD. In 1930, Rafael Trujillo was elected President of the Dominican Republic with more votes than there were voters. Once in place, he set about remaking the country in his own image with all the modesty of your average megalomaniac. The capital, one province, a whole slew of smaller towns and the Caribbean's highest mountain were all renamed after him as he pocketed nearly a billion dollars; those granted an audience spent it standing to attention with four machine guns pointed at their chests. At his inauguration, Trujillo appeared wearing a sash with the words 'God and Trujillo'; by the time he was assassinated 31 years later, the slogan was everywhere—but with Trujillo's name first.

Columbus reaches the Americas (Mk 1)

RESTLESS SPIRIT. History books say Christopher Columbus visited the Americas four times. But the final tally was five—albeit that the last trip was posthumous. Thirty-six years after his death, Columbus's son dug him up and shipped him across the Atlantic from Spain to the Dominican Republic.[2] Here his bones lay until 1795, when they were (probably[3]) moved to Havana to keep them from thieving French invaders. A century later, when Spain lost Cuba too, whatever was left was shifted back one last time to Seville Cathedral, where, since 1898, his remains have remained.

ELOCUTION LESSON. The worst atrocity of the Trujillo era was the Parsley Massacre of 1937, in which over 20,000 people were killed for failing to pronounce the word *perejil* ('parsley') correctly.[1] Compensation of $32 per victim was eventually agreed, but, due to corruption, the sum actually handed over reportedly averaged just two cents.

[1] *The pogrom was aimed at Haitian immigrants who, not being native Spanish speakers, struggled to roll the letter 'r' when asked. Upon getting it wrong, most were hacked to death by machete on the spot.*

IT'S A BOY–GIRL THING. In the Dominican village of Salinas, so many of the girls used to turn into men as teenagers that some families waited until puberty before treating them as either daughters or sons. In the 1970s, researchers found that the children—known locally as *guevedoces* ('testicles at twelve')—suffered from a genetic enzyme deficiency that blocked normal physiological development until the rush of testosterone at puberty rectified the condition.

[2] *Specifically, Santo Domingo. Now the capital of the Dominican Republic, in the 16th century the city was known as the 'Gateway to the Caribbean', and still contains the oldest cathedral, castle, convent, hospital, monastery and university in the Americas.*
[3] *Dominicans say that the Spanish took the wrong body and celebrate their own rival set of remains. Either, both or neither of the claims could be correct.*

BOUNDLESS OCEAN. The Sargasso is the only sea in the world without any shores. (It is circumscribed by ocean currents instead.) Starting 400 miles north-east of the Dominican

BIBLIOPHILE. The Dominican Republic is the only country in the world to display the Bible on its flag.

Republic, it's a nutrient-poor ocean desert whose still waters and seaweed prairies were much feared by early sailors, who knew they could be trapped for weeks if becalmed.

♦ · **GSR**: 59 · **WHS**: Santo Domingo (historic city) · **IHC**: Cocolo Dance Drama □ Villa Mella Congos Brotherhood (drumming)

ECUADOR

'La Carita de Dios.'

—'The Face of God', a nickname for Ecuador's capital, Quito, coined for its beautiful architecture,
setting and claimed proximity to heaven (as the world's highest legally proclaimed capital city)

Chimborazo

ON TOP OF THE WORLD. The peak of Ecuador's Chimborazo volcano is the highest point on the planet (when measured from the Earth's centre). Chimborazo beats the more recognized Mt. Everest by 2,167 m (7,109 ft) because it lies almost on the Equator[1], where the Earth bulges outward most strongly under the inertial centrifugal force created by its daily rotation—similar to the outward pressure felt in a fast-cornering car. The nearby and slightly lower Cayambe volcano lies directly on the Equator and is the only point on its length where snow lies permanently.

[1] *Since 'Ecuador' means 'Equator' in Spanish, the conventional word used by the rest of the world is inherently ambiguous in Ecuador itself—where the term* mitad del mundo *('middle of the world') is sometimes preferred.*

'ALFARO LIVES, YOU PRICK!' is the English translation of ¡Alfaro Vive, Carajo! (or the AVC)—one of South America's more esoteric terrorist organizations. The Nicaraguan-backed, Libyan-trained group emerged from obscurity in 1983 to stage a raid on a Guayaquil museum, liberating Sr. Alfaro's sword. Nine years later, a splinter group captured more headlines by occupying the British embassy. The Alfaro in question was active in Ecuadorian politics a century ago, and is best remembered for commissioning the construction of the Quito–Guayaquil railway in 1897 and, 15 years later, getting sprung from jail by a mob crying 'Death to all Freemasons!', who then promptly murdered him (thereby rendering the AVC's chief ideological premise indubitably false).

HOLD ON TO YOUR HATS. Ecuador is the home of the Panama hat, the best of which are hand-woven in the small town of Montecristi (allegedly by moonlight to stop the fibres drying in the sun). That the hats are known as 'Panamas' is a source of long-term consternation and arose since they used to be shipped through Panama City and were later adopted by workers building the Panama Canal.

HEADING FOR TROUBLE. The Jívaroan peoples of Ecuador's upper Amazon are the only ones to have carried out head-shrinking in modern times. Historically, the practice was rare, and was undertaken to trap the spirit of a powerful enemy warrior in the head and so prevent him from exacting vengeance. But in the 19th and early 20th centuries, heads became fashionable curios in Europe and America, causing a vast upsurge in tribal warfare to meet the commercial demand, while the country's morgues were harvested by *mestizo* counterfeiters flooding the market with fakes.

The Galápagos Archipelago was the first World Heritage Site (WHS) to be listed, and Quito was the first city to gain the status (both in 1978). As of 2010, a further 909 miscellaneous natural and cultural treasures deemed of the utmost international value have been inscribed. World Heritage Sites can now be found in 151 nations, with Italy having the highest number (45, i.e. 5% of the total).

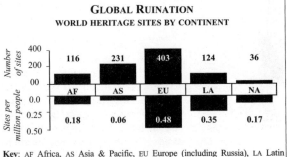

GLOBAL RUINATION
WORLD HERITAGE SITES BY CONTINENT

	AF	AS	EU	LA	NA
Number of sites	116	231	403	124	36
Sites per million people	0.18	0.06	0.48	0.35	0.17

Key: AF Africa, AS Asia & Pacific, EU Europe (including Russia), LA Latin America (including Mexico) & Caribbean, NA North America.

THE EVOLUTION REVOLUTION

THE BIRTH OF DARWINISM: CHARLES DARWIN AND THE BEAGLE IN THE GALÁPAGOS ISALNDS

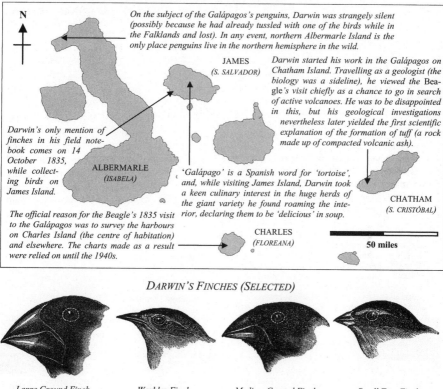

N

On the subject of the Galápagos's penguins, Darwin was strangely silent (possibly because he had already tussled with one of the birds while in the Falklands and lost). In any event, northern Albermarle Island is the only place penguins live in the northern hemisphere in the wild.

JAMES
(S. SALVADOR)

Darwin started his work in the Galápagos on Chatham Island. Travelling as a geologist (the biology was a sideline), he viewed the Beagle's visit chiefly as a chance to go in search of active volcanoes. He was to be disappointed in this, but his geological investigations nevertheless later yielded the first scientific explanation of the formation of tuff (a rock made up of compacted volcanic ash).

Darwin's only mention of finches in his field notebook comes on 14 October 1835, while collecting birds on James Island.

ALBERMARLE
(ISABELA)

'Galápago' is a Spanish word for 'tortoise', and, while visiting James Island, Darwin took a keen culinary interest in the huge herds of the giant variety he found roaming the interior, declaring them to be 'delicious' in soup.

CHATHAM
(S. CRISTÓBAL)

The official reason for the Beagle's 1835 visit to the Galápagos was to survey the harbours on Charles Island (the centre of habitation) and elsewhere. The charts made as a result were relied on until the 1940s.

CHARLES
(FLOREANA)

50 miles

DARWIN'S FINCHES (SELECTED)

| *Large Ground Finch* | *Warbler Finch* | *Medium Ground Finch* | *Small Tree Finch* |

BIRD EAT BIRD. Darwin didn't realize it until well after he returned home, but the 'finches'[1] he collected in the Galápagos provide one of the classic case studies of evolutionary radiation,[2] and in due course helped guide him to his landmark ideas on the origin of species. Of the 13 species of 'finch' found on the islands, the strangest is a subspecies of the sharp-beaked ground finch known as the vampire finch. This pecks at the skin of boobies (and, given a chance, people) with its dagger of a beak to drink the blood it draws.

[1] *Classed today as tanagers.* [2] *The rapid differentiation of a single ancestor species to a number of daughter species—in this case, characterized by modification of beak shape to take advantage of different vacant ecological niches.*

Cartoon of Darwin (1871)

LONG WAY ROUND. After his return home on the *Beagle* in 1836, it was 23 years before Darwin got round to publishing *On the Origin of Species*, in which he set out the idea of natural selection he first conceived on the voyage. During the wait, Darwin spent 8 years on an exhaustive study of barnacles—either to gain a thorough knowledge of one animal before generalizing, or simply to put off getting to work on *Species*. But, whether Darwin was aware of it or not, his choice was an interesting one, since it turns out that, due to their adult immobility, natural selection has pushed barnacles into evolving the longest penises relative to body size of any animal, allowing males to reach right out of their shells to nearby females.

♦ · **GSR**: 51 · **WHS**: Cuenca (colonial townscape) □ Galápagos (wildlife) □ Quito (historic city) Sangay (volcanoes, Amazonian forest and wildlife) · **ICH**: Zápara (Amerindian culture)

EGYPT ● مصر

'Man fears time; time fears the pyramids.'

—Egyptian proverb

OZYMANDIAS[1]

*'I met a traveller from an antique land
Who said: Two vast and trunkless legs of stone
Stand in the desert. Near them, on the sand,
Half sunk, a shattered visage lies, whose frown
And wrinkled lip, and sneer of cold command
Tell that its sculptor well those passions read
Which yet survive, stamped on these lifeless things,
The hand that mocked them and the heart that fed.
And on the pedestal these words appear:
"My name is Ozymandias, king of kings:
Look on my works, ye Mighty, and despair!"
Nothing beside remains. Round the decay
Of that colossal wreck, boundless and bare
The lone and level sands stretch far away.'*

—Percy Shelley (1818)

[1] *Ozymandias was the Greek name for Ramesses II, arguably the greatest of the ancient Egyptians. (He is said to have built more temples, erected more statues and fathered more children than any other pharaoh.) Shelley's quotation comes from an inscription on a statue of Ramesses now in the British Museum: 'King of kings am I, Ozymandias. If anyone would know how great I am and where I lie, let him surpass one of my works.'*

BEER AND SANDWICHES.[2] As ancient civilizations went, Egyptian labourers seem to have had a pretty cushy time. Wages were guaranteed and reasonable, and prices fixed and fair. The working week was six days long, followed by a two-day break, and supervision appears to have been relaxed—hangovers and 'a row with the wife' both appear in scrolls as reasons for time off, seemingly without adverse comment.[3] Nevertheless, in 1170 BCE, workers at Deir el-Medina went on history's first recorded strike. (Their complaint was over a delay to the wheat ration, and after their demands were met, they went back to work.)

[2] *Ancient Egyptian workers lived on a diet of bread and ale. While the pita-like flatbread would be recognizable today, the beer—made from fermented bread—was a lumpy alcoholic gruel made at home.* [3] *Yet another legitimate excuse for time off was, apparently, checking on the homebrew.*

WINDY CITY. The classic Egyptian breakfast of *ful medames* (beans cooked overnight to a pulp with oil, garlic and hard-boiled eggs) goes back over 3,000 years: Ramesses II offered 11,998 jars of the stuff to the God of the Nile, while medieval Cairo was equipped with vast central vats, bubbling through the night, that fed the entire population. Modern Cairenes now cook their own at home on electric hotplates, but, in the villages, people still use traditional embers—and round off their breakfast with a crisp raw onion eaten whole.[4]

[4] *In passing, it might be noted that, according to the WHO, Egypt suffers the world's highest incidence of fatal flatulence.*

Queen Nefertiti

HAIRLESS IN GIZA. For over a millennium, the fashionable ancient Egyptian woman-about-town went around totally bald: she shaved her head daily, and wielded tweezers to pluck out all body hair, (eyebrows too). Men also shaved fully—below as much as above; and children went hairless as well, except for one lone lock that was left to grow down the right side of their heads. Comfort and hygiene dictated these choices, given the hot sun and ever-present lice. However, when dressing up, both men and women donned wigs, while female as well as male pharaohs would also strap on fake beards, fastened by strings around their ears.

Q. *What do you get if you cross an Egyptian mummy with a mechanic?*

A. *Toot and Car man.*

ALL SORTS OF RELICS. Along with gold and jewels, Tutankhamun was buried with box-loads of boomerangs and a huge stockpile of liquorice. Intended to equip the pharaoh for the afterlife, the boomerangs were for hunting evil spirits, while the liquorice was to ward off any that got too close. In the land of the living, ancient Egyptian boomerangs were widely used for hunting waterfowl and liquorice root was regarded as a powerful cure-all.[5]

[5] *Liquorice is indeed a potent drug. In 2004, an English woman was hospitalized for four days with muscle failure after overdosing on it, and eating just 100 g a week in pregnancy measurably lowers an unborn child's later IQ.*

DAWN OF THE GODS—THE ANCIENT EGYPTIAN PANTHEON

The ancient Egyptian gods are among the oldest that are still known. They were worshipped continuously for over 3,000 years, before being supplanted by Christianity. During this time, the fortunes of individual gods rose and fell, with the exception of Aten, within a consistent theological framework. Over 100 major gods are recorded (with countless local deities worshipped also), the most important of which are shown below. Although their images appear to show quasi-human figures, the depictions were symbolic, not representational, and, at least to the priestly class, the actual nature of the gods was recognized to be mysterious and possibly beyond human comprehension.

AMUN

The prime creator, Amun later largely fused with Ra to form Amun-Ra, a majestic Zeus-like deity. Tutenkhamun translates as 'living image of Amun'.

RA (HORUS)

Ra was the sun god, who subsumed Horus, god of the sky. Egyptians believed they were the 'Cattle of Ra', as they had been created from his tears.

OSIRIS

Green-skinned Osiris was brother and husband of Isis. After his murder by Set, he returned as god of the dead (minus his penis, which was eaten by a fish).

ISIS

Fertility goddess Isis was seen as the perfect wife and mother. The annual Nile flood was said to spring from her tears for murdered husband Osiris.

ANUBIS

The jackal-headed Anubis was god of mummification. While preparing a body for mummification, the lead embalmer would wear an Anubis mask.

HATHOR

Hathor, goddess of love and beauty, was variously Ra's mother, daughter and wife. Normally represented as a cow, she could also appear as a hippopotamus.

THOTH

The moon god, Thoth, also invented writing. The lost Book of Thoth holds a spell enabling humans to see the gods, but anyone who finds it will be horribly cursed.

SET

God of darkness, deserts and storms, Set wasn't all bad at first, but by Ptolemaic times had come to be identified with Typhon, the 'father of all monsters'.

The Aten Heresy: *For 15 years in the middle of the 14th century BCE, the old gods of Egypt were supplanted by Aten, previously an obscure aspect of Ra embodying the physical orb of the sun: not only were the traditional gods neglected, their temples were defaced and worship was banned. For this, Atenism is sometimes considered the first monotheistic religion. Shown as a rayed sun, Aten never took human form.*

Rise and Fall: *Atenism was solely down to Pharaoh Amenhotep IV, who, five years into his reign, renamed himself Akhenaten ('Servant of Aten'). Only the pharaoh and his wife, Nefertiti, were actually allowed to worship Aten; everyone else had to worship them and hope they passed the message on. Almost as soon as Akhenaten died, Atenism was ended, the old gods reinstated and his name all but expunged.*

GRANDER THAN THE GRAND CANYON—THE MESSINIAN NILE

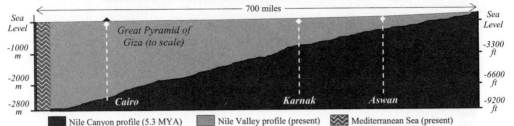

Sea Level	Sea Level
-1000 m	-3300 ft
-2000 m	-6600 ft
-2800 m	-9200 ft

700 miles

Great Pyramid of Giza (to scale)

Cairo — Karnak — Aswan

■ Nile Canyon profile (5.3 MYA)   ■ Nile Valley profile (present)   ▨ Mediterranean Sea (present)

The shallow valley where Cairo now sprawls was, 5.3 million years ago, a sheer-sided gorge half as deep again as the Grand Canyon. Three hundred thousand years previously, the Strait of Gibraltar had sealed up and the ancient Mediterranean dried to salty puddles. In response, the Nile cut its way 8,500 ft down to the barren seabed. Then, triggered by an earthquake perhaps, the strait abruptly ruptured and, in the Zanclean flood, the Mediterranean refilled in two years—the torrent that poured through is estimated to have had 1,000 times the flow of the Amazon and an initial drop (as rapids) almost three times that of Angel Falls; subsequently, silt carried by the Nile refilled the Nile Canyon to the current valley bottom. This cycle of drying and flooding has repeated itself more than once, and given Africa's inexorably drift north into Europe, geologists believe it's inevitable the Strait of Gibraltar will close up once more 'very soon' (thankfully as geologists reckon things—so no need to worry).

SQUARING THE CIRCLE. The 11th-century Arab scientist Alhacen got himself into serious trouble when, in a rash moment, he claimed he could tame the annual Nile flood. Hearing of his boast, the caliph put him in charge of a project to do just that. Alhacen quickly realized the impossibility of the task, and, fearing for his life, came up with the idea of feigning madness, which he did until the caliph died, all the while working in secret on various mathematical topics—including his famous treatise on how to square the circle.

GLASS SANDAL. The original Cinderella is thought to have been Rhodopis, a 'rosy-cheeked' Greco-Egyptian girl who, according to Strabo, lived beside the Nile six centuries before Christ. As first told, an eagle snatched off one of her sandals and deposited it in the lap of the pharaoh, who then sent soldiers to scour the land until Rhodopsis was found and duly married. In various permutations, Cinderella's story has been a favourite ever since—even through the unfortunate period in Victorian times when she was known as 'Cinderslut' (from the grime acquired during housework).

CANOPIC JARS—THE WORLD'S FIRST ORGANIC BURIALS

During the Old Kingdom period, ancient Egyptian embalmers were unable to mummify the wet internal organs of a body. Rather than discard them, they put the four most important,[1] aside from the heart, into stone vessels, so the dead person could retrieve them in the afterlife. The vessels, called canopic jars, were each protected by the appropriate son of Horus, whose head would be inscribed on the stopper. (The heart was kept in the body so that it could be weighed by Anubis, and if found lacking, fed to the Ammit monster.)

NORTH CORNER:	EAST CORNER:	SOUTH CORNER:	WEST CORNER:
Hapi (Baboon)	**Duametef**	**Imseti** (Human)	**Qebehsenuef**
Lungs	(Jackal)	*Liver*	(Falcon)
	Stomach		*Large Intestine*

[1] *The brain did not count as important since ancient Egyptians thought its role was limited to making mucus. Accordingly, they pushed long bronze hooks up through the nostrils, whisked them round to turn the brain matter to mush, and then drained off the gloop through the nose and poured it down the sewer.*

♥♣ · **GSR:** 46 · **WHS:** Abu Mena (Christian ruins) □ Cairo (historic city) □ Giza–Memphis (pyramids and necropolis) □ Luxor (pharaonic ruins of Thebes) □ Nubia: Abu Simbel–Philae (pharaonic monuments and ruins) □ St. Catherine, Sinai (monastery) □ Wadi Al-Hitan (whale fossils) · **ICH:** Al-Sirah Al-Hilaliyyah (Beduin epic poetry)

EL SALVADOR

'I beg you in the name of God: stop the repression.'

—Archbishop Óscar Romero of San Salvador, 23 March 1980.
The next day, he was shot dead while celebrating Mass.

LORD BE PRAISED. For the smallest mainland colony in the Americas, Spain's conquistadores dreamt up a name so long it had to be punctuated: *La Provincia De Nuestra Señor Jesus Cristo, El Salvador Del Mundo*—'The Province of Our Lord Jesus Christ, the Saviour of the World'. Thankfully, this shrank to plain 'El Salvador', though its formal name ('The Republic of El Salvador in Central America') still sounds more like a postal address.

NOXIOUS NIPPERS. All the world's centipedes are venomous, but it is the Salvadorans who suffer the most fatal attacks. Centipedes inject poison through their front feet, and while no species targets prey larger than birds or mice, they are aggressive creatures and, especially in children, their toxins can be powerful enough to induce anaphylactic shock.

LITTLE... Endemic across El Salvador, the world's smallest flea, the chigoe, may also be the itchiest, due to its fondness for burrowing into human feet. On at least one occasion, a

Chigoe after feeding

whole village has been permanently abandoned to leave a severe infestation behind.

... AND LARGE. El Salvador's shallow coastal waters are home to the Pacific seahorse, one of the largest known seahorse species, reaching up to 30 cm in length. Unlike any other animal, it's the male seahorse that gets pregnant and gives birth to the young.

SINGING THE BLUES. The 'blue' in blue jeans is indigo, and 20,000 tons a year are used. The dye historically came from the indigo bush and fetched stellar prices. Luckily for El Salvador, conditions were ideal for indigo cultivation, and the country got rich supplying the Spanish Empire. Unluckily for El Salvador, in 1897 a cheap synthetic version was invented and, overnight, the country was ruined.

PAINT ME A RAINBOW—PRE-INDUSTRIAL COLOUR		
Colour	*Dye*	*Source*
Red	*Carmine* [1]	boiled cochineal insects (Mexico)
Orange	*Lawsone*	henna plant (India, North Africa)
Yellow	*Indian Yellow*	urine of cows fed with mango leaves
Green	*Woad + Weld* [2]	leaves then roots [2] (Lincoln, famously)
Blue	*Woad*	mustard leaves (Western Europe)
Indigo	*Indigo*	rotten leaves (India, El Salvador)
Violet	*Logwood*	tropical wood chips (Belize, Mexico)

[1] *During the Middle Ages, the aristocratic smart set rode horses with bright red teeth and hooves. This effect was obtained by feeding the horses madder roots, another source of red.* [2] *A two-stage process (weld is a yellow).*

UNSUNG SAVIOUR. During WWII, Salvadoran diplomat George Mantello saved the lives of up to a hundred thousand Hungarian Jews. From his Geneva base, Mantello smuggled 10,000 blank Salvadoran citizenship certificates into the Axis country for use by Jewish Hungarians trying to avoid round-up and near-certain death. His biggest coup, however, came in June 1944, when he orchestrated an international press campaign that halted the transfer of Jews from Hungary to Auschwitz for four months. With this reprieve, 140,000 Hungarian Jews survived to the war's end.

♦ · **GSR**: n/a · **WHS**: Joya de Cerén (pre-Columbian ruins)

— EQUATORIAL GUINEA ● GUINEA ECUATORIAL —

'There is no god other than Macias Nguema.'

—Equatoguinean national motto under the presidency of Macias Nguema (1968–79)

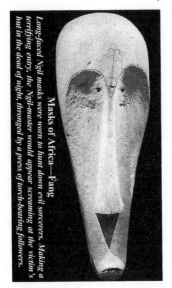

Masks of Africa—Fang

Long-faced Ngil masks were worn to hunt down evil sorcerers. Making a terrifying entry, the Ngil-master would appear screaming at the victim's hut in the dead of night, thronged by a press of torch-bearing followers.

FAMILY FORTUNES. When, in 1996, oil was struck in Equatoguinean waters, the country shot from bumping along the bottom of Africa's wealth league to having a GDP per capita equal to Denmark—not that this is very apparent to the 70% of citizens who still live on less than $2 a day. Meanwhile, over in Kleptocrat Acres, Teodorín Obiang (agriculture minister and president's son) somehow ekes out his $6,400-a-month salary to run a $32m Malibu mansion, private jet and fleet of supercars. However, in June 2011 he did cancel the yacht he'd commissioned for $380m—three times the country's combined health and education budgets.

'I am hugely grateful to President Obiang.'

—Simon Mann, Old Etonian, mercenary and ex-SAS officer, after release from Black Beach prison in 2009

DOGS OF WAR.[2] In 2004, Simon Mann and 66 other mercenaries were arrested in Zimbabwe en route to Equatorial Guinea, where they had planned to overthrow President Teodoro Obiang.[3] Mann was eventually extradited to Equatorial Guinea in 2008 and sentenced to 34 years in jail.

Simon Mann

In 2009, however, he was pardoned after his family paid $320,000. Separately, in 2005, Margaret Thatcher's son, Sir Mark Thatcher, was fined over $400,000 and given a four-year suspended sentence, after admitting his part in financing the same coup plot.

[2] *Equatorial Guinea, thinly disguised as the fictional Republic of Zangora, was the setting for Frederick Forsyth's 1974 novel* The Dogs of War. [3] *A 2003 World Bank study found that the discovery of oil increased a developing country's risk of suffering a coup or violent conflict by 450%—one facet of the so-called 'curse of oil' (gross corruption being another).*

AROUND THE WORLD IN 21,600 MINUTES.[1] The word 'equator' is an abbreviation of the medieval Latin phrase *'aequator diei et noctis'*, meaning 'equalizer of the day and night'. The term was first applied to the celestial equator—the imaginary line in the sky followed by the sun on the dates of the two annual equinoxes, when day and night are of equal length—and appears in English as a terrestrial feature only in the 17th century.

[1] *The equator's 360 degrees of latitude are each divided into 60 angular minutes, each exactly one nautical mile in length.*

NOT TO SCALE

TROPICAL CHILL. *Since the atmosphere bulges outward at the Equator and temperatures drop with altitude, the coldest air temperatures (of –75°C) are found high above the Equator and not at the Poles.*

THE AUSCHWITZ OF AFRICA is what they called Equatorial Guinea under President Obiang's predecessor and uncle, Macias Nguema. Governing while high on hallucinogenic drugs, his 11-year reign was so bad (and mad) that 30% of the country's population either fled overseas or were killed—notably including 150 alleged coup plotters who were executed in the national stadium while Mary Hopkin's *Those Were the Days* was played over the loudspeakers. As a cost-saving measure, at one stage Nguema ordered the capital's electricity generators to be switched off whenever he left town. Then, giving up any attempt at a national budget, he had the governor of the Central Bank killed, stuffed the national reserves into several suitcases and carried them back to his home village, where he kept them in a hut.

♥ · **GSR**: 173 · **WHS**: none

———— ERITREA ● ኤርትራ ————

'It is better to suffer with your own people than to eat porridge by yourself.'

—Tigrinya proverb. (Since seceding from Ethiopia in 1993, Eritrea has steered a savagely autarkic course.)

The Queen of Punt visiting Egypt

PUNT HUNT. Eritrea is the likely location for the lost Land of Punt. To the ancient Egyptians, Punt was the most exotic country their ships ever visited—source of ivory, incense, animal skins and strange tales. But after 1100 BCE, contact was broken and, in later Egyptian chronicles, it faded to their Eldorado and Shangri-La rolled into one.

ERITREA—READ THIS FIRST

★ Eritrea is the only country on Earth where the press is more tightly controlled than North Korea.[1]

★ Eritrea has never in its history had an election.[2]

★ Eritrea is the first nation anywhere planning to make its entire coast into a marine conservation zone.

[1] *Reporters Without Borders Press Freedom Index (2009).* [2] *Regular elections are mandated by law. But, in a brilliant piece of doublethink, the ruling party claims elections must be called by the Electoral Commission, and, if they choose not to act, its hands are tied.*

SECOND ROME. Eritrea was Italy's first colony—its *colonia primogenita*—declared in 1890. After Mussolini ascended to power, and, in 1936, he determined to build its new capital, Asmara, as a city without peer in Africa. Starting almost from scratch, young Italian architects were encouraged to create a bravura fantasia of modernism, from cubism to futurism and streamline deco, unthinkable

back home in Europe—all in the name of fascism. With an extravagant budget and 50,000 Italian settlers, Piccolo Roma ('Little Rome') blossomed over the next five years into one of the world's most modern cities (at the time, one of its grandest boasts was that it had more traffic lights than Rome itself). In 1941, however, WWII intervened, and the British overran the colony,[3] closing the door on Italian involvement and leaving Asmara mouldering ever since.

Image: Asmara's futurist Fiat Tagliero filling station (1938). [3] *During the invasion, the British Army faced its last ever cavalry charge when Italian Amedeo Guillet and his Eritreans tried to ride down a tank column wielding swords and hand grenades. Needless to say, the engagement was one-sided (though Guillet himself, a former Olympic equestrian, lived on to reach 101).*

When it was opened in 1938, the Italian-built Asmara–Massawa cableway was hailed as one of the engineering marvels of the century. Dropping 7,300 ft in 45 miles over precipices, deserts and ravines, it linked Eritrea's capital with the torrid coast by cables strung between 500 giant termite-proof towers. Majestic or not, the enterprise was broken up by Britain as war booty.

FISH STEW. At 32°C in summer, the soupy waters of Eritrea's Dahlak Archipelago form the warmest stretch of the world's warmest sea (the Red). Ticklishly, while divers are unlikely to be troubled by exposure *(right)*, scientists believe excess heat drives sharks to hyper-aggression—and there are plenty.

ALL AT SEA—SURVIVAL TIME BY WATER TEMPERATURE		
Temp. (°C)	*Survival*	*Example*
< 5	10–90 mins	New York (March)
5–10	1–3 hrs	North Sea (January)
10–15	1–6 hrs	Cape Town (July)
15–20	2–40 hrs	English Channel (August)
20–25	3 hrs–indefinite	Costa del Sol (August)
>25	indefinite	Red Sea (October)

Source: USAF 5ᵗʰ Weather Wing.

♥ · **GSR:** 174 · **WHS:** none

ESTONIA • EESTI

'Estonians are economical with their feelings. Instead of polite superficiality, they display a discourteous indifference.'

—The Estonian Institute

YULE LOG. Tallinn's Brotherhood of Black-heads (a guild for bachelor merchants) gave the world the Christmas tree. From 1441 onwards, they erected a fir tree in the city's Town Hall square at Christmas, danced round it with some handy maidens, then set it on fire. The rest of the globe followed later (if without the frolicking or arson[1]).

[1] *Or perhaps not: three times as many homes go up in flames each Christmas Day as burn down on a typical day year-round.*

UNIVERSAL DECLARATION OF HUMAN RIGHTS:[2]

WORD COUNT IN ...

Estonian	(1,421)
Czech	(1,531)
Hungarian	(1,573)
Russian	(1,634)
German	(1,678)
Swedish	(1,717)
Welsh	(1,732)
English	(1,778)
Bulgarian	(1,799)
Portuguese	(1,873)
Greek	(1,942)
Spanish	(1,959)
French	(1,974)
Dutch	(1,995)

1,400   *Number of Words*   2,000

[2] *The Universal Declaration of Human Rights, published in 1948, is the world's most widely translated document. It is currently available in 370 languages.*

WWW.WAR. In April 2007, the Estonian government moved a Soviet war memorial out of the centre of the country's capital, Tallinn. A few days later, Estonia came under a massive and sustained distributed DOS[3] attack which, for two weeks, all but closed down internet, e-commerce and email access across the nation. It was the first time that an entire country had been paralysed electronically, and all leads pointed to Russia. The onslaught shook the West, and taking it as the shape of things to come, NATO moved swiftly to establish a dedicated Cyber Defence Centre—which has been based, appropriately enough, in Tallinn.

[3] *A 'Denial of Service' attack—overloading websites, email servers, etc. using large numbers of external computers until the target crashes.*

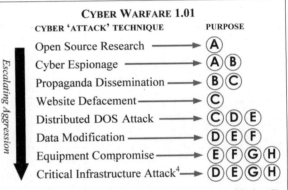

CYBER WARFARE 1.01

CYBER 'ATTACK' TECHNIQUE	PURPOSE
Open Source Research	Ⓐ
Cyber Espionage	Ⓐ Ⓑ
Propaganda Dissemination	Ⓑ Ⓒ
Website Defacement	Ⓒ
Distributed DOS Attack	Ⓒ Ⓓ Ⓔ
Data Modification	Ⓓ Ⓔ Ⓕ
Equipment Compromise	Ⓔ Ⓕ Ⓖ Ⓗ
Critical Infrastructure Attack[4]	Ⓓ Ⓔ Ⓖ Ⓗ

Escalating Aggression

Key: A Gathering intelligence, **B** Recruiting agents (blackmail) and sympathizers, **C** Undermining morale, **D** Damaging adversary's economy, **E** Disrupting enemy's 'Command and Control' capability (its military nervous system), **F** Disabling weapons systems, **G** Causing physical damage to enemy country and its facilities, **H** Inflicting human casualties (fires, explosions, etc.).

[4] *Disrupting or destroying a nation's power grid or other utilities—the cyber equivalent of a nuclear strike.*

SEA LANES. Every winter, Estonia builds ice roads across the sea to its offshore islands. A couple of special rules apply: no driving at 15–25 mph (because resonant vibrations can build up and crack the ice) and seatbelts must *not* be worn—because you don't want to drown if they do.

LEADING LADIES

Counting 118 women for every 100 men, Estonia is the most feminine country in the world (jointly with next-door Latvia.)

♠ · **GSR**: 75 · **WHS**: Old Tallinn (cityscape) ☐ Struve Arc (survey line) · **ICH**: Baltic Song Festivals (folk singing and dance) ☐ Kihnu (island culture) ☐ Seto Leelo (minority group folk singing)

——————— ETHIOPIA ● ኢትዮጵያ ———————

*'Ethiopia is a place to teach patience to a man who has it not,
and to take it away from him who has.'*

—Baron Dablin (*c.* 1862)

LION KING. When, in 1930, Haile Selassie was crowned King of Kings, Emperor of Ethiopia, one of the subsidiary titles he acquired was 'Conquering Lion of the Tribe of Judah'. It was an honorific he took seriously. The founder of his dynasty, King Solomon, had kept lions as pets, and Selassie surrounded himself with them. Even before his coronation, while still regent, he had made headlines around Europe by taking a pride of lions with him on a 1924 Royal tour[1]—giving them away as he went (including one to Britain's King George V and another to London Zoo). Once he was crowned as emperor, black-maned Abyssinian lions remained on guard by his side day and night. On formal occasions, lions would lie either side of the throne, and, to demonstrate his continuing authority to rule, each morning Selassie would walk one around his palace grounds.

In 1930, Haile Selassie became the first black person to appear on the cover of Time *magazine when he was crowned Emperor of Ethiopia.*

[1] *On the same tour, Selassie adopted 40 Armenian orphans, had them trained as musicians and sent to Ethiopia, where they formed his imperial brass band.*

> **BAND AID (1984)**
> **CAST LIST (SELECTED)**
>
> Bob Geldof launched Band Aid to help starving Ethiopian children. On release, the single outsold all other songs in the UK chart combined.
>
> *Bob Geldof ~ Midge Ure*
> *David Bowie ~ Phil Collins*
> *Culture Club ~ Paul Weller*
> *George Michael ~ Bono*
> *Duran Duran ~ Status Quo*
> *Paul McCartney*
>
> Famine deaths 1,000,000
> Money raised $13,000,000

LEGLESS. Ethiopia's national drink, *tej*, is a honey mead sold in two varieties: filtered and unfiltered. The difference comes down to whether you think the bees' legs lend added kick.

Ark of the Covenant

Ge'ez manuscript: infant Jesus

RAIDERS LOST THE ARK. Judaism's Holy of Holies, the Ark of the Covenant, was lost from knowledge nearly 3,000 years ago. According to Ethiopian histories, however, what happened was that it was stolen by a son of Solomon and taken to Aksum, in northern Ethiopia. It's said to be there still, in its own little bungalow, off-limits to all but the generations of priestly guardians who, once appointed, give up their names and never again leave its side until they die. True or not, scepticism is tempered (a little) by the centuries-old presence in Ethiopia of the Beta Israel, a Jewish people of ancient lineage, 80,000 of whom have now been airlifted to Israel.

SPACE RACE. Ethiopian monks had kept vigil on the site of Jesus's crucifixion for over 1,200 years until 1838, when they all died from plague. Before replacements could arrive, Egyptian Coptic monks took over the space and refused to make way. Taking the long view, the fresh Ethiopians (and their successors) doggedly waited until 1970, when the Copts briefly left the area unguarded. The Ethiopians promptly swooped, and an agreement to share the space was eventually hammered out. However, tempers snapped in 2002, when one Copt moved his chair out of the sun and into the Ethiopian zone. In the fistfight that followed, 11 monks were hospitalized.

OUT OF AFRICA—PRE-COLONIAL EMPIRES (SELECTED)

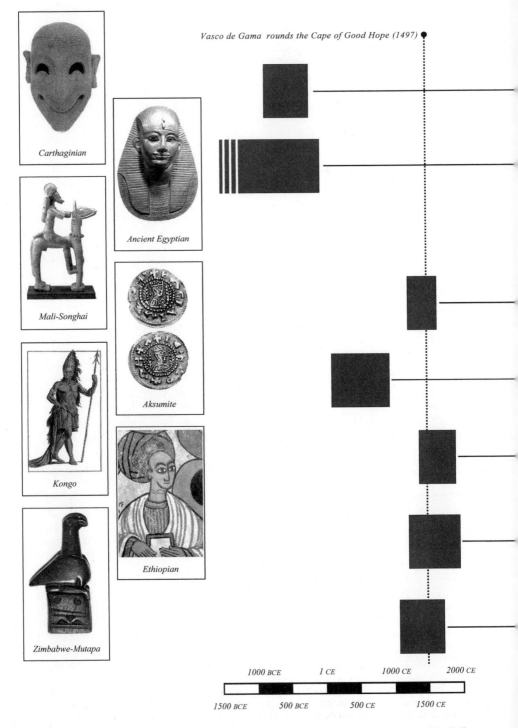

Carthaginian

Ancient Egyptian

Mali-Songhai

Aksumite

Kongo

Ethiopian

Zimbabwe-Mutapa

Vasco de Gama rounds the Cape of Good Hope (1497)

1000 BCE   1 CE   1000 CE   2000 CE

1500 BCE   500 BCE   500 CE   1500 CE

OUT OF AFRICA—PRE-COLONIAL EMPIRES (SELECTED)

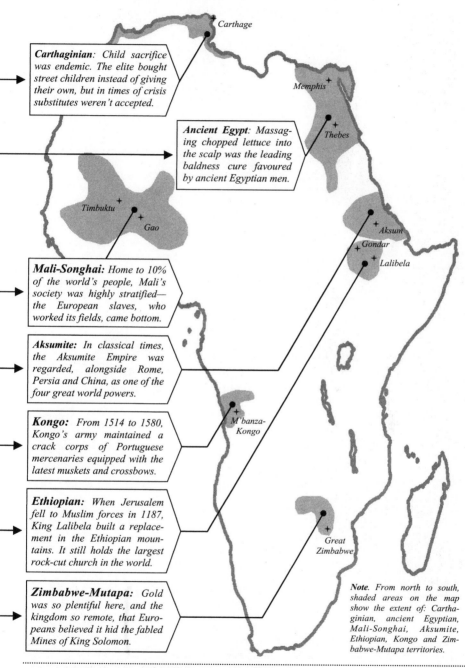

Carthaginian: *Child sacrifice was endemic. The elite bought street children instead of giving their own, but in times of crisis substitutes weren't accepted.*

Ancient Egypt: *Massaging chopped lettuce into the scalp was the leading baldness cure favoured by ancient Egyptian men.*

Mali-Songhai: *Home to 10% of the world's people, Mali's society was highly stratified—the European slaves, who worked its fields, came bottom.*

Aksumite: *In classical times, the Aksumite Empire was regarded, alongside Rome, Persia and China, as one of the four great world powers.*

Kongo: *From 1514 to 1580, Kongo's army maintained a crack corps of Portuguese mercenaries equipped with the latest muskets and crossbows.*

Ethiopian: *When Jerusalem fell to Muslim forces in 1187, King Lalibela built a replacement in the Ethiopian mountains. It still holds the largest rock-cut church in the world.*

Zimbabwe-Mutapa: *Gold was so plentiful here, and the kingdom so remote, that Europeans believed it hid the fabled Mines of King Solomon.*

Note. *From north to south, shaded areas on the map show the extent of: Carthaginian, ancient Egyptian, Mali-Songhai, Aksumite, Ethiopian, Kongo and Zimbabwe-Mutapa territories.*

Map labels: Carthage · Memphis · Thebes · Timbuktu · Gao · Aksum · Gondar · Lalibela · M'banza-Kongo · Great Zimbabwe

♥ · **GSR**: 145 · **WHS**: Aksum (ruined city) □ Awash (human fossils) □ Gondar (castles) □ Harar (walled city) □ Konso Landscape (terracing and fortifications) □ Lalibela (rock churches) □ Omo (human fossils) □ Simien (mountains) □ Tiya (lost civilization)

───── FAROE ISLANDS ● FØROYAR ─────

'The coward believes he will live for ever if he holds back in battle;
but in old age he shall have no peace, though spears have spared his limbs.'

—*Hávamál*, the collected wisdom of Odin (*c.* 10th century)

THE NORTHERNMOST BRITISH ISLES. Far to the north of Scotland's Shetland Islands, the Faroes were reputedly first settled by a Viking called Grímr Kamban. But, as suggested by his Gaelic surname (related to Cameron), Kamban and his early followers probably came from one of the Viking colonies in northern Britain or Ireland, rather than from Denmark or Norway itself. DNA analysis shows that, while 87% of the Faroes' male settlers were of Scandinavian (i.e. Viking) origin, 83% of their willing or unwilling female consorts were Celtic British.

Faroese Coat of Arms. Føroyar means 'Sheep Islands' in Faroese.

In old Norse, the verb 'to go viking' originally just meant 'to go on an expedition'.

SAILOR SPEAK. As well as colonizing the northern Atlantic, the Viking seafarers left a lasting legacy in nautical jargon across northern Europe. An example is the English 'starboard' ('right' to landlubbers), which comes from the Viking practice of fitting rudders to the right-hand side of their ships, causing it to become known as the *styrbord* or 'steer side'. The Viking term for the ship's left-hand side, *ladebord* ('loading side'), also found its way into English—as 'larboard', the former nautical term for 'left'. However, in the 19th century, the scope for confusion with the sound-alike 'starboard' (especially when shouted into the teeth of a gale) persuaded the English world to substitute 'port'.

FISHY BUSINESS. The *grindadráp* is perhaps the Faroes' most entrenched tradition. Several times each summer, islanders encircle schools of pilot whales and dolphins and drive them on to a nearby beach, where they are killed and the meat distributed. The hunts have long been a magnet for international opprobrium, but, in 2008, it looked as if the *grindadráp* would come to an end for a wholly different reason, as the Faroes' chief medical officers said that, due to high mercury levels, the whales had become too toxic to eat. Highly unusually, however, the Faroese government has advised its citizens to ignore its own medical advice pending more 'evaluation' (which three years later has still to appear).

Catch (2010): 1106 whales

GRINDADRÁP—STEP BY STEP

1. When a school of whales and dolphins is sighted, islanders surround it in small boats.

2. At a signal, roped stones are thrown into the sea to drive the school into a bay or fjord.

3. The quarry either beach themselves or are dragged from the shallows by their blowholes.

4. They are then killed by slicing through their spines (and main arteries) with a large knife.

HAVE A HEART. The Faroese are hugely fond of their half a million resident puffins. Their black and white penguin livery, clownlike beaks and lovable friendliness are all appreciated, but what excites the Faroese most of all is the juiciness of their breast meat marinated in milk or ale.[1]

[1] *However, even the Faroese baulk at the Icelandic delicacy of puffin hearts served raw and still warm.*

JUST CALL ME FLIPPER. Humans are not the only animals to go by personal names. In 2006, scientists discovered that bottlenose dolphins choose a name for themselves as infants and keep it for the rest of their lives, using it to alert family members of their location and, when distressed, call for help.

♠ · **GSR**: 182 · **Autonomous country under the Danish Crown**. **WHS**: none

————— FIJI • MATANITU KO VITI • फ़िजी —————

'Eat me.'

—The traditional greeting given by a commoner to his chiefs until Christianization. In the 19th century, the Fijian archipelago was known as the 'Cannibal Islands' due to the ubiquity of the practice. Fear of the local diet significantly delayed European encroachment, with documented instances of opportunistic anthropophagy continuing until at least 1937.

SERVE CHILLED. Going under the slogan 'the anti-energy drink', *kava* is the Pacific's gift to world drinking culture. In Fiji, it's known as 'grog' (or more formally *yaqona*) and forms the centrepiece of village life, drunk daily after work on a strictly men-only basis. Although the thick, grey-green liquid tastes of mud and anaesthetizes the lips and tongue (as well as the stomach—creating a risk of regurgitation in the inexperienced), for grog's many devotees, all this is worth it thanks to its sedative effect—which is described as being like a large dose of liquid diazepam (Valium).

HOTFOOTING IT. Fiji is split roughly evenly between native Fijian and ethnic Indian citizens in a mix that's not always happy. (Friction has led to four post-independence coups.) But a tradition the two communities have in common is fire-walking—by coincidence developed separately by each when still living thousands of miles apart. In both cases, participants step without injury across a bed of glowing embers or coals over twice the temperature of a domestic oven. Those who do it put their apparent immunity down to faith and spiritual purity. Science, however, credits the result to a careful regard to relative thermal effusivity. (In brief, because the human foot is a big, watery bag with a built-in cooling system (the circulation), on first contact with the surface of the small, dry coals, it cools them down far more than they heat it up, thus letting the pedestrian escape with just a mild warming—so long as he or she doesn't hang around.[1])

[1] *When 30 KFC restaurant managers tried fire-walking as a 'leadership skills' exercise during a 2002 management conference in Australia, 20 were hospitalized with burns.*

SEALED WITH A KISS. Found in waters from Fiji to Hawaii, as well as elsewhere in the tropical oceans, the diminutive cookie-cutter shark uses specially adapted suction-grip lips to smooch on to larger animals such as dolphins or tuna (and occasionally humans).[3] Once firmly anchored, it saws out a neat circle of flesh with its outsize teeth,[4] twists its body to extract the prize, and darts away with a swish of its powerful tail before its victim can even think about retaliating.

[3] *Swimmers have had plugs of muscle removed from their legs as they swam. Additionally, in the 1970s, a US Navy submarine was crippled when the sharks bit neat round holes in its rubber sonar dome—leading the military at first to believe the damage had been caused by a new Soviet secret weapon. In consequence, all sonar domes are now fibreglass.* [4] *Cookie-cutters have proportionately the biggest teeth of all sharks. To conserve calcium, the fish eat the old ones each time they grow new sets.*

 The 'Fiji Mermaid' was the name P. T. Barnum gave to one of the 19th century's most notorious 'curiosities', which he exhibited around America as a circus sideshow. Allegedly the mummified corpse of a genuine mermaid, it was, in fact, the head of a baboon sown on to the body of an orang-utan stuffed into the tail of a fish, which, prior to coming into Barnum's possession, had never been closer to the South Pacific than the Boston workshop of Mr. Moses Kimball—from whom Barnum rented it for $12.50 a week.

▪ Although the Fiji Mermaid was an out-and-out fake, human mermaid syndrome (also known as sirenomelia)—in which both legs are fused together in a single tail-like limb—occurs roughly as often as Siamese twins. However, only three such children are known to have survived.

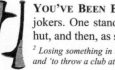 **YOU'VE BEEN BRAINED!** Chiefs in pre-colonial Fiji were noted practical jokers. One standard jape was to invite local commoners to help thatch a hut, and then, as soon as they arrived, hurl volleys of war clubs at them.[2]

[2] *Losing something in translation, this joke is a wordplay on* ulaula *meaning both 'to thatch a hut' and 'to throw a club at'—how anyone fell for this more than once, though, is harder to explain.*

● · **GSR**: 135 · **WHS**: none

FINLAND ● SUOMI

'You won't survive life.'

—Finnish proverb

SANTA WARS. Father Christmas can be fairly described to be an international man of mystery. For the CEO of a major multi-national manufacturing-cum-logistics corporation, his biographical details are extremely brief—sketchy even: under 'age', you won't find closer than 'old'. Even his choice of home is hazy, though plenty fight for the plaudit (and the tourists it brings). Front-runner is Rovaniemi, in Finnish Lapland, with its Santa theme park; but the Norwegians also claim him, as do the Danes—who insist he lives in an earth hut in northern Greenland. The Canadians are certain he runs a North Pole HQ (and have given it the post code H0H 0H0), while America's choice, Santa Claus, Indiana (pop. 2041) seems a little wishful. Finally, 'Father Frost' at Veliky Ustyug, Russia, mustn't be forgotten (even if some whisper this is only a franchise operation).

'A worm-infested turnip is sweet, but bitter the one that a mouse has bitten.'

—Profound Finnish thought

CHILD'S PLAY. In 1910, Finnish folklorist Antti Aarne completed an epic classification of Europe's fairy tales according to content. As extended by Stith Thompson, the Aarne-Thompson Index remains the core tool for comparing folk tales worldwide. Organized hierarchically, the index lists 2,500 numbered 'tale types'. While 'Cinderella' and some others are known to all, many 'tale types' bear obscure, if not downright cryptic, titles. Examples below.

FAIRY FABLE TABLE

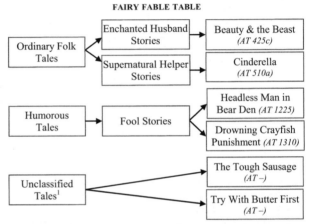

[1] *The coyly named 'Unclassified Tales' are, in fact, bawdy folk stories. Thompson declined to enumerate such 'obscene' gatherings further, and contented himself with merely assigning them the range AT 2400–2499 generically.*

PROTECTING PEOPLE. Nokia may be known today for making more mobile phones than anyone else, but in the 1960s its rather more exotic product range extended to the M61 gas mask, bought by NATO, and used by Finland's own armed forces until 1995.

EASY COME, EASY GO. Fines in Finland rise with income and it's just too bad if you're a multi-millionaire. In 2004, sausage plutocrat Jussi Salonoja was handed a speeding ticket for $185,000.

CRADLE TO GRAVE. Well into the 20th century, many Finns were born in the family sauna.[2] When it was time to die, they often sought it out too—finding solace in its warmth and memories.

[2] *Due to their heat and the tannic acid in wood smoke, saunas are relatively sterile, and so were rightly thought one of the safest places to give birth.*

♠ · **GSR**: 47 · **WHS**: · **Autonomous Province**: Åland Islands · **WHS**: Kvarken Archipelago (receding coastline) □ Petäjävesi (church) □ Rauma (townscape) □ Sammallahdenmäki (burial mounds) □ Struve Arc (survey line) □ Suomenlinna (fortress) □ Verla (paper mill)

FRANCE

'The French are Italians in a bad mood.'

—Jean Cocteau

SIGNS AND PORTENTS—THE FRENCH BURGLARS' CODE

| Burglary planned | Women alone | Can be intimidated | Simple break-in | Nosy neighbours | Nothing of interest |

French housebreakers mark the houses they've cased with a secret code understood by other burglars. According to the French police, the use of these symbols has spread to the UK and Belgium as well.

CORPSE BRIDE. Under the French legal code, it is possible to marry a dead person: but the president has to give his personal consent first. The unusual law was created by President de Gaulle in 1959, after he was touched by the pleas of a distraught young woman whose fiancé was killed in a dam burst. Around 20 such weddings take place yearly (and 30 requests are refused). If permission is granted, the marriage is officially backdated to the day before the death of the deceased partner.

ALIEN JURISDICTION. In 1954, Chateauneuf du Pape passed a by-law banning UFOs from the village. The by-law further ordered the village bobby to arrest any UFO that defied the regulation and landed anyway.

INTRODUCTORY FRENCH LESSON

Monsieur[1] = *Mon Sieur* = 'My Sire'
Madame = *Ma Dame* = 'My Dame'
Mademoiselle = *Ma Damoisele* = 'My Damsel'

[1] *The plural form,* Messieurs (Mes Sieurs *or 'My Sires'), survives unchanged in the English word 'Messieurs', albeit this is almost invariably abbreviated to Messrs.*

Rij-Rousseau portrait (1915)

THE ART OF WAR. France pioneered the development of military camouflage in WWI at the urging of Guirnard di Scévola, an academic artist. Scévola took his inspiration directly from the work of contemporary Cubists and, because colour wasn't an issue (as aerial photography could only be done in black and white),

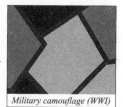

Military camouflage (WWI)

for a brief period the battlefield took on the appearance of an immense sculpture park, with heavy artillery pieces becoming giant art-installations painted in primary playground colours. Catching on fast, the Germans responded with a range of nine camouflage tarpaulins each in a different artistic style (beside Cubist, patterns available included Monet and Kandinsky). The British, meanwhile, took to painting their tanks in a red and green tartan.

MAD AS MARCH HARES. For 12 years from 1793, Revolutionary France ran on a decimal calendar. Hours had 100 minutes, days 10 hours, weeks 10 days, months 3 weeks and, in one disappointing bow to convention, years 12 months. Nevertheless, each month was renamed (*below*) and each day of the year given a unique name of its own—thus, 29 December was 'Manure' and 28 July 'Watering Can'. Today, the calendar lives on mainly through Lobster Thermidor (a dish ultimately inspired by the summary guillotining of Robespierre, an event which took place in the revolutionary month of Thermidor).

FRENCH REVOLUTIONARY CALENDAR MONTHS
(WITH LAMPOONS HELPFULLY SUPPLIED BY THE ANGLO-SAXON NEIGHBOURS)

Vendémiaire ('of Grapes') ..... *Wheezy (October)*
Brumaire ('of Fog') .... *Sneezy (November)*
Frimaire ('of Frost') .... *Freezy (December)*
Nivôse ('of Snow') .... *Slippy (January)*
Pluviôse ('of Rain') .... *Drippy (February)*
Ventôse ('of Wind') .... *Nippy (March)*

Germinal ('of Germination') ..... *Showery (April)*
Floréal ('of Flowers') .... *Flowery (May)*
Prairial ('of Pasture') .... *Bowery (June)*
Messidor ('of Harvest') .... *Wheaty (July)*
Thermidor ('of Warmth') .... *Heaty (August)*
Fructidor ('of Fruit') .... *Sweety (September)*

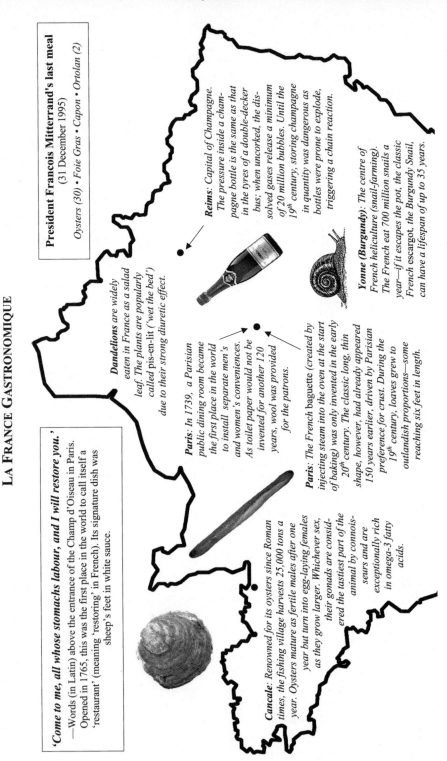

LA FRANCE GASTRONOMIQUE

President Francois Mitterrand's last meal
(31 December 1995)

Oysters (30) • Foie Gras • Capon • Ortolan (2)

'Come to me, all whose stomachs labour, and I will restore you.'

—Words (in Latin) above the entrance of the Champ d'Oiseau in Paris. Opened in 1765, this was the first place in the world to call itself a 'restaurant' (meaning 'restoring' in French). Its signature dish was sheep's feet in white sauce.

Reims: Capital of Champagne. The pressure inside a champagne bottle is the same as that in the tyres of a double-decker bus; when uncorked, the dissolved gases release a minimum of 20 million bubbles. Until the 19th century, storing champagne in quantity was dangerous as bottles were prone to explode, triggering a chain reaction.

Yonne (Burgundy): The centre of French heliculture (snail-farming). The French eat 700 million snails a year—if it escapes the pot, the classic French escargot, the Burgundy Snail, can have a lifespan of up to 35 years.

Dandelions *are widely eaten in France as a salad leaf. The plants are popularly called pis-en-lit ('wet the bed') due to their strong diuretic effect.*

Paris: In 1739, a Parisian public dining room became the first place in the world to install separate men's and women's conveniences. As toilet paper would not be invented for another 120 years, wool was provided for the patrons.

Paris: The French baguette (created by injecting steam into the oven at the start of baking) was only invented in the early 20th century. The classic long, thin shape, however, had already appeared 150 years earlier, driven by Parisian preference for crust. During the 19th century, loaves grew to outlandish proportions—some reaching six feet in length.

Cancale: Renowned for its oysters since Roman times, the fishing village harvests 25,000 tons a year but turn into egg-laying females as they grow larger. Whichever sex, their gonads are considered the tastiest part of the animal by connoisseurs and are exceptionally rich in omega-3 fatty acids.

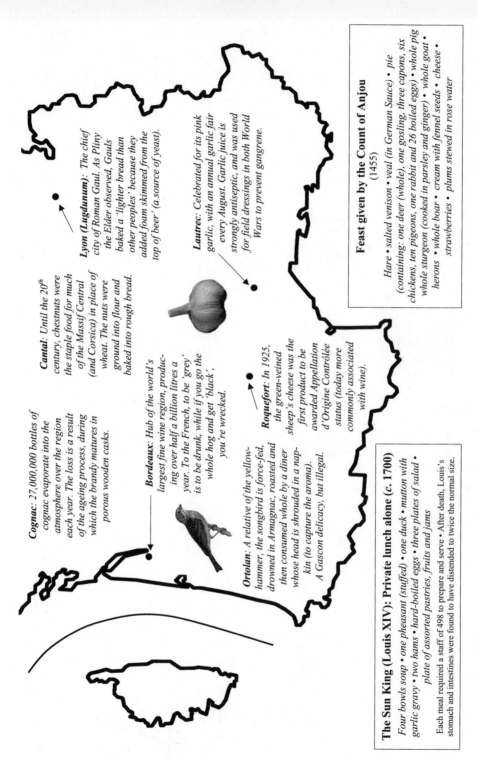

Lyon (Lugdunum): *The chief city of Roman Gaul. As Pliny the Elder observed, Gauls baked a 'lighter bread than other peoples' because they added foam skimmed from the top of beer' (a source of yeast).*

Cantal: *Until the 20th century, chestnuts were the staple food for much of the Massif Central (and Corsica) in place of wheat. The nuts were ground into flour and baked into rough bread.*

Lautrec: *Celebrated for its pink garlic, with an annual garlic fair every August. Garlic juice is strongly antiseptic, and was used for field dressings in both World Wars to prevent gangrene.*

Cognac: *27,000,000 bottles of cognac evaporate into the atmosphere over the region each year. The loss is a result of the ageing process, during which the brandy matures in porous wooden casks.*

Bordeaux: *Hub of the world's largest fine wine region, producing over half a billion litres a year. To the French, to be 'grey' is to be drunk, while if you go the whole hog and get 'black', you're wrecked.*

Roquefort: *In 1925, the green-veined sheep's cheese was the first product to be awarded Appellation d'Origine Contrôlée status (today more commonly associated with wine).*

Ortolan: *A relative of the yellow-hammer, the songbird is force-fed, drowned in Armagnac, roasted and then consumed whole by a diner whose head is shrouded in a napkin (to capture the aroma). A Gascon delicacy, but illegal.*

Feast given by the Count of Anjou
(1455)

Hare • salted venison • veal (in German Sauce) • pie (containing: one deer (whole), one gosling, three capons, six chickens, ten pigeons, one rabbit and 26 boiled eggs) • whole pig • whole sturgeon (cooked in parsley and ginger) • whole goat • herons • whole boar • cream with fennel seeds • cheese • strawberries • plums stewed in rose water

---

The Sun King (Louis XIV): Private lunch alone (c. 1700)

Four bowls soup • one pheasant (stuffed) • one duck • mutton with garlic gravy • two hams • hard-boiled eggs • three plates of salad • plate of assorted pastries, fruits and jams

Each meal required a staff of 498 to prepare and serve • After death, Louis's stomach and intestines were found to have distended to twice the normal size.

THREE THOUGHTFUL FRENCH

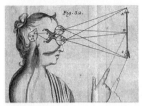

DESCARTES. *'I think, therefore I am.'* ■ An example to students everywhere, Descartes never got out of bed before lunchtime. When he was forced to rise early (at the Queen of Sweden's express summons), it killed him—he got pneumonia and died.

VOLTAIRE. *'A witty saying proves nothing.'* ■ Hence the reason Voltaire's critique of *Hamlet* as 'the work of a drunken savage' has been consigned to the wastepaper bin of history.

PROUDHON. *'Capitalism is the exploitation of the weak by the strong. Communism is the exploitation of the strong by the weak.'* ■ As father of anarchism, Proudhon has done more for spraycan sales than anyone before or since. (The ubiquitous Ⓐ sign makes reference to his slogan: 'Anarchy is Order'.)

FASHION GOD. Paris is synonymous with haute couture. But it was an English draper from Lincolnshire, Charles Worth, who got the French industry started. Opening in Paris in 1858, Worth dressed Empress Eugenie, pioneered the fashion show and was first to sew a 'label' into the clothes he created.

FIRST IMPRESSIONS. When history's most celebrated art movement erupted in the 1860s, it was to universal opprobrium from the Academic art establishment. 'Art sunk so low does not even deserve reproach,' and 'Wallpaper in its embryonic state is more finished,' were two insults levelled at the fresh-faced 'Impressionists'.

THE VOICE OF HISTORY—HIGHEST AUCTION PRICES PAID

Impressionists   *Academic Art*

	Impressionists	
EM	Manet	$35.8m
CM	Monet	$65.4m
PR	Renoir	$73.9m
	Academic Artists	
WB	Bouguereau	$1.9m
AC	Cabanel	$0.3m
JG	Gérôme	$1.1m

2010[1] 2002 1990   2007 2007 2008   *[1]Year sold; historic exchange rates.*

SATAN'S APPLE. Until 1772, the French avoided potatoes as food of the devil, and even had a law banning their cultivation (as they thought they spread leprosy). It took a potato zealot named Antoine-Augustin Parmentier to get them eating their spuds. Step one was to prod the Paris Faculty of Medicine into declaring potatoes edible. After that, his further ploys included handing the Queen a posy of potato flowers and ringing his potato patch with security guards to make the crop look super-valuable (then withdrawing them at night to let curious citizens 'steal' some). Parmentier's potato epiphany came as a POW in Prussia, where he was fed on them despite their contemporary status as animal feed (a standing common to most of Europe with the notable exception of Ireland).

PASCAL'S WAGER. 'In the absence of certainty either that God does or does not exist, the only rational course is to act as if he does—because one has nothing to lose and all to win.' Aside from being very interesting in its own right, Pascal's 1670 contention is the first formally presented use of decision theory.

In mathematical notation, the French philosopher's argument is rendered thus:

DECISION MATRIX		
	God	**No God**
Act is God (Y)	∞	f_1
Act is no God (N)	f_2	f_3

$E(Y) = \infty p + f_1(1 - p) = \infty$

$E(N) = f_2 p + f_3(1 - p)$

Where f_1, f_2 and f_3 are any finite numbers, and p is any non-infinitesimal positive probability.

WHAT IF ... As a teen-ager, Napoleon considered applying to the British Royal Navy for a cadetship. Instead, he tried unsuccessfully to get a berth on the La Pérouse expedition—that later vanished with all hands in the South Seas.

'The Elephant of Triumph'

In 1758, The French government received a proposal from architect Charles Ribart to fill the site where the Arc de Triomphe now stands with a monstrous pachyderm (with work-ing trunk and folding furniture) to symbolize the king. He was declined.

BLUE-BLOODS. Female courtiers at Versailles drew 'veins' on their necks in blue pencil to highlight their nobility.[1]

[1] *'Blue-bloodedness' goes back originally to medieval Spain. The idea came about since only non-working aristocratic women could keep their skin fair enough to allow their veins to be seen.*

Liberté • Égalité • Fraternité

RÉPUBLIQUE FRANÇAISE

BON MOTS. France's national motto was forged in the crucible of the French Revolution. Its first form, however, read more threat than promise:

'Liberty, Equality, Fra-ternity—or Death.'

GETTING THE CHOP. One of the French Revolution's most popular moves was to guillotine every tax collector in the country. Two centuries later, the last person beheaded by France was a one-legged murderer, Hamida Djan-doubi, executed in 1977.

'France has no friends, only interests.'
—Charles de Gaulle

BIG ON THE INSIDE. The 'Napoleon Complex'—the outsize attitude of the overcompensating little guy—has, at best, sketchy support in human studies; but it is very real in other species. Studies with swordtail fish show 78% of fights are started by the smaller male (who usually goes on to lose). As it happens, Napoleon wasn't so short; he was just always seen flanked by extremely tall and strong imperial guards.

LUCKY FOR SOME. Until WWII, *Quatorziens* ('fourteeners') were professional party-goers who could be hired after a late cancellation to avoid having 13 guests at a dinner party.

DOUBLE VISION. The Capgras Delusion, named after the French psychiatrist who first described it, causes sufferers to believe a loved one has been replaced by a doppelganger. The first observed case was a Parisian seamstress, 'Mme M.', who, in 1918, went to the police to complain that the city's cellars were full of imprisoned citizens, while their doubles stalked the streets. Sufferers now number tens of thousands worldwide; causes can include head injuries and strokes.

TOTALLY DELUDED—CONSULT YOUR DOCTOR IF ...	
You Think ...	*Delusion*
your husband/wife/cat is an imposter[2]	**Capgras**
you are already dead and in hell etc.	**Cotard**
the people round you are all the same person	**Fregoli**
the reflection in the mirror is someone else	**Mirrored-Self M.I.**

[2] *Of course, you may be right—it's known as the 'Martha Mitchell Effect' (named after Mrs Mitchell, who tried to report White House staff for breaking the law but was diagnosed as mentally ill—until Watergate broke).*

IN FLANDERS FIELDS. On 1 July 1916, the first day of the Battle of the Somme, the British suffered 3,483 casualties an hour. By midnight, losses stood at 57,470 (over 50% of the headcount of the entire Regular British Army in 2010).

Left margin (vertical): Aide-mémoire • au fait • avant-garde • beau geste • blasé • carte blanche • cri du cœur • déjà vu • éminence grise • fait accompli • film noir

Right margin (vertical): un best-seller • le coming-out • flirter • un has-been • les leggings • overbooké • le self-made man • la sex-symbol • un skinhead • le thriller

LES BARBARES AUX PORTES. To some, it's all that holds back Anglo-Saxon anarchy; to others it's meddling linguistic *dirigisme* to be deplored. Whichever, France's 1994 anti-English Toubon law (aka *la loi AllGood*) has real teeth: in 2006, GE Medical Systems was fined $800,000, plus an extra $27,000 each day it remained in breach, for failing to translate some internal software into French. 'Deserters' from the language get named and shamed too, at Paris's annual English Doormat Awards. One memorable winner was Jean-Claude Trichet, French president of the European Central Bank, who, when taking office in 2004, confusingly announced in English, 'I am not a Frenchman.'

LE CANCAN

'A boisterous and indecorous dance. Its exact nature is unknown to anyone connected with this Companion.'

—*Oxford Companion to Music* (1938)

BISOU BISOU. French kissing fights tooth decay by washing bacteria off a partner's teeth and breaking down their oral plaque; exchanging saliva also boosts the immune system by expanding each side's oral zoo. And it's not just humans that do it. Chimpanzees are immensely fond of a lingering, open-mouthed smooch.

MAN-MAN. In its early days, the cancan was frequently danced by men, such as the all-male troupe that caused a storm in London in 1870.

HOW TO KISS EN FRANCE

Combien?[1]

[1] *But apparently zero if travelling on the railways, as kissing has been illegal since 1910 (when it was banned to end the incessant delays caused by parting lovers).*

ORBITAL VELOCITY. From a near standing start in 1983, France has built traffic roundabouts with the obsession of a zealot. It currently has over 30,000—half the world total.

TIP OF MY TONGUE

AN A–Z OF LESS-OBVIOUS WINE-TASTING ADJECTIVES

Autolytic .... biscuity, often aged *sur lie*
Blowzy .... excessively fruity
Charming .... good—but not great
Dirty .... off-notes from poor hygiene
Edgy .... with flavour-enhancing acidity
Foxy .... American grape aroma (rank)
Green .... overly acid (unripe grapes?)
Hollow .... expected fruitiness absent
Inky .... darkness bordering on opaque
Jammy .... fruit not balanced by tannin
Lightstruck ... with damp cardboard aroma
Mean .... fruit overwhelmed by tannin

Nervy .... acid, but still in balance
Oxidized .... sherry-like (a fault)
Prickly .... very lightly effervescent
Quaffable .... fine for everyday drinking
Racy .... acidic, but in balance
Short .... taste quickly dissipates
Transparent ...... flavour elements distinct
Upfront .... lacking in complexity
Vegetal .... herby, contrast floral
Warm .... high but balanced alcohol
Yeasty .... biscuity
Zesty .... acid with citrus notes

♠ · **GSR**: 5 · **WHS**: Albi (museum town) □ Amiens (cathedral) □ Arles (Roman ruins) □ Avignon (museum city) □ Bordeaux (cityscape) □ Bourges (cathedral) □ Canal du Midi □ Carcassonne (museum city) Chartres (cathedral) □ Fontainebleau (palace) □ Fontenay (abbey) □ Flemish belfries (civic bell-towers) □ Le Havre (concrete) □ Loire Valley (châteaux) □ Lyon (architecture) □ Mt. Perdu (mountain) Mont-St.-Michel (island abbey) □ Nancy (cityscape) □ Provins (museum town) □ Orange (Roman theatre) □ Paris (cityscape) □ Pile Dwellings □ Pont du Gard (Roman aquaduct) □ Reims (cathedral) Santiago Pilgrimage Route (monuments) □ St.-Emilion (cultural landscape) □ St.-Savin (abbey) Salins-les-Bains (saltworks) □ Strasbourg (cityscape) □ Vauban Forts (military engineering) □ Versailles (palace) □ Vézelay (abbey) □ Vézère Valley (cave art) ■ Corsica: Gulf of Porto (*maquis* scrub) **ICH**: Alençon Lace-Making □ Aubusson (tapestry) □ Compagnonnage (apprenticeships) □ Falconry French Food □ Giants and Dragons (effigies) □ Scribing (carpentry) ■ Corsica: Paghjella (singing)

— FRENCH DEPENDENCIES ● LA FRANCE D'OUTRE-MER —

'We could not but compare this happy country to Mohamed's Paradise.'

—G. Forster (1777), on Tahiti

POSITIVE SPIN. At Kourou, a jungle-backed beach in French Guiana, the European Space Agency enjoys the world's best spaceport. Kourou's advantage lies not just in its lush setting but in being just 300 miles from the Equator. This maximizes the slingshot acceleration generated by the Earth's own rotation, worth a 'free' 1,030 mph before even firing the rocket's motors (enough to boost a rocket's payload by 40% compared to the same launch from Russia). In case of disaster, safety cover is provided by the sole South American outpost of the Paris Fire Brigade. Although Europe's spaceport is the world's best-sited, it nearly ended up with the worst—Kourou was chosen from a shortlist that also contained Somalia's Mogadishu.

SPACE RACE—NUMBER OF LAUNCHES INTO ORBIT
(LEADING LAUNCH SITES)

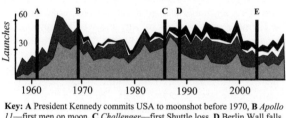

Key: A President Kennedy commits USA to moonshot before 1970, **B** *Apollo 11*—first men on moon, **C** *Challenger*—first Shuttle loss, **D** Berlin Wall falls, **E** China's first astronaut.

Baikanour (USSR/Russia)　　　Xichang/Jiquan (China)

Cape Canaveral (USA)　　　Kourou (ESA/France)

LOST

Strange things happen on ocean specks, and France has more than its fair share:

■ **Clipperton Island**. In 1914, it had 100 settlers, but then it fell off the sea lanes. Three years on, the lighthouse-keeper was the last man alive, along with 15 women and children. Dubbing himself 'king', he forced himself on the women for a year, before they jointly killed him. By fluke, the US Navy rescued the survivors that same day.

■ **Crozet Islands**. In 1887, the crew of the *Tamaris* were shipwrecked here. To alert the world, they tied messages to albatrosses. Seven months later, one was read in Australia. But the sailors had vanished when help arrived.

■ **Alofi Island**. During the course of the 19th century, its 1,500 people were eaten by their neighbours on Futuna.

IRON DISCIPLINE. The first European vessel to reach Tahiti—HMS *Dolphin* in 1767—introduced Tahitians to iron. But after the islanders found they could trade their young women's favours for the metal, so many nails began to go missing, Captain Wallis had to ban his men from shore visits to forestall his ship falling apart.

ISLAND LIFE. As recently as historical times, New Caledonia's reptiles included the last descendents of an armoured turtle as big as a Mini and a type of crocodile that may have jumped on to its prey out of trees. Its plants still include the mother of all blooms—*Amborella*, thought to be the world's most primitive flower.

FIRST FRUIT. Three hours ahead of Paris, Réunion, in the Indian Ocean, was the first place in the world where Euro coins became legal tender (on 1 January 2002). The very first purchase: a bag of lychees bought from a market stall in St. Denis, the capital.

Dependent Territories: Clipperton, Fr. Guiana, Fr. Polynesia, Fr. Southern & Antarctic Lands, Guadeloupe, Martinique, Mayotte, New Caledonia, Réunion, St-Barts, St-Martin, St-Pierre & Miquelon, Wallis & Futuna.

●♦♥★ · **GSR**: n/a · **WHS**: New Caledonia (reefs) □ Réunion (cirques) · **ICH**: Réunion—Maloya (music)

—————— GABON ——————

'Africa without France is like a car without a driver.
But France without Africa is like a car without petrol.'

—President Omar Bongo. Ruler of Gabon for 42 years, Bongo was a staunch ally of France—which in turn provided security and helped exploit Gabon's vast oil reserves. Following his death in 2009, Bongo was replaced by his son Ali.

Masks of Africa—Kwele

The Kwele of north-eastern Gabon have a strongly developed belief in witch-craft, which tends to be blamed for all manners of misfortune. To protect themselves, the Kwele hold beete *rituals to seek purification from benign forest spirits associated with the large, horned antelopes known as bongos. For the purpose of the ritual, the bongo is represented by a participant wearing an* ekuk *mask (above). Then, at its end, the meat of a real captured bongo is eaten.*

FLUID FAITH. In 2006, Pastor Franck Kabele received a divine revelation that he would be able to walk on water. Thus alerted, he gathered his congregation together and took them all to a Libreville beach. Sadly, there must have been a miscommunication, since, as he ploughed resolutely into the Atlantic, the waves closed around him and he was never seen again.

....

'You can't teach an old gorilla the road.'
—Fang proverb

92
U
235

TWO-BILLION-YEAR-OLD POWER STATION. In 1972, a French scientist ran a routine check on some ore being imported from the uranium mines at Oklo, a jungle mining camp in Gabon's interior. To his puzzlement and concern, he found the uranium appeared to have been partly reacted. Follow-up investigations were urgently ordered, and these eventually found that, 2,000,000,000 years ago, sixteen natural nuclear reactors had spontaneously sputtered into life around Oklo. Collectively, these had consumed around 200 kg of uranium (enough for several atom bombs) and created two tons of plutonium—an element supposedly only synthesized in exploding stars or by atomic scientists. Surprised that the reactors could have existed at all, the investigators were even more perplexed as to why the whole thing hadn't simply gone bang. However, further detective work later furnished the answer. The 'reactors' had underlain a river, whose water-flow was necessary to sustain the nuclear chain reactions. But, within 30 minutes of these starting, the heat generated would have boiled off all the water—bringing further reactions to a halt until the rock cooled enough for the river water to flow back and start the cycle once again, in a naturally self-limiting system that had continued for hundreds of thousands of years until the uranium became too depleted.

SCIENTIFIC FRONTIER. Hemmed in by dense rainforest and elephant-grass hills, the sleepy upriver town of Franceville boasts scenic waterfalls, a vibrant bush-meat market, a crumbling 19th-century mission—and one of only two maximum biosafety level 4 containment labs in Africa,[1] whose facilities match those of the UK's Porton Down or the smallpox-holding CDC in Atlanta, USA.

[1] *The independent International Centre for Medical Research of France-ville. Substantially funded by the Total oil group, and run in collaboration with the French and Gabonese governments, research areas include track-ing the origin of HIV and all aspects of the Ebola virus.*

BOXING IN THE BUGS—LAB BIOSAFETY LEVELS		
Level	Extra measures include ...	Example pathogen
1	gloves and face mask	*E. coli* (harmless strains)
2	controlled access	*Salmonella*, influenza
3	safety cabinets, filtered air	TB, SARS, anthrax
4	airlocks, Hazmat suits	smallpox, Marburg, Ebola

♥ · **GSR**: 175 · **WHS**: Lopé-Okanda (rainforest, savannah and Iron Age settlement sites)

GAMBIA

'"Gambia" is said to mean clear water;
surely a misnomer, it is as muddy as the Mersey.'

—Richard Burton (1863)

British Anti-Slavery Society (1795)

GUINEA WORM. The Gambia is a river masquerading as a country. Never more than 30 miles wide, and penetrating almost 200 miles into the heart of Francophone Senegal, English-speaking Gambia is one of the oddest legacies of Britain's colonial rivalry with France. Since independence in 1960 and 1965 respectively, Senegal and Gambia have dabbled with union, but are presently moving further apart.

ON HUMAN BONDAGE. Gambia's capital, Bathurst (now Banjul), was founded by the British in 1816 as a base from which to suppress the slave trade. However, the British met concerted local resistance. When abolition was proposed, Gambian chiefs even made the long journey to London in person to lobby against the change.[1] Their prime motivation was economic. Prior to Britain's intervention, the Gambia River had been one of the biggest sources of slaves in Africa—to the extent that 'Senegambian' was still used informally in the USA to mean 'black' right into the 1950s.

[1] *Although Britain passed the Abolition of Slavery Act in 1833, intra-African slavery within Gambia wasn't ended until 1895.*

PREDATORS ...

For all its wildlife, the 'cougar' was unknown in Gambia until recently, but now around 15,000 single European women a year visit—making it Africa's top 'romance' destination.

... AND PREY
TOY BOYS OF THE WORLD

Gambia .... *bumster ('bum')*
Croatia ...... *galebovi ('seagull')*
Cuba .... *jinetero ('jockey')*
Greece ..... *kamakia ('harpoon')*
Jamaica .... *rent-a-dread*

BE GOOD—or the *ninki-nanka* will get you. That's what Gambian parents tell their naughty children, anyway. Said to have a horse's head and a body like a crocodile but twice as long, the *ninki-nanka* causes all who see it to drop dead. Undaunted, a British team set off in pursuit in 2006. Sadly for science (if not the scientists), they came back without so much as a glimpse.

The president's big idea

MEDICINE MAN. An African leader of the old school, Gambia's president Yahya Jammeh (or President Professor Doctor Jammeh, as he has it) could have come straight from central casting. Across the main road into the capital, he's built an elephantine triumphal arch to himself—under which no one else can drive. Then there are the obligatory diktats: one recent stand-out was the threat to behead every gay. But Jammeh also holds a clinic each Thursday at which he claims to cure AIDS (using herbs and a pair of bananas). A true man of action, the president has now branched out and claims cures for arthritis, diabetes and infertility too.

'However long the log
remains in the river,
it won't become a
crocodile.'

—Mandinka proverb

'Gambia is a country where the ubiquitous display
of the image of one man relegates the North Korean
leader to the backburner.'

—Umaru Fofana (BBC *Focus on Africa* magazine)

♥ · **GSR**: 165 · **WHS**: James Island (ruins) □ Senegambia Stone Circles · **ICH**: Kankurang (initiation)

───── GEORGIA ● საქართველო ─────

*'Georgia is not just a European country, but one
of the most ancient European countries.'*

—Mikheil Saakashvili, President of Georgia

Georgia: *Post-Soviet nation;
pop. 4.6 million.* The name
'Georgia', taken from St.
George, the country's patron,
is used only by foreigners. To
those who live there, it is and
always has been 'Sakartvelo'.

Abkhazia: *Breakaway region under
Russian military protection; pop.
190,000.* Its Krubera Cave is the
deepest in the world, and the only one
known to descend more than 2,000 m.
In 2007, Ukrainian cavers pushed
down to a depth of 2,191 m (7,188 ft).

South Ossetia: *Breakaway
region under Russian military
protection; pop. 72,000.* Os-
setians are the descendants of
the ancient Alans, sidekicks-
in-chief to the Vandals in the
sack of Roman Gaul.

BONE OF CONTENTION. Georgians have the most beautiful
skulls in the world. So thought
Johann Blumenbach, who, in
1779, divided the world into five
races based on skull measurements. Reflecting his enthusiasm for Georgian crania,
he gave the name 'Caucasian' to the broad
swathe of peoples from India to Atlantic.
Blumenbach bore no malice. (He was
explicit that no one race was innately
superior to others.) However, his
work opened the door to two centuries of pseudoscience culminating in
Nazi eugenics, such that, within
science, the term 'Caucasian' is now
deprecated. Meanwhile, in popular
parlance, the name has morphed into a
direct euphemism for 'white' much
favoured by police spokesmen, news
presenters and American bureaucrats.

SHAGGY SHEEP STORY. Georgia's Black Sea
coast was, in ancient times, the site of the kingdom
of Colchis—Jason's destination in his quest for the
golden fleece. Even within living memory, villagers would lay fleeces along streambeds to trap gold
washed down from the Caucasus mountains, and
then hang them to dry from trees—giving a neat,
if unproven, explanation for the famous Greek myth.

**FLUSHING THE TOILET OF
HISTORY**. Without doubt,
Georgia's best-known scion is
cobbler's son and one-time
trainee priest Ioseb Jughash-
vili. Better known as Stalin, the
Georgian's reputation took a nose-
dive after his 1953 death.

Stalin's throne

But in hometown Gori, the citizens kept
the flame alive, even after the Berlin
Wall fell, with a museum stuffed full of
memorabilia. However, the Great Dictator
may finally be about to be airbrushed out of
history. In an irony Stalin wouldn't appreciate,
Gori finished up as the frontline in the 2008
Russo-Georgian war, and Georgia has subsequently announced plans to replace Uncle Joe
with a 'Museum of Russian Aggression'.

*'I wish for you four animals:
a mink on the shoulders, a Jaguar in
the garage, a tiger in the bedroom, and
a jackass to pay for it all.
To you!!'*
—Georgian toast

OLD FRIENDS! Wine is
thought to have been in-
vented in Georgia around 8,000
BCE, thus giving Georgians
time to perfect the world's most
over the top toasting tradition.

2,191 m, depth reached 7 September 2007

♣♣ · **GSR**: n/a · **WHS**: Kutaisi (cathedral and monastery) □ Mtskheta (churches) □ Svaneti (fortified villages) · **ICH**: Polyphonic Singing

GERMANY ● DEUTSCHLAND

'The dumbest farmer harvests the fattest potatoes.'
—German proverb

MARCH OF THE BARBARIANS—WHO'S WHO OF GERMANIC TRIBES			
Tribe	*Tribal Foible*	*Epic Moment*	*Remembered As ...*
Goths	pretty jewellery	sacking Rome (410, 546)	pasty-faced teenagers
Vandals	fine dining	sacking Rome (455)	tearaway teenagers
Huns	not being German	sacking Germany (400, 451)	being German

'Deutschland, Deutschland über alles'
—German national anthem (opening line)

TROUBLED TUNE. Embraced by the Nazis, banned by the occupying powers, then rehabilitated from 1952 (although officially with the lyrics of the plodding third verse only), *Das Deutschlandlied* ('Song of Germany') is perhaps the world's most contentious national anthem. The main trouble stems from the first verse,[1] whose opening line might seem a no-holds-barred assertion of German supremacy (and which then goes on to delimit a national territory notably larger than that enclosed by the current frontiers). In fact, the song was written as a 19th-century appeal for German unification—a then-treasonous call that later forced its author, Professor August Hoffmann, into hiding from the Prussian police for six years.

[1] *The second verse has its own issues, since it consists mainly of two beer hall toasts to German wine, women and song.*

SPRACHRAUM. German has 96 million native speakers, with outposts worldwide (*see table*). In addition, 51 million Americans claim German ancestry, but, except for the Pennsylvania Amish and related communities, virtually all speak only English.

MINOR LEAGUE GERMAN	
Kazakhstan	960,000
Poland	500,000
Italy	230,000
Paraguay	170,000
Pennsylvania	80,000
Belgium	50,000
Other	160,000

PUB TRIVIA. The beer mat (or *bierdeckel*) is a German invention, patented by one Robert Sputh of Dresden in 1892. Herr Sputh later went global with his mats, shipping as far as Brazil. Germans continue to dominate world beer-mat production, with the Katz group in the Black Forest turning out 12 million daily—75% of the world total. For consumption, however, it's the Irish who are the champions: each resident tears, trousers or otherwise does away with 50 a year.

BIRTHDAY SUIT. In 1903, the *Freilicht-park* ('Open Air Park'), near Hamburg, opened as the world's first naturist resort. After WWII, naturism grew to be exceptionally popular in East Germany, where it was cherished as a rare personal freedom: the Proletarian-FKK (naturist) wing of the 'Workers Sports Organization' counted 60,000 members. Today, over 12 million Germans visit naturist beaches each year.

$$\Delta x \Delta p \geq \hbar/2$$

BLURRED VISION. Werner Heisenberg's Uncertainty Principle (*above*) tells us that the more exactly we know something's speed, the less sure we can be about where it actually is.

WEST GERMAN JOKE

Two thick feet are crossing the street. Says one thick foot to the other thick foot: 'Hello!'.

THIS BOOK WILL SELF-DESTRUCT ... The world's first paperback, *Pelham* by Edward Bulwer-Lytton, was published in Leipzig in 1841. To counter concerns that it might damage hardback sales, as a condition of purchase, readers had to agree to throw the paperback away on finishing.

Grundstücksverkehrsgenehmigungszuständigkeitsübertragungsverordnung

TONGUE-TWISTERS. The longest non-contrived German word has 67 letters (*above*). The 18-syllable monster is the short-form name of a regulation concerning the arbitration of property disputes. The runner-up is an anti-mad-cow beef-labelling law (*bottom of page*).

THREE GERMAN MAESTROS

BACH. *'Music is an agreeable harmony for the honour of God and delight of the soul.'[1]* ■ Three of Bach's compositions form part of the most distant human artefact in existence, fixed to the side of the *Voyager 1* probe in interstellar space.

[1] *Bach once also requested: 'Bring me a coffee before I turn into a goat.'*

BEETHOVEN. *'Music should strike fire from the heart of man.'* ■ The playable length of a standard CD (74 minutes) was chosen so as to fit Beethoven's Ninth Symphony on a single disc.

WAGNER. *'Never look at the trombones, it only encourages them.'* ■ Wagner went on to invent 'Wagner tubas' specifically to avoid using trombones in his *Ring* cycle.

'Someone should tell the Germans about hyphens.' —William Cole

PRIVATES ON PARADE. Fourth-ranked in the 1936 women's high jump, Germany's Dora (*né* Hermann) Ratjen became the only confirmed gender cheat in Olympic history when, at the end of a long train journey from a later competition, other passengers grew suspicious of the athlete's five o'clock shadow and a doctor was called.[2] Partly in response, gender-testing became mandatory with the 1966 European Athletics Championships—at which point several Eastern bloc stars abruptly retired. Athletes initially had to disrobe in front of a panel of inspectors; but this was later replaced by a more modest (and accurate) urine test.

[2] *Hermann's later explanation was that he had been told to live and compete as a girl by Hitler Youth officials keen to boost Germany's medal tally.*

'The hole is too large, and too round, owing to the broader bottoms of the Germans.'

—David Garrick (1764), on a German toilet

DOWN THE PAN. In 1945, U-boat *U-1206* was sunk by its captain using the toilet. Ignoring orders that only trained operatives should attempt to flush, he went it alone. Unluckily, the wrong valve got opened, and the outcome was catastrophic.

FRIEND & FOE. The Nazi V-2 rocket bomb was three times more deadly to those who built it than to those who were bombed: on average, six forced labourers died in the making of one rocket, yet it killed just two people on the ground.

FAKE. Disneyland's 'Sleeping Beauty Castle' is modelled on Bavaria's Neuschwanstein Palace, itself a 19th-century fake built by Mad King Ludwig in homage to Wagner.

TOOTH AND CLAW: WORLD OF THE BROTHERS GRIMM	
Tale	Synopsis; [An Academic Deconstruction ...]
Little Red Riding Hood	girl is eaten by wolf, then emerges unscathed [cycles: night swallows day, but dawn follows]
Snow White	stepmother fails to kill daughter, is usurped [puberty: the passage from girl to womanhood]
Hansel and Gretel	two lost children outwit a cannibalistic witch [the triumph of hope: serfs will escape shackles]

Rindfleischetikettierungsüberwachungsaufgabenübertragungsgesetz

<table>
<tr><td>LIGHT ...</td><td>... AND SHADOW</td></tr>
</table>

LIGHT ...	**... AND SHADOW**
'Do what is right, though the world may perish.'	*'Morality is herd instinct in the individual.'*
—Immanuel Kant	—Friedrich Nietzsche

IN A WORD: *Bildungsroman* ... *novel exploring personal development* ● *Gestalt* ... *concept of a whole transcending the attributes of its parts* ● *Götterdämmerung* ... *apocalyptic collapse* ● *Schadenfreude* ... *joy in another's troubles* ● *Sprachraum* ... *area of a language's usage* *Weltschmerz* ... *sadness derived from life's experience* *Weltanschauung* ... *interpretation of the world.*

WHERE THE SAUSAGE IS KING. Germany's food agency diligently categorizes 1,750 varieties of sausage grouped into three broad families. Kochwursts (of which there are 350) are made from fully-cooked meats, while Rohwursts (600 variants) contain raw meat that has been cured to allow it to stand up to long-term storage. In between come the 800 types of Brühwurst, stuffed with part-cooked sausage meat. In every case, ice is the sausage maker's secret weapon, added to stop the meat from cooking in the frictional heat of intense mechanical chopping and stuffing. Best served on dark rye bread with mustard and sauerkraut, sprinkled liberally with caraway seeds.

BEST OF THE WURST	
Bratwurst	a juicy pork griller—the classic street sausage
Frankfurter	pork paste with bacon fat—the hot dog staple
Salami	bacterial fermentation gives the distinctive tang
Saumagen	pig stomach—once served up to Margaret Thatcher
Weisswurst	veal 'ghost' sausage—a perfect Bavarian breakfast
Currywurst	sausage in curry sauce—800m are eaten annually

EAST GERMAN JOKE (I) [1]

- Doors made from cotton.
- 0–60 mph in 21 seconds.
- Waiting list: 14 years.

[1] *Trabant 601 (1964–89)*

EAST GERMAN JOKE (II)

Q. *What's the difference between an HO [the state-grocery chain] sausage and Sputnik Two?*

A. *The party confirmed officially that Sputnik Two had a dog inside it.*

BEASTLY BERLIN. Germany has more zoos (414) than any other country and Berlin Zoo has more animals (23,700) than any other zoo; as a legacy of the Cold War, the zoo comes in two parts—one each side of the long-gone Wall.

NUMBER OF €1 COINS ISSUED BY COUNTRY [2]

German €1   Vatican €1

Germany	*1,700*
Italy	*950*
France	*820*
Spain	*435*
Austria	*200*
Netherlands	*200*
Belgium	*160*
Ireland	*102*
Greece	*98*
Portugal	*68*
Finland	*60*
Slovakia	*43*
Slovenia	*30*
Cyprus	*28*
Malta	*14*
Luxembourg	*10*
Monaco	*1*
San Marino	*0.4*
Vatican	*0.1*

[2] *Initial supply (in millions of coins).*

BANKFURT. Seat of the European Central Bank, Frankfurt is the home of the euro. Quick facts:

■ In October 2006, the euro overtook the US dollar as the world's largest currency by value in circulation. There are now €849 billion sloshing around in cash.

■ Euro banknotes have a lifespan of 18 months, but the coins last for 30 years.

■ Each euro banknote carries a unique serial code, but none of these contains the letter 'J': this has been set aside for the exclusive use of the UK if and when it joins the currency.

HERMANN THE GERMAN was the man who stopped the Roman Empire in its tracks when he annihilated three full legions at the 09 CE Battle of Tuetoburg Forest and forced their commander to commit suicide. With this achievement, he probably had more long-term impact on history than any German king, emperor or *Führer* who came after; since, bruised by their brush with Hermann's Germans, the Romans never again tried to expand their empire across the Rhine— so fixing the great fault line between Germanic north and Latin south that still rules Europe today.

'Sometimes when reading Goethe I have the paralyzing suspicion that he is trying to be funny.'

—Guy Davenport

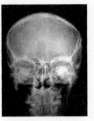

BRAIN POWER. Germans have won 102 Nobel Prizes—more than any other non-English-speaking country. Among the laureates is Wilhelm Röntgen, who won the very first Nobel Prize in physics for his 1895 discovery of X-rays. Though these are conventionally described as invisible, Röntgen reported that if he brought a powerful X-ray source close enough to his eye, he could 'see' a blue-grey glow floating within his eyeball. For obvious reasons, no one has tried to repeat the experiment more recently, and the ghostly glimmering remains a mystery.

BODY IMAGE		
Technology	*First used*	*Good for ...*
X-rays	1895	bones, lungs, guts
Ultrasound	1947	pregnancy, prostates, tendons
Infra-red	1956	breasts
MRI	1977	brains, backs, blood vessels

I-SPY. One in every 66 East German adults spied regularly for the communist regime's Stasi secret police;[1] while an estimated one in seven informed more occasionally. Informers were placed in every workplace and apartment block in the country and included 10,000 children.

[1] *By comparison, the KGB operated with one agent per 580 citizens and the Nazi Gestapo made do with one per 2,000.*

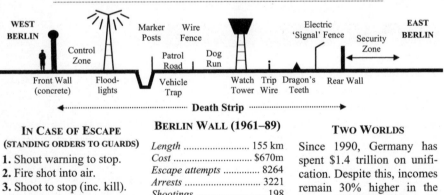

IN CASE OF ESCAPE
(STANDING ORDERS TO GUARDS)
1. Shout warning to stop.
2. Fire shot into air.
3. Shoot to stop (inc. kill).
—*Any guard entering Control Zone is deemed an escapee.*

BERLIN WALL (1961–89)
Length .... 155 km
Cost $670m
Escape attempts 8264
Arrests 3221
Shootings 198
Deaths 136

TWO WORLDS
Since 1990, Germany has spent $1.4 trillion on unification. Despite this, incomes remain 30% higher in the west and unemployment is twice as high in the east.

♠ · **GSR**: 7 · **WHS**: Aachen (Charlemagne's cathedral) □ Alfeld (factory) □ Bamberg (historic town) Berlin (x3) (housing/museums/palaces) □ Bremen (town hall) □ Brühl (castles) □ Cologne (cathedral) Dessau-Wörlitz (gardens) □ Eisleben/Wittenberg (Lutheran sites) □ Essen (industrial complex) Goslar (historic town) □ Hildesheim (churches) □ Lorsch (abbey) □ Lübeck (cityscape) □ Maulbronn (monastery) □ Messel Pit (fossils) □ Muskau (parkland) □ Pile Dwellings □ Potsdam (palaces) Quedlinburg (townscape and church) □ Regensburg (museum town) □ Reichenau (churches) □ Rhine Valley (cultural landscape) □ Roman Limes (border fortifications) □ Speyer (cathedral) □ Stralsund & Wismar (historic towns) □ Trier (Roman monuments) □ Völkingen (ironworks) □ Wartburg (castle) Wattenmeer (mudflats) □ Weimar (historic town) □ Weimar & Dessau (Bauhaus architecture) □ Wies (church) □Würzburg (palace)

GHANA

'We face neither East nor West; we face Forward.'

—Kwame Nkrumah (Ghana's first president). In 1957, Ghana became the first colonial African territory to win independence.

FUNNY BONES. Women often want a hen as a sign of their commitment to motherhood. Men often choose  an emblem of their trade: a hammer for a carpenter or, for a street vendor, a bottle of Coke (*below*). Others are more aspirational: an aeroplane (*above*) for the jet-set they never joined. Whatever the fantasy, the coffin-carpenters of Accra are happy to oblige. Personalized coffins first surfaced in the 1950s among the Ga ethnic group living around the Ghanaian capital. Since then, the practice has become a tradition, despite a typical price tag per casket of $650—about five months' average income. By now, almost every idea has been tried and it is hard to think up a coffin that's truly new. That notwithstanding, the gynaecologist who 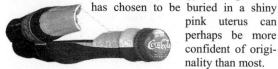 has chosen to be buried in a shiny pink uterus can perhaps be more confident of originality than most.

CURIOUS CONTOURS. In 1923, a group of British Army officers, charged with surveying an especially obscure corner of what is now Ghana, decided to apply their imagination in place of a day spent tramping through tropical brush. If they'd kept it boring, no one would probably ever have known. As it was, their creativity was reprinted on successive editions of the official map until the 1960s (*pictorial clue below*).

IN GHANA: *No one tests the depth of a river with both feet • One should never rub bottoms with a porcupine • If power can be bought, sell your mother to get it • Nature gave us two cheeks instead of one to make it easier to eat hot food • If you are hiding, don't light a fire*

AFRICA'S FINEST. When Sir Charles Mac-Carthy was appointed the soldier-governor of the Gold Coast (now Ghana) in 1821, he decided to expand the new colony into the interior. This was a bad idea. A few weeks later, his gold-rimmed skull was being used as the Ashanti emperor's drinking cup, while his jawbones were doing service as drumsticks. The Ashanti continued to keep the British Empire at bay for the next 70 years with the most powerful indigenous army in Africa (complete with trained medical corps) and a professional civil service whose Foreign Office had desks for each of the colonial powers. When Lord Baden-Powell (later founder of the Boy Scouts) finally secured the territory in 1896, it came about only after the Ashanti emperor ordered his troops not to resist.

BEAT IT. Jungle drums were a staple of *Boy's Own* adventures throughout Africa, but it was the Ashanti who perfected drum telegraphy for long-range communication. Matching the tone and rhythm of spoken language, drums could transmit messages by relay for hundreds of miles if the need arose. In the still of pre-dawn, each drummer might be heard for up to 12 miles, but during the bustle of the day, three miles was more likely. To avoid mistakes, each drummer had his own (often cryptic) call sign—'You'll die of witchcraft at midnight' was one—and messages were kept simple by using fixed codes. Thus: 'Person he not go in house, but outside, outside' was the standard phrase used to warn when a leopard had been spotted on the prowl.

♥ · **GSR:** 99 · **WHS:** Asante Traditional Buildings ▢ Coastal Castles

Greece • Ελλάδα

'We are all Greeks.'

—Percy Shelley, *Hellas* (1821)

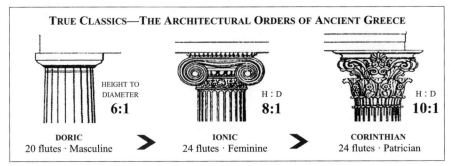

TRUE CLASSICS—THE ARCHITECTURAL ORDERS OF ANCIENT GREECE

HEIGHT TO DIAMETER
6:1

H : D
8:1

H : D
10:1

DORIC
20 flutes · Masculine

IONIC
24 flutes · Feminine

CORINTHIAN
24 flutes · Patrician

IRRATIONAL RESPONSE. The square root of 25 is 5, the square root of 9 is 3, but no numeric value can be written for the square root of two—a fact the ancient Greeks found so upsetting, they drowned the mathematician who proved it (after slaughtering 100 oxen).

HOW WAS IT FOR YOU? Greece leads the world in the post-coital fag. Actually, no such statistic exists. However, since the average Greek enjoys the world's most regular sex (87% of adults partake at least weekly[1]) and smokes the highest number of cigarettes (4,313 a year), the presumption does seem a one-way bet.

[1] *For Greek women, this may be a case of quantity over quality since, at 4.8 inches, the average Greek manhood is the smallest in Europe, and a full 1.5 inches behind the world-beating French. Still, on the bright side, Greek men can cheer themselves up by thinking of the bottom-ranked Koreans, who measure in at just 3.7 inches full stretch.*

LONG AND WINDING ROAD. The Knossos Labyrinth[2] where, in legend, Theseus killed the bull-headed Minotaur is the original after which all others have been named.

[2] *To a pedant, a labyrinth is distinct from a maze. While a labyrinth has only a single, linear path, mazes feature junctions and dead ends. So, whereas navigation through the former can be tortuous, it is never problematic. Exit from the latter, however, can be all but impossible.*

KNOSSOS LABYRINTH, CRETE

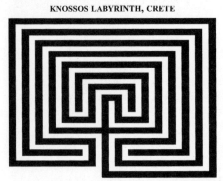

OMPHALOSKEPSIS. Mt. Athos is the Greek male-only monastic state where those who wish to can pass a lifetime in deep religious contemplation—and perhaps obtain a crystallinity of vision that escapes those with more cluttered lives. One example of such work is the exquisite ranking of sin put forth by Nicodemus the Hagiorite in 1794.

THE SEVEN GRADES OF SIN

Pneumatic Peril

GRADE	WORKED EXAMPLE
1. *Pardonable*.....…….becoming irritated
2. *Near-pardonable*..................….shouting
3. *Non-mortal*……......................swearing
4. *Near non-mortal*…......striking with hand
5. *Intermediate*…..striking with small stick
6. *Near-mortal*..........striking with big stick
7. *Mortal*.........................murder (any stick)

CRUEL AND UNUSUAL PUNISHMENTS. Said to lie nine days below the Earth as the anvil fell, Tartarus was, for ancient Greeks, the deepest pit of hell—reserved for those whom the gods truly despised. But even here, some were felt to have transgressed so mightily that worse still was prescribed:

- **Ixion** ... caught playing footsie with Zeus' wife
  Sentence .... tied for eternity to a red-hot wheel
- **Metis** .... Zeus' canoodling (first) wife
  Sentence ...... turned into a fly, then swallowed
- **Prometheus** ,......................... borrowed a light
  Sentence .... liver eaten by a large bird (daily)[3]
- **Tantalus** .... served his own son as ragout
  Sentence .. 'tantalized' for eternity by grapes and water that would recede just out of reach

[3] *This punishment did not take place in Tartarus but on a mountain in the Caucasus.*

A PERFECT THEORY—PLATONIC SOLIDS

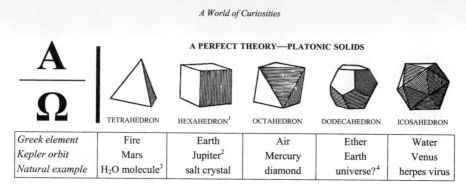

	TETRAHEDRON	HEXAHEDRON[1]	OCTAHEDRON	DODECAHEDRON	ICOSAHEDRON
Greek element	Fire	Earth	Air	Ether	Water
Kepler orbit	Mars	Jupiter[2]	Mercury	Earth	Venus
Natural example	H₂O molecule[3]	salt crystal	diamond	universe?[4]	herpes virus

[1] *Commonly called a cube.* [2] *In addition, Saturn fits around the outside.* [3] *Its tetrahedral shape is the reason why water is a liquid (and not a gas) at room temperature—allowing life on Earth.* [4] *A lack of structure to the temperature of space at vast scales causes some theorists to think the universe has the shape of a twisted dodecahedron which joins up with itself.*

THE UGLY TRUTH—REAL WORLD. As the ancient Greeks found out, there are only five flat-sided solids that are perfectly regular (i.e. they look the same whichever face you lie them on). This discovery so seduced the Greeks, led by Plato, that they convinced themselves they had stumbled on the secret of creation. Although this notion was, in fact, a colossal blind alley, which stymied scientific progress for two millennia, on the positive side, Johannes Kepler did at least get a silver punch bowl out of it by showing that the orbits of each of the six known planets could be fitted to a corresponding solid (*see above*), while Euclid's textbook-writing career also got a boost when his *Elements*—the standard account of the solids' geometry—sold 1,000 editions in a run lasting 2,300 years.

'Any Englishman having the usual knowledge of Ancient Greek will be able to read the Athenian papers with ease.'

—How times change: *Murray's Guide to Greece* (19th century)

AND THE BAND PLAYED ON ... Running to 158 verses in praise of liberty, Greece's national anthem, Ύμνος εἰς τὴν Ἐλευθερίαν, is the longest in the world. Thankfully, only the first two are played at public occasions.

HELP THE HELLENES. Originally named the 'Oxford Committee for Famine Relief', Oxfam was founded in 1942 to supply food to starving Greek civilians affected by Allied naval blockades in WWII.

GODS AMONG MEN. At the ancient Greek Olympic Games, winners were awarded an olive wreath (even at the time, regarded as rather cheapskate), while runners-up got nothing. The tradition of awarding gold, silver and bronze belongs to the modern Olympics, beginning in 1904. The metals were chosen to reflect the first three ages of Greek mythology: gold being the age when men lived alongside the gods, silver the age where youth lasted a century, and bronze the age of heroes. Before 1904, awards were more variegated: the runner-up in the 1900 pole vault was given an umbrella.

OLYMPIC SPORTS—HOW TO RECREATE THE ANCIENT GREEK GAMES	
Event	*Notes for prospective athletes*
Boxing	killing your opponent is permitted, but he then automatically wins
Equestrian	Olympic olive wreaths are awarded to the trainers not jockeys
Total Combat	no holds barred—the only exceptions are biting and eye-gouging
Pentathlon	to show off their (naked) physiques, competitors should oil their skin
Running	the most gruelling race is that run wearing full armour and shield
Wrestling	genital grabs are banned, but breaking fingers is an approved tactic

♠ · GSR: 22 · WHS: Athens Acropolis (temples) □ Bassae (temple) □ Corfu (townscape) □ Daphni (monasteries) □ Delos (ancient ruins) □ Delphi (ancient ruins) □ Epidaurus (ancient theatre) □ Meteora (mountain monasteries) □ Mt. Athos (Orthodox quasi-state) □ Mycenae (ancient ruins) □ Mystras (medieval ruins) □ Olympia (stadia) □ Patmos (monastery) □ Rhodes (townscape) □ Samos (temple and ruins) □ Thessalonika (churches) □ Vergina (Macedonian ruins) · WHS: Mediterranean Diet

—— Greenland • Kalaallit Nunaat ——

'Many times I have thanked God for a bite of raw dog.'

—Robert Peary, two-toed Arctic explorer (he lost the other eight to frostbite in 1898)

At 840,000 square miles, Greenland is the world's biggest island—more than twice as large as second-placed New Guinea, and seven times as big as the British Isles. Although 80% of the island lies beneath an ice sheet (the largest outside of Antarctica), the extreme northern area of Peary Land is a rock and gravel desert too dry for permanent ice cover to form. A Danish dependency since 1814, Greenland achieved internal self-government in 2009, with only defence and foreign policy reserved to Denmark. The island is notable for the Northeast Greenland National Park. Larger than 163 countries, it's the biggest national park in the world.

DOGGED DETERMINATION. For the past 61 years, members of the Danish Army's Sirius Patrol have guarded the empty north-east quadrant of Greenland. In one of the loneliest jobs in the world, two-man teams undertake dog-sled patrols of up to four months at a time, during which they are completely cut off from other human contact. Collectively, the Patrol's 14 personnel aim to visit each stretch of the 10,000-mile coastline at least every three to four years, and, cumulatively, members have sledged over 500,000 miles since the Patrol's inception—a distance greater than that to the moon and back.

While sailing along the Greenland coast in 1736, Hans Egede provided one of the earliest credible first-hand sightings of a sea serpent—drawn left as he described.

SEAL OF SUCCESS. When Lutheran priest Hans Egede set off in 1721 to re-establish contact with the lost Viking colonies on Greenland, he was driven by concern that the colonists would have missed out on the Reformation and thus would still be Catholic—or, after 300 years of isolation, might even have lapsed into paganism. Instead, he found they had disappeared entirely, and so he set about converting the Inuit (and, at the same time, reclaiming Greenland for Denmark). The task of proselytization posed serious challenges since many of the concepts taken for granted in the gospels were entirely alien to the Inuit. Nevertheless, Egede displayed an impressive talent for improvisation—in the absence of bread, he rewrote the Lord's Prayer as: 'Give us this day our daily harbour seal'—to achieve success as the Apostle of the Arctic.

FOOD FOR THOUGHT. While it is widely known that polar bear livers are toxic (30–90 g is fatal), less publicized is the excruciating manner of death. Following large doses, bear-liver-nibblers suffer extreme and sudden desquamation: all their skin falls off.

'He who wears his anorak back to front will catch a polar bear the same day.'

—Greenlandic Inuit proverb

FLAGGING SPIRITS. The earliest documented instance of a flag being flown at half-mast was in 1612, aboard the English ship *Heart's Ease* following the killing of her master, James Hall, by Inuit in West Greenland. One theory is that the practice makes space for the 'invisible flag of death'. However, other sources suggest this is a later rationalization, and that the gesture is instead a hangover from the ancient custom whereby all tasks would be deliberately performed in a half-hearted way as a sign of respect for the dead.

♠♦ · **GSR 164 · Autonomous country under the Danish Crown** · **WHS:** Ilulissat Icefjord

——————— GUATEMALA ———————

'Guatemala is a good place to commit a murder,
because you will almost certainly get away with it.'

—Prof. P. Alston (UN Special Rapporteur on extrajudicial killings)

MAYAN DAYS[1] (1–10)	
1	Imix'
2	Ik'
3	Ak'b'al
4	K'an
5	Chikchan
6	Kimi
7	Manik'
8	Lamat
9	Muluk
10	Ok

2012 AND ALL THAT. Guatemala is the only country on the North American continent with an indigenous majority—the Maya. Apart from building very big pyramids, the forebears of the current Maya devised an intricate calendar that conceived of time as something that repeated itself in cycles, rather than flowed in a straight line (as in the West). Instead of tallying years, the Maya kept a running count of what day it was according to two separate calendar cycles of different length. Specifying a given day in terms of both calendars would then give them a usable date[2] that, in our terms, repeated only every 52 years—good enough for most. But for really serious things, like monuments, the Maya had a third gargantuan cycle, the Long Count, which *may* have repeated itself every 5,126 years. This, according to Mayan myth, was the lifetime of the world that was destroyed to make way for our own. The current Long Count just happens to end on 21 December 2012, which is giving rise to excitable talk among the more mystically inclined that the four horsemen may be about to gallop forth once more.

[1] *Used in the Maya's most important 'Tzolk'in' calendar—a 260-day cycle measured by repeating these 20 named days 13 times.* [2] *The concept is slippery to grasp, but as a very rough analogy, instead of writing that the London Olympics will start on 27 July 2012, the Maya might write that the they will start on the 33rd day after Midsummer's Day next falls on a Sunday.*

MURDER MOST FOUL. After Harvard-trained lawyer Rodrigo Rosenberg was gunned down in Guatemala City in 2009, a video emerged in which he said the president planned to assassinate him. An outcry erupted and the UN was asked to investigate. Their finding: Rosenberg had arranged his own murder to frame the president.

BLEND 101. The first brand of instant coffee was developed in Guatemala by Englishman George Washington in 1906. Known as 'Red-E-Coffee', it dominated world sales for over 30 years. But when WWII broke out, newcomer Nescafé won a contract to supply a million cases to US troops and Red-E-Coffee was left in the dust.

BEWARE THE BOGEYMAN:
GUATEMALAN TALL TALES TO FRIGHTEN CHILDREN

- *If you wear a foreign hat or sandals, you'll go down with cramps.*
- *If you disobey your parents, you'll get hen ticks when you die.*
- *If you walk backwards, you'll grow abnormal testicles/breasts.*
- *If you wear a basket on your head, you'll get eaten by a dog.*

	MAYAN DAYS[1] (11–20)
11	Chuwen
12	Eb'
13	B'en
14	Ix
15	Men
16	Kib'
17	Kab'an
18	Etz'nab'
19	Kawak
20	Ajaw

♦ · **GSR:** 69 · **WHS:** Antigua (museum city) □ Quirigua (Mayan stelae) □ Tikal (ruined Mayan city)
IHC: Garifuna Dance and Music □ Rabinal Achí (Mayan drama)

GUINEA • GUINÉE

'Fifty years of poverty!'

—Anti-government slogan (2008)

SOUNDS FAMILIAR? Dutch Guinea, French Guinea, Portuguese Guinea, Spanish Guinea, Equatorial Guinea, Guinea-Bissau, New Guinea,[1] plus, of course, vanilla Guinea (and that's not counting the British, French and Dutch Guianas); you might have thought the cartographers had run out of words. Morocco's Berbers first got this ball rolling with *aguinaw*—their name for 'black man'; Portuguese sailors then adapted this as a label for the whole of the West African coast. When the scramble for Africa followed, each colonial power had to give

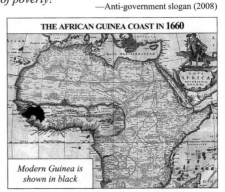

THE AFRICAN GUINEA COAST IN **1660**

Modern Guinea is shown in black

their slice its own title, and finally independence has since added a further layer. As the Republic of Guinea is the biggest chunk, it's the one that gets to be called plain 'Guinea'.

[1] *New Guinea is several thousand miles from West Africa, but it is hot and has a coast—which was good enough for the first European to reach the island, Ynigo Ortiz de Retes, a man who was clearly not one of life's poets.*

MONKEY BUSINESS. The botanical gardens in Guinea's capital, Conakry, were the site of an official Soviet attempt to breed a human–ape hybrid. In 1927, Russian biologist Ilya Ivanov spent nine months catching local chimpanzees and inseminating three females with human sperm. After none of the chimps fell pregnant, he took all the apes back to the USSR with the revised goal of fertilizing human volunteers. Before preparations were complete, however, Ivanov was purged and the research permanently halted.

GUN CONTROL. 'We prefer poverty in liberty to riches in slavery', so said Ahmed Sékou Touré when breaking ties with France in 1958 and leading Guinea to isolationist independence. Sékou Touré delivered on half his vision, but sadly not the half his countrymen would have preferred. Over the next 50 years, power in Guinea changed hands just twice—both times down the barrel of a gun. However, with the world less tolerant of power seized by force (*see right*), the first free and fair presidential elections in Guinean history were held in 2010, making it (hopefully) third time lucky for the people of Guinea.

13
Al
26.98

FLASH IN A PAN. Nearly a quarter of the world's aluminium ore (bauxite) can be found beneath Guinea's soil. Today, its uses include cooking foil, but before modern production methods were discovered, aluminium was worth its weight in gold—at the 1855 Paris International Exhibition, a single bar was prominently displayed beside the French crown jewels.

COUPS D'ÉTAT (GLOBAL TOTAL)

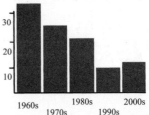

CASHING OUT. Guineas were the main unit of British currency until 1816, when they were replaced by pounds sterling[2]. The name 'guinea' arose because the gold from which one guinea coins were struck initially came from West Africa. Fixed at the value of £1.05, the guinea is now all but obsolete. (The auctioning of rams is one noteworthy exception.)

[2] *Sterling is so called because one pound of the currency was originally worth one pound in weight of sterling silver.*

♥ · **GSR**: 129 · **WHS**: Mount Nimba (highland forest) · **ICH**: Sosso-Bala (musical instrument)

——— GUINEA-BISSAU ● GUINÉ-BISSAU ———

*'Justice does not work. The police do not work. A place where criminals
can do whatever they want is not a country. It is chaos.'*

—Constantino Correia, senior Ministry of Justice official

†

'We are a fragile nation.'

—Lucinda Barbosa, Chief of Police

OUT TO LUNCH. With a mere 62 officers under her command to police a country bigger than Belgium, Barbosa has a point— especially as her force doesn't possess a single pair of handcuffs, nor, until 2010, did Guinea-Bissau have a prison (in case any criminals were actually caught). It's not only law and order that's been neglected. The country's health service boasts a total of 78 doctors, while the navy has just two boats (one of which would sink if put in the water) and the air force not a single aircraft. Nevertheless, as far as the armed forces go, this is arguably to the good, since the US government has placed the heads of the air force and navy respectively on a list of the world's key drugs traffickers (*see right*).

FISHING FOR HUSBANDS. Although Portuguese colonists established themselves on the coast of Guinea-Bissau in 1474 (when they declared the formation of Portuguese Guinea), they didn't subdue the 88 Bijagós Islands, lying within sight offshore, until 1936—when, after 450 years, they finally declared the archipelago 'conquered'. Still aloof from the mainland, the Bijagós have a

*Bijagós villagers c. 1890
(with termite mound)*

matriarchal society, in which it's always the women who choose their husbands. On the island of Orango, the bride-to-be does this by making her intended male an offer he can't refuse (of a traditional fish-eye dinner), before setting off to build the new marital home on her own.

*'The drug traffickers can do anything;
they have money, they have guns, they can
buy the government.'*

—Allen Yero Emballo (2008), Guinea-Bissauan journalist now in France following death threats

COKE OR BROKE. As a single two and a half ton consignment of cocaine has a value equal to Guinea-Bissau's national budget, Emballo's remark (*above*) is no overstatement; even the 600 kg that, in 2006, vanished from the country's treasury following its seizure was enough to run the country's schools for 20 months. From almost nothing in 2005, Guinea-Bissau's drug problem has grown to become virtually overwhelming. Now a key transfer point for smuggling cocaine into Europe, Guinea-Bissau has risen to prominence for a mix of reasons centred on corruption, poverty and the labyrinthine geography of the unpatrolled Bijagós Archipelago. Although this influx has left some bewildered,[1] (slightly) more knowing Guinea-Bissauans have welcomed the chance to earn extra cash in a country where the average monthly wage is less than $30: a 2006 spot check at Amsterdam Airport revealed 32 Guinea-Bissauan drugs mules on just one inbound flight.

[1] *When a cargo of drugs washed up on one beach, many local villagers tried spreading the cocaine on their fields as fertilizer, while others used it to whitewash their huts.*

MAKING WAVES. Orango island hosts the world's only herd of marine hippopotami.

HITTING THE FAN. Possibly to mark out territory, hippos spin their tails like propellers while defecating, thus catapulting their crap far and wide.

♥ · **GSR:** 162 · **WHS:** none

GUYANA

'Georgetown is so hot, rain-clouds form in one's head.'

—Lafcadio Hearn (1887), on Guyana's capital

WHAT LITTLE GIRLS ARE MADE OF. Flowing through sugar cane plantations past Georgetown to the sea, Guyana's fat, chocolate-coloured Demerara river has given its name to the best-known variety of brown sugar. Like its darker cousin, muscovado, demerara is an unrefined cane sugar that's simply boiled and spun; the taste and colour coming from the residue of natural molasses that's been retained. In contrast, sugar that's just labelled 'brown' is usually merely ordinary refined white sugar with a small shot of molasses added at the end.

The evolutionary roots of the human sweet tooth run immensely deep. Studies with E. coli show that even bacteria prefer pudding—swimming up a glucose gradient if given a choice. The biological purpose of this perception of pleasure is to prod organisms towards the energy-rich nutrition provided by natural sugars. To allow the rapid feedback necessary for effective foraging by 'taste and test', nature has also rewarded us with a near instant 'hit': it takes just 4.1 seconds from a grain of sugar hitting our tongues to the sensation of sweetness peaking in our brains.

View from Mt. Roraima to the adjacent tepui *(table-top mountain) of Mt. Kukenán in the Guiana Highlands*

LIZARD MAN. Flat-topped Mt. Roraima is considered the model for *The Lost World*, the 1912 dinosaur yarn by Sir Arthur Conan Doyle that spawned a genre running to *Jurassic Park* and beyond. Sadly, Roraima's summit plateau contains nothing more exotic than clumps of rare heathers and a wasteland of oddly eroded rocks. Nevertheless, the book's chief protagonist, Professor Challenger, was rewarded in 1996 with his own real dinosaur species—the *Irritator challengeri*.

MIND YOUR 'P'S AND 'Q'S. After independence in 1966, one of the early acts of Guyana's first prime minister, Forbes Burnham, was to ban the import of peas (and candied fruit). Part of a strategy of self-sufficiency, Burnham's autarkic policies quickly spawned economic chaos and long queues for food. For such efforts on behalf of his country, he was mummified after death by Dr. Debov, the man who looks after Lenin (*see Russia*).

MAGIC. Guyana's Sir Lionel Luckhoo, amateur magician and world's most successful lawyer, secured an unbroken 245 murder acquittals from 1940 to 1985.

SWEETNESS INDEX[2]

ARTIFICIAL

600 ◄ Sucralose (E955)

400 Saccharin (E954) ◄

200 ◄ Aspartame (E951)

0

NATURAL

1.5 Fructose (fruit sugar) ◄

1.0 Sucrose (sugar) Glucose (grape sugar) ◄

0.5

Lactose (milk sugar)

0.0

THE END IS NIGH—LARGEST CULT SUICIDES SINCE WWII			
Group	Location	Deaths	Why?
People's Temple	Jonestown, Guyana (1978)	909	'revolutionary suicide'
Branch Davidian	Waco, Texas, USA (1993)	74	under tank assault by FBI[1]
Solar Temple	Switzerland/Canada (1994)	53	to 'transit' to a new planet
Heaven's Gate	San Diego, USA (1997)	39	to catch an alien spaceship

[1] *There remains much dispute as to whether the deaths (mainly in a fire) were suicide, accident or murder.*

[2] *The human perception of sweetness is not entirely objective: for example, soft drinks are rated 11% sweeter when tinted with red food colouring.*

♦ · GSR: 155 · WHS: none

—————— HAITI • AYITI • HAÏTI ——————

'It is the destiny of the people of Haiti to suffer.'

—Jean-Claude 'Baby Doc' Duvalier, Dictator of Haiti (1971–86)

Veves of Haiti (see below): Top row from left—Papa Legba (gatekeeper of the spirit world), Baron Samedi (master of the dead), Maman Brigette (foul-mouthed, pale-skinned consort of Baron Samedi, a reinterpretation of St. Brigitte of Ireland). Descending columns from top—The Marassa (the divine twins, although they number three), Damballa (creator), Ayizan (the first priestess), Erzuli Dantor (avenger of abused women), Ayizan: alternative veve, Baron Cimetière (keeper of cemeteries), Ogoun (spirit of war).

VOODOO NATION. Haitian Vodou acknowledges a supreme god—Bondye ('good God', from the French *bon Dieu*), but he is far beyond human comprehension. So practitioners instead focus prayers and entreaties on the *loa* or spirits beneath him. Not only are these more accessible, but with the correct *veves* (symbols) they can be compelled to attend those who summon them.

BAD MEDICINE. From 1957 to 1971, François 'Papa Doc' Duvalier ruled Haiti with a reign of terror. Literally. He asserted he was the Baron Samedi, Vodou Lord of the Dead. Although this may just have been a sophisticated psychological ploy, the dictator gave every indication of actually believing it. When, in 1963, advisors told him that a certain fugitive had transformed himself into a black hound, he ordered Haitian police to shoot every black dog on sight; while later, after President Kennedy's assassination, Duvalier allegedly sent an agent on a secret mission to collect soil and air from the gravesite in a plan to influence US foreign policy by capturing Kennedy's soul and forcing it to do his will.

DEADLIEST NATURAL DISASTERS OF THE 21ST CENTURY (2000–2010)	
Disaster (Year)	*Deaths*
1. Haiti Earthquake (2010)	316,000
2. Asian Tsunami (2004)	230,000
3. Burma Cyclone (2008)	146,000
4. Pakistan Earthquake (2007)	75,000
5. Sichuan Earthquake (2008)	69,000

SHARK ALERT. Bucking the national economic collapse, Haiti's security chief Luckner Cambronne made millions in the 1960s selling corpses to the US. Arriving in a sharkskin suit, he would demand funeral parlours hand over their cadavers (loved ones would find coffins emptied), then export the bodies for dissection.

THE LORD'S PRAYER (HAITIAN VERSION)

'Our Doc who art in the National Palace for life, hallowed be Thy name by present and future generations, Thy will be done at Port-au-Prince and in the provinces. Give us this day our new Haiti and never forgive the trespasses of the enemies of the Fatherland, who spit every day on our country. Let them succumb to temptation and under the weight of their own venom. Deliver them not from any evil. Amen.'

—Authorized by François 'Papa Doc' Duvalier, dictator of Haiti (1957–71), excommunicated 1961

··

♦ · **GSR:** 95 · **WHS:** Citadelle Henry (castle)

—————————— HONDURAS ——————————

'These Central American Republics are queer concerns. I do not precisely know what a last-year's-calf's ideas of immortal glory may be, but probably they are about as lucid as those of a Central American in regard to government.'

—Artemus Ward (Charles Farrar Browne), *Complete Works, Pt 4* (*c.* 1867)

UNITED FRONT. There are few areas of endeavour in which Honduras can be said to have led the world, but with nearly 300 wars and rebellions since inde-

Honduran Army rolls out its big gun.

pendence, civil unrest is one. It is, in fact, the original 'banana republic'—a term coined by US writer O. Henry, in 1904, after an extended sojourn in the country.[1] The banana reference was literal, since, at their peak, bananas made up 88% of Honduran exports[2]— and, as Henry realized, the clout of American banana companies, such as United Fruit, was as a result immense. Nicknamed El Pulpo ('The Octopus'), United ran its own railways, ports, shipping lines and even police, as well as wielding huge influence over the government. And if that wasn't enough, companies like United were able to call on successive sympathetic American administrations to 'protect their interests'. Following such requests, US troops landed in Honduras in 1903, 1907, 1911, 1912, 1919, 1924 and 1925, while in 1910 the Cuyamel Fruit Company paid a mercenary army to overthrow the Honduran president directly.

[1] *Henry was necessarily an acute observer of the Honduran political and judicial scene since he was hiding out in the country having skipped bail in Texas the day before he had been due to stand trial for embezzlement from the bank where had worked.* [2] *Benefiting from dirt-cheap land prices and miserly wages, the big banana companies were able to push production costs so low that, in 1913, a Boston housewife could buy six bananas for the price of a single local apple—thus fuelling insatiable demand.*

ASKING FOR THE MOON. On 18 November 1998, a US special agent recovered 1.14 grams of Honduran moon rock from a bank deposit box in Miami. The recovery was the culmination of a sting operation that had started some months previously with a 'Moon Rocks Wanted' ad in the US press, and gathered steam when would-be moon rock dealer Alan Rosen responded, offering a specimen for $5m. In the subsequent court case,[3] it came out that Mr. Rosen had bought his rock from a retired Honduran colonel (for a payment of one second-hand delivery truck and $14,000), and that the colonel had pilfered it from the Presidential Palace in Tegucigalpa around 1994. Originally a gift from President Nixon, the recovered lunar sample was returned to Honduras in 2003.

[3] *United States of America vs. One Lucite Ball Containing One Moon Rock And One Ten By Fourteen Inch Wooden Plaque (almost certainly the first time anyone has sued any part of the moon).*

The city state of Copán, in west Honduras, lay at the extremity of the Mayan world. Despite this, the elaborate carvings and steles it left behind are considered to represent a pinnacle of Mayan art.

AIN'T NO CURE FOR THE FASHION BLUES. In Classic Mayan society, the size of headdress was viewed as a badge of status. Perhaps inevitably, millinery inflation set in, so that the headdresses of nobles eventually grew to become taller than their wearers. (Conversely, petty criminals were punished by being sent to the barber for a short back and sides.) What you put on your head wasn't the only affectation of rank. When in public, a noble would be accompanied by a slave whose job it was to hold a cloth in front of the noble's face, thus preventing anyone from speaking to him or her directly. On special occasions, social position could be further shown using body paint: warriors would arrive daubed with red and black, while those about to be sacrificed got painted duck-egg blue.

♦ · **GSR**: 78 · **WHS:** Copán (Mayan ruins) □ Rio Plátano (rainforest) · **ICH**: Garifuna Culture

—— HUNGARY • MAGYARORSZÁG ——

'A légpárnás hajóm tele van angolnákkal.'

—'My hovercraft is full of eels' in Hungarian (apparently).
(Source: Omniglot.com, with thanks to *Monty Python*.)

As the earthy Hungarian saying has it, 'good paprika burns twice'—key grades include: 'Special' (*Különleges*), mild, sweet, bright red • 'Delicate' (*Edes*

N Night **W** Set **E** Rise **S** Noon

In Hungarian, the four cardinal directions are named for the time of day that the sun shines there (note the sun is never in the north).

PLAIN SPEAKING. Unless you happen to be a native speaker, Hungarian poses a major challenge: not just for the exotic spelling but from the sheer oddness of the language's structure. Born on the plains somewhere between the Caspian and the Urals, and isolated for 3,000 years, it, for example, feels no need for the word 'have', but nevertheless requires each noun to take one of 18 cases, every verb to use one of 72 forms and has a rule that word endings have to be chosen to rhyme with the word's first vowel.

GAME THEORY AND PRACTICE. It's widely thought that the cerebral challenge of mastering Hungarian does strange things to the growing brain. Certainly, a wholly implausible share of the world's top physicists and mathematicians has been Hungarian, including the 'fathers' of both the atom and hydrogen bombs, and János (John) von Neumann, perhaps the 20th century's finest mathematical thinker. The oddest, though, was Paul Erdös. He had no home or possessions, survived by sleeping on colleagues' floors and referred to God as the 'Supreme Fascist'. He also wrote more maths papers than anyone in history (1,475). Mathematicians still make a game of tracking each other's academic standing through their 'Erdös Number'—the number of steps needed to link their work back to a paper written by Erdös; and, more than once, the chance to improve one's Erdös Number has been auctioned on eBay.

STEP BY STEP
HOW TO SOLVE
RUBIK'S CUBE

▶ Do top face (edges before corners)
▶ Do edge pieces of middle layer
▶ Form a cross on bottom face
▶ Rotate bottom face cross as needed
▶ Position bottom face corner pieces
▶ Rotate cube corner pieces to finish

—*Invented 1974, Ernö Rubik*

NOBEL SPICE. Hungarian scientist Albert Szent-Györgyi won a Nobel Prize in 1937 for isolating Vitamin C, using paprika as his source. The spice is twice as rich in the substance as lemon juice: one bowl of goulash can give 37% of the recommended daily dose.

BLOODY END. After slaughtering much of Europe and extorting an annual tribute of one tonne of gold not to sack Constantinople, Attila the Hun died at his Tápiószentmárton palace in 453 CE of a nosebleed. Still, he remains something of a hero at home, with Attila ('the Hungarian'?) a popular boy's name and 10 Attila Streets in Budapest.

'This is Prime Minister Imre Nagy speaking. At daybreak, Soviet troops attacked our capital.'

Hungary's 1956 Revolution marked the first Soviet use of force to impose its will in Eastern Europe. After it was crushed, Nagy was hanged on Khrushchev's secret orders, and his body bound in barbed wire and buried. Thirty-one years later, in 1989, Nagy was reinterred a hero before a crowd of 100,000. The day's last speaker was a student, who demanded free elections and the departure of Soviet troops. Three months later, Hungary opened its Western borders—breaching the Iron Curtain; two months after that, the Berlin Wall fell; and as of 2011, that student, Viktor Orbán, is prime minister.

aromatic, pink • 'Noble Sweet' (*Édesnemes*), slightly spicy, bright red (the export grade) • 'Strong' (*Érös*), fiery, brown • 'Half-Sweet' (*Félédes*), blended

♠ · **GSR:** 64 · **WHS:** Aggtelek (caves) □ Budapest □ Fertö (lake) □ Hollókö (village) □ Hortobágy (steppe) □ Pannonhalma (abbey) □ Pécs (tombs) □ Tokaj (viticulture) · **ICH:** Mohács (carnival)

csemege), mild, rich, red • 'Exquisite Delicate' (*Csemegepaprika*), like'Delicate', but spicier • 'Rose' (*Rósza*),

————— ICELAND ● ÍSLAND —————

'If the Italian landscape is like Mozart; and if in Switzerland the sublimity
corresponds to Beethoven; then we may take Iceland as the music of the moderns
—say Schumann at his oddest and wildest.'

—Elizabeth Oswald, *By Fell and Fjord* (1882)

'Better wise language
than well-combed hair.'

—Icelandic proverb

ICELANDIC CULINARY DICTIONARY ...		
Dish	**Means**	**Tasting note**
Blóðmör	sheep's blood pudding	'wheaty and slightly beefy'
Hákarl	putrefied shark cubes	first-timers often vomit
Hrútspungar	pickled ram's testicle	'balloons of cold spaghetti'
Lundabaggar	fermented sheep's colon	'fatty—to be savoured'
Selshreifar	milk-cured seal flipper	'like slimed calamari rings'
Sviðasulta	sheep's-head jam	'texture of chilled eyeballs'

... OR MAYBE NOT. The Viking forebears of modern Icelanders took personal grooming very seriously, leaving more Viking combs preserved than swords (or any other artefact). Blondeness was especially prized, so warriors used special lye soap to bleach their hair.

... AND TRADITIONAL ETIQUETTE MANUAL

'Neither is it lawfull to rise from the Table to make water, but for this purpose the daughter of the house gives the chamber-pot under the Table with her owne hands; the rest in the meane while grunt like Swine, lest any noise bee heard.'

—Dithmar Blefkens (1563)

COVER UP. Iceland is the only Western democracy in which pornography is totally illegal. Within Europe, the only other countries where it is banned entirely are Belarus and Ukraine (albeit with a cryptic exemption for 'medical purposes').

ASHES TO ASHES. Although it might have caused the worst travel disruption since WWII, Europe got off lightly when Eyjafjallajökull erupted in April 2010. After nearby Laki erupted in 1783, clouds of sulphuric acid killed 23,000 people in the UK alone and shipping had to stay in port as the fogs were too thick to navigate, while ice floes were spotted in the Gulf of Mexico. The bad news is that, as of early 2011, geologists are warning that a new Icelandic eruption is building that could make even Laki look like a popgun.

Icelandic ash ...

0.1 mm

... and where it fell

14–25 April 2010

MUSHROOM MECHANICS. It's not only nuclear weapons that create mushroom clouds: volcanoes, meteorites, fire-storms and even conventional explosions can, if sufficiently large, produce them too. In all cases, the principle is the same—a column of super-heated air, steam and debris rises rapidly, but stalls and spreads out when it reaches the tempera-ture of the surrounding atmosphere. A mush-room cloud can easily reach the jet stream (starting at 7,000 m) to send ash—or fall-out—worldwide, but, unless replenished by fresh activity, will dissipate within around one hour.

♠ · **GSR**: 106 · **WHS**: Surtsey (volcanic island) □ Þingvellir (site of Viking-era parliament)

INDIA • भारत

'Here, activity prevailed when even Greece did not exist. Ideas after ideas have marched from India, but every word has been spoken with peace. We, of all nations, have never been a conquering race, and that blessing is on our head.'

—Swami Vivekananda

DEMOLITION MAN. In an 1835 economy drive, the British Governor of India, Lord Bentinck, drew up plans to pull down the Taj Mahal and auction the marble in London as decoration for English stately homes.[1] Demolition equipment was said to be already in place when news arrived from England that a prior sale of Indian marble had flopped and, as a result, the Taj was reprieved.

[1] *Although frequently dismissed as black propaganda, the planned sale has been confirmed by the Archaeological Survey of India.*

HINGLISH—BE A P3P NOT A COUNTRY FELLOW

Backside ... behind (e.g., the sofa)	*Ladies bar* ...... pole-dancing club
Chuddies ……….….. underpants	*Long-cut* .... opposite of short-cut
Clean-chit …………... not guilty	*Military hotel* ..... non-veg. eatery
Country fellow/brute...yokel/boor	*Miscreant* .... petty criminal
Deadly …..…….…..... very good	*Native place* .... hometown
Dickey .... car boot	*No encumbrances* ..... no children
Doodwallah .... milkman	*Non-veg. joke* .... adult joke
Enjoy (to) .... have sex with	*Nose-cut* .... insult
Eve-teasing .... sexual harassment	*Offs* .... holidays
Godman ... living saint (or nutter)	*On the anvil* .... imminent
Goonda .... hired thug	*Page Three Person* ..... It-girl/boy
Half-ticket .... small child	*Prepone* .... to bring forward
Healthy .... overweight	*Stepney*..spare tyre (also mistress)
History sheeter ... career criminal	*Updation* ..... process of updating
Kitty party .... ladies at lunch	*Would-be* .... fiancé(e)

ADOLF HITLER MARAK is a member of Meghalaya's State Assembly and a past forests minister. Meghalaya politicians also include a Frankenstein, Lenin, Stalin, Churchill and Tony Curtis.

TICKET TO RIDE[2]—HOW FAR CAN YOU GO ON $1?

India	*(21.8 miles)*
China	*(12.0 miles)*
USA	*(6.6 miles)*
France	*(3.2 miles)*
Germany	*(2.6 miles)*
UK	*(2.3 miles)*

[2] *Standard second-class, long-haul, inter-city, express rail journey (2009).*

MASS TRANSIT. At 6,700,000,000[3], the annual number of passengers on Indian Railways equals the population of the planet; train services include two hospitals and four hotels.

[3] *Excludes a billion or so assorted fare-dodgers, roof-riders and toilet-hiders.*

INSTANT KARMA. For a teaching aid to convey the metaphysics of reincarnation, look no further than snakes and ladders. First developed by Indian priests in the 2nd century BCE, the game was devised to use ladders to represent virtuous deeds and snakes to depict vices. With the basics grasped, it's child's play to see that good deeds lead to heaven, while bad condemn the soul to the risks of reincarnation. Cockroach next time round, anyone?

UNLUCKY FOR SOME. The swastika[4] is one of the ancient symbols created by humanity, and, in India, remains ubiquitous as a powerful talisman of good fortune. A century ago, the swastika sign was also fashionable across Europe (and originally uncontroversial), but, for obvious reasons, it has fallen into disuse—except in Finland, where it is still proudly flown as the symbol of both the country's president and air force.

[4] *'Swastika' comes from the Sanskrit words su-asti-ka, 'well-being-maker'.*

INTENSIVE ISLAM. With over 300,000, India has more mosques than any other country in the world.

'India has two million gods and worships them all. In religion all other countries are paupers; India is the only millionaire.'

—Mark Twain

1500 BCE

1000 BCE

500 BCE

2000 CE

1500 CE

1000 CE

500 CE

1 CE

LDS

DEALING WITH DEATH—WHAT'S IN STORE FOR THE NEARLY DEPARTED		
Religion	**Earthly Remains**	**Hereafter**
Buddhism ✡	cremated—can up to one year later	reincarnated (but no soul)
Christianity ⸙	buried—now often cremated instead	heaven, or hell (downplayed)
Confucianism 木	buried—called the 'white happy-event'	of secondary interest
Hinduism ॐ	cremated—except infants and monks	reincarnated (with soul)
Islam ☾	buried—with head pointing to Mecca	paradise or hell
Judaism ✡	buried—takes place on day of death	heaven or purgatory
Zoroastrianism	exposed to be picked clean by vultures	an ordeal by molten metal

ASHES TO ASHES. The dead have been burnt in India for at least 4,000 years. According to Hindu tradition, flame purifies a person's remains and helps free the soul. In contrast, the Abrahamic religions have all historically opposed the practice. In part, this was because cremation was favoured by the Romans, and so considered pagan; but mainly it was a taboo inherited from the ancient Egyptians, who believed cremation blocked the migration of the soul. By the Middle Ages, views had hardened to the extent that, in some areas of Europe, cremating a body became punishable by death. More recently, however, Christianity has softened its stance, not least due to cremation's advantages where space is at a premium: on average, an adult male body reduces to 2.7 kg of ash and a female to 1.8 kg.

HOLY COW. Distilled cow urine has a hallowed role in Ayurvedic Indian medicine. Practitioners suggest preparing your own at home (using a pressure cooker) to treat everything from coughs to cancer. More ambitiously, in 2009, a Hindu nationalist group set out plans for 'Cow Water'—a cow-urine soft drink—with, it believes, the potential to outsell Pepsi and Coke. Mixed with milk, ghee and dung, cow urine becomes known as 'Five Cow Nectar', a tonic said to soothe stomachache and heartburn. Cow dung pure and simple serves as a disinfectant, mosquito repellent and fuel (replacing 43m tons of coal yearly), although dung prices have now climbed beyond the reach of the poorest. It is also made into toothpaste.

WEIGHTY SENTENCE. The Indian punishment of death by elephant was commonplace until the 19th century and could be ordered for everything from military desertion to tax evasion—or sometimes just the maharaja's pleasure. Especially large elephants were bred for the purpose, weighing up to nine tons.

TARGET PRACTICE. Sentinel Island is home to Asia's last uncontacted people. When an Indian coastguard helicopter overflew to assess damage after the 2004 tsunami, islanders shot at it with bows and arrows.

THE BIG SMOKE. Thanks to its pollution-laden smog, living in Delhi is as risky as smoking 20 cigarettes a day.

Timeline Key (*other faiths and doctrines not in table at top*): ✺ Bahá'í, 🖐 Jainism, יהוה Jehovah's Witnesses, **LDS** Mormonism, ⚙ Protestant schism, ⛩ Shinto, ☬ Sikhism, ☯ Taoism.

COLONEL KENNEY-HERBERT'S ANGLO-INDIAN CURRY POWDER (1885): chillies · coriander · cumin seed · fenugreek · ginger · mustard seed · peppercorn (black) · poppy seed · turmeric.

BURNING QUESTION. Though native to the tropical Americas, chillies are so central to Indian food that, until 1868, Europeans believed the plant had originated there. Properly speaking, chillies aren't hot but 'piquant'. Piquancy isn't a flavour at all, but a pain response—as will be blindingly obvious to anyone who has rubbed their eyes after chopping chillies. Bypassing the taste buds, chilli works directly on pain-sensing nerves, and shares the same biochemical pathway as tarantula venom. Chilli's active ingredient, capsaicin, is concentrated in the pith around the seeds, and may have evolved to deter browsing animals. Birds, on the other hand, can't sense chilli's fire and, feasting on the peppers, spread the seeds in their droppings. As to why humans like the pain that comes from chilli, one theory argues its effect on the nervous system stimulates the body to produce pain-killing endorphins, which, being opium-analogues, would make chilli a truly addictive taste.

RED HOT CHILLI PEPPERS
THE SCOVILLE SCALE

SCOVILLE UNITS	FOUND IN
15,000,000	*pure capsaicin*
5,000,000	*police-grade pepper spray*
1,000,000	*Naga Jolokia*
200,000	*Jamaican pep.*
80,000	*Thai pep.*
30,000	*Cayenne pep.*
7,000	*Jalapeño pep.*
2,500	*Tabasco sauce*
100	*pimento*
0	*red pepper*

Log scale

ELEPHANT STRENGTH. The world's hottest chilli is generally considered to be the *Naga Jolokia* from Assam. In its native region, the chilli is pounded into paste and daubed on fences as an elephant repellent, but India's Defence Research Organisation is working to develop a wider use by incorporating it into a hand grenade. Hot as the *Naga Jolokia* may get, even it is blown away by the sap of *Euphorbia resinifera*, a Moroccan spurge. This plant contains a substance known as resiniferatoxin, with a Scoville score of 16 billion: ingesting it causes severe chemical burns to the mouth and all points down.

> **PUTTING OUT THE FIRE.** *Water fails to quench a burning curry since the capsaicin in chilli doesn't dissolve in it. Milk (or the Indian yoghurt drink lassi) works better, as dairy proteins have a detergent effect. But best of all, if you can avoid gagging, is to quaff neat cooking oil.*

ROOT CAUSE. In order to avoid unnecessary violence to plants, Jains won't eat potatoes, onions or other root vegetables as harvesting kills the whole organism. Strict Jains go further and take a vow never to eat after sunset to prevent moths being drawn to the cooking flame; neither may food be kept overnight since, during storage, bacteria and other microorganisms will have started to multiply, and their deaths too must be minimized.

SYMBOLS OF DEMOCRACY—A SELECTION OF INDIAN BALLOT SLIP GRAPHICS

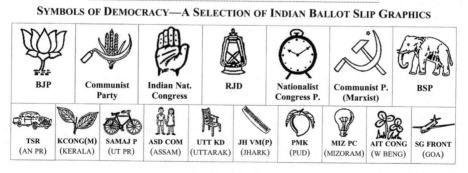

BJP	Communist Party	Indian Nat. Congress	RJD	Nationalist Congress P.	Communist P. (Marxist)	BSP

TSR (AN PR)	KCONG(M) (KERALA)	SAMAJ P (UT PR)	ASD COM (ASSAM)	UTT KD (UTTARAK)	JH VM(P) (JHARK)	PMK (PUD)	MIZ PC (MIZORAM)	AIT CONG (W BENG)	SG FRONT (GOA)

lapis lazuli · onyx · tiger's eye · garnet · jasper ● ● zen · yoga · veranda · toddy · thug · shampoo ·

Left margin (vertical): lapis lazuli · onyx · tiger's eye · garnet · jasper · cornelian · malachite · turquoise · jade · coral · bloodstone · agate · slate · red sandstone · white marble **Stones adorning the Taj Mahal (selected):**

Right margin (vertical): pyjamas · pundit · pariah · loot · jungle · juggernaut · guru · doolally · chit · cot · catamaran · bungalow · bangle **English words from Indian languages:**

Rank[2]	Country	Estd. Pop.
ON TOP OF THE WORLD:		
LARGEST POPULATIONS (2050)		
1 (2)	**India**	**1.75bn**
2 (1)	China	1.44bn
3 (3)	USA	439m
4 (4)	Indonesia	343m
5 (6)	Pakistan	335m

[2] *Current rank in brackets.*

TOGA PARTY. The classic single-piece woman's sari, worn draped about the body, is thought to have arrived in India around two thousand years ago along the silk route from ancient Rome. Stylistically, the modern garment remains very close to the Roman *palla*, the feminine version of the male toga.

PRINCE CHARMING. Observant Sikhs always take the name Singh, meaning 'lion', for men and Kaur, which means 'prince', for women.

RED TAPE. Kamathipura in Mumbai is the world's largest red-light district. It was originally set up by British colonial administrators as an official facility to service British troops.

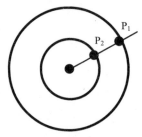

POINT OF PRINCIPLE—at least as far as the scientists are concerned. If you sit on a single nail, 70 kg or so of you pushing down on the point of one nail a fraction of an inch across will ensure a trip to your local A&E. But sit on a *bed* of nails (say 1,000) and now the tip of each only has to support a skin-safe 70 g. A leathery hide still helps, even so.

'I think it would be a good idea.'

—Mahatma Gandhi, when asked for his thoughts on Western civilization

MENTAL ARITHMETIC. Indian mathematicians were the first to talk about infinity (around 400 BCE). Not a number but a concept, infinity is slippery to grasp. Thus, for example, there is the same (infinite) quantity of points on the perimeters of the inner and outer circles above—even though the perimeter of the outer one is plainly longer.[1] One philosopher claimed puzzles like this had driven him to contemplate suicide.

[1] *A line from the centre of the outer circle to any point P_1 on its perimeter must also pass through a point P_2 on the inner one. So for each point on the large circle, there must be a corresponding one on the small circle too.*

HERE KITTY. India is famous for its man-eating big cats, but usually people don't have the catfish in mind. However, a super-sized variety known as the *goonch* is thought to be behind at least three incidents where bathers have been dragged beneath the surface on one stretch of the Kali river. No remains were found, and it's speculated *goonchs* may have got a taste for human flesh after feeding on part-burnt remains discarded from cremation piles. At the other end of the size scale, another type of catfish, the *candiru*, is feared for its odd habit of swimming into bodily orifices. In 1997, one had to be surgically removed in Brazil after it swam up a fisherman's penis.

♣ · **GSR**: 12 · **WHS**: Agra Fort □ Ajanta Caves (carvings) □ Bhimbetka (rock art) □ Bodh Gaya (temples) □ Chhatrapat Shivaji Terminus (station) □ Chola Temples □ Elephanta (cave art) □ Ellora Caves (temples) □ Fatehpur Sikri (deserted city) □ Goa (churches) □ Hampi (ruined city) □ Humayun's Tomb □ Jantar Mantar (observatory) □ Kaziranga (wildlife) □ Keoladeo (birdlife) □ Khajuraho (temples) □ Konârak (temple) □ Mahabalipuram (temples) □ Manas (wildlife) □ Mountain Railways Nanda Devi (landscape) □ Red Fort □ Pattadakal (temples) □ Pavagadh (ruined city) □ Qutb Minar (tower) □ Sanchi (ruins) □ Sunderbans (mangroves) □ Taj Mahal (mausoleum) · **ICH**: Chhau Dance Kalbelia (songs and dances) □ Kutiyattam (theatre) □ Mudiyettu (theatre) □ Navruz (New Year festival) Ramlila (epic narrative) □ Ramman (theatre) □ Vedic Chanting

INDONESIA

*'We need the children of Indonesia
to manufacture our freedom of choice.'* —Marc Maron, on footwear

W ◄━━━━━━━━━ I N D O N E S I A ━━━━━━━━━► **E**

◄---------------------------- *3,180 miles* ---------------------------►

●◄━**London** (UK) ━━━━━━━━━━━━━━━━━━ **Kashgar** (China) ━►●

ISLANDS OF THE WORLD (LARGEST BY POPULATION)		
1	**Java (Indonesia[1])**	**131m**
2	Honshu (Japan)	103m
3	Great Britain	57m
4	**Sumatra (Indo)**	**47m**
5	Luzon (Phil)	46m

[1] Total population of Indonesia is 230m—the fourth largest in the world after China, India and the USA.

MADE IN ENGLAND. The word 'Indonesia'[3] was invented by 19th-century English academics. Prior to this, the immense island chain sprawling from Asia to Australia was known (rather vaguely) as the East Indies or Spice Islands.
[3] A doggerel mix of Latin and Greek, the name means 'Indian archipelago'.

PULLING THE PLUG. Indonesia straddles more of the Equator than any other country, which should make it ideal to demonstrate the well-known fact that bathtubs drain clockwise in the Southern Hemisphere but anti-clockwise in the Northern. Sadly, it's untrue. While correct in theory (due to the Earth's rotation), the effect is tiny, and, in practice, swamped by extraneous factors—such as which side you climb out of, or even the gunk down the hole.

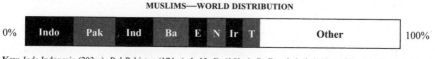

HERE BE DRAGONS. Locally, they call them 'land crocodiles', but 'snakes on stilts' might be more apt. Like many snakes, the 10-ft Komodo dragon comes with two penises, a mouth oozing venom and articulated jaws that let it swallow almost its own body-weight in one feed.[2] Rampant cannibalism makes dragon sex a risky proposition, which may explain why females can give virgin birth.

[2] Komodo dragons consume every part of a kill except its stomach contents (and, in the case of one tourist, apparently, the spectacles and camera).

BRAIN PAIN. The Indonesian form of the 'scissors, paper, stone' game pits an earwig against an elephant and a human. For those wishing to play at home, the rules are as follows: elephant crushes man, man crushes earwig, earwig crawls into elephant's brain and drives it insane.

INFLATION. President Suharto ruled as an authoritarian strongman for 32 years, until overthrown by students in 1998. In this time, his wife, Tien, became known as 'Madame Tien Per Cent' for the rake-offs she allegedly skimmed from public contracts. Near the end, however, she got greedy and her nickname had to be upgraded to 'Madame Fifty-Fifty'.

BLOODY TOURISTS. When, in 1597, the first European ship arrived in Bali, the sailors liked what they saw so much they promptly jumped ship. The impression they made seems to have been less positive. Three centuries later, when a Dutch army landed, 4,000 members of Bali's ruling elite marched up to the foreign troops and, led by the Rajah, committed mass suicide rather than put up with yet more Europeans.

THE EAST IS GREEN. Indonesia is the most populous Muslim nation on Earth. It has over two-and-a-half times as many Muslims as Egypt, and nearly three times as many as Iran.

MUSLIMS—WORLD DISTRIBUTION

0% | Indo | Pak | Ind | Ba | E | N | Ir | T | Other | 100%

Key: *Indo* Indonesia (203m), *Pak* Pakistan (174m), *Ind* India (161m), *Ba* Bangladesh (145m), *E* Egypt (79m), *N* Nigeria (78m), *Ir* Iran (74m), *T* Turkey (74m). *Other* (583m)—of which largest share is Europe (38m). **Total**: 1.57 billion.

Left margin (top to bottom): Seram • Halmahera • Timor (part) • Java • Sulawesi • Sumatra • Borneo (part) • New Guinea (part): Indonesian islands larger than 1,000 square miles in area

Right margin (top to bottom): Nias • Siberut • Wetar • Yamdena • Waigeo ■ Other Indonesian islands: Ambon • Bandanaira • Batam • Bintan • Ternate • Tidore ... and 17,479 more

LAVA LAMPS. More than half of all Indonesians live in sight of a volcano. Of the 1,500 active volcanoes in the world, 10% are in Indonesia—by far the greatest single country total. Around 10 of these erupt every year.

BIG BANGS—VOLCANIC EXPLOSIVITY INDEX (VEI) [1]

VEI Rating [2]	V	VI	VII	VIII
Description:	**Paroxysmal**	**Colossal**	**Super-Colossal**	**Mega-Colossal**
Example:	Vesuvius (Italy) 79 CE	Krakatoa (Indon.) 1883	Tambora (Indon.) 1815	Toba (Indon.) 74,000 BCE
Size: [3]	<1 cubic mile	5 cubic miles	40 cubic miles	700 cubic miles
London/UK drawn to scale.				
Comment:	Roman cities of Pompeii and Herculaneum buried.	The last wave circled the Earth seven times.	Global famines; no summer in the following year.	Near-extinction of humanity—perhaps just 2,000 survivors.
Frequency: [4]	~ every 50 yrs	~ every 100 yrs	~ every 1,000 yrs	~ every 10,000 yrs

[1] *The VEI measures the violence of a volcanic eruption, based on the total amount of rock and ash that is ejected.*
[2] *Lesser eruptions are described as: non-explosive (0), gentle (I), explosive (II), severe (III) or cataclysmic (IV); such eruptions eject up to 100 million m^3 of material and occur globally from daily (I) to every 10 years (IV).*
[3] *Volume ejected; map shows area that would be covered to an even depth of 3 m (10 ft).* [4] *Worldwide occurrences .*

MOCHA, LATTE OR CAT POOH? *Kopi Luwak* is coffee retrieved from the dung of the Asian palm civet, a small cat-like animal that's fond of Sumatran coffee berries. Gourmets divide on whether it's the civet's ability to sniff out the sweetest berries or the 36 hours within the animal's gut that counts—but, either way, they are prepared to pay up to $80 a cup.

'About two weeks upriver, stay with the Dutch priest ... cross rapids and whirlpools ... three days from this village, you must begin the overland trek ... eat speared lizards and boar fat ... from the longhouse, it's 10–15 days walk to the turning ... no maps for this section ... next, build a raft ...'

—Instructions for crossing Borneo on foot, *Indonesia* (Moon Handbooks, 1985)

EDIBLE EXCRETA		
Ingredient	Source	Use
Yàn wo	saliva (swift)	bird's nest soup
Honey	vomit [5] (bee)	sweetening
Civet oil	anal glands	flavouring [6]
Lant	urine (human)	flavouring [7]

[5] *Honey is regurgitated from the honey-stomach. 'Honeydew honey' is a variety of honey produced by bees out of the faecal waste of aphids and is thus, uniquely, a twice-excreted foodstuff.* [6] *Found in some brands of cola.* [7] *Stale urine was formerly used to flavour ales, and as a pastry glaze and breath freshener.*

SWEET AND SOUR. In 1667, the Dutch struck a deal with Britain which gave them control of the Indonesian spice island of Run. In return, the British were fobbed off with some place called Manhattan.

WITH THE BENEFIT OF HINDSIGHT ...		
	Run	Manhattan
Area (sq. miles)	1	23
Population (2010)	1,000	1,635,000
GDP ($, 2010)	1 million	800 billion

~ Indonesia's Puncak Jaya is the highest peak between the Himalayas and the Andes ~

♣ · **GSR**: 9 · **WHS**: Borobudur (Buddhist temple) □ Komodo (lizards) □ Lorentz (alpine mountains, rainforest, coral reefs) □ Prambanan (Hindu temple) □ Sangiran (human fossils) □ Sumatra (rainforest) Ujung Kulon (human fossils) · **ICH**: Angklung (musical instrument) □ Batik (craft) □ Kris (weapon) Wayang (puppet theatre)

IRAN ● ایران

'Neither West nor East nor Arab.'

—Mehdi Akhavan Sales, poet (1928–90). Despite being jailed by the Shah, Sales wrote under the pen-name 'Hope'.

'I cannot believe that the purpose of all these sacrifices was to have less expensive melons.'

—Grand Ayatollah Khomeini

GRAVELY POPULAR. Famously ascetic, Khomeini was a man who also possessed intense charisma.[1] He needed it, since, while he adopted a masterly approach to building his new Islamic society, once in power, Khomeini was disastrous at workaday issues such as economics. Nevertheless, despite the stratospheric cost of cantaloupes, his 1989 burial was arguably the funeral of the century. On the first attempt, the cortege was simply overwhelmed by more than two million mourners. Once finally at the gravesite, Khomeini's wooden coffin was knocked to the ground and broken open by people desperate to grab a piece of his shroud. His body was lost to the crowd before shots were fired into the air, and it was retrieved and evacuated by helicopter. A second funeral took place five hours later, by which time the ex-leader's body had been transferred to a steel casket and ringed by armed security personnel. Although, this time, the ayatollah was buried successfully, the organizers were still forced to lower a shipping container over the newly filled grave to protect it from being dug open by mourners.

[1] *Analysts have put the secret of Khomeini's success down to a few simple rules: he never looked at his audience, never acknowledged anyone else and never, ever smiled—after all, as he said himself: 'There are no jokes in Islam.'*

BANNER OF BELIEF. The emblem of the Islamic Republic of Iran was chosen by Ayatollah Khomeini in 1980 to replace the lion and sun of the Shah. Pictorially, it shows four crescents and a sword. Collectively, these stand for the five articles of Shia Islam, while the four crescents alone spell out the word 'Allah'. The double cup above the central sword (technically a *shadda*, a sign of emphasis) represents the tulip, the ancient (and pre-Islamic) Persian symbol of martyrdom.

BOTANIC BLISS. Paradise is a walled garden—literally. The ultimate root of the word is the phrase *pairi daêza* ('walled enclosure'), which appears in the sacred texts of Zoroastrianism. Striking a chord in the arid Middle East, this promise of paradise caused Islam to adopt green as its emblematic colour.

CHOPPY WATERS. The 2010 Islamic Solidarity Games ran into trouble when the host nation, Iran, insisted that the arm of the Indian Ocean separating it from Arabia be shown as the 'Persian Gulf' on all medals. The Arab countries disagreed and dug their heels in for 'Arabian Gulf', until, in the end, the whole event had to be cancelled. It's a matter Iran feels passionate about: airlines are only allowed to fly into the country if their in-flight monitors show the Gulf as Persian, and nothing to do with Arabs.

NAME YOUR POISON—A WHO'S WHO OF GOVERNING CLASSES		
Government	*Who's the boss?*	*Examples*
Theocracy	God (typically by way of clerics)	Iran, Deseret (now Utah), Tibet (to 1950)
Gerontocracy	an aged (often enfeebled) generation	USSR, Cuba, China (late 20th century)
Kleptocracy	criminals (before or once in office)	Indonesia (Suharto), Equatorial Guinea
Timocracy	property owners (over a threshold)	Athens (classical), UK (in part until 1928)
Kakistocracy	those who are the most unscrupulous	many would say always and everywhere

3200 BCE

◄ *Iranians claim the Persian nation has a history going back to 3200 BCE, making theirs the oldest country in the world. This is debatable. But even a conservative assessment gives a foundation date of 559 BCE—still the world's third earliest (after Egypt and Ethiopia).*

◄ The earliest antecedent of the Easter egg can be found in Zoroastrianism, originating in Persia 2,500 to 3,000 years ago and formerly the world's largest religion. To mark Nowruz (the ancient New Year, celebrated on the spring equinox), painted boiled eggs were prepared as an offering symbolizing rebirth. From this, it was a small step for early Christians to adapt the association to signify the Easter resurrection.

625 BCE

◄ *In Media, women could have as many husbands as they wished. Those with fewer than five were treated with scorn.*

559 BCE

The ancient Greeks were accustomed to ridiculing the Persians ◄ as unmanly for fighting in trousers—they themselves favoured a pleated miniskirt and tunic with nice snug hose.

'Here with a loaf of bread beneath the bough A flask of wine, a choice kebab[1]—and thou ...'

—*Rubaiyat of Omar Khayyam (c.1100)*

LUNCH. Iran is the home of the kebab, which, for romantics, was invented by the nameless Persian soldier who first skewered lumps of meat with his sword to toast over a campfire. Spoilsports, however, claim that the kebab was just an obviously efficient way to cook in a land where wood for European-style roasts was perennially scarce.

[1] *Other translations have* kitab *('book').*

CASPIAN CATS. Think 'jungle' and images of Borneo, Brazil and tropical Africa may well spring to mind, but possibly not Iran. However, the mountains flanking the southern shore of the Caspian Sea are cloaked with dense sub-tropical rainforests conventionally referred to as the 'Jungles of Iran'. Even now, some parts have scarcely been penetrated, and large areas remain the demesne of leopards, jungle cats and, until recently, both lions and tigers (1944 and 1959 respectively being the last widely accepted sightings in Iran).

In 636 CE, Arab invaders brought Islam to Iran, and over the next 150 years it eclipsed the traditional Zoroastrianism almost completely. Because the cooked teeth of pigs are highly resistant to decomposition, archaeologists are able to track the spread of Islam in great detail by timing the disappearance of pig teeth from local rubbish heaps.

Iran is currently the ► *only country where it's legal to buy and sell human organs (mostly kidneys). As a result, there is no waiting list for transplants. But purchasers must be Iranian—so everyone else with cash to flash must still rely on the likes of Liver4you.com.*

When the second Qajar ► shah of Persia, Fat'h Ali, completed his reading of the entire 3rd edition of the *Encyclopaedia Britannica* (a feat he began in 1797), he expanded his royal title to add: 'Most Formidable Lord and Master of the *Encyclopaedia Britannica.'*

Persia sacked repeatedly by Mongol Hordes, from Genghis Khan to ► *Timur: population only recovered in the 1950s.*

1387 CE | 1218 CE

Based at their mountain fortress of Alamut in northern Iran, the original Assassins were an Ismaili terrorist sect, active between 1092 and 1265 CE, that specialized in murdering high-profile individuals through often suicidal attacks by dagger-wielding adepts. Their name likely derives from ► 'hashish-eater', which may or may not have been disinformation. But, in any event, they were so feared that, when the Crusaders returned with tales of their exploits, the term came to be applied to all murderers ▼ of political figures.

1979 CE

---

636 CE

ACHAEMENIDS ～ SELEUCIDS ～ PARTHIANS ～ SASSANIDS | ARAB CALIPHATES

(left margin top to bottom) Timeline not to scale · ELAMITE KINGDOMS · MEDES · CYRUS · DARIUS I · XERXES I

(right margin top to bottom) ISLAMIC REP. · QAJARS ～ AFSHARIDS ～ PAHLAVIS · SAFAVIDS · KHWARAZMIDS · SAMANIDS · TAHIRIDS

♣ · **GSR**: 57 · **WHS**: Ardabil (religious buildings) □ Armenian Monasteries □ Bam (citadel) □ Bisotun (bas-relief memorial) □ Esfahan (monumental square) □ Pasargadae (ruined city) □ Persepolis (ruined city) □ Persian Gardens □ Shushtar (ancient waterworks) □ Soltaniyeh (mausoleum) □ Tabriz (bazaar) Takht-e Soleyman (Zoroastrian ruins) □ Tchogha Zanbil (ruined city) · **ICH**: Bakhshis (music) □ Fars (carpet weaving) □ Kashan (carpet weaving) □ Nowruz (New Year celebrations) □ Pahlevani (ritual gymnastics) □ Radif (Iranian classical music) □ Ta'zīye (ritual drama)

———— IRAQ ● العراق ————

'Unfortunate is the man who has no nails with which to scratch his head.'

—Iraqi (Arab) proverb

COS OF DEATH. Lettuces are taboo for Iraq's Yazidi minority—they are forbidden to grow, sell, eat or even touch the salad leaf. Followers of Yazidism, a synthesis of Sufi Islam, Mithraism and traditional Kurdish folk beliefs, the Yazidi hold that the Earth is watched over by seven magical beings, led by the Peacock Angel,[1] and that, uniquely among mankind, they themselves are descended without the intervention of Eve from some sperm Adam stored in a jar—hence they never marry outsiders or accept them as converts. The origin of the aversion to lettuce is obscure. One story states that it arose in the 18th century, after Ottoman soldiers slaughtered thousands of Yazidi believers while they were tending their lettuce fields. However, another theory claims it is much older—arising after the body of a Yazid martyr was pelted with lettuces in 13th-century Mosul, while a third explanation claims it's because of the vegetable's alleged resemblance to the human ear.

[1] *Muslims consider the Yazidi to be devil-worshippers, largely because one of the names the Peacock Angel goes by is Shaytan, the Islamic term for Satan. The Yazidis deny this, however, and point out that the Peacock Angel's tears have, in any case, already extinguished the fires of Hell.*

PHANTOM MENACE. As US forces made their final push into Baghdad in 2003, they were confronted by the random sight of hundreds of Darth Vader lookalikes stepping out of the shadows to engage them—or that's what it seemed from the rear. When the Vaders

turned round, it was clear they were, in fact, ultra-loyalist Fedayeen militia wearing Darth Vader-styled black Kevlar helmets. Rumours later suggested the helmets had been commissioned by Saddam Hussein's son Uday to resemble that worn by the *Star Wars* character because he thought it would make their wearers more intimidating. If accurate, it's a case of reality imitating art imitating reality, as George Lucas chose to model Darth Vader's helmet on those of *samurai* for the same reason. In any event, any threat in Iraq was illusory as the helmets gave no protection in actual combat, and the Fedayeen melted away almost as soon as they had appeared.

BLOODY BOOK. In 1997, Saddam Hussein had a Qu'ran written with (he claimed) 27 litres of his own blood. The book still exists, and what to do with it is now causing a major headache. While using blood for the text makes Saddam's Qu'ran an abomination, it nonetheless remains forbidden to destroy any copy of the holy book.

DESERT SWARM. Of the stories Western troops sent back from Iraq during both recent wars, some of the most startling concerned the fearsome camel spider. Emails, which soon went viral, reported the beasts roamed in hordes, grew as big as dinner plates, outran Humvees, jumped as high as a man's face, laid their eggs inside a camel's belly and fed on the flesh of sleeping soldiers. None of this is true. But the reality is grim enough. Equipped with outsize fanglined pincers (which they rub together when agitated with a disconcerting rattle), they do attack rodents, lizards and even snakes. Once their prey is dead, they use the pincers to chop up the body, before liquefying it with digestive fluid and slurping the juices. Humans are far too big to tackle, but, nevertheless, camel spiders will bite when cornered, and have caused deep and dirty wounds. Frequent stories of being chased by a camel spider can be explained by the creature's attempts to hide in a person's shadow to escape the sun—an especially unnerving experience, since, while no match for a jeep, camel spiders can indeed scuttle as fast as a soldier weighed down for battle can comfortably run.

IRAQ—THE LAND WHERE CIVILIZATION BEGAN

4000 BCE	3000 BCE	2000 BCE	1000 BCE	01 CE	1000 CE	2000 CE

Iraq has been home to the world's largest city of its era five times: Ur (2000 BCE), Nineveh (650 BCE), Babylon (400 BCE), Ctesiphon (600 CE) and Baghdad (800 CE).

● **POLE POSITION.** Humanity's earliest recorded striptease comes in the Sumerian creation myth explaining the four seasons. As part of the story, the goddess of fertility, Inanna, makes a journey to the underworld, during which she is forced to remove one item at each of its seven gates until she arrives at her destination stripped naked. Although direct proof is absent, many have taken this as the origin of biblical Salome's Dance of the Seven Veils, which, in turn, has been one of the classic inspirations for contemporary ecdysis.

Inanna

● **21ˢᵀ-CENTURY MEDICINE.** Records suggest the Sumerians were the first to discover the pain-killing potency of salicylic acid compounds, found naturally in willow bark.[2] The synthetic analogue, aspirin, is today the world's favourite medicine—with 40,000 tonnes of the pills popped each year.

[2] *Willow is listed in an inventory of medicinal materials found on a 21ˢᵗ-century (BCE) tablet from Ur. However, the use to which it was put is not explicitly recorded, so it is conceivable that it was instead known in its alternative capacity—as a treatment for teenage acne.*

● **ZAP.** In 1938, a dozen unusual pots surfaced just outside Baghdad. Each contained an iron rod and copper sheath and, despite being dated to 200 BCE (2,000 years before Volta invented his pile), are thought by many scholars to be ancient batteries.

● **WHODUNIT?** History's first murder mystery is 'The Three Apples', one of the *1,001 Arabian Nights* tales. Set in Baghdad around 800 CE, the story begins when a young woman's dismembered body is found in a chest, and the caliph orders his vizier to solve the crime in three days or face execution himself. Plot twists, flashbacks and a liberal sprinkling of clues all follow, until a lifesaving surprise denouement is supplied by the vizier's daughter just as he is facing the sword.

Lord Gilgamesh: fifth ruler of Sumerian Uruk,[1] beloved father to his people and epic protagonist of the world's oldest great work of literature. Ruled 2500 BCE.

[1] *The word 'Iraq' is believed to derive ultimately from this 6,000 year-old city state.*

CITY OF ERIDU
(founded 5400 BCE)

SUMERIANS

'*If a fire break out in a man's house and a man who goes to extinguish it cast his eye on the furniture of the owner of the house, and take the furniture of the owner of the house, that man shall be thrown into the fire.*'

—Law 25 (out of 282) in the *Code of Hammurabi*, c. 1700 BCE. The Sumerians and Babylonians were the first to adopt formal written laws. Most laws were general, and along the lines of 'an eye for an eye'; but others were notably specific.

SUM

AK

AM

BAB

ASSYRIANS

BAB

● **HOLY HOPHEADS.** Starting from around 3400 BCE, the Sumerians were the first people to cultivate opium poppies—which they named *hul gil* ('plants of joy'). Usage was probably initially confined to the priestly class, who either inhaled the fumes given off from heated bowls or took the opium by mouth as a euphoriant in religious rituals.

بيت الحكمة: (**'House of Wisdom'**)
The world's foremost library and research institute of the era.

PER · SEL · PERSIANS · ARAB CALIPHATES · OTT · IR

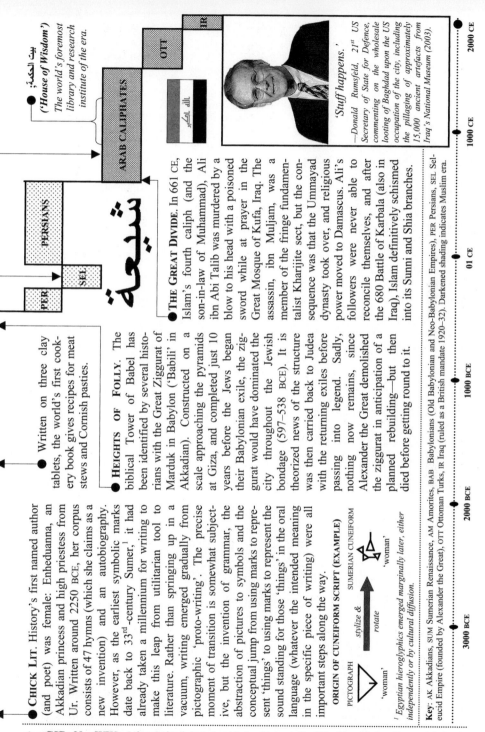

الله أكبر

'Stuff happens.'

—*Donald Rumsfeld, 21st US Secretary of State for Defence, commenting on the wholesale looting of Baghdad upon the US occupation of the city, including the pillaging of approximately 15,000 ancient artefacts from Iraq's National Museum (2003).*

شيعة

Timeline: 3000 BCE · 2000 BCE · 1000 BCE · 01 CE · 1000 CE · 2000 CE

● **CHICK LIT.** History's first named author (and poet) was female: Enheduanna, an Akkadian princess and high priestess from Ur. Written around 2250 BCE, her corpus consists of 47 hymns (which she claims as a new invention) and an autobiography. However, as the earliest symbolic marks date back to 33rd-century Sumer,[1] it had already taken a millennium for writing to make this leap from utilitarian tool to literature. Rather than springing up in a vacuum, writing emerged gradually from pictographic 'proto-writing'. The precise moment of transition is somewhat subjective, but the invention of grammar, the abstraction of pictures to symbols and the conceptual jump from using marks to represent 'things' to using marks to represent the sound standing for those 'things' in the oral language (whatever the intended meaning in the specific piece of writing) were all important steps along the way.

ORIGIN OF CUNEIFORM SCRIPT (EXAMPLE)

PICTOGRAPH		SUMERIAN CUNEIFORM
'woman'	*stylize & rotate*	'woman'

[1] *Egyptian hieroglyphics emerged marginally later, either independently or by cultural diffusion.*

● Written on three clay tablets, the world's first cookery book gives recipes for meat stews and Cornish pasties.

● **HEIGHTS OF FOLLY.** The biblical Tower of Babel has been identified by several historians with the Great Ziggurat of Marduk in Babylon ('Babili' in Akkadian). Constructed on a scale approaching the pyramids at Giza, and completed just 10 years before the Jews began their Babylonian exile, the ziggurat would have dominated the city throughout the Jewish bondage (597–538 BCE). It is theorized news of the structure was then carried back to Judea with the returning exiles before passing into legend. Sadly, nothing now remains, since Alexander the Great demolished the ziggurat in anticipation of a planned rebuilding—but then died before getting round to it.

● **THE GREAT DIVIDE.** In 661 CE, Islam's fourth caliph (and the son-in-law of Muhammad), Ali ibn Abi Talib was murdered by a blow to his head with a poisoned sword while at prayer in the Great Mosque of Kufa, Iraq. The assassin, ibn Muljam, was a member of the fringe fundamentalist Kharijite sect, but the consequence was that the Ummayad dynasty took over, and religious power moved to Damascus. Ali's followers were never able to reconcile themselves, and after the 680 Battle of Karbala (also in Iraq), Islam definitively schismed into its Sunni and Shia branches.

Key: AK Akkadians, SUM Sumerian Renaissance, AM Amorites, BAB Babylonians (Old Babylonian and Neo-Babylonian Empires), PER Persians, SEL Seleucid Empire (founded by Alexander the Great), OTT Ottoman Turks, IR Iraq (ruled as a British mandate 1920–32). Darkened shading indicates Muslim era.

♣ · **GSR**: 28 · **WHS**: Ashur (ruined Assyrian city) □ Hatra (ruined Parthian city) □ Samarra (ruined Abbasid city) · **ICH**: Maqam (music)

——————— IRELAND • ÉIRE ———————

'Being Irish, he had an abiding sense of tragedy, which sustained him
through temporary periods of joy.'

—W. B. Yeats

MUNSTER PLUMS, Smiling Murphys, Irish apricots, bog-oranges or simply spuds; potatoes were brought to Ireland by Sir Walter Raleigh. By the 19th century, the potato had become firmly established as the staple of Irish households. From 1845 to 1848, however, the potato crops failed, as blight turned the tubers into pulpy black sacks. Ireland starved: by the time the famine eased, one million had died, another million had emigrated and the Irish population had fallen by a quarter.

FORTY SHADES OF GREEN. The emerald in the 'Emerald Isle' is down to the rain, which just happens to be perfect for grass. Steady, persistent and reliable, in places it rains nearly two days out of three. It was while looking down on Ireland from a plane that Johnny Cash was inspired to write his classic 'Forty Shades of Green'. In fact, there are closer to an infinite number, and naming them can be quite a challenge. X11 (a computer-display protocol) lists 23, while upmarket paint-makers Farrow & Ball manage a lowly 18. Somebody at Dulux must have been working through the night, however, with a grand total of 213 green gradations. The more inventive include: *Dublin Bay ~ Peppermint Beach ~ Kiwi Burst ~ Melon Sorbet ~ Gooseberry Fool ~ Minted Glory ~ Japanese Maze ~ Indian Ivy ~ Moorland Magic.*

PILE 'EM HIGH. From 5,000 passengers in 1985, Irish budget carrier, Ryanair, has grown into the world's biggest international airline. In 2009, it flew 65m international passengers—enough for every person in Ireland to take 15 flights each.

RECORD-MAKERS

Artist	Albums Sold
U2	170,000,000
Enya	70,000,000
Van Morrison	55,000,000
Cranberries	43,000,000
Corrs	30,000,000

LUCK OF THE IRISH. One for hope, two for faith, three for love—and four for luck. The odds on finding a four-leafed clover are around 10,000 to 1. Five- and more leafed clovers can also be found—the current record, from Japan, is 21 leaves.

■ In the 1840s, an Irish peasant family of six was typically consuming 252 pounds of potatoes each week—and very little else.

■ In the 1950s, both the USA and USSR cultivated potato blight mould for future use as a biological weapon.

IRISH POPULATION
(% OF ENGLISH POPULATION)

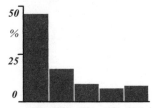

| 1841 | 1881 | 1921 | 1961 | 2001 |

'I showed my apprecia-tion of my native land in the usual Irish way: by getting out of it as soon as I possibly could.'

—George Bernard Shaw

GOOD CRAIC?
YOU'RE HAVING A LAUGH. Until the 1970s, 'craic' was plain old 'crack', as in 'wise-crack' or 'to crack a joke'. Then Irish Gaelic got trendy and a new pseudo-old spelling was devised. If you must use it, be very careful—the genuine Irish Gaelic word *cráic* (with the accent carefully noted) is a most impolite way of referring to the human fundament.

YOUR HEALTH. Packing a mere 210 calories per pint, Guinness is less fattening than half-fat milk, orange juice or dry white wine.

CONNAUGHT:
*Galway, Leitrim,
Mayo, Roscommon,
Sligo.*

THOROUGHBRED. The Curragh, Ireland's premier race course, has hosted the Irish Derby since 1866. But the racetrack's pedigree goes back much further—to the 3rd century, when the site was used for chariot racing.

BLUE-SKY THINKING. Irishman John Tyndall was the first person to work out why the sky is blue, even though air itself seems transparent. As he realized, it's because the atmosphere scatters the blue component of sunlight more than the other colours, so that, if you look in any direction other than straight at the sun, most of the light reaching your eye is blue that has already been scattered at least once. If it were not for this, the sky would be as black as on the moon and, looking away from the sun, the stars would remain visible throughout the day.

MUNSTER:
*Clare, Cork, Kerry,
Limerick, Tipperary,
Waterford.*

NEVER TRUST A TORY. In the time of Oliver Cromwell, 'Tory' (or *Tóraidhe*) described a type of Irish brigand who specialized in killing English settlers. Later, the term was widened to any militant Papist. A generation later, the word jumped the Irish Sea as a nickname for a group of politicians supporting the rule of James II (England's last Catholic king). Finally, it became attached to the Conservatives as the party seen to be closest aligned with tradition and the Crown.

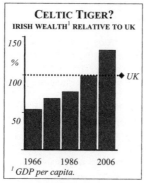

CELTIC TIGER?
IRISH WEALTH[1] RELATIVE TO UK

← UK

1966   1986   2006
[1] *GDP per capita.*

BLACKBORED. Ireland's schools deliver the rich world's most mind-numbingly dull lessons—or so say Ireland's pupils.

SCHOOL PUPIL BOREDOM		
-	*Country*	*%*
1	**Ireland**	**67**
2	USA	61
3=	Australia	60
3=	Finland	60

DEEPEST SYMPATHIES. Irish Taoiseach (prime minister) Éamon de Valéra was the only non-fascist leader to present formal condolences upon Adolf Hitler's suicide.

ULSTER: *Cavan, Donegal, Monaghan, Antrim[2], Armagh[2], Down[2], Fermanagh[2], Derry/ Londonderry[2], Tyrone[2].*
[2] *Counties of Northern Ireland (UK).*

GOSPEL. The world's oldest surviving version of the New Testament is found on a set of Egyptian papyri kept in Dublin's Chester Beatty Library. Dating as early as 180 CE, the papyri were written as much as a century before Rome's *Codex Vaticanus*, the source of the modern text in use today.

'DANNY BOY'. This maudlin anthem of the Irish diaspora was actually written in Somerset by an English barrister, Fred Weatherly, in 1910.

MASS PRODUCTION. Come rain or shine, mass has been said in Ballintuber Abbey, County Mayo, every Sunday without exception since 1216—that's 41,366 Sundays (if you're counting). The reference to rain is worth noting, since, until 1966, the abbey had stood roofless for 236 years.

LEINSTER: *Carlow, Dublin, Kildare, Kilkenny, Laois, Longford, Louth, Meath, Offaly, Westmeath, Wexford, Wicklow.*

THE IRISH QUESTION

'Ireland, Ireland!
That cloud in the west,
that coming storm.'
—W. Gladstone (1845)

'My mission is to pacify
Ireland.'
—W. Gladstone (1868)

'One prayer absorbs all
others: Ireland, Ireland,
Ireland.'
—W. Gladstone (1877)

'Gladstone spent years
trying to guess the answer
to the Irish Question;
unfortunately whenever he
got warm the Irish secretly
changed the Question.'
—W. Seller & R. Yeatman
(*1066 and All That*)

SAINTS AND SINNERS

▪ **St. Brendan**: A wanderer celebrated for his voyage in search of the Isle of the Blessed. Tales relate he landed on a sea monster (and possibly Iceland and America too).

▪ **St. Brigid**: Compassionate Mary of the Gael, Ireland's best-loved saint.

▪ **St. Patrick**: Brought as a slave and credited with introducing Christianity; his famous banishment of 'snakes' from Ireland may actually refer to the serpent symbols of Druidism.

▪ Philip Twysden, **Bishop of Raphoe**: shot dead while moonlighting as a highwayman on Hounslow Heath, London.[1]

[1] *The Church's official version of events was that he had gone for a saunter on the Heath by moonlight (as you do), and had been mysteriously gripped by a sudden and fatal 'inflammation of the bowels'.*

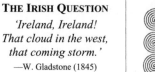

Newgrange spirals

Celtic cross knot

OLD STONES. Cairns, tombs and barrows erupt across the Irish countryside. Newgrange appears the most magnificent, but Carrowmore is older by far. Trifling to look at, the site's Tomb 4 has been radiocarbon dated at 7,400 years. If correct, that could make it the most ancient building in the world.

FAIRY TALES. Rationalized as fallen angels, neither good enough for heaven nor bad enough for hell, Ireland's fairy folk are best left alone. *Leanan sídhe* are sirens who suck the life from human lovers; *pooka*, hobgoblins that roam the night; leprechauns come tricksy as snake-oil salesmen; while death stalks in the wake of a banshee's wail. Most feared of all are the fairy changelings: mean-spirited cuckoos-in-the-nest who drain all luck from a home. A (high-risk) traditional test is to heat a shovel and cast the suspect baby into a fire. If a changeling, it will scuttle up the chimney and return the true child unharmed.

RECORD-BREAKERS. Conceived in 1951 as a PR stunt by the then MD of Guinness breweries, *Guinness World Records* has gone on to become the world's biggest-selling copyrighted book, with 120 million copies sold.

PRETTY DITTIES
EUROVISION WINS

-	Country	Wins
1st	Ireland[2]	7
2 =	France	5
2 =	Lux.	5
2 =	UK	5
3 =	Holland	4
3 =	Sweden	4

[2] *Ireland's Johnny Logan is the only performer to have won twice (1980 and 1987).*

HEROES AND VILLAINS
(OR VICE VERSA)

▪ **American Presidents**: At least 21 have Irish ancestors, including Washington and every president since JFK.

▪ **Neil Armstrong**: The first man on the moon boasts Fermanagh roots.

▪ **Ned Kelly**: Australia's best-known bushranger was the son of a transported Irish convict.

▪ **Che Guevara**:[3] A scion of the Galway Lynches. In the words of his father: 'The blood of the Irish rebel flowed in my son's veins.'

[3] *On 13 March 1965, Che himself stopped off for an evening tipple at Hanratty's Bar, in Limerick, while en route back from Moscow to Havana.*

CONSTRUCTION TIMELINE

Carrowmore
5400 BCE

Pyramids
4300 BCE

Parthenon
2500 BCE

Aachen Dom
805

Eiffel Tower
1889

♠ · **GSR**: 27 · **WHS**: Boyne Valley Tombs—inc. Newgrange □ Skellig Michael (monastic ruins)

—————— ISRAEL • יִשְׂרָאֵל ——————

> *'Let me tell you something we Israelis have against Moses. He took us
> 40 years through the desert to bring us to the one spot in the Middle East
> that has no oil.'*
>
> —Golda Meir

The Egyptian Stele of Merneptah (c. 1210 BCE) contains the first written reference to 'Israel' (shown above). The relevant part reads: 'Israel lies wasted, its seed gone.' The phrase was a stock one, and meant that an enemy's grain stores had been destroyed, so leaving it open to famine in the following year and nullifying it as a military threat.

TWELVE TRIBES—NEW BEGINNINGS. When Jacob, grandson of Abraham, reached Canaan after 20 years of exile, an angel of the Lord barred his entry. All night they wrestled until the angel, seeing he could not prevail, gave way. Jacob then demanded a blessing, and the angel declared that, henceforth, Jacob should be known as *Israel*: 'he who has prevailed with God'. Many years went by and, eventually, the descendents of Jacob's twelve sons (the 'children of Israel') were driven into exile. More years passed[1] until, in 1947, the modern state was founded and Israel was chosen as its name.[2]

[1] *2,514 years to be exact.* [2] *Alternative proposals that were rejected included Zion, Judea, Ivriya and the Land of Ever.*

DEAD RICH. When Einstein died, in 1955, he bequeathed his estate to Jerusalem's Hebrew University. This was a more substantial gift than it might at first seem, since, in recent years, Albert has been lending his name so diligently to everything from Disney toys to McDonald's Happy Meals, that he has become one of the world's 10 top-earning dead celebrities—and all royalties go to Jerusalem.

DEAD CELEBRITIES: TOP-EARNERS (2009)

1. Yves Saint Laurent ...... $280m[7]
2. Rodgers/Hammerstein...$260m[7]
3. Michael Jackson $95m
4. Elvis Presley $55m
5. J. R. R. Tolkien $50m
6. Charles Schulz $30m
7. John Lennon $15m
8. Dr. Seuss $15m
9. Albert Einstein $11m
10. Michael Crichton $10m

Source: Forbes Top-Earning Dead Celebrities (2009). [7] Annual earnings inflated by one-off asset sales.

THE ATTENTIVE AIRLINE. Every passenger checking in to fly on El Al, Israel's national airline, is interviewed alone by security staff and psychologically profiled. Prior to flying, all hold bags are put through a decompression chamber. Each El Al pilot is trained in unarmed combat and weapons handling. Two armed sky marshals travel on every flight. No El Al plane has been hijacked or blown up in service since 1968.

TWELVE APOSTLES—BITTER ENDS

	Apostle	Cause of Death[3]	Location
1	Peter	crucifixion[4] (upside down)	Rome
2	James	decapitation	Judea
3	John	old age (retired)	Turkey
4	Andrew	crucifixion (diagonal cross)	Greece
5	Philip	crucifixion (upside down)	Turkey
6	Bartholomew	flaying then decapitation	Caspian
7	Matthew	spearing (with halberd)	Persia
8	Thomas	spearing	India
9	James the Less	crucifixion then clubbing	Egypt
10	Thaddeus	crucifixion	Beirut
11	Simon	sawing in half(?)	Persia[5]
12 }	Judas Iscariot	suicide (hanging)[6]	Jerusalem
12 }	Matthias	stoning then decapitation	Jerusalem

[3] *Most commonly held tradition.* [4] *Crucifixion was particularly valued as a means of capital punishment in the ancient world for the deterrent given by the victim's lingering and immensely painful death. (Hence the English word 'excruciating'.)* [5] *Alternatively, he was crucified in Lincolnshire.* [6] *Alternatively, 'his bowels gushed out' after he was either hit by a chariot or fell.*

Epistles *(28)* • Job *(23)* • Acts *(22)* • Exodus *(18)* ■ **Least Discussed**: Kings II *(2.5)* • Isaiah *(2.2)* •

READY FOR THE WEEKEND (BUT WHICH ONE?)

JEWISH. The Torah's fourth *mitzvot* (commandment) mandates the *Shabbat* as a day of rest. It reflects God's repose after the six days of Creation (which started on a Sunday) and lasts from sunset on Friday until such time as 'three small stars' are visible on Saturday evening. Adding the balance of Friday makes a two-day weekend.

M	TU	W	TH	F	SA	SU

Two's company ... Adam, Eve and Lilith carved on to Notre-Dame Cathedral in Paris

CHRISTIAN/WESTERN. Setting aside a day for worship as the *Lord's Day* dates back to the 2nd century. Sunday was selected as the day on which Jesus was resurrected. In 321 CE, Emperor Constantine I independently decreed that Sunday should become the Roman day of rest; but the two aspects of Sunday's special significance have long since become fused. In 1926, Henry Ford pioneered the idea of giving workers Saturday off too, correctly reasoning that a well-motivated workforce could achieve as much in five days as six, and still have a day off in which to drive around in the cars he wanted to sell them.

M	TU	W	TH	F	SA	SU

MUSLIM. The Qu'ran requires all male Muslims to attend the *Jumuah* (Friday-noon prayers) that mark Allah's giving life to Adam on the sixth day of Creation. While there is no historic tradition of a day of rest, many Arab nations use this to fix a Friday and Saturday weekend.

M	TU	W	TH	F	SA	SU

SARACENS V. CRUSADERS—SEASON END SCORECARD

Crusade	Result	Goal of the Match	Man of the match
1	away win	Jerusalem captured (1099)	Godfrey Bouillon
2	score draw	Lisbon captured (1147)	Atabeg Zangi
3	away win	Acre recaptured (1191)	Richard Lionheart
4	diverted	Sack of Constantinople	Doge Dandalo
5	home win	crusaders captured (1221)	Sultan Al-Kamil
6	away win	Jerusalem leased (1229)	Frederick II
7	home win	Louis IX ransomed (1250)	Sultan Baibars
8	abandoned	Louis IX died (dysentery)	the local water
9	home win	Holy Land lost (1291)	Sultan Khalil

[1] *Based on relative number of Google search results returned for each book.*

ADAM'S EX. Jewish folklore tells that Eve was Adam's second wife. His first was Lilith, who, like Adam, was created by God out of dust. As Lilith considered herself Adam's equal, she refused to submit to his will and left. Only then did God fashion Eve from Adam's rib. As children of Eve, Jewish infants wore amulets well into the 19th century as a ward against Lilith's spite-filled attentions.

'If an expert says it can't be done, get another expert.'
—D. Ben-Gurion

NEW MOON. History's first recorded mooning occurred in Jerusalem in 66 CE, when a Roman soldier took it upon himself to expose his buttocks to the crowd as a signal of his disdain. Triggering a riot, the action led ultimately to the city's destruction and the razing of Jerusalem's Temple to the ground.

♣ · **GSR**: 29 · **WHS**: Acre (museum town) □ Haifa (Bahá'i monuments) □ Jerusalem (historic city) Masada (fortress ruins) □ Megiddo, Hazor, Beer Sheba (Iron Age ruins) □ Negev Incense Route (classical ruins) □ Tel Aviv (architecture—modernism)

———————— ITALY • ITALIA ————————

'It's all about good taste.'

—Giorgio Armani

SPENDING A PENNY. The 1st century Roman emperor, Vespasian, earned enduring ignominy by imposing a tax on urine. The tax was actually paid by entre-

preneurs who drew the liquid off from public latrines to use for laundering togas and tanning leather. However, some things are beyond forgiveness, and to this day Italian urinals are called *vespesiani*. By all accounts, Vespasian was in all other respects regarded rather well.

TRIVIAL PURSUIT. When, in 1088, a group of teachers banded together in Bologna, they had to coin a word to describe their new undertaking. The title they fixed on was *universitas magistorum et scholarium* ('the entirety of masters and scholars')— quickly shortened to just 'university'. It was the world's first (and still remains open for business). Setting a pattern for all Europe's medieval universities, students first had to study the *trivium* ('three ways') before moving on to tackle the four-part *quadrivium*.[1] Courses added in subsequent centuries included 'natural magic' (science).

MEDIEVAL UNIVERSITY SYLLABUS

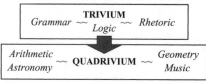

TRIVIUM
Grammar ~ Logic ~ Rhetoric

Arithmetic ~ **QUADRIVIUM** ~ Geometry
Astronomy ~ Music

[1] *The sense that the* trivium *was more elementary than the* quadrivium *gives us the words 'trivial' and 'trivia'.*

THE CHEESE THAT WALKS. Sardinian Casu Marzu cheese comes with quite a USP: it's alive with maggots. The larvae are no garnish, it's their digestive juices that transform ordinary pecorino into the desired oozing, weeping goo. Some say the cheese is dangerous, but the local view is it's fine so long as the maggots are still moving. (If dead, the cheese is too ripe.)

BAD DADS. Roman law furnished fathers with rather sweeping powers over their household. *Inter alia*, they could:

- sell children into slavery
- discard unwanted infants
- help themselves to any property owned by their adult children[2]
- force adult children to get divorced
- kill family members (though they were supposed to consult their friends first).

[2] *By the same token, a father kept responsibility for any debts his children ran up even after they had left home.*

SWAMPED. Malaria was endemic in Italy until WWII, and it was 1970 before the country was malaria free. The city of Rome, in particular, was so badly affected[3] that the medieval Church sometimes struggled to fill the papacy (many potential candidates regarded moving to the Vatican as akin to a death sentence). By the late 19th century, much of the countryside surrounding Rome had been abandoned to the disease entirely, and lay uninhabited until Mussolini drained the Pontine marshes in the 1930s.

[3] *Until the 16th century, the disease was known as 'Roman Fever'. The later 'malaria' is itself from the early Italian* mala aria *('bad air'), by association with stinky swamps.*

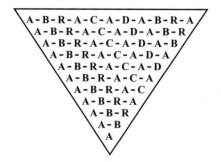

HOCUS POCUS. The first recorded use of 'abracadabra' was by the Roman Serenus Sammonicus, who gave Emperor Caracalla an amulet with the letters arranged in a triangle to protect him against malaria.

'Is it worthwhile to observe that there are no Venetian blinds in Venice?'

—W. D. Howells

> *'Without mathematics there is no art.'* —Luca Pacioli

ACCOUNTING FOR BEAUTY. Pronounced 'phi', φ is the near-mystical number that, since the Renaissance, has underpinned much of Western aesthetics—from the shape of credit cards to the self-portraits of Rembrandt. Known as the Golden Ratio, φ was discovered by the ancients, but its cultural significance exploded after the publication in 1509 of a book entitled *De Divina Proportione* ('On the Divine Proportions') by Luca Pacioli, the father of double-entry book-keeping. Pacioli had asked his friend Leonardo da Vinci to do the illustrations and the work da Vinci produced was so beautiful (and novel) that Pacioli's book was taken up by artists as well as accountants—allowing φ to make the leap from mathematics to art.

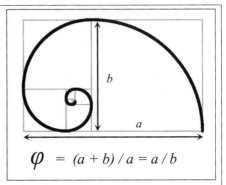

$$\varphi = (a + b) / a = a / b$$

Golden Ratio with Construction of Golden Spiral

What's so special? If you cut a square from a rectangle with sides in proportion to the Golden Ratio, you get a rectangle with sides in proportion to the Golden Rectangle, and if you cut a square from that you get yet another ... and so on to infinity. The Golden Ratio is also used to make the Golden Spiral, a type of logarithmic curve, which, it turns out, crops up all over nature—from the structure of galaxies to the shape of hurricanes to the paths flown by birds of prey as they stalk their quarry.

HANGING UP YOUR HAT. In Italy, it's considered very bad luck to leave a hat on a bed. The superstition arises because priests take off their hats and place them on the bedside while administering last rites.

BREATH-TAKING. At a Roman deathbed, it was traditional for the near-deceased's oldest male relative to lean over his stricken kin and inhale as he or she expired, in an attempt to catch their last breath. They needn't have bothered—with every breath we take, we breathe in an average of one molecule from the dying breath of each person who has ever lived[1] without trying .

[1] *To allow for atmospheric mixing, this is only strictly correct for those who died more than 10 years ago.*

HIGH-CLASS HARLOT. Platform heels go back to the prostitutes of 16th-century Venice, who wore them to signal their profession (and keep their toes clean). Known as *chopines*, the shoes grew to ludicrous heights before being banned due to the lofty death rate among those who stumbled.

UP THE BUM OF A WHALE
& OTHER ITALIAN IDIOMS

square balls............................nerves of steel
speak outside your teeth........say your mind
outside like a balcony.....out to lunch, crazy
put the horns on.......cheat on [your partner]
Up the bum of a whale![2]..........Break a leg![3]

[2] *To which the reply is, 'Hope it doesn't pooh!'* [3] *Said in the theatrical sense before a performer goes on stage.*

GETTING SCREWED. Of the 600 varieties of pasta, spaghetti was one of the last to appear. It took until the mid 19th century for spaghetti to take off because it has to be extruded and, until then, the long screws needed to do so mechanically were prohibitively expensive.

PASTA SAUCES—SOURCED			
Name	*Invented*	*Means*	*Note*
Bolognese	1500s	from Bologna	Bolognese serve their *ragù* with tagliatelle—*never* spaghetti
Carbonara	1944	charcoal grill	created for American GIs to use up their egg and bacon ration
Marinara	1550s	'sailor-style'	acidity in tomatoes preserved it well on long sea voyages
Pesto	Antiquity	pounded	evolved from *moretum*—a Roman cheese spread, with basil
Puttanesca	1960s	'whore-style'	a spicy sauce allegedly easy to knock up between clients

'"See Naples and die." Well, I don't know one would necessarily die after merely seeing it, but to try to live there might turn out a little differently.'

—Mark Twain

COSA NOSTRA[1]
ORGANOGRAM

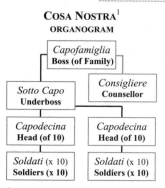

```
        ┌─────────────────────┐
        │     Capofamiglia    │
        │   Boss (of Family)  │
        └─────────────────────┘
   ┌──────────────┐  ┌──────────────┐
   │  Sotto Capo  │  │  Consigliere │
   │   Underboss  │  │   Counsellor │
   └──────────────┘  └──────────────┘
   ┌──────────────┐  ┌──────────────┐
   │  Capodecina  │  │  Capodecina  │
   │ Head (of 10) │  │ Head (of 10) │
   └──────────────┘  └──────────────┘
   ┌──────────────┐  ┌──────────────┐
   │ Soldati (x 10)│ │ Soldati (x 10)│
   │Soldiers (x 10)│ │Soldiers (x 10)│
   └──────────────┘  └──────────────┘
```

[1] *'Mafia' is used by outsiders; insiders refer to Cosa Nostra ('our thing'). Membership is estimated at 5,000.*

'He who walks with his head held high dies only once.'

—Giovanni Falcone,
Anti-Mafia Investigative Magistrate[2]

[2] *In 1992, Falcone, his wife and three bodyguards were killed outside Palermo when the motorway beneath their armoured Fiat was blown up with half a tonne of dynamite. Salvatore 'The Beast' Riina and Giovanni 'The Pig' Brusca were later convicted of the murders.*

FASCIST FALLOUT. On 10 April 1938, Mussolini secretly asked Pope Pius XI to excommunicate Hitler (who had been born and brought up a Catholic). Piling on the pressure, he added that, if the pope wouldn't act, Italy might have to declare war on Germany. Mussolini's anger had been aroused by the German annexation of Austria, and he was concerned that Hitler might move against Italy's German-speaking Alpine regions next. As it turned out, Hitler fixed his sights on Czechoslovakia's Sudetenland and, within three weeks, Hitler and Mussolini were cementing their alliance with a parade through the streets of Rome.

NICE ICE. It's not just the setting, Italian *gelato* really is tastier than ice cream in other countries—because it has half the fat and whipped-in air. Both kill flavour, but in different ways: fats clog your taste buds as you eat, so dulling your perception of flavour; while air dilutes the concentration of other ingredients and so reduces the intensity of their tastes.

BLEEDING DOCTORS. The greatest doctor of the Roman era, and physician to three emperors, Galen got much right (he was the first to take his patients' pulse), but he got it wrong when he held that illness was caused by an imbalance in four bodily fluids he called 'humours'. Going further, he taught that a patient's temperament ('humour') was the key symptom from which to make diagnoses. Galen's blunder was monumental: his dogma stymied medical progress into the 19th century. Not just useless, some of his 'cures' were dangerous. Thus, Galen instructed that, where illness arose from an excess of blood, bleeding would rebalance the body—if the patient didn't expire first. Parallel reasoning prescribed the use of enemas, emetics and expectorants. While Galen's theory has long since been swept aside, his 'humours' survive alive and well in everyday language.

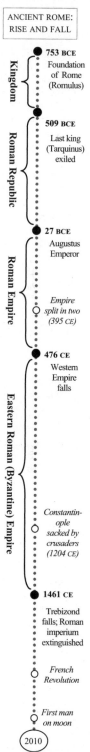

Kingdom	● **753 BCE** Foundation of Rome (Romulus)
Roman Republic	● **509 BCE** Last king (Tarquinus) exiled
Roman Empire	● **27 BCE** Augustus Emperor
	○ *Empire split in two (395 CE)*
	● **476 CE** Western Empire falls
Eastern Roman (Byzantine) Empire	○ *Constantinople sacked by crusaders (1204 CE)*
	● **1461 CE** Trebizond falls; Roman imperium extinguished
	○ *French Revolution*
	○ *First man on moon*
	(2010)

FUNNY FACES—A 'HUMOUROUS' GUIDE TO DIAGNOSIS

SANGUINE	CHOLERIC	MELANCHOLIC	PHLEGMATIC
Excess blood	Excess yellow bile	Excess black bile	Excess phlegm
Reckless, dissolute	*Explosive, irascible*	*Doleful, anxious*	*Quiescent, ponderous*

TWO LATIN LOVERS

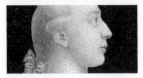

GIACOMO CASANOVA. History's most important source on the early use of condoms,[1] Casanova records that one of his most effective seduction techniques was to whip an 'English Overcoat'[2] from his pocket and then blow into it until it was fully inflated—much to a lady's entertainment. (More pragmatically, the Venetian clergyman also took the opportunity to discreetly check for holes.)

[1] *An article entitled 'The Medical Interests of Casanova's Memoirs' appears in* The British Medical Journal. [2] *Casanova's device was a reusable sheep gut tied by a ribbon.*

RUDOLPH VALENTINO. The Italian silent-movie heart-throb may have had America's women swooning in the aisles, but its men were less impressed. After a piece headed 'Pink Powder Puff' appeared in the *Chicago Tribune*, Valentino challenged its writer to a boxing match. The journalist never responded and Valentino died abruptly a few weeks later from an ulcer. But the jibe must have really hurt. On his deathbed, Valentino still summoned the energy to demand: 'Am I a pink powder puff now?'

'I have offended God and mankind as my work did not reach the quality it should.'

—Leonardo da Vinci (last words)

A NEW SLANT. Venetian printer, Aldus Manutius, invented *italics*[3] in 1501. Emphasis had nothing to do with it. His big idea was to print books that would fit inside a gentleman's pocket—a radical departure from the monster tomes that were then the norm. This proved impossible with the gothic typeface of the time (which became an illegible tangle when miniaturized). So Aldus copied the elegant and compact handwriting of a secretary called Poggio Bracciolini—who has thus achieved immortality in the italic lettering of today.

[3] *From* italicus—*Latin for 'Italian'.*

OPERA-TIVE TONGUE
OPERAS BY LANGUAGE[4]

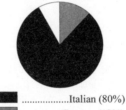

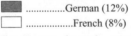

................Italian (80%)
..............German (12%)
.................French (8%)

[4] *The 25 most frequently staged operas (1981–2001); original libretto.*

6-6-6

NAME AND NUMBER. The 'number of the beast' in the Bible's Book of Revelation is thought to be code for the arch-persecutor of Christians Emperor Nero, whose name and title sum to 666[5] in Hebrew numerology.

[5] *A hexakosioihexekontahexaphobe is someone who fears or avoids the number 666. Examples include Nancy and Ronald Reagan, who, in 1989, had their house address changed from number '666' to '668'.*

HANDBALL. In 2008, Italy's Supreme Court struck down the ancient right of Italian men to grab their crotches (generally exercised when discussing ill health or death, or to ward off bad luck as a hearse passes by). It was, they deemed, an affront to decorum and public decency. With this ruling, it seems the law may have moved full circle, since a long-standing tradition has it that Roman courts once required witnesses to clasp their right hands to their vitals while giving sworn testimony—which is why testicles are so named.[6]

[6] *A differing derivation suggests that testicles 'testify' to a man's virility.*

CAFFÈ CULTURE—THE ITALIAN WAY WITH COFFEE

- ■ *Americano*....'**American**': a WWII creation of GIs, who added water to *espressos* for coffee more like home.
- ■ *Cappuccino*....'**Capuchin**': named for the shade and hood of the monkish robes. (Foam helps keep drink hot.)
- ■ *Espresso*....'**Pushed out**': so called because the coffee is extracted under pressure—invented in Milan in 1901.
- ■ *Latte*....'**Caffelatte**' is the more accurate term—ask for a *latte* in Italy and you'll get a glass of milk.
- ■ *Macchiato*....'**Marked**': *espressos* with a drop of milk got 'marked' with foam so waiters could tell them apart.

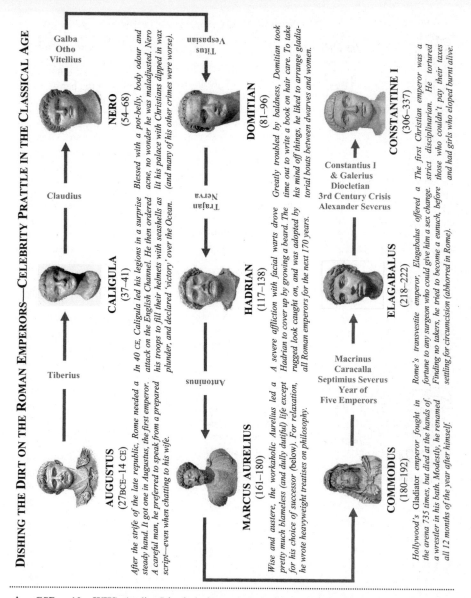

DISHING THE DIRT ON THE ROMAN EMPERORS—CELEBRITY PRATTLE IN THE CLASSICAL AGE

AUGUSTUS (27BCE–14 CE)
After the strife of the late republic, Rome needed a steady hand. It got one in Augustus, the first emperor. A careful man, he preferred to speak from a prepared script—even when chatting to his wife.

Tiberius

CALIGULA (37–41)
In 40 CE, Caligula led his legions in a surprise attack on the English Channel. He then ordered his troops to fill their helmets with seashells as plunder, and declared 'victory' over the Ocean.

Claudius

NERO (54–68)
Blessed with a pot-belly, body odour and acne, no wonder he was maladjusted. Nero lit his palace with Christians dipped in wax (and many of his other crimes were worse).

Galba Otho Vitellius

Titus Vespasian

DOMITIAN (81–96)
Greatly troubled by baldness, Domitian took time out to write a book on hair care. To take his mind off things, he liked to arrange gladiatorial bouts between dwarves and women.

Nerva Trajan

HADRIAN (117–138)
A severe affliction with facial warts drove Hadrian to cover up by growing a beard. The rugged look caught on, and was adopted by all Roman emperors for the next 170 years.

Antoninus

MARCUS AURELIUS (161–180)
Wise and austere, the workaholic Aurelius led a pretty much blameless (and dully dutiful) life except for his choice of successor (below). For relaxation, he wrote heavyweight treatises on philosophy.

COMMODUS (180–192)
Hollywood's Gladiator emperor fought in the arena 735 times, but died at the hands of a wrestler in his bath. Modestly, he renamed all 12 months of the year after himself.

Macrinus
Caracalla
Septimius Severus
Year of Five Emperors

ELAGABALUS (218–222)
Rome's transvestite emperor, Elagabalus offered a fortune to any surgeon who could give him a sex change. Finding no takers, he tried to become a eunuch, before settling for circumcision (abhorred in Rome).

Constantius I & Galerius
Diocletian
3rd Century Crisis
Alexander Severus

CONSTANTINE I (306–337)
The first Christian emperor was a strict disciplinarian. He tortured those who couldn't pay their taxes and had girls who eloped burnt alive.

♠ · **GSR**: · 10 · **WHS**: Aeolian Islands (volcanoes) □ Agrigento (Greek ruined city) □ Alberobello (dry-stone houses) □ Amalfi (coast) □ Aquileia (basilica) □ Assisi (basilica) □ Barumini (Bronze Age ruins) □ Casale (mosaics) □ Caserta (palace) □ Castel del Monte (castle) □ Cerveteri & Tarquinia (Etruscan cemeteries) □ Cinque Terre (museum towns) □ Crespi d'Adda (company town) □ Dolomites (mountains) □ Florence (cityscape) □ Ferrara (townscape) □ Genoa (townscape) □ Longobards (Lombard buildings) □ Mantua (townscape) □ Matera (rock churches) □ Milan—Santa Maria delle Grazie (mural) □ Modena (cathedral) □ Mt. San Giorgio (fossils) □ Naples (cityscape) □ Padua (botanical garden) □ Paestum (Greek ruined city) □ Pienza (townscape) □ Pile Dwellings □ Pisa (monuments) □ Pompeii (ruined Roman city) □ Ravenna (Greco-Roman monuments) □ Rhaetian Railway □ Rome (classical & baroque monuments) □ Sacri Monti (chapels) □ San Gimignano (museum town) □ Siena (museum town) □ Syracuse (townscape) □ Tivoli (x2) (Roman ruins/gardens) □ Turin (Savoyard palaces) □ Urbino (museum town) □ Val di Noto (townscapes) □ Val d'Orcia (landscape) Valcamonica (rock art) □ Venice (museum city) □ Verona (cityscape) □ Vicenza (cityscape) · **ICH**: Canto a Tenore (Sardinian folk singing) □ Mediterranean Diet □ Opera dei Pupi (Sicilian puppetry)

JAMAICA

'Hog say, "De first dutty water mi ketch, mi wash."'

—Jamaican proverb (another way to say *'Carpe diem'*)

Pirate not prostitute, Anne Bonny was sentenced to death in Port Royal in 1720. Pleading 'the belly' (an unborn child), she got execution deferred and then slipped silently from history.

THE WAGES OF SIN. Its people had more coin in their pockets than Londoners, there was one rum shop for every 10 inhabitants and every second man was a pirate (while most of its women were whores). In the 17th century, Jamaica's Port Royal was the biggest English port outside England until, in 1692, the town was struck by an immense earthquake that turned the ground to quicksand and—much to the satisfaction of Spanish admirals and English moralists—sucked the entire settlement into the sea.

NUTCRACKER. The wood of Jamaica's national plant, the lignum vitae, is so heavy it sinks in water and so tough it was chosen for use in the bearings of the first nuclear submarine. But its most outstanding attribute is its extraordinary hardness—a property that did not go unnoticed when it was selected as the wood from which to make the traditional British policeman's truncheon.

'They shall not make baldness upon their head, neither shall they ... make any cuttings in their flesh'

—Leviticus 21:5

JAH RULES. The dreadlocks of an observant Rasta are worn in obedience to 2,500-year-old rules for ancient Israelite priests contained in the Old Testament. The further prohibition on cutting the flesh was the reason Bob Marley refused amputation when diagnosed with skin cancer on his toe—so allowing the cancer to spread, and three years later kill him.

GRITTY GRANNY. Wearing bracelets strung with white men's teeth and catching British bullets with her hands,[2] Jamaica's female national hero, Queen Nanny, kept the British at bay for 20 years, until 1739, at the head of a community of escaped slaves known as the Maroons.[3]

LANGUAGE OF RASTAFARI—AN IYARIC GLOSSARY

Babylon .... *Western society—by extension its agents, police*
Baldhead .... *Non-Rastafari, since their hair is cut*
Gideon .... *the troubled state of the world in recent times*
I and I .... *since God is in everyone, we are one, hence 'we'*
Jah[1] .... *God, shortened form of Jehovah (YHWH)*
Zion .... *redeemed Africa (esp. Ethiopia), also state of mind*

[1] *Jah is also used by the Jehovah's Witnesses movement. More generally, the word survives in Hallelujah!, which literally means 'Praise Yahweh', and is normally Anglicized as 'Praise the Lord'.*

---

[2] *So say the more colourful stories.*
[3] *Hence 'to be marooned' (because of the remoteness of the Maroon settlements, which were sited to escape detection by the British).*

BOLTS AND BOBS. The world's fastest man, Usain Bolt of Jamaica, reaches a top speed of 27.3 mph when in a flat-out sprint. Though not as fast as a Jamaican bobsled, that is how he covers 100m of track in the time it has taken you to read this paragraph.[1]

[1] *Based on average adult reading speed (300 words per minute).*

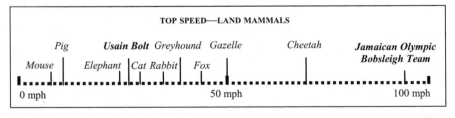

TOP SPEED—LAND MAMMALS

Pig · *Usain Bolt* Greyhound Gazelle · Cheetah · *Jamaican Olympic Bobsleigh Team*

Mouse · Elephant · Cat Rabbit · Fox

0 mph · 50 mph · 100 mph

♦ · **GSR:** 96 · **WHS:** none · **ICH:** Moore Town (Maroon heritage)

—————————— JAPAN ● 日本 ——————————

'If you understand, things are just as they are;
if you do not understand, things are just as they are.'

—Zen saying

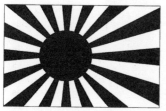

SUN-DAY LUNCH. The solar disc has been the symbol of Japan since at least 607 CE, when the country's ruler styled himself 'the Emperor of the Rising Sun' in a letter to his Chinese counterpart. Although most modern forms show a simple orb, the Japanese Navy still retains the 16 rays of the Imperial War Flag. Usage of both remains controversial due to the intense nationalism fomented during WWII. In occupied countries, schoolchildren were made to sing the Japanese national anthem in a daily flag-raising ceremony; while at home eating 'flag meals' (of boiled rice with a ball of pickled plums in the centre) became a near-universal display of patriotic support for the soldiers fighting abroad.

行春や鳥啼魚の目は泪

—Matsuo Bashō, in *Oku no Hosomichi* (*Narrow Road to the Interior*, 1694). 'Spring departing: the birds cry out and the eyes of the fish are full of tears.' Traditionally written in a single vertical column, *haiku* are the best-known Japanese poetic form in the West. Each has a length of precisely 17 sounds (*onji*) and holds an abrupt change of sense and (sometimes oblique) seasonal reference.

WAGE SLAVE. For Japan's millions of salarymen, *karoshi*—meaning 'death by overwork', is a very real risk, claiming the life of one overburdened executive every second day on average.

SOUND PURCHASE. When buying traditional wooden shoes, Japanese women listen as well as look—wearing a pair with a discordant click-clack is considered the epitome of bad taste.

SHORT, SHARP, SHOCK. Executions are kept secret from the condemned until an hour (or less) beforehand; their families only find out when called and given 24 hours to collect the corpse.

INADEQUATE. At 0.7 babies per 100 persons per year, Japan has the world's lowest birth rate. Notably, Japanese also report the world's worst sex lives, with just 15% claiming to be 'satisfied'.

SERIOUSLY SEAFOOD—JAPANESE COOKING STYLES

Name	Means	On the plate
Sashimi	pierced flesh[1]	thinly sliced fresh raw fish
Sushi	it is sour	vinegared rice with topping[2]
Tempura	fast time (Latin)[3]	deep-fried battered morsels[4]

[1] *The term may come from the* ike jime *technique in which the fish is killed by spiking through the brain immediately on landing, in order to maximize freshness and minimize bleeding.* [2] *Typically fish or other seafood.* [3] *Ad tempora quadragesimae.* [4] *Deep-frying in batter was introduced by Portuguese missionaries in the 16th century as their preferred way of preparing fish (and vegetables) on Catholic fast days, when meat was forbidden.*

PARTY GOBLETS. The earliest form of *sake*, known as *kuchikami no sake*, was created around 300 BCE, when villagers took to chewing mouthfuls of rice and spitting them into a communal tub, following which one enterprising individual discovered that the sour-tasting slush became mildly alcoholic if left to stand for a few days. (It's now known that the enzymes in saliva break rice starch down into sugars, which then ferment to alcohol.)

BODY OF EVIDENCE. When Midori Naka died on 24 August 1945, 18 days after her home was reduced to rubble by the Hiroshima atom bomb, her death certificate was the first in history to give radiation poisoning as the cause of death. Shortly after, her remains were confiscated by the US Army and sent to America, for intensive study where, together with statistical evidence gathered on atom-bomb survivors, they were eventually used to set the maximum radiation exposure limits, still relied on today, for everything from dental x-rays to permissible flying hours for pregnant aircrew.

SOUL SHINES NAKED

~~~

THREE JAPANESE PURSUITS

According to its Cultural Affairs Agency, *karaoke*[1] is Japan's most popular 'cultural' activity. However, more traditional recreations also persist ...

YUKIGUSSEN. Literally, 'snow battle', organized snowball fighting involves two teams, snow walls for shelter and flags to be captured.

HANAMI. 'Flower viewing' is synonymous with the spring cherry-blossom season, when the whole country heads outside to picnic under cherry trees.

KINGYO-SUKUI. A sport that's harder than it sounds, goldfish-scooping requires great delicacy as scoops are made of paper and a player is eliminated once their scoop breaks.

[1] *Meaning 'empty orchestra'. Sociologists suggest its popularity is down to the lack of any human interaction while singing, answering Japanese reticence perfectly.*

'It is a matter of regret to let the moment one should die pass by.'
—Shiba Yoshimasa (1383)

HACKED OFF. The end of the *samurai* dominance of Japan can perhaps be traced to 1877, when they lost the right to cut down any commoner who, they felt, had shown them insufficient respect. Prior to this, Japan's elite warrior caste lived for centuries by the *bushido*, a code of conduct that placed absolute emphasis on loyalty to one's lord at whatever cost. The value placed on honour and disdain of death within the code was extreme: on one occasion, the powerful 16th-century warlord Takeda Shingen executed two of his followers for brawling—not for the brawl itself, but because they had failed to fight to the death. Despite this, from an early stage *samurai* valued the pen as highly as the sword, striving to outdo each other in poetry and Zen commentary—which proved handy when the end of their era finally came, as many went off and got jobs as Japan's first reporters.

HARD TO STOMACH. A *samurai*'s suicide was considered a final opportunity to retrieve his family's honour following defeat or other shame. Known as *seppuku* ('stomach-cutting') or, more colloquially, *harakiri*, it was performed before an audience by a sideways disembowelling cut to the abdomen. Generally, a chosen second would then step up and perform a decapitation. *Samurai* women had their own suicide ritual, *jigai*, in which they cut their jugular vein after tying their knees together to preserve modesty as a corpse. Though rare, *seppuku* has been performed into the 21st century.

万歳!!!!! Supposedly the WWII battle cry of Japanese *kamikaze* pilots, '*Banzai*' translates as '10,000 years' and was understood to mean 'May the Emperor live for ten thousand years'. More recently, the phrase has reappeared in 'Banzai skydiving'—the modern 'sport' of jumping from a plane without a parachute. While extreme, it is survivable—so long as you manage to find someone with a parachute on the way down. The current Guinness World Record holder is Japan's Yasuhiro Kubo, who waited 50 seconds before following his partner (and the necessary parachute) out of the hatch.

LAST RESORT. Almost 100 Japanese kill themselves every day, and scenic Aokigahara Forest, at the foot of Mt. Fuji, is the world's number-two suicide spot.[2] In Tokyo, jumping in front of trains has grown so common, rail companies now bill relatives for the disruption costs.

[2] *The Golden Gate Bridge is first, Beachy Head third.*

HOW'S IT HANGING IN HARAJUKU?[1]
A FIELD GUIDE TO JAPANESE YOUTH FASHION

Style: *aristocrat*

Look: androgynous Victorian dandy—black frock coat, black maxi skirt, black gloves, black top hat, corset (optionally black).

Accessory: black PVC teddy bear.

Style: *Lolita (classic or sweet)*

Look: pink or peach make-up, girly Victorian clothing, pastel shades, skirt, knee socks—emphasis is cute (not erotic).

Accessory: toy stuffed animal.

Style: *cosplay* ('costume play')

Look: fancy dress—*anime* and *manga* (Japanese animation and comics) characters especially, but also Western sci-fi and fantasy.

Accessory: photographer in tow.

Style: *yamanba* ('mountain hag')

Look: dyed pink-orange-white hair, ultra-heavy fake tan, white lipstick and eye shadow, garish plastic clothing, platform shoes.

Accessory: huge junk-jewellery.

[1] *The Tokyo district nationally renowned for its trend-setting street scene (especially visible on Sundays).*

WATER MUSIC. In the beginning, the Japanese made do with an open drain and a stash of fresh seaweed. Later, a simple long drop sufficed. But after WWII, modesty set in, and women took to repeated flushing while in the toilet in order to mask more natural sounds. To address the waste this caused, public toilets have, since the 1980s, been fitted with electronic 'Sound Princess' devices that broadcast the sound of flushing without the flush. Going even more hi-tech, manufacturers are now promoting smart toilets that carry out a urine analysis after each use and automatically alert a doctor if any abnormality is found—a major boon in Japan, since the Japanese are also the world's biggest hypochondriacs.[2]

[2] *By number of visits to a doctor per person per year.*

NOODLE POTTY. In a survey in 2000, instant noodles were voted the best Japanese invention of the 20th century. According to the World Instant Noodles Association, 90bn packets are eaten each year (including in North Korea, where they're a prime perk of the party elite); there's even a zero-gravity formulation for use in space.

REALITY NASTY. *Susunu! Denpa Shōnen* was one of Japan's most popular reality TV shows until it was taken off the air in 2002 in a government crackdown on torture. In its most famous stunt, a contestant was stripped naked and locked in an empty flat with a supply of magazines, but no food. He was then told he could only eat what he won in magazine competitions and would only be released after he had clocked up $8,000 in prizes. It took him over a year, after which he was taken to Korea for a 'holiday'—and locked into an identical flat until he had won enough to fly home.

NOBODY NOSE. Until they were returned to Korea in 1992, the Okayama Nose Tomb used to house 20,000 anonymous Korean noses removed by *samurai* as war trophies in 1597. While understandably a cause of resentment in Korea, Okayama has a vanishingly low profile in Japan, with most Japanese unaware of its existence. Despite this, Japan still seems determined to keep the Mimizuki Ear Mound's 75,000 pickled ears, stored in Kyoto for 400 years after arriving from Korea in barrels of brine.

♣ · **GSR**: 4 · **WHS**: Gusuku (Ryukyuan ruins) ☐ Himeji-jo (castle) ☐ Hiraizumi (Buddhist landscape) Hiroshima (peace memorial) ☐ Horyu-ji (Buddhist monuments) ☐ Itsukushima (Shinto shrine) ☐ Iwami Ginzan (silver mines) ☐ Kii (sacred landscape) ☐ Kyoto (historic city) ☐ Nara (historic city) ☐ Nikko (temples) ☐ Ogasawara (islands) ☐ Shirakami-sanchi (forest) ☐ Shirakawa-go and Gokayama (villages) Shiretoko (land and marine preserves) ☐ Yakushima (forest) · **ICH**: Ainu Dance ☐ Akiu no Taue Odori (dance festival) ☐ Chakkirako (dance festival) ☐ Daimokutate (ceremony) ☐ Dainichido Bugaku (dance) ☐ Gagaku (music) ☐ Hayachine Kagura (ritual dances) ☐ Hitachi Furyumono (cherry blossom parade) ☐ Kabuki (theatre) ☐ Koshikijima no Toshidon (folk ritual) ☐ Kumiodori (musical theatre) Ningyo Johruri Bunraku (puppetry) ☐ Nogaku (theatre) ☐ Ojiya-chijimi, Echigo-jofu (cloth-making) Oku-noto no Aenokoto (harvest ritual) ☐ Sekishu-banshi (paper-making) ☐ Yamahoko (parade floats) Yuki-tsumugi (silk production)

JORDAN • الأردنّ

'Dotted with the ruins of empires once great,
Jordan is the last resort of yesterday in the world of tomorrow.'
—King Hussein I

COVER UP. Worn alike by the stone-throwing teenagers of the *intifada* and British soldiers in the Gulf War, but most traditionally associated with Arab merchants and elders, the cotton *keffiyah* is the emblematic headgear of the Middle East. Ubiquity comes from its usefulness—the white cloth reflects the desert sun and, at need, masks the face from dust and sand. Its distinctive chequering goes back to ancient Mesopotamia and symbolizes ears of corn.

READING THE *KEFFIYAH*	
Colour	*Affiliation*
Red/white	Jordanian (or Hamas)
Black/white	Palestinian (esp. Fatah)
Blue/white	Israeli
Plain white	Saudi Arabia, Gulf States

ARABIAN KNIGHT. The epic desert valley of Wadi Rum, Jordan, served as the wartime lair of T. E. Lawrence, better known as Lawrence of Arabia. From here, he organized the WWI revolt against Ottoman Turkey that eventually secured Arabia's independence and negated Turkey's threat to the Suez Canal. Just weeks after leaving military service, Lawrence was thrown over the handlebars of his motorbike and fatally injured. His death so affected the surgeon who treated him that the doctor began a search for better protection for motorcyclists—leading, thirty years later, to crash helmets being made compulsory in Britain.

'Nine-tenths of tactics are certain, and taught in books: but the irrational tenth is like the kingfisher flashing across the pool, and that is the test of generals.'
—T. E. Lawrence

Kufic (9th C)   Naskh (hand)   Kufic (11th C)   Naskh (print)

بسم الله الرحمن الرحيم

SCRIPT CHANGE. Arabic script has its roots in the Nabatean alphabet of ancient Petra, now in Jordan. From 4th-century origins, the script has evolved through a number of styles, and can today be written in several distinct ways: all the above are the same phrase—the Bismillah (the invocation of Allah at the start of all but one Qur'anic chapters).

PLUMBING THE DEPTHS

At -422 m below sea level, the shore of the Dead Sea is the lowest dry land on earth.

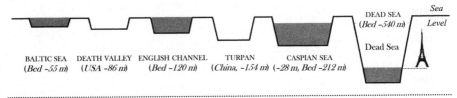

BALTIC SEA (Bed –55 m)   DEATH VALLEY (USA –86 m)   ENGLISH CHANNEL (Bed –120 m)   TURPAN (China, –154 m)   CASPIAN SEA (–28 m, Bed –212 m)   DEAD SEA (Bed –540 m)   Sea Level   Dead Sea

♣ · **GSR:** 48 · **WHS:** Petra (ruined city) □ Quseir Amra (castle) □ Um er-Rasas (ruined city) · **ICH:** Bedu (nomad culture) □ Wadi Rum (historic desert valley)

——— Kazakhstan • Қазақстан ———

'I am God sent.'

—The traditional words used to announce one's arrival at a Kazakh home. (To which the host should respond by asking about the health of one's livestock, followed, if all is satisfactory, by an enquiry about one's family and a glass of *kumys*—fermented mare's milk.)

Calais

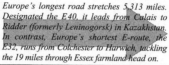

E40 (setting out): Calais docks

Europe's longest road stretches 5,313 miles. Designated the E40, it leads from Calais to Ridder (formerly Leninogorsk) in Kazakhstan. In contrast, Europe's shortest E-route, the E32, runs from Colchester to Harwich, tackling the 19 miles through Essex farmland head on.

E40 (last lap): Kazakh steppe

Риддер

WAS GOD A KAZAKH? The consensus view is that God was born 7,000 years ago to the north of the Caspian Sea, somewhere on the formless steppes that spread from the west of Kazakhstan into eastern Ukraine. This is the best guess for the original homeland of the earliest Proto-Indo-Europeans, who chose the name 'Dyeus' for their supreme deity—the god of the daytime sky. By the dawn of written history, their later migrations had already spread linguistic echoes of Dyeus' memory eastwards to India, and as far west as Ireland (*dia* means 'god' in Irish). Both the Greek Zeus and Roman Jupiter (*Ious pater*) also come from Dyeus—as does the French *dieu* (and hence the English 'deity' and 'divine'). Although the word 'God' derives from *guđan*—the term chosen by Ulfilas the Goth when he translated the Gospels into German, it can also be traced to the same primal Kazakh campfire, since it descends from the Proto-Indo-European *gutom*, meaning 'he who has been invoked'—presumably yet another reference to Dyeus.

STRAIGHT FROM THE HORSE'S MOUTH. The Bitoi of northern Kazakhstan have recently been pinpointed as the people who probably first domesticated the horse—some time around 5,500 years ago. Evidence includes ancient stable dung and potsherds holding traces of mare's milk fats, but the clincher comes from bit marks worn into preserved teeth, which could only have come from harnessing. Archaeologists think the first use the Bitoi made of domesticated horses was to help hunt herds of their wild kin, since up to 99% of the meat eaten by the Bitoi was horseflesh.

On 15 November 1988, the other Space Shuttle, Buran, made a flawless maiden flight into orbit and back again from the Baikonur spaceport in Kazakhstan. It was to be a one-off, as the craft was mothballed by Gorbachev and, in a classic instance of post-Soviet decline, destroyed in 2002, when its hanger collapsed through lack of maintenance.

BUT WHAT ABOUT *BORAT*? For the urban sophisticates of Almaty, *Borat* was about as funny as *Monty Python* and *Austin Powers* combined (it was Amazon's top-selling export to Kazakhstan that year); while over in the capital, Astana, they were too busy banking petrodollars and building skyscrapers to notice much, beyond commenting that surely there was a typo, and the film meant Tajikistan (*see Tajikistan*). As far as these audiences were concerned, the film was pure and unadulterated fantasy—except, of course, for the hair, the prostitution and the Uzbek grudge match—oh, and the abduction of brides using a marriage sack.[1]

[1] *In the interest of balance, mention should perhaps also be made here of the popular Kazakh horseback sport of Kyz Kuu, ('girl-chasing')—for more on which, see Kyrgyzstan (whose people share the pastime).*

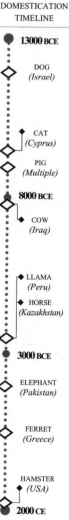

FOUR-LEGGED FRIENDS

DOMESTICATION TIMELINE

13000 BCE

DOG
(Israel)

CAT
(Cyprus)

PIG
(Multiple)

8000 BCE

COW
(Iraq)

LLAMA
(Peru)

HORSE
(Kazakhstan)

3000 BCE

ELEPHANT
(Pakistan)

FERRET
(Greece)

HAMSTER
(USA)

2000 CE

♣♠ · **GSR**: 43 · **WHS**: Saryarka (steppe) □ Tamgaly (rock art) □ Yasi (mausoleum)

KENYA

'God's Resting Place.'

—Original literal meaning of Mt. Kenya in local languages; the
mountain, in turn, gave its name to the country

ROGUE ELEPHANT. If you're charged by an elephant, experts advise standing your ground and shouting. If the elephant's ears stay flattened, its attack is probably a sham. But if its ears flare, it's in earnest and your chances may be slim. Running isn't much of an option, as elephants hit 25 mph once into their stride—although a tip from one flint-hearted tracker may help you to survive: never venture into elephant country on foot unless you are absolutely certain you can outrun at least one member of your group.

LONG IN THE TOOTH. Kenya is the leading African opponent of the worldwide trade in elephant ivory. Biologically, ivory is precisely the same as dentin, the substance out of which our own teeth are made (dentin may completely correctly be referred to as 'human ivory').[1] Ivory or dentin, tusk or tooth, all ultimately derive from the body armour of ancient fish, which, hundreds of millions of years ago in the Devonian period, migrated into their mouths—giving rise, no doubt, to the primordial toothache.

[1] *In the classic 'hot pin' test, used to distinguish genuine elephant ivory from fake, pressing with a heated pin is said to cause ivory—unlike plastic or bone—to give off the unmistakable whiff of the dentist's drill.*

KENYA WILDLIFE SERVICE SEIZURES & CONFISCATIONS (2008)	
Ivory	857 kg
Bush meat	7445 kg
Animal skins	240
Firearms	30
Snares & traps	3708

ILLICIT IVORY TRADE (2008)	
Tusk (Nairobi)	$2,500[2]
Tusk (Shanghai)	$180,000
Kenyan elephants poached	98

[2] *In comparison, Kenyans have an average annual income of $800 per person.*

DESERT SWARM. The largest insect swarm ever recorded was one of desert locusts that invaded Kenya in 1954. As surveyed by plane, it covered 80 square miles, numbered 10 billion insects and weighed 20,000 tons.

HOME STRETCH. Making up just 0.05% of global population, the Kalenjin people of Kenya's Central Highlands take home around 40% of the world's distance running honours. Altitude helps, but the Kalenjin also possess a physiological adaptation that lets them resist fatigue and use oxygen more efficiently—squeezing 10% extra distance out of every lungful.

**BEIJING 2008 OLYMPICS
DISTANCE RUNNING MEDALS**

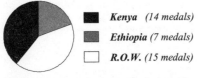

Kenya (14 medals)

Ethiopia (7 medals)

R.O.W. (15 medals)

Total: 36 medals (includes all non-sprints)

OUR TURN TO EAT. The typical urban Kenyan pays 16 bribes a month, while nearly 50% of people live on less than 75 cents a day. Politics makes a good alternative: Kenya's 40 cabinet ministers each earn $215,000 p.a. (plus $30,000 in allowances), while the government spends $3m a year importing luxury cars—S-Class Mercedes-Benz are preferred. No coincidence, then, that ordinary Kenyans mock their political masters as the *Wa-Benzi* ('Benz tribe').

MAN BITES SNAKE. When Ben Nyaumbe was grabbed by a 13-foot python in 2009, he had the presence of mind to use his mobile phone to summon help. He next bit on to the snake's tail to stop it eating him and waited. After Nyaumbe's rescue, the python fled, and the police issued an arrest warrant.

♥ · **GSR**: · 89 · **WHS**: Lake Turkana (wildlife and fossils) □ Lamu (museum town) □ Mijikenda Kayas (sacred forests) □ Mombasa (fortress) □ Mount Kenya (landscape) □ Rift Valley Lakes · **ICH**: Mijikenda Kaya Practices (rituals and legends)

—— KOREA (NORTH) •조선 ————

'In essence, North Korea has become the Sopranos state—a government whose actions resemble those of an organized crime family more than a normal nation.'

—David Asher, Head of US North Korea Working Group (2005)

FLOWER POWER. North Korea's late president, Kim Jong Il, was apparently something of a begonia fancier—or at least he had a big red one, the Kimjongilia, named after him. Each year, thousands of the plants[1] starred at the Annual Pyongyang Kimjongilia Flower Show, held on his 16 February birthday,[2] and, before his death, foreign embassies wishing to curry favour competed to donate the finest flower.

[1] The North Korean Army runs its own dedicated Kimjongilia Cultivation and Research Centre (and has published a 100-page book devoted to the flower). [2] The date on which the begonia has been bred to bloom.

Satellite photograph of the Korean peninsula at night. (Coastlines and Chinese border added for clarity.)

MARGERY DAW. North Koreans stand rather than sit while riding on a seesaw. See-saw jumping (acrobatic leaps launched from repeated upstrokes of a springy see-saw) and competitive swinging are both major adult sports.

Participants at North Korea's annual Arirang Festival: tens of thousands of performers create intricately and (mostly) exquisitely choreographed effects full of cryptic propaganda in the world's biggest mass games.

M*A*S*H. The first US Mobile Army Surgical Hospital was deployed in 1950, at the outbreak of the Korean War. Required to be operational within four hours of arrival, and ready to move again on six hours notice, it brought professional medical treatment to the front line for the first time and, combined with the first use of helicopters for Medevac, reduced the fatality rate for wounded soldiers by 55% compared to WWII. The final MASH unit left Korea in 1997, and the last MASH anywhere disbanded in 2006 after treating victims of Pakistan's 2005 earthquake.

PLUS ÇA CHANGE ... For 1,000 years until the 1850s, up to half of Koreans were slaves in their own country.

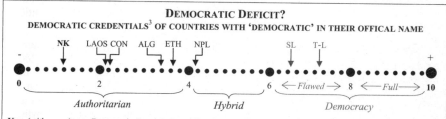

DEMOCRATIC DEFICIT?
DEMOCRATIC CREDENTIALS[3] OF COUNTRIES WITH 'DEMOCRATIC' IN THEIR OFFICAL NAME

NK LAOS CON ALG ETH NPL   SL   T-L

-                    +

0   **2**   **4**   **6** ←*Flawed*→ **8** ←*Full*→ **10**

Authoritarian   *Hybrid*   *Democracy*

Key (with score): NK Democratic People's Republic of Korea (North Korea) (1.1), LAOS Lao People's Democratic Republic (2.1), CON Democratic Republic of Congo (2.2), ALG People's Democratic Republic of Algeria (3.4), ETH Federal Democratic Republic of Ethiopia (3.7), NPL Federal Democratic Republic of Nepal (4.2), SL Democratic Social-ist Republic of Sri Lanka (6.6), T-L Democratic Republic of Timor-Leste (7.2). (Democratic Republic of São Tomé and Principe—no data.) ❖ *[3] Democracy Index Score (2010).* **Source**: *Economist Intelligence Unit. Most democratic coun-try: Kingdom of Norway (9.8); least democratic country: Democratic People's Republic of Korea (North Korea) (1.1).*

NEXT OF KIM

MEET THE FAMILY: NORTH KOREA'S LEADERS—PAST AND PRESENT.

'Eternal President'
Kim Il Sung (1–83[1])
Leader (36–83)

Despite his death over 18 years ago, Kim Jong Il's father remains North Korea's president, with the Presidential Palace in the centre of Pyongyang now a giant mausoleum. The great man's birth was heralded by a double rainbow and the birth of a bright star (according to officials).

'Great Successor'
Kim Jong Un (b. 72)
Leader (100—?)

Hailed by official sources as 'a lighthouse of hope' and 'born of heaven', Kim Jong Il's youngest son and chosen heir is a man so enigmatic his existence wasn't confirmed in the West until he was 20 years old. Following a radical change in appearance, he is widely thought to have had plastic surgery to make him look more like Grandpa.

'Dear Leader'
Kim Jong Il (30—100)
General Secretary of Worker's Party of Korea and de facto ruler (83—100)

PARTY ANIMAL. With his 5'2" stature in mind, analysts put Kim Jong Il's remarkable bouffant hairstyle (and the 4-inch platform shoes he wears) down to vanity and a desire to stretch his arguably modest natural assets as far as vaguely plausible.[2] Certainly, Kim apparently achieved an indefinable magnetism for the opposite sex:[3] his marital status was a state secret, but it's reckoned he had one official wife and three live-in mistresses—a film star, a dancer and his secretary. However, Kim didn't just look after himself. He showed a touching sensitivity towards North Korea's other paunchy middle-aged men by relaxing the national short-hair rule to allow an extra ¾ inch for comb-overs (only if aged above 50). Naturally, Kim wasn't all work. In his spare time, he liked to kick back and watch one of his 20,000 DVDs—Bond movies and Daffy Duck were favourites. And as an enthusiastic patron of the screen arts, he had leading South Korean film director Shin Sang Ok and his actress wife kidnapped and held prisoner for eight years while Shin was forced to make *Pulgasari*—a North Korean version of *Godzilla* based on a screenplay dreamt up by Kim himself.

[1] *All dates are according to North Korea's official Juche calendar, which takes the year of Kim Il Sung's birth as 'year 1'. To convert to the Gregorian calendar, add 1911.* [2] *Kim was acutely aware of his lack of height. Greeting a foreign VIP, he once commented that he was 'as small as a midget's turd'.* [3] *Absolute life and death power might perhaps have helped here too.*

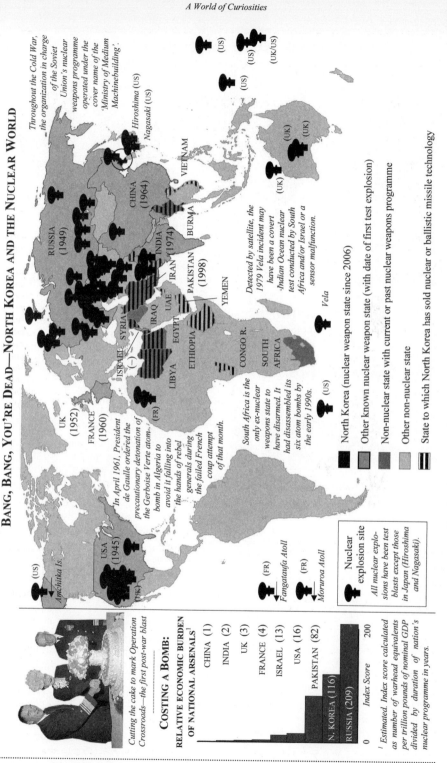

—— KOREA (SOUTH) • 한국 ————

'Rivers and Mountains Embroidered on Silk.'
—Ancient Chinese name for Korea

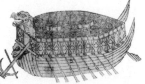

ADMIRABLE. Admiral Yi's greatest moment came at Myeongnyang in 1597, when he defeated a Japanese invasion fleet of 333 vessels with just 13 ships of his own. Japanese casualties were estimated at 12,000; those on the Korean side are believed to have been ten. Even modern historians are left describing the outcome as 'miraculous'. But it was no fluke: during his career, Yi fought 23 battles and won them all—a record not even Nelson can match. Yi combined brilliant tactics with a genius for creativity. His best-known innovation was 'turtle-ships': 16th-century sea-going tanks. Covered in iron plate to deflect enemy fire and studded with spikes to impale boarders, they bore dragon figureheads that belched sulphur fumes (an early smokescreen), concealed four cannon, served as battering rams and terrified the Japanese. In a Nelsonian echo, Yi was killed by a single shot during a final climactic battle that saw off the Japanese for 300 years. Mortally wounded, Yi bade his nephew change into his armour, beat his war drum, and keep his death secret until victory was won.

MIRACLE ON THE RIVER HAN

In 1961, average incomes in South Korea were below those in Congo. Today, they are poised to overtake the West.

GDP PER CAPITA—RELATIVE TO UK

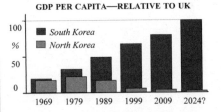

South Korea / North Korea
100 % / 50 / 0
1969 1979 1989 1999 2009 2024?

MARCH OF THE TITANS. South Korea's economic miracle has been delivered through its mighty *chaebols* (literally 'business families'). The annual revenue of the largest, Samsung, exceeds the GDP of the world's 57 smallest nations combined. However, it wasn't always this way ...

■ **Samsung** (*founded 1938*). First manufactured noodles. Big break came in 1977 when its engineers dismantled televisions from Japan to figure out how to make them.

■ **LG** (*founded 1947*). First product was Lucky face cream. Moved into plastics to produce its own jars, and then radios after making plastic radio casings for other firms.

■ **Hyundai** (*founded 1946*). Originally a car repair shop. Founder Chung Ju Yung ran away from home three times to escape a future as a farmer—once selling one of his father's cows to raise the train fare.

GAME ON. South Korea sends out more Christian missionaries than any other nation except the USA. Furthermore, since South Korea is training 1,200 new missionaries each year—more than the West combined, it's expected that, in a few years, Korean missionaries will form an absolute majority worldwide.

GAME OVER. Helped by the world's fastest internet speeds (twice those of second-place Japan and almost four times as fast as the US), South Korea is the world centre of online gaming—30% of the country's population are registered players. There is, however, a dark side. One young Korean died from heart failure after a gaming session of 86 hours with nothing more than toilet breaks. Another killed his mother after she asked him to spend less time online. Sadder still, in 2010 a couple from the city of Suweon were arrested for the fatal neglect of their 3-month-old baby daughter after they spent 12 hours at a time raising a virtual daughter named Anima online. An autopsy showed their real daughter had starved to death.

KAL 007. When Korean Airlines Flight 007 was shot down on 1 September  1983 after straying over the USSR en route to Seoul, the loss of 269 innocent lives caused a worldwide outcry. However, the night's most lasting consequence passed almost unnoticed at the time: to avoid similar navigation errors in future, US President Ronald Reagan decided to authorize civilian access to a secret new military satellite navigation system—now known as GPS.

FAST FORWARD. Korean babies are born aged one as Koreans count the time in the womb as 'year zero'. Koreans are also unusual in all having the same birthday— New Year's Day, which is the day the whole country is deemed to age one additional year in unison. Taken together, this explains how a Korean baby born on 31 December can become a two-year-old before it's even seen out its first 24 hours. Sadly for Korean teenagers, however, the age thresholds for driving and drinking are calculated the Western way.

SAUSAGE DOG. Koreans eat only 8,500 tons of dog a year (with a further 90,000 tons reportedly going into medicinal tonics). Nevertheless, for cultural reasons, the meat is often regarded as a pillar of Korean cuisine. While opposition is growing, many remain perplexed by Western attitudes. Certainly, dog was widely eaten in both France and Germany into the 20th century. The Germans, however, may have been less than keen consumers: one report described boiling dog meat as 'giving off the odour of a neglected zoo' (but did go on to admit that roast Dachshund was 'succulent').

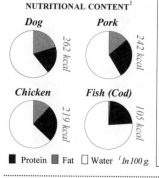

NUTRITIONAL CONTENT[1]

Dog	Pork
262 kcal	242 kcal

Chicken	Fish (Cod)
219 kcal	105 kcal

■ Protein ■ Fat □ Water [1] *In 100 g.*

'THE SCARIEST PLACE ON EARTH'[3]

KOREAN DEMILITARIZED ZONE · 한반도 비무장지대

SOUTH KOREA		NORTH KOREA		
US & SOUTH KOREAN		*NORTH KOREAN*		
38,000	690,000	1,200,000		
300,000[4]	4,500,000	7,700,000	3–12?	
300	2,400	4,100		
100	750	1,200	4	1

155 miles

Per capita, South Korea is the world's second most militarized country.

2.5 miles

Per capita, North Korea is the world's most militarized country.

🔫 Active military	▰ Tanks	💣 Atom bombs		
🔫 Active reserve	✈ Aircraft	⛏ DMZ coal mines[5]	🚩 Flagpoles[6]	

P Panmunjom Joint Security Area (JSA)—the only place the two Koreas come face to face (across a wooden table set on the precise border, marked out by a line of three microphones.)

[3] *US President Bill Clinton (1993).* [4] *US Pacific Command.* [5] *Four covert tunnels have been found crossing from North Korea under the border into the South. According to the North Koreans, these are 'coal mines'. However, given they run through solid granite miles from the nearest known coal seams, most observers have their doubts.* [6] *Towering an intimidating 525 ft, one of the world's tallest flagpoles supports a North Korean flag as big as a tennis court that flies above its side of the DMZ at Kijong-dong.*

CHOPPED. When two US soldiers went to trim a poplar inside the JSA in 1976, they were hacked to death with their own axes by North Korean guards. To get the job done, the UN then decided upon 'overwhelming force'. Three days later, 813 troops deployed—supported by seven helicopter gunships, B-52 bombers and an aircraft carrier just offshore. In 42 minutes, the tree was down.

♣ · **GSR:** 11 · **WHS:** Gochang (dolmens) □ Gyeongju (historic city) □ Haeinsa Temple (books) Hahoe and Yandong (clan villages) □ Hwaseong (fortress) □ Jeju Island (lava tubes) □ Joseon Tombs Mount T'oham (grotto) □ Seoul (palace, shrine) · **ICH:** Cheoyongmu (dance) □ Daemokjang (wooden architecture) □ Falconry □ Gagok (songs) □ Ganggangsullae (harvest festival) □ Gangneung Danoje (shaman festival) □ Jeju Chilmeoridang Yeongdeunggut (sea festival) □ Jongmyo Rites (Confucian rituals) □ Namsadang Nori (clowning) □ Pansori (Korean opera) □ Yeongsanjae (Buddhist dance)

——————— KOSOVO ● KOSOVA ———————

'Serbia, of course, will never recognize the unilaterally
proclaimed independence of Kosovo.'

—Boris Tadic (President of Serbia, 2010)

HISTORY LESSON. Few countries have a touch-stone to match the symbolism of Kosovo for the Serbs. So epic was the 1389 Battle of Kosovo—the word literally means 'blackbird field'—that it even gave the province, now (disputed) country, its name. This was the place where the cream of medieval Serbia was annihilated, but not before fighting the Turks to a military standstill, with one knight (Miloš Obilič) even breaking through the royal bodyguards to kill the Ottoman sultan—an achievement unique in history. No matter that the Serbs were so weakened they were forced to accept the sultan's son as their overlord, nor, more problematically, that Kosovo is now 90% Muslim Albanian and Serbs have been in a minority for a century; when, in 1999, NATO threw its air power behind the Albanian KLA rebels, the Serbs took it as an unspeakable act of betrayal on the very site where, as they saw it, they had sacrificed them-selves for the sake of the whole of Christendom.

THE CURSE OF KOSOVO

'Whoever is of Serb blood and comes not to the Battle of Kosovo, may he never have the progeny his heart desires, may nothing grow that his hand sows, and let him be cursed from all ages to all ages.'

—Serb Prince Lazar (1389)

Kosovo Liberation Army (KLA) insignia

TOUGH GIRLS. Under the *Kanun* code, women in Kosovo and northern Albania may choose to be men by taking a solemn oath before local elders. Known as 'sworn virgins', they thereafter dress as men, own property, wear watches and carry guns.

CRICKET BALLS. The male tuberous bush cricket has the largest testes of any animal relative to its weight. Scaled up to human size, each testicle weighs one stone. The crickets, which are endemic to Kosovo and much of southern Europe, are thought to have equipped themselves with such monstrous gonads to provide supercharged stamina when chancing upon a glut of available females.

WAR NOT PEACE. NATO's air war on Serbia to force it to relinquish Kosovo was the last major conflict to begin in the 20th century. The campaign cost around 1,000 lives; a tragedy for those affected, it barely registers beside the loss of life through war for the century overall.

WORLD AT WAR[1]:
20TH CENTURY DEATH TOLL BY YEAR[2]

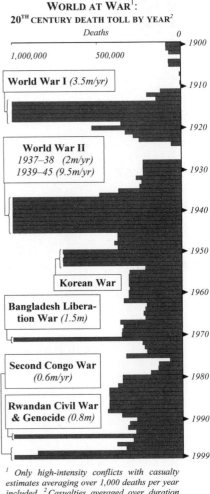

[1] *Only high-intensity conflicts with casualty estimates averaging over 1,000 deaths per year included.* [2] *Casualties averaged over duration of each war (WWII=1937–45 in China, 1939–45 in other theatres).*

♠ · **GSR** 178 · **Recognition**: Kosovo is recognized by 72 sovereign states · **WHS**: Medieval Monasteries

————— KUWAIT ● الكويت —————

'We were supposed to be going on holiday at 10 a.m. Seeing as the airport was the first thing that got bombed—that obviously wasn't going to happen.'

—Sonia Afroz, 12-year-old eye-witness to the Iraqi invasion of Kuwait on 2 August 1990

LIQUID ASSETS. Discovered in 1938, Kuwait's vast Burgan Oilfield—a place where the oil flows so freely it virtually oozes from the ground—was where Arabia's oil bonanza first got going; and although Kuwait is barely bigger than Yorkshire, it still holds 10% of world reserves. Over the years, the nation has used its oil to put $240bn in the bank, but also to give its citizens the freest press and most established parliament in Arabia and the Gulf.

The Kuwait Towers (left): a Kuwaiti icon, and the best-known water tanks-cum-revolving restaurant in the Middle East

NOBODY HOME. Out of around 3.5 million Kuwaitis, around 100,000 are stateless—known locally as *bedoun* ('without [citizenship]'). Often, this was simply a case of somebody's great-grandfather being out in the desert, or illiterate, when registration came round in the 1920s. But, almost a century on, their descendents cannot travel (no passport), drive (no licence), get a job (no identity card), access public health care and education (no birth certificate) or even legally get married (no marriage certificate without valid ID).

• Although a generally undesirable status, a number of well-known people have at one time or another found themselves without any nationality, including: Albert Einstein · Karl Marx · Friedrich Nietzsche · Aristotle Onassis · Nicholas Romanov, Prince of Russia.

HERE'S LOOKING AT YOU, KID. Kuwait's Bedouin are not to be confused with the *bedoun*, but the two categories do overlap. When it comes to cooking, the desert nomads are most notorious for the esteem they reserve for eyeballs (lamb or goat)—which, while nutritious, present other cultures with a challenge.[1] But the aspect of Bedouin life of which squeamish visitors should perhaps be yet more wary is that pertaining to dysentery, for which the Bedouin prescribe a diet of fresh, warm camel faeces.[2]

[1] *'A consistency between squid and pure fat' is the view of one Western foodie, while another warns it's not the eyeball itself that's the biggest hurdle, but the cord of optic nerve dangling from the back.* [2] *German soldiers stationed in North Africa during WWII have confirmed this is a successful cure (probably due to the presence of hay bacilli, which were widely used worldwide as an effective treatment for gastrointestinal disease before they were superseded by antibiotics).*

SCORCHED EARTH. When Saddam Hussein retreated from Kuwait in 1991, his forces torched 600 oil wells. Until capped, these burnt 6m barrels of oil every day—more than was released by the entire three-month *Deepwater Horizon* oil spill.

SEAWEED JUICE. Crude oil is a soup of organic detritus that was once mainly algae. Buried in sediment, the dead material was very slowly compressed into a waxy gunk known as kerogen, which, in turn, became either oil (if the temperature was between $65°C$ and $150°C$) or natural gas (if above $150°C$). A thick, black (or occasionally dark red, green or brown) liquid, crude oil is itself a mix of different-sized molecules that, to be useful, must first be separated according to the number of carbon atoms they have. The smallest come off as gases, while the biggest clog up the pipes as toxic, tacky crud.

HOW CRUDE IS USED

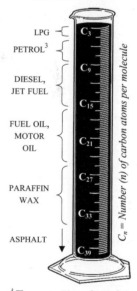

LPG — C_3
PETROL[3]
C_9
DIESEL, JET FUEL
C_{15}
FUEL OIL, MOTOR OIL
C_{21}
C_{27}
PARAFFIN WAX
C_{33}
ASPHALT
C_{39}

C_n = Number (n) of carbon atoms per molecule

[3] *The composition of petrol is varied according to the time of the year. Winter petrol is made with more small, volatile molecules to help with cold starts.*

♣ · **GSR**: 84 · **WHS**: none

———— KYRGYZSTAN ● Кыргызстан ————

'Horses are a man's wings.'

—Kyrgyz proverb. Kyrgyzstan is one of six modern nations founded by the nomadic Turkic tribes who originally inhabited China. (The other five are: Azerbaijan, Kazakhstan, Turkey, Turkmenistan and Uzbekistan.)

HORSING AROUND—THE WORLD OF KYRGYZ EQUESTRIANISM

GO-AT 'EM! Kyrgyzstan's national sport of *kökbörü* ('grey wolf') has been described as 'goat polo'. Two teams, each mounted on horseback, compete to grab the carcass of a headless goat and throw it into a scoring receptacle (known as the 'Circle of Justice'). The use of guns and knives on opponents is banned, and deliberate whipping increasingly discouraged, but apart from that, there are few rules, and traditional matches can last for days—or until the goat disintegrates, after which the players retire to their homes to eat it.

GIRL WHIPS BOY. *Kyz kuumai* or 'girl-chasing' is a popular Kyrgyz sport that one can easily try at home without the need for special equipment (like a decapitated goat). Play is simple. A girl gallops past a boy and, from a standing start, he has to try to catch up with her before she reaches the finishing line. If he succeeds, he then has to lean over and steal a mid-gallop kiss to clinch victory; if he fails, the girl chases him back to the start, landing at least one blow with her whip to win.

Best of the Rest*: Further traditional Kyrgyz equestrian events that have yet to make it to the Olympics include* oodarysh *(horseback wrestling),* tyin Emmei *(plucking a coin from the ground while riding at a gallop) and at* chabysh *(long-distance horse-racing covering distances of 30 miles or more).*

⊟ Hampstead Heath

STAN-DARD USAGE. The suffix *-stan* has come in English to connote a far-off, little-known and almost certainly unappetizing land,[1] but it is, in fact, related to some of the most familiar and domestic of English words. Deriving from the Indo-European root *-sta* ('to stand'), it shares a common origin with 'state', 'statue' and 'stand' itself, among many others. Denoting in its proper sense merely 'place of', *-stan* also shares both meaning and origin with the Anglo-Saxon *-stead*, thus making the likes of Kyrgyzstan etymological first cousins to the English word 'homestead' or, indeed, Hampstead Heath.

[1] *These value judgements depend, of course, on one's perspective. From the time of the Crusaders until the 17th century, the Arabs and Persians referred to the whole of Western Europe simply as Frangistan—'place of the Franks'.*

PLANELY POISON. The world's last remaining source of fresh mercury is Kyrgyzstan's Khaidarkan Mine.[3] Mercury is a material that's notoriously hazardous to handle,[4] and alongside its toxicity and insidious vapour, part of the reason is that the liquid metal can 'eat' aluminium without itself ever getting used up. One important consequence is that even a tiny trace of mercury can, given time, eat right through the walls of an aircraft fuselage—which is why, together with bombs, knives and scissors, mercury thermometers are banned from the cabin of every commercial passenger aeroplane.

[3] *China also mines mercury, but does not export it.* [4] *The United Nations is currently trying to find ways of replacing mercury in all its uses, with a view to banning it entirely after 2013.*

COSMIC CRAPSHOOT:		
READING THE FUTURE IN SHEEP DUNG AND OTHER TECHNIQUES		
Technique	*Society*	*Future is revealed in ...*
Kumalak	Kyrgyzstan	41 dried sheep droppings[2]
Haruspicy	Babylon	features of an animal's liver
Kau cim	China	100 numbered bamboo slivers
Moleosophy	Ancient Greece	location of moles on one's body

[2] *A shaman puts all 41 droppings on a cloth, then touches each to his forehead. After this, he recites various spells until a spirit arrives. At this stage, droppings are gradually removed and those remaining are placed in a grid and linked to the elements of fire, water, wind and earth for the divination.*

♣ · **GSR**: 148 · **WHS**: Sulaiman-Too (sacred mountain on the Silk Road) · **ICH**: Akyns (reciters of Kyrgyz epics) □ Nowruz (New Year celebrations)

LAOS • ລາວ

'Lao—Please Don't Rush'

—Expat synonym for Lao P.D.R. (Lao People's Democratic Republic)

LAOSY SPELLING. The Lao language doesn't even have an 's'. As far as Laotians are concerned, they live in Lao—proud heir to the rather randomly named kingdom of *Lan Xang*, 'Land of a Million Elephants and a White Parasol'. But when France came along, the country had temporarily split into three: *les* Laos. While French bureaucrats soon sorted the politics, no one has ever got round to updating the name—which says it all about Laos really.

'France did nothing for Laos. I say this proudly—we preserved it with our neglect.'

—French official, quoted by Norman Lewis (1959)

PULLING THE STRINGS. Laos is conventionally described as a Buddhist nation. But this is true only of the 50% who are Lowlanders; Highlanders are animist spirit-worshippers. Even among the Lowlanders, animist beliefs lie just below the surface. Almost all believe they have 32 guardian spirits (*khwan*) and, since illness can result if any leave, they tie cotton strings around their wrists to keep them from straying.

'He who walks behind an elephant may feel secure, but will get covered in dung.'

'Say yes when nobody asked.'
—Lao proverbs

'The brothels are cleaner than the hotels, marijuana is cheaper than tobacco, and opium easier to find than a cold beer.'

—Paul Theroux, on Vientiane (capital of Laos) in 1975

MAKING MUD, NOT WAR. The official US history rates the Truong Son Supply Route as one the most impressive military engineering achievements of the 20th century. Better known as the Ho Chi Minh Trail, by 1965 the corridor hacked through the Laotian jungle was supplying 90 tons of material a day to the Vietcong guerrillas in South Vietnam. Desperate to stem this flow, American forces blitzed the trail repeatedly. But they also got creative. In 1968, three CIA-sponsored missions bombed sections with a special 'soap' that was supposed to turn it into a morass of mud. Results were mixed—not least since hundreds of Vietnamese would materialize to clear the 'soap' before it could cause damage. More successful was Project Popeye, an attempt to change the local climate by prolonging the rainy season indefinitely. Seeding clouds with chemicals, the USAF claimed an 85% success rate, and Popeye ran for five years until 1972. To monitor traffic, the US Navy's 'Ghost Squadron' also littered the trail with thousands of 'Turdsids'—movement detectors disguised as lumps of excrement.

THE SERPENT'S BREATH. On certain nights, crowds gather to watch luminous red balls of flame as they erupt high into the air above the Mekong River. Called Naga fireballs, they're snorted by a giant water snake—or so say locals. More likely is that they are bubbles of phosphine, a gas occasionally produced by the action of bacteria on putrefying organic matter, which spontaneously ignite in the air. However, even this explanation is uncertain.

SEEING THE LIGHT—GHOSTLY GLOWS OF THE WORLD		
Light	*Manifests as ...*	*Cause*
St. Elmo's Fire	hissing violet glow that plays around masts, spires, etc.	plasma field
Will-o'-the-wisp	elusive, dancing bogland flames	burning marsh gases?
Ball Lightning	spherical lightning bolt moving erratically through the air	unknown
Earthquake Lights	aurora-like glowing clouds seen during earthquakes	unknown

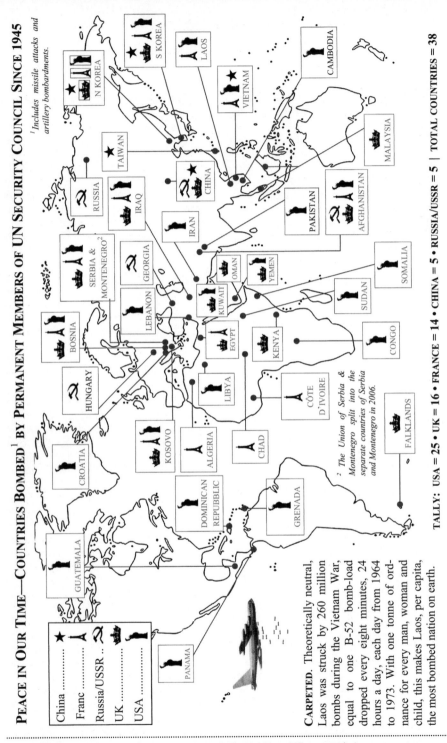

PEACE IN OUR TIME—COUNTRIES BOMBED[1] BY PERMANENT MEMBERS OF UN SECURITY COUNCIL SINCE 1945

[1] Includes missile attacks and artillery bombardments.

S KOREA

LAOS

CAMBODIA

N KOREA

VIETNAM

MALAYSIA

TAIWAN

CHINA

RUSSIA

IRAQ

PAKISTAN

AFGHANISTAN

IRAN

SERBIA & MONTENEGRO[2]

GEORGIA

OMAN

YEMEN

SOMALIA

LEBANON

KUWAIT

SUDAN

BOSNIA

EGYPT

KENYA

CONGO

HUNGARY

LIBYA

CÔTE D'IVOIRE

CROATIA

KOSOVO

ALGERIA

CHAD

FALKLANDS

GUATEMALA

DOMINICAN REPUBLIC

GRENADA

[2] The Union of Serbia & Montenegro split into the separate countries of Serbia and Montenegro in 2006.

PANAMA

China ....
Franc ....
Russia/USSR ...
UK ....
USA ....

TALLY: USA = **25** · UK = **16** · FRANCE = **14** · CHINA = **5** · RUSSIA/USSR = **5** | TOTAL COUNTRIES = **38**

CARPETED. Theoretically neutral, Laos was struck by 260 million bombs during the Vietnam War, equal to one B-52 bomb-load dropped every eight minutes, 24 hours a day, each day from 1964 to 1973. With one tonne of ordnance for every man, woman and child, this makes Laos, per capita, the most bombed nation on earth.

♣ · **GSR**: 91 · **WHS**: Luang Prabang (museum city) □ Vat Phou (Khmer temples)

LATVIA • LATVIJA

'Never wrestle with a strong man nor bring a rich man to court.'

—Latvian proverb

Riga: 'Europe's finest art nouveau.'
—UNESCO

BEAR HUG. At the close of the 17th century, Latvia was an integral part of Sweden, and its present capital, Riga, was Sweden's biggest city—larger than Stockholm. Disastrously, though, Tsar Peter the Great invaded in 1710, and Latvia was drawn into a bleak Russian embrace that endured—with one short interlude—until 1991. After WWII, some Latvians tried to fight back by disappearing into the forests and waging a guerrilla war. Most were killed or captured within a decade, but one, Jānis Pīnups, outlasted the Soviet Union and only walked out of the woods in 1994.

BLOTTO. In 2003, a resident of Riga became the world's worst drunk when found with twice the normal lethal level of alcohol in his blood. This was extreme, but inebriation isn't unusual in Latvia. Losing heart after Russia's 18th-century reinstatement of feudalism, the entire country effectively gave up and went on a year-long bender known as the 'Days of Liquid Bread'.

BIONIC BUG. Not many other countries have a national insect (in fact, just one[2]); but Latvians are fond of theirs, the two-spotted ladybird. Although said to be 'rather slow', it can apparently defend itself ferociously (how isn't explained)—an obviously appealing trait for a small country with a grumpy and immensely more powerful neighbour.

[2] *Sri Lanka. Americans have also shown great enthusiasm, with partisans presenting petitions in favour of the honeybee and Monarch butterfly. Neither has succeeded.*

Flag of Courland Empire

PAX COURONIA. Both Gambia in West Africa and Tobago in the Caribbean were once Latvian colonies—or, more precisely, outposts of the Duchy of Courland, since swallowed by Latvia. The tiny Duchy's muscular pursuit of global glory—which pitted the statelet against the greatest European powers of its day—was cut short by the Dutch, who, by 1659, had seized both Courlandish colonies (although by 1666 they had themselves lost both to Britain).

602,201,417,930,000,000,000,000

One mole—the number of molecules in a teaspoon of water (give or take the odd ten sextillion)

COLD HARD SCIENCE. Since atoms and molecules are far too small to study individually without vast difficulty, scientists need a way to link the results of their human-sized experiments to events going on at a microscopic scale. In 1893, Latvian Wilhelm Ostwald forged that link with the mole[1]. Essentially, a system to scale atomic quantities up by a large fixed number (*above*), Ostwald's mole has since become the cornerstone of chemistry and bane of decades of schoolchildren. A multi-talented researcher, Ostwald was also the man who discovered that, given time, big ice crystals grow at the expense of small ones, even if the ice stays firmly frozen—which is why ice cream gets unpleasantly crunchy if kept much beyond its sell-by date. (The same process, known as 'Ostwald ripening', can also take place in liquid mixtures, such as between oil drops suspended in water, and, in 2005, was shown to be the reason ouzo and pastis turn milky after dilution.)

[1] *Nothing to do with furry animals or skin blemishes, mole is here a contraction, via German, of 'molecular weight'. The mole measures 'amount of substance' such that a mole of, say, gold contains the same number of atoms as a mole of, say, carbon—despite being 16 times heavier.*

♠ · **GSR**: 100 · **WHS**: Riga (Jugendstil cityscape) □ Struve Arc (survey line) · **ICH**: Baltic Song Festivals (folk singing and dance) □ Suiti (minority culture)

LEBANON • لُبْنَان

*'The righteous shall flourish like the palm tree
and grow like a cedar in Lebanon.'*

—Psalms 92:12. Appearing on the national flag and emblem, Lebanon's cedars have symbolized the land since deepest antiquity. Lebanese cedar groves were the abode of the gods according to the ancient Sumerian *Epic of Gilgamesh*, while Moses commanded the application of the resinous bark as a salve immediately following circumcision. In 1876, Queen Victoria personally paid for a wall to be built around the finest remaining grove, the 'Cedars of God', to stop it being eaten by goats—the grove has since become a World Heritage Site.

A+B. 'Alphabet' comes from *alf* and *bet*, the first two letters of the *abjad*[1] developed by the ancient Phoenicians of the Lebanese coast. Ultimately derived from Egyptian hieroglyphics, the Phoenician *abjad* was taken up and adapted in the 9th century BCE by the ancient Greeks, who, by adding vowels, transformed it into the Greek alphabet—the first true alphabet in the world. Two centuries later, the early Romans borrowed the Greek's handiwork, changed the shape of some of the letters and created the Latin alphabet, currently the most widespread scripting system in the world.

A, B, C, D, E ... There's no real logic in the ordering of an alphabet's letters, but it seems that, once established, any given alphabetical order remains very stable. A cache of 3,000-year-old clay tablets found in Syria in 1928 gave two alphabetical orders. One, A, B, G, D, E, is found today in all Latin languages; while the other, H, M, Heth, L, Q, is still used in Ethiopian Ge'ez.

[1] *An abjad is a lettering system that consists only of consonants, leaving readers to guess for themselves which vowel sounds should be used.*

PHOENICIAN *ABJAD*

**THE ANCIENT MEANINGS OF
OUR MODERN LETTERS**

A	*Alf* ('ox')
B	*Bet* ('house')
G	*Gaml* ('camel')
D	*Delt* ('door')
E	*He* ('window')
F, V, W	*Wau* ('hook')
Z	*Zai* ('weapon')
H	*Het* ('wall')
I, J	*Yod* ('hand')
K	*Kaf* ('palm'[2])
L	*Lamd* ('cattle prod')
M	*Mem* ('water')
N	*Nun* ('snake')
X	*Semk* ('fish')
O	*Ain* ('eye')
P	*Pe* ('mouth')
C	*Sade* ('hunt')
Q	*Qof* ('monkey')
R	*Rosh* ('head')
S	*Shin* ('tooth')
T	*Tau* ('mark')

[2] *Palm of a hand (not a tree).*

Note: Although letters A, E, I and O were used, these had consonantal sounds (such as the glottal stop).

ARAB IN-JOKE

A Lebanese woman, a Syrian woman and a Sudanese woman go to hospital to give birth. Each has a baby boy. But there's a disaster: before being tagged, the babies get mixed up. Hospital staff decide that each 'mother's heart' will know which is her son. So they put the three boys in a room, and tell the women to go in and pick their true natural babies. But the Lebanese woman insists on going first. 'I can't wait a minute longer to hold my son,' she says. She goes in, and comes out with the Sudanese baby. 'What on earth are you doing?' a nurse asks. 'That baby obviously isn't yours—look at him—he's clearly a Sudanese child.' 'Yes—but one of those other two is Syrian,' the Lebanese mother tells her, and quickly makes her escape.

HUMMUS BE JOKING. In 2008, the Association of Lebanese Industrialists petitioned their government to apply for EU Protected Geographical Status limiting hummus production to Lebanon (and, not unconnectedly, excluding Israelis). The bid remains pending; but sadly for both sides, the first reference to hummus appears to be from 18th-century Damascus.

The world's biggest blocks of cut stone can be found in the Roman quarries of the Bekaa Valley town of Baalbek. The largest weighs 1,240 tonnes and the site's second largest (right) has a weight of 1,000 tonnes. It's not known how the Romans intended to move such enormous masses, and perhaps they didn't know either as the blocks still lie where they were cut.

Baalbek's largest stone is almost twice as heavy as all of the standing stones at Stonehenge combined.

♣ · **GSR**: 88 · **WHS**: Anjar (ruined Umayyad city) □ Baalbek (ruined Phoenician and Roman city) Byblos (Phoenician city) □ Tyre (ruined Phoenician city) □ Wadi Qadisha (monasteries and cedars)

———————— Lesotho ————————

'The Kingdom in the Sky.'

—Colloquial name for Lesotho

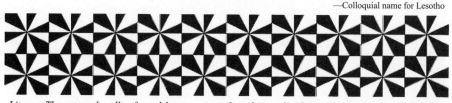

Litame: The external walls of rural houses across Lesotho are brightened by Litame murals built up from repeating patterns based on the furrows of a ploughed field. Applied by hand, the designs are made in a plaster of soil and cow dung, with purists insisting only earth from a termite mound will do.

The 'hole' in the middle of South Africa, Lesotho came about in 1867, after its king petitioned Queen Victoria for protection from the Boers. The country's perilous geo-political position gives Lesotho its other nick-name—the Hostage State.

AFRICA'S ATTIC. By one measure, Lesotho is the world's highest state, since, uniquely, nowhere in the country lies below 1,000 m.[1] Combined with a latitude to the south of the Tropic of Capricorn, this gives July temperatures down to -18°C, snow showers year-round, an abundance of Sloggett's ice rats and the distinctly un-African sight of a population permanently swathed in thick mohair blankets (*right*).

[1] Lesotho's lowest point is 1,400 m (4,600 ft).

A QUESTION OF SCALE. To keep the country securely stocked with mohair blankets, Lesotho keeps a flock of nearly one million angora goats. Considered a luxury yarn elsewhere, mohair's superior softness arises because, whereas the fibres of sheep's wool are covered with small scales, in mohair (and cashmere) these have been reduced to vestigial stubs.

SESOTHO RIDDLE TIME

A. I'm the nest of a bird overhanging an abyss: what am I?
B. I'm a bird that leaves its eggs and runs away: what am I?

Answers: A. Cow's udder; B. Smoke (which leaves the fire).

JEWEL IN THE CROWN. The Lesotho Promise, unearthed in a Lesotho mine in 2006 and sold for $12m, is the biggest diamond discovered so far this century and has since been cut into 26 separate jewels. But while diamonds may, we are told, be for ever, throughout most of history both sapphires and rubies have been more valued.[2] The contemporary fascination with diamonds comes about chiefly for their 'brilliance' (the amount of light they reflect) and 'fire' (the degree to which they disperse light into colours), but it requires special cuts to bring these out. Until the late Middle Ages, rough diamond crystals were renowned more for their hardness, and it was considered taboo to attempt to cut them at all (which, in any case, was all but impossible with the technology to hand). Only in the 14th century did German craftsmen start to 'improve' the uncut stones by smoothing and polishing their natural octahedral shape. More sophisticated cuts gradually evolved, but it was not until 1919, when Marcel Tolkowsky used optical modelling to standardize the modern 'round brilliant' cut, that diamond jewels truly caught alight—though thankfully not literally since, unlike other gems, diamonds burn happily to a mere puff of carbon dioxide.

[2] For example, rubies were worth eight times more than diamonds, carat for carat, in 1550 Florence.

LIGHTING THE FIRE—THE EVOLUTION OF DIAMOND GEMS

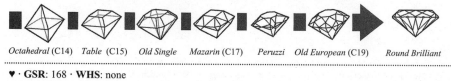

Octahedral (C14) *Table* (C15) *Old Single* *Mazarin* (C17) *Peruzzi* *Old European* (C19) *Round Brilliant*

♥ · **GSR**: 168 · **WHS**: none

LIBERIA

'The love of liberty brought us here.'

—National motto (strictly accurate only for the 5% of the population
who are members of the Americo-Liberian elite)

*Liberian
wooden
spoon*

A LIGHTER SHADE OF BLACK. Uniquely among African nations, Liberia was never conquered by a European power. Instead, it was bought by an American charity for a mixed bag of goods including four umbrellas, a box of soap, a barrel of rum and 12 spoons. The charity—the American Colonization Society—used the land to 'repatriate' emancipated slaves who wished to return to Africa. Once across the Atlantic, however, the returnees decided they were more American than African, and created a settler society modelled on European norms that kept aloof from the 'natives', who were systematically oppressed and exploited. Conditions were so bad that both Britain and the USA broke off diplomatic relations in 1930, after a League of Nations report found the government was exporting captured indigenous Liberians to Fernando Po as slave labour. In Liberia itself, the native Liberians didn't get the vote until 1963 (later than in all three of the adjoining European colonies)—not that it was of much use, since no one was allowed to oppose the Americo-Liberian president.

*'He killed my ma, he killed my pa,
but I will vote for him.'*

—Charles Taylor's election slogan for Liberia's 1997 presidential elections. Taylor's unique approach to electioneering won him 75% of the vote and made him almost certainly the first head of state to have previously escaped from an American top security jail (in 1985) by sawing through the bars on a laundry window and shimmying to freedom down a rope of knotted bed linen.

Nations never colonized by a European power:
Liberia, Thailand, Tonga, Korea, Afghanistan, Bhutan, China, Japan, Iran.

8,483 miles: the greatest distance you can travel in a straight line without crossing the sea

GREENVILLE (LIBERIA) · NIAMEY (NIGER) · CAIRO (EGYPT) · Suez Canal · JERUSALEM · TEHRAN (IRAN) · SAMARKAND (UZBEKISTAN) · XIAN (CHINA) · WENZHOU (CHINA)

CURSE OF THE CROSS-DRESSING CANNIBAL KILLERS!

When fighters of Charles Taylor's rebel NPFL stormed Cuttington University in 1989, they wore wedding dresses, Halloween wigs and high school graduation gowns. During the civil war that followed, Taylor's soldiers went on to accessorize their wardrobe with shower caps, feather boas and sequined purses. Paid to fight on the government side, General Butt-Naked went into battle as good as his name, and shared the heart of a freshly killed child with his teenage troops before each combat. While profoundly strange to outsiders, there was a logic (of sorts) to this: cross-dressing was believed to confuse enemy bullets, while human sacrifice rituals were to ensure victory. General Butt's nakedness, however, is still unexplained.

Samuel Doe, President of Liberia (1986–90). During Liberia's civil wars, cannibalism wasn't just limited to the lower ranks. In 1990, rebel faction leader Prince Johnson had himself videoed drinking a chilled Budweiser while nibbling on the captured president's severed ear as he oversaw Doe's torture and murder. (Doe himself had earlier won power by breaking into his predecessor's bedroom and disemboweling him while he slept.) Johnson is currently a Liberian senator and is a candidate in the October 2011 presidential election.

LIBYA ● ليبيا

'God damn America.'

—Muammar Gaddafi (1973)

GADAFFI ON ...

■ **AL QAEDA**: *Against*—In 1998, Libya issued an international arrest warrant for Osama bin Laden (for the murder of two German agents)—the first country to do so.

■ **THE SWISS**: *Against*—In 2009, Gaddafi submitted a draft UN resolution calling for Switzerland to be abolished. Still disgruntled, in 2010 he declared *jihad* on the nation.

■ **ROYALTY**: *For*—Rather at odds with his distaste for political or military rank (*see right*), Gadaffi had himself crowned 'King of Kings of Africa' in 2008 by an assemblage of 200 traditional African kings and chiefs.

LIVE FOR THE MOMENT. Cyrene was the chief city of ancient Libya and the home of the Cyrenaics, an influential school of ultra-hedonist philosophers who thought that the only good was pleasure, that pleasures of the moment trumped anything anticipated, and that bodily gratification outweighed anything in the mind. Cyrene grew rich as the sole source of *silphium,* the miracle contraceptive of the classical world, until the city harvested the plant to extinction (the last stalk was given to Emperor Nero) and its people slowly drifted away, leaving Cyrene a lifeless shell.

THE HEAT IS ON

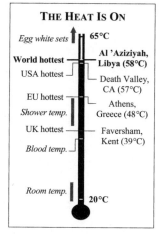

Egg white sets	65°C
World hottest	Al 'Aziziyah, Libya (58°C)
USA hottest	Death Valley, CA (57°C)
EU hottest	Athens,
Shower temp.	Greece (48°C)
UK hottest	Faversham,
Blood temp.	Kent (39°C)
Room temp.	20°C

'From the Halls of Montezuma
to the shores of Tripoli' —'Marines' Hymn'

FIRST BLOOD. As name-checked in the US Marine Corps' anthem, the infant USA's first overseas combat victory was in Libya, at the 1805 Battle of Derne. The action saw 10 Americans march a mercenary army across the Sahara for 50 days, then storm a walled city full of corsairs.

ZERZURA. Rumours of a fabulously wealthy Lost City of Zerzura somewhere in the Libyan Desert have circulated for 800 years. By the 1930s, the deep desert was the very last blank on the map, and the search for Zerzura became a cause célèbre among explorers. After extraordinary efforts, four new oases were found, but, sadly, no city and no treasure.

THREE THINGS YOU DON'T NEED TO KNOW ABOUT THE COLONEL

1 RANK. Despite running Libya for 42 years until 2011, Colonel Gadaffi was never president, resigned as prime minister within three years, and never promoted himself to general.

2 AMAZONS. Gadaffi's forty-strong personal security detail was made up entirely of women; a smart move in an Arab nation, where a female leader would be unthinkable. What's less clear is why they had to wear lipstick and, it's said, be certified as virgin.

3 CAMPING. Gadaffi took his Bedouin nomad tent everywhere. On his trip to the US in 2009, he pitched it in Donald Trump's garden (apparently without permission) after protests forced a move from New York's Central Park. No sign, though, of the camel he took on his visit to Paris in 2007.

♥ · **GSR**: 80 · **WHS**: Cyrene (Hellenic ruins) □ Ghadamès (museum town) □ Leptis Magna (Roman ruins) □ Sabratha (Roman ruins) □ Tadrart Acacus (petroglyphs)

———————— LIECHTENSTEIN ————————

'The jewel at the pulse of Europe, Liechtenstein is like a book.
Once you've started reading, you can't put it down.'

—Liechtenstein Tourism Authority, on the country's unique proposition to prospective visitors

CHOMP. Liechtenstein is the world's biggest exporter of false teeth. It also has the world's highest per capita income. (The two

facts are not necessarily connected.) Throughout most of recorded history, dentures have been constructed from human or animal teeth—George Washington had one hippopotamus ivory pair and another made from donkey teeth. But modern false teeth are fabricated from acrylic, plastic and porcelain. Until the 1980s, depleted uranium was also usually added. The material, a by-product in the manufacture of nuclear fuel rods, was included to give wearers a healthy glowing smile.[1] However, even with the radiation removed, the technology remains far from perfect—even good falsies provide only 12% of the chewing power of real teeth.

[1] *As human teeth fluoresce, dentists found non-fluorescent dentures gave their wearers a lifeless smile.*

THOSE RAMPANT SWISS. Belying its sober image (not to mention conventional notions of neutrality), Switzerland launched a rocket attack on Liechtenstein in 1985, inflicting millions of pounds of damage to the country's national forest. In 2007, the Swiss Army followed this up with an 'accidental' land invasion by almost 200 infantry soldiers toting assault rifles. The Liechtensteiners themselves downplayed the incident, claiming nobody in the country had actually noticed.

JOB DONE. The Liechtensteiner Army last fought in 1866, when it played a minor role in the Austro-Prussian War. This final action appears to have been successful—the entire 80-man force came through unscathed (and they also brought home an Italian 'friend'). Nevertheless, the soldiers hung up their helmets for good in 1868, when, as a cost-cutting measure, the country decided to rely on a force of 485 boy scouts and being too small to find instead.

ON YOUR BIKE. A third of Liechtenstein's workforce commutes from abroad daily.

MONEY MATTERS. Patronized by crooks and tax-evaders (but also by legitimate investors with well-heeled advisors), tax havens shelter an estimated $4–6 trillion worldwide. Of this, Liechtenstein manages $180 billion. The country is also home to 73,700 'letter-box' companies—established for foreign interests, but not actually doing anything. Taken together, this keeps Liechtensteiners very gainfully employed, with an average of $5m and two companies to look after per Liechtensteiner.

OAK TO ACORN. The only country to be named after the people who bought it (the Liechtensteins), Liechtenstein is, by a cosmic joke, also the only surviving territory of the Holy Roman Empire (out of 1,800). Historically, its non-liquidation

Charlemagne

has been due to its unmitigated unimportance; to the extent that, after their 1712 purchase, the Liechtenstein family didn't visit for 106 years (preferring their far grander estates in long-vanished Moravia, Silesia and Bohemia).

LOST REALMS OF THE HOLY ROMAN EMPIRE		
Realm	*Swallowed into*	*Gave world ...*
Bohemia	Czech Republic	exotically loose morals
Lorraine	France	eggy flans
Pomerania	Poland/Germany	yappy little dogs
Prussia	Germany	its first world war

♠ · **GSR**: 118 · **WHS**: none

——— LITHUANIA • LIETUVA ———

'We address all those who hear us. It is possible that the army can close our mouths, but no one will make us renounce freedom.'

—Last broadcast from Lithuanian radio as the country's main radio and TV centre was stormed by Soviet troops on 13 January 1991, killing 14 civilians and injuring 140 more. On 11 March 1990, Lithuania had been the first Soviet Republic to declare its independence from the USSR, presaging the communist superpower's total collapse. The dying Soviet state finally recognized Lithuania's secession on 7 September 1991 and its last soldiers left two years later.

'There is a herb for every sort of sickness, but not for death.'

—Lithuanian proverb

FEMME FATALE. Death, unlike taxes, is certain.[1] But the manner of his (or her) imagining is definitely a matter of choice. Although the grim reaper, with cloak and scythe, is the modern standard, many cultures also had, or have, their own. Of these, the Lithuanian vision is unusually vivid: to them, death descends as 'the Stinger'—an ugly old crone with poisonous tongue and long, blue nose. Alas, however, death's sting does not seem much of a deterrent, since Lithuania suffers the highest suicide rate in the world.

[1]*Nauru is an entirely tax-free jurisdiction (except for airport departure tax, a bed tax for those staying at the hotel and an import tax on sugary foods).*

NATURAL ENEMIES. To its great misfortune, Lithuania straddled the Eastern Front in both World Wars. But for a short time in the winter of 1916, the German and Russian combatants were forced to agree a truce to face a common foe—Lithuania's wolves.[2] Driven by hunger, packs had begun to attack the front-line trenches of both sides (despite attempts to drive them off using grenades and machine guns). Acting together, the two armies killed several hundred of the predators before turning their guns back on each other.

[2] *When attacking humans, wolves target lone children 85% of the time. They usually stalk their victim from behind to deliver a first bite to the back of the neck.*

LOOKING DEATH IN THE FACE—A SELECTION OF GLOBAL PSYCHOPOMPS			
Culture	*Name*	*Translation*	*Description*
Hellenic	Thanatos	'Death'	winged and beautiful youth, implacable but not evil
Hindu	Yama	'Lord of Death'	the colour of a storm cloud, with a soul-swiping lasso
Islamic	Azra'il	'whom God helps'	huge but gentle angel with four faces and 4,000 wings
Japanese	Izanami	'she who invites'	maggot-ridden corpse sworn to take 1,000 lives a day
Kono	Sa	[the supreme god]	filthy child-snatcher with a grudge against humans

LIVING ON THE EDGE. In places only 400 yards wide, the Curonian Spit stretches 60 miles along the south-east coast of the Baltic Sea. Made entirely of sandy beaches backed by dunes up to 200 ft high, the World Heritage Site is shared by Lithuania, Russia and thousands of German holidaymakers.

LINE IN THE SAND—A TYPICAL BEACH IN CROSS-SECTION

As with other beaches, those on the Curonian Spit have distinct summer and winter profiles. In summer, sand piles up onshore, making a broad strand. In winter, however, storms remove much of it to an offshore bar, where it is stored until spring—when the cycle repeats.

Intelligence agencies analyse shore profiles to determine the rough date of images and videos containing a beach.

Winter sand bar

Sea

Summer beach

Frontal dune

Winter profile

Back dune

Marsh

♠ · **GSR:** 67 · **WHS:** Curonian Spit (sand spit) □ Kernavė (hill forts) □ Struve Arc (survey line) □ Vilnius (cityscape) · **ICH:** Baltic Song and Dance Celebrations □ Cross-Making □ Sutartinės (multipart singing)

—— LUXEMBOURG • LËTZEBUERG ——

'We want to remain what we are.'

—Luxembourgish national motto

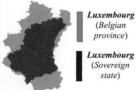

Luxembourg (*Belgian province*)

Luxembourg (*Sovereign state*)

DUCHY ORIGINAL. The world's sole remaining Grand Duchy,[1] the sovereign nation of Luxembourg can fit comfortably inside the neighbouring Belgian province of the same name (which split off in 1839).

[1] *Other former European Grand Duchies included Finland, Lithuania and Transylvania. Within the German sphere of influence (which included Luxembourg), a sovereign duke normally outranked a prince.*

FIVE FAST FACTS

- There are more Michelin-starred restaurants per head than in any other country.

- For a few hours on 9 November 1918, Luxembourg was taken over by communist revolutionaries.

- NATO's entire fleet of early-warning aircraft is registered in Luxembourg.

- Europe's busiest petrol station is Luxembourg's Aire de Berchem Services.

- After the 2001 census, one in eight people in Luxembourg were found to be Portuguese.

THE GREAT LUXEMBOURG OBSTACLE COURSE

Infant School: Luxembourgish
(*the language of the home*)

Junior School: German
(*the language of the media*)

Secondary School: French
(*the language of the office*)

Proficiency required in all three languages to get School Leaver's Certificate

50% of children in Luxembourg **FAIL SCHOOL**

TICKLED. The origin of the Prince of Wales's feathers lies with John the Blind—Count of Luxembourg since 1309 and sightless for a decade when, aged 50, he got himself strapped on to his horse for the Battle of Crécy and, not surprisingly, rapidly killed. Tradition has it that Edward, the Black Prince, came across John's body while surveying the vanquished slain, and, impressed by his stupendous—not to say lunatic—chivalry, decided to adopt his personal motto (*Ich dien*, 'I serve') as his own, while taking the ostrich feathers of John's helmet as inspiration for his crest as the Prince of Wales.

JAW-JAW. When, in 1932, Radio Luxembourg began to beam commercial programmes across the North Sea to Britain, an apoplectic British government coined a new phrase by storming that the broadcasts 'pirated' its wavelengths. Matters got truly serious in WWII, however, after the station was forced to carry Lord Haw-Haw's Nazi propaganda.

SCI-FI DE LUXE. With H. G. Wells and Jules Verne, Luxembourger Hugo Gernsback is regarded as the father of science fiction—he invented the term, although he himself preferred 'scientifiction'; and his name has been memorialized in the annual science fiction awards, known as 'Hugos'. His main contribution came in America, where he published the first 'pulp' science fiction—initially in his popular science titles, but from the 1926 *Amazing Stories* onwards, in dedicated magazines. Gernsback also wrote his own fiction (said to be dire): blasting coffins into space to clear cluttered graveyards and electronic mating were favourite themes.

Luxembourg is the wealthiest country in the world. In 2010, the average income of each citizen was 600 times that of a citizen of Burundi (the poorest nation).

Luxembourg: Nominal GDP per capita (2010).

Burundi: Nominal GDP per capita (2010).

♠ · **GSR**: 65 · **WHS**: Luxembourg City (fortifications) · **ICH**: Echternach Hopping Procession

$106,000

Source: IMF

$180

————— MACEDONIA ● МАКЕДОНИЈА —————

'We are Macedonians but we are Slav Macedonians. That's who we are.'

—President Kiro Gligorov (1992)

THE FRUITS OF VICTORY. From his Macedonian home, Alexander the Great (*right*) fought his way to Afghanistan and India, conquering everything in his path. Though he lived 2,300 years ago, his deeds still echo across the ages in the homage paid daily by elevated restaurants with their *Macédoine de fruits* (fruit salad)—a name coined in the 18th century in remembrance of the polyglot empire Alexander briefly threw together.

PULL THE OTHER ONE. After the Persians won a string of battles by hauling Alexander's troops off their horses by their beards, Alexander ordered his whole army to shave.

NICE ONE, CYRIL! St. Clement of Ohrid is by tradition credited with the invention of the Cyrillic alphabet, used in Russia and across the Balkans and Central Asia. Adapted from Greek script, Cyrillic was developed as a political project to undermine Byzantium's influence amongst the Slavs. The name is said to be a tribute to St. Cyril, St. Clement's mentor and former boss.

IDENTITY CRISIS. Nowhere is there a terminological dispute as bitter as that between Greece and Macedonia. After Yugoslavia imploded in the early 1990s, the constituent republic of Macedonia quietly declared independence. Up went a flag emblazoned with the Star of Vergina (*see left*)—symbol of Alexander the Great's royal House of Macedon—and the celebrations began. The Greeks, however, were not amused. Slapping on a trade embargo and blocking UN membership, they insisted that they were Alexander's heirs, and that their neighbours to the north were no more than opportunistic Slavs engaging in a spot of cultural larceny. Strong words were spoken on both sides, but, eventually, the infant state redrew its flag and entered the UN under the cumbersome interim title of 'Former Yugoslav Republic of Macedonia'. Even so, the dispute still festers: in 2008, Greece vetoed Macedonia's NATO accession and, until a new name is found, threatens the same for any bid to join the EU.

WRETCHED LIVES. In 1913, the British-run Macedonian Relief Fund engaged a young woman named Eglantyne Jebb to deliver famine-relief money to Macedonia. Despite her personal dislike of children (she referred to them as 'wretches'), Jebb's experiences spurred her both to found the Save the Children charity and to write a 'Children's Charter'. This later formed the basis of the UN Convention on the Rights of the Child—since adopted by every member of the United Nations except Somalia and the USA.

LATIN	GREEK	CYRILLIC
C	K	K
L	Λ	Л
E	E	И
M	M	М
E	'E	E
N	N	Н
T	T.ю	Т
Oof	Oτης	O
H	X	Х
R	P	Р
I	'I.	И
D	Δας	Дски

♠ · **GSR**: 108 · **WHS**: Ohrid (lake, Byzantine churches and icons)

—— MADAGASCAR ● MADAGASIKARA ——

'The Eighth Continent.'

—Epithet for Madagascar; given due its isolation (it is separated from Africa by a 300-mile-wide channel), size (it's the world's fourth largest island) and, above all, the distinctiveness of its flora and fauna (80% of its species are endemic)

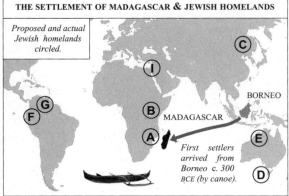

THE SETTLEMENT OF MADAGASCAR & JEWISH HOMELANDS

Proposed and actual Jewish homelands circled.

BORNEO

MADAGASCAR

First settlers arrived from Borneo c. 300 BCE (by canoe).

Key to proposed Jewish homeland locations: **A**. Madagascar Plan (*see below*). In 1937, Polish officials had also visited Madagascar with a view to implementing a similar scheme for Polish Jews. **B**. In 1903, Britain offered Jewish settlers 5,000 sq. miles of Uganda as an independent homeland. **C**. In 1934, Stalin created the 14,000-sq.-mile Autonomous Jewish Oblast near Khabarovsk. **D**. A private plan in the 1940s for a Tasmanian homeland won the support of the state premier, but the proponent died. **E**. Starting in 1939, the Freeland League tried to buy 11,000 sq. miles in Australia's Kimberley region, but in 1944 was blocked by the government. **F & G**. In 1935, the Freeland League investigated buying a homeland in Ecuador or Surinam. **I**. Israel—8,000-sq.-mile state founded 1948 in the former British Mandate of Palestine.

ONE OF A KIND. Madagascar is a huge chunk of India lying off the coast of Africa, inhabited by people from Borneo, and named by mistake by Marco Polo (who thought he was writing about Mogadishu in Somalia). Isolated for the past 88 million years, the island was left behind when the rest of India began to drift north, ultimately to crash into Asia. Its location far from any other land mass then kept it undisturbed until it was colonized by people from Borneo around 300 BCE. It's not clear what prompted them to make their epic 5,000-mile voyage in open canoes, but the cultural links—ranging from an Asian rice-based cuisine[1] to a language similar to Malay—remain unmistakable.

[1] *The Malagasy are the world's biggest rice-eaters, consuming 135 kg annually each, and often drinking a thin toasted rice gruel (*ranon'ampango*) instead of water.*

UNLUCKY FOR SOME. Malagasy are traditionally extremely superstitious: for example, one Sakalava clan formerly killed all children born on Tuesdays.

MADAGASCAR PLAN. Before fixing on its 'final solution', Nazi Germany planned to force all 4 million non-Russian European Jews to emigrate to Madagascar. In preparation, the head of the Reichsbank travelled to London in 1938 in an attempt to arrange bank loans to cover the cost (the plan was later changed to become self-funding through confiscation of Jewish property), while, in 1939, Nazi Foreign Minister von Ribbentrop tried to secure support from the pope. The scheme, however, always had a delusive quality, not least in a German lack of shipping. It relied on the use of British vessels and failure to defeat Britain removed any slim chance of the plan becoming real.

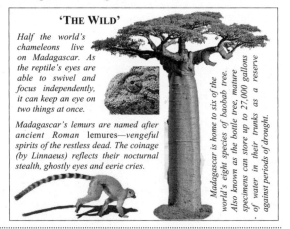

'THE WILD'

Half the world's chameleons live on Madagascar. As the reptile's eyes are able to swivel and focus independently, it can keep an eye on two things at once.

Madagascar's lemurs are named after ancient Roman lemures—*vengeful spirits of the restless dead. The coinage (by Linnaeus) reflects their nocturnal stealth, ghostly eyes and eerie cries.*

Madagascar is home to six of the world's eight species of baobab tree. Also known as the bottle tree, mature specimens can store up to 27,000 gallons of water in their trunks as a reserve against periods of drought.

♥ · **GSR**: 138 · **WHS**: Ambohimanga (ruins and tombs) □ Atsinanana (rainforest) □ Tsingy de Bemaraha (lemurs) · **ICH**: Zafimaniry (woodworking skills)

———————— MALAWI ————————

'Female passengers will not be permitted to enter the country if wearing trousers.
Skirts and dresses must cover the knees to conform with Government regulations.
The entry of 'hippies' and men with long hair and flared trousers is forbidden.'

—Visa regulations for entry to Malawi, (1970s—in practice, men with hair
below their collars were forcibly given a haircut at the airport or border crossing)

Helping to hold Malawi together, the MV Ilala *has plied the waters of 300-mile-long Lake Malawi for the last 60 years, and still completes one circuit weekly. Named for Livingstone's burial place, the 620-ton steamer was built in Glasgow in 1949, disassembled into 780 crates, shipped to Beira in Mozambique, transported to Central Africa by rail, and finally reassembled on the lakeshore.*

AFRICA ON A SHOESTRING. When, in 1891, Britain reluctantly set up British Central Africa (now Malawi) in order to keep the Portuguese out, the Colonial Office allocated the newly acquired territory a budget of $16,000 a year—enough for 10 European civil servants, 2 officers, 70 Indian soldiers and 85 African porters—to govern an area half the size of Britain.

ORPHANS OF HISTORY

Moses b.1446 BCE

Santa Claus b.270 (a.k.a. St. Nicholas)

Muhammad b.571

Leo Tolstoy b.1828

Ella Fitzgerald b.1917

Nelson Mandela b.1918

NO BATTLE OF HASTINGS. Dressed like a tropical undertaker with a wardrobe of 60 sober suits, 32 pairs of dark glasses, 14 fly-whisks and uncounted Homburg hats, Dr. Hastings Banda was Malawi's president from independence in 1964 until 1994. A Church of Scotland elder, he ruled his 'children' with a rod of iron, and, while not outright mad (unlike some other leaders), he was capable of considerable eccentricity: when his relations with 'official hostess' Cecilia Kazamira hit a sticky patch, he banned the Simon & Garfunkel song 'Cecilia'. Despite doubt as to whether he even came from the country (he didn't speak the language), Malawians were largely tolerant of Banda—and he returned the favour by going quietly when finally pushed.

BIG STINK. In 2011, Malawi's justice minister introduced a bill which he said would make farting in public illegal. Calling it an affront to 'public decency', he proposed offenders should just go to the toilet. However, the solicitor general reacted angrily, curtly dismissing the idea as nonsense.

AMERICAN LIFE. Madonna's adoption of David Banda and Chifundo James highlighted the plight of Malawi's two million orphans—over 10% of the total population. But, despite the controversy, there's every chance their lives will turn out better than those of most other orphans in history. Roman orphans could be enslaved, while adoption was reserved for patrician adults—usually to manage inheritance. (Many who became Roman emperors were adopted.) In the Middle Ages, adoption was banned entirely because it disrupted blood lines, and orphans were given to the Church to become lay brothers if lucky, or farmed out as cheap labour if not—a practice continued by orphanages and 'guardians' into the 20th century. It was only in 1917, in Minnesota, that checks on those taking children in were instituted, and adoption in the modern sense began. By the 1960s, the proportion of US orphans adopted had soared from 2% to 30%, but, even so, their status appears to remain unequal: research shows households with adopted children spend less on food than equivalent ones where the children are natural-born, while suicide rates and mental illness are both much higher.

♥ · **GSR:** 156 · **WHS:** Chongoni (rock art) □ Lake Malawi (fish) · **ICH:** Gule Wamkulu (cult) Vimbuza (healing dance)

———————— MALAYSIA ————————

*'The Malays are easy-going; the non-Malays, and especially the Chinese, have an appetite
for work. For equality to come about, these contrasting races must adjust to each other.'*
—Dr. Mahathir Mohamad (*The Malay Dilemma*, 1970)

PHANTOM WORRIES. Ghosts are taken very seriously by both Chinese and Malays in Malaysia, where the connection with the dead—for good or, more often, ill—is keenly felt. Property around cemeteries is significantly discounted due to the perceived danger of living in such a location, while the biggest-grossing Malay movie of all time is a 2007 horror flick about an evil spirit in a jar. Of the many varieties of Malay ghost, one of the most feared (and film-scripted) is the *orang minyak* ('oily man'), a supernatural serial rapist who goes naked except for a layer of grease that makes him impossible to hold. Mingling fact and fantasy, several *orang minyak* attacks have been reported in recent years, most often around student and nurses' hostels. Although presumably the work of human impostors or overcooked rumour, belief in the *orang minyak* is such that, following each, a number of female students took to sleeping in the sweaty cast-offs of male friends (since the fiend only ever preys on virgins).

RUBBER BANNED. For most of the 20th century, Malaya was the world's chief source of rubber, a fact not lost on the Japanese, who prioritized the seizure of the peninsula's rubber plantations early in WWII. Quickly accomplishing this, they gained control of 95% of the world production and the American war effort was thrown into crisis. To buy time for an alternative, the US immediately banned all non-war uses of rubber, imposed a national speed limit of 35 mph (to conserve tyres) and established 400,000 rubber collection points in history's biggest ever recycling exercise—even President Roosevelt's pet dog, Fala, had to sacrifice his toys. Despite being Japan's ally, Germany faced a similar problem, since it was blocked from getting supplies. Ever inventive, the country's scientists turned to lettuce, the sap of which contains up to 2% rubber. Both the American and German measures held the line until each country discovered economic ways to make synthetic alternatives. However, although the development of lettuce rubber stopped at that point, researchers have recently started to look at it once more, not least to help the 7% of people who are allergic to rubber tree latex.

OFF WITH THEIR HEADS! After a childhood spent on the edge of Bracknell, Sylvia Brett married the last White Rajah of Sarawak in 1911 to become Sylvia, the self-styled 'Queen of the Headhunters'. While she was an outrageous self-publicist, there was indeed some truth in the name. After WWII, one of her last acts before her husband's abdication[1] was to accompany him up the Rajang River to inspect some of the 1,500 smoked Japanese heads his Dayak subjects had kept as trophies from their wartime fight on behalf of the Allies. As one chief put it: 'nice round heads with good hair and gold teeth' (and, it should be added, some still wearing their original glasses).

[1] *In favour of the British Crown on 1 July 1946 in return for a fat pension. This made Sarawak, alongside adjoining Sabah, the British Empire's final colonial acquisition.*

DEADLY WEAPON. Under Malaysia's strict legal code, the unauthorized possession of any firearm carries the mandatory death sentence (as does the taking of hostages).

♣ · **GSR**: 44 · **WHS**: Gunung Mulu (tropical karst, biodiversity and caves) □ Kinabalu (rainforest) Melaka & Penang (colonial townscapes) · **ICH**: Mak Yong Theatre

————— MALDIVES ● ‏ދިވެހިރާއްޖެ‎ —————

'To speake truly, the men are halfe-fishes, they are so used to the sea.'

—F. Pyrard de Laval (1602)

BOWING OUT—COUNTRY SUBMERSION TIMETABLE

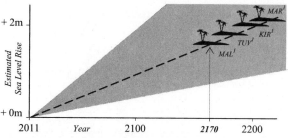

Key (estd. inundation date in brackets): MAL *Maldives (2170)*, TUV *Tuvalu (2190)*, KIR *Kiribati (2210)*, MAR *Marshall Islands (2220).* [1] *Mean elevation. Grey area indicates range of uncertainty, dashed line mid-case scenario.*

BAILING OUT. On 17 October 2009, the government of the Maldives held the world's first underwater cabinet meeting. But on current trends, every such meeting will be a wetsuit-and-tie affair within 160 years. More than 99.7% ocean, the Maldive atoll chain is home to the world's lowest country (1.6 m above sea level on average, and nowhere above 2.4 m). With its main island, Malé, already the second most crowded place on Earth, options in the face of rising sea levels are constrained. Malé has now been entirely ringed by a Dutch-style concrete sea-wall, but with another 1,200 islands to protect, this can only be a stop gap. As a last resort, the country has started to put tourist revenue aside to buy a new home in Sri Lanka or Australia. Next down for dunking, dirt-poor, off-the-grid Tuvalu has fewer options—faced with a choice between drowning and leaving, its people have already begun to drift away to New Zealand as climatic refugees.

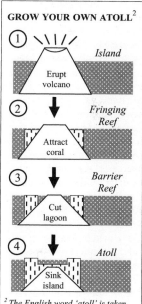

GROW YOUR OWN ATOLL [2]

① Island — Erupt volcano

② Fringing Reef — Attract coral

③ Barrier Reef — Cut lagoon

④ Atoll — Sink island

[2] *The English word 'atoll' is taken from the Dhivehi (Maldivian) atolu.*

MAKING OUT. According to a 2010 UK survey, the Maldives—with its romantic mix of sun, sand and seclusion—is the most popular long-haul honeymoon destination. The origins of 'honeymooning', however, appear anything but romantic. Separate strands of thought suggest the word originally conveyed recognition that, as in the waning of the full moon, the initial sweet ardour of married life is fast doomed to fade; while the custom recalls the Norse practice of abducting the object of one's lust for one month, by which time she would be presumed to have conceived, making 'marriage' a fait accompli.

SHELLING OUT. Collected by the million from Maldivian lagoons, cowrie shells were once the staple currency of the West African slave trade[3] —in 1747, the going rate was 25 kg per slave. Between Malé and Timbuktu, the shell's value increased a thousand-fold, giving the Arab merchants who acted as middlemen every reason to refer to the Maldives as the 'Money Islands'.[4]

[3] *Ghana's modern currency, the* cedi, *means 'cowrie' in the local Akan language.* [4] *For their own use, Maldivians preferred silver fishhooks imported from Iran as currency.*

♣ · **GSR**: 160 · **WHS**: none

MALI

'Salt comes from north, gold from south and silver from the land of Whites;
but the Word of God, the famous things, histories and fairy tales,
we only find them in Timbuktu.'

—Sahelian saying

Mansa Musa—from a 1375 map

HOW TO MAKE WATER IN A DESERT[2]

1. Dig pit until you reach moist subsoil.
2. Place cup or tin can in bottom.
3. Cover pit with clear plastic wrap.
4. Seal edges of wrap with piled sand.
5. Weight centre with a stone.

Notes: *Dry wadi beds are a good place to dig; to be effective, the site must be in full sun. Digging at night will conserve sweat. This is especially useful for recycling urine (pee into the hole or into a second cup). Several pits are needed to support one person—survival is not guaranteed.* [2] *The Tanezrouft ('Land of Thirst'), shared by Mali and Algeria, is the most desolate region of the Sahara.*

EMPIRE IN THE SUN. At its 14th-century peak, the Mali Empire far surpassed all contemporaneous European kingdoms in extent, population and—especially—wealth: Mali's mines produced over half the known world's supply of gold, and, instead of coins, Malians used bags of gold dust for currency.[1] Much of this was hardly known outside West Africa until 1324, when Mali's pious tenth emperor, Mansa Musa, decided to undertake a pilgrimage to Mecca. Setting out with a retinue of over 60,000 and a camel train loaded with an estimated six tonnes of gold, Musa was generous to a fault—the fault being that, wherever he went, he gave away so much of the metal that he left a trail of financial chaos. Thus, the economies of both Medina and Makkah were temporarily ruined, while in the metropolis of Cairo it took at least 12 years for gold to recover its former value.

[1] *Salt was used in Mali as a parallel second currency. Its value varied by region: in the north, it was worth its weight in gold; but in the south, it was considerably more expensive.*

AFRICAN STUDIES. The catalyst for trans-Saharan trade was the introduction of the camel in the 7th century. Fattened for months on rich pastures and travelling in caravans of up to 12,000, camels could cross in eight tough weeks from the Maghreb to Timbuktu—which soon developed into West Africa's commercial hub. With international commerce came new ideas, and the city became known across the Islamic world as a centre of learning too. From 1300 until its sack by the Moroccans in 1591, Timbuktu's Sankoré University was one of the world's biggest, with 25,000 students;[3] while its library—holding 700,000 volumes—was Africa's greatest since the Ancient Library of Alexandria.

[3] *In comparison, Oxford University had roughly 1,500 students at this time.*

EMPEROR IN THE SUNSET. The circumstances by which Mansa Musa (*see left*) ascended the throne of Mali were somewhat unusual. In 1311, his predecessor as emperor, Abubakari II, became curious as to what lay beyond the Atlantic and decided to investigate personally. Accordingly, he fitted out a fleet of 1,000 ships, each towing a barge with two years of supplies, declared Musa regent and set off west into the sunset—never to be seen again.

Dogon dancers

UNKINDEST CUT. According to Dogon belief, children are born ambisexual, and can only acquire their 'proper' gender after their 'female' foreskin (in the case of boys) or 'male' clitoris (in the case of girls) has been removed. The procedure for girls is discreetly out of sight, but for ten-year-old boys, it's a trip to the village blacksmith and then a month of parading naked to let friends and family applaud their new and hard-won status.[4]

[4] *Across the world as a whole, it's estimated that 30% of men and 4% of women have been circumcised.*

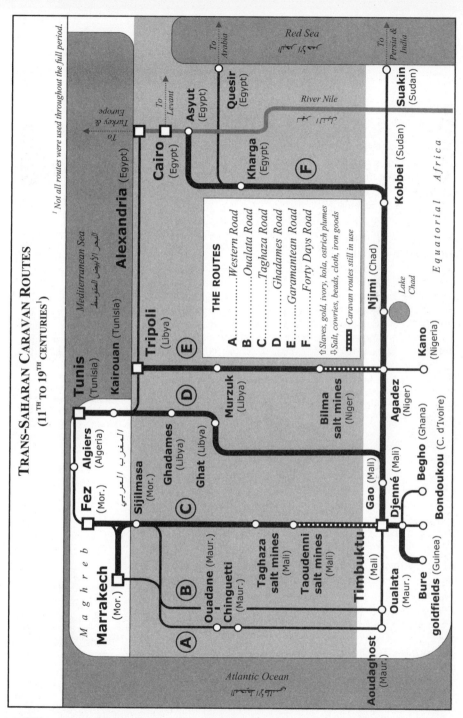

♥ **GSR** · 104 · **WHS**: Bandiagara Cliff (traditional villages) □ Djenné (townscape) □ Gao (tomb) Timbuktu (historic city) · **ICH**: Kamablon Re-Roofing (ceremony) □ Manden Charter (oral constitution) □ Sanké Mon (fishing ceremony) □ Yaaral and Degal (cattle drover festivals)

————————MALTA————————

'By God's help Malta will not weaken, but endure until victory is won.'

—Maltese reply when accepting the George Cross (*left*)
for collective bravery during WWII (1942)

THINKING (I): OUTSIDE THE BOX.
Maltese-born Edward de Bono coined
the phrase 'lateral thinking' in his book
New Think, published in 1967. **Q.** *New
Think* sold over 270,000 copies, yet
never earned de Bono a penny—why?

A. Published in America, it was priced in dollars.

*'You cannot dig a hole
in a different place by digging
the same hole deeper.'*

—Edward de Bono

PUZZLE CORNER

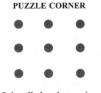

Join all the dots using
no more than four
straight lines without
taking your pen off the
page (*answer below*).

CROSSES TO BEAR

MALTESE CROSS
Worn by crusader
knights and St. John
Ambulance volunteers.
The four arms symbol-
ize the four virtues of
prudence, temperance,
justice and fortitude;
the eight points, the
eight beatitudes.

PETRIFYING. Since antiquity, Malta has been
the source of strange triangular stones known
as *glossopetrae*. The Romans thought they fell
from the sky during lunar eclipses. Medieval
Europeans believed they were the tongues of
serpents petrified by St. Paul when ship-
wrecked on the island. In 1667, Danish scholar Niels Stensen
was the first to realize they were actually fossilized shark teeth,
and, in doing so, lay the foundations for modern palaeontology.

Megalodon

Great White Shark

Among the fossil shark teeth found on Malta are those of the Megalodon
*('big tooth' in Greek), whose teeth could reach the size of a human face.
Able to swallow a cow whole, it was the biggest predatory fish of all time.*

MALTASHIRE. In 1955, Britain offered Malta union as a full
member of the UK. In a referendum, the Maltese voted 3 to 1
in favour, but as the 'yes' vote total fell just short of an absolute majority, this was insufficient. Shortly afterwards, redun-
dancies at Malta's Royal Naval dockyard soured relations and
Malta moved towards independence instead.

THINKING (II): ON ANOTHER PLANET. In 1999, Edward de
Bono was invited to the British Foreign Office to lecture its
Middle East section on ways to solve the Arab–Israeli conflict.

De Bono duly attended and advised feeding both
sides Marmite. (Apparently, Marmite is rich in zinc,
which, if absent, renders humans over-aggressive.)

PAPAL CROSS
Worn exclusively by
the pope. The three
cross-bars signify his
authority in faith, the
Church and the world.

MARINER'S CROSS
Outwardly an anchor,
it's worn by Christians
who need to hide their
faith due to persecution.

♠ · **GSR**: 73 · **WHS**: Hal Saflieni (underground temple) □ Megalithic Temples □ Valletta (historic city)

───── MAURITANIA ● موريتانيا ─────

'It's a normal thing, to have slaves in Mauritania.'

—Mohamed, runaway Mauritanian slave (2004)

The port of Nouadhibou, in northern Mauritania, has the world's biggest ships' graveyard—at the latest count, there were over 300 rusting hulks from all over the world lining its beach. The ships are dumped in this remote location since, with the advent of tough waste disposal and recycling regulations in the developed world, getting rid of an old ship can be very expensive, while word has got around that the port officials in Nouadhibou will accept anything in return for a small bribe. Since Nouadhibou has absolutely no facilities to do anything with the hulks (although local families have moved into some as informal housing), their numbers have just increased over the years. Given the toxic hazard the ships pose, the EU has recently announced plans to start towing them away or, if unseaworthy, to blow them up in situ.

SOLD. With 20% of the population enslaved, Mauritania is the biggest slave-owning society in the world today. As in many other cultures, slavery in Mauritania has a racial dimension: the 'white moor' elite are mostly the slave-owners and the dark-skinned 'black moors' mostly the enslaved. (There is black-on-black slavery too.) In theory, this is all illegal, since slavery was banned (for the third time) in 2007. But despite there being 600,000 slaves to choose from, the first prosecution wasn't brought until April 2011—when all five defendants were acquitted.

SHADES OF GREY
SKIN COLOUR IN ARAB SOCIETIES

Abyad/Asfar[1]	*white/yellow*
Ahmar	*red*
Asmar	*shades of brown*
Dahabi	*golden brown*
Gamhi	*light brown*
Khamri	*maroon brown*
Akhdar[2]	*green*
Azrag[3]**/Aswad**	*blue/black*

Decreasing prestige ↓

[1] *Slaves at Cairo slave market that were graded as being* abyad *or* asfar *attracted a price premium.* [2] *Visually identical to black, but used to refer to those with some noble blood.* [3] *Euphemism for 'black'.*

The trains hauling iron ore to the coast from Mauritania's desert mines at Zouerate are reputedly the longest in the world, stretching for a mile and a half from end to end. The line itself, built at the twilight of the French colonial era, is also modestly famous for one of the most arrant bits of nonsense thrown up by Europe's African scramble. Near Choum, a corner of Spain's Rio de Oro protruded for just a mile or so into the track's natural route across the stony desert plains. But despite the land being of no conceivable use, the Spanish and French were unable to agree terms to allow the railway a right of passage, so in the end the French blasted a one-mile tunnel through a solid granite mountain simply to keep on its side of the border. Today, the tunnel has been abandoned and the trains take their chances with the Polisario guerrillas by taking a brief shortcut through what is now the contested territory of Western Sahara.

....

♥ · **GSR**: 161 · **WHS**: Banc d'Arguin (birdlife) □ Ouadane, Chinguetti, Tchitt and Oualata (townscapes)

———————— MAURITIUS ————————

'A daintie Island of good refreshing and the best provided
for man's use of any other under the Sunne.'
—P. Mundy (1634)

DEAD AS A [....]—CELEBRITY EXTINCTIONS COURTESY OF *HOMO SAPIENS*

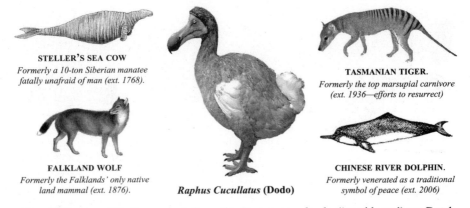

STELLER'S SEA COW
Formerly a 10-ton Siberian manatee
fatally unafraid of man (ext. 1768).

TASMANIAN TIGER.
Formerly the top marsupial carnivore
(ext. 1936—efforts to resurrect)

FALKLAND WOLF
Formerly the Falklands' only native
land mammal (ext. 1876).

CHINESE RIVER DOLPHIN.
Formerly venerated as a traditional
symbol of peace (ext. 2006)

***Raphus Cucullatus* (Dodo)**

GOT KNOTTED. Whether named from the Portuguese *doudo* ('stupid one') or Dutch *dodaars* ('knot-arse'), it's clear that early European sailors didn't think much of this three-foot walking pigeon with a comedy beak. Within a century of their landfall on Mauritius the dodo was extinct—not so much from hunting (dodo meat was described as 'loathsome' and 'tough') but from the depredations of the cats, pigs and rats that jumped ship. The last complete dodo was pitched on to an Oxford bonfire during a 1755 museum clear-out; but dodo eggs remain, and a recent discovery that DNA can be extracted from eggshells raises just a glimmer of hope that one day the dodo will waddle once more. (*Extinct 1690.*)

DROP OF THE BLACK STUFF. Mauritius specializes in molasses[1], exporting 65,000 tons of the goo each year. Apart from use in the kitchen and as cattle food, molasses puts the 'dark' in dark ales and stouts, while engineers use it by the vat to de-rust iron and steel.

R.I.P.
EXTINCT ISLAND NAMES

Île de France	**Mauritius**
Île Bourbon	Réunion (Fr.)
Candy	Crete (Gr.)
Celebes	Sulawesi (Indon.)
Ceylon	Sri Lanka
Cipango	Japan
Disko	Qeqertarsuaq (Grn.)
Fernando Pó	Bioko (Eq. G.)
Formosa	Taiwan
Ilha de Vera Cruz	Brazil
New Holland	Australia
Pines	Youth (Cuba)
Sandalwood	Sumba (Indon.)
Sandwich	Hawaii (USA)
Sorlinges	Isles of Scilly (UK)
Staten Landt	New Zealand

NOTHING LASTS FOR EVER:
AVERAGE LIFESPAN OF SPECIES[2]

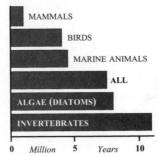

MAMMALS
BIRDS
MARINE ANIMALS
ALL
ALGAE (DIATOMS)
INVERTEBRATES

0 *Million* 5 *Years* 10

[2] *Expected lifespan of a typical species before extinction, based on long-term background rates. Current extinction rates are estimated at 50 to 500 times higher than background (and up to 35,000 times higher for amphibians).*

[1] *Molasses is the residue from the refining of sugar. Blackstrap, the strongest grade, is sold as a health supplement and can also be used to make improvised explosive devices.*

AS GOOD AS IT GETS
IBRAHIM INDEX[3] (2009)

1. **Mauritius** .... **(83%)**
2. Cape Verde .... (78%)
3. Seychelles .... (77%)
4. Botswana .... (74%)
5. South Africa .... (69%)
....
51. Zimbabwe .... (31%)
52. Chad .... (30%)
53. Somalia .... (15%)

[3] *The leading index measuring civic governance for all African countries: 100% is a perfect score, 0% is a kleptocratic charnel house.*

♥ · **GSR**: 133 · **WHS:** Aapravasi Ghat ('coolie' complex) □ Le Morne (runaway slave shelters)

—————— MEXICO • MÉXICO ——————

'Poor Mexico, so far fom God and so close to the United States.'

—Porfirio Diaz (Mexican president 1884–1911)

ADIÓS—MEXICO'S SHRINKING STATE

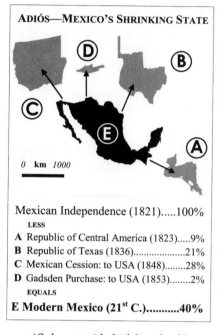

0 km *1000*

Mexican Independence (1821).....100%
LESS
A Republic of Central America (1823).....9%
B Republic of Texas (1836)....................21%
C Mexican Cession: to USA (1848).......28%
D Gadsden Purchase: to USA (1853)........2%
EQUALS
E Modern Mexico (21st C.)...........40%

'Only men with thick lips should smoke cigars.'
—Mexican proverb

LUNAR BUNNY. The Aztecs believed that there was a rabbit, not man, in the moon (a view still shared by much of Asia).

HOT DOGS
LITTLEST AND LARGEST COMPARED

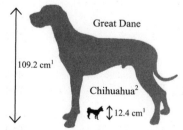

Great Dane

109.2 cm[1]

Chihuahua[2]

12.4 cm[1]

[1] *Heights of record-holding largest and smallest adult members of the Great Dane and Chihuahua breeds respectively.* [2] *Scientifically speaking, the Mexican Chihuahua is a grey wolf. As members of the same wolf sub-species (Canis lupus familiaris), the two animals shown should be capable of cross-breeding successfully—if, that is, they weren't both male and the Great Dane wasn't hungry.*

HEROES OF THE REVOLUTION

PANCHO VILLA
'Centaur of the North'

EMILIANO ZAPATA
'Tiger of the South'

The 1910–20 Mexican Revolution laid the foundations of modern Mexico and ushered in the left-leaning PRI[3] government that kept itself in power until 2000. The revolution's twin poster boys, Robin-Hood-like Emiliano Zapata and bandit-made-half-good Pancho Villa,[4] remain huge national heroes.

[3] *The aptly named Institutional Revolutionary Party.*
[4] *Media-savvy from the start, Villa part-funded his rebellion by selling the film rights to Hollywood in 1914. Four cameramen from the Mutual Film Company subsequently accompanied Villa on his campaigns, but contrary to a widely circulated story, the contract did not require Villa to repeat attacks if the light or camera angles were bad.*

SPIRIT OF DISCOVERY. Mexican researchers have found that heating tequila to 800°C turns it into sheets of pure diamond. Although the individual diamond crystals that form are far too small for jewellery, they are ideal for industry. The scientists involved are now working their way through as many of the 2,000 tequila brands as possible—ostensibly to decide which one works best.

MORBID CURIOSITY. Every 2 November, the people of Pomuch buff up the bones of their parents before laying them on a fresh, clean cloth. The ritual starts three years after death, when the recently deceased are dug up and given a thorough clean. It may be extreme, but, on the Day of the Dead, families all over Mexico travel to cemeteries to reminisce with their dead relatives and perhaps share a tequila, while the children play and nibble on sugar skulls.

EMPIRES IN THE BALANCE

DISPOSITION OF FORCES—CONQUISTADOR LANDFALL IN MEXICO (1519)

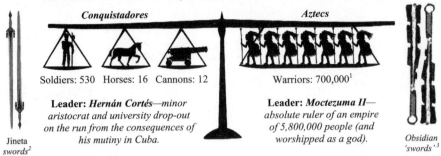

Conquistadores	*Aztecs*
Soldiers: 530 Horses: 16 Cannons: 12	Warriors: 700,000[1]

Leader: *Hernán Cortés*—minor aristocrat and university drop-out on the run from the consequences of his mutiny in Cuba.

Leader: *Moctezuma II*— absolute ruler of an empire of 5,800,000 people (and worshipped as a god).

Jineta swords[2]

Obsidian 'swords'[3]

[1] *Estimated maximum Aztec forces.* [2] *Spanish swords, such as the* jineta, *were made from tempered steel. The best came from Toledo, which possessed probably the finest weapon-smiths of the era outside Japan.* [3] *Lacking iron, the Aztecs used* macuahuitl *('hungry wood') staves set with shards of obsidian glass; though clumsy looking, they were razor sharp.*

AGAINST ALL ODDS. Within two and a half years of first setting eyes on Mexico, Hernán Cortés toppled the Aztec Empire and captured its capital, Tenochtitlan—a city larger than any in Europe apart from Constantinople. For Spain, it ushered in the Golden Century that saw the country at the head of the first empire on which the sun never set; for 80% of Mexico's people, it meant death from disease, massacre or maltreatment.

SOLAR POWER. If you think the sun is fuelled by human blood,[4] procuring enough victims to keep it burning soon becomes a pressing concern. Faced with such a problem, the Aztecs agreed with neighbouring states to fight the semi-continuous Flower Wars, where the object was to capture enemy soldiers for later sacrifice rather than kill outright. To this end, fighters would aim not for head or chest but for their opponents' legs—to sever their hamstrings so that they could be picked up by the roping crews that worked to the rear. The Spanish tactic of actually trying to slaughter people in battle thus caused initial bafflement (and may temporarily have helped even the long odds the Spaniards faced). Soon enough, however, the Aztecs learned to respond in kind.[5]

[4] *Before relations ruptured, the Aztecs gave the Spanish a feast of welcome in which the food was served splattered with human blood; the assumption being that if the Spaniards were gods this would best sate their hunger. (The Spanish were sick.)* [5] *With exceptions: at one point, the Aztecs took 70 Spanish prisoners and later pulled out their hearts in front of their comrades as sacrifices.*

LA COCINA MEXICANA—ORIGINS AND MEANINGS

- **Burrito** (*c.* 1910)... 'little donkey': invented by street-vendor Juan Mendez, who carried them by donkey.
- **Nacho** (*c.* 1943) .... created by waiter Ignacio Anaya, 'Nacho' to his friends, when facing an empty kitchen.
- **Taco** (Aztec) ...'wadding': as in plugging the hole in your stomach (tacos were first filled with minnows).
- **Tortilla** (10,000 BCE) ....'little cake': in Spain, it means 'omelette' and early Spanish settlers made the analogy.

MUMMY'S BABY, DADDY'S MAYBE

'Non-paternity events' occur when DNA tests show the identity of biological father is not that told to child. Frequent causes are infidelity (by the mother) and hidden adoptions. Less common are some forms of fertility treatment and neonatal hospital mix-ups. Whatever the cause, Mexico leads the field:

Population	NPE Rate
Mexico (1999)	12%
Amazon Indians[7] (1975)	9%
UK (1957)	4%
France (1992)	3%
UK (1999)	2%
USA (Hawaii, 1980)	2%
Switzerland (1994)	1%
Global (estimated)	4%

[7] *Yanomamo.*

MARGARITA. Chill glass, rub rim with lime slice and coat with salt crust. Shake 35 ml Tequila, 20 ml Cointreau and 15 ml fresh lime juice together with ice. Strain into glass and add lime segment garnish.

IT CAME FROM OUTER SPACE ... THE DAY THE EARTH NEARLY DIED

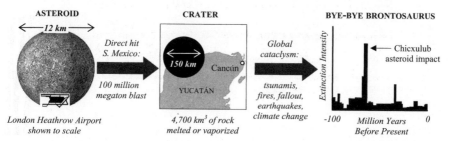

ASTEROID

← 12 km →

Direct hit S. Mexico:

100 million megaton blast

London Heathrow Airport shown to scale

CRATER

150 km   Cancún ○

YUCATÁN

4,700 km³ of rock melted or vaporized

Global cataclysm:

tsunamis, fires, fallout, earthquakes, climate change

BYE-BYE BRONTOSAURUS

← Chicxulub asteroid impact

Extinction Intensity

-100   *Million Years Before Present*   0

LUCKY BREAK. Faster than a speeding bullet,[1] more powerful than a locomotive,[2] a long time ago[3]—but not far, far away, three trillion tonnes of space rock smashed head-on into what would later be Chicxulub ('Flea Devil'), an otherwise unexceptional Mayan village in Mexico's Yucatán. After the dust had settled (which took several years), the world had been transformed. For the next decade or so, fungi dominated the land, followed by ferns. Later, insects, mammals and amphibians all bounced back, but anything too big to hide in a hole had no chance to survive: the dinosaurs—except for the birds—were gone.[4] Oddly though, the Chicxulub impact may still count as a narrow escape. Follow-up studies have suggested that the Chicxulub asteroid was just a small splinter of a 170-km-diameter parent that broke up in a space collision 100 million years earlier. Other, potentially larger, fragments spattered Mars, Venus and the Moon, and if one of those had hit the Earth, it really could have been life's big goodbye. As it was, the scale of the carnage is still hard to grasp—see the calculated effects of the impact if today and on London (*below*).

[1] *At 20 km/s, more than 20 times faster than a round fired from a M16 assault rifle.* [2] *Incomparably so: proportionately, the explosive yield of the Chicxulub asteroid exceeded that of the Hiroshima atom bomb by as much as the latter exceeded a fire cracker.* [3] *About 65,000,000 years.* [4] *Explaining the extinction of the dinosaurs has generated a great deal of controversy. However, in March 2010, an exhaustive multidisciplinary review concluded that Chicxulub was indeed the cause.*

MEXIBABBLE. Mexico has more languages than Europe.

CHICXULUB IMPACT—IF IT HAD HIT LONDON ...	
Location	*Damage*
London	Gone: hole bored 30 km deep into ground
Brussels (*250 km*)	Fireball limit: everything to here incinerated
Moscow (*2,400 km*)	Falling debris coats city in layer 10 cm thick
Baghdad (*4,000 km*)	Blast wave flattens all wooden buildings

HEAVY WATER. The Gulf of Mexico has many underwater lakes dotted across its bed. The lakes can be up to 12 miles long, have their own waves and shorelines, and hold hypersaline brine that is too dense to mix with normal seawater. Submarines can't penetrate and bounce off their surfaces.

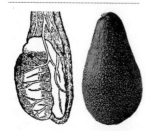

FORBIDDEN FRUIT. The word 'avocado' comes from the fruit's Nahuatl name, *ahuakatl*—which literally means 'testicle'. Native to Mexico, the fruit was highly esteemed among the Aztecs as a sex stimulant as much as a food staple. Because of this, many Catholic priests forbade their congregations from partaking when it was brought back to Europe, and even in more modern times, avocados had to be procured nefariously to avoid heinous damage to a gentleman's—or, worse, lady's—reputation.

FRENCH STICK. After Monsieur Remontel's Mexico City pâtisserie was damaged by drunken soldiers, the French embassy submitted his colossal compensation request of 600,000 peso ($45m today). When this claim was ignored, France acted and launched the 1838 'Pastry War'. A fleet was despatched, Mexico's navy captured, the whole country blockaded, and its main port, Veracruz, stormed. Shortly after, Mexico paid up in full.

MEXICO

* 9% of Mexicans live in USA
* 500,000 illegal crossings yearly
* 500 migrants die crossing per year
* 87% of all illegal guns are smuggled from USA

MEXICO–USA: WORLD'S BUSIEST BORDER
(350 million legal crossings per year)

Tijuana–San Ysidro: World's Busiest Crossing Point
(17 million vehicles and 50 million pedestrians each year)

USA

* 0.3% of Americans live in Mexico
* 20,000 border guards deployed
* 25 incursions by Mexican soldiers and police yearly
* 90% of illegal drugs are smuggled from Mexico

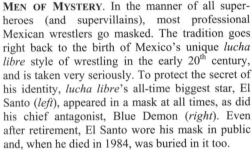

MEN OF MYSTERY. In the manner of all super-heroes (and supervillains), most professional Mexican wrestlers go masked. The tradition goes right back to the birth of Mexico's unique *lucha libre* style of wrestling in the early 20th century, and is taken very seriously. To protect the secret of his identity, *lucha libre*'s all-time biggest star, El Santo (*left*), appeared in a mask at all times, as did his chief antagonist, Blue Demon (*right*). Even after retirement, El Santo wore his mask in public and, when he died in 1984, was buried in it too.

El Santo

Blue Demon

LA OLA. Adapting techniques developed to study heart attacks and forest fires, scientists have found that a typical Mexican wave travels at 20 seats a second, is 15 seats wide and needs 30 fans working together to get launched. American spectators started doing 'The Wave' (as it is known in the US) in 1981, but it took the 1986 Mexican World Cup for the mass gesture to go global—thus giving it its worldwide name. The wave's chief nemesis is the VIP box.

REINVENTING THE WHEEL. When Europeans reached Mexico, it seemed none of the civilisations had invented the wheel. Later, it was found that this wasn't true. Wheels had been known since 500 CE, but were used only for pull-along toys. The failure to use the device more is baffling. An absence of draught animals is often cited—but wheelbarrows and hand-carts are man-powered.

> '¡Viva México! ¡Viva México! ¡Viva México!'
> —Miguel Hidalgo (1810)
>
> *The battle cry of the Mexican War of Independence is repeated on 15 September each year by the serving Mexican president in front of up to half a million Mexicans.*

FOR THE HIGH JUMP. Acne kills more Mexicans than any other nationality. For non-teenagers, however, a greater concern might be the prospect of death by being pushed from a high place, which is 600% more likely than in any other country.

♦ · **GSR**: 8 · **WHS**: Calakmul (ruined Mayan city) □ Camino Real (colonial trade route) □ Campeche (colonial townscape) □ Chichen-Itza (ruined Mayan city) □ El Tajin (pyramids) □ El Vizcaino (whales) Guadalajara (building) □ Guanajuato (historic town) □ Gulf of California Islands □ Mexico City (x3) & Xochimilco (historic city & lake village/Barragán studio/university) □ Monarch Butterfly Reserve Morelia (colonial townscape) □ Oaxaca & Monte Alban (colonial townscape, Zapotec ruins) □ Palenque (Mayan ruins) □ Paquimé (adobe ruins) □ Popocatepetl (monasteries) □ Puebla (townscape) Querétaro (townscape) □ San Miguel (church, townscape) □ Sian Ka'an (mangroves) □ Sierra de San Francisco (rock art) □ Sierra Gorda of Querétaro (missions) □ Teotihuacan (ruins and pyramids) Tequila (distilleries) □ Tlacotalpan (colonial townscape) □ Uxmal (Mayan ruins) □ Xochicalco (pre-Columbian ruins) □ Yagul and Mitla Caves (prehistoric remains) □ Zacatecas (historic town) **ICH**: Day of the Dead (festivities) □ Mexican Cooking □ Otomí-Chichimecas Traditions (cultural landscape) Parachicos (dance) □ Pirekua (song) □ Voladores (flying ceremony)

———————— MOLDOVA ————————

*'Moldova's role is that of a country
so obscure it can safely be ridiculed.'*
—*Economist* (2007)

SOURCE OF
THE DANUBE

BLACK
SEA

BLUE DANUBE—River, waltz ... and atom bomb. Britain's first nuclear weapons, deployed in 1953, were officially referred to as Blue Danubes. (The civil servant who dreamt the name up was apparently confident his wheeze would succeed in throwing the Russians off the scent.) Blue Danubes were later replaced in turn by Red Beards, Green Grasses, Yellow Suns, Red Snows and, finally, the disappointingly pedestrian WE 177s (scrapped in 1998). The river—as opposed to the bomb—is distinguished by being the world's most international, beating the Nile's nine countries by one—thanks to Moldova's modest but game-winning 1,600 ft of left-bank frontage.

ULM

D

REGENSBURG

UNCLE JOE'S FABLES. There isn't really any country by the name of Moldova—or rather there was, but it merged with sundry other Balkan bits and pieces 150 years ago. The state now bearing the title is a sliver of land that Stalin grabbed from Romania after WWII and then retro-rebranded. Europe's poorest people (20% living off $2 a day), many, if not most, Moldovans are anxious to ditch Stalin's make-believe and amalgamate once more with their fellow Romanians.

UA

MD

RO

GALAȚI

A

Organ Gun, as drawn by Leonardo da Vinci

STEPHEN'S ORGAN. Moldova's national hero is Stephen the Great, a one-time ally of Dracula. In his wars against the Turks, Stephen was noted for his enthusiastic use of the 'organ gun'—a cumbersome medieval multiple-rocket-launcher-cum-machine-gun.

VIENNA

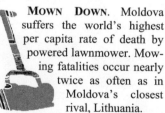

MOWN DOWN. Moldova suffers the world's highest per capita rate of death by powered lawnmower. Mowing fatalities occur nearly twice as often as in Moldova's closest rival, Lithuania.

SK

BRATISLAVA

H

SK

*'For connoisseurs of truly dismal
Soviet-style rudeness, apathy,
squalor and clashing shades of
muddy pastel, it is unmissable.'*

—E. Lucas on the Hotel Friendship, Tiraspol,
Transnistria (*Economist* online)

GUNSHOP. Moldova's pro-Russian breakaway statelet of Transnistria describes itself as 'nearly twice the size of Luxembourg with almost the population of Guyana'. 'The black hole of Europe' is the name most outsiders use. Their concern is arms-smuggling: for all its obscurity, Transnistria sits on 22,000 tons of weaponry (possibly Europe's largest arms dump) and its president, Igor Smirnov, is said to be the godfather of Transnistria's organized crime. Items that have gone 'missing' include 70 SAM missiles and 38 dirty-bomb rocket warheads.

RUSE

BG

Key (International Vehicle Registration Codes): A Austria, BG Bulgaria, D Germany, H Hungary, HR Croatia, MD Moldova, RO Romania, SK Slovakia, SRB Serbia, UA Ukraine.

BUDAPEST

H

SRB

Iron Gates

RO

HR

SRB

BELGRADE

♠ · **GSR** 136 · **Territorial Note**: Transnistria claims independence · **WHS**: Struve Arc (survey line)

——————— MONACO • MÚNEGU ———————

'In Monte Carlo, and especially among tax exiles, one does not choose friends.
It's a bit like being in prison. You talk to the people you're thrown in with.'

—'Taki' (1980)

GILDED CAGE. Only one person in five in Monaco is actually Monegasque. The remaining 80% of the principality's residents are a motley mix of tax exiles and superrich drawn chiefly from France, Italy and Britain (and referred to as 'Monacans').

POLICE STATE. Monaco is the most heavily policed country on Earth, with a police headcount of 517 (one for every 59 inhabitants). However, in case that isn't enough, Monaco arms its 130 firemen too. Not surprisingly, crime rates are low.

 A RIGHT ROYAL LEMON. Whereas American colonialists reached breaking point over tea, for the 19th-century Monegasque it was lemons. When, in 1848, Prince Florestan I tried to tax the lemon crop, the people exploded and 95% of the national territory seceded, leaving just the current 2-km^2 rump.

HOLLYWOOD ROMANCE. When American screen goddess Grace Kelly married Monaco's ruling Prince Ranier in 1956, it was dubbed 'the wedding of the century'. But her parents had still had to stump up a $2,000,000 dowry before Grace and her 80 trunks of baggage were able to cross the Atlantic to the homeland of her true love.[1] Nine months later, the birth of the couple's first daughter, Caroline, was celebrated with a 21-gun fusillade and free champagne in the streets. But when Albert, their only son (and the current ruler), was born a year later, 101 guns were fired—since, by treaty, the country would have reverted to France without a male heir. Following her marriage, all of Grace Kelly's films were banned in Monaco and she never acted again up to her 1982 death at the wheel of her car.

[1] *Even at their first meeting, Prince Ranier was thinking of Kelly as a candidate wife, and, to woo her, deployed the unusual strategy of thrusting his hand into his pet panther's cage—apparently in the belief that she would be impressed.*

WHEN THE CHIPS ARE DOWN

MONTE CARLO CASINO TABLE GAMES: BACCARAT (PUNTO BANCO & CHEMIN DE FER) • BLACKJACK • CRAPS • ROULETTE

If you flip three straight heads, and then ask someone watching to call the next toss, many will be tempted to say 'tails'. But the odds remain, as ever, 50:50. Known as the Monte Carlo fallacy, the idea that past outcomes can somehow influence a future random event is one of the most elementary errors a gambler can make.

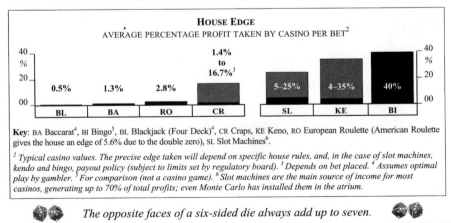

HOUSE EDGE
AVERAGE PERCENTAGE PROFIT TAKEN BY CASINO PER BET[2]

BL	BA	RO	CR	SL	KE	BI
0.5%	1.3%	2.8%	1.4% to 16.7%[3]	5–25%	4–35%	40%

Key: BA Baccarat[4], BI Bingo[5], BL Blackjack (Four Deck)[4], CR Craps, KE Keno, RO European Roulette (American Roulette gives the house an edge of 5.6% due to the double zero), SL Slot Machines[6].

[2] *Typical casino values. The precise edge taken will depend on specific house rules, and, in the case of slot machines, kendo and bingo, payout policy (subject to limits set by regulatory board).* [3] *Depends on bet placed.* [4] *Assumes optimal play by gambler.* [5] *For comparison (not a casino game).* [6] *Slot machines are the main source of income for most casinos, generating up to 70% of total profits; even Monte Carlo has installed them in the atrium.*

The opposite faces of a six-sided die always add up to seven.

♠ · GSR: 90 · WHS: none

MONGOLIA • МОНГОЛ УЛС[1]

'May your moustache grow like brushwood!'

—Mongolian exclamation after a sneeze

TAMING THE LION. Fought without weight or age restrictions, wrestling is Mongolia's favourite sport.[2] Victories earn wrestlers the titles falcon, elephant, lion and, ultimately, titan.

[2] *Scissors, Paper, Stone is probably more popular nationwide but is not officially deemed a sport.*

[1] *The Cyrillic script imposed by Russia in 1941 is being replaced (slowly) by the historic Uighur script. The word 'Mongolia' is above.*

'The greatest joy for a man is to defeat his enemies, to take from them all they possess, and to hold their wives and daughters in his arms.'

—Genghis Khan

The Soyombo (above) is Mongolia's very popular national symbol. Its intricate symbolism includes references to unity, honesty and Mongolia enduring as long as its famously wide blue skies.

PATERNAL INSTINCT. His name might be a byword for terror, but the 13th-century Mongolian warlord Genghis Khan was also an astonishingly good father; or, more precisely, an exceptionally successful one. In fact, from an evolutionary perspective, he is probably the most successful human of recorded time. DNA tests show that, from Caspian to Pacific, he has 16 million male descendents alive today.[3] This compares with a statistical norm of 20 for his peers, making his genes 800,000 times more successful than average and him history's ultimate alpha male.

[3] *To be pedantic, the tests show that someone living in his part of Mongolia at his epoch was their common ancestor, but given his legendary sexual appetite and stamina, and unparalleled access to women, the scientists do not doubt it was he.*

STEPPE-ING OUT

NATIONAL POPULATION DENSITIES

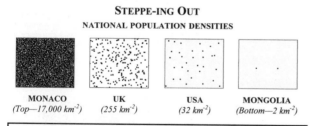

MONACO	UK	USA	MONGOLIA
(Top—17,000 km⁻²)	*(255 km⁻²)*	*(32 km⁻²)*	*(Bottom—2 km⁻²)*

SOULLESS. Stalin stole Genghis Khan's soul—or, at any rate, his agents may have done. In 1937, they ransacked and torched the Shankh monastery, a remote bastion of Buddhism where a thousand Yellow Hat monks had kept watch for 400 years over Genghis Khan's spirit banner. Made from the hairs of his favourite black stallions tied around the shaft of a spear, the spirit banner had been Genghis Khan's totem in life and, in accordance with Mongol custom, had afterwards given a home to his soul. Some say the banner was smuggled away before the atheists arrived, but its whereabouts—if it still exists—are now unknown.

AMERICAN INVASION. The Bactrian camel was once an American animal, but, at some point, a herd migrated over the land bridge to Asia and got marooned when the Bering Strait flooded after the last Ice Age. This was just as well, since America's herds died out 8,000 years ago. Around 1,000 wild camels still survive in Mongolia's Gobi Desert, shared with China.

MR. OCEAN. When Mongolia's 16th-century ruler Altan Khan wished to convert to Buddhism, he invited Tibet's supreme monk, Sonam Gyatso, to visit him. On Gyatso's arrival, Altan mistook his name for a title, and greeted him with the Mongolian translation—*Dalai Lama* ('Ocean of Wisdom'). The phrase has stuck ever since.

WORLD DOMINATION—BEST EFFORTS TO DATE

*'With Heaven's aid, I have conquered a huge empire.
But my life was too short to achieve the conquest of the world.'*

—Genghis Khan

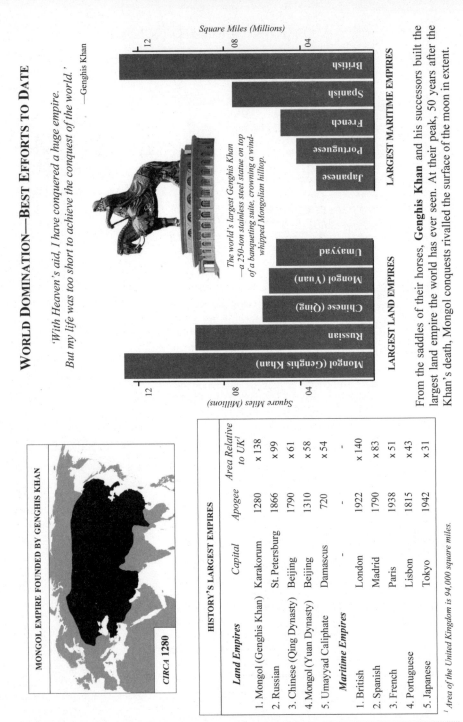

Square Miles (Millions)

LARGEST MARITIME EMPIRES

British · Spanish · French · Portuguese · Japanese

The world's largest Genghis Khan
—a 250-ton stainless steel statue on top
of a banqueting suite, crowning a wind-
whipped Mongolian hilltop.

LARGEST LAND EMPIRES

Umayyad · Mongol (Yuan) · Chinese (Qing) · Russian · Mongol (Genghis Khan)

Square Miles (Millions)

From the saddles of their horses, **Genghis Khan** and his successors built the largest land empire the world has ever seen. At their peak, 50 years after the Khan's death, Mongol conquests rivalled the surface of the moon in extent.

MONGOL EMPIRE FOUNDED BY GENGHIS KHAN

CIRCA **1280**

HISTORY'S LARGEST EMPIRES

Land Empires	Capital	Apogee	Area Relative to UK[1]
1. Mongol (Genghis Khan)	Karakorum	1280	x 138
2. Russian	St. Petersburg	1866	x 99
3. Chinese (Qing Dynasty)	Beijing	1790	x 61
4. Mongol (Yuan Dynasty)	Beijing	1310	x 58
5. Umayyad Caliphate	Damascus	720	x 54
Maritime Empires	–	–	–
1. British	London	1922	x 140
2. Spanish	Madrid	1790	x 83
3. French	Paris	1938	x 51
4. Portuguese	Lisbon	1815	x 43
5. Japanese	Tokyo	1942	x 31

[1] *Area of the United Kingdom is 94,000 square miles.*

♣ · **GSR**: 132 · **WHS**: Altai (petroglyphs) □ Karakorum-Orkhon Valley (ruins) □ Uvs Nuur (salt lake) **ICH**: Biyelgee (dance) □ Falconry □ Khöömei (throat singing) □ Morin Khuur (fiddle music) Naadam (festival) □ Tsuur (pipe music) □ Tuuli (oral epic) □ Urtiin Duu (song)

———— MONTENEGRO • CRNA GORA ————

'At the moment of the creation of our planet, the most beautiful merging of land and sea took place at the Montenegrin coast.'

—Lord George Byron

Orthodox icon of the Virgin Mary. The use of characteristically two-dimensional iconic imagery in Orthodox worship first arose as a reaction against the classical Greek tradition of statuary—seen as glorifying the aesthetics of the human form at the expense of the divine spirit. Having Roman not Greek roots, the Western Catholic church grew up unencumbered by such concerns, and instead developed a strong tradition of religious sculpture, which has often served as a corresponding focus for devotional veneration.

Serb traditional costume. Although ethnically Serb, Montenegro became the final ex-Yugoslav republic to declare its independence, when, in May 2006, a national referendum on secession cleared the EU-designated threshold of 55% by just 2,300 votes—leaving Serbia on its own as the sole Yugoslav successor state.

DIVINE GUIDANCE. Montenegro has historically been a bastion of the Orthodox Church, and, in 1516, provided a unique example of a European monarchy choosing to convert to a full-blown theocracy when Prince Đurađ V Crnojević handed over all power to Montenegro's Orthodox bishop and retired to Venice (thus preserving the country's autonomy in the face of Ottoman expansion). Dynasties of hereditary prince-bishops[1] then ruled until 1852, when the ruling house decided to focus definitively on the 'prince' at the expense of the 'bishop'.

[1] *Since Orthodox bishops were bound to celibacy, dynastic succession rather unusually passed from uncle to nephew.*

NOTHING TO BE SNEEZED AT. While Montenegro's coast has been lauded for centuries as one of the world's most beautiful, the Adriatic waters just offshore have recently emerged as a global hotspot for sea-snot formation. Believed to be created by the coagulation of marine snow (the biological detritus that constantly falls through the water column), blobs of sea snot have appeared over the last 20 years at an exponentially increasing rate. Deeply unwelcome (and very smelly), sea snot is a nuisance to fishermen and is causing rising concern as a health hazard— harbouring viruses and bacteria such as *E. coli*.

Sea snot blob to scale

BOMBS AWAY. Despite a population of under one million, Montenegro is a world force in water polo—maintaining a first-class professional domestic league and winning the European Championships in 2008 and World League in 2009. Although now something of a Balkan speciality, the sport was originally a late-19th-century British invention,[2] initially known as 'water rugby' and played in Britain's rivers and canals. In this incarnation, unlike in the modern sport, brute strength was king (not to mention a healthy disregard for personal mortality). Wrestling and holding one's opponents under water were both encouraged, while goalkeepers stood on the bank and attempted to launch themselves through the air so as to land on top of any member of the opposite side trying to score.

[2] *Under British influence, water polo was one of the original team games in the Olympic programme (alongside cricket, rugby, football, polo, rowing and the tug of war). Britain then won gold in the first four Olympics in which it took part.*

♠ · **GSR**: 102 · **WHS:** Durmitor (mountains and canyons) □ Kotor (historic region)

—————— MOROCCO ● المغرب ——————

'Little by little, the camel goes into the couscous.'

—Moroccan proverb

ROOTS. Morocco is known in Arabic simply as 'The West' (*al-Magrib*). In Turkish, it bears the title 'Fas',

ⵍⵎⵖⵔⵉⴱ

The Berber 'Moor Akush' ('Land of God')—origin of the word 'Morocco'

after the city of Fez. In contrast, the English name 'Morocco' honours a different city, coming from 'Marrakesh' (via Latin and Portuguese). Tracing the origin of the word back even further, 'Marrakesh' (and so also 'Morocco') is derived from 'Moor Akush', which means 'Land of God' in Berber. The word 'Berber' itself comes from the same Greek source as 'barbarian' (as is plain in the region's old label—'Barbary Coast'), which at first was just a neutral word for 'foreigner'.

El Peñón de Vélez de la Gomera— one of a handful of rocks and islands (as well as the towns of Ceuta and Melilla) that Spain retains along Morocco's northern coast, despite the latter's protests. Vélez de la Gomera is notable for having the world's shortest international border (just 12 metres).

OLD SKOOL. Al Karaouine in Fez is the world's oldest university. Founded in 859 CE, its library holds Malik ibn Anas's *Muwatta*, one of the earliest source texts of Islamic law.

WORLD'S OLDEST UNIVERSITIES	WORLD'S TOP-RANKED UNIVERSITIES
1.. *Al Karaouine* (Fez, Morocco) 859	1 .... *Cambridge* (UK) 100%
2 .... *Al-Azhar* (Cairo, Egypt) 972	2..*Harvard* (Cambridge, USA) 99.2%
3 .... *Bologna* (Italy) 1088	3 ..... *Yale* (New Haven, USA) 98.7%
4 .... *Oxford* (UK) 1096	4 .... *UCL* (London, UK) 98.5%
5 .... *Salamanca* (Spain) 1134	5 .... *MIT* (Cambridge, USA) 98.2%
6 .... *Modena* (Italy) 1175	6 .... *Oxford* (UK) 98.2%
7 .... *Vicenza* (Italy) 1204	7 .... *Imperial* (London, UK) 97.8%
8 .... *Cambridge* (UK) 1209	8 .... *Chicago* (USA) 97.5%
9 .... *Padua* (Italy) 1222	9 .... *Caltech* (Pasadena, USA) 96.5%
10 .... *Naples* (Italy) 1224	10 .... *Princeton* (USA) 96.0%

QS World University Rankings (2010)

'Never cover any road a second time.'

—Ibn Battuta

KING OF THE ROAD. History's greatest traveller has to be the medieval Moroccan judge ibn Battuta, who notched up 75,000 miles at a time when most people never ventured further than 20. Along the way, he was outraged at Malian women's (lack of) costume, married six wives in the Maldives (divorcing all before leaving) and moaned about the Chinese taste for frogs.

POLO V. BATTUTA
(No contest)

20 countries[1]
24 years

44 countries[1]
29 years

15,000 miles

75,000 miles

Marco Polo

Ibn Battuta

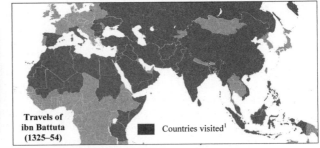

Travels of ibn Battuta (1325–54)

Countries visited[1]

[1] *Based on the national boundaries in effect in 2011.*

ROCK AND ROLL. Visible from space, the world's longest conveyor belt carries phosphorite rock (for fertilizer) 62 miles from the Bu Craa mines in Western Sahara to the sea.

♥ · **GSR**: 77 · **Disputed Territory**: Morocco occupies most of Western Sahara · **WHS**: Ait-Ben-Haddou (walled village) □ Essaouira (townscape) □ Fez (historic city) □ Marrakesh (historic city) Mazagan (fort) □ Meknes (historic city) □ Tétouan (townscape) □ Volubilis (ruined city) · **ICH**: Falconry □ Jemaa el-Fna (street life) □ Mediterranean Cooking □ Moussem of Tan-Tan (nomad gathering)

———— MOZAMBIQUE ● MOÇAMBIQUE ————

'The rich man's dog gets more vaccination and medical care than do the workers upon whom the rich man's wealth is built.'

—President Samora Machel, FRELIMO leader and first president of Mozambique

Although Mozambique is now a moderate and democratic state, in a nod to its 25 years of struggle for independence and civil war it retains the original revolutionary crossed hoe and AK-47 on its emblem and flag. It is one of only two countries to put a gun on its flag (the other being Guatemala, which has a pair of Remington rifles).

SPECIAL NEEDS. Only half of Mozambique's teachers have any qualifications, while, in 2006, only 2% of girls finished primary school (up from 1% in 2002).

PIPED MUSIC. With supplies now limited to Mozambique and Tanzania, African Blackwood has become the world's most expensive timber (fetching $24,000 per cubic metre). It's best known as the only wood suitable for bagpipe chanters,[2] but its superb tonal resonance finds it used for top-quality clarinets and oboes too.

[2] *In the 1970s, Idi Amin banned African Blackwood exports from Uganda in an effort to develop a Ugandan bagpipe industry.*

TAP TAP TAP. When firing guns, regular soldiers and police the world over are trained to aim at their opponent's 'centre of mass' (i.e. chest). But when it comes to close-quarters combat, this simply isn't good enough.[3] Instead, special forces, assassins, elite bodyguards and the like—all those who need their man down *now*—practise something called the 'Mozambique Drill'. Developed from an instinctive response by mercenary Mike Rouseau, when he rounded a corner at Lourenço Marques[4] Airport and found himself 10 paces from a FRELIMO guerrilla with AK-47, it is now regarded worldwide as the fastest and most reliable way of killing someone instantly using a handgun.[5]

[3] *According to the FBI, the brain holds sufficient oxygen to maintain full, voluntary control of the body for 10–15 seconds after the heart has been destroyed—and a fanatical, psychotic or drug-fuelled opponent will use this time to continue to fight.* [4] *Now Maputo, the capital of Mozambique.* [5] *For those that need to know, the Mozambique consists of two fast rounds fired at the chest followed by a focused head shot aiming for an area of the brainstem known as the* medulla oblongata *(referred to in the trade as the 'apricot').*

'Never marry a woman with bigger feet than your own.'

—Sena proverb

BULLSEYE. The Mozambique Spitting Cobra is considered Africa's second most dangerous snake (after the mamba). Nervous and easily spooked, the cobras deliberately aim for the eyes when spitting,[1] causing agonizing burns to the cornea and often permanent blindness. In order to project the venom effectively, the snake's fangs have evolved small nozzles through which it is squirted with the speed and range of a powerful water pistol.

[1] *Mozambique cobras achieved a 100% hit rate up to 8 ft away when tested in captivity. For this reason, zookeepers must always wear masks or goggles.*

NUTTY. Mozambique's chief cash crop is the cashew nut, harvesting 100,000 tonnes a year. On the tree, the cashew 'fruit' has a bizarre appearance, with the seed (i.e. cashew 'nut') found in the green boxing-glove shaped 'drupe' that protrudes below the much larger yellow 'cashew apple' (a false fruit).

♥ · **GSR**: 128 · **WHS**: Mozambique Island (town) · **ICH**: Gule Wamkulu (cult) □ Timbila (xylophones)

NAMIBIA

'There is no bird that never gets ripe fruit on its lips.'

—OshiWambo proverb ('All things come to those who wait'). In 1990,
Namibia became the last African country to be formally decolonized.

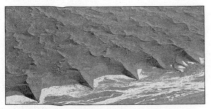

Sand dunes in the Namib desert viewed from space

SANDS OF TIME. Created more than 55 million years ago, the Namib (literally 'vast place') is the oldest desert in the world. It also features the Earth's tallest sand dunes, rising to 1,000 feet in places. Due to their age, the dunes have turned a vivid orange colour as the iron in the sand has reacted with atmospheric oxygen. In other words, they've gone rusty.

SONG OF THE DUNES
The Namib Desert's 'booming dunes' are one of around 40 locations worldwide where the sand dunes sometimes begin to growl, giving off a low droning sound (a bit like a distant light aircraft in flight). The noise can get very loud—comparable to the music level at a night club—and, though usually started by sand slumping from the dune crest, can persist for minutes. Scientists are still not able to fully explain the cause, but it's thought the movement of the sand grains somehow becomes synchronized, causing the dunes to emit a strong and coherent acoustic signal—which would make the dunes, in some ways, natural sonic analogues of lasers.

SPOT THE SPRINTER. Namibia has the world's greatest number of cheetahs, by far the world's fastest animal. Although a top speed of 71 mph helps it a lot, what the cheetah really relies on is a fearsome acceleration of 0–60 mph in 3 seconds (outpacing a Ferrari) and an ability to turn in midair, using its tail as a rudder. However, because a cheetah's muscles produce so much heat, if it sprinted for more than a minute or so its body temperature would spiral irreversibly and fatally out of control.

SNOWBALL EARTH. In 1998, geologists examining an exotic type of rock in Namibia known as banded iron found the first strong evidence suggesting that around 710 million years ago,

The Jovian moon Europa may give a glimpse of how the 'Snowball Earth' looked.

and again around 635 million years ago, the whole of the Earth froze over. Eventually, it is believed, volcanoes pumped enough greenhouse gases into the atmosphere to trigger thaws, but for millions of years life must have clung on by its fingertips (or more likely flagella)—surviving in cracks under the ice or possibly in a narrow band of slush at the Equator. Picking up the story, some biologists have argued that the extreme evolutionary stress of the later event triggered the appearance of the first multi-celled organisms (which enter the fossil record at about the same time). The move from single-celled organisms—like bacteria—to multi-celled ones—like polecats—has always been hard to explain since coming together as a single entity requires almost all of the cells involved to abandon any chance of passing on their genes. However, in very small populations, the proportion of genes shared by member organisms soars (i.e. they are likely to be closely related). This makes the altruistic sacrifice required to help another organism reproduce much more attractive, and so the big freeze may have been just what the doctor ordered to get the world of animals and plants kick-started.

FOUR-WAY SPLIT. The world's only international quadripoint may exist in the Zambezi river, where Namibia, Botswana, Zambia and Zimbabwe all touch—perhaps.[1]

[1] *This might seem the ultimate in geographical trivia. But the South Africans, while they were still running Namibia, cared enough about the point (in both senses) to start shooting at people. In any event, to this day, nobody is sure whether all four borders meet exactly, or just get very close.*

♥ · **GSR** 97 · **WHS**: Twyfelfontein (petroglyphs)

NEPAL ● नेपाल

*'Do not dwell in the past, do not dream of the future,
concentrate on the present moment.'*

—Gautama Buddha, born in Lumbini, Nepal, *c.* 563 BCE.
(Nepal is nonetheless a predominantly Hindu country today.)

YUCK. Strictly speaking, yaks are all male. The proper term for a female is 'nak'. Yak or nak, Nepalese use the animals' milk, meat, wool, dung (for fuel) and even sweat (as a folk medicine).

KING AND COUNTRY. Nepal is the only country with a non-rectangular flag. Its twin triangles now denote Himalayan peaks but come historically from a fusion of the royal and prime ministerial pennants, one flown above the other.

ODD NUMBER. When the British first surveyed Mt. Everest in 1856, after Herculean efforts they determined it to be 29,000 ft—precisely. But the mapmakers were worried the public would think this just a rounded estimate, so they added two spurious feet to produce a published figure of 29,002 ft instead.[1]

[1] *The true value is 29,029 ft; not bad given the British couldn't enter Nepal, so had to work from 100 miles away.*

'You don't have to be a fantastic hero. You can be just an ordinary chap, sufficiently motivated.'

—Sir Edmund Hillary, on being the first, with Tenzing Norgay, to climb Mt. Everest (in 1953)

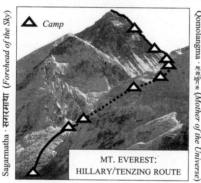

△ Camp

Sagarmatha · सगरमाथा *(Forehead of the Sky)*

Qomolangma · ཇོ་མོ་གླང་མ *(Mother of the Universe)*

MT. EVEREST:
HILLARY/TENZING ROUTE

WORD OF WARNING. Climbing Mt. Everest has historically been more dangerous than committing suicide.[2] But, with guiding and equipment improvements, it's now merely as risky as a drugs overdose.[3] As a result, climbers on their way to the top today must pass over 150 frozen corpses, which are too cumbersome to move.

[2] *The fatality rate to 1990 was 32%, against 9% for attempting suicide (in the USA).* [3] *A 4% fatality risk versus 1.8%.*

LOVE THINE ENEMY. When the Nepali kingdom of Gorkha fought Britain to a stalemate in the 1815–16 Anglo-Nepalese War, British officers were so impressed they negotiated the right to recruit their own 'Gurkha' volunteers as part of the peace treaty. The Nepalese have been a fixture of the British Army ever since and, as encapsulated in their battle cry (*below*), their exceptional loyalty, bravery and fortitude have been demonstrated beyond doubt through many campaigns.

THE QUEEN'S TRUNCHEON. In place of regimental colours, Gurkhas in the British Army parade the Queen's Truncheon—a 6-foot-tall silver staff topped with three Gurkhas supporting Queen Victoria's crown.

ONCE MORE UNTO THE BREACH—WAR CRIES OF THE WORLD

Duchy of Bar: *Fire! Fire!* ● Britain (Parachute Regiment): *Wahoo Mohammed!* ● Canada: *Allegedly none, since it's considered impolite.* ● Crusader: *Heaven at Last!* ● Finland: *Shoot for their testicles!* Gurkha: *Victory to Goddess Mahakali, the Gurkhas are coming!* ('Huj, Huj, Hajrá!') ● Ireland (FitzGerald family): *I will burn!* ● Nazi Germany: *Hail Victory!* (*Sieg Heil!*) Scotland (Clan Cameron): *Sons of the hounds, come feed on flesh!* ● Sioux Nation (and Klingons): *Today is a good day to die!* ● Spain (Foreign Legion): *Long live death!* ● USA: *Hooah!*

♣ · **GSR**: 94 · **WHS**: Chitwan (rhinoceros and tigers) □ Kathmandu Valley (temples and monuments) Lumbini (Buddhist pilgrimage site) □ Sagarmatha (Mt. Everest region)

———— NETHERLANDS ● NEDERLAND ————

'From Sea, Spaniard and the Devil, Lord deliver me.' —Old Dutch prayer

NAME GAME. In the beginning, there was the province of **Batavia**—the land of the Batavi tribe; but after the Romans left, things got trickier. The **Netherlands** used to be synonymous with the **Low Countries**. But when Belgium split off, it came to apply only to the bit most call **Holland**—itself yet another way of saying low country (literally 'hole-land'). Technically, however, Holland is only a single region of the Netherlands, though the **Dutch**[1] themselves use both terms interchangeably.

[1] *And the word 'Dutch' used simply to refer to any speaker of a Germanic (*Deutsch*) language.*

BLOOM AND BUST. Pretty, but worth $800,000? In the 1630s, Holland was gripped by tulip mania. Prices spiralled until a single bulb could cost more than a townhouse at a prime Amsterdam address. The crash came in 1637, when prices plummeted 99% in a few weeks. Its cause was complex, but it seems to have been triggered by a new round of the Thirty Years War, which forced Germany's princes to dig up their tulip gardens to preserve them from rampaging peasants.

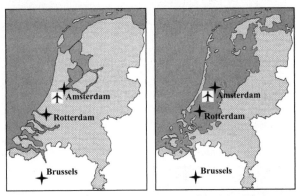

The Netherlands ...   ... if the dykes failed.

AND MAN MADE HOLLAND. Before the Dutch got involved, the territory of the Netherlands was a miserably marginal place of shifting estuaries and reeking fens. The earliest inhabitants built themselves high mounds (*terpen*) to retreat to when the going got choppy. But from around 1200 onward, the Dutch set to more boldly, using dykes to reclaim the sea bed and wind-pumps to drain it dry. Today, around 60% of Dutch people live below sea level: if the dykes were to give way, the results would be unthinkable.

'Very slight authority would persuade me there was a period when Holland was all water, and the ancestors of the Dutch fish. A certain oysterishness of eye, and flabbiness of complexion, are almost proofs sufficient of this aquatic descent.'

—W. Beckford, during the Fourth Anglo-Dutch War (1780–84)

LIQUID AIR. The Netherlands are the epicentre of European waterspout activity, with over a third of the continent's spouts appearing off the Dutch coast. Contrary to appearances, the water in a spout doesn't come from the sea (or lake), but is condensed out of humidity present in the atmosphere.

LONG AND SHORT OF IT. The Dutch are the world's tallest people. The average Dutch man stands 6 ft exactly, the average Dutch woman 5 ft 7 in. The corresponding heights for Indonesians—the shortest nationality reported—are 5 ft 2 in for men and 4 ft 10 in for women.

DUTCH WIT. *A bearded man is a woman provided for ~ He who has butter on his head should stay out of the sun ~ Every little bit helps said the mosquito pissing into the sea ~ Break my clog!*

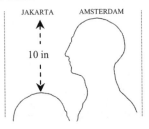

THREE DUTCH MASTERS

REMBRANDT. As someone who lived chronically beyond his means, Rembrandt was forced to sell his wife's grave in order to pay for the burial of his mistress.

VERMEER. The 17th-century painter's sublime mastery of detail may have been aided by use of a camera obscura, an optical device that projects a pin-sharp image on to a screen. The link is unproven, but Vermeer's choice of lens-maker and father of microscopy van Leeuwenhoek as his executor is highly suggestive.

VAN GOGH. The archetypal tortured artist: insane, insolvent and ignored. Despite painting 900 pictures during his lifetime, Van Gogh managed to sell just one.

'Apart from cheese and tulips, the main product of Holland is advocaat, a drink made from lawyers.'
—Alan Coren

WHY DO BABIES CRY?
This is not as simple as it might seem. Setting out the four basic questions to ask about any sort of animal behaviour helped win Dutch biologist Niko Tinbergen the 1973 Nobel Prize for physiology. His four questions—with answers for baby-crying—are:

- What causes it?
  Hunger/pain/loneliness
- How does it alter with age?
  Follows cognitive capacity
- Why has it evolved?
  Extends mother contact range
- What is its survival value?
  Elicits care, but costs energy

Combining Tinbergen's four questions with the hierarchy of life[1] gives a 'periodic table' by which to organize biological studies.

[1] *That is: molecule < cell < organ < individual < family < group < society.*

KIND TO KIDS
CHILD WELL-BEING IN RICH COUNTRIES[2]
1. Netherlands.............100%
2. Sweden.....................94%
3. Denmark..................79%
4. Finland....................76%
5. Spain.......................73%
20. USA..........................1%
21. UK.............................0%

[2] *UNICEF Innocenti Report (2007). Scores indexed with top (Neth.) = 100%; bottom (UK) = 0%.*

'By God, I think the Devil shits Dutchmen!'
—Reaction of the Surveyor of the English Navy on learning the size of the attacking Dutch fleet, as reported by Samuel Pepys (1667)

ALMOST ENGLISH. Frisians[3] from Friesland in the northern Netherlands speak Frisian—the closest living relation to English. When not nearly speaking English, Frisians can be found indulging in their traditional pastimes of *wadlopen* (hiking through mudflats in gum boots) or *fierljeppen* (vaulting their drainage ditches on wooden poles).

[3] *The people, that is, not the area's celebrated black and white cows .*

ENGLISH–FRISIAN LEXICON	
bite..........*bite*	salt...........*salt*
dust........*dust*	what.........*wat*
ear............*ear*	wife.........*wiif*
fruit........*fruit*	you......*jimme*
man ....*man*	leg........*skonk*

GULP. Dutch cooking is known for its honest lack of pretension:

- *Patatje oorlog*—'Chips at war': chips with curry, ketchup, mayonnaise and satay sauces (or a subset thereof), plus raw onions.

- *Paling broodjes*—bread rolls baked with a surprise inside (an eel).

- *Maatjesharing*—raw herrings. (To eat: grip by tail and lower the fish headfirst into your mouth.)

- *Snert*—pea and pig's foot gruel with sausage.

KING CARROT. Carrots were purple until 17th-century Dutch growers cultivated an exotic new orange variety as a horticultural tribute to their king—William of Orange.

♠ · **GSR:** 26 · **Associated Territories**: Aruba, Bonaire, Curaçao, Saba, Sint Eustatius, Sint Maarten
WHS: Amsterdam (x2) (townscape/amphibious fort network) □ Beemster Polder (historic landscape) Kinderdijk-Elshout (windmills) □ Rietveld Schröderhuis (architecture) □ Schokland (drowned island) Waddenzee (mudflats) □ Woudagemaal (pumping station) ■ Curaçao: Willemstad (townscape)

———— NEW ZEALAND ● AOTEAROA ————

'God's own country.'

—Thomas Bracken (1890)

Invercargill

'Invercargill—the Last Lamp-post in the World.'

—Rudyard Kipling

FRUITFUL. One of the Cold War's odder victims was the Chinese gooseberry. In the era of McCarthy, it was a brave American housewife who bought a fruit so redolent of the Yellow Peril—even if it had been grown in New Zealand. A rebrand was required, and after a brief spell as the dud 'melonette', the kiwi fruit was launched upon the waiting world in 1959.

LIFE AND DEATH. The *Ka Mate haka*, performed by New Zealand's All Blacks before rugby matches, was composed in 1821 by a Māori chief[2] after escaping his enemies by hiding in a hole with his wife seated on top. *Ka mate!* means 'I may die', to which the response is *Ka ora!* - 'I will live'.

[2] *In 1998, a group of his descendants tried to trademark the chant but, to the dismay of teams squaring up to the All Blacks, ultimately failed.*

MARKED MEN. 'Tattoo' comes from the Polynesian word *tatau*. Like other Polynesians, New Zealand's Māori have for centuries decorated their bodies with intricate designs. The practice was taken back to Europe by British sailors, who valued a tattoo as identification if lost at sea. It was later adopted enthusiastically by Britain's upper classes (Churchill had an anchor on his forearm), before latterly becoming a mark of youthful rebellion. In the US, however, a tattoo is seen as more sexy than angry; 49% of all young Americans wear one. In both the US and the UK, around 17% of tattoo-bearers regret having gone under the needle.

NORMAL PEOPLE. *Māori* means 'ordinary' in the Māori language; in contrast, European New Zealanders are *pākeha*—'pale shadows'.

INEXCUSABLE. On 10 July 1985, French agents sank the Greenpeace ship *Rainbow Warrior* in Auckland harbour, with the loss of one life. The operation was personally authorized by the president of France.

At up to 1.3 m, Spenceriella gigantea, found in North Auckland, is the world's longest earthworm. A common earthworm gives scale.

TOOTHLESS. None of New Zealand's 33 million sheep possess top front teeth. Like all ruminants,[1] the sheep instead have a dental pad against which the lower teeth bite.

[1] *Except llamas, which grow four sharp fighting fangs in adulthood.*

HEALTHY GLOW. New Zealand's Waitomo Caves are famously lit by the glimmer of myriad glow-worms. In order to lure prey, the glow-worms emit a particularly strong light, but all living things give off bioluminescence to some degree. Humans emit light mainly from their cheeks, forehead and neck, and shine most brightly around 4 p.m.—though, even then, their glow remains about 1,000 times too dim for the naked eye to see.

BRIGHT LIGHTS—BIOLUMOINESCENCE SPECIALISTS IN NATURE (SELECTED)

Source	Colour	Miscellanea
Fungus gnat	green	Waitomo glow-worms are the gnat's larvae, get brighter when hungry
Honey fungus	green	used to light *Turtle*, the world's first military submarine
Marine bacteria	blue	areas of glowing sea the size of Devon have been spotted from space
Vampire squid	blue	strobes its lights to daze predators and spurts out globs of glowing goo
Christmas trees	green	genetically modified self-lit trees don't yet exist—but are planned

MIGHTY MOA. Isolated for 65 million years, New Zealand went its own way when it came to fauna—or, more accurately, birdlife. In place of the herds of deer, antelope and bison found elsewhere, great flocks of flightless birds grazed the NZ turf. King was the moa, the biggest of which reached a quarter tonne; while the fearsome Haast's Eagle, with 10-foot wingspan, was the apex predator. Both were extinct by 1500 CE, after the arrival of Māori hunters.

*Kiwi
(to scale)*

Dinornis robustus: At 12 feet, the largest moa and tallest ever bird.

MINI MOA. The kiwi is a pint-size cousin of the moa. A strange, shaggy-feathered bird, it lays an egg 25% of its body weight[3] and has nostrils at the end of its beak that let it smell grubs, even underground. The kiwi first appeared on regimental badges of the early New Zealand Army and, during WWI, its soldiers came to be nicknamed for their badges. Since then, Kiwis of all stripes have proudly borne the name.

[3] *An evolutionary throwback to the moa, which laid an egg with a circumference of one metre.*

AT EASE: MOST PEACEFUL STATES[1]	
1 New Zealand	100[2]
2 Iceland	99
3 Japan	97
4 Austria	95
5 Norway	94

[1] *Global Peace Index (2010).* [2] *Index score: NZ = 100; bottom (Iraq) = 0.*

KIWIS ON AUSSIES
'New Zealanders who go to Australia raise the IQ of both countries.'
— Sir Robert Muldoon, while New Zealand's prime minister

GONE TO POT: ADULT CANNABIS USE[4]	
1 New Zealand	22%
2 Australia	18%
3 USA	12%
4 UK	9%
5 Switzerland	8%

[4] *Percentage of adults who state they have used cannabis. (Source: OECD)*

BUSY MUM. New Zealander Jayne Bleackley holds the record for the most closely spaced separate births—a boy and a girl just 208 days (less than 7 months) apart.

TIP OF THE ICEBERG. New Zealand is the visible pinnacle of the drowned continent of Zealandia, 93% of which remains under the Pacific Ocean. Beneath the waves, Zealandia covers an area as large as India.

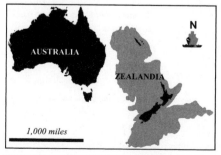

WONDER LOST. Known to the 19th century as the 'Eighth Wonder of the World', the Pink and White Terraces at Lake Rotomahana were New Zealand's premier tourist attraction, drawing visitors from as far as Europe. Sparkling staircases of crystal pools, the terraces were as extraordinary to look at as they were perfect for bathing; but, on the night of 9 June 1886, they were obliterated as Mt. Tarawera exploded. All was then quiet until 1900, when the Waimangu geyser (A) erupted in the same valley. Dwarfing the tallest geyser active today (Yellowstone's Steamboat (B)), Waimangu was the biggest geyser ever known, shooting up steam and rock 1,500 feet, until it too ceased activity in 1904.

● · **GSR** 19 · **Dependency**: Tokelau · **WHS**: Te Wahipounamu [Fiordland, Mt. Cook, Westland] (mountains, glaciers and coast) □ Tongariro (volcanoes, sacred sites) ■ Sub-Antarctic Islands (wildlife)

NICARAGUA

'Somoza may be a son of a bitch, but he's our son of a bitch.'

—Franklin D. Roosevelt (1939, attributed—quite possibly by Nicaraguan strongman Anastasio Somoza himself)

A 60-ft statue of the man who posthumously gave his name to the Sandinista movement stands today on the site of President Somoza's ruined palace on the edge of Nicaragua's capital, Managua.

AUGUSTO SANDINO AND HIS HAT

SEASONAL ADJUSTMENT. Despite being in the northern hemisphere, Nicaraguans call October to May 'summer' and April to November 'winter'.

WALKERAGUA. The first American to invade Nicaragua did so with the purest of capitalist motives at heart. Aged 31, and with one prosecution for illegal war-waging already under his belt, one-time child prodigy William Walker's big idea was to conquer as much of Central America as possible, and then to use it as a nursery to raise and sell a limitless stream of black slaves to the plantations of the southern US states. Landing in Nicaragua in 1855 at the head of a private army of 60 US freebooters, Walker took advantage of a civil war to gain control of the country within five months. Once in power, he quickly restored slavery and switched the national language to English. But before he could take his plans further, he got distracted by starting another war—this time with Costa Rica, which he lost. Burning the capital behind him, Walker turned tail and fled back to the USA, where he received a hero's welcome upon arrival.[1]

[1] *In 1860, Walker tried the same stunt in neighbouring Honduras. However, this time he ran afoul of the British Royal Navy, who handed him over to the Hondurans, who promptly shot him.*

GIVING IT A SHOT. When, in 1955, animosity between Nicaragua and Costa Rica threatened to turn into a shooting war, Nicaraguan President Anastasio Somoza challenged his Costa Rican counterpart, José Figueres, to a duel to settle things. Figueres's response: 'He's crazier than a goat in the midsummer sun.'

Baird's Tapir—the largest land mammal in Central America. Although a herbivore, the gawky-looking beast can be ferocious. In 1998, one ripped the arm off a zookeeper in Oklahoma, while, in a separate incident, the Costa Rican environment minister was ambushed and almost killed by another.

WINDS OF THE WORLD—A SELECTION OF EXOTICALLY NAMED BREEZES		
Wind	*Where?*	*What?*
Papagayo ('Parrot')	Nicaragua	hurricane-strength gale blowing over Lake Nicaragua
Barber	Canada/NE USA	frigid wet wind that encrusts hair and beards with ice
Brickfielder	SE Australia	hot, dusty desert wind that leaves the soil brick-hard
Chinook	Canada/US Plains	sudden winter blast of hot wind[2]—turns over trucks
Doctor	W. & S. Africa	cooling onshore wind named for supposed healthiness
Loo	N. India/Pakistan	hot afternoon wind—causes heatstroke and kills crops
Williwaw	Cape Horn	erratic hurricane-force gusts that whip the sea to a froth

[2] *A 1943 Chinook in South Dakota raised the temperature by 27°C in two minutes—the fastest natural temperature change ever recorded. After the Chinook had passed, the temperature fell back by 32°C in less than half an hour.*

♦ · **GSR**: 92 · **WHS**: León Cathedral □ León Viejo (early colonial ruins) · **ICH**: El Güegüense (satirical folk drama) □ Garifuna Culture

NIGER

'Before one cooks, one must have meat.'

—Nigerien proverb

Tree of Ténéré, pre-1973

TRAFFIC HAZARD. The Ténéré Desert is one of the severest stretches of the Sahara, with only barren sand and gravel for hundreds of miles—except, once, for a tree. The Tree of Ténéré famously stood in the middle of the vast nothingness. Perhaps 200 miles from its nearest neighbour, it was even marked on maps. In 1973, however, a spectacularly hapless Libyan lorry driver managed to crash into it and knock it flat. Attempts were made to plant a replacement but nothing would grow—the tap roots of the original reached 120 feet down. Eventually, the Nigeriens gave up, and travellers now make do with a post assembled from discarded exhaust pipes.

RIVER OF RIVERS. Giving its name to Nigeria as well as Niger, the Niger is Africa's third great river after the Nile and Congo. Rising in Guinea, with the Atlantic just 150 miles to the south, the Niger instead heads north and east for 2,500 miles to skirt the Sahara and pass Timbuktu before emptying into the ocean through Nigeria's oil-drenched Delta. The name probably comes from the Tuareg *ngher* meaning 'the river of rivers' (and so has nothing to do with black).

MEN IN BLUE. Although the Tuaregs of Niger's Sahara are Muslim, their women don't wear a veil. That's reserved for the men. The *tagelmust*, as the covering is known, can be over 15 ft long and is never taken off except among close family. Traditionally dyed indigo, it's replaced only when it has rotted through.

HUMAN DEVELOPMENT INDEX: BOTTOM FIVE		
Rank	Country	HDI (%)
178	Mali	37
179	C.A.R.	37
180	S. Leone	37
181	Afghan.	35
182	Niger	34

WOODEN SPOON. Based on life expectancy, wealth and access to education, the UN's Human Development Index (HDI) attempts to give a more rounded view of life prospects than GDP figures alone. Of the 182 countries included, Niger ranks bottom—making the country officially the world's worst place to live.

LIVE FAST ... Niger has both the world's highest teenage pregnancy rate (20% of girls aged 15–19 give birth each year) and largest family size—an average of seven children per woman. Nearly one in five children die before they reach five; of those that survive, 40% are malnourished and 70% are set to work. Only a little over one in three ever sees inside a school.

Sarcosuchus ('flesh crocodile'). Human and modern Nile crocodile to scale.

THE MONSTER OF THE SAHARA. Niger's Gadoufoua fossil beds have disgorged the remains of a truly terrifying crocodilian as heavy as a small whale. Living 110 million years ago, the bus-sized *Sarcosuchus* had 6-foot jaws filled with 132 teeth, each as big as a dagger. While *Sarcosuchus* may have snacked on dinosaurs, the very earliest crocodilians (twice as ancient still) were cat-sized reptiles with canine faces and the spindly legs of a gazelle.

♥ · **GSR**: 141 · **WHS**: Aïr-Ténéré (desert) □ W NP (savannah/forest ecosystem)

NIGERIA

'People create stories create people;
or rather stories create people create stories.'

—Chinua Achebe (1988)

Igbo woman in the 1920s, with ankle plates marking upper-class status

CROWDED OUT. The Igbo 'Women's War' of 1929 was largely successful in improving the lot of Igbo women. It was, however, also notable for 'sitting'— the novel non-violent method the women devised to achieve their goals. Up to 10,000 women simply invaded the personal space of the petty colonial officials they objected to, and dogged their every step until they could bear it no more, and either gave into the demands or resigned.

FRUIT ON NUT GANG. From just 290,000 people in 1950, Lagos, Nigeria's commercial capital, has grown into the world's wildest and most chaotic mega-city, with a population that's expected to reach 25m in 2015 (and stood at 15m in 2006). Cutting a path through this mayhem are a fraternity of anarchic motorcycle taxi drivers, known as *okada* riders, without whom the city's near-gridlocked streets would probably already have ground to a halt. Thus, in 2009, there was despair when Governor Babatunde Fashola made unaffordable helmets mandatory. Happily, however, the *okada* riders rose to the challenge magnificently by donning painted melon rinds.

THE TICKLER TEST. Nigeria's Cross River rainforest boasts the world's greatest diversity of butterflies, with over 1,000 species found. Telling butterflies from moths is tricky, but the most reliable means is to look at the antennae: those of butterflies are smooth and clubbed, while moth antennae are not (often looking like tiny feathers). Night flight is a less useful guide, since there are very many day-time moths and some butterflies also take wing at night, notably the homely garden red admiral.

419 Section 419 of the Nigerian criminal code deals with the crime of 'cheating', but has come to be synonymous with the revival of a classic 19th-century scam once known as the 'Spanish Prisoner'.[1] Stripped of the story-telling, 419 fraud dangles an ever-receding—and often avowedly ill-gotten—prize as bait to lure the dupe into advancing multiple lumps of facilitation money (hence its more formal name of 'advance fee fraud'). The scam's explosive reappearance was a consequence of the invention of email, which made international communication at once anonymous and virtually costless. Spewed at target addresses in the West as a wall of spam, in 2003 the fraud was estimated to have netted $240m from gullible Britons alone; and while the classic mark is perceived as a mildly befuddled pensioner bilked of their $30,000 life savings, the stakes can be far higher—from 1995 to 1998, Brazilian banker Nelson Sakaguchi was stung for $243m of his bank's cash, chasing a non-existent contract to build the new Abuja Airport.

HEART OF DARKNESS: WORLD'S BLACKEST ECONOMY[2,3]

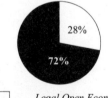

28%

72%

☐ .... *Legal Open Economy*

■ ...... *Illegal Black Economy*

[2] *Share of total GDP.* [3] *Joint with Egypt.*
Source: Fleming, J. Int. Affairs (2000)

THE LANGUAGE OF 419
Catcher ..... scammer who hooks the mark
Guyman .... scammer who works the mark
Oga .... boss who 'owns' the mark
Mugu .... the mark, 'fool'

[1] *In the 'Spanish Prisoner' the mark was asked to ransom an undisclosed aristocrat who had been falsely imprisoned in Spain, on the understanding that he would be handsomely rewarded later and, in a chivalric twist, would receive the grateful blue-blood's very eligible daughter's hand in marriage.*

ON SCRAMBLING FOR AFRICA—AND BEING BLOWN BACK OUT AGAIN:
THE RISE AND FALL OF WHITE COLONIALISM ON 'THE DARK CONTINENT' (1850–2010)[1]

'Take up the White Man's burden—
Send forth the best ye breed—
Go bind your sons to exile
To serve your captive's need;'

—Opening of Rudyard Kipling's 'The White Man's Burden' (1899). Kipling wrote the lines as a poetic plea to America to take on the governance of the Philippines. Nevertheless, they have since been taken as the acme of the imperialist ethic in general, and, in particular, as applied to Africa.

Cape Verde was the first European colony of the modern era in Africa (if the Canary Islands are excluded). Previously uninhabited, it was settled by the Portuguese in 1462.

'It is quite customary to ask in the morning, how many died last night?'
—Opening quotation in *The White Man's Grave: A Visit to Sierra Leone in 1834* by F. H. Rankin

In 1990, Namibia became the most recent African country to achieve nationhood. After a long struggle, independence came from white South Africa, which had inherited the colony from Germany in 1920 as a trust territory.

Namibia's North Korean-built monument to the Unknown (but the spitting image of SWAPO leader Sam Nujoma) Soldier, throwing a hand grenade

European territories in African region (2011): Mayotte (Fr.), Réunion (Fr.), St. Helena, Ascension and Tristan da Cunha (UK), Ceuta and Melilla (Sp.).

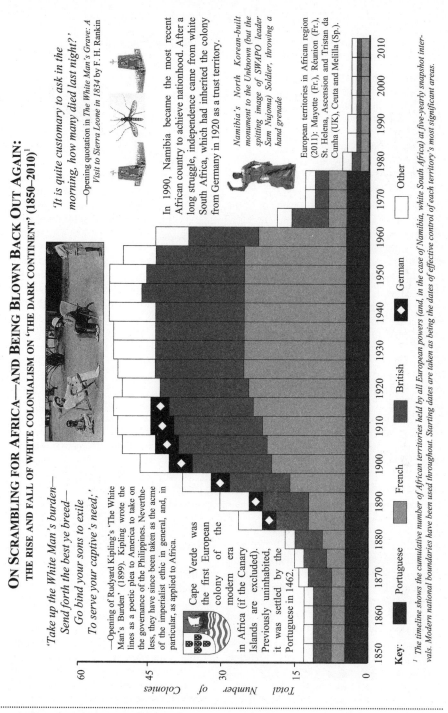

Key: Portuguese · French · British · German · Other

Total Number of Colonies (y-axis: 0, 15, 30, 45, 60)
(x-axis: 1850, 1860, 1870, 1880, 1890, 1900, 1910, 1920, 1930, 1940, 1950, 1960, 1970, 1980, 1990, 2000, 2010)

[1] The timeline shows the cumulative number of African territories held by all European powers (and, in the case of Namibia, white South Africa) at five-yearly snapshot intervals. Modern national boundaries have been used throughout. Starting dates are taken as being the dates of effective control of each territory's most significant areas.

♥ · **GSR:** 82 · **WHS:** Osun-Osogbo (sacred forest) ☐ Sukur (ruins) · **ICH:** Gelede (masked singing) Ifá (divination) ☐ Ijele (masquerade)

—————— NORWAY • NORGE ——————

'The strongest man in the world is he who stands most alone.'

—Henrik Ibsen

ON TOP OF THE WORLD. Norway is the world's most stable, peaceful and trusting country, with the highest quality of life, freest press, most humane prisons and most generous unemployment benefits—but they do eat whales.

SCANDINAVIAN SOLIDARITY

Q. *Why did the Norwegian take a ladder to the supermarket?*

A. *Because he'd heard prices in Oslo were extremely high.*

—Swedish Norwegian joke[3]

[3] *For what the Norwegians say about Swedes, see Sweden.*

HOLD ON. The Vikings never wore horned helmets for the rather persuasive reason that, when facing an angry Anglo-Saxon, the last thing you wanted to do was give him a handy handle to hold you by while he slit your throat.

KISS OF LIFE. Kissing under the mistletoe first gave thanks for a Norse god's resurrection. According to the ancient stories, Baldr, god of light and love, was immune to everything except mistletoe. On learning this, Loki, the cosmic troublemaker, arranged for him to be killed with a spear fashioned from the plant. Without Baldr, the world fell into winter, until the other gods resurrected him. His mother, Frigg, then decreed that, in future, mistletoe should be a symbol of love, not hatred.

EXTREME IRONING. If all Norway's fjords were ironed flat and its coastline was stood up on to its edge, it would stretch a quarter of the way to the moon.

NIGHTLIGHT. Seasons happen because the Earth's axis, around which the Earth turns each day, isn't quite at right angles to the circle that the planet sweeps each year around the sun. It's 23.3° off, and the tilt[1] means that the length of time any place spends facing the sun in any 24 hours (and hence how much warmth and light it receives) depends on the time of year. In some months, some places near the poles face the sun for the full 24 hours: the 'midnight sun'. Conversely, during the winter, the sun may never rise at all: the 'polar night'. The phenomenon is best known in Norway, where the Gulf Stream enables settlement further north than anywhere else in the world. In northern regions, and most particularly on the island of Spitsbergen, there can be up to four months between sunrise and sunset (and, in winter, almost as long between sunset and dawn).

[1] *No one knows for sure why the Earth's tilt is at the angle it is. Not all planets are so lucky; Uranus, for instance, lies on its side. If the Earth were to do this, its climate would be bizarre to the point of being non-survivable, with poles warmer than the Equator and each hemisphere 'enjoying' six months of tropical day followed by six months of polar night.*

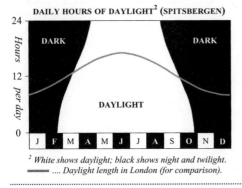

DAILY HOURS OF DAYLIGHT[2] (SPITSBERGEN)

Hours per day

24 / 12 / 0

DARK — DARK

DAYLIGHT

J F M A M J J A S O N D

[2] *White shows daylight; black shows night and twilight.*
═══ *.... Daylight length in London (for comparison).*

DATELINE DOOMSDAY. Longyearbyen, the chief town on Norway's Arctic island of Spitsbergen, lies almost literally at the end of the Earth. Just the place, then, to build the Global Seed Vault—an anti-apocalypse insurance policy to reboot the planet with life should the unthinkable occur. Dug into a mountain, behind air locks and blast doors, its deep-frozen chambers hold samples of over 430,000 seed varieties and there's room for 4,000,000 more.

♠ · **GSR: 50** · **Dependent Territory:** Bouvet Island · **WHS:** Alta (rock art) □ Bergen (waterfront) Fjords □ Røros (townscape) □ Struve Arc (survey line) □ Urnes (church) □ Vega (duck houses)

———————— OMAN ● عُمان ————————

'Muscat was clearly designed by Allah for piracy and slave-running.'
—C. Belfrage (1936), on Oman's capital

ONE-STOP SHOP. Gold, frankincense and myrrh: Oman produces all three, but the latter two are its specialities. Collected as 'tears' of yellow resin exuded from a thorny desert tree, Oman's Hojari frankincense is the world's finest. Although burnt for its vapours in the West, frankincense is mainly chewed in Arabia as gum. Myrrh is a related resin, but bitter where frankincense is spicy. Its ruby chunks were used by the ancients for everything from embalming corpses to rubbing on piles, while every Greek soldier carried a piece into battle as a natural wound-cleansing antiseptic.

WISEMANGIFTS.COM INVOICE	
Ship to: *E&OE.*	
HRH Caspar & Associates.	
Product	*Price ($)*
Gold Bar (1 kg) 50,000	
Frankincense (1 kg) 100	
Myrrh (1 kg) 78	
TOTAL **50,178**	

SWEET SURPRISE. Above the gate to each of Oman's 500 forts is a small hole from which guards would pour boiling honey on uninvited guests. The effect of the liquid is reminiscent of napalm: it sticks like glue and burns to the bone.

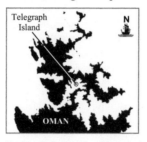

Telegraph Island

OMAN

DEATH-DEFYING. Between 1970 and 2003, Omani life expectancy rose from 40 to 74. As a result, death was outpaced and the expected lifespan remaining to an average Omani grew greater as he or she aged.

Enclosed by walls of naked rock, the Arabian fjords of Omani Musandam are so stiflingly hot and soul-sappingly lifeless that British soldiers posted to Telegraph Island, deep within the most tortuous, were often driven insane—thus giving us the phrase 'round the bend'.

RAIN ON ME. Each summer, thousands of Arab holidaymakers descend on Salalah, in Oman's far south, to enjoy days of unremitting drizzle under a blanket of steel-grey cloud.[2] After the obligatory photo beside a frankincense tree, the next most popular excursion is a picnic in the rain—an event of presumably greater novelty value for those with home skies of a perpetual and searing blue.

[2] *Salalah owes its tourism to a climate quirk, which sees it, exceptionally for Arabia, catch the Asian monsoon.*

THE MAN WHO BANNED THE 20TH CENTURY. Said bin Taimur didn't like radios, books, glasses or education, all of which he banned. But most of all, Oman's previous sultan didn't approve of travel. Until 1970[1], coastal Omanis were not allowed inland, while inland villagers couldn't even visit the next valley. The gates to the capital, Muscat, were locked every night and foreigners, except for his British advisors, forbidden. Like most countries, Oman now promotes itself to tourists; elsewhere in the world, a handful of hermit hold-outs remain (*see below*).

[1] *When Said's son, who had been imprisoned in a castle by his father since 1964, launched a successful coup.*

KEEP OUT—LEAST WELCOMING DESTINATIONS FOR TOURISTS

Recluse	*What's the issue?*	*For the really determined ...*
Bhutan	cultural contamination	paying the $225 daily minimum spend gains entry
Eq. Guinea	magnet for mercenaries	very hard, its few hotels block-booked by oilmen anyway
North Korea	Cold War paranoia	take a group tour (two minders shadow you at all times)
Saudi Arabia	defilement by infidels	no issue for Muslims, others can try for an expat job
Turkmenistan	egregious oddness	try, try, try again for a visa—they really don't want you

♣ · **GSR**: 98 · **WHS**: Aflaj Sites (antique irrigation systems) □ Bahla (fort) □ Bat (ancient ruins) Frankincense sites (trees, oasis and ports) · **ICH**: Al-Bar'ah (music and dance)

—————— PACIFIC ISLANDS ——————

*'You could drop all the dry land on our planet into the Pacific
and still have room for another continent the size of Asia.'*

—David Stanley, *South Pacific* (Moon Handbooks)

HARD CASH. Until the 1960s, the islanders of Yap, in Micronesia, used discs of limestone, known as *rai* stones, as currency. Since the rock wasn't found on Yap, they were quarried from stalactites on Palau, 200 miles away, and imported by canoe—no mean feat given the largest denomination coins were 10 ft across and weighed four tons. Size wasn't the only determinant of value; history mattered just as much. In particular, a given stone's worth would be boosted substantially if lives were lost in its production. *Rai* stones weren't usually moved physically when they changed hands and many were deposited permanently on the bed of a channel known as the 'money bank'.

LIFT OFF. Flying fish really do fly: their outstretched pectoral fins have evolved the same aerodynamic shape as wings and their tails, beating at 70 strokes a second, can accelerate the creatures to almost 40 mph underwater before breaking the surface. Once in the air, the fish can remain airborne for up to a quarter of a mile. In the Solomon Islands, fishermen hunt flying fish by paddling offshore at night and hoisting paraffin lamps on their canoes. Swarms of the fish are soon attracted by the lights and, using devices much like butterfly nets, the islanders proceed to swat the airborne animals out of the air until their boats are full.

POLITICAL HEAVYWEIGHT. Despite a youth spent as Tonga's top-ranked pole-vaulter, King Taufa'ahau Tupou IV went on to become the world's weightiest monarch—peaking at 31 stone (half as heavy again as Henry VIII). But, by the time of his death in 2006, the King had shed 11 stone through a unique fitness plan that combined a diet of soup with closing the country's airport once a week so he could ride his bicycle up and down the runway flanked by six jogging bodyguards.

WHITE MAGIC. On the Vanuatuan island of Tanna, young men still conduct parade drills with bamboo 'rifles' over their shoulders and 'U.S.A.' daubed in white across their bare chests. They are members of the John Frum cargo cult and believe

GOD ON EARTH? *The villagers of Yaohnanen on Tanna worship the Duke of Edinburgh as a god, believing him the son of a mountain spirit. Over the years, the duke has given the elders a number of signed portraits and gifts, which are all deeply revered.*

that, through such rituals, the spirits will one day favour them with more 'cargo' (advanced technology goods) of the sort that briefly became so abundant when the US Army passed through during WWII. Elsewhere in Melanesia, other cults have in the past built mock airstrips, straw 'aircraft', dummy lighthouses and coconut 'radios' in efforts to attract similar cargo.

ROYAL FOOL. In 1999, King Taufa'ahau Tupou IV appointed Jesse Bogdonoff his court jester—the only one anywhere in modern times. Unfortunately, the last laugh appears to have been on the king (or his people) since, on his jester's advice, the king then invested Tonga's national wealth fund in an obscure US company—which promptly went bust.

Includes: Cook Is., Federated States of Micronesia, Kiribati, Marshall Is., Nauru, Niue, Palau, Samoa, Solomon Is., Tonga, Tuvalu and Vanuatu. *See separate entries for Fiji and Papua New Guinea.*

HAPPY SLAPPING. The Samoan slap dance is thought to have originated in efforts to ward off hungry mosquitoes. Performed exclusively by men, the traditional dance is undertaken without music, with the rhythmic slapping of skin and stomping of feet providing the dancers with their own accompaniment.

JUST NOT CRICKET. *Kilikiti*, a sport played on Tuvalu and several nearby island groups, has grown up locally since the 19th century, when British missionaries introduced cricket to the South Pacific as an alternative to tribal warfare. Now only very loosely based on its conventional roots, *kilikiti* features a three-sided bat shaped like a Toblerone bar, a single stump and a rubber ball the size of an egg. Any number of people can play and a match lasts until the ball is irretrievably lost (potentially after several days). Reports suggest the precise rules are unknowable other than to those involved—except that the hosting village automatically loses if the catering runs out.

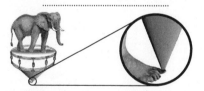

The Challenger Deep, off the Micronesian island of Fais, is the deepest known point in any ocean. At its maximum depth of 10,971 m, the pressure is 1.25 tonnes per square centimetre—the same as that exerted by an elephant balancing on your big toenail. Despite this, probes have filmed shrimps and worms living normally.

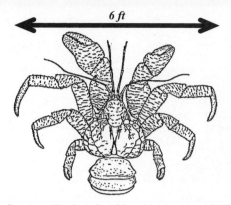

6 ft

CLAWS. Equipped with pincers powerful enough to snap a broom handle, the coconut crab is the world's largest land arthropod, and pretty much at the theoretical limit for any exoskeleton-bearing creature in an Earth-like atmosphere—extreme specimens have measured 6 feet across. Both a scavenger and a predator (as well as a coconut-crusher), it's found on islands across the tropical Pacific and Indian Oceans, including, in large numbers, on uninhabited Nikumaroro Atoll in Kiribati. This is the place it's thought Amelia Earhart probably crash-landed when she disappeared in 1937 while attempting to fly round the world, and, given this, if anything of Amelia still remains, according to those who are still searching for her, it's almost certainly to be found down a crab hole.

TITLES OF TEMPTATION. The name of the island nation of Niue translates as 'Behold the coconut!', while that of Nauru is a contraction of *Anáoero*—which, according to the original German colonial authorities, meant 'I am going to the beach'.

TOYS FOR BOYS. Between 1946 and 1962, the Marshall Islands hosted 105 US nuclear tests, including, in 1952, the world's first hydrogen bomb blast, Ivy Mike, which showed the new weapon could vaporize an entire island (*right*). But the name linked for ever with the programme is Bikini—the site of the first test (held in July 1946), since just two weeks later, French engineer Louis Réard adopted it to describe his radical new two-piece swimsuit. While Réard insisted he chose the name as his costume 'split the atom' when it came to the smallest possible piece of clothing, the Paris press less kindly suggested it was because wearers looked like they had just emerged in tatters from an atomic explosion.

SPOT THE DIFFERENCE[1]

[1] *'Before' and 'after' aerial photos taken over Bikini Atoll.*

• · **GSR**: n/a · **WHS**: Kiribati—Phoenix Islands (coral reefs) □ Marshall Islands—Bikini Atoll (nuclear test site) □ Solomon Islands—East Rennell (lake and forest) □ Vanuatu—Chief Roi Mata's Domain (historic sites) · **ICH**: Tonga—Lakalaka (dance) □ Vanuatu—Sand Drawings (writing system)

PAKISTAN ● پاکِستان

'Blood speaks.'

—Balochi proverb

B.I.R.T.H. Pakistan was invented in a terraced house in Cambridge in 1932—the name, certainly, but also, in good measure, the will to carve a new Muslim state out of north-west India. Conceived by Cambridge student Rahmat Ali, the word 'Pakistan' is an acronym for the five Indian provinces which then occupied the territory—**P**unjab, **A**fghan/North-West Frontier, **K**ashmir[1], **S**indh and Balochi**stan**—that, felicitously, also means 'Land of the Pure' in Urdu. (The 'i' arrived later to ease pronunciation.)

[1] *In the event, the greater part of Kashmir stayed with India at the behest of its maharajah, poisoning relations between the two countries ever since.*

1944: The twin pillars of Subcontinental independence, Pakistan's Al-Jinnah (l) and India's Gandhi (r), stand shoulder to shoulder against the British Raj.

BROTHERS IN ARMS
AN INDO-PAK. TIMELINE[2]

1947 Partition...........*14m displaced*
1947 Indo-Pak. War I.....*6,000 dead*
1965 Indo-Pak. War II....*7,000 dead*
1971 Indo-Pak. War III *13,000 dead*
1974 .... **India tests atom bomb**
1984-2003 Siachen War *2,000 dead*
1998 ... **Pakistan tests atom bomb**
1999 Indo-Pak. War IV..*2,000 dead*
2008 Mumbai terror raid.. *164 dead*
[2]*All totals: Pakistani & Indian combined.*

KISSING COUSINS. Pakistan has the world's highest rate of marriage between cousins, at 61% of all unions.[3] While scientific studies bear out the Western belief that such consanguinity can cause birth defects, the effect is nonetheless quite modest: a 3% excess risk—the same as in giving birth at 40 relative to 30.

[3] *In comparison, first-cousin marriages run at 0.4% among UK non-Asians.*

'There is nothing we cannot copy.'

—Haji Munawar Afridi, Darra Adam Khel shopkeeper

ARMS BIZARRE. Darra Adam Khel is a scruffy one-street town on the edge of Pakistan's tribal belt. Unusually, though, that street is lined with front-room shops selling the biggest choice of firepower outside the US Strategic Reserve. Everything from knock-off anti-aircraft cannons to pen-guns (popular with the assassin niche market) can be had over the counter; and since the town's back-room workshops turn out 700 new weapons daily, waiting lists are kept refreshingly short.

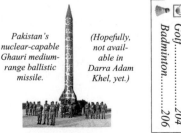

Pakistan's nuclear-capable Ghauri medium-range ballistic missile.

(Hopefully, not available in Darra Adam Khel, yet.)

Rawalpindi Express

In 2003, Shoaib Akhtar became the world's fastest bowler when he delivered a ball at 100.2 mph. While cause for celebration in cricket-obsessed Pakistan, Akhtar's efforts are still leisurely, compared to almost every other sport—as can be seen, right.

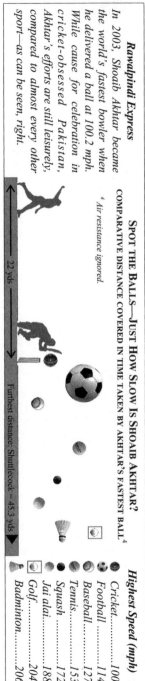

SPOT THE BALLS—JUST HOW SLOW IS SHOAIB AKHTAR?
COMPARATIVE DISTANCE COVERED IN TIME TAKEN BY AKHTAR'S FASTEST BALL[4]

[4] *Air resistance ignored.*

— 22 yds —

Furthest distance: Shuttlecock = 45.3 yds ▼

Highest Speed (mph)

Cricket................100
Football 114
Baseball..............127
Tennis.................153
Squash................172
Jai alai...............188
Golf....................204
Badminton.........206

Aside from unicorns, the ancient cities of the Indus Valley are known for inventing the sewer. As early as 2600 BCE, domestic kitchens and bathrooms had channels leading outside to covered drains running on either side of each street, cleaned out periodically by a man from the council.

ONE-SPIKE PONY. Not just a horse with a horn, the historic unicorn had the beard of a goat, the tail of a lion and the hooves of a deer. The earliest depiction goes back 4,000 years to Pakistan's Indus Valley civilization, which produced seals bearing a unicorn-like image (*left*). However, it was only much later, in the early Christian period, that the association with chaste nobility sprang up, after a popular allegory linked the magical beast to the Virgin Mary. As the centuries wore on, the connection widened until, by the era of chivalry, every swain worth his sword knew that to catch a unicorn, all one had to do was to lead a virgin into the forest, whereupon one would come and lay its head in her lap. Despite this, unicorns remained stubbornly rare, and genuine unicorn horn fetched several times its weight in gold. All of which made for a lucrative market for unicorn-faking, which, as it happens, is (and often has been) easily achieved by grafting together the horn buds of any newborn goat or cow—after which a single, centred horn will sprout naturally.

'The size defies all reason. It stands in the middle of nowhere defending nothing.'
—Isobel Shaw

STONY SILENCE. The world's largest fortress, Ranikot Fort, sprawls across a dusty range of hills 20 miles west of the Indus. Also known as the Great Wall of Sindh, its 26 miles of massive masonry guard—on the face of it—absolutely nothing. Inside, there's no city (ruined or otherwise), the site isn't strategic and no road passes through; its purpose (if any) remains wholly obscure. Furthermore, no one knows who built it, and estimates of its age vary by 1,500 years.

SWAT—A PRINCELY STATE

Flag of Swat

Swot up on Swat: *An isolated and scenic valley in the Hindu Kush mountains roughly half the size of Wales, and, until 1969, a feudal principality with its own ruler—notwithstanding incorporation into Pakistan in 1947. Swat's current population is 1.2 million.*

FOUR FAMOUS FANS OF SWAT

■ **QUEEN ELIZABETH II**. Following her 1964 holiday in Swat, she declared it 'the Switzerland of the British Empire'. Her words were (to a limited extent) prophetic as it's home to Malam Jabba, now Pakistan's premier ski resort.

■ **GAUTAMA BUDDHA**. Many scholars believe Swat is the ancient Uddiyana, birthplace of Tantric Buddhism. If correct, the valley furnished a vital sanctuary that let the religion survive and spread into East Asia after being displaced from India.

■ **WINSTON CHURCHILL**. Participation in the 1897 Malakand Expedition pacifying Swat taught him the killing power of modern rifles and later led him to push development of the tank.

■ **TALIBAN**. Overran Swat from March to May 2009.

AKOND OF SWAT

'Who, or why, or which, or what, Is the Akond of Swat?'
—Edward Lear (1877)

Edward Lear's Akond (today 'Akhund') of Swat was no mere runcible but a real theocratic ruler, who held power from 1857 to 1877, and, along the way, played a bit part in the Anglo-Russian Great Game. More generally, an Akhund is a bumpkinish rank of Islamic cleric. There are, however, exceptions: the best known is the current leader of the Taliban, who, on formal occasions, should be addressed as: 'Mullah Mohammed Omar Akhund'.

♣ · **GSR**: 52 · **WHS**: Lahore Fort □ Makli (necropolis) □ Mohenjo-daro (Bronze Age city ruins) Rohtas Fort □ Takht-i-Bahi (Buddhist ruins) □ Taxila (Buddhist city ruins) · **ICH**: Novruz (New Year)

PANAMA • PANAMÁ

'A man, a plan, a canal—Panama.'

—Anon. (hint: read backwards)

TOP BANANA. Until the 1950s, Gros Michel was the world's undisputed top banana cultivar. But then it was laid low by a global plague of Panama Disease (an incurable fungal wilt). Since then, we have all made do with a new banana known as the Cavendish, discovered in Saigon's Botanical Gardens. But, as all true bananaphiles agree, in size, handling, aroma and above all flavour, the Cavendish is a shadow of the glorious fruit that was once 'Big Mike'.

A 'hand' of bananas. Each individual fruit is properly known as a 'finger'.

Famous for geometric appliqué panels known as molas (above), the Kuna Indians won autonomy fighting under their chosen symbol of a swastika in a successful 1925 revolt.

MIND THE GAP. When it came to founding a colonial empire, Scotland could hardly have chosen worse than Panama's Darien. Today, it's an almost uninhabited swathe of tropical jungle, swamps, mountains and mosquitoes, notorious as the impenetrable 'gap' between Central and South America still uncrossed by any road.[1] But in 1698 it was to be the site of 'New Edinburgh', as 1,200 Scottish would-be colonists hid below-decks from hostile English warships on their first leg outbound from Leith. Within a year, however, all but 300 were dead, with nothing to show except the loss of the quarter-share of Scotland's national wealth that had been sunk into the project—a financial disaster so dire it's credited as having driven Scotland to agree the Act of Union with England nine years later.

[1] *The only all-land crossing of the Darien Gap by four-wheeled vehicle took 741 days to cover the 125 miles in 1985–87.*

THE CANAL ZONE

In 1513, Vasco Núñez de Balboa made the first recorded crossing of the isthmus of Panama and so became the first European to lay eyes on the Pacific Ocean.

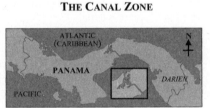

• Transiting from the Atlantic to the Pacific via the Panama Canal, you travel east (not west).

• Sea level on the Atlantic side of the Panama Canal is 20cm below that on the Pacific side.

Based on a midstream jungle island in the Panama Canal, the Smithsonian Tropical Research Institute is the world's top centre for tropical biology. Animals studied include Panama's golden frogs, which wave their hands at each other to 'talk' in noisy mountain streams.

BIG DIGS—PANAMA AND SUEZ COMPARED

Traffic (ships/year)............14,700; *Suez: 21,000*   **Toll** ('Panamax' ship)...$330,000; *Suez: $270,000*
Transit Time ....…...10 hours; *Suez: 11 hours*   **Wars**...........1903, 1989; *Suez: 1956, 1967, 1973*

Construction Deaths....27,600 (mostly due to yellow fever and malaria); *Suez: number unknown but far fewer. (President Nasser cited a figure of 120,000 Egyptian lives lost as justification for his 1956 nationalization of the Suez Canal. However, he was being disingenuous, since this number related to the deaths incurred in the attempted construction of a canal under Pharaoh Necho around 600 BCE.)*

PANAMA CANAL[2]   SUEZ CANAL[2]

[2] *Minimum dimensions; drawn to scale. The container ship (also shown to scale) is Panamax-rated (i.e. built specifically to fit through the Panama Canal—just).*

♦ · **GSR**: 79 · **WHS**: Coiba (tropical islands and reefs) □ Darien (rainforest) □ Panama City (historic city) □ Portobelo (fortifications) □ Talamanca Range (mountains)

—— PAPUA NEW GUINEA • PAPUA NUIGINI ————

'A long time ago, our people discovered the secret of life:
live well, love well and die a happy death.'

—Bernard Narokobi, *The Melanesian Way* (1980). A lawyer, philosopher and advocate for traditional Melanesian values, Narokobi was one of Papua New Guinea's most eminent citizens and part-author of its constitution.

A Komunive Mudman from Asaro district with traditional clay mask. The Mudmen wear these heavy masks to perform a dance celebrating how they once caked themselves in mud to defeat an enemy village by fooling them into thinking they were demons. When, in 1957, the Mudmen first did the dance in front of other villages, many watchers were so terrified they got up and fled.

ONE-MAN ARMY. Before WWI, eastern New Guinea was split between German New Guinea and Australian Papua. Then, at the start of the war, Australia occupied the entire territory. Oberleutnant Hermann Detzner—who was surveying the German colony's interior—wasn't aware of this, however, and when he found out, declined to capitulate. Instead, he eluded the Australians until the war's end, when he surrendered in dress uniform. In the interim, he marched around singing German patriotic songs, flying the German flag and exploring. Afterwards, he was awarded both the Iron Cross and the German Geographical Society's Nachtigal Medal for exploration—in all probability a unique pairing.

NUMBA WAN TOK.[1] Papua New Guinea is the most multicultural country on Earth. Despite a population of under seven million, it's home to at least 832 separate languages—over three times as many as are native to the whole of Europe. Given the formidable challenge this presents, the creole language of Tok Pisin—based very loosely on English—has grown up as the lingua franca.

[1] *Meaning 'very good language' (literally 'number one talk') in Tok Pisin.*

THE MELANESIAN WAY—SELECTED IDIOMS OF PAPUA[2] NEW GUINEAN TOK PISIN

Tok Pisin	English	Meaning	Note
bun baik	bone bicycle	thin person	referring to the long, thin shape of many bones
lewa bilong mi	liver of mine	my true love	the liver is thought to be the seat of emotions
namba ileven	number eleven	running nose	a visual pun on the shape of the figures
pos opis	post office	toilet	arising since to defecate is 'to send a letter'
susok man	shoe sock man	town dweller	one who wears shoes and socks

[2] *'Papua' is taken from the Malay word* papuah, *meaning frizzy-haired—referring to the characteristic Melanesian hairtype, and, by extension, to Melanesian people. Beyond New Guinea, Melanesian populations extend east as far as Fiji.*

Papua New Guinea's national emblem: the bird of paradise

FLIGHT OF FANCY. Bird of paradise skins have been traded within New Guinea for 2,000 years, and from the 16th century onwards were carried back to Europe by explorers. Obtained through trade, these specimens had been prepared with their wings and feet cut off, bringing about the idea that the birds never came to earth but floated perpetually in a celestial paradise supported by their fabulous feathers—so giving rise to their English name.

• · **GSR**: 144 · **WHS:** Kuk (ancient agriculture excavation site)

———————— PARAGUAY ————————

'Paraguayans, Republic or death!'
—Paraguayan national anthem

GRAND THEFT AUTO. Up to 50% of the cars on Paraguay's roads are thought to be stolen. In 2001, when it was noticed that the presidential BMW was itself hot (having been taken from a Johnson & Johnson office in Brazil), the Interior Minister simply pointed out that in Paraguay, journalists, priests and the police all drove stolen cars. Ciudad del Este, on the Brazilian frontier, is the country's contraband hub—in the 1990s, the city saw more cash change hands than anywhere except Hong Kong or Miami. (Fittingly, *Miami Vice* was also partly filmed in the town.)

'America's health care system is second only to Japan, Canada, Sweden, Great Britain ... well ... all of Europe. But you can thank your lucky stars we don't live in Paraguay!'
—Homer Simpson

TAKE YOUR PICK. Paraguay's flag is almost[1] unique in having a different appearance depending on which side you face. The front (*top*) has the national coat of arms between red and blue bands, while the back (*bottom*) has the lion seal of the treasury.

[1] *Moldova's flag officially shows the national arms on one side only, but this is generally ignored. On either side of Saudi Arabia's flag, the holy script is reversed in order to prevent it from ever reading backwards.*

WHAT A DIFFERENCE A DAY MAKES. One day in 1864, the leader of Paraguay (current population 7m), Solano Lopez, woke up and decided it would be a good idea to declare war on the neighbouring countries of Brazil, Argentina and Uruguay (combined current population 235m) all at the same time. Despite having enemies on three sides, the Paraguayans fought like badgers at bay for six years and, against all odds, held out until 1870. But the War of the Triple Alliance, as it was known, ended in utter defeat: by the time Lopez was finally killed, the majority of Paraguay's people lay dead—including 90% of its adult men. In many ways, over a century on, Paraguay has yet to recover.

MOTORMOUTH. The size of a pilchard with the teeth of a shark, the piranha is an ugly sight. Its reputation was made by Teddy Roosevelt, who first came upon the fish on the River Paraguay and later wrote of a shoal stripping a cow to a skeleton in 60 seconds. (Recent research suggests this ferocity has been somewhat overcooked.)

BANGED UP. For the innocent, Paraguay is the world's worst place to be arrested: 93% of the country's prison population is still awaiting trial.

LOCAL LINGO. Paraguay is the only American country where an indigenous language (Guaraní) has been adopted by the incoming settlers. English borrowings include both 'jaguar' and 'piranha'.

SS-O-S. After WWII, Latin America provided a refuge for a number of vanishing Nazis. Frederick Forsyth's 1972 thriller, *The Odessa File*, was the fictionalized tale of the hunt for one such—Eduard Roschmann. Four years later, Roschmann turned up dead in Paraguay's steamy river port capital for real.

♦ · **GSR**: 87 · **WHS:** Jesús de Tavarangue & Santísima Trinidad Missions (Jesuit ruins)

PERU • PERÚ

*'Since it is impossible to know what's really happening,
we Peruvians lie, invent, dream and take refuge in illusion.'*

—Mario Vargas Llosa

[1] *El Niño events in grey.*

1950

1960

1970

HAM-STERS. Guinea Pig was an Inca staple. The rodents were disembowelled, cooked from the inside with fire-hot stones and eaten with a chunk of rock salt that each diner licked, then passed on; popular sauces included various types of clay and toasted mayfly grubs ground up with chilli. Guinea pig is still an Andean favourite. Two males and 20 females will produce one pup a day—enough to keep a family in meat. And, as local manuals note, since guinea pigs are unable to climb over a sturdy threshold, they are self-penning when grown inside the home.

'A sleeping lobster gets taken by the current.'

—Peruvian proverb

PLANE PLEASE. The world's first hijack ended in a stand-off at Arequipa Airport in 1931, when pilot Byron Rickards refused to take a band of armed revolutionaries to Lima. He relented 10 days later—by then they were the Peruvian government.

PERU'S CURSE OF THE CHRIST-CHILD. Typically appearing in the weeks around Christmas (and, hence, bearing the Spanish name for the infant Jesus), El Niño is an erratic warming of the Pacific Ocean off Peru that disrupts weather worldwide, bringing flood and famine. A 1789 event is mooted to have caused the European crop failures that spurred the French Revolution, while another El Niño in 1997 killed one in six of the world's coral reefs.

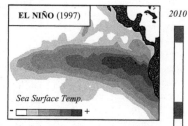

EL NIÑO (1997)

Sea Surface Temp.
− +

2010

STREETS AHEAD. A network of 25,000 miles of road linked the limits of the empire with the Inca capital Cuzco ('belly button of the world' in the Inca Quecha language). Though not designed solely for the purpose, it enabled the ruling Inca to enjoy fresh fish from the Pacific within two days of being landed. A century later, the same journey took the Spanish two weeks. Most roadway has long since gone, but one short segment still in use is the Inca Trail to Machu Picchu.

Km 82   **INCA TRAIL (CLASSIC ROUTE)**   Machu Picchu

DAY 1   DAY 2   DAY 3   DAY 4   4,200 m ⌐
2,600 m ⌐

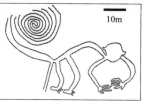

10m

NAZCA GEOGLYPH 'THE MONKEY'

Cut into the desert near Nazca, in southern Peru, lie 70 immense stick figures predating the Incas by 800 years. What they were for, no one knows.

PRE-SCHOOL MUM. In 1939, Lina Medina entered the medical record books by becoming the youngest mother ever known—at the age of five. After the healthy 6-lb boy was born in a Lima hospital, another 33 years went by before she had her second child.

DARKEST PERU. Paddington Bear almost came from 'Darkest Africa'. Peru, home to the Andean spectacled bear, was only substituted when author Michael Bond's agent pointed out no bears live in Africa.

2000

1990

PRE-COLUMBIAN CULTURES (SELECTED)

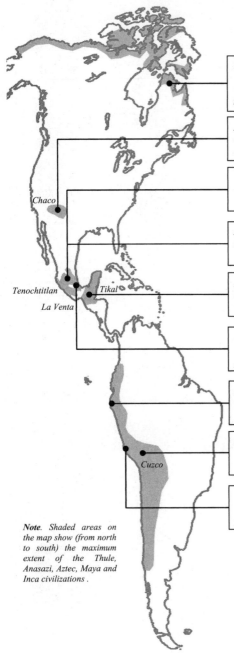

Chaco

Tenochtitlan

Tikal

La Venta

Cuzco

Thule: *Naming their descendents is a problem. 'Inuit' is usual in Canada and Greenland, but 'Eskimo' is preferred in Alaska. One distinction is that Inuit build igloos, while Eskimo don't.*

Anasazi: *Cautious builders—villages were often only accessible by rope climbing; houses were entered by a ladder though a hole in the roof.*

Teotihuacáno: *The largest pyramids in history were built at this time. The Great Pyramid of Cholula is twice the size of Egypt's biggest.*

Aztec: *Along with 'shack', other Aztec words now found in English include: 'chilli', 'chocolate', 'coyote', 'guacamole' and 'tomato'.*

Maya: *Being cross-eyed was a sign of beauty among the Maya. To foster the trait, mothers would hang a bead in front of their baby's eyes.*

Olmec: *Domestic dogs played a key role in the rise of the first urban society in the Americas by providing the principal source of dietary protein.*

Moche-Chimú: *In their religious ceremonies, Moche priests performed a hugely imaginative range of ritual sex acts and played badminton.*

Inca: *To demonstrate his prestige, Emperor Atahualpa wore a cord woven from the finest vampire bat hair coiled around his forehead.*

Nazca: *Some graves hold cross-legged human skeletons whose heads have been replaced by painted jars; their significance is unknown.*

Note. *Shaded areas on the map show (from north to south) the maximum extent of the Thule, Anasazi, Aztec, Maya and Inca civilizations.*

PRE-COLUMBIAN CULTURES (SELECTED)

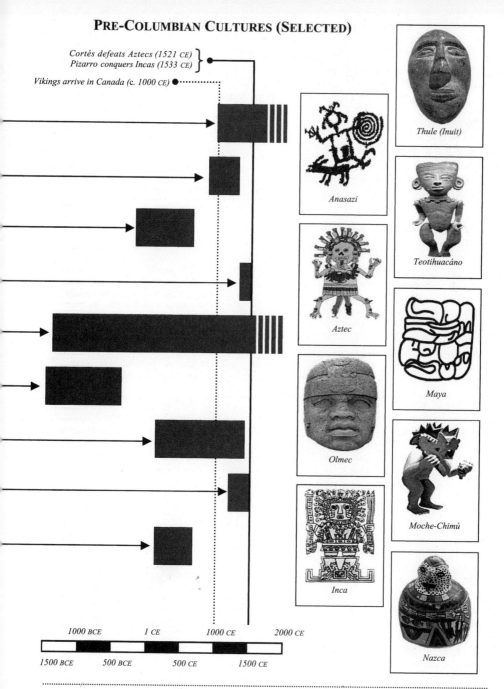

Cortés defeats Aztecs (1521 CE)
Pizarro conquers Incas (1533 CE)

Vikings arrive in Canada (c. 1000 CE)

Thule (Inuit)

Anasazi

Teotihuacáno

Aztec

Maya

Olmec

Moche-Chimú

Inca

Nazca

1000 BCE   1 CE   1000 CE   2000 CE

1500 BCE   500 BCE   500 CE   1500 CE

♦ · **GSR**: 60 · **WHS**: Arequipa (cityscape) □ Caral-Supe (ruined city) □ Chan Chan (ruined city) Chavín (ruined city) □ Cuzco (museum city) □ Huascarán (mountains) □ Lima (historic city) □ Machu Picchu (Inca ruins) □ Manú (tropical forest) □ Nazca Lines (geoglyphs) □ Río Abiseo (mountain forest) **ICH**: Aymara (indigenous culture) □ Huaconada (ritual dance) □ Scissors Dance (competitive dance) Taquile (textiles) □ Zápara (myths and language)

Philippines • Pilipinas

'If you know how much you've got, you probably haven't got much.'

—Imelda Marcos (1986)

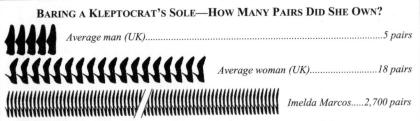

Baring a Kleptocrat's Sole—How Many Pairs Did She Own?

Average man (UK)...*5 pairs*

Average woman (UK)........................*18 pairs*

Imelda Marcos.....2,700 pairs

First Secretary Khrushchev in happier mood

The Filipino Shoe Moment. For many veteran observers, the United Nations' most sublime piece of theatre came on 12 October 1960, when Filipino delegate Lorenzo Sumulong made a seemingly routine criticism of Soviet policy. It was in a session at which Nikita Khrushchev was present, and, clearly, the Russian premier was having a bad day—or simply didn't like Filipinos. In any event, he start heckling from the floor, shouting 'Imperialist lackey!' and, less socio-theoretically, 'Jerk!', then, really getting into his stride, he fished off his right shoe and began pounding it into his desk. No more was said at the time; but when Khrushchev was removed four years later in a Kremlin putsch, it was amid much muttering about 'absurd antics' and 'barbarian manners'.

Divine Inspiration. Cardinal Sin obviously wasn't born that way, but the memorable moniker of the Philippines' most famous cleric is part of an honourable tradition of unusual, inventive and plain far-out names given to Filipino children with seemingly no thought as to how they will wear.[1] Other choice selections include Girlie, Bumbum and John F Kenneth Dee; while the president—'Noynoy'—has sisters called Pinky and Ballsy. But probably most common of all are Bing, Bong, Ding and Dong.

[1] *The Filipino prelate relished his notable name: his usual greeting when receiving visitors at his home was: 'Welcome to the House of Sin.'*

Emblem of Empire. The pith helmet, or sola topi, was created by blending the traditional Filipino rattan *salakot* with the spiked German *Pickelhaube*.

Language Lovers. Hanunóo, used by the Mangyan peoples, has a number of oddities. For a start, it's written vertically—but from the bottom of the page upwards. Also, there's no alphabetical order. The letters may be learnt in any sequence; a feat mastered by memorizing as many love songs as possible.

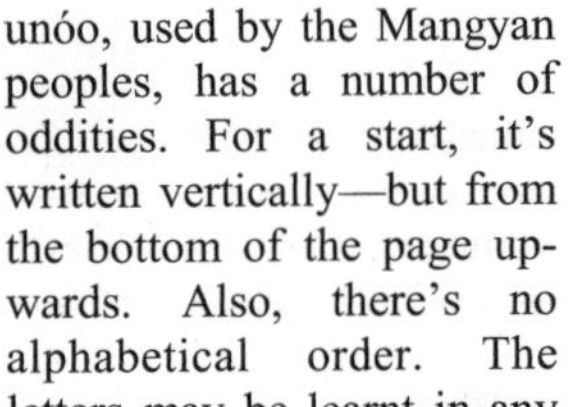
Short-hop transport in the Philippines is in jeepneys. Devised after WWII, these were originally discarded US Army jeeps—now usually pick-up trucks—pimped with chrome and ghetto-blaster, and bolted up with two benches (for the lucky).

Brief Snack. When, in 1994, Renato Arganzo was rescued at sea after drifting for some time on a lifebuoy following the loss of his boat, the fisherman attributed his survival to his strategy of eating his underpants.

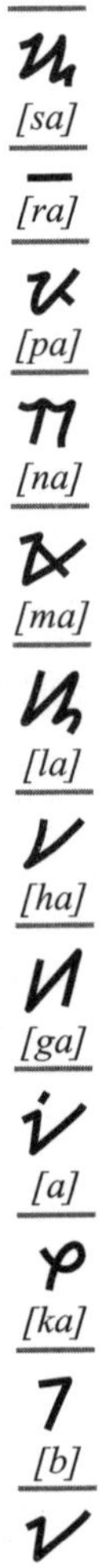

Hanunóo lettering (selected):

♣ **GSR** · 51 · **WHS**: Baroque Churches □ Ifugao (rice terraces) □ Puerto-Princesa (subterranean river) Tubbataha (reefs) □ Vigan (colonial townscape) · **ICH**: Darangen (epic song) □ Hudhud (chants)

POLAND ● POLSKA

'W Szczebrzeszynie chrząszcz brzmi w trzcinie i Szczebrzeszyn z tego słynie.'

—Popular Polish tongue-twister ('In the town of Szczebrzeszyn a beetle buzzes in the reed, for which Szczebrzeszyn is famous')

EASTERN EUROPEAN 'SKI' GUIDE

		EXAMPLE
👉	IF '-SKI' → POLISH	**Sikorski, Władysław** *Polish national hero, wartime leader in WWII.*
👉	IF '-SKY' → RUSSIAN[2]	**Sikorsky, Igor** *Russian engineer, developed Sikorsky helicopters.*

[2] *Or possibly Ukrainian or Czech.*

When the Nazi Reich invaded Poland on 1 September 1939, it triggered WWII. Although fighting spread worldwide, Poland suffered proportionately more than any other nation, counting 5.9m dead, including 90% of Poland's 3.3m Jews.

'I want to make love to the Polish people.'

—US President Jimmy Carter, on arriving in Warsaw (1977)[3]

[3] *The English text of the speech, used to open Carter's ground-breaking détente tour of the USSR's Eastern Europe satellites, said: 'I have come to learn the desires of the Polish people ...' However, due to cost-cutting, the US State Department had hired a non-native interpreter from New York for the trip. Other gaffes in the same speech included the apparent claim that Carter had 'fled' the US and that he thought Poland's historic constitution (the second oldest in the world, preceded only by America's) was an object of 'ridicule'. The New Yorker was replaced by a native speaker overnight.*

'Mi amas vin.'

—Esperanto: 'I love you.'

LINGVO. Esperanto, which means 'hopeful' in Esperanto, was created in 1887 by Polish-born Ludwig Zamenhof. Designed to be easy to learn, it has up to two million occasional users and 1,000 native speakers.

LEARNING TIME[1]

SWEET SMELL OF SUCCESS. The world's first sugar beet mill was opened in 1801 in the Polish town of Konary, after growers selectively bred a strain of mangelwurzel containing 6% sugar.[4] Europe was under British blockade at this time, and Napoleon seized on the new 'sugar beet' with gusto to replace the blockaded cane sugar. His zeal was such that, by the time of Waterloo, Europe had 300 mills, and since then, sugar beet has spread to supply 30% of sugar worldwide.[5] Extraction is simplicity itself—in effect, just boiling, filtering and drying; with perhaps the key outstanding technical issue being the rank stench sometimes discernable downwind for miles (described as a mix of molasses, boiled cabbage and rotten eggs).

Key: D *German*, EN *English*, I *Italian*, EO *Esperanto*. [1] *Average required by French students to reach same level.*

[4] *Up from 1.5% in normal mangelwurzels; modern varieties now contain 20% sugar.* [5] *Poland is still a major sugar beet producer, growing 11m tons a year.*

TOUGH GUY. In the seventeenth century, Poland was home to 100,000 Lipka Tatars; today just 400 remain. Descendants of Genghis Khan's Mongol Hordes who decided to stay, many eventually took up gardening (but not Charles Bronson, the best-known Lipka Tatar of modern times).

STRONG GUY. When it comes to food, the world's strongest man, Mariusz Pudzianowski, puts his success down to his Polish diet. Breakfast of 10 eggs and bacon is followed by Polish pork chops, *sauerkraut* and potatoes for lunch, with more potatoes and Polish sausage at dinner.

EAR GUY. After watching his wife grappling with a wooden toothpick to clean out their baby's ears, Polish-born Leo Gerstenzang felt the time had come for the cotton bud. He originally named his invention, launched in 1923, the 'baby gay'.

MARCHE FUNÈBRE.

Fr. Chopin.

PIANO.

SKELETON IN THE CLOSET. Chopin's *Funeral March* has been played at funerals as varied as John F. Kennedy's and Stalin's, and indeed Chopin's own. It seems there's something about it that flawlessly sets the tone. That something may just have been the skeleton the Polish composer was clutching as it was composed. According to the artist Félix Ziem, who claimed to be present, after attending a dinner party, Chopin wrapped himself in a shroud, sat at the piano and called for the skeleton (which the host kept in a cupboard); clasping it to his chest, he then laboriously pounded out the notes.

SPECIAL DELIVERY. Poland has the most storks in Europe (about 50,000 pairs) and, as in other countries, they are considered lucky. The special association with babies seems to have come about for a whole bundle of reasons, ranging from the symbolic (pairs of storks tend to be faithful) to the practical (even to a child, it's obvious not many other birds could carry a newborn). But the deepest connection appears to go back to the heathen tribes of Pomerania (now split between Poland and Germany), who believed the souls of yet-to-be-born infants dwelt in marshes and fens. As water birds, storks frequented such lonely places, and it was thought that whenever a stork (and originally also a swan) came across a child's soul it would deliver it to human parents.

PAPA PAUL. One of the earlier reforms made by Karol Wojtyła (Pope John Paul II) was abolition of the Devil's Advocate, the priest charged with opposing the canonization of new saints. Making full use of the change, John Paul II went on to canonize 483 people (more than the total over the previous 400 years) and is now on the fast-track to sainthood himself.

Pope John Paul II (aged 12)

84
Po
210

POLISH POISON. Named by its discoverer, Marie Curie, for her native Poland, Polonium-210 is spectacularly nasty stuff that came to prominence in 2006, when it was used to kill Russian émigré Alexander Litvinenko in London. More than 4,000 times as intensely radioactive as radium and 250,000 times as toxic as cyanide, 0.1 µg—a thousandth the weight of a grain of sugar—is a lethal dose. Less than 100 g are produced globally each year, 97% of which is in Russian state nuclear reactors. But then polonium's uses are murky and few. Aside from silencing troublemakers (and, in the past, acting as antifreeze for Russia's moon buggies), it's principally valued as a trigger for atom bombs. Of course, none of this was known to Marie Curie, who carried out her early research innocent of danger, with the result that her lab records (and even recipe book) were so heavily contaminated they are too dangerous to hold in any library. Instead, they are kept in lead-lined boxes and must be read wearing protective clothing.

HOLY HEROES—HOW SAINTS GET MADE

D	Ⓐ **Servant of God**		Ⓑ **Venerable**		Ⓒ **Blessed**		S
E	*1. Life and works scrutinized; and*	IF OK	*Martyrdom OR*	IF YES	*Two miracles confirmed in*	IF YES	A I
A T	*2. Body exhumed and relics taken.*		*Miracle due to prayer by them.*		*their name after death.*		N T
H							

♠ · **GSR**: 23 · **WHS**: Auschwitz (Nazi death camp) ◻ Białowieża (forest) ◻ Jawor and Świdnica (churches) ◻ Kalwaria Zebrzydowska (park) ◻ Krakow (historic city) ◻ Little Poland (wooden churches) ◻ Malbork (castle) ◻ Mużakowski Park ◻ Toruń (historic town) ◻ Warsaw (historic city) Wieliczka (salt mine) ◻ Wroclaw (exhibition hall) ◻ Zamość (Renaissance townscape)

PORTUGAL

'Lisbon plays, Braga prays and Porto gets the job done.'

—Traditional Portuguese saying

TSUNAMI! On 1 November 1755, Lisbon was shaken by a colossal earthquake. As it was All Saints' Day, most people were at worship, and thousands were crushed by masonry as the city's great churches fell. Survivors made for the open space of the waterfront, but arrived to see the sea vanishing beyond the horizon. Forty minutes later, the water returned in three huge tsunami that engulfed the bewildered crowds. Through earthquake, tsunami and fires that raged for the next five days, 85% of Lisbon was razed. Elsewhere, the tsunami reached 65 feet in height and swept as far as the West Indies. In Britain, a 10-foot wave scoured Cornwall's coast, and in Ireland, it tore down part of Galway's city walls.

AFTER THE DELUGE—MAJOR TSUNAMI OF THE MODERN ERA (SELECTED)			
Year	Location	Death toll[1]	Note
1755	**Lisbon**	80,000	shook European faith in God; gave birth to seismology
1792	**Kyushu (Japan)**	15,000	5,000 killed by echo tsunami that bounced back to source
1883	**Krakatoa**	36,000	human skeletons washed on pumice rafts as far as Africa
1908	**Messina (Italy)**	70,000	many emigrated to USA, boosting Italian-American numbers
1958	**Lituya (Alaska)**	2	1,720-ft wave (highest recorded) was ridden out by fishing boat
2004	**Indian Ocean**	300,000	wave reached Antarctica, but was only 2 ft in open ocean

[1] *Fatalities include those from associated causes, including earthquakes, fires and post-disaster epidemics.*

'Be their business ever so urgent, or the rains ever so violent, they never hasten their pace and seem to number each step.'

—C. Brockwell on the Portuguese (1726)

KING FOR (LESS THAN) A DAY. According to the *Guinness Book of Records*, history's shortest reign was that of Portugal's King Luís II—who, in 1908, ruled for 20 minutes before succumbing to the head wound he sustained in the assassination that killed his father outright. His mother, Queen Amélia, struck back at the assassins with a large bouquet of flowers and survived unharmed.

MAKE MINE A VINDALOO. The super-hot lads-night-out favourite started life in Portugal as Carne de Vinha d'Alhos, an innocuous pork stew flavoured with nothing more challenging than wine (*vinho*), vinegar and garlic (*alhos*). Portuguese merchants then took the dish to Indian Goa, where chillies were added with a shovel, before it finally travelled west again to the Indian restaurants of Britain.

MOTHER TONGUE. Written like Spanish but sounding like Russian, Portuguese is the world's sixth most widely used language—almost wholly due to Brazil.

GLOBAL PORTUGUESE SPEAKERS

- Brazil
- Portugal
- Other

Total: 178 million

REVERSE TAKEOVER. From 1808 to 1821, the capital of Portugal was moved to Rio de Janeiro, making it the only European country to have been ruled from its colonies.

FOREVER FRIENDS. The 1386 Treaty of Windsor between Portugal and Britain cemented the world's longest-standing alliance—and it's still in force. In WWII, Winston Churchill successfully invoked the 600-year-old agreement to gain use of ports and airfields in Portugal's mid-Atlantic Azores, despite the country's official neutrality. The bases proved a

devastating weapon in the hunt for German U-boats, helping to turn the tide in the Battle of the Atlantic and secure the sea lanes between America and Britain. More recently, Portugal gave help to Britain in both the Falklands Conflict and the first Gulf War.

GLAZE WHEREVER YOU GAZE
PORTUGUESE *AZULEJOS* THROUGH THE CENTURIES

From the largest cities to the smallest towns, the Portuguese urban landscape is immediately set apart from every other in Europe through the prolific use of ceramic tiling for both interior and exterior decoration. Churches, palaces and domestic homes, as well as shops, factories and even railway stations are clad in thousands of little blue and white tiles known as *azulejos* (from the Arabic for 'polished stone'). The Portuguese first acquired a taste for the ceramics from the Moors, via Spanish Andalucía, as an effective method to keep walls (and floors and ceilings) cool in the country's hot and sunny climate. But the *azulejo* has long since transcended utilitarian reasoning and is today, above all, a badge of Portuguese national identity (shared with other Lusophone countries, especially Brazil).

C15 *During the 15th century, Portugal relied on imported tiles from Moorish craftsmen in North Africa and Seville. Reflecting their Islamic provenance, decoration of the tiles was restrained, consisting of geometric designs and floral patterns.*

National Palace, Sintra

National Tile Museum, Lisbon

C17 *By the 17th century, azulejos were made in Portugal and technological improvements allowed intricate images to be painted directly on to the tiles before firing. Polychromatic tiles also became available, giving rise to a vogue for richly florid picture panels.*

C18 *The first half of the 18th century is considered the Golden Age of azulejo art, with commissions for huge baroque compositions on a massive scale. After the Lisbon earthquake of 1755, these were replaced by mass-produced tiling for quick and cheap rebuilding.*

Lisbon before 1755, National Tile Museum

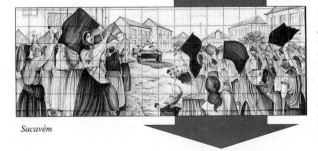

Sacavém

C20 *After the economic stagnation of the 19th century, the Portuguese azulejo was reinvigorated in the early 20th century, when the medium was adapted to a new range of modern styles. As previously, however, tiles were usually restricted to blue and white—the standard azulejo colours ever since the import of large quantities of Delftware tiles from Holland in the late 17th century.*

BEACH BOOBOO. The Moors held sway over Portugal's top beaches for 500 years (*Al-Gharb* is Arabic for 'The West'). Today, it's tourists—who often arrive thinking they're on the Mediterranean. Sadly for them, it's the chillier Atlantic that laps this shore (*see below*).

BIG TOE TEST—ATLANTIC ALGARVE HEAD TO HEAD WITH CYPRUS IN THE MED												
Sea Temp. (°C)	JAN	FEB	MAR	APR	MAY	JUN	JUL	AUG	SEP	OCT	NOV	DEC
Algarve (Albufeira)	14	15	15	16	17	19	21	22	21	19	17	16
Cyprus (Limassol)	18	17	16	18	19	23	26	26	29	24	22	20

NUN'S HABIT. Portugal's national dessert, the *pastel de nata*, is a sticky custard tart built on a nun's guilty secret. It was created at the Jerónimos Monastery in the 18th century by a nun who needed to dispose of the embarrassing surplus of yolks that accumulated through the use of egg white to starch their habits. The recipe, a secret, was sold in 1820 when the monastery closed, and the confection's wider success was assured since egg white was also used on an industrial scale to clarify port and other wines.

FADO is to Lisbon what *flamenco* is to Seville. An embodiment of the Portuguese soul, *fado* is *saudade*, melancholic unrequited yearning, set in song. After the 1974 socialist revolution, the genre was initially banned, ostensibly for spreading 'listlessness and fatalism'—but its earlier co-option by the toppled fascists hadn't helped either.

STING IN THE TAIL. Named for its surface resemblance to a Portuguese caravel, the Portuguese man o' war packs a powerful venom. Though seldom fatal to humans, it is excruciatingly painful. If threatened, the man o' war can deflate its float and submerge like a submarine.

If stung: apply salt, then hot water, then ice.

PASSING THE PORT—GLOBALIZATION'S FIRST STIRRING

Globalization arguably shapes the modern world more profoundly than any ideology or religion. In the last 30 years, the idea that nations should produce only what they're best at, and trade for the rest, has gained apparently irreversible momentum. But the theoretical underpinning goes back to David Ricardo's 1817 Law of Comparative Advantage, and his observation that Portugal traded port for English cloth, even though cloth could be made more cheaply in Portugal. Upon reflection, Ricardo realized that, whereas Portugal could easily produce both port and cloth, England found it very hard to produce wine and only moderately difficult to weave cloth. Therefore, while it was cheaper to make cloth in Portugal than England, it was nevertheless cheaper still for the Portuguese to make excess port and trade that for English cloth. The trade simultaneously benefited England as the cost of cloth stayed unchanged, but it could now get wine much more cheaply (at the price of cloth).

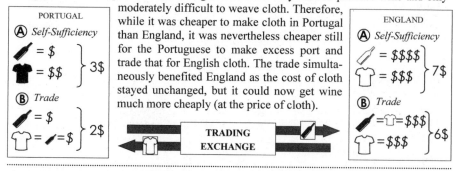

♠ · **GSR**: 24 · **WHS**: Alcobaça (monastery) □ Alto Douro (vineyards) □ Batalha (monastery) □ Côa Valley (rock art) □ Évora (museum city) □ Guimarães (townscape) □ Jerónimos Monastery & Tower of Belém (monument) □ Porto (cityscape) □ Sintra (palaces) □ Tomar (convent) ■ Azores: Angra do Heroismo (museum city) □ Pico (landscape) ■ Madeira: Laurisilva (forest)

QATAR ●قطر

'Is Doha one of the most boring places ever?'

—Qatarliving.com discussion thread about life in the Qatari capital

MEN ONLY. With 77% of its population male and a mere 23% female, Qatar has more than three men for every woman. This makes it both the most male society on Earth and a bad place for a Saturday night out for the unattached man.

ORIGINS. In Arabic, *Qatara* means 'to wrangle camels into a line and halter them'.[1]

[1] *Less colourfully, it's also 'to drip'.*

LIFE'S A GAS. Where Saudi Arabia has oil and South Africa gold, Qatar has gas: enough to supply a country the size of the UK for 260 years. Shared around, what's in the ground makes every Qatari a millionaire (on paper).

PER CAPITA GAS RESERVES[2]

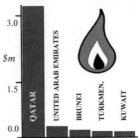

[2] *Monetary value, Henry Hub spot.*

'And Cain went out from the presence of the Lord, and dwelt in the Land of Nod, on the East of Eden.'

—King James Bible (Genesis 4:16)

OH, MR SANDMAN. If Bahrain was the Garden of Eden (*see Bahrain*), then Qatar, just to its east, must have been the biblical Land of Nod—fitting, since there's nothing but sand.

SPELLING IT OUT. Doha International Airport is (arguably) lucky in that its IATA airport code of 'DOH' is both obvious and memorable. The same is true for a relative handful of others (see examples *below*), but most of the other 17,576 three-letter codes used by IATA are to varying degrees impenetrable. (Even London Heathrow's LHR seems easy beside the YYZ of Toronto.) Used worldwide on baggage tags and tickets, IATA codes are not limited to airports: QQP is London's Paddington Station, while FFA ('First Flight Airport') is preserved for the Carolina sand dune where the Wright brothers first flew in 1903.

IATA AIRPORT CODE SCRABBLE

DOH SEXPOT! BIN THE SAD GIT! CRY NOT—I'LL TRY AND FLY OUT (FOG BIT BAD). MAD FOR HUG FUN. LUV. BIG BUM (TOM).

Doha (Qatar) ~ Sembach (Germany) ~ Port Antonio (Jamaica) ~ Bamiyan (Afghan.) ~ Teresina (Brazil) ~ Safford (US) ~ Geita (Tanz.) ~ Carlton Hill (Australia) ~ Novato (US) ~ Willmar (US) ~ Tororo (Uganda) ~ Anderson (US) ~ Finley (Australia) ~ Bousso (Chad) ~ Foggia (Italy) ~ Baitadi (Nepal) ~ Barksdale (US) ~ Madrid (Spain) ~ Fortaleza (Brazil) ~ Huehuetenango (Guat.) ~ Funafuti (Tuvalu) ~ Langgur (Indon.) ~ Big Delta (US) ~ Butler (US) ~ Timbuktu (Mali).

Al-Jazeera was sent the bin Laden videos.

SHOOTING THE MESSENGER. Qatar-based Al-Jazeera TV launched in 1996 with $140m from the Emir and a clutch of ex-BBC employees. However, it was only after broadcasting statements by Osama bin Laden and later reporting from Baghdad in the Iraq War that the station became a worldwide phenomenon. In 2004, it was voted the world's fifth most effective brand, and it remains the only Arab brand with global recognition. Since President Bush started his 'War on Terror', relations with the US have often been fraught. During the Afghanistan and Iraq invasions, the local Al-Jazeera bureaux were struck directly by an American bomb and missile respectively. ('Accidents,' say the US.) Then, in December 2003, six Air France flights were cancelled after the CIA briefed the White House that Al-Jazeera programmes had displayed bar codes containing secret targeting instructions for Al-Qaeda bombers. Tests later showed this was nonsense—the agency had been duped by a con artist in a scam to sell it bogus software.

♣ · **GSR**: 86 · **WHS**: none · **ICH**: Falconry

———— Romania • România ————

'Better a healthy donkey than a consumptive philosopher.'

—Romanian saying

HAPPY FAMILIES. By the time he was shot in the revolution of 1989, Romania's Communist strongman Nicolae Ceauşescu probably had no idea just how awful his country had become—thanks to the diligence of apparatchiks. Thus, the state kept a herd of cows well-nourished solely to window-dress any farm Ceauşescu decided to visit, while every shop he

'The Genius of the Carpathians'
(1918–89)

entered was pre-stocked with 'food' that often turned out be polystyrene. One policy area that was Ceauşescu's own, however, was an obsession with increasing the country's population. To achieve this, he banned both contraception and abortion (and stationed Securitate secret police agents in every gynaecological ward to ensure it was enforced). Taking no chances, he also compelled all women of child-bearing age to have regular gynaecological examinations, punished childless couples and unmarried women over 25, and had all books on sex education and human reproduction reclassified as state secrets.

'Dear Mr. President, you have held the highest political office in Romania for 18 years, a fact for which we warmly congratulate you. What has made you so popular with the Romanians?'

—Robert Maxwell, transcript of his interview included in his book *Nicolae Ceausescu: Builder of Modern Romania* (1983). (During the 1980s, Maxwell wrote similarly hard-hitting tomes on Honecker (GDR), Jaruzelski (Poland), Kadar (Czech.) and Zhivkov (Bulgaria).)

WHICH CAME FIRST: THE CHICKEN OR THE EGG?[1]

Romania is home to the fossilized remains of *Hatzegopteryx thambema*, the largest creature that has ever flown. Three times heavier than a man, its wingspan exceeded the length of a bus.

[1] *Answer at bottom of page.*

FANCY FOOTWORK. The real-life Dracula, Transylvanian-born Prince Vlad III, is renowned for having been an enthusiastic impaler (with perhaps 50,000 speared). But he was far from a one-trick pony. His punishment for thieves was to skin their feet, rub their wounds with salt, then bring in goats to lick it off.

BLOOD-LETTING BULB. As everyone knows, garlic is highly effective as a vampire repellent. Or is it? Garlic is a natural anti-coagulant (so much so that patients are warned not to eat it before certain types of surgery and just before childbirth), leading some conspiracy theorists to wonder if this bit of folklore might not perhaps have been planted by the Count himself—after all, what a good way to make a quick bite that bit more thirst-quenching?

Impalement, usually with a sword, is one of the most death-defying illusions modern magicians perform. To work the effect, the impalee wears a specially engineered corset beneath their costume, which, when he or she is placed on to the sword tip, catches and deflects the blade, while springing a second, dummy sword from its neckline.

A. The egg, of course. Chickens—and all other modern birds—evolved from the classic dinosaurs, which were already laying eggs. Pterosaurs, such as *Hatzegopteryx*, evolved separately from dinosaurs, although they lived at the same time.

♠ · **GSR**: 58 · **WHS**: Danube Delta (wetlands) □ Horezu (monastery) □ Maramureş (wooden churches) Moldavian Churches □ Orastie Mountains (Dacian fortresses) □ Sighişoara (medieval townscape) Transylvanian Fortified Churches · **ICH**: Căluş Ritual (games, dances and songs) □ Doina (chanting)

RUSSIA • РОССИЯ

'Russia is not a nation, but a world.' —Old Russian saying
'Woollen underwear is recommended.' —*Baedeker's Russia* (1914)

MOSCOW TORONTO LONDON

Mon 08:00

Trans-Siberian—Rossiya

Flying Scotsman

EDINBURGH Mon 12:30

PEOPLE'S HEROES. The USSR's highest award, the Order of Lenin, was given 430,000 times. Recipients included Kim Philby, Fidel Castro, Armand Hammer, Yuri Gagarin, Josip Tito, Mikhail Kalashnikov, James Bond (in *A View to a Kill* anyway) and Trade Minister Nikolay Patolichev—a record 12 times (for services to bureaucracy).

'Liberty is precious—so precious it must be rationed.' —V. I. Lenin

CORPSE LIFE. Vladimir Ilyich Lenin receives visitors five mornings a week in Moscow's Red Square. Now 124 years young, the spookily enduring corpse is kept fresh by a dip every 18 months in potassium acetate and glycerol, plus quinine as a disinfectant. Between soakings, Lenin is dabbed with the same fluid twice weekly and bacterial growths are scraped off by hand.

CASPIAN GOLD. To some, salted fish eggs; to others, the ultimate luxury edible; caviar is sturgeon roe. The finest comes from the Caspian Sea and is found in three grades: *beluga* (the best), *sevruga* (the commonest) and *osciotr* (source of the ultra-rare 'golden caviar'). Around 100 tonnes a year are exported, but overfishing is a critical concern. In imperial Russia, anyone other than the tsar caught eating it had their right hand removed. In Britain, sturgeon are 'reserved to the Crown'. The flesh is said to taste of veal—but royal assent is required before you sample it.

COKESKY. Catering for the masses, *kvass*—a feebly alcoholic drink made from fermented dry (or sometimes fried) bread—was a mainstay of Russian life in

the Soviet era. For a few kopeks, ordinary Russians could get a shot of the murky brown brew from any of the tractor-towed tankers found on almost every street corner. *Kvass* sales are now on the rebound as a 'patriotic' alternative to Western drinks like Pepsi and Coke. In 2008, Coca-Cola responded by setting up its own *kvass* plant, and, in 2010, launched the drink in the US too.

THE PRICE OF PLEASURE: MOST EXPENSIVE FOODSTUFFS[1]		
Bonne bouche	$[2]	kcal[3]
Caviar (beluga)	500	250
Truffle (white)	200	20
Jamon Iberico[4]	30	130
Foie gras	26	460
Kobe beef	17	190
Gull's egg	10[5]	140
Lobster[6]	9	105
Fugu (pufferfish)	n/a[7]	85
E175 (gold)	5,000	nil

[1]*Excludes spices and seasonings.* [2]*Cost per 100 g.* [3]*Calories per 100 g.* [4]*'Bellota' (off the bone).* [5]*Per egg (90 g).* [6]*Meat only.* [7]*Illegal in EU due to the risk of poisoning.*

ASIA'S ATTIC. Meaning 'Sleeping Land' in Tatar, the sparsely inhabited Russian region of Siberia is, on its own, larger than every country in the world except Russia.

[Zd`rastvuyte!]*     214     *[Da svi`daniya]

HOW LOW CAN YOU GO?

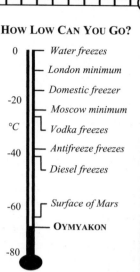

0	Water freezes
	London minimum
	Domestic freezer
-20	
	Moscow minimum
°C	Vodka freezes
-40	Antifreeze freezes
	Diesel freezes
-60	Surface of Mars
	OYMYAKON
-80	

Oymyakon in Siberia is the coldest inhabited place on Earth with a recorded lowest temperature of -71.2°C.

BACK TO THE FUTURE. At the height of the Cold War, US spy satellites snatched grainy images of a bizarre aircraft afloat on the Caspian Sea. Twice as big as any existing plane and with mere stubs for wings, analysts dubbed it the 'Caspian Sea Monster'—while desperately trying to work out what the thing was. They had, in fact, spotted the KM: the world's largest *ekranoplan*—a machine that simply didn't exist in the West. Capable of skimming at 300 mph just 10 feet above the sea with a payload of 500 tons, this secret weapon was seen by Soviet generals as the ultimate high-speed troop-carrying landing craft. Later, American spooks fretted over a latter-day Spanish Armada—with a fleet of *ekranoplans* flying beneath radar cover in a surprise attack on US shores. They needn't have worried: the Soviets could never keep the KM stable and the sole prototype crashed in 1980.

LONG AND WINDING ROADS—WORLD'S TOUGHEST DRIVES

Route	Location	Miles	Challenges
Kolyma Highway	NE Siberia	1,300	fuel freezes (winter)/impassable rivers (summer)
Canning Stock Route	W Australia	1,100	thirst (no water for 1,000 miles)/heatstroke
Trans-Africa 8	Congo	1,000	much of the 'road' has been swallowed by jungle
Karakoram Highway	China–Pakistan	800	rockfalls can block road for years at a time
Dempster Highway	NW Canada	600	washouts/mosquitoes/falling through the ice

'One death is a tragedy, a million deaths a statistic.'
—J. Stalin

'History is on our side. We will bury you.'
—N. Khrushchev

'My conscience is clear. I gave the people freedom.'
— M. Gorbachev

POSTHISTORIC MAMMOTHS. Schools have long taught that mammoths became extinct by the end of the last Ice Age. But, in 1991, scientists discovered that a race of pygmy mammoths had survived on Arctic Wrangel Island until 1700 BCE—over 800 years after the Great Pyramid of Giza was finished. Some biologists now hope living mammoths could be cloned from preserved DNA within two decades.

WHITE RUSSIAN. Mix 50 ml of vodka with 20 ml of coffee liqueur and pour into a lowball glass filled with ice cubes. Pour over 30 ml of fresh cream and stir gently.

BEAR ESSENTIALS. Around 120,000 brown bears roam Russia's forests. The biggest and fiercest animals reach 10 ft and are found in Kamchatka. In 2008, a pack of 30 trapped workers in a remote platinum mine after eating two of the guards—it took several days before help arrived and the men could be freed.

GIFT-WRAPPED. The 19th century had no doubts, the Circassian women of the Caucasus were the world's fairest. Poets eulogized their slender grace, while Oriental despots enslaved them for concubines. Part of the fascination came from the custom that, at puberty, Circassian girls were bound in laced leather corsets so tight they stopped breasts from swelling. So they stayed until their wedding night, when, to consummate the marriage, the groom unwrapped his prize by cutting her out with a knife.

BACK IN THE USSR

Q. Why did the Politburo invade Afghanistan?

A. They wanted to begin alphabetically.

★ ★ ★

Q. Why do KGB men always come in threes?

A. One to write a report, one to read it, and one to check up on the two intellectuals.

RUSSIAN ROULETTE. If the cylinder of the gun isn't spun between trigger pulls, the odds of taking a bullet are, in turn: 17%, 20%, 33%, 50% and 100%.

'I would prefer to have invented a lawnmower.'

—M. Kalashnikov

LIBERATION CHIC. The Soviet AK-47 can make a strong claim to be the most iconic weapon of the 20th century—even featuring on the flag of a country (Mozambique). Over 60 years after its introduction, it remains the most widely used assault rifle in the world, with an estimated 100,000,000 in circulation.

COMRADE CREWMAN. The USS *Enterprise*'s Russian navigator, Pavel Chekhov, popped up in *Star Trek*'s second series after its creator, Gene Rodenberry, heard the Soviet newspaper *Pravda* had complained about the lack of any Russian crew members in the first series. Taking no chances, Rodenberry also sent a formal letter of apology to the Soviet Ministry of Culture.

BIG BANG ...
On 30 June 1908, a monstrous explosion blasted a remote area of Siberia near the Tunguska River. Witnesses spoke of the sky splitting in two, heat like a furnace and the sound of the end of the world; 800 sq. miles of forest were levelled. Much remains mysterious, but the consensus is that a meteor 50 m across exploded in mid-air—an event predicted to occur somewhere on earth every 300 years or so.

EXPLOSIVE POWER

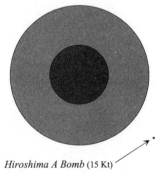

Hiroshima A Bomb (15 Kt)

Tunguska Event (15 Mt) ....■

Tsar Bomba (50 Mt) ....■

... BIGGER BANG.
On 30th October 1961, the Soviet Air Force dropped the world's most powerful hydrogen bomb, the 'Tsar Bomba', on Novaya Zemlya island. Upon detonation, the mushroom cloud rose 40 miles, windows shattered 600 miles away and the shock wave circled the Earth three times. Soviet scientists had originally planned a bomb double the size—but realized in time that testing it would turn much of Russia into a nuclear wasteland.

♠♣ · **GSR**: 16 · **WHS**: Altai (mountains) □ Baikal (lake) □ Caucasus (mountains) □ Curonian Spit (dunes) □ Derbent (citadel) □ Ferrapontov (monastery) □ Kamchatka (volcanoes) □ Kazan (monuments) □ Kizhi (churches) □ Kolomenskoye (church) □ Komi (taiga) □ Moscow (Kremlin & Red Square) □ Novgorod (museum city) □ Novodevichy (convent) □ Putorana (mountains) □ St. Petersburg (cityscape) □ Sergiev Posad (monastery) □ Sikhote-Alin (forest) □ Solovetsky Islands (monasteries) Struve Arc (survey line) □ Uvs Nuur Basin (steppe) □ Vladimir & Suzdal (museum cities) □ Wrangel Island (wildlife) □ Yaroslavl (cityscape).· **ICH**: Old Believers (culture) □ Olonkho (epics)

RWANDA

'The Hutu should stop having mercy on the Tutsi.'

—Commandment no. 8 of the 'Hutu Ten Commandments' featured in the December 1990 issue of *Kangura*, a Rwandan magazine published from 1990 to 1994 with sponsorship from the MRND—the Hutu-dominated ruling party at that time. From April to July 1994, 800,000 members of Rwanda's Tutsi minority (as well as moderate members of the Hutu majority) were slaughtered in a genocide that was halted only by the military defeat of the MRND by Tutsi rebels.

KING PONG. A farting gorilla is a happy gorilla, and Rwanda is the most popular place for visitors to catch a flavour of simian satisfaction firsthand. But while sustained farting is the main tool by which mountain gorillas communicate contentment to fellow group members, chest thumping, screaming and tearing at vegetation all signal trouble. In such circumstances, local advice is to crouch, avert one's eyes and act submissively. If this doesn't work, one last-ditch option is to brandish a caterpillar—as gorillas are all terrified of the little grubs.

LEADING LADIES. In 2008, Rwanda became the first country anywhere to elect a majority female parliament, with 56% of seats held by women. Furthermore, the speaker, chief justice and chief of police are all female, as are one-third of cabinet posts, including the foreign minister.

LOUSY LUCK. One special bond of brotherhood shared by humans and gorillas alone is infestation by pubic lice. From DNA extracted from gorilla lice harvested in Rwanda and Uganda, it appears we caught the parasites from gorillas around 3 million years ago (possibly by sleeping in gorilla nests). As we also share head lice with chimpanzees (but not gorillas), we are the only animal to have attracted more than one variety of louse.[1]

[1] *To round out the happy picture, a third species, the body louse, is all our own, having evolved 100,000 years ago when we first started to wear clothes.*

DARKNESS OF HEARTS—THE 1994 RWANDAN GENOCIDE

Cover of the December 1993 issue of Kangura *magazine. The vertical text to the right of the machete reads: 'What weapons shall we use to triumph over the cockroaches once and for all?' ('Cockroaches' was the term Hutu extremists used for Tutsi.)*

LEBENSRAUM. No one can doubt the viciousness of Rwanda's genocide—many Tutsis ended up bribing their Hutu attackers to shoot them in preference to slow dismemberment by machete; but more elusive is the cause. While described as an ethnic conflict, 25% of Rwandans had grandparents on both sides, which has led some to argue ethnicity was instead merely the fault line along which Rwandan society fractured, driven by what is still the highest rural population density in Africa (*see below*).

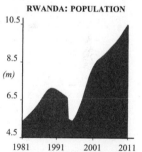

RWANDA: POPULATION

One unforeseen problem following the 1994 genocide was a surge in Rwanda's prison population, peaking at 120,000 (1.5% of the population). Most notorious was Gitarama prison, where 7,000 genocidaires were locked up in a space half the size of a soccer pitch. Standing barefoot in their own filth, 40% succumbed to footrot—causing the toes of many to drop off.

THE BEHAVIOURAL SINK. *In a classic series of 1960s experiments widely adopted as a model of human society, American academic John B. Calhoun set up various rodent colonies with unlimited food and water, but only fixed space. In all cases, populations quickly rose until, at a certain level of overcrowding, normal social behaviour collapsed into mortal hyper-agression and reclusive passivity.*

♥ · **GSR**: 146 · **WHS**: none

———————— SAN MARINO ————————

'An unashamed tourist trap. There is a crummy waxworks museum, a stamp museum and places where you can view suits of armour.'

—*Rough Guide to Italy* (1999), the San Marino paragraph

PROUD TO BE PUNY—EURO-MIDGETS COMPARED[1]									
—	VATICAN		LEICHTENSTEIN		ANDORRA		MONACO		**SAN MARINO**
Area (square miles)	0.2	(5)	62	(2)	181	(1)	0.8	(4)	**23** (3)
Population ('000)	0.8	(5)	35	(2)	84	(1)	33	(3)	**30** (4)
GDP ($ bn)	0.3^2	(5)	4.8	(1)	2.7	(2)	0.8	(4)	**1.0** (3)
Adjoining territories	1	(4)	2	(1)	2	(1)	2^3	(1)	**1** (4)
Embassies to nation	20	(1)	3	(4)	5	(2)	4	(3)	**1** (5)
Head of state's rank	pope	(1)	prince	(2)	bishop	(4)	prince	(2)	**minimal** (5)
Chief industry	religion	(1)	banking	(2)	skiing	(4)	casino	(3)	**philately** (5)
Notable attribute	holiness	(1)	wealth	(3)	health	(2)	glamour	(4)	**tourist tat** (5)
Visitor profile	world leaders	(1)	billionaires	(2)	easyJet-set	(4)	celebs	(3)	**bus trippers** (5)
***Puniness** (points)*	5th (14^4)		4th (19)		3rd (21)		2nd (27)		**1st (39)**

[1] *Puniness ranked according to aggregate scores on selected measures (1=least, 5=most).* [2] *Revenue.* [3] *France, Mediterranean Sea.* [4] *10 points arbitrarily, but reasonably, deducted for being global HQ of the world's largest religion.*

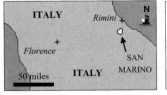

PARENTAL PARADISE. San Marino has both the world's lowest child mortality rate and the lowest incidence of teenage pregnancy.

ROMAN RELIC. Founded in 301 CE, San Marino is the world's oldest sovereign state, with a system of government handed down from ancient Rome. Known as Captains Regent, its two heads of state are modelled on Roman consuls and are elected for six-month terms by a Great Council based on the Roman senate. After each six-month government, three days are then set aside to allow Sanmarinese citizens to submit complaints about their outgoing rulers.

RETURNING THE FAVOUR. Hemmed in on all sides by Italy, San Marino's continued existence is neither logical nor likely. It should have been swept away in Italy's 1861 unification—like every other scrap of territory. But, 12 years earlier, it had briefly sheltered Garibaldi (hunted by the Austrians) so, in gratitude, he uniquely left it alone.

A FORCE TO BE RECKONED WITH. The Sanmarinese military is a well-oiled parading machine with an annual budget exceeding $650,000. Defence, as such, has been contracted out to Italy, but San Marino still retains full responsibility for changing the guard and marching nicely.

SANMARINESE ARMED FORCES—CORE MILITARY UNITS

Crossbow Corps .... wears doublet and hose, flag-waving auxiliaries.
Guard of the Rock .... natty in red and green, key guard-changers.
Guard of Nobles ..... kitted out with pompom hats, sabres and tassels.
Military Ensemble .... 50-strong brass band, more pompoms.

AGONY AND ECSTASY. San Marino holds the record for scoring the fastest World Cup goal ever (achieved eight seconds after kick-off against a hapless England in a 1993 qualifier). On the other hand, in 2006, they were hammered 0–13 by Germany in the European Championships—itself a record, albeit a far less attractive one.

♠ · **GSR**: 101 · **WHS**: San Marino (museum city)

————— SÃO TOMÉ & PRINCIPE —————

'The Chocolate Islands.'

—Nineteenth-century nickname

FLAKED OUT. Africa's second smallest country (after the Seychelles) clings to two volcanoes skimming the Equator far out in the Atlantic. Although today of profound unimportance, São Tomé entered the 20th century as the world's leading cocoa producer, with a third of its crop being taken by Messrs. Cadbury. In 1908, however, stories of slave labour conditions surfaced in the London press. This prompted William Cadbury to travel to the islands to inspect for himself— following which, the firm switched its vast custom to the Gold Coast (Ghana).

RELATIVITILY SIMPLE
$$G_{\mu\nu}+\Lambda g_{\mu\nu}= 8\pi Gc^{-4}T_{\mu\nu}$$
Where: $G_{\mu\nu}$ = Einstein tensor, Λ = cosmological constant, $g_{\mu\nu}$ = metric tensor, G = gravitational constant, c = speed of light, $T_{\mu\nu}$ = stress-energy tensor.

NEWTON ECLIPSED. In 1919, Sir Arthur Eddington sailed to the island of Principe, São Tomé's little brother, to make the first experimental test of Einstein's new 'General Theory of Relativity' (*above*). Timing his trip for a solar eclipse, he successfully observed starlight bending round the edge of the sun—exactly as Einstein had predicted, but at odds with the old Newtonian description. Once back in London, Eddington made headlines worldwide with his results, and hoisted Einstein into the pantheon of science's immortals.

NO BUTTS. São Tomé's post-independence communist government made it illegal to smoke cigarettes along the seashore after dusk. Nothing to do with health concerns, the purpose was to make life hard for covert 'imperialist infiltrators' who—so the thinking went—might otherwise have been tempted to use the glowing stub to signal to any hostile submarines that happened to be passing by.

(VERY) G.P. After all of São Tomé's Portuguese colonists fled as a group at independence in 1975, the country was left with precisely one (locally trained) doctor.

AFRICAN ARK. With monster begonias ten times as tall as those found anywhere else, the only mammal with different numbers of teeth in its upper and lower jaws (the São Tomé collared fruit bat) and the only snail in the world that has a hinged shell (the São Tomé door snail), São Tomé is a hotspot of unique species as varied and exotic as the Galápagos Islands. However, the island's isolation, tiny

The São Tomé Giant Land Snail. Found only on the island, it's such a popular source of protein for islanders it is now threatened with extinction.

size and poverty also make São Tomé a potential hotspot of extinction: at least four of its endemic species are currently listed as critically endangered, and most of the rest are either endangered or vulnerable—often with populations estimated in no more than dozens.

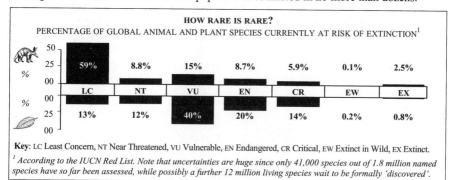

HOW RARE IS RARE?
PERCENTAGE OF GLOBAL ANIMAL AND PLANT SPECIES CURRENTLY AT RISK OF EXTINCTION[1]

	LC	NT	VU	EN	CR	EW	EX
% (animals)	59%	8.8%	15%	8.7%	5.9%	0.1%	2.5%
% (plants)	13%	12%	40%	20%	14%	0.2%	0.8%

Key: LC Least Concern, NT Near Threatened, VU Vulnerable, EN Endangered, CR Critical, EW Extinct in Wild, EX Extinct.

[1] *According to the IUCN Red List. Note that uncertainties are huge since only 41,000 species out of 1.8 million named species have so far been assessed, while possibly a further 12 million living species wait to be formally 'discovered'.*

♥ · **GSR**: 179 · **WHS**: none

—— SAUDI ARABIA ● المملكة العربية السعودية ——

'If the King says it is night in the middle of the day, look up at the stars.'

—Arabian proverb

	GATEWAYS TO GOD—ISLAM'S HOLIEST SITES		
	Location	*Reason*	*Note*
1	**Makkah**[1] *(S. Arabia)*	Muhammad ordained it so	prayers said to be boosted up to 50,000-fold
2	**Medina**[1] *(S. Arabia)*	burial site of Muhammad	an empty grave nearby is reserved for Jesus
3	**Jerusalem** *(Disputed)*	Muhammad's gate to heaven	Muslims originally prayed facing Jerusalem
4	**Kairouan** *(Tunisia)*	linked in legend to Makkah	Seven pilgrimages said to be worth one Hajj
5	**Mt. Sinai** *(Egypt)*	associations with Moses	Moses is revered second only to Muhammad

[1] *Since 1986, the kings of Saudi Arabia have discarded all former regal honorifics and, in their place, adopted the exclusive title of 'Custodian of the Two Holy Mosques'—echoing the office formerly held by Islam's early caliphs.*

RELATIVE PLENTY. The Saudi royal family numbers over 5,000 princes. Adding princesses and those who have married commoners, the total roster of royals in the kingdom may amount to over 25,000.

THE PRICE OF BELIEF. Under Saudi law, blood money must be paid to the families of those killed either intentionally or negligently (such as in a road accident). The sum is calculated according to the victim's faith and gender,[2] and the degree of fault.

SAUDI BLOOD MONEY TARIFFS[3] (2010)

Muslim (male) ....…......... $27,000
Muslim (female) ....…........ $13,500
Christian or Jew (male) ......…............. $13,500
Christian or Jew (female) ......…........... $8,800
Other religions or atheist (male) $1,750
Other religions or atheist (female) ....… $880

[2] *Iran has a similar system, but the time of year is also important: during the four months of* haram, *all rates are doubled.* [3] *Levels for 100% culpability.*

HOTHEADS. In 2009, a Medina man sued a local *djinn* (genie) for harassment, after it allegedly took over his home. Found more usually in wild and desolate places (very rarely lamps or bottles), *djinn* are recognized in Muslim theology as one of the three classes of being, alongside angels and humans. Whereas angels were made from light and men from clay, the Qu'ran says *djinn* were created from flame. Although invisible, *djinn* share our world. Marriage to a *djinn* is permitted by some clerics (and sex during menstruation is likely to result in a *djinn* child); like humans, *djinn* can be good, bad (or neither)—but all can be irascible and share an aptitude for magic.

BEHIND THE VEIL—THE WHATS & WHYS OF ARABIAN DRESS

TUNNEL VISION. Clothing that hides the entire body (head included) has been worn by Arabian women since the Roman era. However, with the rise of Islam, this ethnic custom has been conflated with the notion of *awrah* (modesty). Saudi Arabia takes a strict view, enforcing the *niqab* (1). Nevertheless, this isn't enough for some clerics: Sheikh al-Habadan is now calling for women to expose just one eye—as the sight of two, he feels, is too alluring.

DESERT SHIELD. The Islamic concept of *awrah* (modesty) applies to men as well as women—albeit far less restrictively. Males must conceal their bodies behind shapeless clothing between navel and knees—often with the loose ankle-length shirt known as the *thawb* (3). Although not mandatory, it is seen as more modest also to cover one's head with a *ghutra* (4) and *agal* (5).

(2) *Abaya (*cloak*)*   (6) *Bisht (*robe*)*

واذن في الناس بالحج ياتوك رجالا وعلى كل ضامر ياتين من كل فج عميق

'Proclaim thou unto all the duty of Hajj. They will come to thee on foot and every kind of mount, from every far point.'

—Qur'an 22:27

THE FIFTH PILLAR OF ISLAM—A HOW-TO OF HAJJ[1]

Known as the Hajj, a pilgrimage to Makkah during the second week of the last Islamic month of the year is a sacred duty for all Muslims with the necessary physical, mental and financial capacity at least once in their adult lifetime. In 2010, 2.8m did so, suggesting that, at current rates, broadly 10% of Muslims will achieve this ideal in practice.

[1] *The Hajj described here is the Hajj al-Ifrad. This is the simplest valid form.*

Day 1 — Enter Ihram

Ihram: On arrival, pilgrims bathe. Men then put on Ihram clothing (essentially two white hem-less towels) for the rest of their Hajj.

Once in a state of Ihram, pilgrims may not wear sewn clothes, carry weapons or clip their nails, and women may not cover their faces. Marriage proposals are also forbidden.

Day 2 — First Tawaf

First Tawaf: Entering Makkah's Sacred Mosque, pilgrims kiss the Black Stone (if able), then circle the Ka'aba seven times.

The Ka'aba is the holiest structure in Islam. Reputedly first built by Adam, it held 360 idols (including an image of Jesus and Mary) before it was cleansed by Muhammad.

Day 3 — Day of Arafat

Day of Arafat: This day is spent in quiet contemplation until sunset on Mt. Arafat—the site of Muhammad's final sermon.

Muhammad means 'be greatly praised' in Arabic ('Ahmed', and 'Mahmud' share the same root). With an estimated 150m 'Muhammads', it is today the world's most popular name.

Days 4–5 — Ramy

Ramy al-Jamarat: Literally 'Stoning the Devil'; each pilgrim throws 70 pebbles at three stone walls signifying Shaitan (Satan).

According to Islam, Satan is the most powerful djinn. Out of pride, he rebelled against God when commanded to bow down before Adam, and now whispers sin into human hearts.

Day 5 — Tawaf al-Ifadah

Tawaf al-Ifadah: After cutting (women) or shaving (men) their hair, pilgrims repeat the Tawaf undertaken on the second day.

In 1979, the Sacred Mosque was seized by armed zealots. It took the Saudis two weeks to dislodge them (finally resorting to gas, drowning or electrocution depending on the source).

Day 5 — Sa'y

Sa'y: To finish the Hajj, pilgrims run seven times between two mounds (Safa and Marwa), then drink from the Zamzam spring.

Although it is illegal to export Zamzam water from Saudi Arabia, there is an overseas black market. In 2010, the UK warned that counterfeits were often laced with arsenic.

ISLAM'S FIRST LADIES

Muhammad had 11 (or perhaps 13) wives. The majority were political arrangements or widows married out of charity, but his first two wives, Khadijah and Aisha, appear to have been true love matches. Domestically, Muhammad was a man centuries ahead of his time, helping with the cooking and household chores, valuing his wives' opinions, and spending many hours engaging them in debate.

خديجة بنت خويلد

Khadijah bint Khuwaylid was traditionally fifteen years older than Muhammad when they married, and during their 24 years together, and for two years after her death, Muhammad refused to take any other wives. Khadijah is known as the first convert to Islam and so the first Muslim after Muhammad himself.

عائشة بنت أبي بكر

When Muhammad was 52, he got engaged to the seven-year-old Aisha bint Abu Bakr, marrying her two years later.[2] Described as prodigiously clever and eloquent, Aisha went on to become probably the most respected interpreter of Muhammad's teachings after the prophet's death.

[2] *These are the dates given in the Hadith. Certain modern Islamic writers argue Aisha was approximately four years older.*

♣ · **GSR**: 30 · **WHS**; Al-Diriyah (historic town) □ Madâin Sâlih (rock tombs) · **ICH**: Falconry

─────SENEGAL • SÉNÉGAL─────

'Everyone strum your koras, strike the balafons.'

—Opening line of the Senegalese national anthem (written by its first president, Léapold Senghor)

PLANET OF THE APES. One trait that has long been thought to separate humans from every other species has been the manufacture of weapons. However, a group of chimpanzees in southeast Senegal has recently learnt to make and use spears to hunt bush babies (a smaller primate). The apes have been observed tearing off branches and sharpening them with their teeth, before stabbing the freshly made weapons repeatedly and with great force into likely bush baby hiding places—an action described by the lead researcher as reminiscent of a scene from Alfred Hitchcock's *Psycho*. Noting that female chimps seem to have been the first to make the spears (despite the males being the primary hunters), the primatologists believe the behaviour also hints that women may have played a similar part in human evolution by filling the role of lead innovators.

....

'The jungle is stronger than the elephant.'

—Senegalese proverb

PLANT POWER. Senegal's key cash crop is the goober pea; production runs at nearly one million tonnes a year, enough to earn Senegal a

place in the global Goober Big Five. Although, like runner beans and garden peas, goobers are legumes, the unusually nutty texture and oily richness of the goober's seeds have led to their alternative descriptive name of 'pea-nuts'. (The additional term 'ground-nut' comes from the plant's strange habit of burrowing its flowers into the soil after pollination, so that the peanuts that develop from them mature underground like mini potatoes.) Aside from making butter, peanuts have been used extensively to manufacture explosives (as peanut oil can readily be converted into nitroglycerine—a vital component of dynamite and cordite), while at the 1900 Paris World Fair one of Rudolf Diesel's new combustion engines was run exclusively on peanut oil—making it the world's first biodiesel.

Made from skin, gourd and bamboo, the ekonting *is the most likely origin for the American banjo. Traced to Senegal's Casamance river, not only does the* ekonting *look like a banjo, it's played by 'stroking' as the banjo can be.*

DAKAR DETOUR. Crossing the toughest terrain the Andes has to offer, the epic Paris–Dakar rally is one of the world's harshest challenges. Until 2007, it was run—as might be guessed—from Paris to the Senegalese capital, through the Sahara. But then threats from Al Qaeda forced a cancellation, followed by long-term relocation to South America. In 2008, one of Osama bin Laden's sons announced plans for a replacement race on horseback along the original route, with the proceeds going to war orphans. His comment: 'I heard the rally was stopped because of Al Qaeda. I don't think they're going to stop me.'

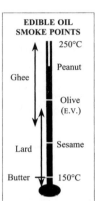

EDIBLE OIL SMOKE POINTS	
	250°C
Ghee	Peanut
	Olive (E.V.)
Lard	Sesame
Butter	150°C

Oriental cooks use peanut oil for stir-frying because its elevated smoke point allows the use of high cooking temperatures. This crisply seals the food's surface, so preventing the penetration of oil turning it greasy.

....

♥ · **GSR** 139 · **WHS**: Djoudj (birdlife) □ Gorée Island (slave station) □ Niokolo-Koba (wildlife) □ Saint Louis (museum town) □ Saloum Delta □ Senegambia Stone Circles · **ICH**: Kankurang (initiatory rite)

SERBIA • СРБИЈА

'Before him trembled Constantinople, father of plague and gore;
And even the Turks swore by his sword, no other oath they swore!'

—Prince-Bishop Petar II Petrović-Njegoš, *The Mountain Wreath* (1847). The lines eulogize Karađorđe Petrović ('Karageorge' to Anglophones), leader of the First Serbian Uprising against Ottoman Turkey.

Detail from Serbia's Miroslav Gospels, *the earliest extant document in Old Church Slavonic (c. 1190). Like all of Europe's late medieval manuscripts, it is written with ink made from the galls that grow on oaks (Serbia's emblematic tree)—replacing the soot used before the 12th century.*

CHRISTIAN BROTHERS. The only cathedral to have been used as a truck park by both the German and Red armies, St. Sava, the largest Orthodox church in the world, is now inching towards completion in Belgrade. Serbia was converted by Byzantine missionaries around 863 and the bonds between Greece and Serbia remain strong—1,136 years on, Greece was the only NATO member to refuse an active role in the 1999 air war in support of Muslim Kosovo.

THE TIES THAT BIND. Christmas is celebrated with great elaboration across Serbia, and has a central place in family life. Despite this, Serbian children do not traditionally receive presents. Instead, they get tied up with ropes three Sundays before Christmas and have to ransom their freedom with gifts to their parents. On the next Sunday, it is their mothers who get bound, and they likewise have to give gifts to be freed. Finally, on the Sunday immediately before Christmas, wives and children unite to tie down their menfolk until they too pay their assailants off. Over Christmas itself, fir trees don't play any traditional role. Instead, families burn an oak log (*badnjak*) in the hearth, taken from a tree that is by custom felled on Christmas Eve morning after having first been greeted and kissed.

MAD, BAD AND DANGEROUS TO KNOW

NIKOLA TESLA (1856–1943)
The man who brought us AC (without which electricity would essentially be limited to batteries) was mostly very sane, but a few of his ideas were fairly 'out there'—his patent electric laxative being a case in point. When he died, Tesla was working on a death ray he claimed could destroy 10,000 aeroplanes at a distance of 200 miles.

ARKAN (1952–2000)
Before Arkan founded his Serb Volunteer Guard (*above*) and became the most feared individual in the Yugoslav Wars, the former international bank robber, purse-snatcher and sadist escaped from jail as a hobby—having broken out of prisons in Belgium, Holland, Germany and Switzerland.

ARNOLD PAOLE (d. 1726 ?)
Paole's life became interesting only after he broke his neck and went to his grave. A little later, locals exhumed his body, found it drenched in blood, and, concluding he was a vampire, drove a stake through his heart. Nothing unusual there, except that, by chance, news reached Britain, sparking the interest in Balkan vampires that still lives today.

♠ · **GSR**: 85 · **Serbia does not recognize the independence of its former Autonomous Province of Kosovo**. **WHS**: Gamzigrad-Romuliana (fortified Roman palace) ▢ Stari Ras & Sopócani (medieval building ensemble and monastery) ▢ Studenica (monastery)

———————— SEYCHELLES ————————

'Twice as nice as Waikiki Beach.'

—Anonymous American visitor

RAINBOW BEACH. The beaches of the Seychelles are some of the world's most alluring—thanks to porcelain-white sands of finely crushed coral. Globally, striking beach hues have many causes, including:

Silver .... *pure quartz*
Green .... *olivine*
Yellow ... *iron-rich quartz*
Pink .... *coral*
Red .... *iron deposits*
Purple...*manganese garnet*
Black ... *basalt or obsidian*
Tan .... *mixed quartz*
White ..... *coral or gypsum*

UGLY DUCKLINGS. In 1981, a planeload of mercenaries attempted a coup while posing as members of the Ancient Order of Frothblowers (a genuine but defunct British drinking club). Leading the group was Colonel 'Mad Mike' Hoare, previously technical advisor to the successful 1978 mercenary film *The Wild Geese*, starring Roger Moore. The mercenaries were rumbled when a customs officer spotted an AK-47 assault rifle in one man's luggage, but after a firefight, most escaped to South Africa on a hijacked jet.

ISLANDS IN THE SUM. The Seychelles is the only country named after an accountant—Moreau de Séchelles, controller of finances for Louis XV of France.

TEMPTING TASTE. At over 17 lb, the largest seed in the world is that of the *coco de mer*, a palm unique to three islands in the Seychelles. Its admittedly suggestive shape got Victorian colonialists seriously hot under the collar. Noting a resemblance to 'the true seat of carnal desires', General Gordon (later of Khartoum) declared the *coco de mer* to be the 'forbidden fruit' and, by extension, the Vallée de Mai, where it grows, the original Garden of Eden. The fruit's flesh is said to taste of minted coconut and, not surprisingly, is regarded as a potent aphrodisiac. Its original botanical name, *callipyge*, translates as 'beautiful rump'.

SHARK CHUTNEY. *Boil 2 lbs shark with fresh* bilimbi[1] *juice and lime. Mash and fry with onion and turmeric, then season.* One of the best-known Seychellois dishes, shark chutney was created to make use of some of the sharks caught by the country's shark-finning fishery (which are otherwise thrown overboard to bleed to death[2]).

[1] Bilimbi *is a close relative of the starfruit. If unavailable, substitute tomato or tamarind.* [2] *As the fins are the only bit of a shark that are sought after, fisherman hack them off, then throw the wounded sharks overboard to save space for more valuable catches such as tuna.*

TOTALLY TORTOISE. Over 150,000 strong, the world's largest creep of giant tortoises roams the remote Seychellois atoll of Aldabra. Within the islands, tortoises occupy a similar ecological niche to that of elephants on the African mainland. They are the primary consumers of vegetation and depositors of seeds and fertilizer, clear paths through the bush that can be used by other animals (even knocking down small trees),

THE GIANT TORTOISE OF SOUTH ALDABRA ISLAND.

and modify the environment to suit themselves through the creation of special 'tortoise prairies'. Individually, Aldabran tortoises can weigh up to 800 lbs and live far beyond the human span. 'Adwaita', a tortoise once owned by Clive of India, may have been as old as 255 when he died in March 2006 of liver failure brought on by a shell infection.

♥ · **GSR**: 166 · **WHS**: Aldabra (atoll and tortoises) □ Vallée de Mai (palm forest)

———————— SIERRA LEONE ————————

'They cut off my hands so that I couldn't vote for democracy any more. They told me to go to the international community to give me new hands. I suffered for democracy, so I have to support democracy until the end of my life.'

—Ishmael Daramy (2002). During Sierra Leone's 1991–2002 civil war, between 4,000 and 10,000 people had arms, legs and sometimes noses amputated by militia forces—mainly the RUF rebels (ultimately defeated following the intervention of British forces), who typically assigned child soldiers to do the task. Unlike many RUF victims, Daramy wasn't given the choice of 'short sleeves' or 'long sleeves'—arms amputated above or below the elbows.

CAPITAL IDEA. Britain's first African colony, Sierra Leone was founded around its capital Freetown, built from scratch in 1787 as a place to resettle poor black Londoners. In 1819, Freetown also became the base for the Royal Navy's West Africa Squadron, tasked with suppressing the Atlantic slave trade. At its height, the squadron encompassed a sixth of the Royal Navy's ships and by 1860 it had rescued 150,000 African slaves—most of whom chose to stay in Sierra Leone, where they knew they would be safe from recapture.

SOLE TRADERS. Until 1940, Kissi 'pennies' circulated as legal tender in northern Sierra Leone. Each was a locally made twisted rod of iron about a foot long. However, if it was accidentally snapped, a penny couldn't be spent again until a *zoe* (witchdoctor) had conducted a special ceremony to rejoin it and reincarnate the penny's soul—hence, Kissi currency was known as the money with a soul. For larger purchases, Kissi pennies were tied in bundles of twenty: 100 bundles bought a cow and 300 a slave, while a bride was between the two at 200.

COAST TO COAST. While the Gold Coast exported gold and the Slave Coast slaves, the Rice Coast, based around Bunce Castle in modern Sierra Leone, exported not rice but more slaves. However, these were experienced rice farmers (coming from communities that may have grown native African rice for 3,000 years) and could therefore be sold at a premium to the plantation owners of America's Carolinas coast, who often lacked rice-growing expertise themselves. Later becoming known as the Gullah, the descendents of the Rice Coast slaves managed to retain a unique degree of cohesion in later generations and, still living on the coast of the Carolinas, are now regarded as having preserved the most complete African heritage of any of the USA's black communities.

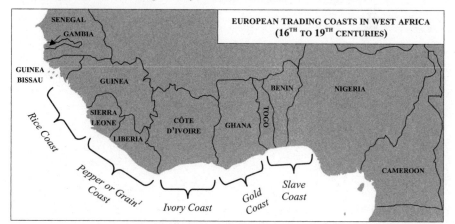

Modern states are shown for identification purposes only as most were established after the end of the period.

[1] *'Pepper' and 'grain' both refer to grains of paradise, also known as guinea pepper. Now largely forgotten in the West, the spice was originally used as a substitute for the more expensive Asian black pepper. After Asian pepper became more affordable, culinary demand declined and grains of paradise found their chief use in the adulteration of beer (making it taste more potent). Another continuing use is as a 'botanical' flavouring added to some gins (such as Bombay Sapphire).*

♥ · **GSR**: 105 · **WHS**: none

——————— SINGAPORE ———————

'Disneyland with the death penalty.'

—William Gibson

SINGAPORE—A FINE CITY

Offence	Penalty
Toilet (not flushing of)....$120
Jaywalking.....................$800
Chewing gum...................$800
Dropping litter.................$800
Vandalism....................Caning
Drugs..............................Death

HAPPY DAYS. When, in 2006, the government of Singapore launched a Four Million Smiles campaign[1] to improve the welcome received by foreign visitors, the country's main newspaper, the *Straits Times*, ran a splash feature briefing readers on smiling etiquette. It included a list of circumstances when smiling might be inappropriate—such as at the scene of a car crash.

[1] *When activist and musician Seelan Pillai tried to launch a parody '400 Frowns' website, he was arrested and his computer was confiscated.*

TRUE BRIT. The founder of Singapore, Sir Stamford Raffles, was also an ardent naturalist and eminent opponent of slavery. After his return to the UK in 1824, he co-founded London Zoo, but on his death three months later, he was refused burial in his local parish church because of his abolitionist views.

STAYING ALIVE. The world's lowest annual murder rate is found in Singapore—less than 1 death per 100,000 people.

MELTING POT

Chinese ■ Indian ▨
Malay ■ Other □

Total pop. of Singapore: 4.8m

	PREMIER-LEAGUE PREMIERS[2]		
1	Lee[3]	(*Sing*)	$2.7m
2	Tsang	(*HK*)	$510,000
3	Obama	(*US*)	$400,000
4	Merkel	(*Ger*)	$390,000
5	Gillard	(*Aus*)	$375,000
6	Harper	(*Can*)	$330,000
7	Sarkozy	(*Fr*)	$320,000
8	Kenny	(*Ire*)	$280,000
9	Noda	(*Jap*)	$240,000
10	Cameron	(*UK*)	$230,000

[2] *National leaders' annual salaries (2011).* [3] *A further 28 Singaporean ministers earn at least $1,000,000— over twice the salary of the world's second-best-paid leader.*

'I want a world-class opposition, not a riff-raff.'

—Lee Kuan Yew,
(ex-prime minister)

SEA SERPENTS. In 1932, the crew of a steamer in the Malacca Strait, off Singapore, spotted a continuous column of sea snakes 60 miles long. Similar sightings have been made elsewhere, but why the snakes occasionally mass in such huge numbers is still unknown.

SINGAPORE SLING. Shake 40 ml gin, 20 ml cherry brandy, 5 ml each Cointreau and Benedictine, 10 ml Grenadine, 80 ml fresh pineapple juice (pref. from Sarawak), 30 ml fresh lemon juice and a dash of Angostura bitters with ice. Strain into a highball glass.

WHITE FLAG. Britain's WWII defence of Singapore—touted as the 'Gibraltar of the East'—lasted just six days. When Lt. Gen. Percival capitulated to the Japanese, 60,000 troops were taken prisoner—the biggest surrender in British military history.

PLONKERS. In 1967, Singapore was gripped by an epidemic of *koro*, a form of mental illness found only in Asia, in which the sufferer believes his penis is retracting into his body, and that, when fully gone, he will die. At the outbreak's peak, 100 patients presented at Singapore's General Hospital each day. According to Professor Kua: 'The panic-stricken man often clutched on to his penis with bewildered spouse and relatives assisting.' By the time they reached help, many had tied chopsticks to their organ to arrest further shrinkage.

♣ · **GSR**: 18 · **WHS**: none

————— SLOVAKIA • SLOVENSKO —————

'He who doesn't steal from the state steals from his family.'

—Communist-era Slovak saying

THE BALTIC–BALKAN PROBLEM. Slovakia is not one of the world's higher-profile nations. Given that its only flicker of independent existence, prior to 1993, was as a Nazi puppet state, this isn't perhaps altogether surprising. However, national brand recognition is made infinitely more challenging by sharing the first four letters of its name with Slovenia—a place on the Med that people actually visit on holiday. Confusion is even worse in the local languages. Slovaks talk in *slovenčina* while Slovenes speak *slovenščina* (spot the difference).

A RICH HERITAGE OF AGRICULTURAL ACUMEN

** When it's dark, all cows look black **
** Even a dog can't crap fast **
** I love you like a horse[2] **
** To the kale![3] **
** Cabbage is best reheated seven times **

[2] *The ultimate Slovak lover's compliment.*
[3] *'Damn it, I've just stubbed my toe.'*

VELVET DIVORCE

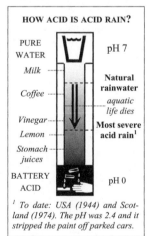

CZECH— o — SLOVAKIA

SLOVAKIA'S NATIONAL AXE

An important symbol of nationhood

BUZZED OFF. Slovakia is the global epicentre of death by overexposure to vibration. Official figures show just over 0.5 Slovaks per million get wobbled to death annually.

On 1 January 1993, the Czech and Slovak Republics officially separated. This brought to an end their 76-year marriage as the state of Czechoslovakia, begun in a civil ceremony at the Moose Hall, Pittsburgh, Pennsylvania, in 1918.

CORROSION PROBLEM. A toxic mix of Soviet-era heavy industry and rain-soaked mountain forests has given Slovakia some of Europe's worst acid-rain damage. In the mid 1990s, loss of leaf cover was measured at 28%, while 40% of the country's pine forests have been classed as poisoned. Emission controls now help, but the legacy remains.

HOW ACID IS ACID RAIN?

PURE WATER	pH 7
Milk	
	Natural rainwater
Coffee	
	aquatic life dies
Vinegar	
Lemon	Most severe acid rain[1]
Stomach juices	
BATTERY ACID	pH 0

[1] *To date: USA (1944) and Scotland (1974). The pH was 2.4 and it stripped the paint off parked cars.*

IT'S RAINING MEN. In 1913, Slovak Štefan Banič invented the first military parachute. Looking like an umbrella with the wearer as the handle, it nonetheless worked—as Banič proved by jumping off a 41-storey building in front of the patent examiners.

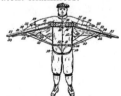

MY LITTLE DUMPLING. Slovak cuisine is one of the sturdiest in Central Europe. *Bryndzové halušky*, a favourite, offers potato dumplings, sour cream and cheese heaped with diced pork fat. Such high-calorie cooking may help Slovak farmers through snowbound winter days but keeps Slovakia second in Europe's obesity league—just behind the UK.

♠ · **GSR**: 55 · **WHS**: Banská Štiavnica (historic mining town) □ Bardejov (museum town) □ Carpathians (x2) (beech forests/wooden churches) □ Slovak Karst (caves) □ Spišsky Hrad (museum town) Vlkolínec (museum village) · **ICH**: Fujara (shepherd's flute)

————————SLOVENIA • SLOVENIJA ————————

'All resistance will be broken.'

—Yugoslav General K. Kolsek (1991), after Slovenia declared independence

STARTING GUN. Slovenia's June 1991 declaration of independence triggered the first war on European soil since 1945. The Ten-Day War, as it is known, cost 76 lives. Though fairly modest in itself, the brief conflict opened the door to Yugoslavia's 10 years of dismemberment with the death of 130,000 and displacement of 3.7 million.

'God knows why he has made the wings of some birds shorter.'
—Slovene proverb

HORSEFLESH. Arguably the world's finest dressage horses,[1] Lipizzaners were developed in Slovenia from 1580 onwards at the Hapsburg imperial stud at Lipica[2]. During WWII, the entire herd was rustled by the Nazis (part of a plan to breed an equine master race), then snatched back by the US Army's Operation Cowboy from under the noses of the advancing Soviets—who, the Germans and Americans alike feared, were going to convert them into sausage.

[1] *Used most famously by the Spanish Riding School in Vienna.* [2] *Lipizza in Italian—hence the breed's name.*

HERE BE DRAGONS. For centuries, Slovenes have known that hosts of foot-long flesh-coloured 'worms akin to lizards' would wash out from certain underground springs after spells of heavy rain. Putting two and two together, they believed these to be the offspring of giant dragons living deep underground. They are not dragons, but the scientific explanation is hardly less strange. Known as olms, the 'worms' are troglodyte amphibian larvae that never grow up, live for over a century and can survive for a decade without food.

STICK IN THE MUD. Slovenia's Kras plateau gave the world the word 'karst' to describe limestone landscapes across the globe. Formerly covered with oak, two-thirds of the region was deforested in the Middle Ages to supply the estimated 100 million wooden piles that underpin Venice.

TRUE BELIEVERS. The gods of antiquity died at the 394 CE Battle of the Frigidus, in Slovenia. With 100,000 troops on each side, the pagan Western Roman Empire, marching under the banner of Hercules, took on the Christian East, and lost. Within a generation, Italy's patrician pagan families had pragmatically turned to supplying popes instead.

STAR PERFORMER—NATION-BUILDING SCORES OF POST-COMMUNIST EU MEMBERS[3]

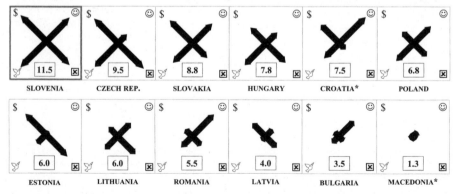

SLOVENIA	CZECH REP.	SLOVAKIA	HUNGARY	CROATIA*	POLAND
11.5	9.5	8.8	7.8	7.5	6.8

ESTONIA	LITHUANIA	ROMANIA	LATVIA	BULGARIA	MACEDONIA*
6.0	6.0	5.5	4.0	3.5	1.3

[3] *Nation-building is shown by relative ranking in four measures: $ average income, ☺ life satisfaction and sustainability of society, ☒ commitment to democracy, ⅋ freedom from conflicts. Boxed figure gives average score. Sources: GDP per capita (nominal), IMF (2009); Happy Planet Index, New Economics Foundation (2009); Democracy Index, Economist (2008); Global Peace Index, Institute for Economics and Peace (2010).* *Candidate members.*

♠ · **GSR:** 74 · **WHS:** Pile Dwellings □ Škocjan Caves

——————— SOMALIA • SOOMAALIYA ———————

'Speak not to me with a mouth that eats fish.'

—Somali nomad insult. Most Somali clans have a taboo against eating fish. Clan members will refuse to marry anyone from one of the few clans that do eat seafood.

SHIPS OF THE DESERT. Somalia is the place where the camel was first domesticated over 4,000 years ago, and the country still retains the world's biggest herd: around one in four camels worldwide are found on Somali territory.[1] As a beast of burden adapted to desert terrain, the camel is, of course, unmatched, and it can boast the unique achievement of having been the only pack animal ever to have displaced the wheel as the preferred means of transport (which it did across much of Arabia and the greater Sahara until well into the 20th century and the arrival of reliable motor vehicles).

[1] *Somalia's camels are exclusively one-humped dromedaries, which outnumber two-humped Bactrian camels by around ten to one on a global basis.*

SHALL I COMPARE THEE TO EXHIBIT A? Poems are a highly valued art form in Somali society, to the extent that litigants are customarily expected to present their case in court using poetry. Even among fighters, standing is determined in part by the ability to converse concisely, allude alliteratively and sprinkle one's speech with similes as sparkling as stardust.

EATS SHOOTS AND LEAVES. Ten planeloads of *khat* each day are flown into Somalia. Containing a natural stimulant related to amphetamine, the shoots and leaves of the *khat* bush are eaten by 60% of Somalis, and, when Somalia still had an army, were even included in soldiers' rations to make them more aggressive (since k*hat*-chewing reduces inhibitions). The Somalis (and Yemenis across the Red Sea) weren't the first to enjoy the plant, however. The ancient Egyptians were fond of *khat* too, and referred to it as 'divine food'. Going even further, they believed anyone who chewed it acquired the attributes of a god.

MAD, BAD & DANGEROUS TO KNOW
AFRICA'S FIVE MOST PERILOUS COUNTRIES

Safest African country is Mauritius (Danger Index Score = 15)

Danger Index Score[2]: MRTA 78, ZIMB 78, SUDAN 80, CONGO DR 84, SOMALIA[3] 94

Key: MRTA Mauritania, ZIMB Zimbabwe. [2] *Inverse of Ibrahim Index score for Personal Safety (2009).* [3] *The danger in some parts of Somalia is both extreme and random. After evading the FBI for a decade with a $5m bounty on his head, al-Qaeda's chief of East African operations, Fazul Abdullah Mohammed, was shot dead in Mogadishu in June 2011 simply due to taking a wrong turning. (His importance was only realized later when his vehicle was found to be full of cash and computers.)*

WHEELS OF WAR. Poor man's tanks, 'technicals' are today paraded by warlords  from Congo to Pakistan and Iraq to Sudan, but it was in 1990s Somalia that the now-ubiquitous pick-up with anti-aircraft gun acquired its unusual *nom de guerre*. The name arose after aid agencies were prevented from bringing in their own security and so, to plug the gap, hired local militia with what euphemistically went into the accounts as 'technical assistance grants'. The guards and their vehicles quickly got labelled 'technicals' and, from this, the term was soon applied to anyone's battlewagons.

> *According to Transparency International's 2010 Corruption Perceptions Index, Somalia is the world's most corrupt country, scoring just 1.1 out of a possible 10 for probity.*
>
> **A BEGINNER'S GUIDE TO BRIBERY**
> If it ever becomes imperative to offer a bribe, there is just one golden rule: ensure plausible deniability. Whether you slip notes with the paperwork or ask to pay the fine on the spot, always, always do so in a way that lets you deny the cash was intended as a bribe.

• *Handily for Somalis of a piratical bent, their homeland has the longest coastline of any African nation.* •

♥ · **GSR**: 140 · **WHS**: none

———————— SOUTH AFRICA ————————

'When the missionaries came to Africa, they had the Bible and we had the land.
They said, "Let us pray." We closed our eyes. When we opened them,
we had the Bible and they had the land.'

—Archbishop Desmond Tutu

NATURAL HIGHS. South Africa is home to more species of mammal than Europe and Asia combined. It's also the only nation with its own botanical kingdom, holding 10% of the world's flowers.

BLACK AND WHITE. Given that they're both grey, the names of Africa's two rhino species seem pretty silly. One theory is that the 'white' rhino's name arose from a mistranslation of the Dutch *wijd* ('wide')—referring to the broadness of its mouth. True or not, it's agreed that its narrow-jawed relative was then called 'black' to distinguish it. One of conservation's greatest successes, white rhino numbers have risen from 100 in 1895 to 17,500, with 90% of these found in South Africa.

'The sun never sets without fresh news.'

—Xhosa proverb

CUT AND PASTE. The first successful heart transplant was performed by Christiaan Barnard in Cape Town on 3 December 1967. His patient survived for 18 days. The current record is 31 years, but innovations continue to be made—one notable milestone, passed in 2006, was the first transfer of a heart while it was still beating.

HEART TRANSPLANT TIMESPANS[1]	
MEASURED IN HEARTBEATS[2]	
Waiting time (UK)	18,000,000
Operation duration	18,000
Post-transplant survival	500,000,000
Human lifespan	2,500,000,000

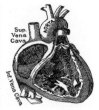

[1] *Average lengths.* [2] *At a rate of 70 beats per minute.*

MISPLACED HOPE. While exceedingly beautiful and grandly imposing, the Cape of Good Hope is neither Africa's southernmost tip nor the point where the Atlantic and Indian Oceans meet. The stunningly anticlimactic and almost unknown Cape Agulhas ('Cape of Needles'), 100 miles to the south-east, claims both accolades.

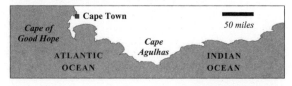

SKIN DEEP. From 1950 to 1994, apartheid assigned every person in South Africa to one of several 'population groups'. In 'borderline' cases, race was determined by such arbitrary tests as measuring lip size and running a pencil through a person's hair to see if it snagged. Local race examiners were also free to dream up their own tests. One swore he could decide if someone was 'coloured' by the way they spat. The results lasted for life and controlled everything from who you could sleep with to where you got lowered into the ground.

APARTHEID ERA	
POPULATION GROUP CODES[3,4]	
White 00	*Chinese* 04
Cape Coloured...01	*Indian* 05
Malay 02	*Other Asian* 06
Griqua[5] 03	*Other Coloured*..07

[3] *After 1958, there were officially no black South African citizens as they had all been transferred to notionally self-governing Bantustan homelands.* [4] *Version in force in 1980.* [5] *A sub-group of 'Coloured'.*

LODED. At least half of all the gold amassed in human history has been mined

in South Africa. Two-thirds goes into jewellery, but much is now also used in electronics, where its price is offset by extreme ductility—a single ounce can be stretched into 50 miles of wire. And the future's golden too: scientists claimed in 2010 to have made the first prototype invisibility cloak out of gold-plated silk.

BOYS' OWN. Air ace Adolph 'Sailor' Malan was the classic South African hero and son of the Empire. Joining the RAF in time for WWII, he ended his fighting career as its top-ranked fighter pilot (with 27 kills). Even more significantly, he used the experience he gained to draw up his 'Ten Rules for Air-Fighting', which, posted in every RAF mess hall, became the dog-fighting bible for all Battle of Britain pilots. After the war, Malan became an early leader of the anti-apartheid cause, addressing rallies of up to 75,000 until he died in 1963.

BILTONG[1] RECIPE

Trim beef (or game—zebra works best) to size, rub well with salt, black pepper and coriander, marinate in vinegar, then air-dry for four days.

▪ Said to be notably good for teething babies.

[1] *Biltong is derived from Dutch, and means 'buttock strip'.*

FIREARMS HOMICIDES

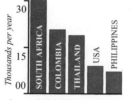

Source: *Eighth UN Crime Survey.*

MAKE MY DAY. Some ATMs in South Africa are now 'weaponized'. If tampering is detected, they fire a disabling pepper spray into the eyes of the would-be thief. An automatic alarm then summons a rapid-response SWAT team to arrest the incapacitated villain.

Deepest metro tunnels ➤ ○
(Pyongyang, 110 m/360 ft)

Empire State Building
(New York, 449 m/1,470 ft)

HOT AS HELL. TauTona Mine, near Johannesburg, is the deepest in the world. With a 2½-mile maximum vertical drop, it's also the furthest below the Earth's surface humans have yet visited. The extreme depth makes for immensely challenging working conditions: TauTona's ore seams are too hot to handle—at a temperature of 60°C, the rock can blister unprotected skin in 30 seconds.

TauTona Goldmine (3,902 m/2,800 ft)

TEN RULES FOR AIR-FIGHTING

1. *Wait until you see the whites of his eyes.*

2. *Whilst shooting, think of nothing else.*

3. *Always keep a sharp look-out.*

4. *Height gives you the advantage.*

5. *Always turn and face the attack.*

6. *Make your decisions promptly.*

7. *Never fly straight for more than 30 seconds.*

8. *When diving to attack, leave a top guard.*

9. *Initiative, Aggression, Discipline, Team Work.*

10. ***Go in quickly. Punch hard. Get out!***

PRETTY PEBBLE. Three million years ago, one of our pre-human ancestors recognized a face in a striking but natural stone and carried it off to Makapansgat cave. In so doing, he or she left us evidence of the first known symbolic thought.

76
Os
190.23

HEAVYWEIGHT. South Africa has the world's largest reserves of osmium, the heaviest substance on Earth (and used for pen nibs). A melon-sized lump weighs more than a man, but that's still angel's breath beside neutron-degenerate matter, the densest stuff in the galaxy—a teaspoonful weighs 10 times more than mankind.

SKEWERED. The heaviest ever defeat of a modern army by indigenous forces occurred at Isandlwana in 1879, when 20,000 Zulus overwhelmed a British column, killing 1,300 men. The victory proved Pyrrhic, as the humiliation made Zululand's conquest a national priority for the British public, replacing their previous indifference.

♥ · **GSR**: 20 · **WHS**: Cape Floral Region (Fynbos plants) □ iSimangaliso (wetlands) □ Mapungubwe (ruins) □ Richtersveld (desert and pastoralists) □ Robben Island (prison) □ Sterkfontein, Swartkrans, Kromdraai (early human fossils) □ uKhahlamba Drakensberg (mountains) □ Vredefort (meteor crater)

SOUTH SUDAN

'Death of one son; glory of another.'

—Dinka proverb

HAPPY BIRTHDAY! On 9 July 2011, South Sudan became the world's newest sovereign nation.

Daddy?

CATTLE BREEDING. Even more than other African pastoralists, the Nuer of South Sudan prize their cattle—to the extent that it is their exchange, not biology, that determines a child's paternity. The transfer is made at the time of marriage, when a groom gives the family of his bride a certain number of cows as 'bride wealth'—without which the groom will not be considered the father of any children that may result. The converse also applies, so even where the biological dad is not the husband, with the cows in place, the latter would still be both legally and culturally the father. Two unusual consequences can, and do, follow. First, a bride may marry a dead man to give him children (usually through the biological agency of his brother)[1]; and, secondly, an infertile woman can choose to take a wife and, with suitable biological assistance, become a father herself.

[1] *Such marriages are nearly as common as 'ordinary' ones, and usually occur where a man has been killed in a blood feud. Their purpose is to continue his blood line so that one of his posthumous 'sons' can later avenge his death.*

BATTLE OF THE NILE II. When Charles de Gaulle wrote his memoirs, he listed the disasters that had befallen France in his youth. Top was the name of a dusty Nile-side village now known as Kodok. In his day, it was Fashoda, and the place where Major Marchand's east–west march of conquest across Africa ran into five British gunboats steaming south from Khartoum. After six tense weeks, Marchand had given way, leaving Sudan to Britain. Prior to this check, however, France had secretly drawn up a plan to divert the Nile into the Red Sea and turn British Egypt into a dustbowl.

'There is no more formidable swamp in the world.'

—Sir Samuel Baker, Nile explorer

SEA OF GAZELLES. Alive with hippos, crocs and mosquitoes, and choked by rafts of rotting reeds 20 miles long, South Sudan's Sudd is a swamp as big as England. Almost unknown to outsiders, it's visited every dry season by two million antelope in the world's greatest mammal migration (larger than that of the Serengeti).

—SO, HOW MANY COUNTRIES ARE THERE?

This is not such an easy question to answer. The obvious place to start is the list of UN members. This has grown from the original 51 who, in 1946, gathered at a Methodist church in London for the first General Assembly to the current tally of 193. But membership isn't obligatory, and though considered sovereign, the Holy See (Vatican) chooses to remain an observer. Partially recognized states are more contentious. The Republic of China (Taiwan) was expelled from the UN in 1971 to make way for the People's Republic, but is nonetheless still recognized by 23 nations and plainly exercises sovereignty over its own territory. Other partially recognized states in descending order of international acknowledgement are: Palestine (recognized by at least 112 nations), Kosovo (76), Western Sahara (57), Abkhazia (4), South Ossetia (4) and North Cyprus (1). In addition, there are at present 16 territories listed by the UN as 'non-self-governing'—places like Bermuda or the US Virgin Islands. On a day to day basis, most of these, in fact, run their own affairs. Thus, from the above, anything from 194 to 217 might be a reasonable answer. But even this doesn't address other constitutional entities such as, for example, the Channel Islands or Greenland; nor the legal fiction that places like Tahiti and the South American jungles of French Guyana are metropolitan France.

♥ · GSR: 184 · WHS: none

—————————— SPAIN • ESPAÑA ——————————

'In Spain, the dead are more alive than the dead of any other country.'

—Federico García Lorca

HANDY HELP. After Spanish dictator General Franco came to power in 1939, he requisitioned the 357-year-old left hand of Saint Teresa of Ávila[1]—less the little finger (which had been sawn off long before by Jeronimo Gracian).[2] The Generalissimo then slept with the mummified appendage beside his bed each night until his eventual death in 1975.

[1] *Patron saint of Spain and those suffering from a headache.* [2] *The blessed digit was later captured by Barbary pirates.*

HERE COMES THE SUN—COSTA WEATHER PICKER

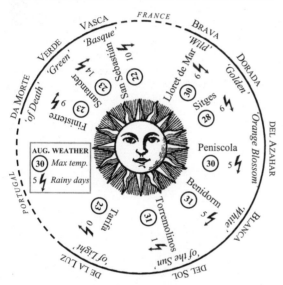

AUG. WEATHER
30 Max temp.
5 Rainy days

Madrid is unique among European capitals for having been founded with disregard for comfort or convenience. Set on a high plateau that bakes for nine months of the year and freezes for the other three, its all-commanding virtue has been its location at the dead centre of Spain—the best place from which to wield absolute authority, or so thought Philip II, the king who, in 1561, made it his capital and who, in his time, was the most powerful man in the world. At the city's centre is the Puerto del Sol ('Gate of the Sun'), the 'kilometre zero' from which the Spanish road system still radiates.

TIME TRAVEL. Juan Sebstián Elcano was the first person to circumnavigate the globe.[3] But, when the Spaniard finally dropped anchor back in Sanlúcar on a quiet Saturday morning three years after having set off, he was amazed to find that, despite a meticulous log, it was actually Sunday. This apparent discrepancy is readily understood today since Elcano crossed what would become known as the Date Line[4] when he sailed westward across the Pacific. However, at the time, the disappearing day seemed so unnatural that a mission was sent to notify the Pope.

[3] *Elcano was Ferdinand Magellan's second in command on his 1519 expedition to sail around the world. Since Magellan was killed in the Philippines, it was Elcano who was in command at the end of the voyage.*
[4] *Formally speaking, the International Date Line has no legal standing even today, it is merely a widely accepted and convenient convention.*

QUESTION TIME. When Pope Sixtus IV was pressured by King Ferdinand II into establishing the Spanish Inquisition in 1478, he regretted the move almost at once; under the direct authority of Spain's monarchs, the Inquisition undercut his own authority at a stroke. Six years later, Sixtus attempted to create a right of appeal to Rome, but the king quickly nullified this by decreeing the death penalty for anyone tempted to take it up. Feared and hated, the Inquisition wasn't abolished until 1831, trying bigamists and freemasons, as well as Protestants, Muslims and Jews.

During its 350 year history, the Spanish Inquisition is thought to have heard around 150,000 cases and used torture in about 30% of these (typically hanging from the arms, water-boarding or stretching on the rack). An estimated 5,000 people were executed, most by being burnt at the stake. This was both a deterrent and an extra punishment, since the condemned was corporeally consumed, so depriving them of a body in the afterlife.

'THE RAIN IN SPAIN FALLS MAINLY ON THE ...' north-west Atlantic coast—but most of all on the village of Grazalema, high in the mountains between Málaga and Cádiz.

'Dar gato por liebre.'

—'To give cat for hare'; Spanish
idiom meaning to swindle

MORE THAN ONE WAY TO SKIN A CAT. Once head and paws are removed, the skinned carcass of a cat is indistinguishable from that of a rabbit or hare except by an expert. This difficulty has been exploited by unscrupulous vendors throughout Europe for centuries, particularly during wars[1] and other times of hardship. The opportunities for subterfuge, however, are especially abundant in Spain—as rabbit (along with snail) is an essential ingredient in authentic *paella*[2]— such that, even now, savvy housewives insist on seeing the carcass with the head still on before buying from a butcher.

[1] *During WWII, cat was eaten in Germany as 'roof-hare' and in England as 'roof-rabbit' (or, for those with more delicate stomachs, 'Australian rabbit'). [2] At least in recipes from the 19th century onwards. Before this, the meat was traditionally marsh rat.*

LIKE FATHER LIKE SON
EUROPEAN SURNAMES MEANING 'SON OF'

Spain: *-ez .... Gonzalez = son of Gonzalo*
Denmark: *-sen .... Andersen = son of Anders*
England: *-s .... Williams = son of William*
France: *-ot .... Pierrot = son of Pierre*
Ireland: *Mc- ...... McDonald = son of Donald*
Italy: *-i .... Garibaldi = Garibaldo*
Romania: *-escu ..... Ceauşescu = son of Ceauşe*
Russia: *-ov .... Ivanov = son of Ivan*

MONSTER NUT. Coconuts take their name from the Spanish *coco*—a malevolent child-eating bogeyman with which generations of Iberian mothers terrified their errant youngsters. The link comes from the strange pits on a coconut's shell, which sailors fancied resembled the evil face of a bugbear.

THE WAR OF JENKINS' EAR. was waged for nine years between Spain and Britain from 1739. The bone (or, more accurately, cartilage) of contention was that of master mariner Robert Jenkins, whose ship was boarded by a Spanish patrol off Havana in 1731. After loosing off a few choice expletives, Jenkins had been bound to the mast and his ear sliced off with a sword. Nothing much happened next. But seven years later, Jenkins was summoned to parliament by MPs looking to pick a fight with the Spanish, and his ear (by now pickled in a bottle) was passed round for inspection. Suddenly aggrieved, Britain rushed to take up arms. Something of a damp squib, the war itself was perhaps most memorable for occasioning the first public performance of *Rule, Britannia!*

*Scooped from the surf of Galicia, the goose barnacle (*percebe*) is Spain's most esteemed crustacean. It is said to blend the taste of lobster with the texture of oyster (and the looks of the devil).*

LATIN LIAISON. When King Philip II of Spain dispatched the Spanish Armada in 1588, he already knew England well as he had previously ruled as king for four years before losing the crown to Elizabeth I.[3] During his time as ruler, Philip had been unable to understand English, so, by law, all important government business had also to be translated into Spanish (or Latin).

[3] *Philip acquired the English throne in 1554 upon his marriage to Mary I, Queen of England and daughter of Henry VIII. Under the terms of the marriage contract that was negotiated, Philip and Mary essentially became co-rulers during Mary's lifetime, each with the power of veto, but Philip was barred from succeeding her in his own right. Thus, when Mary died in 1558, the crown went not to Philip but to her sister Elizabeth.*

WORLD'S UNLUCKIEST GOAT. On 6 January 2000, the Pyrenean ibex became the first recorded extinction of the third millennium when a tree fell on top of the lone surviving individual. In 2009, the Pyrenean ibex also became the first animal ever to become 'unextinct', albeit briefly, after a cloned kid was born and survived for seven minutes.

THE GRINGO TALE. Long before sunburnt 'gringos' became an object of scorn across Latin America, the word was in use in Spain. In 18th-century Málaga it meant any foreigner who spoke rotten Spanish, while in Madrid it was oddly reserved for the Irish.

Cro-Magnon man—but is he Basque too?

CORRIDA DE TOROS: SPANISH BULLFIGHT

CAST LIST

1 *Matador* ('killer')
2 *Picadores* ('prickers') ⎱ v 1 *Toro Bravo*
3 *Banderilleros* ('darters') ⎰ ('fighting bull')

....

PROGRAMME

ACT 1	*Picadores* spear bull's neck to weaken it
ACT 2	*Banderilleros* goad bull with barbed darts
ACT 3	*Matador* kills with sword thrust to heart

....

SCORECARD
Successful Kills (2010)

Bulls 0   Bullfighters..........13,300 (est.)

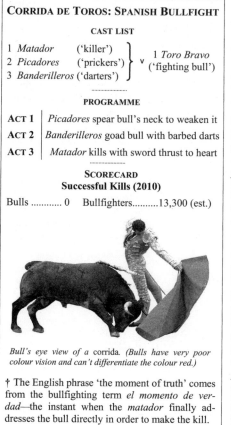

Bull's eye view of a corrida. *(Bulls have very poor colour vision and can't differentiate the colour red.)*

† The English phrase 'the moment of truth' comes from the bullfighting term *el momento de verdad*—the instant when the *matador* finally addresses the bull directly in order to make the kill.

NOR ZARA ZU?[1] Europe, it appears, can be divided into two: the Basques and the rest. With their language unconnected to any other, and largely unadulterated over millennia,[2] the origin of the Basques has long been a mystery. But DNA studies now suggest they are Europe's sole surviving indigenous natives, already installed in the cloud-streaming mountains of northern Spain before the end of the last Ice Age. Somehow, it would seem, they alone resisted absorption by the Indo-European invaders of 6,000 years ago, who are the forebears of almost all other Europeans.[3]

[1] *'Who are you?' in Basque.* [2] *For example, the Basque for 'axe' (aitzkor) comes from 'stone' (aitz), suggesting it was coined when axes were made from stone—i.e. in the Stone Age.* [3] *The Uralic-speaking Finns, Estonians, Sami and Hungarians arrived separately, but no earlier.*

TIME AND PUNISHMENT. When, in 1972, Mallorcan postman Gabriel Granados was charged with not delivering his mail, the prosecutor wanted to make an example of him, so asked for jail time of 384,912 years (calculated as the maximum penalty applied to each of the 42,768 non-delivered items of mail). The judge was evidently a more forgiving soul, however, as he sent Granados down for just 7,109 years.[4]

[4] *This is not quite the longest prison sentence ever imposed. Alabama triple-murderer Dudley Wayne Kyzer is currently 34 years into a stretch of 10,000 years plus two life terms (all to be served consecutively). Although Kyzer did subsequently seek permission to appeal, leave was refused because the 30-day time limit to lodge such an application had already expired.*

'Spanish for love, Italian for song, French for diplomacy and German for a horse.'
—Spanish saying

....

♠ · **GSR**: 15 · **WHS**: Alcalá de Henares (university) □ Alhambra (palace) □ Altamira (cave paintings) Aragon (Mudejar architecture) □ Aranjuez (gardens) □ Atapuerca (human fossils) □ Ávila (museum town) □ Barcelona (x2) (art nouveau/work of Gaudi) □ Bilbao (transporter bridge) □ Burgos (cathedral) Cáceres (townscape) □ Cordoba (mosque/cathedral) □ La Coruña (lighthouse) □ Cuenca (townscape) Doñana (wetlands) □ Elche (palm groves) □ El Escorial (palace) □ Guadalupe (monastery) □ Ibiza (island) □ Lugo (Roman walls) □ Mediterranean Rock Art □ Las Médulas (Roman mines) □ Mérida (Roman ruins) □ Mt. Perdu (mountain) □ Oviedo (churches) □ Poblet (monastery) □ Salamanca (historic city) □ San Millán (monasteries) □ Santiago de Compostela (museum city) □ Santiago Pilgrimage Route □ Segovia (museum town) □ Serra de Tramuntana (landscape) □ Seville (cathedral) Siega Verde (rock art) □ Tarragona (Roman ruins) □ Toledo (museum town) □ Úbeda & Baeza (townscapes) □ Valencia (silk exchange) □ Vall de Boí (churches) ■ Canaries: La Gomera (laurel forest) □ Tenerife—La Laguna (townscape) □ Tenerife—Teide (volcano) · **ICH**: Berga (festival) Elche (mystery play) □ Falconry □ Flamenco □ Human Towers □ Mediterranean Diet □ Pusol (school museum) □ Sybil Chant □ Water Tribunals (courts) ■ Canaries: La Gomera (whistling language)

—— SRI LANKA ● ශ්‍රී ලංකා ● இலங்கை ——

'Blow, blow, ye spicy breezes, O'er Ceylon blow your breath;
Where every prospect pleases, save only that of death.'

—Bishop Sheber. Former names for Sri Lanka include Ceylon, Taprobane and Serendib (whence
the English word 'serendipity'); Sri Lanka itself means 'resplendent isle' in Sanskrit.

Reclining Buddha at Polonnaruwa, Sri Lanka. The granite figure was carved
in the 12ᵗʰ century and depicts the Buddha
having reached ultimate nirvana
*(*parinirvana*) after the death of his*
body.

Head to toe length=46 ft

KEEPING THE FAITH. Sri Lanka is the world's oldest Buddhist country, with a continuous history of worship going back beyond 245 BCE—when a branch from the original Bodhi-Tree, under which the Buddha attained enlightenment, was planted at Anuradhapura.[1] Sri Lanka still adheres to the original Theravada branch of Buddhism (unlike Bhutan, the only other remaining Buddhist nation in the Buddha's native South Asia), and, like the Hinduism of the Tamil minority, the faith is in rude health, with 99% of Sri Lankans saying religion is an important part of their daily lives (making Sri Lanka the third most religious country in the world).

[1] *The tree, which is still alive, is considered the world's oldest documented plant.*

VENOMOUS SNAKEBITES (PER MILLION PEOPLE, 2007)		
1	Sri Lanka	1,650
2	Nepal	670
3	Vietnam	345
4	Mexico	261
5	Brazil	155

Sri Lankan snakebites are often due to cobra infestations in the tea gardens. But, in addition, Sri Lanka's skink lizards like to sneak between sleepers' sheets at night, inconveniently luring hungry cobras and kraits in after them.

UNDIPLOMATIC IMPUNITY. The concept of diplomatic immunity exists for a very good reason. (In the classical period executing a country's ambassadors was a recognized way of declaring war.) However, it is also subject to abuses. One of the most flagrant occurred in 1979, when the Burmese ambassador to Sri Lanka shot his wife in plain sight as she arrived home after an assignation with a night club singer, and the next morning set about constructing a funeral pyre in his back garden. The Sri Lankan police tried to intervene, but the ambassador merely reminded them of his immunity and calmly got on with his task. The official was eventually recalled to Burma, but only after an awkward pause.

THE WORLD OF BUDDHISM

▶ **Theravada School**
'Orthodox' Buddhism with an emphasis on an individual's own reasoning and experience to attain insight.
▪ *Burma · Cambodia · Laos · Sri Lanka · Thailand.*

▶ **Mahayana School**
Many strands, with greater flexibility in the canon, trust in faith and (in Zen) a central role for meditation.
▪ *China · Japan · Korea · Singapore · Taiwan · Vietnam.*

▶ **Esoteric School**
Noted for its elaborate rituals and use of yoga. Practitioners must abide by various tantric vows.
▪ *Bhutan · Ladakh · Mongolia · Nepal · Tibet.*

BELIEF IN NUMBERS

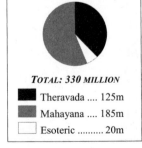

TOTAL: 330 MILLION

■ Theravada 125m
■ Mahayana 185m
□ Esoteric 20m

♣ · **GSR**: 54 · **WHS**: Anuradhapura (Buddhist holy city) □ Central Highlands (wildlife and flora) Dambulla (cave monastery) □ Galle (colonial townscape) □ Kandy (historic city) □ Polonnaruwa (ruined city) □ Sigiriya (ruined stronghold) □ Sinharaja (rainforest)

SUDAN • السودان

'When Allah made the Sudan, he laughed'

—Traditional Arabic saying

'Blemmye'
c. 250 CE

◄ KNOW YOUR FOE ►

'Fuzzy-Wuzzy'
c. 1890

The Beja of the Sudan's Red Sea coast have the unhappy distinction of having picked fights with both 19th-century Britain and the Roman Empire. Against each, they gave an excellent account of themselves before being overwhelmed. The Victorians called them Fuzzy-Wuzzies, after their extravagant hairstyles (held in place with butter). To the Romans, they were the Blemmyes—bizarrely portrayed as headless cannibals, for no known reason.

OF MONSTROUS MEN. Blemmyes may look laughable today, but in a world where knowledge grew very ragged round the edges, who knew what lay over the next hill? Besides, they were by no means alone:

SCIAPODS. Hailing from India, Sciapods allegedly hopped agilely on a foot that doubled as a shade.

CYNOCEPHALI. Sightings of dog-heads came from India, Iran, Libya and, strangely, Edinburgh. (Scotland aside, the dog-heads may have been inspired by real baboons.)

BLACK POWER. The kings of Kush in Sudan conquered ancient Egypt in 750 BCE and, for 100 years, ruled the country as black pharaohs.[1] At their peak, the Kushites even took control of Jerusalem, over 1,000 miles north of their homeland in the African savannah, before being driven back and ultimately out of Egypt by the Assyrians.

[1] *Egypt's 25th dynasty (750–656 BCE)*

TRIANGULATED. Sudan is home to more pyramids than anywhere else in the world—including Egypt

OVERALL SCORE
Sudan 228–138 Egypt

Ruled: 690–664 BCE

Taharqa—greatest of the Kushite pharaohs and the 'Tirhakah King of Ethiopia' of the Book of Isaiah.

SOFT POWER. When, in 2007, the USA slapped sanctions on Sudan over the Darfur conflict, the Sudanese had their retaliation in hand—they threatened to cut America's jugular: its Coca-Cola supply. It turns out one vital additive is gum arabic, which allows soft drinks to contain more sugar than can be dissolved in water alone—and Sudan is the world's biggest supplier. Perhaps because 5,000,000 Sudanese depend on the gum for a living, the threat has not yet been followed through—but Coke addicts might nevertheless still wish to stockpile against a day their world suddenly turns sour.

FLESH-CRAWLING. Sudan has 75% of the world's cases of guinea worm, a truly gruesome parasite that erupts, *Alien*-like, out of the skin. A further horror is the treatment, which consists of winding the 80-cm-long worm around a stick until fully emerged—a month-long process of piercing pain. Dracunculiasis, the name of the disease it causes, gives an indication—it means 'affliction with little dragons' in Latin.

♥ · **GSR**: 130 · **WHS**: Gebel Barkal Area (pyramids and temples) □ Meroe (ancient ruined city)

SURINAME

'If you like okra, you have to like the seeds as well.'

—Surinamese proverb

The Central Suriname Nature Reserve World Heritage Site. *The Reserve, funded by Conservation International, protects an area of pristine rainforest larger than Northern Ireland, inhabited by jaguars, giant armadillos, giant river otters, harpy eagles and macaws. Overall, around 80% of Suriname is still undisturbed tropical forest and savannah, as away from a narrow strip along the northern Atlantic coastline, the country remains almost completely undeveloped.*

UNITED NATIONS. Despite the lowest population of any South American country (having less than half a million inhabitants), Suriname is one of the most heterogeneous nations on Earth. From the 16th century until 1975, the territory was part of the Kingdom of the Netherlands, and the Dutch imported many Indian and Indonesian labourers, as well as West African slaves. In addition, there are large numbers of Brazilian gold miners and Chinese, and smaller communities of indigenous Amerindians, Jews and Christian Lebanese (who call themselves Phoenicians).

Suriname's coat of arms. The five-pointed star references the five continents the Surinamese hail from.

FEARSOME FROGS. There are 175 species of poison dart frog found across northern South America, including many in Suriname. All are poisonous to the touch to some degree[1] due to the presence of toxin-secreting glands over the whole of the skin. However, if a frog is taken into captivity, it eventually loses its toxicity, while captive-born frogs are never poisonous at all. From this, biologists believe that the amphibians do not manufacture their own poison but ingest it as part of their diet— although the source, presumably an insect of some sort, is still unknown. With bold colour patterns to advertise their toxicity widely, the poison dart frogs are diurnal and can feed alongside potential predators unmolested, unlike non-toxic frog species, which are forced to be nocturnal.

[1] *The skin of a single specimen of one of the most potent species, the golden poison frog, contains enough toxins to kill 10–20 humans.*

NO COMMENT. With a total of just 340 recognized words, Taki-Taki— an English-Dutch creole that serves as Suriname's lingua franca—is believed to have the most limited vocabulary of any living language.

LAW AND ORDER. Elected in 2010, Suriname's current president, Dési Bouterse, is a convicted drugs smuggler wanted for questioning over the killing of 15 people in 1982. On top of this, in 1990 he once seized control of the country by telephone.

♦ · **GSR**: 170 · **WHS**: Central Suriname Nature Reserve (rainforest) □ Paramaribo (cityscape)

———————— SWAZILAND ————————

'We are a mystery.'

—Swazi national motto

SWAZILAND—HIGHS & LOWS

- World's **highest** HIV infection rate .... 25%[1]
- World's **highest** death rate .... 3%[2]
- World's **highest** share of households
  headed by a child .... 10%[3]
- World's **lowest** life expectancy .... 32 years[4]

[1] *Adults over 15 (2007).* [2] *2008 (60% of deaths are due to AIDS).* [3] *More-over, 30% of all Swazi children have lost both parents.* [4] *At birth (2008).*

Swazi Coat of Arms

THE LION AND THE SHE-ELEPHANT. The twin pillars of the Swazi nation are the king (the 'Lion') and the queen mother (the 'She-Elephant'). Each holds court in a separate capital and maintains a separate power base. When the king dies, succession goes not to his eldest son but is decided by a family council headed by the She-Elephant. Since a young (and pliable) candidate is usually selected, the new king's mother then becomes She-Elephant, and rules until her son is of age.

'I am being overworked, but I have to do everything to satisfy my people.'
—King Mswati III

FATHER OF THE NATION. King Mswati III of Swaziland currently has 14 wives, but in due course is expected to take at least one from each of the country's clans. (He still has a long way to go to match his predecessor's final tally of 70.) Wife selection takes place at the annual Reed Dance (*Umhlanga*), a bare-breasted beauty pageant at which 50,000 girls dance to honour the She-Elephant and to advertise their virginity. When not doing his bit for population growth,[5] the king rules as Sub-Saharan Africa's last absolute monarch with a trademark blend of extravagance[6] and whim[7].

[5] *When he died, the last king's 1,000-plus grandchildren made up 0.2% of the national population.* [6] *In the middle of Swaziland's 2002 famine, King Mswati III ordered a royal jet for his own exclusive use—claiming he needed one to 'scout for food'; the cost was $50m—twice the country's annual health budget. (The purchase was eventually aborted, but only after intense pressure from the IMF.)* [7] *In 2004, the king closed Swaziland's schools for a week when he ordered the nation's schoolboys to weed his royal fields.*

IDEAL HOME EXHIBITION. Optimizing for local needs and materials, African huts exhibit huge regional diversity. Across the continent, nine broad styles are found:

- Beehive
- Cone on cylinder
- Pyramidal cone
- Cone on ground
- Square
- Box—with rounded roof
- Box—with flat roof
- Gabled roofed
- Quadrangle—enclosing yard

SWAZILAND *beehive (thatch)*

BENIN *cone on cylinder*

MALI *box—flat roof*

CAMEROON *beehive (mud)*

IT'S CRYING. Swazi babies are 'unpersons' until reaching 'personhood' at three months old. Prior to this, they are traditionally kept unnamed, referred to as 'things' and left untouched by men.

OLD TIMER. On the throne from 1899 to 1982, King Sobhuza II had the longest confirmed reign in history. At 82 years, it was over 2½ times the lifespan of a typical Swazi subject.

....

♥ · **GSR**: 172 · **WHS**: none

————— SWEDEN • SVERIGE —————

'I have never seen more perfect physical specimens, tall as date palms,
blond and ruddy; they wear neither tunics nor caftans, but each man
has an axe, a sword and a knife, and keeps each by him at all times.'

—Ibn Fadlan, on encountering Swedish Rus Vikings while travelling on the River Volga (*c.* 922 CE)[1]

EUROPEAN ENLIGHTENMENT: PERCENTAGE OF BLONDS

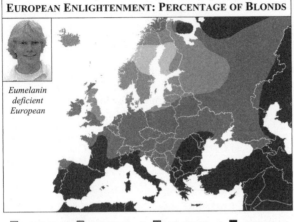

Eumelanin deficient European

■ >80% Blond   ■ 50–79% Blond   ■ 20–49% Blond   ■ <20% Blond

NICHE FAITH. Of the gods venerated by the Vikings, possibly the most specialist was Ull—the God of Snowshoes.

GINGER SPICE. Post-war children's writer Astrid Lindgren is the best-selling Swedish author of all time, with 100 million books sold. Her central protagonist, the carrot-haired Pippi Longstocking, has recently resurfaced in the massively successful *Millennium* crime series by fellow Swede Stieg Larsson. According to the author, he created his red-headed heroine, Lisbeth Salander, as a dark, grown-up Pippi (and, in homage, he put an abbreviation of Pippi's address, 'V. Kulla', in the nameplate of Salander's apartment door).

LAPPING IT UP. As all Sami reindeer herders know, the quickest way to catch a reindeer is to pee in the snow—upon which the animals will come to you at a trot (to lick up the scarce salt contained in urine). But, even once caught, reindeer can still throw up challenging questions of delicacy. On one pre-Christmas Shuttle launch, Swedish astronaut Christer Fuglesang was banned by NASA from taking dried reindeer meat with him for fear of upsetting millions of American children. He had to make do with venison instead.

KINGS OF DARKNESS. The Goths most probably first emerged on the Swedish Baltic island of Gotland and nearby parts of the mainland between 300 BCE and 100 CE. From there, they fought their way south to the Black Sea, split into two, and led the barbarian charge in snuffing out the European Golden Age of classical Rome. While some might have wished to distance themselves from such events, not so almost a millennium of Swedish kings, who chose to style themselves 'King of Sweden, the Goths and the Wends' right up until 1973.

Goth (2006 CE)[2]

[2] *Modern Goths look nothing like their ancient namesakes, nor, in the main, do they share the proclivity for extreme acts of wanton barbarism.*

A STATE OF DISBELIEF. Despite atheism having been technically illegal as recently as 1951, surveys show Sweden is the world's most disbelieving country.

'DON'T BELIEVE IN GOD'

1. Sweden ……..………. 85%
2. Vietnam ………………...81%
3. Denmark ……..……….. 80%
4. Norway …………......... 72%
5. Japan …...…………. 65%
15. UK ………………….. 44%
44. USA …………………… 9%

Source: *P. Zuckerman,* Cambridge Companion to Atheism *(2007).*

---

[1] In the interests of balance, it should be noted that ibn Fadlan further observed: 'They are the filthiest of God's creatures. They have no modesty in defecation and urination, nor do they wash after pollution from orgasm, nor do they wash their hands after eating. Thus, they are like wild asses.'

ᛁᚻ ᚱᛁᚱᚷᛈᚻᚻᛁᚲ ᚳᛋᛁᛁᛁᛏᛋᚾᛈᛁᚱᛟᛞᚬᛉ

Kylver Stone inscription, Gotland, listing all 24 Elder Futhark runes in sequence; Sweden has Europe's highest concentration of such rune-stones. Runic alphabets were used by all Europe's Germanic peoples from around 100 CE, and runes were later adopted in a simplified form by the Vikings. After the 11th-century Christianization of Scandinavia, Latin script replaced rune-writing for everyday use, but runic calendars could still be found in rural homes until the early 20th century. Runes were derived from early Italian alphabets, possibly brought by a mercenary returning from service in the Roman Army. Their original use seems to have been to write graffiti, but more orthodox applications soon developed. Runes have a lingering, if poorly substantiated, association with magic. The Kylver Stone runes were found on the underside of a grave slab, and possibly had the purpose of pacifying the corpse beneath.

ROLLING START. Swedish company AB SKF originally planned 'Volvos' to be their new line of ball bearing (hence the name: it means 'I roll' in Latin). But then two of the staff got fed up with the failure of US cars to survive Sweden's fierce winters and gravel roads, and, in 1924, decided to build their own—so the brand became a car. After a few teething problems,[1] Volvos were a success, and the cars have since built a global reputation for safety and reliability.

[1] *The very first car to roll out of the factory would only go backwards as a gear had been fitted the wrong way round.*

CAR BRANDS AND THEIR MEANINGS[2]

BMW .... acronym of 'Bavarian Motor Works'
Fiat ...... acronym of 'Italian Car Factory of Turin'
Kia ... acronym of 'arising to the world from Asia'
Mazda ...... the ancient Zoroastrian god of wisdom
Mitsubishi .... 'three water chestnuts'
Saab...acronym of 'Swedish Aeroplane Company'
Toyota (initially *Toyoda*) ...... 'fertile paddy fields'
Volkswagen .... 'people's car'

[2] *When translated from their home languages.*

SECRET OF THE SEXES. The 18th-century Swedish taxonomist Carl Linnaeus was the great organizer of life. Among his many achievements was the introduction of the male and female symbols now in universal use. Linnaeus didn't just pluck these from the air; he borrowed the old alchemical glyphs for Mars and Venus. In alchemy, the circle signified 'spirit' or 'mind', while crosses or arrows signified 'physical matter'. Thus, to those who can read alchemy's secret code, the sign for female actually means 'more brain than brawn', while that for male means 'more brawn than brain'.

EUROPEAN EXPANSION. After Swedish soldier Johan von Strahlenberg was captured by the Russians in 1709, he was taken as a POW to Siberia. He then spent his next 10 years of captivity pondering exactly where European Russia ended and Asia began.[3] Following his eventual release, he wrote up his observations in book and map form, giving the crest of the Urals as the border throughout their length. His determination was subsequently formally accepted by Tsarina Anna, and has stuck as Europe's eastern border ever since.[4]

[3] *Strahlenberg also studied a variety of other Siberian topics new to science, including the use of magic mushrooms by shaman for 'mental flying' excursions and a description of Vogul rituals which may have later served as the source for Goldilocks's three bears.* [4] *Although the Urals may now seem obvious, in earlier times the River Don, flowing into the Black Sea, was typically held to be the dividing line, while the Urals themselves were thought mythical as late as 1549 (and their highest summit, Mt. Narodnaya, wasn't discovered until 1927—16 years after the South Pole was reached).*

♠ · **GSR:** 34 · **WHS:** Birka (Viking site) □ Drottningholm (palace) □ Engelsberg (ironworks) □ Falun (mining town and pit) □ Gammelstad (traditional village) □ Karlskrona (naval base) □ Kvarken Archipelago (rising coastline) □ Laponia (Sami culture and landscape) □ Öland (landscape) Stockholm (cemetery) □ Struve Arc (survey line) □ Tanum (rock art) □ Varberg (radio transmitter station) □ Visby (townscape)

──SWITZERLAND • SCHWEIZ • SUISSE • SVIZZERA──

> *'The only excitement in Switzerland is that you can throw a stone*
> *a frightfully long way down—and that is forbidden by law.'*
>
> —D. H. Lawrence

W◄──── THE ALP-SPOTTER'S GUIDE TO SWISS PEAKS ────►E

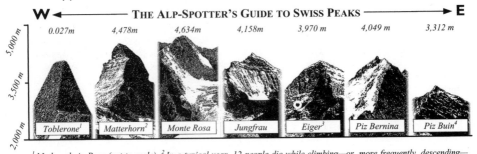

0.027m	4,478m	4,634m	4,158m	3,970 m	4,049 m	3,312 m
Toblerone[1]	Matterhorn[2]	Monte Rosa	Jungfrau	Eiger[3]	Piz Bernina	Piz Buin[4]

[1] Made only in Bern (not to scale). [2] In a typical year, 12 people die while climbing—or, more frequently, descending—the Matterhorn. [3] Unusually, a railway station (marked by white circle) has been installed part of the way up the sheer North Face. [4] The sun cream is named for the mountain and not vice versa. (The cream's creator, Franz Greiter, had the idea for his invention—the world's first effective sunscreen—after he got severe sunburn while climbing the mountain, and named his product after it. Greiter later went on to devise the Sun Protection Factor scale now used worldwide.),

ROCKS OF AGES: HOW OLD ARE THE HILLS?

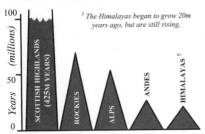

[5] The Himalayas began to grow 20m years ago, but are still rising.

GAME OF TWO HALVES. Home to 47 international federations, Switzerland is the world capital of sport—trouncing next-place Monaco's five. Football's FIFA is biggest, with 208 members (16 more than the UN). Despite this, it only gets a half-say in setting football's rules. Changes need the approval of at least half the Home Nations (England, Scotland, Wales and Northern Ireland) too.

HOLE TRUTH. The holes in Swiss Emmental cheese are made by carbon dioxide during fermentation. The gas is a by-product in the making of all cheeses, but in most, the gas escapes. However, Emmental's dense texture and thick rind traps the bubbles of bacteria burp *in situ*.

SWITZERLAND—NEED TO KNOW:
PT (I): HOW TO SURVIVE AN AVALANCHE

Presuming you can't ski out of trouble:

- Discard skis, dig in with ice axe, and grip.
- When (inevitably) you're swept up, 'swim' for it—double backstroke is best.
- Cover nose and mouth (use your clothes).
- Save energy for last Herculean effort as avalanche slows, and strike for surface. [6]

[6] Don't try this at home.

PT (II): HOW TO OPEN A NUMBERED SWISS BANK ACCOUNT

Presuming you are in funds:

- Fill in application form.
- Give name, date of birth, passport and proof of address.
- If they like the look of you,[7] you're in.

Disappointed? Swiss bank accounts haven't been anonymous since 1980. Numbered accounts give privacy when dealing with tellers, but the account holder's name is known to senior staff.

Not good enough? Several internet sites offer 'banking passports' at 'surprisingly low cost' (in practice, around $10,000) by which various helpfully flexible African nations will provide a passport with any name desired.

[7] Known international criminals, especially shifty dictators and outspoken activists need not apply.

BLOOM AND GROW. Where other armies award their senior soldiers stars, the Swiss gives them flowers—or, to be more specific, edelweiss. Thus, a major-general, who in a NATO country would wear two stars on his epaulettes, gets two edelweiss in Switzerland instead.

THE SWISS INQUISITION. Swiss psychologist Hermann Rorschach took a childhood fascination with inkblot pictures[1] and turned it into the world's most popular open-ended personality test. Participants are asked to give responses to 10 intrinsically meaningless inkblot images, which the psychologist then interprets. Nearly half of clinical psychologists apply the Rorschach Test routinely, and 80% make use of it at least occasionally—particularly if faced with an uncooperative subject. Although deployed since 1921, controversy over the tests has never died. One problem is cultural bias: for example, Scandinavians often see Card IV (*below*) as a troll. Another thorny issue is objectivity. Some studies have suggested testers may be more likely to label normal respondents as 'pathological' when issues are raised with them beforehand. Unknown to the subject, when applying the test, psychologists are taught to pay as much, if not more, attention to external factors (such as the time taken to answer, or whether or not the subject asks permission before rotating the card) as to what the subject says the cards actually look like.

[1] *Rorschach was so obsessed as a boy that his schoolfriends nicknamed him 'Inkblot'.*

LIFE'S WHAT YOU MAKE IT

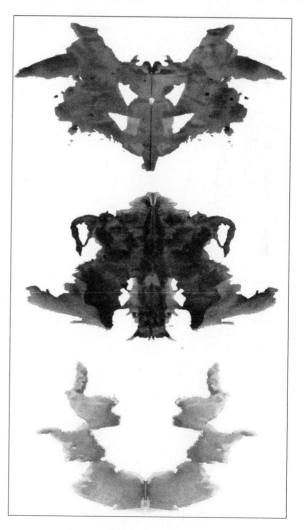

RORSCHACH CARD I

What[2]? Bat.

Why? The opening card. It gives an initial insight to the way in which the respondent reacts to stress or new situations. As the image is fairly well delineated, it is considered an 'easy' card.

[2] *The most common answer—there are no 'right' or 'wrong' responses.*

RORSCHACH CARD IV

What? Animal hide.

Why? A challenging card for the respondent, often perceived as dominant or threatening, and almost invariably masculine. Responses may give clues to feelings towards males and/or authority.

RORSCHACH CARD VII

What? Human head.

Why? Frequently called the 'mother card'. This is often linked with femininity and sometimes more specifically female sexuality (referencing the centre detail). Respondents who have difficulty here may have issues with a female figure in their life.

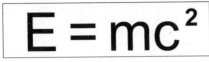

$$E = mc^2$$

BIGHEAD. When Albert Einstein was born, his head was so big his mother thought he was deformed. A few years later, the child Albert's promise as a violinist was checked after he threw a chair at his teacher and she fled, refusing to return. But all came good when he thought up the world's most famous scientific equation in his spare time while working as a patent clerk in Bern.

WHAT DOES IT MEAN? Formally speaking, Einstein's $E=mc^2$ is a statement of mass–energy equivalence. More usefully, its gist is that matter can turn into energy and vice versa. (In practice, extreme conditions are needed for this to occur on any real scale.)

NUCLEAR WEAPON

LARGE HADRON COLLIDER

The explosion of the Hiroshima atom bomb was due to matter with the weight of a paper clip turning into energy.

OUR TUNE	
NATIONAL INSTRUMENTS	
Switzerland	Alphorn[1]
Brazil	Musical Bow
Bulgaria	Bagpipes
Russia	Spoons
UK	Handbells[2]
USA	none[3]

[1] *The alphorn has been criticized as old-fashioned—yodelling is considered an alternative.* [2] *According to Handel, who called the British Isles the 'Ringing Isles'.* [3] *While no official instrument is designated, Kazoo America has vigorously lobbied every new president since Nixon.*

BILLY THE BOLT. William Tell's apple-splitting exploits are known by all. What often goes unsaid is that Tell had a second bolt, which he planned to use on Gessler (the villain) if his first went awry. When this was found, Tell was hauled off in irons. He soon escaped, however, and dispatched bolt two through the tyrant's heart.

'For thirty years under the Borgias, Italy had warfare, terror, murder and bloodshed, but produced Michaelangelo, Leonardo de Vinci and the Renaissance. In Switzerland, they had 500 years of democracy, brotherly love and peace, and what did they produce—the cuckoo clock.'[6]

—Orson Welles (as Harry Lime)

[6] *Unfortunately, not even that. The cuckoo clock was invented in Germany's Black Forest around 1730.*

(SOME) SWISS JUST WANT TO HAVE FUN

Swiss inventions and discoveries include:

- **Absinthe** .... *psychoactive liquid*
  —invented 1792, banned 1910–2005.
- **Laudanum** [4] .... *psychoactive liquid*
  —invented 1520, banned 1921.
- **LSD** .... *psychoactive solid*
  —discovered 1943, banned 1973.
- **Diazepam**[5] .... *psychoactive solid*
  —discovered 1963, restricted 1971.
- **Milk Chocolate** .... *psychoactive solid*
  —invented 1876, no ban yet.

[4] *Opium dissolved in alcohol.* [5] *Originally sold as Valium.*

LAND OF THE UN-FREE

In Switzerland, you are not allowed to:

- flush the toilet or urinate upright after 10 p.m. (if in an apartment);
- wash your car, mow the lawn or hang out washing on a Sunday;
- name your boy Sue, your daughter Billy, Paris, Brooklyn or Chelsea.[7]

[7] *Names have to be approved by a civil registrar, who will turn down place names, brands, wrong-sex names and anything that's offensive, a joke or mad; Cain and Judas are banned outright. Which means 'Number 16 Bus Shelter', 'Talula Does The Hula From Hawaii' or 'Benson' and 'Hedges' (for twins)—all real names from New Zealand—wouldn't stand a chance.*

'I've always wanted to go to Switzerland to see what the army does with those wee red knives.'

—Billy Connolly

♠ · **GSR**: 40 · **WHS**: Bellinzona (castles) □ Berne (museum city) □ La Chaux-de-Fonds (watch-making town) □ Jungfrau-Aletsch (mountains) □ Lavaux (vineyards) □ Monte San Giorgio (fossils) □ Müstair (monastery) □ Pile Dwellings □ Rhaetian Railway □ St. Gall (monastery) □ Swiss Tectonic Arena Sardona (geology)

SYRIA ● سورية

'An easy country over which armies have marched since the first days of mankind.'

—Freya Stark (1937)

A Syrian war elephant helping to crush the Jewish Maccabean revolt at the Battle of Beth-Zachariah in 164 BCE

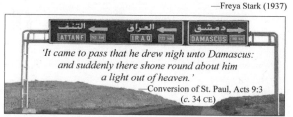

'It came to pass that he drew nigh unto Damascus: and suddenly there shone round about him a light out of heaven.'
—Conversion of St. Paul, Acts 9:3
(*c.* 34 CE)

St. Paul is known for his profound influence on the early Church, including his hard-fought doctrinal victory securing approval for gentiles to convert directly to Christianity without first becoming Jews. Control by former gentiles soon followed, with consequences—not least in 2,000 years of European anti-Semitism—that can hardly be overstated. Thus, as well as being a personal epiphany, Paul's divine road-to-Damascus conversion holds huge significance as the moment when Christianity became destined to turn away from its Jewish roots and to strike out instead as a freestanding and often hostile faith.

PIGGY IN THE MIDDLE. Due to its huge size, the now-extinct Syrian elephant was the preferred war elephant of the classical world. Hannibal's personal animal, Surus ('the Syrian'), was one, as may have been the lone elephant that Caesar used to force a crossing of the Thames when he conquered Britain. The disciplined Romans also worked out ways to counter the beasts. Soldiers were trained to cut off their trunks, which sent them out of control in a maddened fury; they would also sometimes deploy 'war pigs' against them, as it was said elephants were driven crazy by the hogs' high-pitched squeals.

Fat-tailed sheep predominate in the Fertile Crescent. The tail-fat from such sheep is an essential ingredient in top-quality baklava.

MADE IN YORKSHIRE. Sharing red, white and black stripes, the flags of five Arab states—Syria, Iraq, Egypt, Sudan and Yemen—differ only in their detailing. This commonality arises because they are all variants of the flag of the Arab Revolt, dreamt up in 1916 by Yorkshire landowner Sir Mark Sykes at the request of the British War Office. His brief was to make a flag that conveyed the maximum possible amount of 'Arabness' in order to help T. E. Lawrence recruit more men for his fight against the Ottoman Turks. Accordingly, Sykes chose a design combining Mohammad's black banner with the white and red flags of the Arab Umayyad and Hashemite dynasties respectively. (A fourth colour, green, stood for the Egyptian Fatamids.) While Lawrence's intended monolithic Arab union soon fizzled, the pan-Arab ideal lives on, most visibly in the flags of daughter states.

Quiz Time: The flags of Syria, Iraq, Egypt, Sudan and Yemen are shown below—but which is which? And for extra kudos, what do the unique details on each national flag represent? (*Answers below.*)

Answers: A. Egypt (Eagle of Saladin), B. Sudan (green triangle—Islam), C. Syria (two stars—the defunct 1958–61 union with Egypt), D. Iraq (Allahu Akbar—'God is Great'), E. Yemen.

♣ · **GSR**: 117 · **WHS**: Aleppo (historic city) □ Bosra (ruined classical city) □ Crac des Chevaliers (crusader castle) □ Damascus (historic city) □ Northern Syria (ancient villages) □ Palmyra (ruined classical city) · **WHS**: Falconry

——— TAIWAN (ROC) • 台灣 ———

'In the end, you care more about Los Angeles than Taipei.'

—Chinese General Xiong Guangxi to a senior US defence official (1995), explaining
none too subtly that if the US tried to defend Taiwan it would be inviting World War III

FIDDLEFINGERS. Taiwan has one manufacturing company for every 18 inhabitants—the highest density found anywhere.

'Children of the Sweet Potato.'

—Taiwanese nickname for themselves

'Chinese Taipei' (aka Taiwan) Olympic emblem

CHINESE TAIPEI. Beijing and Taipei don't agree on much, but are unanimous that there's only a single China. The question is whose? Plainly, in 1950, the Communists won the Civil War, sweeping the Nationalists off the mainland. But, since then, the Republic of China (in Taiwan) has firmly upheld the fiction that its troops are just taking a breather and will be popping back to finish off the Communists shortly. The make-believe gets more surreal, since the ROC still officially claims Mongolia and dares not stop for fear of upsetting Beijing. The ultimate taboo remains for Taiwan to renounce its claim to be China and declare independence. To do so would make invasion all but inevitable.

MADE IN TAIWAN. Studies of bacteria in stomach samples have shown that Taiwan's aborigines are the ancestors of all of the modern Polynesian peoples. Supported by DNA analysis and research on linguistic evolution, the gut bacteria

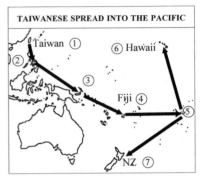

TAIWANESE SPREAD INTO THE PACIFIC

Taiwan ① ⑥ Hawaii
②
③
Fiji ④
⑤
NZ ⑦

show the ancient Taiwanese set off by canoe around 3,000 BCE and settled the Pacific in several stages (*see above*), eventually reaching New Zealand (as the Maoris) four millennia after first having set out in their tree-trunk dugouts.

MAN PORK. Until the 1890s, the flesh of Taiwanese aborigines could be bought in the island's markets alongside pork and other meats. Even after that trade was halted, hostile aboriginal groups were confined to a number of mountain valleys by a cordon of electric fences many miles long.

PING-PONG. From 1958 to 1978, China and Taiwan shelled each other across the narrow channel between the mainland and Taiwan's Kinmen archipelago. By a gentleman's agreement, China shelled Taiwan on odd days, while even days were reserved for Taiwanese retaliation. Enough shells landed the Taiwanese side for Kinmen's blacksmiths to forge a worldwide reputation among Chinese restaurant chefs for the top-end meat cleavers they pound from the high-grade steel of the Chinese Army shell casings.

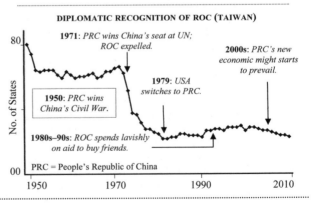

DIPLOMATIC RECOGNITION OF ROC (TAIWAN)

1971: PRC wins China's seat at UN; ROC expelled.

2000s: PRC's new economic might starts to prevail.

1979: USA switches to PRC.

1950: PRC wins China's Civil War.

1980s–90s: ROC spends lavishly on aid to buy friends.

No. of States

PRC = People's Republic of China

1950   1970   1990   2010

♣ · **GSR:** 35 · **WHS** none

———— TAJIKISTAN • ТОҶИКИСТОН ————

'Gamble everything for love, if you are a true human being.'
—Jalal ad-Din Muhammed Balkhi ('Rumi'), Tajikistan-born poet and Sufi theologian (1207–73)

DOMESTIC BLISS. World Bank figures show that Tajiks are the world's least experienced travellers. In 2002 (the latest year available), just 2,700 outward tourists were recorded. Put another way, this means the typical Tajik ventures abroad once every 2,500 years.

> **WHY SACHA BARON COHEN FINGERED THE WRONG STAN**
> (OR TOUCHING TAJIK TRADITIONS TO MAKE BORAT PROUD)
> - *When entertaining guests, the host drinks some tea before serving it to anyone else to show he hasn't poisoned it.*
> - *A female does not become a woman until she has successfully given birth. If she is still single after the age of 23, she is considered unmarriageable except as a second wife.*
> - *The morning after a wedding, the conjugal bed is inspected by the groom's mother to check the purity of the bride.*
> - *Abducting young women is customary, as is wife-beating.*

PENTHOUSE LIVING. Half of Tajikistan lies above 10,000 ft, making it one of the highest countries on Earth. The name of the range it straddles—the Pamir—is probably Persian, meaning 'Roof of the World'.[1] Likely origins for other major range names include:

Alps .... 'White' (from Latin *albus*)
Andes ..... 'High Crest' (from Incan Quechua *anti*)
Himalayas .... 'Abode of the Snow' (Sanskrit)
Rockies[2] .... translated from Native American

[1] *The Chinese call it Congling—the Onion Range.* [2] *Their original European name was the 'Shining Mountains'.*

BIG SQUEEZE. In the heart of the Pamirs, Tajikistan's 48-mile Fedchenko Glacier is the world's longest away from the Poles. While in a gentle setting ice may form exquisite crystals (*above*), under the brutal conditions inside a glacier its properties alter radically. Below 160 ft, the pressure is intense enough to bend ice like plastic and squeeze it like toothpaste (even sometimes uphill)—which is the primary way most large glaciers, like the Fedchenko, move.

SHAGGY SHEEP STORY. In the late Middle Ages, a tale sprang up in Europe of a curious wonder known as the 'Vegetable Lamb of Tartary' that was cultivated in Central Asia. Sprouting from a seed like that of a melon, the plant grew a lamb tethered to the tip of the stem by its navel. This lamb would then graze upon all the pasture within reach until there was none left and both plant and animal parts died. At this point, the lamb's sweet flesh could be eaten, while its soft fleece could be spun into yarn. In later centuries, several travellers searched in vain for this peculiar hybrid until, by the time of Napoleon, the story was accepted as fable. In retrospect, vegetable lamb was almost certainly cotton, which arrived in northern Europe during the 14th century, and which thrives in the hot, sunny summers of Central Asia—cotton is, by far, Tajikistan's biggest agricultural export. Even now, while 'cotton' in English comes from the Arabic *al-qutn*, in German the fibre is known as *baumwolle*—literally, 'tree wool'.

Tajik policeman

'In dealings with government officials, a bribe is usually offered. The payer must be polite or the price may increase.'
—everyculture.com
(Tajikistan: Political Officials)

....

♣ · **GSR**: 167 · **WHS**: Sarazm (Bronze Age ruins) · **ICH**: Shashmaqom (classical music)

———————— TANZANIA ————————

*'The British Empire at present covers a quarter of the globe, while the
German Empire consists of a small sausage factory in Tanganyika.'*

—Edmund Blackadder on the relative merits of the British and German imperial holdings at the time of the First World
War. Following the war's end, Tanganyika was transferred to Britain under a League of Nations mandate. In 1964, three
years after it became independent, Tanganyika merged with the offshore sultanate of Zanzibar to form Tanzania.

WHAT DID THE BRITISH EVER DO FOR TANZANIA?
While Tanganyika was ruled by Germany, the colonial
authorities adopted an exemplary educational policy with
standards unmatched anywhere else in Sub-Saharan Africa. However, by 1920, two years after the British takeover, the country's education department consisted of one
official and two clerks, and the education budget came to
less than the running costs of the governor's residence.

PLUGGED. At puberty, 19th-
century Chagga men stop-
pered their anuses and
claimed never to defecate
again. Nonsense, obviously;
but the men pretended otherwise, holding it to be proof of
their superiority over women.

SHORT, SHARP SHOTS. The shortest war
in history was fought between Britain and
Zanzibar in 1896. Given Britain had a
fleet of warships and Zanzibar just one
medieval cannon, it's perhaps surprising
the conflict lasted 45 minutes—which is
how long it took Zanzibar to surrender.

....

*'A frog can kill an elephant by
climbing into its trunk.'*
—Swahili proverb. (Don't neglect little problems.)

OTHERWISE KNOWN AS ...
ETYMOLOGY OF AFRICAN CAPITALS (SELECTED)

Dodoma (Tanzania) .... *'It has sunk'*[1]
Banjul (Gambia) .... *'Making rope matting'*
Cotonou (Benin) .... *'Estuary of death'*
Khartoum (Sudan) ..... *'End of the elephant's trunk'*
Luanda (Angola) .... *'Tax'*
Mbabane (Swaz.) .... *'Something sharp and bitter'*
Nairobi (Kenya) .... *'Cold water'*
Nouakchott (Maur.) ..... *'Place of floating seashells'*
[1] *Apparently a reference to an elephant stuck in a waterhole.*

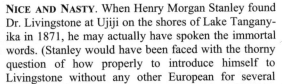

'Dr. Livingstone, I presume?'
—H. M. Stanley

David Livingstone,
Scottish missionary

NICE AND NASTY. When Henry Morgan Stanley found
Dr. Livingstone at Ujiji on the shores of Lake Tanganyika in 1871, he may actually have spoken the immortal
words. (Stanley would have been faced with the thorny
question of how properly to introduce himself to
Livingstone without any other European for several

H. M. Stanley,
Welsh rogue

hundred miles to effect an introduction, and this phrasing would have satisfied the social
niceties.) However, some doubt is cast on the incident, since Stanley tore out the relevant
pages from his diary and Livingstone never mentioned the phrase in his own account.
Nevertheless, the episode brought Stanley great fame and some fortune. The former was
later substantially squandered, in part due to his association with Belgium's King Leopold
II in Congo, but especially as a result of a second 'rescue' expedition he mounted in 1886–
90 to relieve Emin Pasha, the beleaguered governor of Equatoria. Stanley's expedition was
successful, but (probably largely true) rumours later emerged that one of his immediate
subordinates, James S. Jameson (of the whiskey family), had procured a 10-year-old girl
and given her to cannibals for the pleasure of sketching her being killed and cooked.

♥ · **GSR**: 113 · **WHS**: Kilimanjaro (volcano) □ Kilwa Kisiwani (Swahili ruins) □ Kondoa (rock art)
Ngorongoro (caldera and wildlife) □ Selous (wildlife) □ Serengeti (wildlife) □ Zanzibar (townscape)

————— THAILAND ● เมืองไทย —————

'Goodness is something that makes us serene and content; it is magnificent.'

—King Bhumibol of Thailand

หากที่ราบสูงทิเบตคือหลังคาโลก ทวีปแอนตาร์กติกาก็จะเปรียบเสมือนใต้ถุนโลก [1]

CHAIN LETTERS. Thai words don't get separated by spaces, but are strung together until an idea changes. Although it may seem alien, the system held sway in European languages as well, until 7th-century Irish scribes invented white spaces between every word.

[1] *Translation: If the Tibetan plateau is the roof of the world, then Antarctica can be compared to the basement.*

FRIARING TONIGHT. A young male Thai who has not spent time as a Buddhist monk is colloquially spoken of as 'raw'. Only after he has worn saffron robes for at least one rainy season is he considered to be 'cooked' and a suitable marriage or employment prospect. Some Thais lead a monastic existence for much longer; boy monks are allowed to join up once they reach eight.

PUSSY POLICE. Under a 2007 scheme, Bangkok police officers who committed minor transgressions such as parking violations or reporting late for work were shamed by being made to wear high-visibility pink 'Hello Kitty' armbands (set off with paired embroidered hearts) for several days. Serious offences remained subject to formal disciplinary procedures and punishment.

KNEE-JERK REACTION. Thailand's national sport, kick-boxing, delivers the most powerful blow of any form of unarmed combat. As feet are too vulnerable to injury, fighters hit mainly with their shins (traditionally toughened up by kicking banana trees as often as 1,000 times a day); it is the knee, however, that delivers the killer stroke. Using crash-dummy tests of the type performed to assess vehicle safety, kick-boxing's Kao Trong knee-strike at the chest has been shown to depress an opponent's breastbone by up to five centimetres—inflicting the same damage as a 35mph car crash, and potentially sending him into cardiac arrest.

BODY POLITIC—THAI TABOOS

- *Heads*. The most sacred part of the body. Never touch a Thai's head. In any group, the most senior person's head should be highest. (To make life easier, monks usually sit on a dais.)
- *Feet*. The basest part of the body. Toes must never point toward anyone else.
- *Royalty*. The most exalted personages. Even accidental disrespect is heinous.
- *Head & feet & royalty*. A triple-whammy. Whenever the king travels, all bridges over his route are cleared to ensure no feet pass above his head.

MAGIC BUBBLE. In 2006, Thailand was swept by a craze for lucky Jatukam Ramathep amulets, championed by an allegedly 103-year-old policeman. Bearing names like Money-Falling-like-Water, the amulets supposedly made their wearers supremely rich and, by 2007, sales reached $480m. Sadly, not everyone enjoyed good fortune—one woman was trampled to death in the rush for a new consignment, while amulet thefts sent crime rates soaring. But the biggest losers were the traders, who, in 2008, were left with millions of dollars of junk when the Thais finally noticed they weren't all billionaires.

LUCKY THAIS—AUSPICIOUS COLOURS TO DRESS IN EACH DAY OF THE WEEK

Day	Thai	Colour	Day	Thai	Colour
Monday	วันจันทร์	*yellow*	**Thursday**	วันพฤหัสบดี	*orange*
Tuesday	วันอังคาร	*pink*	**Friday**	วันศุกร์	*blue*
Wednesday (day)	วันพุธ	*green (dark)*	**Saturday**	วันเสาร์	*purple*
Wednesday (night)	วันพุธ	*green (light)*	**Sunday**	วันอาทิตย์	*red*

BRIDGE OVER THE RIVER KWAI

In 1942–43, the Japanese Army used Allied POWs and Asian civilians as slave labour to construct the 415km Thailand-Burma Railway along a jungle route that British surveyors had earlier dismissed as infeasible. Built at a cost of 106,000 lives, the route has come to symbolize Imperial Japan's wider mistreatment of POWs (*below*), later judged a war crime.

TOURIST TRAP. Hard up against Thailand's border with Burma, a series of 'tourist villages' exhibit the Kayan women, who wear brass coils around their necks. Starting in childhood, their collarbones are forced downwards as more coils are gradually added, eventually giving the impression of a swan-like neck. The Kayan originally arrived in the 1980s, as refugees from Burma, but, despite offers of resettlement from New Zealand, many have not since been allowed to leave. Various bureaucratic excuses are mumbled, but it's an open secret that the Kayan have become too valuable as a crowd-pulling tourist lure: visitors are charged $6 to view the women (although the Kayans themselves are paid just $35 a month).

POW MORTALITY RATES (WWII)					
Captor	**Captive**				
-	*Chinese*	*German*	*Japanese*	*US/UK*	*USSR*
GERMANY				4%	58%
JAPAN	~100%[1]			27%	
US/UK		4%	4%		
USSR		19%	10%		

[1] *Only 56 Chinese survived the war as POWs; almost all Chinese soldiers were killed after capture (including 57,500 after the sack of Nanjing alone).*

WEIGHING ANGELS. Thailand's capital is known the world over as Bangkok. To Thais, however, it's Krung Thep, the 'City of Angels'—a title shared with its smaller Californian cousin, Los Angeles. Parallels go further since in both cases the name is an abbreviation; but there the similarities end. Impressive though LA's original El Pueblo de la Reina de Los Angeles ('Village of the Queen of the Angels') is, it's blown out of the water by Bangkok's full ceremonial title, the longest place name on Earth, which in English reads:

'The City of Angels, the Great City, the Eternal Jewel City, the Impregnable City of God Indra, the Grand Capital of the World Endowed with Nine Precious Gems, the Happy City, Abounding in an Enormous Royal Palace that Resembles the Heavenly Abode where Reigns the Reincarnated God, a City Given by Indra and Built by Vishnukarma.'

WHY WAI? Performed with a slight bow, the prayer-like *wai* greeting is so ingrained into Thai life that even the most culturally inflexible of foreigners soon find themselves asking, 'why not?'

JOINED AT THE HIP or head, but most commonly the chest, 1 in 200 sets of identical twins are born conjoined. Although sets of conjoined twins are recorded going back over 1,000 years, it was the 19th-century Chang and Eng Bunker twins from Thailand who first achieved international celebrity— hence 'Siamese twins'. The underlying cause of linkage remains obscure, but is probably connected with a delay before the embryo splits; sadly only around 25% of such twins survive early infancy. Amongst all births, the incidence of conjoined twins is around 1 in 100,000. Rare though this is, conjoined triplets are much rarer; only a handful have ever been reported. As to Chang and Eng themselves, they prospered: after travelling America as showmen, they bought themselves a farm, married sisters and fathered 21 children.

GRUB'S UP. Fried insects are a popular street food in north-east Thailand. Salted and topped with a squirt of Golden Mountain sauce, they're *the* classic munchies to go with a beer. Fried insects are wholesome too. A 100g portion contains 37 to 60g of protein and 30g of fat (thus providing the same nutritional value as pork). Thai researchers are now campaigning to boost insect-eating worldwide. Requiring only 15% of the fodder needed by cattle per kg of 'meat' produced, insects increasingly look like the green alternative for ethical meat-eaters unwilling to embrace vegetarianism.

Mangda

CRUNCHY MUNCHIES—STREET FOOD FAVOURITES		
Thai	**English**	**Flavour Notes**
Jing Leed	Cricket	mild popcorn/prawn
Kudjee Yak	Dung Beetle	best fed on buffalo dung
Non Pai	Bamboo Worm	'express trains'; cheesy with a hint of chew.
Mangda	Giant Water Beetle	9 cm long; only males have 'ripe gorgonzola' taste (from pheromone sacs in belly); grind essence with chillies for *namprik* dipping sauce.

BEETLEJUICE. Thailand, along with India, is the main source of shellac, a sticky insect secretion. Known casually in the food industry as beetlejuice (but sold as 'confectioners' glaze'), it gives a shiny gloss coat to pills, fruit (especially apples) and certain sweets. Look out for E904 on the list of ingredients.

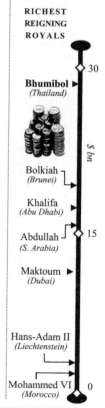

LONGEST RULING CURRENT LEADERS

HOW TO KILL A KING? Regicide is always a ticklish affair. So when the most revered king in Thai history, Taksin the Great (*left*), had to go, they decided at least to give him a VIP send-off; avoiding any bloodshed, they used a scented sandalwood club to beat him to death inside a velvet sack.

TRENCH WARFARE. In 1975, the US drew up plans to explode a line of 139 atomic bombs across southern Thailand. The idea was to blast a Panama-style canal from the Indian Ocean to the South China Sea as a 1,000-mile short cut to the Pacific. A no-nuke version of the same plan is now being studied by China.

PANTS! In Thailand, it's illegal not to wear a shirt outside the home (men too), or to go about in a public place without underwear (although spot checks are infrequent).

MEN ONLY. Over the last three decades, Thailand has enjoyed a phenomenal tourist boom. Unusually, however, the ratio of male to female arrivals from the West (and Japan) is almost 2:1; a surplus of 950,000 men a year. The official explanation is golf. But strangely, Thailand's 200 golf courses only record 350,000 foreign players, leaving 600,000 males who inexplicably disappear before reaching the first tee.

UK TOURIST VISITS TO THAILAND[1]

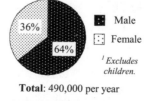

36%

64%

■ Male

▦ Female

[1] *Excludes children.*

Total: 490,000 per year

RICHEST REIGNING ROYALS

Bhumibol
(Thailand)

Bolkiah
(Brunei)

Khalifa
(Abu Dhabi)

Abdullah
(S. Arabia)

Maktoum
(Dubai)

Hans-Adam II
(Liechtenstein)

Mohammed VI
(Morocco)

$ bn

30

15

0

Years

60

50

40

30

Bhumibol
(Thailand)

Elizabeth II
(UK)

Bolkiah
(Brunei)

Margrethe II
(Denmark)

Carl XVI Gustaf
(Sweden)

Juan Carlos I
(Spain)

♣ · **GSR:** 31 · **WHS:** Ayutthaya (ruined city) □ Ban Chiang (prehistoric site) □ Dong Phayagen-Khao Yai (wildlife) □ Sukhothai (ruined city) □ Thungyai-Huai Kha Khaeng (wildlife)

—— TIMOR-LESTE ● TIMÓR LORO SA'E ——

'It is important that whatever you do succeeds quickly.'

—Dr. Henry Kissinger, speaking to President Suharto of Indonesia on 6 December 1975 to signal US acquiescence to the invasion of Timor-Leste, which had declared independence from Portugal nine days previously. Indonesia attacked the following day and occupied the country for the next 24 years—fighting a drawn-out insurgency that led to the deaths of at least 103,000 Timorese (10% of the current population).

LAND OF THE RISING TAUTOLOGY. Previously known in English as East Timor, Timor-Leste occupies the eastern half of the island of Timor. However, as Timor comes from the Malay word *timur* meaning 'east', East Timor literally meant 'East East'. Unfortunately, the current name is no real improvement as *leste* is simply 'east' in Portuguese. The only variant that almost escapes this tautological trap[1] is the local Tetum form of 'Timór Loro Sa'e'—but not really, since *lorosa'e* means 'rising sun' and, hence, 'east' as well.

[1] *Under Indonesian rule, the territory was known as Timor Timur ('East East' again), snappily contracted to Timtim.*

TREE OF DESTINY. With a heady, bright fragrance that lingers for decades, sandalwood has arguably been the most precious and sought-after aromatic wood throughout history. But on Timor, it was formerly commonplace to the point that villagers chopped it for firewood (leaving their houses so thick with the exotic fragrance that outsiders would get physically ill). Once Chinese and Indian traders discovered the island's sandalwood forests, however, Timor amassed so much wealth that the legend later grew up of the Noil Noni, a river of gold that was said to flow through the interior. Even today, the remoter hill villages form one of the best places in the world to find pieces of antique ivory—brought to the island centuries ago by merchants trading for sandalwood, and still circulating as the traditional form of dowry.

HOLY SMOKE. Sandalwood is essential to the practice of Zoroastrianism. Proffered by a mask-wearing priest using a pair of silver tongs, it is prescribed as an offering to all three grades of sacred fire: 'appointed place fires', 'fires of fires' and the very holiest, 'fires of victory'[2].

[2] *Each such fire must be lit using flames collected from 16 different sources (including lightning and a funeral pyre) and then subjected to purification rituals that take a team of 32 priests up to a year.*

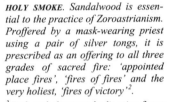

Members of Australia's 'Sparrow Force' in East Timor in 1942. Evacuated in February 1943 after 12 months of fighting, they were the last Allied troops in South-East Asia to hold out against the Japanese during WWII.

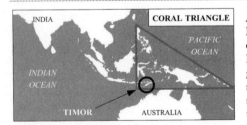

THE BLUE AMAZONIA. Timor-Leste enjoys a prime position inside the Coral Triangle—the global epicentre of marine diversity. At the meeting point of the Indian and Pacific Oceans, the Triangle holds 76% of the world's coral species and nearly 40% of reef fish despite occupying just 1% of the surface of the Earth.

ADVANCED FLUID DYNAMICS FOR MARINE INVERTEBRATES. Like reefs in other regions of the tropics, Timor-Leste's 40 square miles of offshore coral gardens are exquisite to the eye but scalpel-sharp to the touch. More than simply a hazard for inattentive divers, the hard, jagged surface of coral is actually fundamental to its survival as it introduces turbulence into the water flow, so diverting nutrients into the interiors of the living polyps and enabling the reefs to grow.

♣ · **GSR**: 183 · **WHS**: none

———— TOGO ————

'Anyone who has been bitten by a snake fears even the earthworm.'

—Gilchrist Olympio (opposition leader), while in exile after assassination attempt

MAN OF THE MOMENT. Togo's Gnassingbe Eyadema was by no means worst, but he was first. Participating in Africa's earliest post-colonial coup, in 1963, and hanging onto power until death in 2005, Eyadema blazed the trail that Mobuto, Amin and the other 'big men' across the continent would follow. Eyadema's personal foibles included a retinue of 1,000 dancing girls and a novelty watch, issued to all Togo's security personnel, that featured the presidential visage flashing on and off four times every minute.

TOGO—RELIGION	
Animist[2]	51%
Christian	29%
Muslim	20%

[2] *Majority: Vodun (2.5m believers).*

TOGOLESE TRUISMS

Every rhinoceros is proud of its horn · With gold you can build a road to heaven, but it will end in hell · When all men say you are a dog, it is time to bark.

TRADE MUST BE PAID. The Togolese capital lent its name to the Lomé Conventions—the rules governing aid from Europe to Africa via preferential trade access going back to 1975. In 2000, however, US lawyers claimed American farmers were suffering unfairly, and forced Lomé to end. It has now been replaced by the much less generous 'Cotonou' (negotiated in next-door Benin).

BIZARRE BAZAAR. Lomé's Akodessewa Market is the best place in Africa to buy animal skins, bones and body parts. Known as fetishes, the objects are used to focus the divine power that, according to Vodun religion, infuses the natural world.

A FETISH CURE[3]

Grind monkey head with chosen herbs; roast on fire and reduce to black ash. Cut patient three times in the chest or back and rub the powder into the flesh.

[3] *For all-purpose use on serious maladies, especially those that conventional medicine can't cure.*

WORLD AID BY DONOR[1] (2007)

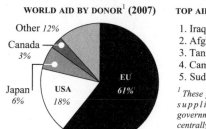

Other *12%*
Canada *3%*
Japan *6%*
USA *18%*
EU *61%*

TOTAL $114bn

TOP AID RECIPIENTS (2007)

1. Iraq $9.0bn
2. Afghanistan $3.0bn
3. Tanzania $1.8bn
4. Cameroon $1.8bn
5. Sudan $1.6bn

[1] *These figures are only for aid supplied by national governments (and the EU centrally). Private money from charities, NGOs, etc. adds 15% to state spending, giving a grand total of $140bn annually.*

'Aid is a method for transferring money from poor people in rich countries to rich people in poor countries.'

—P. Bauer

VALUE FOR MONEY? Research studies repeatedly turn up no link between aid and economic growth. The cause—if indeed this is so—is unclear. Ideas include:

- Aid reflects the donor's values not recipient's needs.
- Aid allows needed economic reform to be delayed.
- Aid fosters a culture of corruption and/or dependency.

ZIPS, WHIPS & JUMBO NAPPIES. In Western contexts, fetishism is normally associated with sexuality, an extended usage first adopted by Alfred Binet in 1887. Binet further divided sexual fetishism into 'spiritual loves'—fixation on an abstraction: dominance or humiliation, for example; and 'plastic loves'—fixation on a category of object: leather perhaps.[3]

[3] *A 1980s UK study found the most common such fetishes were: clothing (58%), rubber (23%) and shoes (15%).*

♥ · **GSR**: 109 · **WHS**: Koutammakou (mud tower-houses) · **ICH**: Gelede (animistic ceremony)

———— TRINIDAD & TOBAGO ————

*'Everything that makes a Trinidadian an unreliable citizen makes him
a quick, civilized person whose values are always human ones.'*

—V. S. Naipaul, *The Middle Passage* (1962)

LOWERING THE BAR

The world limbo record is held by Dennis Walston, who has shimmied his way under a six-inch bar (gap shown actual size below).

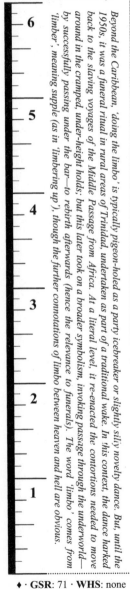

Inches

6

5

4

3

2

1

Beyond the Caribbean, 'doing the limbo' is typically pigeon-holed as a party icebreaker or slightly silly novelty dance. But, until the 1950s, it was a funeral ritual in rural areas of Trinidad, undertaken as part of a traditional wake. In this context, the dance harked back to the slaving voyages of the Middle Passage from Africa. At a literal level, it re-enacted the contortions needed to move around in the cramped, under-height holds; but this later took on a broader symbolism, invoking passage through the underworld—by successfully passing under the bar—to rebirth afterwards (hence the relevance to funerals). The word 'limbo' comes from 'limber', meaning supple (as in 'limbering up'), though the further connotations of limbo between heaven and hell are obvious.

BURIED MEANING

'She was a mother without knowing it, and a wife without letting her husband know it except by her kind indulgence to him.'

—The famously enigmatic epitaph on Betty Stiven's tomb, Plymouth, Tobago. No one is quite sure what it means, but Betty was an African slave who died in 1783.

CRASH IN THE PAN. Trinidad's oil-based economy has borne unlikely fruit in the steelpan: the cannibalized 55-gallon oil drum that Trinidadians have made their national instrument. This creativity was spurred by the British, who, in 1868, banned traditional drumming for fear of subversion. In response, young men soon took to hitting *tamboo-bamboos* (lengths of bamboo

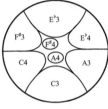

'Centre Three Cello' Pan, showing tuning

cane) and empty bottles with sticks. By the 1930s, carnival marchers were also banging large biscuit tins ('booms') and brake hubs ('basses'); and, from around 1935 onwards, the tops of oil drums. At this point, the sounds were still random bangs—it was the rhythm that mattered. But in 1942, Winston 'Spree' Simon found the pitch of his oil drum could be varied by hammering, opening the ability to play a melody. Quickly, tuneful oil drums swept away all other 'instruments'; and, in 1951, the first ever all-drum steelband (the 'Trinidad All Steel Percussion Orchestra') was assembled specifically to travel to London to represent Trinidad at the Festival of Britain.

SEA SERPENTS. Anacondas regularly swim across the 7-mile sea channel separating Trinidad from the mouth of the Orinoco River and the South American mainland. By most measures the biggest snake in the world, anacondas are extravagantly muscular. The longest ever caught in Trinidad (in the 1930s) was over 30 ft, making it among the biggest anywhere. For over a century, however, there have been persistent rumours of truly immense specimens deep in the Amazon, leaving trails 6 ft wide and growing over 60 ft in length— but nothing approaching this size has ever been trapped.

Safety Note: Anacondas should always be handled by their tails.

It's widely known that constrictors, such as the anaconda, don't crush their prey to death; but now it seems they don't suffocate them either (they kill too fast). Instead, they squeeze so hard they stop the blood from circulating—forcing a fatal heart attack in seconds.

♦ · **GSR**: 71 · **WHS**: none

TUNISIA ● تونس

'If the full moon loves you, why worry about the stars?'

—Tunisian proverb

CONTINENTAL DRIFT. The Afrigi were once a Berber clan living in the hills of northern Tunisia. After subduing them, the Romans took their name, Latinized it to 'Africa' and used it to describe the region. As Rome extended its holdings, 'Africa' grew, until ultimately it applied to the entire continent (displacing the previously preferred names of 'Libya' or 'Ethiopia').

HOW THE CONTINENTS GOT THEIR NAMES		
Name	*Source*	*Meaning*[1]
Africa	Afrigi	Folk of the Dusty Land
America	Amerigo	Italian explorer's name
Antarctica	Arktikos[2]	Land of the Great Bear
Asia	Asu	Land of the Rising Sun
Europe	Ereb	Land of the Setting Sun
Oceania	Oceanus	World-Girdling Stream

[1]*Tentative, other roots may exist.* [2] *Plus 'anti' = opposite.*

CALL ME KONG. Around 500 BCE, Hanno the Navigator set out from Carthage, just outside today's Tunis, to explore Africa's coast. At the limit of his voyage, he encountered a savage and hairy 'people', whom local guides named as the 'Gorillae'. Intrigued, Hanno captured three females and tried to persuade them to accompany him back home. They, however, refused all entreaties, so he had them killed and took their flayed hides instead. Nothing more was heard of the Gorillae for two millennia, until 1847, when Thomas Savage, an American missionary working in West Africa, came upon a huge ape unknown to science. Guessing that the ape and Hanno's hirsute 'wild women' were one and the same, Savage resurrected the ancient name, giving us the gorillas we know today.

MAKING WHOOPEE. In Tunisia, you have to be 20 to engage in sexual activity—the world's highest minimum age of consent.

NASAL STEREO. Tunisia's national drink, mint tea, must be prepared with spearmint for an authentic flavour and aroma. The chemical responsible is carvone—but it is also carvone that gives caraway its (very different) smell. Puzzled, scientists found right-handed carvone smells of spearmint, while the left-handed form has a caraway odour. This, in turn, has led them to discover that our noses are equipped with both left and right-handed odour detectors.

AFRICA RISING. When the Carthaginian general Hannibal inflicted the Roman Republic's most serious ever defeat at Cannae, he was the first in centuries to make Rome feel fear. Facing the numerically superior Roman army, Hannibal ordered his infantry into a measured retreat. As the Roman troops took up pursuit, the Carthaginian flanks and cavalry wheeled round and sprang a carefully laid trap, plunging savagely into the Roman sides and rear. It was history's first recorded pincer movement and perhaps its most brutal: after encirclement, 600 legionaries were cut down each minute until darkness fell. With nothing between Hannibal and the gates of the city, Rome's terrified citizens were reduced to human sacrifice, burying four victims alive in the Forum in an attempt to placate the gods.

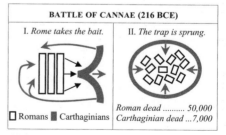

BATTLE OF CANNAE (216 BCE)	
I. *Rome takes the bait.*	II. *The trap is sprung.*
□ Romans ■ Carthaginians	Roman dead 50,000
	Carthaginian dead ...7,000

FRIENDS. In 1985, the mayors of Tunis and Rome signed a treaty finally ending the Third Punic War (149–146 BCE).

♥ · **GSR**: 68 · **WHS**: Carthage (ruined city) □ Ichkeul (wetlands) □ El Jem (amphitheatre) □ Kairouan (mosque) □ Kerkuane (ruined city) □ Sousse (townscape) □ Thugga (ruins) □ Tunis (historic city)

—————— TURKEY • TÜRKIYE ——————

'There is no love like a mother's, nor a place like your homeland.'
—Turkish proverb

SIMPLON
ORIENT
EXPRESS
(1936)

LUNAR ATTRACTION. The world's largest transcontinental city is now known as Istanbul; prior to 1930, it was Constantinople and, before that, Greek Byzantium. While Byzantium, the city put the crescent moon on its banners, adding the Star of the Virgin Mary when it became Christian Constantinople. After the Ottoman Turks conquered Constantinople and made it their capital, they adopted Byzantium's star and crescent as their own.[1] As Ottoman power grew to dominate the Middle East, the Empire's symbol came to be seen as synonymous with Islam and, for most,[2] it remains so today.

[1] An alternative theory holds the Turks adopted the symbol from Siberia.
[2] Devout Muslims often reject the crescent and star due both to the link to the Ottomans and to Hadithic injunctions against symbols or images.

BOWING OUT. The Turks were once the world's greatest turban-wearers, sporting huge balloon creations wrapped around a frame. In 1826, they were banned as too Oriental and Turks took to Western hats instead. However, the hats had to have their brims removed to allow kneeling at prayer—and this resulted in the fez.

FRAMED. Many pubs in England display the sign of the Turk's Head. The majority of these refer back to the Crusades[6]—but they're wrong-headed: the foes that the Crusaders battled were mainly Arabs from Egypt, and their greatest commander, Sultan Saladin (*above*), was an Iraqi Kurd.

[6] Others reference instead the 'Turk's Head' nautical knot, named for its resemblance to a Turkish turban.

'Men, I am not ordering you to fight, I am ordering you to die.'
—Kemal Atatürk, at Gallipoli, 1915
(his troops died, but the line held)

BOLDLY GOING. Aside from an unlikely appearance in deep space on board the USS *Enterprise*, the *Orient Express* has materialized in *Dracula*, *Around the World in 80 Days*, one *Flashman* adventure, two Graham Greene stories, *From Russia, with Love* and, naturally, *Murder on the Orient Express*—written by Agatha Christie[3] at the train company's Istanbul hotel.

[3] According to UNESCO, Agatha Christie is the most translated author of all time. She has 6,589 works in translation, beating Jules Verne (4,223), Shakespeare (3,674), Enid Blyton (3,544) and Lenin (3,517).

SCENIC ROUTE. When the Ottoman Empire gave German entrepreneurs a contract to build a rail network across its territory, it guaranteed them a minimum return per kilometre of track laid—thus resulting in some impressively meandering[7] journeys.

[7] The Meander (now Menderes) is a river in western Turkey that follows a notably curvaceous course.

BULGARIA TO ISTANBUL: ROAD V. RAIL

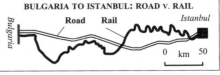

GIVING THE JOB A BAD NAME—LABELLING HISTORY'S BAD GUYS

-	First Usage	First Meaning	Note
Despot	Byzantium	senior official[4]	remains a title for bishops in the Orthodox Church
Dictator	Roman Empire	magistrate	Julius Caesar first to adopt name in sense of 'ruler'
Junta	Spain	committee	in Spain, *junta* means simply 'board of directors'
Tyrant	Ancient Greece	self-crowned king	an early tyrant, Cleisthenes, notably banned poets[5]

[4] Usually one rank below the emperor—who, to avoid confusion, further styled himself Kosmokrator (Master of the Universe) and Kronokrator (Lord of Time). [5] Cleisthenes also gave his daughter away as a competition prize.

Paris: 23:50
Lausanne: 07:00 +1
Milan: 12:23 +1
Venice: 17:05 +1
Istanbul: 12:30 +3
Sofia: 18:56 +2

Zagreb: 03:10 +2   *Belgrade: 09:00 +2*

THREE EMPERORS ON THE GOLDEN HORN

CONSTANTINE (272–337). The man who founded the Byzantine Empire and converted the Roman world to Christianity was indubitably acclaimed emperor while living in York. But English chroniclers claim more, saying his maternal grandfather was Old King Cole of Colchester—lending Byzantium a very British bloodline.

SÜLEYMAN (1494–1566). The magnificently crowned ruler of the Ottoman Empire at its apogee was checked only at the gates of Vienna. In his spare time, Süleyman enjoyed making jewellery.

ATATÜRK (1881–1938). The father of modern Turkey was an ardent Westernizer. One radical move, in 1925, was to ban the fez as too Islamic. Atatürk also pioneered ballroom dancing at all official gatherings to set a cutting-edge tone.

HAPPY DAYS. After Evagirus (later 'the Solitary') misspent his youth sampling all 4th-century Constantinople had to offer, he became a hermit and drew up a list of eight 'evil thoughts'. Tweaking these slightly, Pope Gregory I republished Evagirus' list in 590 as the *Seven Deadly Sins*. For those wishing to avoid perdition, the Catholic Church conveniently provides a list of seven opposing virtues.

I'LL BE DAMNED—A SHOPPING LIST FOR SINNERS

Evil Thoughts	Seven Deadly Sins	Seven Virtues
Pride / Vainglory	Pride (the gravest sin)	Humility
Avarice	Greed (for wealth/power)	Charity
Gluttony	Gluttony (of food)	Temperance
Fornication	Lust (sexual)	Chastity
Despair / Torpor	Sloth (the mildest sin)	Diligence
Wrath	Wrath (inc. at self: suicide)	Patience
	Envy (wishing others ill)	Kindness

THE DAY HISTORY BEGAN. On Wednesday 28 May 585 BCE, the Lydian and Mede armies marched up to the river Halys in central Turkey and began to battle. Then the sun went out, and the two terrified kings agreed a peace treaty on the spot. The date is the earliest in history that can be given with absolute precision and we know it so exactly because the eclipse timing can be calculated retrospectively.[1] From this foundation, ancient historians can then calculate the passage of time to recorded events that happened later, making the Battle of the Eclipse truly the day history began.

[1] *The eclipse was also the first one to be correctly forecast in advance (by Thales in the Greek city of Miletus). His feat is itself regarded as the earliest scientific prediction—and, so, the first appliance of science.*

NAKED CHEFS. By the mid 17th century, the Ottoman emperor's kitchens at the Topkapi Palace employed 1,370 staff. Sophistication was so great, there was a master chef for each type of *halva*. Nevertheless, however elevated, all cooks were still expected to work in their underwear.

BLOOMING TURBANS. Although linked with Holland, tulips were first cultivated in Turkey, and they remain the country's national plant. The word 'tulip' comes from the Turkish for muslin and ultimately derives from 'turban'—describing the shape of the flower.

♣♣ · **GSR**: 38 · **WHS**: Cappadocia (troglodyte houses) □ Divriği (mosque) □ Edirne (mosque) Hattusha (Hittite ruins) □ Hierapolis (classical ruins) □ Istanbul (historic city) □ Nemrut Dağ (mausoleum) □ Safranbolu (Ottoman town) □ Troy (classical ruins) □ Xanthos (classical ruins) · **ICH**: Âşıklık (minstrels) □ Karagöz (puppetry) □ Kirkpinar (oil wrestling) □ Meddah (storytelling) □ Mevlevi Sema (whirling dance) □ Nevruz (New Year) □ Semah (ritual) □ Sohbet (village meetings)

—— Turkmenistan ● Türkmenistan ——

'Ruhnama *must be the centre of this universe.*
In this universe, all the current and the future cosmic matters should go on spinning,
in Ruhnama*'s attraction, centripetal force and orbits. '*

—Late President Saparmurat Niyazov (*Ruhnama*, 2001). For more on this, see Myway Code (*below*).

Mr. January. The sun always shines on Saparmurat Niyavoz, whose 49-ft-high gold-covered statue rotates in the centre of Turkmenistan's capital, Ashgabat, so as to permanently face the sun. Not so on many other Turkmen, who, until the dictator's sudden death in 2006, had to endure the most repressive and erratic regime of any post-Soviet country—and there was some stiff competition. Aside from renaming January after himself (and April after his mum), Niyavoz redefined old age to start at 85 and discontinued the pensions of 100,000 pensioners (ordering them to reimburse the state for the previous two years of money received). More idiosyncratically, he banned lip-synching, libraries, circuses and news reporters with make-up; gold teeth were also outlawed, with the command that people should instead gnaw on bones. This last may have been on the advice of his dentist, Gurbanguly Berdymukhammedov, who, despite in 2004 overseeing the dismissal of all the country's midwives (and their replacement with teenage conscripts), was welcomed as a return to sanity when he ascended to the presidency following his ex-patient's death.

Hothouse Hell. The villagers of Derweze call the vast flame-licked pit outside their hamlet the 'Door to Hell'. Less apocalyptically, it apparently opened under a gas drilling rig in 1971 and has been burning ever since. While some might care about the squandering of resources, in Turkmenistan it's no big deal, as gas is free anyway—and so, perversely, Turkmen keep their gas stoves lit 24/7 to save the price of a match.

Myway Code. On top of the usual three-point-turns and clutch control, passing a Turkmen driving test requires 16 hours' study of the *Ruhnama*—ex-president Niyavoz's rambling autobiography and miscellany of musings. The silver lining is that, according to the late president, those who manage three readings are guaranteed entry into heaven. What is truly miraculous, however, is how Niyavoz came to write it, given that he was illiterate.

Turkmenistan lies on the eastern shore of the Caspian, smallest of the three geological oceans.

From a geological perspective, the world has a total of just three distinct oceans (separate areas of oceanic crust): the Black Sea, the Caspian Sea and the rest.

Queen of the River. Reaching 99 lbs in European fisheries and living for 200 years as Japanese *koi*, the common carp is a Caspian Sea native that has gone on to conquer the globe. Of greater significance still, 2.8m tonnes are farmed each year for food, more than salmon and trout combined.

Mongol Matricide. Now just walls of crumbling mud where the mountains of Afghanistan run into the Kara Kum Desert, the ancient city of Merv was once known in Arabic as 'the mother of the world', and is thought to have been the largest city on Earth from 1145 to 1153, with a population of 200,000.[1] Its glory days were traumatically ended only 68 years later, when, in 1221, it opened its gates to Tule, son of Genghis Khan, who then ordered the slaughter of all but 400 of its inhabitants, as well as hundreds of thousands of refugees[2]—a total of up to 1,000,000 people, and one of the bloodiest massacres in history.

[1] *In comparison, the population of London at the time was no more than 20,000.* [2] *Who had taken shelter inside its walls.*

♣ · **GSR**: 171 · **WHS**: Kunya-Urgench (ruined city) □ Merv (ruined city) □ Nisa (ruined fortress)

———————— UGANDA ————————

'I ate them before they ate me.'

—Idi Amin Dada, President of Uganda (1971–79), in darkly metaphorical mood—probably

---

BITE-SIZE BRIEFINGS

- Uganda's pornography laws include one banning the playing of 'erotic music'.
- Idi Amin's fifth wife, Sarah, was formerly part of the Ugandan Army Revolutionary Suicide Mechanized Regiment Band.
- Uganda's police force operates a special Anti-Human-Sacrifice Task Force.

MELTING MOON. Separating the Nile and Congo rivers, Uganda's Rwenzori mountains were hazily known to the ancients as the Mountains of the Moon. Since they were first surveyed 100 years ago, the range's glaciers have shrunk by 80%.

BAD JOKE. 'Tough but benevolent' was the crisp assessment of Britain's security services when former King's African Rifles assistant cook Idi Amin seized power in Uganda in a 1971 coup. There was satisfaction too: a keen rugby player[1] and former boxing champion, Amin was 'their' man through and through. Even when things started to go off the rails—an appearance at a Saudi state funeral dressed in a kilt, the self-awarded CBE ('Conqueror of the British Empire')— Amin seemed merely an entertaining buffoon. Eventually, however, there was no hiding he had turned Uganda into a charnel house, killing up to 500,000. When the grave-diggers couldn't keep up, they started throwing the bodies to the crocs, and when even they were sated, the flow of body parts kept on coming until they clogged the inlets at the Owen Falls hydroelectric plant, causing nationwide blackouts.

[1] *While in the British Army, Amin was notorious for getting teammates to hit him on the head with a hammer before games to fire him up—inspiration, perhaps, for his later penchant for the 'hammer punishment' (execution by sledgehammer).*

'Women are like fresh banana leaves: they never come to an end in the plantation.'

—Luganda proverb[3]

OOOPS! *Matooke* means both 'banana' and 'food' in Luganda, Uganda's main language. Not surprisingly, Ugandans are the world's biggest banana-eaters, with banana skins making up 40% of Kampala's rubbish.

[3] *Despite the swaggering talk, recent surveys suggest that 95% of Ugandans aged between 15 and 50 now either adhere to monogamous relationships or abstain. This behaviour has helped reduce the country's HIV rate from 30% in the 1980s to 6% in 2008—the sharpest drop in Africa.*

✖✖✖✖✖✖✖✖✖✖✖✖✖✖✖✖ † ✖✖✖✖✖✖✖✖✖✖✖✖✖✖✖✖

'The LRA has no political program or ideology, at least none that the population has heard or can understand.'

—R. Gersony, reporting on the LRA for the US embassy in Kampala (1997)

DELIVER US FROM EVIL. After Joseph Kony first heard the voices of angels, he decided to form an army. Twenty-four years on, no one has any real idea what his Lord's Resistance Army is fighting for (beyond the fire-and-brimstone enforcement of the Eleven Commandments[2]). Nevertheless, his recruitment methods—abducting an estimated 104,000 children into his army while killing their families to make sure they have no home to escape to—ensured that, in 2005, he became the first person to be indicted by the new International Criminal Court. (Despite this, Kony remains at large.)

[2] *The regular Ten, plus an 11th added by Kony: 'Thou shalt not ride a bicycle.'*

The LRA shouldn't be confused with the Movement for the Restoration of the Ten Commandments of God, another Ugandan millennial group, which took the Ten Commandments so literally it communicated by sign language to avoid accidentally bearing false witness (and so breaking the Ninth Commandment). The sect imploded in March 2000, when 800 members were murdered by its leaders after questioning why the world hadn't ended yet as they had forecast.

♥ · **GSR**: 111 · **WHS**: Bwindi (gorillas) ▢ Kasubi (tombs) ▢ Rwenzori (mountains) · **ICH**: Barkcloth

UKRAINE ● УКРАЇНА

'C'est magnifique, mais ce n'est pas la guerre.'

—Marshal Pierre Bosquet, on the British Army's Charge of the Light Brigade (1854) during the Crimean War. Despite the best efforts of an incompetent British High Command (the Charge is still taught at staff colleges as an example of how not to give orders), the Light Brigade survived, albeit with casualties of 40%, and Britain and its allies ultimately went on to win the war. In 1954, Khrushchev transferred the whole of the Crimea to Ukraine as an anniversary present.

'With Every Passing Day, Life Gets Better!'—Poster from the Ukrainian SSR (1952). During the Soviet era, non-representational art was rejected as incomprehensible to the proletariat and hence useless for propaganda (art's obvious purpose). The Socialist Realist style approved in its place instead glorified Stalin's New Soviet Man (and woman) and was described by Stalin as 'engineering for the soul'. Western art critics called it 'girl meets tractor'.

Per dollar of GDP, Ukraine's economy is the biggest producer of greenhouse gases on Earth. (The chief culprits are the Kryvbas and Donbas—respectively, iron and coal-based heavy industrial regions.) Pollution of another sort was released in 1986, when Reactor 4 of the V. I. Lenin Nuclear Power Plant at Chernobyl exploded, releasing 25 to 900 times the radioactivity of the Hiroshima bomb depending on the radioisotope measured.

 MR. MEDAL. Ukraine's most famous son, Leonid Brezhnev, ran the USSR from 1964 to 1982. A vain man, he gave himself so many medals that it took a file of 44 soldiers following his coffin to carry them.

SMOKE OF BATTLE. Originally known as *papirossi*, cigarettes were first popularized in Britain by returning Crimean War veterans who had adopted them from the allied Turks.

LOCAL COLOUR. When the Mongol nomads swept west to settle in the steppes of Ukraine and Kazakhstan, they brought with them the ancient Chinese system of naming their five cardinal directions after colours (*see below*). Later adopted by the Turks, the system has been indelibly preserved in the geographical and historical vocabulary shaping Europe's Eastern fringes.

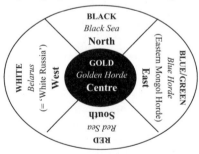

ON A ROLL. Staple of a thousand Westerns, tumbleweed is native to Ukraine. It made the leap to America in 1877 as a stowaway in a consignment of flax.

TOAST OF CRIMEA

'To Premier Stalin, whose foreign policy manifests a desire for peace ... [continuing in an undertone]... a piece of Poland, a piece of Hungary, a piece of Romania ...'

—Winston Churchill, at the Yalta Conference (1945)

NO TURKEY. In 1979, chicken Kiev became Marks & Spencer's first chilled prepared meal ('microwave dinner'). The launch heralded a new era in British cooking as, previously, ready-meals had been either frozen or dried (notably the Vesta range) and seen as resolutely downmarket. Backed by Marks & Spencer, however, exotic but easily cooked concoctions like chicken Kiev became the darlings of middle-class shoppers; such that, by 2010, 80% of Britons ate chilled prepared foods, spending $15bn on them yearly.

♠ · **GSR:** 56 · **WHS:** Carpathians (beech forests) □ Chernivtsi (seminary complex) □ Kiev (cathedral) L'viv (historic East European cityscape) □ Struve Arc (survey line)

— UNITED ARAB EMIRATES ● دولة الإمارات العربية المتحدة —

*'Most people talk; we do. They plan; we achieve. They hesitate; we advance.
Dubai is a living example of that.'*

—Sheikh Mohammed bin Rashid Al Maktoum, Prime Minister of the UAE and Emir of Dubai

▶ In order of population, the seven federated emirates are: **Dubai** (pop. 1.6m, holds veto power) • **Abu Dhabi** (pop. 1.1m, capital and holds veto power)

Dubai 1959 / Dubai 2009

Al-Fahidi Fort, the emir's residence and Dubai's seat of government. It would be two more years before Dubai got electricity, and five before the first piped water arrived.

Ski Dubai, with the world's only indoor black run, is one of the attractions at the Mall of the Emirates. With 520 stores, it's currently Dubai's second-ranked retail mall.

GETTING THE HUMP. The world's biggest beauty pageant for camels[1] takes place annually at the Al Dharfa festival, held in Abu Dhabi's remote western desert. Almost all contestants are cows (widely accepted to be better-looking than bulls), and the key attributes judges look for are large heads with shapely nose and lips, well-separated toes, shiny coat and, of course, a large hump. Losers may go away disgruntled, but the supreme champion collects over $240,000 in prize money, and can go on to fetch as much as $2.7m in the auction ring.

[1] *The English word 'camel' has the same derivation as the Arabic* gamal, *which can mean either camel or beauty.*

SACRED COW. Akab island in Umm al Quwain emirate contains Arabia's oldest known religious site. Dated to 3500 BCE, the sanctuary consists of an oval bone mound topped with rows of dugong skulls, each facing due east—suggesting the first Arabians worshipped the sea cow.

FLUSHED WITH SUCCESS. Based in the emirate of Ras al Khaimah and founded by the emir, RAK Ceramics is the world's largest manufacturer of toilets (thanks largely to a stranglehold on the Bangladeshi market).

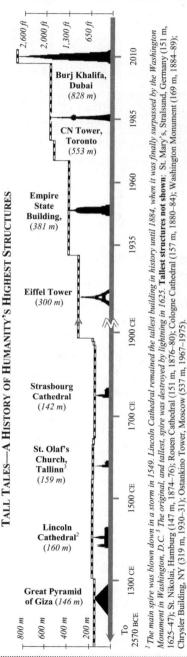

TALL TALES—A HISTORY OF HUMANITY'S HIGHEST STRUCTURES

2,600 ft / 2,000 ft / 1,300 ft / 650 ft

2010

Burj Khalifa, Dubai (*828 m*)

1985

CN Tower, Toronto (*553 m*)

1960

Empire State Building, (*381 m*)

1935

Eiffel Tower (*300 m*)

1900 CE

Strasbourg Cathedral (*142 m*)

1700 CE

St. Olaf's Church, Tallinn[3] (*159 m*)

1500 CE

Lincoln Cathedral[2] (*160 m*)

1300 CE

Great Pyramid of Giza (*146 m*)

To 2570 BCE

800 m / 600 m / 400 m / 200 m

The main spire was blown down in a storm in 1549. Lincoln Cathedral remained the tallest building in history until 1884, when it was finally surpassed by the Washington Monument in Washington, D.C. [3] *The original, and tallest, spire was destroyed by lightning in 1625.* **Tallest structures not shown:** St. Mary's, Stralsund, Germany (151 m, 1625–47); St. Nikolai, Hamburg (147 m, 1874–76); Rouen Cathedral (151 m, 1876–80); Cologne Cathedral (157 m, 1880–84); Washington Monument (169 m, 1884–89); Chrysler Building, NY (319 m, 1930–31); Ostankino Tower, Moscow (537 m, 1967–1975).

[2] *The main spire was blown down in a storm in 1549. Lincoln Cathedral remained the tallest building in history until 1884, when it was finally surpassed by the Washington Monument in Washington, D.C.*

Sharjah (pop. 900,000) • **Ajman** (pop. 240,000) • **Ras al Khaimah** (pop. 120,000) • **Fujairah** (pop. 90,000) • **Umm al Quwain** (pop. 30,000)

♣ **GSR xxx · ICH**: Falconry

———— UNITED KINGDOM ————

'I didn't know he was dead; I thought he was British.'

—Woody Allen

LONDON—SUNSHINE CITY

WE ARE NOT AMUSED.

Queen Elizabeth I was a long-term user of ceruse, a toxic lead-based face-whitener imported from Venice. Over time, the poison ravaged her facial features so badly, Elizabeth eventually banned all mirrors from her palace.[1] Following this, the Queen's servants sometimes painted a red dot on her nose as an in-joke to make fun of her comically transformed visage.

[1] *The lead also rotted the Queen's teeth, turning them black and worsening her already notorious halitosis.*

BLIMEY. The British are called 'limeys' since Royal Navy rations included limes to prevent scurvy. However, they could have been 'krauts', as Captain Cooke tried *sauerkraut* first, but his men refused to eat it.

HOW THEY SAY 'BRIT' AROUND THE WORLD

■ **France—*Les Rosbifs***: *the 'roast beefs', a Gallic commentary on the national cuisine, not just the sunburn.*

■ **Malaysia—*Mat Salleh***: *'mad sailor', the crews of British sailing ships got pickled as newts in port and the name has stuck.*

■ **Roman Empire—*Brittunculus***: *translates from Latin as 'wretched little Brit'.*

■ **South Africa—*Soutie***: *from Sout Piel meaning 'salt penis' in Afrikaans. The idea is that Brits have one leg in South Africa and one in Britain, leaving a certain appendage dangling in the brine.*

TARTAN ARMY. The Romans were the first to call Scotland 'Caledonia'. The word is thought to have been taken from the Celtic *caled*—'hard', possibly via a tribe called the Caledonii. Scotland's poetic title may thus ultimately mean 'land of the hard men'.

NAUTICAL SALUTE. When Scottish-born Alexander Graham Bell invented the telephone, he proposed answering with a crisp 'Ahoy!'; but 'Hello' (previously used to summon boatmen) was championed by his rival Edison and caught on instead.

SCUTTLING TALL. The world's most northerly scorpions live on the Isle of Sheppey in Kent. Equipped with a venomous sting as painful as a bee's, they reach 2 inches in length. However, 300 million years ago, Scottish scorpions were over 6 feet long by 3 feet wide, and lorded over the landscape as the original top predators.

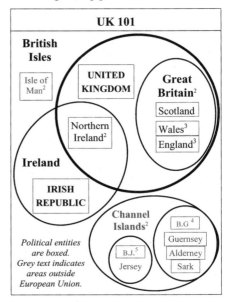

UK 101

[2] *The official name for Great Britain, Northern Ireland, the Channel Islands and the Isle of Man collectively is the 'British Islands'.* [3] *England and Wales (but not Scotland) form a single legal jurisdiction.* [4] *The Bailiwick of Guernsey: comprises Guernsey, Alderney and Sark. The latter two are self-governing and Bailiwick-wide laws only apply if their legislatures assent.* [5] *The Bailiwick of Jersey: comprises Jersey itself and uninhabited outliers.*

'I like pigs. Dogs look up to us. Cats look down on us. Pigs treat us as equals.'

—Sir Winston Churchill [1]

[1] *Churchill contrived to keep a herd of pigs at his Chartwell estate throughout WWII, entering into a contract with a unit of the Canadian army camped on his land to buy their slops for pig food (at the rate of $4 per 100 men per month). Despite his professed porcine preference, Churchill at various times also kept cats (including a favourite named Nelson), dogs, horses, sheep, waterfowl, tropical fish, budgerigars, swans, kangaroos, a lion named Rota and a duck-billed platypus.*

DEAD FAMOUS HISTORY'S BIGGEST FUNERALS		
Personage	Atten-dance	TV audience
Diana, Princess of Wales (1997)	2m	2,500m
Pope John Paul II (2005)	4m	2,000m
Michael Jackson[2] (2009)	18,000	2,000m

[2] *Michael Jackson figures are for the memorial service.*

DUTY DONE. The most decisive victory in British naval history was won by Admiral Nelson at Trafalgar in 1805. For over a century afterwards, the Royal Navy kept an unprecedented global pre-eminence. During the intervening *pax Britannica*, Britain's navy extinguished the slave trade, drove piracy to the edge of the map and charted the world's oceans. But all of this hinged on one bold decision taken at Trafalgar that turned the naval rule book on its head: when closing for battle, Nelson led his ships in at right angles, instead of sailing parallel to the enemy fleet. The tactic exposed the British vessels cruelly for their full approach. But, crucially and decisively, having ridden through the fire, they were then able to land a killing blow as they cut through the Franco-Spanish line. Victory, of course, came at the cost of Nelson's own death, commemorated most notably by Nelson's Column—still in Trafalgar Square, despite Hitler's pet plan to remove it and re-erect it in Berlin as a permanent memorial to his triumph over Britain in WWII.

LIFELINE. In 1866, four successive crews refused to take a cargo ship named the *Harkaway* across the Atlantic, claiming she was manifestly unseaworthy. (Even at anchor, the *Harkaway* was shipping three feet of water per day.) As a result, all four crews were sent to prison for desertion. The incident was far from unusual. At the time, 75% of the prisoners in some English counties were sailors who had refused to put to sea in vessels they feared unsafe. Their peril arose due to the availability of 100% insurance, which made ship-owners indifferent as to whether their ships sailed the ocean waves or rested on its bed. By 1876, over 1,000 British ships were sinking each year at an appalling cost in lives, and the situation was plainly untenable. After nine years battling vested interests, Samuel Plimsoll MP finally won a law compelling ship-owners to paint a maximum loading line on the hulls of all ships. In 1930, this safeguard became international, when Plimsoll's familiar load lines became mandatory worldwide.

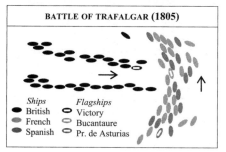

BATTLE OF TRAFALGAR (1805)

Ships	Flagships
● British	○ Victory
● French	○ Bucantaure
● Spanish	○ Pr. de Asturias

Fleet	Ships in Action	Losses
British	27	0
Franco-Spanish	33	22

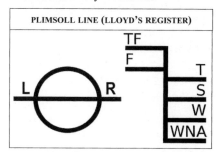

PLIMSOLL LINE (LLOYD'S REGISTER)

Reading the Plimsoll Line: The line bisecting the circle is the original Plimsoll line and provides the benchmark setting the lowest the ship may lie in the water. To the right, subsidiary lines adjust this for different water conditions.
Key: TF *Tropical freshwater,* F *Freshwater,* T *Tropical,* S *Summer,* W *Winter,* WNA *Winter North Atlantic.*

TWO LITERARY TITANS

CHAUCER. On St. George's Day 1374, King Edward III granted Chaucer an awe-inspiring daily gallon of wine for the rest of his life to reward his poetic efforts. Geoffrey Chaucer is, in consequence, considered England's first poet laureate. The post's alcoholic munificence persists today, since modern laureates each receive a more modest 140 gallons of sherry.

SHAKESPEARE. The only thing Shakespeare left in his will to his wife of 34 years, Anne Hathaway, was his 'second best' bed. This was not quite as mean as it might seem, as, in Shakespeare's era, a good bed could be worth as much as a cottage, and the 'second bed' was, in fact, the matrimonial one.

FROZEN IN TIME. The oldest words found in modern English are 'two', 'three' and 'five' and 'I', 'we' and 'who'. Researchers believe these were already in use with their modern meaning during the last Ice Age 15,000 years ago—millennia before English or England had even been thought of.

STICKY END. In the Great London Beer Flood of 1814, a bursting brewery vat sent a tsunami of beer washing down Tottenham Court Road. Over 300,000 gallons later, two houses stood ruined and eight people lay drowned; a ninth succumbed later to self-administered alcohol poisoning. Bad as this was, it was capped by the Boston Molasses Disaster of 1919, in which a 15ft wave of exploding treacle lifted a train from its tracks and gummed 21 passers-by to death.

FLAMING CELTS. Scots are the most redheaded people on Earth, with 13% against 1% globally. Others included Judas Iscariot (allegedly), Lenin and Genghis Khan.

FIREPOWER. The red dragon of Wales is a rare positive depiction of the mythic reptile. According to fable, a Celtic red dragon fought and defeated the white dragon of the despised Saxons. As further related by legend, it now sleeps under the hill of Dinas Emrys by Snowdon, and will waken one day to retake Lloegr (England) from the invaders.

PROUD TO BE SQUARE. The City of London fills just one square mile of metropolitan London's area, but it generates 20% of the capital's wealth. One translation of the City's motto, '*Domine dirige nos*', is 'God help us'!

MONEY MACHINE: ECONOMIC FOOTPRINT	
-	*GDP/sq. mile* [1]
City	$100 billion
London	$1 billion
UK	$25 thousand

[1] *2008, PPP GDP figures.*

MAKING HISTORY. The world's largest preserved human coprolite was unearthed at a branch of Lloyds TSB Bank in York. Found during 1972 renovations, the 9-inch deposit was made by a visiting Viking in clear need of a privy.

FULL ENGLISH—THE BREAKFAST OBESITY CORRELATION			
Breakfast	*% of daily rec. calories*	*Fat*	*Obesity (ranked)*
American—Diner [a]	99% (2240 kcal)	113 g	1
English—Fry-up [b]	**40% (910 kcal)**	**64 g**	**2**
German [c]	18% (400 kcal)	26 g	3
French—Continental [d]	13% (290 kcal)	11 g	4
Japanese [e]	9% (210 kcal)	4 g	5

[a] *Ham, 2 bacon, 2 fried egg, hash browns, muffin, 3 pancake, maple syrup, coffee.* [b] *Bacon, 2 sausage, 2 fried egg, mushrooms, tomato, beans, fried bread, tea.* [c] *Boiled egg, 2 cold meat, 2 rye bread, butter, coffee.* [d] *Croissant, orange juice, coffee.* [e] *Miso soup, boiled rice, grilled fish, pickles, green tea.*

MEMORABLE REGAL EPITHETS (SELECTED)			
Name	*Nickname*	*Reign*	*Need to know …*
Edgar	*The Peaceable*	959–75	raped nun, seized Northumbria, plundered Thanet
William	*The Bastard*	1066–87	1066 and all that (he was illegitimate son of Robert I)
John	*Softsword*	1199–1216	lost France, crown jewels and, finally, life (to dysentery)
Mary	*Bloody Mary*	1553–58	burned with religious zeal (300 Protestants at the stake)
Cromwell	*Queen Dick*	1658–59	Oliver's son, Richard—utterly useless, ditched by coup

ARMED TO THE TEETH. In 892, Orkney's Sigurd the Mighty was slain by the head of his vanquished foe, Máel Brigte the Bucktoothed. After binding it to his saddle as a trophy, Sigurd was nicked by a tooth on the ride home and later succumbed to blood poisoning. While fatal tooth-ache is merely a rarity, such a death by contagion may be unique.

HOME RUN TO ENGLAND Reading printer John Newbery published the world's first successful children's book, *A Little Pretty Pocket Book*, in 1744. To boost sales, Newbery included either a ball (for boys) or a pincushion (for girls) with each copy—so also pioneering the publishing 'giveaway'. The *Pocket Book* is further notable for having the first reference in print to baseball, strongly suggesting an English origin to the sport.[1] (This is supported by another early reference in Jane Austen's *Northanger Abbey*—which has the teenage heroine a keen player.)

RELIGIOUS EDUCATION. The Puckle Gun, invented in 1718 by London lawyer James Puckle, was a revolving pre-loaded flintlock often described as the first working machine gun. Unusually, it was designed to fire two sorts of bullets:

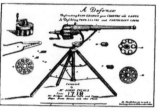

Puckle Gun

conventional round ones for fellow Christians, and more damaging square bullets for Turks and other Muslims. Apparently, in the words of the patent, this was to teach them 'the benefits of Christian civilization'.

FUNNY WAY TO GO. In 1975, Alex Mitchell of King's Lynn died of laughter while watching a kilted Scotsman using bagpipes to do battle against a black pudding. Laughing can kill through either cardiac arrest or asphyxiation due to loss of muscle tone control.

SMOOTH AS A … Cambridge biotech company Intercytex Ltd. has invented a novel skin rejuvenating treatment called Valvelta. First supplied as an injection through private clinics in 2007 and now under trial for the US Army, Vavelta is grown in the lab from baby foreskins.

[1]*Much to the chagrin of certain Americans, the earliest printed reference to baseball in the US is a 1791 bylaw from Massachusetts restricting where it can be played.*

STATE OF PLAY—A SELECTION OF BRITISH WEEKLY WAGE PACKETS

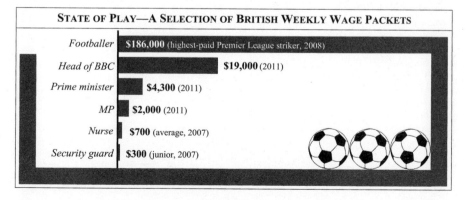

Footballer	**$186,000** (highest-paid Premier League striker, 2008)
Head of BBC	**$19,000** (2011)
Prime minister	**$4,300** (2011)
MP	**$2,000** (2011)
Nurse	**$700** (average, 2007)
Security guard	**$300** (junior, 2007)

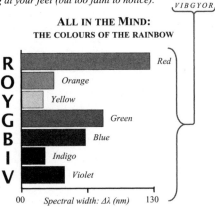

RAINBOW RISING. *If you know the date and your location, you can use a rainbow as a clock to tell the time. During the morning, all rainbows shrink towards the horizon, and then, as the afternoon progresses, they rise ever higher back into the sky. Measuring the height of the arc allows you to calculate the exact time. Whenever the sun climbs above 42°, rainbows can't be seen at all (except from a mountain or a plane), as they are effectively lying at your feet (but too faint to notice).*

COLOUR BLIND. When not catching apples, Sir Isaac Newton took a keen interest in vision[1] and was responsible for deciding on the English language list of colours of the rainbow. (Newton originally chose five colours, then added orange and indigo later as he felt seven was a more auspicious number.) However, other cultures see their colours differently. The Japanese perceive the light of a 'Go' traffic-signal as blue, while the Vietnamese consider blue and green to be the same. Italians and Russians acknowledge green, but say sky blue and navy are not just different shades, but entirely separate colours—which is equivalent to the English habit of treating pink as a different colour from red (itself a nuance that escapes the Chinese).

[1] *In one not-to-be-repeated-at-home experiment, Newton inserted a darning needle as far as he could between his eyeball and its socket and coolly noted that he saw coloured circles as long as he kept 'stirring ye bodkin'.*

ANIMAL MAGIC. In 1726, Mary Toft reported she had been sexually assaulted by a giant bunny in a field near Guildford. Her claim was ignored until, six months later, she gave birth to a rabbit. Various increasingly eminent doctors were called, and over the following days they witnessed the birth of 11 more (dead) rabbits. The story caused a national sensation, and King George I despatched the Surgeon Royal to investigate. Abruptly, the rabbit births stopped, and Toft finally confessed that she had inserted the animals into her womb when no one was looking. As no money was involved, her reasons remain unclear, but the careers of the 'eminent' doctors were finished.

ALL IN THE MIND:
THE COLOURS OF THE RAINBOW

R — Red
O — Orange
Y — Yellow
G — Green
B — Blue
I — Indigo
V — Violet

00   *Spectral width: Δλ (nm)*   130

Newton's division of the rainbow into seven colours (*above*) may seem uncontroversial (give or take indigo). But 'colours' exist only in the human head. When looking at a rainbow, what our eyes actually record are three black and white snapshots of electromagnetic frequencies we call green, violet and chartreuse[2]. This meagre information is then processed by our brain to conjure up an entire—but wholly imagined—palette of fantasy colours. Ancient convention rules how we describe these, but as shown above, the colour names we have settled upon are distributed very unevenly—such that, for example, shades of 'red' take up six times as much of the spectrum as shades of 'yellow'. By contrast, in the real world outside our heads, rainbows vary smoothly across their breadth to sparkle in a near-infinite gradation of hues. The only pity is, we can't see them.

[2] *The addition of chartreuse is a recent evolutionary trick, shared with African primates, that came in useful when we were searching out tender new leaves and tropical fruit.*

ONE FOOT IN THE GRAVE. In the 1970s, the BBC developed plans to follow any all-out nuclear attack with a medley of light entertainment repeats—which, apparently, would have taken viewers' minds off things.

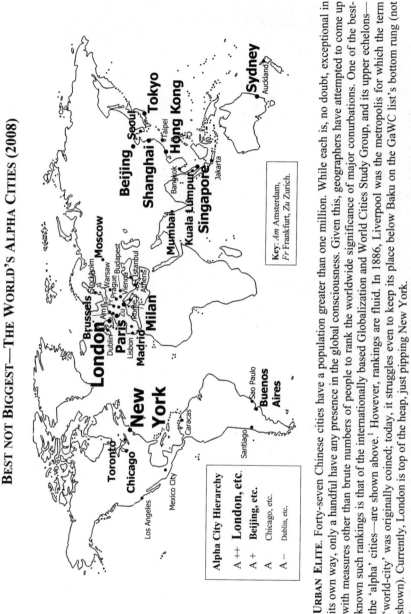

BEST NOT BIGGEST—THE WORLD'S ALPHA CITIES (2008)

Alpha City Hierarchy

A ++ **London, etc.**

A + **Beijing, etc.**

A Chicago, etc.

A − Dublin, etc.

Key: *Am* Amsterdam, *Fr* Frankfurt, *Zu* Zurich.

URBAN ELITE. Forty-seven Chinese cities have a population greater than one million. While each is, no doubt, exceptional in its own way, only a handful have any presence in the global consciousness. Given this, geographers have attempted to come up with measures other than brute numbers of people to rank the worldwide significance of major conurbations. One of the best-known such rankings is that of the internationally based Globalization and World Cities Study Group, and its upper echelons—the 'alpha' cities—are shown above.[1] However, rankings are fluid. In 1886, Liverpool was the metropolis for which the term 'world-city' was originally coined; today, it struggles even to keep its place below Baku on the GaWC list's bottom rung (not shown). Currently, London is top of the heap, just pipping New York.

[1] Attributes taken into account in assessing alpha-city status include head-office presence of international organizations or major multinationals, financial trading volumes, city GDP, size of expat community, presence of global media, cultural and sporting institutions, tourist numbers and scope of transport and communications links.

♠ · **GSR**: 3 · **Constituent Countries**: England, Northern Ireland, Scotland, Wales · **WHS**: ■ England: Bath (townscape and ruins) □ Blenheim Palace □ Canterbury Cathedral □ Cornwall (tin mines) □ Derwent Valley Mills (cotton mills) □ Durham (castle and cathedral) □ Greenwich (historic buildings) Ironbridge (industrial archaeology) □ Jurassic Coast (landscape, fossils) □ Kew (botanical gardens) Liverpool (historic city) □ Roman Limes (Hadrian's Wall) □ Saltaire (planned village) □ Stonehenge (Stone Age monument) □ Studley Royal (gardens and ruins) □ Tower of London (fortress) □ Westminster (abbey and palace) ■ Northern Ireland: Giant's Causeway (coastline) ■ Scotland: Edinburgh (townscape) □ New Lanark (planned village) □ Orkney (Stone Age monuments) □ St. Kilda (islands, wildlife) ■ Wales: Blaenavon (industrial archaeology) □ Gwynedd Castles □ Pontcysyllte (aquaduct)

———— UNITED KINGDOM DEPENDENCIES ————

'God Save the Queen.'

—Anthem of all British Territories and Crown Dependencies

HONOURED EMBLEMS—THE DEPENDENCIES' MOST TREASURED ASSETS ...

Falklands	*Tristan da Cunha*	*BVI*	*Isle of Man*	*Chagos Arch.*	*South Georgia*
Sheep	**Crustaceans**	**Virgins**	**Strange freaky things**	**Turtles**	**Penguins**

SUITS YOU, SIR! Worn with long socks, blazer and tie, short trousers are donned by small schoolboys in Britain and big businessmen in Bermuda, where they were introduced by British military personnel at the turn of the 20th century. Rather mysteriously, Bermuda shorts are reportedly illegal in Iraq.

TILTING TO SPAIN. Gibraltar is a perennial irritant in Anglo-Spanish relations. In 1981, the King and Queen of Spain boycotted Prince Charles' and Lady Diana's wedding because their honeymoon included the Rock. But an end is in sight. In 1967, just 0.4% of Gibraltarians voted to join Spain; 35 years later, the share was up to 1%. Union is therefore confidently predicted for the year 4560.

BIG BLUE. The largest blue whale ever recorded was landed at Gryvitken on South Georgia in 1912. Weighing 180 tonnes and stretching 33.6 m from tip to tail, it was over 30 times heavier than a *T. rex* and two and a half times as long. Needing three million calories a day, each blue whale eats four times as much as the combined populations of Tristan da Cunha and Pitcairn Island.

STRONG LANGUAGE. Faced with an imminent misdeed, residents of Jersey and the other Channel Islands have the right—still actively taken up—to drop to their knees, clasp hands, and shout *'Haro! A l'aide, mon Prince, on me fait tort,'* followed by the Lord's Prayer in French.[1] At this, the miscreant must instantly desist until the matter is heard in court, or face a fine even if ultimately otherwise cleared.

[1] *On Sark, the crier can't wear a hat, while on Guernsey he must add Grace.*

CHIP AND FAG. Until the end of WWII, Tristan da Cunha used potatoes for currency (later supplemented by cigarettes). Tristan also printed postage stamps that were denominated in the root.

TOOT TOOT. When the Vikings settled the islands off northern Britain, they divided them into two kingdoms: Nordr (the 'Northern Isles', i.e. Shetland and Orkney) and Sodor (the 'Southern Isles', i.e. the Hebrides and the Isle of Man). In 1266, Viking control of the south was broken. The name 'Sodor', however, was preserved by the Church in its Diocese of Sodor and Man. Seven centuries later, the Reverend Wilbert Awdrey had to visit on church business, and, on the lookout for a fictional setting, was struck that, while there was an Isle of Man, Sodor was nowhere to be found. On the spot, he decided to reinvent it, which is how an ancient Viking kingdom came to be home to Thomas the Tank Engine and his friends.

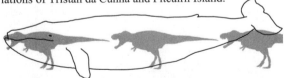

Dependent Territories: Akrotiri & Dhekelia, Anguilla, Ascension Island, Bermuda, British Virgin Islands (BVI), Cayman Islands, Chagos Archipelago, Falkland Islands, Gibraltar, Guernsey, Isle of Man, Jersey, Montserrat, Pitcairn Islands, St. Helena, South Georgia, Tristan da Cunha, Turks & Caicos Islands.

♥♣♦♠★ · **GSR**: n/a · **WHS**: Bermuda—St. George (historic town) □ Pitcairns—Henderson Island (coral atoll) □ Tristan da Cunha—Gough Island (seabirds)

———— UNITED STATES OF AMERICA ————

'The preservation of the sacred fire of liberty, and the destiny of the republican model of government, are justly considered as deeply, perhaps finally, staked on the experiment entrusted to the hands of the American people.'

—George Washington (First Inaugural Address, 1789)

LAST HURRAH. Cheerleading is the USA's most dangerous female sport, causing 71% of all college-level female sports injuries.

SPORTING CHALLENGE. Americans eat almost a ton of pizza each minute (enough each hour to cover three soccer pitches). Pepperoni is much the commonest topping.

FORCE BE WITH YOU. The Washington National Cathedral has Darth Vader chiselled into the stone of its north-west tower.

NUMBER'S UP. More Americans died in the American Civil War than World Wars I and II together (558,000 against 524,000).

PARK AND RIDE. A car park containing all America's parking spaces would be bigger than El Salvador; add roads, and the area under tarmac exceeds England and Wales.

ONE IN A HUNDRED. With more than 1% of adult Americans in jail, the USA leads the world in the incarceration of citizens.

'George Washington's brother, Lawrence, was the Uncle of Our Country.'

—George Carlin

AMERICA—LAND OF THE FREE ... TO EXPRESS YOURSELF EXACTLY AS YOU PLEASE

Biggest Chicken (GA)   *Biggest Donut (CA)*   *Biggest Basket (OH)*   *Biggest Duck (NY)*

MEAN, LEAN AND NOT VERY GREEN. First launched in 1967, the Saturn V rocket is, even now, the most powerful machine ever built. At full throttle, it burnt fuel at 15 tons per second and produced as much power as the entire electricity output of India.

COWABUNGA! Hawaii's 18th-century surfers took their sport religiously—the Ku'emanu Heiau is the only temple known to have been dedicated to a God of Surfing. Apart from this, many aspects haven't changed much even now[1]—although, in ancient Hawaii, those who thumbed their nose at surfing etiquette did risk becoming a human sacrifice.

[1] *Ethnologists note Hawaiian surfers displayed their skills to win 'mates'.*

110 m

To scale

'If you even dream of beating me, you'd better wake up and apologize.'

—Muhammad Ali

DISARMING LIBERTY. In 1916, while America was still neutral in WWI, German agents blew up 2 million pounds of dynamite, TNT and gunpowder stored on a New Jersey wharf while awaiting shipment to Britain. The blast measured 5.5 on the Richter Scale and was felt in five states; windows shattered for 25 miles around. Just offshore, Lady Liberty's arm burst 100 rivets, forcing its immediate closure. (It has never since been reopened.)

BALL BREAKING. The average lifespan of a Major League baseball is six pitches before it is retired.

MOTHER ROAD
Chicago
US ROUTE 66

URBAN AMERICA. Cahokia, Illinois, is deserted today, but 150 years before Columbus 'discovered' the Americas, it was bigger than London. Estimates suggest that in 1250 CE up to 40,000 people may have been living in the settlement, which would have made it the USA's largest city until finally surpassed by Philadelphia at the beginning of the 19th century.

PRESIDENTIAL PETS

G. W. Bush....Cow ('Ofelia')
H. Hoover.......Alligators (2)
A. Johnson..............No pets [1]
T. Jefferson............Bears (2)
C. Coolidge........Dogs (12) [2]

[1] *But he did put out flour and water each day for a family of mice living in his bedroom.* [2] *Also two raccoons, two lions, a hippo, a wallaby and an antelope.*

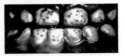

TOP TEN GLOBAL BRANDS[5]

-	Brand Name		Value[6] ($bn)
1	Coca-Cola	(US)	72
2	IBM	(US)	67
3	Microsoft	(US)	62
4	Google	(US)	45
5	GE	(US)	44
6	McDonald's	(US)	35
7	Intel	(US)	34
8	Nokia	(Fin.)	30
9	Disney	(US)	30
10	HP	(US)	27

[5] *Source: Interbrand (2010).* [6] *Estd. stand-alone asset value of brand.*

Santa Monica (2,381 miles)
Los Angeles

Cherokee Man (1762)

'GERONIMO!' When anxious amateurs throw themselves from aircraft, they shout out the name of history's most renowned Apache warrior. But the professionals of the US Army's 101st Airborne Division do things differently. They yell 'Currahee!'—which means: 'Where the watercress grows!' in Cherokee.

'In America, anyone can be president. That's one of the risks you take.'
—Adlai Stevenson

FINISHING TOUCHES. In the early 20th century, it was commonplace for fathers to pay for their daughters' teeth to be removed as a wedding gift, to save their husbands the expense later on. While this would now be seen as eccentric, a recent dramatic rise[3] in the number of teenage girls having breast enlargement surgery—overwhelmingly paid for by parents[4]—is worrying women's groups and professional bodies alike.

[3] *8,199 girls aged 13–19 in 2009 against 978 in 1992.* [4] *The treatment is typically bought as a high-school graduation present.*

PLAY IT AGAIN, SAM. American artist Samuel Morse invented his dot-and-dash telegraphic code in 1837, and while you might think it's long since been abandoned to the steam age, there's life in the keys yet. In 2004, the International Telecommunications Union added the first new character since WWI: the '@' (*below*), responding to the demand to be able to send emails by Morse code.

● ▬ ▬ ● ▬ ▬ ●

US ROUTE 66

BRAINY BEN BAFFLED BY BOLTS. Founding father of the Republic Benjamin Franklin was also fascinated by lightning and his best-known scientific achievement was to show it to be an electrical discharge (although he may never have been so foolhardy as actually to fly a kite in a storm). One observation he had no answer for, however, was why lightning victims are often found with their clothes or shoes blown off. The explanation that eluded Franklin is sweat: if skin is damp, lightning will flow along its surface, instantly vaporizing all moisture present. The steam explosions thus caused are frequently powerful enough to shred fabric and blow stitching apart.

St. Louis
Tulsa
Oklahoma City
Flagstaff

THE WORLD ACCORDING TO RAYMOND CHANDLER

'I knew one thing: as soon as anyone said you didn't need a gun, you'd better take along one that worked.'

'I do a great deal of research—particularly in the apartments of tall blondes.'

Rods: Equalizers • Saturday-Night Specials • Heaters • Roscoes • Persuaders • Biscuits • Iron • Blasters • Hardware • Pieces • Negotiators • Gats • Bean-Shooters

Broads: Bims • Dames • Janes • Twists • Ankles • Babes • Roundheels • Tomatoes • Chicks • Dolls • Molls • Dishes • Frails • Chippies • Canaries • Floozies • Skirts

COURTED. In 1938, Frank Sinatra was arrested in New Jersey for seduction. Though now legal, seduction is still a crime in other states (e.g. Michigan); while elsewhere (e.g. Missouri) a father can sue in court to enforce his 'property interest in his daughter's chastity'.

OLD BLUE EYES. A century ago, half of Americans had blue eyes; by 2006, the figure had dropped to one in six. The loss is real, as light eyes have been scientifically proven to be sexier than dark.[1]

[1] *Blue eyes contrast most vividly with the dark of pupils, so allowing pupil dilation, a key 'come-on' signal in sexual attraction, to be most emphatically displayed.*

SEEING THINGS. American psychologist Joseph Jastrow was a pioneer in the study of optical illusions, and made the drawing above. Images like this play on the brain's instinctive programming to try to organize patterns into shapes, even where they are inherently ambiguous or random: the Martian 'canals' seen by the Victorians[2] are another classic example.

[2] *Beginning in 1877, many astronomers reported seeing a network of canals on Mars, just visible at the limit of human observation. Popular excitement over little green men quickly followed. But, by 1910, scientific advances had proved the canals to be optical illusions.*

NAME THAT TUNE	
Genre	*Originally meant ...*
Blues	short for 'blue devils'—melancholia
Disco	discotheque—a radio record library
Funk	tobacco smoke and sweat pong
Punk	harlot, as used by Shakespeare
Rap	strike smartly—as in 'rap the door'
Rock...	stir things up—as in 'rock the boat'
... Roll	in the medieval sense: have sex

MAKE LOVE NOT WAR. In 1994, the US Air Force sought $8m development funding for a 'gay' bomb that would make enemy soldiers irresistibly attractive to each other and hence too busy to fight. Other ideas out of the same lab were halitosis and flatulence bombs, and sprays to enrage bees from hives that special forces had surreptitiously secreted nearby.

I-SPY. During WWII, American radio stations were banned from broadcasting weather forecasts or reporting hurricanes. Listeners' requests and game shows were likewise barred, in case they contained coded messages. But birthday requests were allowed—so long as they were not broadcast on the date requested.

DOUBLE TROUBLE. Tobacco was the plant that gave birth to the USA, being America's most valuable export for 175 years until 1793—when it was eclipsed by cotton. America still remained the world's biggest cigarette manufacturer until the 1960s. When the health concerns surrounding smoking first surfaced in the 1950s, its tobacco companies responded by promoting filtered cigarettes. One such was Kent, which, in 1952, advertised its new 'Micronite' filter as 'the greatest health protection in cigarette history'. Unfortunately, the filter's special ingredient was crocidolite—the deadliest form of asbestos known. Modern tests show those smoking a pack of Kent a day inhaled an estimated 1.24 billion carcinogenic asbestos fibres a year.[3]

[3] *The asbestos filter was withdrawn in 1956. Contemporary Kent cigarettes use an activated charcoal filter.*

'What? Dodging for single bullets? They couldn't hit an elephant at this distance.'

—Last words of Major General John Sedgwick, the most senior Union casualty of the American Civil War

FROM NEW YORK TO LA—THE MUSIC OF AMERICA

Jimi Hendrix *(1942–70)*
Born in Seattle, his first booking was the city's Temple De Hirsch Synagogue. Unfortunately for him, he was fired by his band-mates midway through the gig for over-excitable playing.

Native American Music
*can be traced back to the 7th century. Featuring singing and drumming, it plays a central role in various ceremonies including the **Ghost Dance**. An attempt by the US Army to suppress this ritual led to the Wounded Knee Massacre of Lakota Sioux (1890).*

Liberace *(1919–87)*
Based in Las Vegas, the showman-pianist was the world's highest paid enter-tainer from the 1950s to 1970s. In 1956, he won $12,000 damages from the Daily Mirror *after it described him as 'fruit-flavoured'.*

'White Christmas' *(1940)*
The world's best-selling song was composed poolside at a Phoenix hotel. The writer, Irving Berlin, didn't himself enjoy the festive season.

'Good Vibrations' *(1966)*
*At the time, the most expen-sive single ever made, the **Beach Boys'** first million-selling hit captured the sound of the South Californian surf scene.*

Katajjaq
Competitive throat-singing was practised by Inuit women until the 20th century; judg-ing was assessed by endurance.

'Dallas Blues' *(1912)*
First blues song to be published.

US BEST-SELLING ALBUM OF THE YEAR	

1960   **1970**   **1977**   **1978**   **1980**

Bridge Over Troubled Water   *Rumours*
Sound of Music   *Saturday Night Fever*

FROM NEW YORK TO LA—THE MUSIC OF AMERICA

Bob Dylan *(b. 1941)*
Born Robert Zimmerman; Duluth, Minnesota.

'If You See My Savior'
Sung at the 1930 National Baptist Convention in Chicago, the song launches modern gospel

Rhapsody in Blue *(1924)*
Composed by George Gershwin; inspired by the clackety-clack of the rails on a Boston-bound train.

'The Day the Music Died'
Don McLean's **'American Pie'** *(1971) recounts the 1959 death of Buddy Holly and Ritchie Valens in a plane crash near Clear Lake, Iowa.*

'Yankee Doodle'
State song of Connecticut. Sung by British to mock American revolutionaries. ('Doodle' meant fool.)

Marshall Mathers *(b. 1972)*
Born St. Joseph, Missouri, Eminem is the biggest-selling rapper ever with over 90 million records sold.

'Please Mr. Postman'
(1961). The first No. 1 single for Detroit's Motown Records, sung by the Marvelettes.

Hip Hop
Earliest roots lie in South Bronx block parties of the 1970s.

'Rocket 88' *(1951)*
Recorded in Memphis, first rock and roll record (Rock and Roll Hall of Fame).

Appalachian Spring *(1944)*
Aaron Copland's masterpiece of Americana has at its core a traditional Shaker melody.

'Star-Spangled Banner' *(1814)*
The US anthem was inspired by the Stars and Stripes flying battered but unbowed after the British bombardment of Baltimore.

Elvis Presley *(1935-77)*
In the last year of his life, Presley received prescriptions for 10,000 doses of drugs.

Congo Square
18th -century New Orleans' slave-owners let their slaves gather here each Sunday to dance and sing—so preserving African musical traditions that would later reignite as **jazz.**

'Jingle Bells'
(1857) This American-written tune was the first song sung in space (1965).

'I Wish I Was in Dixie' *(1860)*
Played by the band in Charleston at South Carolina's vote to secede from the Union (the first Confederate state to do so).

Cajun music
The Mississippi delta is the home of cajun; add a vest-frottoir (washboard) and you have **zydeco***—the ultimate swamp stomp.*

Gloria Estefan *(b. 1957)*
The USA's biggest Latin artist. The CIA tried to recruit her while she was working at Miami Airport.

Ukulele
The ukulele comes from Hawaii, where it was developed from guitars brought by Portuguese. The name means 'jumping flea' in Hawaiian.

1980	1983	1985	1991	1996	2000	2006	2010
	Thriller		*Ropin' the Wind*		*High School Musical*		
	Born in the USA		*Jagged Little Pill*		*No Strings Attached*		

THREE COLOSSI OF CAPITALISM

ANDREW CARNEGIE (STEEL). *'Put all your eggs in one basket, then watch that basket.'* ■ In 1898, Carnegie tried to buy the Philippines. (He failed, but his generous intent had been to give the islands the gift of their independence.) **Peak wealth**: 6 Gates.[1]

HENRY FORD (AUTOS). *'It is the customer who pays the wages.'* ■ When designing his Model T, Ford moved the driver's seat to the off-side. Before this, car drivers had been seated beside the curb.

Peak wealth: 3.5 Gates.

JOHN D. ROCKEFELLER (OIL). *'The way to make money is to buy when blood runs in the streets.'* ■ On 29 September 1916, Rockefeller became the first man to amass one billion dollars. At its height, his fortune equalled 1.5% of US GDP.

Peak wealth: 12.5 Gates.

[1] *A convenient measure of extreme wealth: 1 Gate = the wealth of Bill*

$$$$$

QUICK BUCK. When, in 1792, Congress gave birth to the US dollar, instead of inventing a new symbol, it simply appropriated the '$' that already stood for piratical pieces of eight.[2] The '$' probably first came about as shorthand for 'P[s]', an abbreviation of *peso*—the name pieces of eight held in their native Mexico.

[2] *Pieces-of-eight remained legal tender in America, alongside the dollar, until outlawed in 1857.*

THE GREAT AMERICAN NOVEL

'One thing's sure and nothing's surer; the rich get richer and the poor get—children.'
—F. Scott Fitzgerald
(*The Great Gatsby*)

WHAT'S THE MATTER? Everything we touch is made from atoms. But every atom is composed of nucleons[3] and every nucleon is a collection of quarks. However, quarks, so far as we know, are where it stops: they are truly the fundamental fabric of matter. Named in 1963 by US scientist Murray Gell-Mann after the squawk of seagulls (via a reference in *Finnegans Wake*), quarks were first detected five years later, 25 miles outside San Francisco.

[3] *Atomic nucleons are enrobed in a haze of electrons (themselves indivisible).*

THE SIX FLAVOURS[4] OF QUARK   **NUCLEONS**

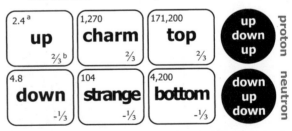

[4] *This is the technical term physicists use to refer to the different varieties of quark.* [a] *Rest mass (MeV).* [b] *Fraction of the charge on an electron.*

THE LAST PLACE. Attu in the Alaskan Aleutians is the most westerly island before the Date Line—and, therefore, the last land on Earth to see the sun set each day.[5]

[5] *But since Attu also happens to have one of the world's most miserable climates, this is only literally true perhaps eight times a year.*

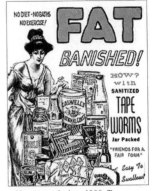

Slimming ad. circa 1900. Tapeworm treatment is still offered online today.

SAN FRANCISCO'S WEED-FUELLED HAZE. The city's fogs are not just down to climate. Colossal seaweed forests off San Francisco's coast release iodine gas that encourages water droplets to seed. Coming together by the trillion, these form the blankets of white that regularly billow in from the ocean.

It Could All Have Been So Different—Defeated Presidential Candidates

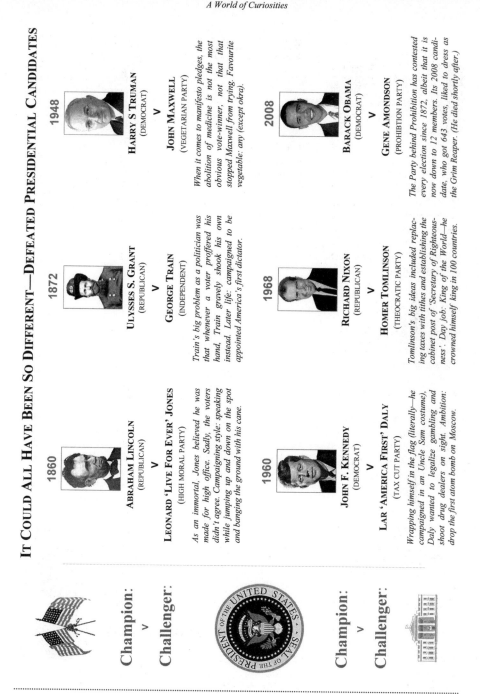

1860

ABRAHAM LINCOLN
(REPUBLICAN)

v

LEONARD 'LIVE FOR EVER' JONES
(HIGH MORAL PARTY)

As an immortal, Jones believed he was made for high office. Sadly, the voters didn't agree. Campaigning style: speaking while jumping up and down on the spot and banging the ground with his cane.

1872

ULYSSES S. GRANT
(REPUBLICAN)

v

GEORGE TRAIN
(INDEPENDENT)

Train's big problem as a politician was that whenever a voter proffered his hand, Train gravely shook his own instead. Later life: campaigned to be appointed America's first dictator.

1948

HARRY S TRUMAN
(DEMOCRAT)

v

JOHN MAXWELL
(VEGETARIAN PARTY)

When it comes to manifesto pledges, the abolition of medicine is not the most obvious vote-winner, not that that stopped Maxwell from trying. Favourite vegetable: any (except okra).

1960

JOHN F. KENNEDY
(DEMOCRAT)

v

LAR 'AMERICA FIRST' DALY
(TAX CUT PARTY)

Wrapping himself in the flag (literally—he campaigned in an Uncle Sam costume), Daly wanted to legalize gambling and shoot drug dealers on sight. Ambition: drop the first atom bomb on Moscow.

1968

RICHARD NIXON
(REPUBLICAN)

v

HOMER TOMLINSON
(THEOCRATIC PARTY)

Tomlinson's big ideas included replacing taxes with tithes and establishing the cabinet post of 'Secretary of Righteousness'. Day job: King of the World—he crowned himself king in 100 countries.

2008

BARACK OBAMA
(DEMOCRAT)

v

GENE AMONDSON
(PROHIBTION PARTY)

The Party behind Prohibition has contested every election since 1872, albeit that it is now down to 12 members. Its 2008 candidate, who got 643 votes, liked to dress as the Grim Reaper. (He died shortly after.)

Champion:

v

Challenger:

Champion:

v

Challenger:

♦ · **GSR**: 1 · **WHS**: Cahokia (pre-Columbian earthworks) □ Carlsbad Caverns □ Chaco Canyon (Pueblo ruins) □ Everglades (wetlands) □ Grand Canyon □ Great Smoky Mountains (forests) □ Hawaii Volcanoes □ Independence Hall (building) □ Kluane (mountains, icefield) □ Mammoth Cave □ Mesa Verde (Pueblo ruins) □ Monticello (architecture) □ Olympic (temperate wilderness) □ Papahānaumokuākea (reefs) □ Pueblo de Taos (village) □ Redwood (forests) □ Statue of Liberty (monument) □ Waterton Glacier (landscapes) □ Yellowstone (geysers, wildlife) □ Yosemite (glaciated landforms)

—— UNITED STATES DEPENDENCIES ——

'John is his name.'

—Official motto of Puerto Rico

THROUGH THE LOOKING GLASS.
It is neither the USA nor somewhere else. Puerto Rico is, to use the legal jargon, 'a territory appurtenant to the United States, but not a part of it'. What this means in practice is that those living in Puerto Rico can vote in US presidential primaries but not in the elections themselves,[1] and Puerto Rico's representative in Washington gets a vote in Congress but not if this would affect the final outcome. Guamanians, Virgin Islanders and Samoans all enjoy similar qualified privileges.

[1] *Unless, in the past, resident in the US proper, in which case they are treated as Americans overseas.*

GITMO.
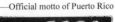

Home to Cuba's one and only McDonald's restaurant, Guantanamo Bay is held by the US on a perpetual lease that was granted in 1903 by Cuba's first president (an American citizen). Rent, set in 1934 at $4,085, is paid annually by cheque sent to Havana. However, since the revolution, these have never been banked[2] (and Fidel Castro once revealed that he has kept them all, unpresented, stuffed into a drawer of his office desk.) At 45 square miles, Guantanamo's territory outranks five sovereign states; and its facilities include schools, hospital, dental clinic, jail (for US personnel) and O'Kelly's Irish Pub—said to offer 'all the warmth of the Emerald Isle' around its faux fireplace.

[2] *Apart from the 1959 one, which was—due to 'confusion', according to Castro. Nevertheless, the US maintains this constitutes ratification of the lease by Cuba's Communists.*

OWN GOAL.
During a 2001 World Cup qualifying game against Australia, American Samoa's soccer team entered the record books when they suffered the worst ever defeat in an international match. It took a recount to confirm, but the final tally was 31–0. To be fair, many of American Samoa's first-choice players were unavailable because of a clash with their school exams, while others had the wrong sort of passport.

E.T., PLEASE PHONE.
Puerto Rico's Arecibo Observatory is the world's biggest single telescope, with a radio dish 1,000 feet across. Its day job is astronomy (it spotted the first planets outside the solar system), but it has also been at the heart of the hunt for extraterrestrial life. In 1974, it made humanity's first attempt to contact alien civilizations, when it beamed a message (*right*) at the Messier 13 Globular Cluster. Since 1999, it has been listening too—feeding data to 250,000 home PCs in a so far unsuccessful search for incoming calls.

The Arecibo Message contains seven pieces of information that, it was thought, any intelligent being would understand. How many can you tease out? (Answers below.)

HUNCHBACKS OF EARLY GUAM.
Before European contact, only Guam's upper-class Matao could fish or even touch the sea. This condemned the lower-class Manachang to generations of shrinkage due to protein deficiency—not that this was obvious, since the Manachang had, in any case, to creep around bent double whenever near a Matao.

Answers: The information is in seven bands. From top: 1–10 (in binary); 2. Atomic numbers of H, C, N, O and P (the elements in DNA); 3. Formulae of the DNA nucleotides; 4. Length and double helix structure of DNA; 5. Size and shape of a human being and (then) population of earth; 6. Sun and (then) nine planets; 7. Shape and size of the Arecibo dish.

Dependent Territories: American Samoa, Baker Island, Guam, Guantanamo Bay Naval Base, Howland Island, Jarvis Island, Johnston Atoll, Kingman Reef, Midway Islands, Northern Mariana Islands, Palmyra Atoll, Puerto Rico, United States Virgin Islands, Wake Island.

◆● · **GSR** n/a · **WHS**: Puerto Rico—San Juan (fortifications) □ Papahānaumokuākea—Midway (reefs)

URUGUAY

'Liberty or death!'

—Uruguayan national motto, shared with Greece and New Hampshire (as 'Live free or die')

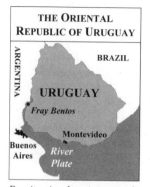

THE ORIENTAL REPUBLIC OF URUGUAY

ARGENTINA — BRAZIL — URUGUAY — Fray Bentos — Montevideo — Buenos Aires — River Plate

Despite its location on the north bank of the River Plate, Montevideo lies marginally to the south of Buenos Aires, making it the southernmost capital in the Americas.

FAR EAST. Uruguayans are known within South America as 'Orientals'. This refers to the country's full title of 'The Oriental Republic of Uruguay', which, in turn, comes from the nation's location on the east bank of the River Plate.[1]

[1] *Thanks to a sand bar limiting the encroachment of seawater, the River Plate is the widest in the world, with a breadth of 140 miles as it empties into the Atlantic at its mouth.*

CELESTIAL. Uruguay has won the World Cup twice despite having fewer people than Scotland. Their greatest triumph was in Rio in 1950, when they came from behind to beat Brazil 2–1 with just moments to go in front of 200,000 spectators (still the biggest sporting crowd of all time). The shock of losing was so great it prompted Brazil to abandon their white strip for the famous green and yellow.

COW JUICE. Concerned that meat was out of reach for Europe's urban poor, in 1865 Baron Justus von Liebig invented a way to produce a liquid 'meat extract'. However, since it took 3 kg of meat to produce 100 g of extract, the cost in Europe was still prohibitive. So the Baron relocated his operation to Fray Bentos in Uruguay, where beef was so cheap it was being thrown away. Able to process a cow every 5 minutes, the Fray Bentos plant was one of the largest factories in South America, and helped bring the industrial revolution to the continent. Liebig's company later launched a cheaper version: 'Oxo'[2], and in 1873 added canned 'Fray Bentos' corned beef[3] to their range. The products were huge successes and, with arch-rival 'Johnston's Fluid Beef'[4], based across the river in Argentina, became staples of the British kitchen throughout much of the 20th century.

[2] *In 1910, Oxo was reformulated as a dehydrated cube with a salt content of 65%.* [3] *In Britain, corned beef is finely minced pre-cooked beef cured in brine and saltpetre (also a key component of gunpowder).* [4] *Now known as Bovril.*

SHIP'S BISCUIT. Before going on to unify Italy, Guiseppe Garibaldi cut his teeth commanding the Uruguayan Navy during the nine-year Siege of Montevideo, starting in 1842.

STARS IN THEIR EYES. Astronauts in orbit over Uruguay see stars shooting across their sight. The 'stars' are actually the tracks left by particles accelerated to 10 million electron volts as they crash into

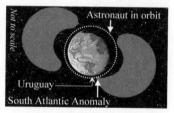

Van Allen Radiation Belts

the astronauts' eyeballs; and they are therefore a natural warning of bombardment by intense radiation. Fortunately, astronauts cross the country in under two minutes; but, even so, the cumulative dose from a week-long stint on the space station is as much as a year spent at sea level. Uruguay is such a radiation hotspot because it lies beneath the so-called South Atlantic Anomaly, the zone where the Van Allen Radiation Belts (formed by the effect of the Earth's magnetic field on cosmic rays) dip closest the ground—and so inconveniently into the path of orbiting spacecraft.

♦ · **GSR:** 61 · **WHS:** Colonia (colonial architecture) · **IHC:** Candombe (drumming) □ Tango (dance)

UZBEKISTAN • O'ZBEKISTON

'The Centre of the Universe.'
—Timur, on his capital, Samarkand

TRUNK ROAD. Through the Great Wall of China by the Jade Gate and across the breadth of Eurasia to imperial Rome, the Silk Route stretched 5,000 miles: the longest road of its era and the most fabled in history. The midpoint was marked by the Stone Tower of Osh; Samarkand, its most exotic city, stood nearby—in today's Uzbekistan. Traffic peaked around 200 CE, then dropped with the fall of Rome, before reviving once more in the Middle Ages. Very few people covered the whole length. Instead, goods were sold on from merchant to merchant, getting ever more expensive by the mile. A party of travellers who did make the whole trip, a group of Chinese officials received by Emperor Augustus, claimed that their journey had taken four years.

■ During the 1st century, Pliny the Elder calculated that the Roman Empire was spending 100 million *sesterces*[1] a year importing silk; cause enough—along with grumbles about wanton Roman maidens wearing transparent dresses—for the Senate to try in vain to ban it.

■ Despite the weight of trade, extreme distance meant Roman and Chinese troops clashed only once. The Chinese came out on top: their crossbow bolts didn't even notice the Roman armour as they sank home.

[1] *Approximately $150 million today.*

> **ROME**
> *silk · musk · rubies*
> *porcelain · perfumes*
> *rhubarb · halos*

> **CHANG'AN**
> *gold · silver · jade*
> *wool · glass · saffron*
> *incense · Christianity*

MAGIC NUMBERS. Khiva-born Muhammed al-Khwarizmi was a leading sundial fancier and the founder of modern algebra. His books gave Europe decimal fractions as well as quadratic equations (and, more usefully, their systematic solution). His name has achieved immortality in the word 'algorithm' (an IT term meaning 'time for non-initiates to tune out').

Registan

'The Registan of Samarkand is the noblest public square in the world. I know of nothing in the East approaching it, and nothing in Europe which can even aspire to enter the competition'
—Lord Curzon

GOD'S SCOURGE. Leader of the last great nomad horde to swoop upon the settled world, Timur the Lame (Marlowe's Tamburlaine) is remembered chiefly for razing almost every city from the Aegean to India, and then usually stacking the severed heads of the slaughtered citizenry into piles as an afterthought. He is the Uzbek national hero, nevertheless; and his statue now graces the main square of the capital, Tashkent, in place of Marx.

ADIEU AND GOODBYE. Once the size of Ireland, the Aral Sea has shrunk since the 1960s to little more than a string of salty puddles, its waters diverted to irrigate cotton. Before the end of this century, the Uzbek half will dry up altogether, to be replaced by a poisonous dust-bowl desert. Already, pesticide residues from the exposed seabed blow as far as Antarctica.

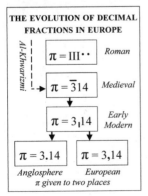

THE EVOLUTION OF DECIMAL FRACTIONS IN EUROPE

$$\pi = III \cdot \cdot \quad \text{Roman}$$
$$\pi = \overline{3}14 \quad \text{Medieval}$$
$$\pi = 3{,}14 \quad \text{Early Modern}$$
$$\pi = 3.14 \quad \pi = 3{,}14$$

Al-Khwarizmi

Anglosphere — European
π *given to two places*

2010 shore

ARAL SEA

1960 shore

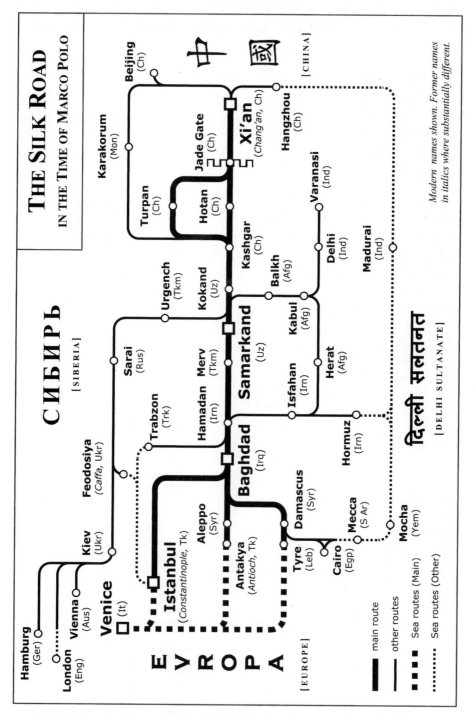

THE SILK ROAD
IN THE TIME OF MARCO POLO

Modern names shown. Former names in italics where substantially different.

[CHINA]

Beijing (Ch)

Karakorum (Mon)

中 國 [CHINA]

Jade Gate (Ch)

Xi'an (*Chang'an*, Ch)

Hangzhou (Ch)

Turpan (Ch)

Hotan (Ch)

Varanasi (Ind)

Kashgar (Ch)

Delhi (Ind)

Madurai (Ind)

СИБИРЬ [SIBERIA]

Urgench (Tkm)

Kokand (Uz)

Balkh (Afg)

Sarai (Rus)

Samarkand (Uz)

Kabul (Afg)

Herat (Afg)

Trabzon (Trk)

Hamadan (Irn)

Merv (Tkm)

Isfahan (Irn)

Feodosiya (*Caffa*, Ukr)

Baghdad (Iraq)

Hormuz (Irn)

दिल्ली सल्तनत [DELHI SULTANATE]

Kiev (Ukr)

Aleppo (Syr)

Damascus (Syr)

Mecca (S Ar)

Mocha (Yem)

Hamburg (Ger)

London (Eng)

Vienna (Aus)

Venice (It)

Istanbul (*Constantinople*, Tk)

Antakya (*Antioch*, Tk)

Tyre (Leb)

Cairo (Egp)

E V R O P A [EUROPE]

main route
other routes
Sea routes (Main)
Sea routes (Other)

♣ · **GSR**: 121 · **WHS**: Bukhara (museum city) □ Khiva (historic town) □ Samarkand (museum city) Shakhrisyabz (historic town) · **ICH**: Boysun (traditional rituals) □ Katta Ashula (choral singing) Navruz (New Year festivaties) □ Shashmaqom (classical music)

—VATICAN & HOLY SEE • VATICANUS ET SANCTA SEDES—

'Stupidity is a gift of God, but one mustn't misuse it.'

—Pope John Paul II

THREE PAPAL PORTRAITS

1285   1287

MARRIED: HONORIUS IV. The one-time rector of Barton Mills in Suffolk was the last pope to have been married. By the time he made it to the papacy, he was so infirm his hands had to be lifted on strings.

1032   1048

MULTIPLE: BENEDICT IX was the only man to have been pope more than once—managing three reigns in total. He is also the only person to have sold the Papacy (to his godfather after reign two).

1492   1503

DAMNED: ALEXANDER VI. The Borgia Pope was so wicked,[1] when he died his successor forbade anyone to hold a requiem mass, saying, *'It is blasphemous to pray for the damned.'*

[1] *In between the incest, orgies and murder, he did, however, find time to carve South America up between Spain and Portugal—why Brazilians now speak Portuguese.*

Pride

MIND & BODY. Of the seven deadly sins, women are most prone to pride followed by envy, while men are most guilty of lust and then gluttony—or so a 2009 Vatican survey of sins admitted during penance (confession) reported.

GRAZIE IL DUCE. The Vatican City was a present from Benito Mussolini to the pope given in 1929. Mussolini's gift was made to settle the so-called 'Roman Question', which arose in 1870, after Italian troops blasted through the walls of Rome and occupied the city as the final act of Italian unification. The Italian takeover left the pope without any physical territory for the first time in 1,200 years, and although most states still treated the Holy See as a sovereign entity (notwithstanding its notable lack of physical domains), the position was uncomfortable for all concerned. A tricky situation was made worse when Pope Pius IX declared he was a prisoner, locked himself in his palace and refused to come out. This papal protest was maintained by his successors for the next 59 years until Mussolini's grand gesture finally tempted the pontiffs out into the open.

LIBERATION THEOLOGY. Set at 12 years, the Vatican City's age of both heterosexual and homosexual consent is the lowest of any country in Europe.

Lust

'I will give you the Keys of Heaven; whatever you bind on Earth will be bound in heaven, and whatever you loose on Earth will be loosed in heaven.'

—Jesus to Peter, Matthew 16:19

KEY ROLE. As depicted by the papal insignia (*above*), the pope holds the Keys of Heaven. The silver key has power to 'bind and loose' on Earth, while the gold does the same in heaven. This double action—effective in heaven as well as on Earth—is the basis upon which the Catholic Church claims authority to absolve spiritual sin.

'INSERITO SCIDULAM QUAESO UT FACIUNDAM COGNOSCAS RATIONEM.'[2]

PECUNIA MACHINA. Vatican ATMs are the only ones in the world that display screen instructions in Latin.

[2] *Insert card (literally, thin strip of bark) to view available transactions.*

♠ · **GSR**: 120 · **WHS**: Rome (extraterritorial papal churches) □ Vatican (uniquely, the entire nation)

VENEZUELA

'Ten years from now, twenty years from now, you will see:
oil will bring us ruin ... Oil is the devil's excrement.'

—Juan Pablo Pérez Alfonso, Venezualan Minister for Mines and Hydrocarbons and the man who created OPEC. When Pérez Alfonso made his statement in 1973, Venezuela's oil boom was just starting, the country was fully democratic and Venezuelans enjoyed the highest standard of living in Latin America. Today, despite the biggest oil reserves in the Americas, 30% of people live on less than $2 a day, Caracas is the murder capital of the world (the country as a whole is four times more violent than Iraq) and Transparency International ranks Venezuela as more corrupt than Congo.

LIFE'S A GAS

At 2.2 cents a litre, Venezuela has the world's cheapest fuel.

World Forecourt Petrol Prices—April 2011 ($/litre)

- $2.40 — UK
- SPAIN
- AUSTRALIA
- $1.60 — CANADA
- USA
- $0.80 — MEXICO
- IRAQ
- VENEZUELA
- $0.00

Born in 1783, Venezuelan soldier and statesman Simón Bolívar was responsible for the independence of six Latin American nations (Bolivia, Colombia, Peru, Ecuador, Panama and Venezuela). He is also the only person to feature in the names of two countries: Bolivia and, since 1999, Chávez's 'Bolivarian Republic of Venezuela'.

'I chew coca every day—and look how I am.'

—President Hugo Chávez discussing his coca habit with the Venezuelan National Assembly (2008)

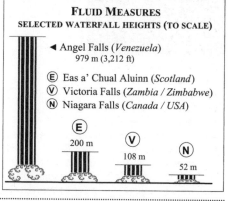

SUPERCHAV. Love him or loathe him (and in the 1998 presidential election campaign he was forced to specifically deny that he ate fried babies for breakfast), Chávez has brought the classic *caudillo* into the 21st century. Combining popularism with muscle—the army as well as the biceps he flashed to parliament during his chat about coca—Chávez has broken new ground for a Latin American strongman by setting up his own Twitter call centre, allegedly employing a full-time staff of 200 to respond to his 1.4 million (as of May 2011) followers.

FERTILE IMAGINATION. When explorer Amerigo Vespucci sailed into tidal Lake Maracaibo in 1499, he saw the native villages were built on stilts over the water. Fancying a similarity to Venice, he called the area 'Venezuela' (literally 'Little Venice'), which term later came to be applied to the whole country.

'That's not the way you spell 'C-a-r-a-c-u-s' anyway.'

—closing lines of *Gregory's Girl* (1981)

RIGHT TIT. A generation of adolescent boys—now middle-aged men—weren't misled. If beauty pageants are a guide, Venezuela is indeed the place to go: its overall tally of 11 Miss Universes and Miss Worlds outstrips even arch-enemy USA (ranked second with 10). But this may be about to change. In early 2011, President Chávez (a former beauty show judge himself) declared that 'monstrous' breasts did not 'square with his revolutionary priorities'.

The world's highest waterfall, Angel Falls, is named after pilot Jimmie Angel, who first spotted it from the air in 1933. Four years later, he landed at the fall's summit, but when his plane bogged in mud, it took Angel 11 days to hike off.

FLUID MEASURES
SELECTED WATERFALL HEIGHTS (TO SCALE)

◄ Angel Falls (*Venezuela*)
   979 m (3,212 ft)

Ⓔ Eas a' Chual Aluinn (*Scotland*)
Ⓥ Victoria Falls (*Zambia / Zimbabwe*)
Ⓝ Niagara Falls (*Canada / USA*)

Ⓔ
200 m

Ⓥ
108 m

Ⓝ
52 m

♦ · **GSR**: 41 · **WHS**: Canaima (rainforest and table mountains) □ Caracas (modernist university campus) □ Coro (colonial townscape)

—————— VIETNAM ● VIỆT NAM ——————

'You will kill ten of our men, and we will kill one of yours,
and in the end it will be you who tire of it.'

—Ho Chi Minh, referring to the French during the First Indochina War (1946–54). From his perspective,
he was being unduly pessimistic, since the overall ratio of military fatalities suffered by each side in that
conflict and its successor, the 1955–75 Vietnam War, was not 10:1, but around 3:2.

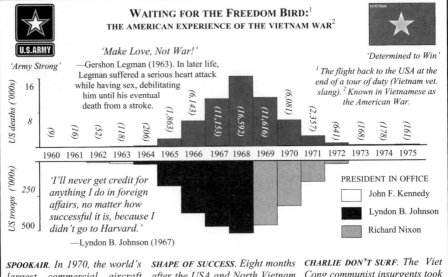

WAITING FOR THE FREEDOM BIRD:[1]
THE AMERICAN EXPERIENCE OF THE VIETNAM WAR[2]

'Make Love, Not War!'
—Gershon Legman (1963). In later life,
Legman suffered a serious heart attack
while having sex, debilitating
him until his eventual
death from a stroke.

'Army Strong'

'Determined to Win'

[1] *The flight back to the USA at the end of a tour of duty (Vietnam vet. slang).* [2] *Known in Vietnamese as the American War.*

US deaths ('000s): 16, 8

(9) (16) (52) (118) (206) (1,863) (6,143) (11,153) (16,592) (11,616) (6,081) (2,357) (641) (168) (178) (191)

1960 1961 1962 1963 1964 1965 1966 1967 1968 1969 1970 1971 1972 1973 1974 1975

US troops ('000s): 250, 500

'I'll never get credit for anything I do in foreign affairs, no matter how successful it is, because I didn't go to Harvard.'
—Lyndon B. Johnson (1967)

PRESIDENT IN OFFICE
☐ John F. Kennedy
■ Lyndon B. Johnson
▨ Richard Nixon

SPOOKAIR. In 1970, the world's largest commercial aircraft fleet belonged to Air America, the ostensibly civilian airline supplying US forces in Vietnam. Later, however, it turned out that the carrier had in fact been owned and run by the CIA.

SHAPE OF SUCCESS. Eight months after the USA and North Vietnam opened their first direct peace negotiations in Paris in 1968, the parties finally managed to agree the shape of the negotiating table (a round one surrounded by square side tables).

CHARLIE DON'T SURF. The Viet Cong communist insurgents took their American nickname of 'Charlie' from the phonetic rendering of V. C.—'Victor Charlie'. Although they claimed autonomy, the VC were directly controlled by North Vietnam.

WAXING LYRICAL. 'Like an orgasm for the ear' is how true believers describe the joy of ear-cleaning. While not many would go so far, scraping out a partner's ear while cradling their head in one's lap is a well-recognized sensual experience in East Asia's ear-cleaning strongholds of Vietnam, Japan and Thailand. (Taking advantage of the ear's rich supply of nerve endings, the Vietnamese also use a tool called a ball-head to give stress-busting ear massages.) Sadly, Europeans are excluded from the fun, as, unlike the dry, easily flaked Asian earwax, a different gene makes theirs wet and sticky and unsuitable for extraction.

PEP[3] AT A PINCH. Pepper is the world's most traded spice, and Vietnam is currently by far the biggest supplier, producing over a third of the global crop. Pepper's dominance dates back to at least the Romans, who were addicted to its pungent potency. It would *Black pepper is the dried fruit of the pepper vine. White pepper is just the seed with the fruit removed.* seem their nemesis, the barbarians, were fans too: when Attila the Hun demanded a ransom not to sack Rome in the 5th century, his ultimatum called for a ton of pepper.

[3] *Pep is a 20th-century shortening of 'pepper'. The world's first recorded 'pep talk' was apparently given in 1926.*

....

♣ · **GSR**: 49 · **WHS**: Ha Long Bay (karst islands) ☐ Hanoi (citadel) ☐ Hoi An (townscape) ☐ Huế (historic city) ☐ My Son (Hindu ruins) ☐ Phong Nha-Kẻ Bang (karst caves) ☐ Tây Giai (citadel) · **ICH**: Ca Trù (singing) ☐ Gióng (festival) ☐ Gongs ☐ Nha Nhac (music) ☐ Quan Họ Bắc Ninh (folk songs)

— WEST BANK[1] & GAZA STRIP[2] ● الضفة الغربية و قطاع غزة —

'O little town of Bethlehem / How still we see thee lie.'

—P. Brooks (Christmas carol, 1868)

Wandering Star

AND PEACE TO MEN ON EARTH. When Catholic priests installed a silver star on the exact spot in Bethlehem on which Jesus was said to have been born, Orthodox monks took exception and, in 1847, prised the star out and stole it—or so the Catholics alleged. Matters escalated, and France's Napoleon III jumped to champion the Catholic cause. Naturally, Tsar Nicholas I responded on behalf of the Orthodox side, and wrongly surmising that he had tacit British support, ultimately invaded Ottoman Turkey. Britain and France then backed the Ottomans and all concerned fought the Crimean War. In 1853, the Turks eventually fitted a new star, but even today neither the Catholics nor the Orthodox (nor the Armenians, who are also present) can agree on any aspect of the upkeep of the Church of the Nativity, where the star is found. One result is that worshippers now have to put up umbrellas whenever it rains, and there are fears that the entire leaking roof could fall in at any time.

TERMINAL BRANDING. Named after the PLO's leader at the time the organization led the world in hijacks and aircraft bombings, Yasser Arafat International Airport was Gaza's air gateway—until it was comprehensively blown up, rocketed and bulldozed in 2001. Other airports with winning names include the Imelda R. Marcos (Philippines) and the Genghis Khan International (Ulan Bator, Mongolia).

A SLICE OF THE PIE: BETHLEHEM'S BIG FAMILY[3]

Total: 48

Italy (14)

Other[4] (20)

France (4)

Spain (3)

Brazil (3)

USA (4)

[3] *Towns that are officially twinned with Bethlehem.* [4] *Includes Glasgow, its sole twin in Britain.*

SCARLET WOMAN. When one of the world's earliest professionals, Rahab, betrayed the world's oldest city, Jericho, to the Israelites, she chose a red cord as her sign—so fixing the link between the colour and prostitution that continues today.

Young Philistines

NEVER-ENDING STORY. 'Palestine' shares its root with *Philistia*, land of the Philistines—the cartoon bad guys for much of the Old Testament (clocking 250 derogatory mentions). Of the many clashes related in the Bible, perhaps the most Hollywood takes place on the site of modern Gaza City, when Samson, the blinded and beaten Israelite superhero, uses his bare hands to pull the idolatrous temple of Dagon, the fish god, down on thousands of crowing Philistines (and himself). Cue closing credits.

Samson bringing the house down

MASTERS OF THEIR UNIVERSE		
Superhero	*Personality*	*Achilles Heel*
Samson .... Israel	dumb—ask Delilah	barber shops
Achilles .... Greece	sulky supermodel	heel
Lancelot, Sir ..... England	deucedly chivalrous	posh totty
Skywalker, A. .... Jedi	hormonal teenager	Dark Side

[1] *A plurality of international bodies considers the West Bank territory under the occupation of Israel. Administration is divided (by area) as follows: Palestinian National Authority (PNA) 17%, PNA (civil only, security retained by Israel) 24%, Israel Military Administration 59%.* [2] *Gaza's legal status has been contentious since Israeli disengagement in 2005 (the nub being whether Israel remains in occupation); since 2007 the Hamas movement has been de facto administrator.*

♣ · **GSR**: 63 · **WHS**: none · **IHC**: Palestinian Hikaye (storytelling)

—————— YEMEN ● اليَمَن ——————

'When the Queen of Sheba heard about Solomon, she came to Jerusalem with a great display of pomp. She gave King [Solomon] 120 talents [5 tonnes] of gold, spices and precious gems. The quantity of spices the Queen gave Solomon has never been matched.'

—*New English Bible* (I Kings 10:1–10). Scholars consider Yemen to be the most probable homeland of the Queen of Sheba (according to ancient legend, descended from a dynasty of 60 female rulers). The Queen also figures in the Islamic tradition but, while rich and powerful, she is said to have had hairy legs and a goat's hoof in place of one foot.

MANHATTAN OF THE DESERT. Built for protection from Bedouin raiders, the walled city of  Shibam, in southern Yemen's isolated Wadi Hadramut, is the world's oldest high-rise settlement, with a history going back 1,800 years. Within its walls, the mud-brick houses rise up to eight storeys—the tallest such structures in the world—and, for convenience, are linked at high level to save residents the effort of having to descend to the ground.

STORM IN A COFFEE CUP. The cup of coffee first enters history in Yemen, as the preferred brew of 15th-century Sufi monks—to be drunk while chanting 'Allah' 116 times. Later, the clerical authorities tried to ban it (arguing roast beans were coal), before it arrived in Italy as 'Arabian wine'.

POISONOUS PLEASURES—THE LD50[1] OF SELECTED SINS

4 grams	15 grams	220 grams	600 grams	2.2 kg
NICOTINE	CAFFEINE	SALT	ALCOHOL	SUGAR
50 mg/kg	*200 mg/kg*	*3 g/kg*	*8 g/kg*	*30 g/kg*

[1] *Mean lethal dose. The headline figure is for an adult of average weight (75 kg).*

HERE BE DRAGONS. Its name derives from 'Isle of Bliss' in Sanskrit and it was conquered by the Portuguese explorer Tristan da Cunha, fresh from his discovery of his eponymous island, but Yemen's Socotra Archipelago is most renowned today for having the most alien landscape on Earth, an accolade earned mostly on the strength of its sci-fi flora. There's the cucumber tree (actually related to the salad staple) and the desert rose—described as resembling an elephant's leg with pink flowers on top; but most famous is the dragon's blood tree (*above*). Its ruby resin is used by Socotrans as both lipstick and glue, but in medieval Europe it commanded high prices as 'dragon's blood',[2] an essential ingredient in inks for writing magical texts and spells, and, more constructively, as violin varnish (for which it is still employed).

[2] *Resin from the related Tenerife dragon tree later became available. Both are sold as dragon's blood today.*

ON A WING AND A PRAYER. Yemeni Judaism goes back more than two millennia, and for a time in the 6th century CE, the territory was even a Jewish kingdom (until overrun by Christian Axum). But after anti-Jewish riots in Aden killed 82 people in 1947, the US and UK secretly airlifted almost all of Yemen's Jewish community to the new state of Israel in Operation Magic Carpet. Lasting for 15 months in 1949–50, this carried some 49,000 of Yemen's 50,000 Jews on a total of 380 flights. However, as most of the evacuees had never even seen a plane, many at first refused to enter the aircraft until rabbis coaxed them aboard by quoting prophecies from the Book of Isaiah.

HEALTH AND SAFETY. Travellers to Yemen should be aware that, while there should be no problem bringing your nine-year-old child bride into the country, attempts to import a ham sandwich (or any other pork product) attract the death sentence.

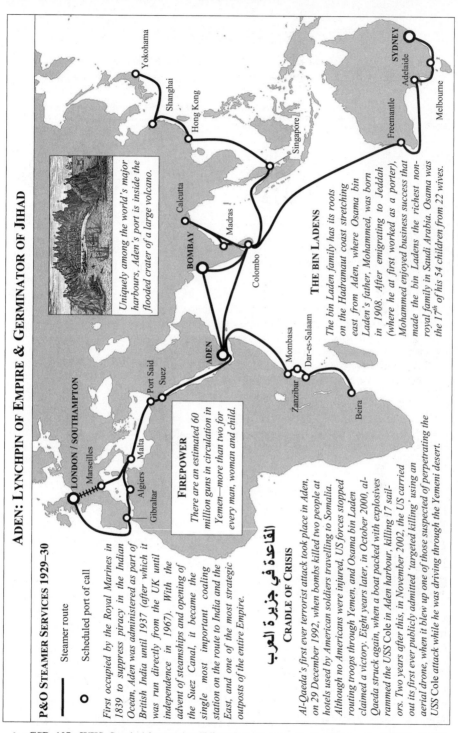

ADEN: LYNCHPIN OF EMPIRE & GERMINATOR OF JIHAD

P&O STEAMER SERVICES 1929–30

— Steamer route

o Scheduled port of call

First occupied by the Royal Marines in 1839 to suppress piracy in the Indian Ocean, Aden was administered as part of British India until 1937 (after which it was run directly from the UK until independence in 1967). With the advent of steamships and opening of the Suez Canal, it became the single most important coaling station on the route to India and the East, and one of the most strategic outposts of the entire Empire.

Uniquely among the world's major harbours, Aden's port is inside the flooded crater of a large volcano.

FIREPOWER

There are an estimated 60 million guns in circulation in Yemen—more than two for every man, woman and child.

THE BIN LADENS

The bin Laden family has its roots on the Hadramaut coast stretching east from Aden, where Osama bin Laden's father, Mohammed, was born in 1908. After emigrating to Jeddah (where he at first worked as a porter), Mohammed enjoyed business success that made the bin Ladens the richest non-royal family in Saudi Arabia. Osama was the 17th of his 54 children from 22 wives.

القاعدة في جزيرة العرب

CRADLE OF CRISIS

Al-Qaeda's first ever terrorist attack took place in Aden, on 29 December 1992, when bombs killed two people at hotels used by American soldiers travelling to Somalia. Although no Americans were injured, US forces stopped routing troops through Yemen, and Osama bin Laden claimed a victory. Eight years later, in October 2000, al-Qaeda struck again, when a boat packed with explosives rammed the USS Cole in Aden harbour, killing 17 sailors. Two years after this, in November 2002, the US carried out its first ever publicly admitted 'targeted killing' using an aerial drone, when it blew up one of those suspected of perpetrating the USS Cole attack while he was driving through the Yemeni desert.

Map labels: Yokohama · Shanghai · Hong Kong · Calcutta · Madras · Colombo · Singapore · BOMBAY · ADEN · Port Said · Suez · Marseilles · LONDON / SOUTHAMPTON · Malta · Algiers · Gibraltar · Zanzibar · Mombasa · Dar-es-Salaam · Beira · Freemantle · Adelaide · SYDNEY · Melbourne

♣ · **GSR**: 107 · **WHS**: Sana'a (cityscape) ▢ Shibam (townscape) ▢ Socotra (flora and wildlife) ▢ Zabid (townscape) · **ICH**: Song of Sana'a (ballads sung to the accompaniment of lute and copper tray)

———————— Zambia ————————

'I am because we are; we are because I am.'

—*Ubuntu*: the Bantu philosophy of community widely practised throughout Zambia

Noughts & Crosses—Scrambling for Africa

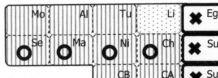

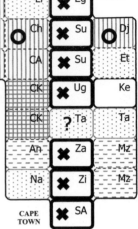

The Colossus of Rhodes.

For Cecil Rhodes, Zambia (or Northern Rhodesia as it was immodestly named at the time) marked the end of the road. An imperialist's imperialist at the height of Britain's Empire, Rhodes dreamt of linking Cape Town to Cairo with British territory all the way in between (*see* '✖'s). His passion (and wealth) was such that he bankrolled the establishment of British colonies north of South Africa out of his personal fortune, in order to cajole a reluctant Colonial Office into cooperation. Although a competing French east west trans-continental ambition (*see* 'O's) was successfully thwarted (as was another coast-to-coast attempt by Portugal in the south), German expansion in Tanganyika (Tanzania) blocked Rhodes' vision in his lifetime. Ironically, the transfer of Tanganyika to Britain after WWI finally made the project feasible, but by then Britain had lost the will to drive it through. To this day, there's no continuous north–south route across Africa, but the main street in Lusaka, Zambia's capital, retains the name 'Cairo Road' in optimistic anticipation.

'I would annex the planets if I could. I often think of that.'

—Cecil Rhodes (1902)

Key: ☐ **British**: *Eg* Egypt, *Ke* Kenya, *SA* South Africa, *Su* Sudan, *Ug* Uganda, *Za* Zambia, *Zi* Zimbabwe; ▯▯▯ **French**: *Al* Algeria, *CA* Cent. Afr. Rep., *Ch* Chad, *CB* Congo-B., *Dj* Djibouti, *Ma* Mali, *Mo* Morocco, *Ni* Niger, *Se* Senegal, *Tu* Tunisia; ▦ **Belgian**: *CK* Congo-K.; ⌐⌐⌐ **Portuguese**: *An* Angola, *Mz* Mozambique; ⣿ **Other**: *Et* Ethiopia, *Li* Libya, *Na* Namibia, *Ta* Tanzania. ***Note***: modern names and borders; not all states shown.

Batty.

Every November, five million fruit bats fly from across Central Africa to roost in three acres of swamp at Kasanka, Zambia. It's the world's largest gathering of mammals, but why it occurs is unknown.

Hi Pops.

Zambian culture respects the elderly. To greet an elder, drop to one knee, bow the head, clap three times, then politely say hello.

True Feelings.

Among the Bemba, it's the custom at a wedding for the groom to show his new mother-in-law how much she's appreciated by feasting on a chicken, then giving her the bones.

Ultimate Victory.

The final German success of WWI was the seizure of the Zambian town of Kasama on 13 November 1918—two days after the war ended. In the action, the Germans stormed the golf course, causing the British to flee. They returned a little later, when news of the armistice arrived on the district's only telephone.

♥ · **GSR**: 147 · **WHS** Victoria Falls · **ICH**: Gule Wamkulu (dance) Makishi Masquerade (initiation)

—————— ZIMBABWE ——————

'I do not believe in black majority rule—not in a thousand years.'

—Ian Smith, as prime minister of Rhodesia (1976)

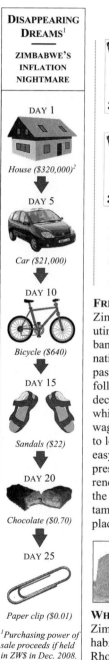

DISAPPEARING DREAMS[1]

ZIMBABWE'S INFLATION NIGHTMARE

DAY 1

House ($320,000)[2]

DAY 5

Car ($21,000)

DAY 10

Bicycle ($640)

DAY 15

Sandals ($22)

DAY 20

Chocolate ($0.70)

DAY 25

Paper clip ($0.01)

[1]*Purchasing power of sale proceeds if held in ZW$ in Dec. 2008.*
[2] *Sterling value.*

LAST, AND SADLY LEAST:
BOTTOM TEN COUNTDOWN—THE WORLD'S MOST BENIGHTED COUNTRIES[3,4]

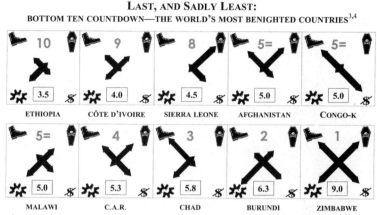

10	9	8	5=	5=
3.5	4.0	4.5	5.0	5.0
ETHIOPIA	CÔTE D'IVOIRE	SIERRA LEONE	AFGHANISTAN	CONGO-K
5=	4	3	2	1
5.0	5.3	5.8	6.3	9.0
MALAWI	C.A.R.	CHAD	BURUNDI	ZIMBABWE

[3] *Misery index calculated by relative ranking in four measures:* A. **Boot**—*Political collapse;* B. **Coffin**—*Average years of premature death;* C. **$**—*Poverty of citizens;* D. **Broken Cogwheel**—*Collapse of business and commerce. Boxed figure gives average score.* Sources: A. *Failed States Index, Fund for Peace (2010);* B. *Life expectancy at birth, UN (2005–10);* C. *GDP per capita (PPP), IMF (2010);* D. *Global Competitiveness Index, World Economic Forum (2010–11).* [4] *Somalia and Eritrea would find berths in the bottom ten but for the lack of statistical data.*

FREEDOM OF THE PRESS. In January 2009, Zimbabwe's Central Bank resorted to distributing 100 trillion Zimbabwe dollar (ZW$) banknotes (numerically, the largest denomination in history) as annual inflation surged past 650 million googol per cent: that's 65 followed by 107 noughts. Zimbabwe's hyperinflation arose from the bank's decision, against all known laws of economic gravity, to print money at will, which in turn was triggered by President Mugabe's need to pay soldiers' wages, after having run out of all other options—including sending his army to loot the Democratic Republic of Congo. Even so, printing money wasn't as easy as it might seem, since it became all but impossible to keep the printing presses turning fast enough, especially after the bank ran out of foreign currency to pay for ink, and the presses themselves began to break down from the strain of their round-the-clock pounding. In the end, the madness was only tamed when, in April 2009, Zimbabwe abandoned its own currency and replaced it with a free for all of US dollars, Rand, pounds and Euros.

'The first time since 1930s Germany that archaeology has been so censored.'

—Paul Sinclair, site archaeologist at Great Zimbabwe during white Rhodesian rule

NO LADY. What is now Zimbabwe was first named Rhodesia after founder Rhodes. But it was nearly named Cecilia instead—after his forename: Cecil.

WHITE LIE. The largest pre-colonial ruined city in Sub-Saharan Africa, Great Zimbabwe was built from 1200–1500 by ancestors of the current Shona inhabitants. However, under secret orders issued in the 1960s by Ian Smith's Rhodesian government, any state employee admitting as much was to be sacked. Instead, Phoenicians, Jews and the Queen of Sheba were all proposed.

A FEW LAST WORDS

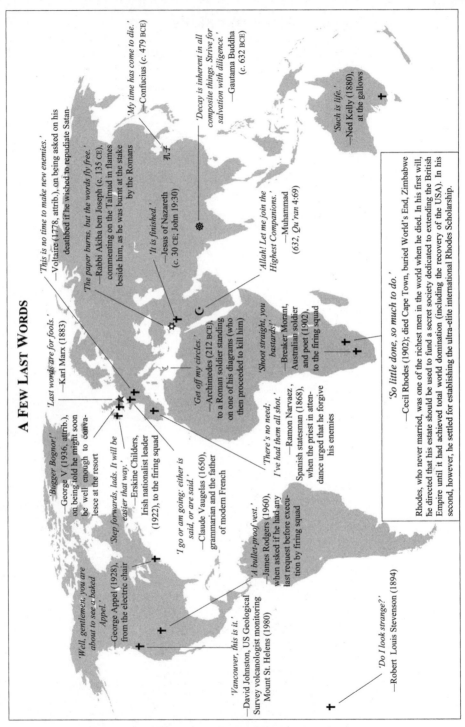

'My time has come to die.' —Confucius (c. 479 BCE)

孔子

'Decay is inherent in all composite things. Strive for salvation with diligence.' —Gautama Buddha (c. 632 BCE)

'Such is life.' —Ned Kelly (1880), at the gallows

'This is no time to make new enemies.' —Voltaire (1778, attrib.), on being asked on his deathbed if he wished to repudiate Satan

'The paper burns, but the words fly free.' —Rabbi Akiba ben Joseph (c. 135 CE), commenting on the Talmud in flames beside him, as he was burnt at the stake by the Romans

'It is finished.' —Jesus of Nazareth (c. 30 CE; John 19:30)

'Allah! Let me join the Highest Companions.' —Muhammad (632, Qu'ran 4:69)

'Last words are for fools.' —Karl Marx (1883)

'Get off my circles.' —Archimedes (212 BCE), to a Roman soldier standing on one of his diagrams (who then proceeded to kill him)

'Shoot straight, you bastards!' —Breaker Morant, Australian soldier and poet (1902), to the firing squad

'There's no need; I've had them all shot.' —Ramon Narvaez, Spanish statesman (1868), when the priest in attendance urged that he forgive his enemies

'Bugger Bognor!' —George V (1936, attrib.), on being told he might soon be well enough to convalesce at the resort

'Step forwards, lads. It will be easier that way.' —Erskine Childers, Irish nationalist leader (1922), to the firing squad

'I go or am going: either is said, or are said.' —Claude Vaugelas (1650), grammarian and the father of modern French

'Well, gentlemen, you are about to see a baked Appel.' —George Appel (1928), from the electric chair

'A bullet-proof vest.' —James Rodgers (1960), when asked if he had any last request before execution by firing squad

'Vancouver, this is it.' —David Johnston, US Geological Survey volcanologist monitoring Mount St. Helens (1980)

'Do I look strange?' —Robert Louis Stevenson (1894)

'So little done, so much to do.' —Cecil Rhodes (1902); died Cape Town, buried World's End, Zimbabwe

Rhodes, who never married, was one of the richest men in the world when he died. In his first will, he directed that his estate should be used to fund a secret society dedicated to extending the British Empire until it had achieved total world domination (including the recovery of the USA). In his second, however, he settled for establishing the ultra-elite international Rhodes Scholarship.

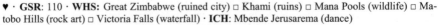

♥ · **GSR:** 110 · **WHS:** Great Zimbabwe (ruined city) □ Khami (ruins) □ Mana Pools (wildlife) □ Matobo Hills (rock art) □ Victoria Falls (waterfall) · **ICH:** Mbende Jerusarema (dance)

—————— LOCATOR MAPS ——————

'If geography is prose, maps are iconography.'

—Lennart Meri, President of Estonia (1992–2001) and one-time professional
potato peeler while exiled to Siberia by General Secretary Stalin

*The 9,288-kilometre post at Vladivostok
Station, marking the eastern end of the
Russian Trans-Siberian Railway*

AFRICA

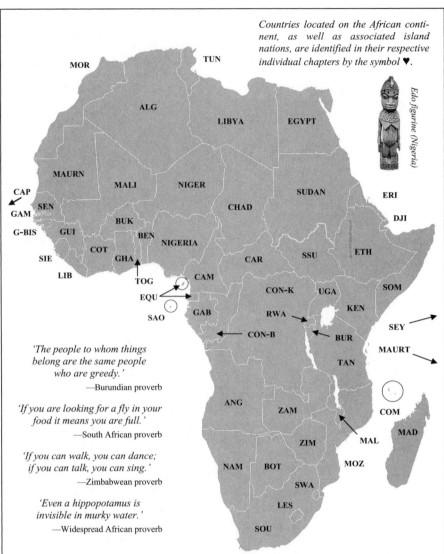

Countries located on the African continent, as well as associated island nations, are identified in their respective individual chapters by the symbol ♥.

Edo figurine (Nigeria)

'The people to whom things belong are the same people who are greedy.'
—Burundian proverb

'If you are looking for a fly in your food it means you are full.'
—South African proverb

'If you can walk, you can dance; if you can talk, you can sing.'
—Zimbabwean proverb

'Even a hippopotamus is invisible in murky water.'
—Widespread African proverb

Key: **ALG** Algeria · **ANG** Angola · **BEN** Benin · **BOT** Botswana · **BUK** Burkina Faso · **BUR** Burundi · **CAM** Cameroon · **CAP** Cape Verde · **CAR** Central African Republic · **CHA** Chad · **COM** Comoros · **CON-B** Congo-Brazzaville · **CON-K** Congo-Kinshasa · **COT** Côte d'Ivoire · **DJI** Djibouti · **EGYPT** Egypt · **EQU** Equatorial Guinea · **ERI** Eritrea · **ETH** Ethiopia · **GAB** Gabon · **GAM** Gambia · **GHA** Ghana · **GUI** Guinea · **G-BIS** Guinea-Bissau · **KEN** Kenya · **LES** Lesotho · **LIB** Liberia · **LIBYA** Libya · **MAD** Madagascar · **MAL** Malawi · **MALI** Mali · **MAURN** Mauritania · **MAURT** Mauritius · **MOR** Morocco · **MOZ** Mozambique · **NAM** Namibia · **NIGER** Niger · **NIGERIA** Nigeria · **RWA** Rwanda · **SAO** São Tomé & Principe · **SEN** Senegal · **SEY** Seychelles · **SIE** Sierra Leone · **SOM** Somalia · **SOU** South Africa · **SSU** South Sudan · **SUDAN** Sudan · **SWA** Swaziland · **TAN** Tanzania · **TOG** Togo · **TUN** Tunisia **UGA** Uganda · **ZAM** Zambia · **ZIM** Zimbabwe

—————————— AMERICAS ——————————

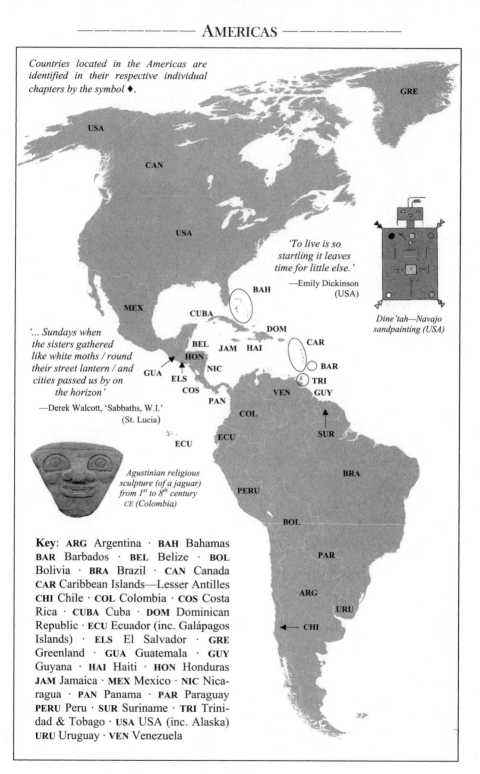

Countries located in the Americas are identified in their respective individual chapters by the symbol ♦.

GRE

USA

CAN

USA

'To live is so startling it leaves time for little else.'
—Emily Dickinson
(USA)

BAH

MEX
CUBA

DOM

Dine'tah—Navajo sandpainting (USA)

'... Sundays when the sisters gathered like white moths / round their street lantern / and cities passed us by on the horizon'
—Derek Walcott, 'Sabbaths, W.I.'
(St. Lucia)

BEL JAM HAI
HON
GUA ELS
COS
PAN

NIC

CAR

BAR

TRI

VEN GUY

COL

ECU ECU

SUR

Agustinian religious sculpture (of a jaguar) from 1ˢᵗ to 8ᵗʰ century CE (Colombia)

BRA

PERU

BOL

PAR

ARG

URU

CHI

Key: **ARG** Argentina · **BAH** Bahamas **BAR** Barbados · **BEL** Belize · **BOL** Bolivia · **BRA** Brazil · **CAN** Canada **CAR** Caribbean Islands—Lesser Antilles **CHI** Chile · **COL** Colombia · **COS** Costa Rica · **CUBA** Cuba · **DOM** Dominican Republic · **ECU** Ecuador (inc. Galápagos Islands) · **ELS** El Salvador · **GRE** Greenland · **GUA** Guatemala · **GUY** Guyana · **HAI** Haiti · **HON** Honduras **JAM** Jamaica · **MEX** Mexico · **NIC** Nicaragua · **PAN** Panama · **PAR** Paraguay **PERU** Peru · **SUR** Suriname · **TRI** Trinidad & Tobago · **USA** USA (inc. Alaska) **URU** Uruguay · **VEN** Venezuela

———— Asia—West & Central ————

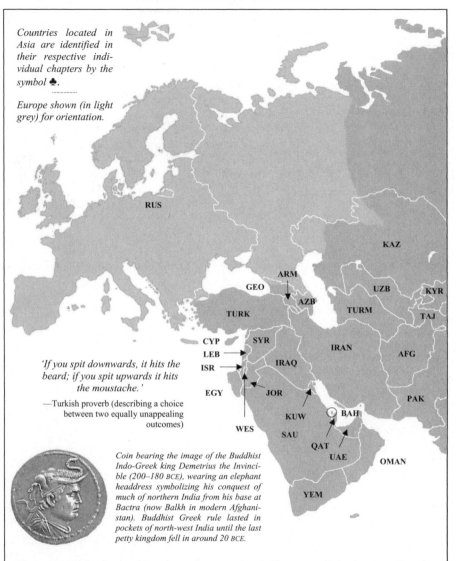

Countries located in Asia are identified in their respective individual chapters by the symbol ♣.

Europe shown (in light grey) for orientation.

'If you spit downwards, it hits the beard; if you spit upwards it hits the moustache.'

—Turkish proverb (describing a choice between two equally unappealing outcomes)

Coin bearing the image of the Buddhist Indo-Greek king Demetrius the Invincible (200–180 BCE), wearing an elephant headdress symbolizing his conquest of much of northern India from his base at Bactra (now Balkh in modern Afghanistan). Buddhist Greek rule lasted in pockets of north-west India until the last petty kingdom fell in around 20 BCE.

Key: **AFG** Afghanistan · **ARM** Armenia · **AZB** Azerbaijan · **BAH** Bahrain · **BAN** Bangladesh · **BHU** Bhutan · **BRU** Brunei · **BUR** Burma · **CAM** Cambodia · **CHINA** China · **CYP** Cyprus · **EGY** Egypt (Sinai) · **GEO** Georgia · **HON** Hong Kong · **INDIA** India · **INDO** Indonesia · **IRAN** Iran · **IRAQ** Iraq · **ISR** Israel · **JAP** Japan · **JOR** Jordan · **KAZ** Kazakhstan · **KOR (N)** Korea (North) · **KOR (S)** Korea (South) · **KUW** Kuwait · **KYR** Kyrgyzstan **LAO** Laos · **LEB** Lebanon · **MAC** Macao · **MALAYSIA** Malaysia · **MALD** Maldives · **MON** Mongolia · **NEP** Nepal · **OMAN** Oman · **PAK** Pakistan · **PHI** Philippines · **QAT** Qatar **RUS** Russia (inc. Kaliningrad Oblast exclave) · **SAU** Saudi Arabia · **SIN** Singapore · **SRI** Sri Lanka · **SYR** Syria · **TAI** Taiwan · **TAJ** Tajikistan · **THA** Thailand · **TIM** Timor-Leste **TURK** Turkey · **TURM** Turkmenistan · **UAE** United Arab Emirates · **UZB** Uzbekistan **VIE** Vietnam · **WES** West Bank & Gaza Strip · **YEM** Yemen

ASIA—EAST & SOUTH

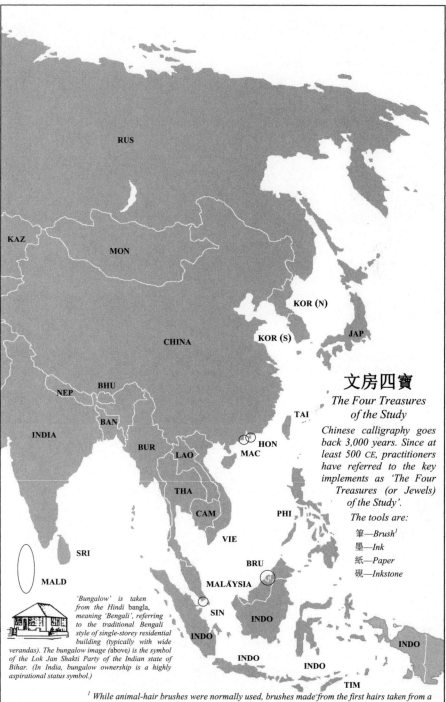

RUS

KAZ

MON

KOR (N)

CHINA

KOR (S)

JAP

NEP

BHU

TAI

BAN

INDIA

BUR

HON

MAC

LAO

THA

CAM

PHI

VIE

SRI

BRU

MALD

MALAYSIA

SIN

INDO

INDO

INDO

INDO

INDO

TIM

文房四寶
The Four Treasures of the Study

Chinese calligraphy goes back 3,000 years. Since at least 500 CE, practitioners have referred to the key implements as 'The Four Treasures (or Jewels) of the Study'.

The tools are:

筆—Brush[1]
墨—Ink
紙—Paper
硯—Inkstone

'Bungalow' is taken from the Hindi *bangla*, meaning 'Bengali', referring to the traditional Bengali style of single-storey residential building (typically with wide verandas). The bungalow image (above) is the symbol of the Lok Jan Shakti Party of the Indian state of Bihar. (In India, bungalow ownership is a highly aspirational status symbol.)

[1] *While animal-hair brushes were normally used, brushes made from the first hairs taken from a baby's head were favoured as bringing good luck to those attempting the imperial examinations.*

EUROPE

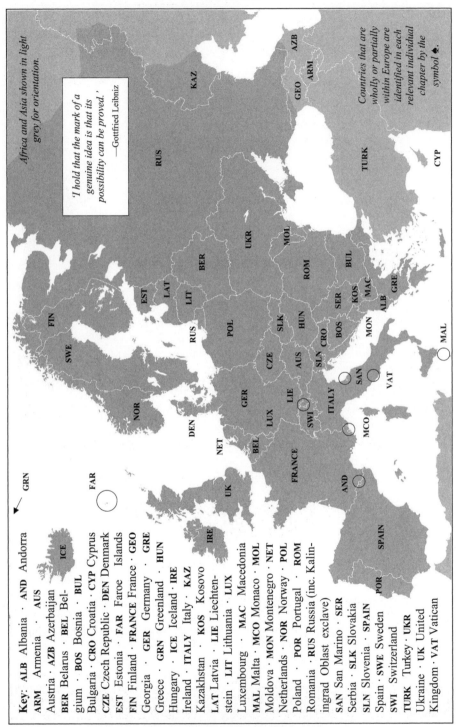

Africa and Asia shown in light grey for orientation.

'I hold that the mark of a genuine idea is that its possibility can be proved.'
—Gottfried Leibniz

Countries that are wholly or partially within Europe are identified in each relevant individual chapter by the symbol ♠.

Key: **ALB** Albania · **AND** Andorra · **ARM** Armenia · **AUS** Austria · **AZB** Azerbaijan · **BER** Belarus · **BEL** Belgium · **BOS** Bosnia · **BUL** Bulgaria · **CRO** Croatia · **CYP** Cyprus · **CZE** Czech Republic · **DEN** Denmark · **EST** Estonia · **FAR** Faroe Islands · **FIN** Finland · **FRANCE** France · **GEO** Georgia · **GER** Germany · **GRE** Greece · **GRN** Greenland · **HUN** Hungary · **ICE** Iceland · **IRE** Ireland · **ITALY** Italy · **KAZ** Kazakhstan · **KOS** Kosovo · **LAT** Latvia · **LIE** Liechtenstein · **LIT** Lithuania · **LUX** Luxembourg · **MAC** Macedonia · **MAL** Malta · **MCO** Monaco · **MOL** Moldova · **MON** Montenegro · **NET** Netherlands · **NOR** Norway · **POL** Poland · **POR** Portugal · **ROM** Romania · **RUS** Russia (inc. Kaliningrad Oblast exclave) · **SAN** San Marino · **SER** Serbia · **SLK** Slovakia · **SLN** Slovenia · **SPAIN** Spain · **SWE** Sweden · **SWI** Switzerland · **TURK** Turkey · **UKR** Ukraine · **UK** United Kingdom · **VAT** Vatican

—————— OCEANIA & ANTARCTICA ——————

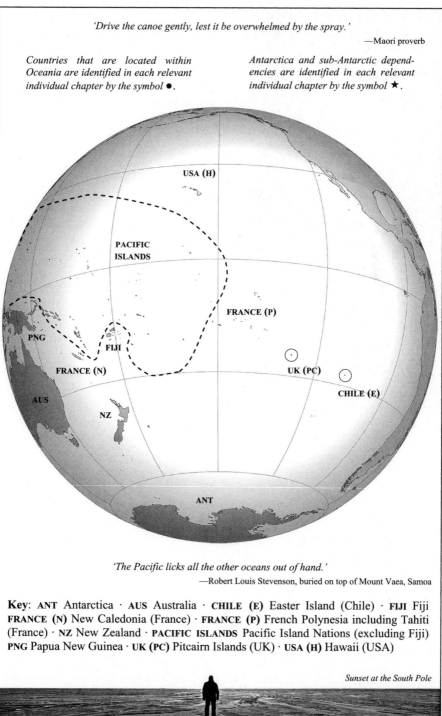

'Drive the canoe gently, lest it be overwhelmed by the spray.'

—Maori proverb

Countries that are located within Oceania are identified in each relevant individual chapter by the symbol ●.

Antarctica and sub-Antarctic dependencies are identified in each relevant individual chapter by the symbol ★.

'The Pacific licks all the other oceans out of hand.'

—Robert Louis Stevenson, buried on top of Mount Vaea, Samoa

Key: ANT Antarctica · AUS Australia · CHILE (E) Easter Island (Chile) · FIJI Fiji FRANCE (N) New Caledonia (France) · FRANCE (P) French Polynesia including Tahiti (France) · NZ New Zealand · PACIFIC ISLANDS Pacific Island Nations (excluding Fiji) PNG Papua New Guinea · UK (PC) Pitcairn Islands (UK) · USA (H) Hawaii (USA)

Sunset at the South Pole

———— GLOBAL SIGNIFICANCE RANKINGS ————

The Global Significance Rank (alternatively 'Google Search Rank') gauges each country's contemporary prominence in the eyes of the world by measuring its internet footprint as a proxy. More specifically, it ranks each nation according to the number of results returned by entering its name as a search term on the Google website.[1] Not surprisingly, the USA dominates (returning more than four times the results of second-placed China). The United Kingdom's prominence is evidence that the internet remains a disproportionately anglophone resource. However, the high positions of several East Asian countries—which are boosted by notably large numbers of local language results—suggest that the dominance of English as the language of the net won't last for ever.

[1] *Calculated as the number of search results returned for the ordinary name in English and in the chief local language combined. In both cases, websites that contain listings of every country in the world are filtered out and discarded.*

1	United States of America	31	Thailand
2	China	32	Belarus
3	United Kingdom	33	Chile
4	Japan	34	Sweden
5	France	35	Taiwan
6	Canada	36	Belgium
7	Germany	37	Bulgaria
8	Mexico	38	Turkey
9	Indonesia	39	Czech Republic
10	Italy	40	Switzerland
11	Korea (South)	41	Venezuela
12	India	42	Colombia
13	Australia	43	Kazakhstan
14	Hong Kong	44	Malaysia
15	Spain	45	Costa Rica
16	Russia	46	Egypt
17	Brazil	47	Finland
18	Singapore	48	Jordan
19	New Zealand	49	Vietnam
20	South Africa	50	Norway
21	Argentina	51	Philippines
22	Greece	52	Pakistan
23	Poland	53	Denmark
24	Portugal	54	Sri Lanka
25	Austria	55	Slovakia
26	Netherlands	56	Ukraine
27	Ireland	57	Iran
28	Iraq	58	Romania
29	Israel	59	Dominican Republic
30	Saudi Arabia	60	Peru

61	Uruguay	102	Montenegro
62	Ecuador	103	Cyprus
63	West Bank & Gaza Strip	104	Mali
64	Hungary	105	Sierra Leone
65	Luxembourg	106	Iceland
66	Afghanistan	107	Yemen
67	Lithuania	108	Macedonia
68	Tunisia	109	Togo
69	Guatemala	110	Zimbabwe
70	Cuba	111	Uganda
71	Trinidad & Tobago	112	Bahamas
72	United Arab Emirates	113	Tanzania
73	Malta	114	Algeria
74	Slovenia	115	Bosnia
75	Estonia	116	Albania
76	Croatia	117	Syria
77	Morocco	118	Liechtenstein
78	Honduras	119	Azerbaijan
79	Panama	120	Vatican & Holy See
80	Libya	121	Uzbekistan
81	Bangladesh	122=	Congo[1]
82	Nigeria	122=	Congo[1]
83	Bolivia	124	Angola
84	Kuwait	125	Andorra
85	Serbia	126	Armenia
86	Qatar	127	Benin
87	Paraguay	128	Mozambique
88	Lebanon	129	Guinea
89	Kenya	130	Sudan
90	Monaco	131	Cambodia
91	Laos	132	Mongolia
92	Nicaragua	133	Mauritius
93	Bahrain	134	Côte d'Ivoire
94	Nepal	135	Fiji
95	Haiti	136	Moldova
96	Jamaica	137	Barbados
97	Namibia	138	Madagascar
98	Oman	139	Senegal
99	Ghana	140	Somalia
100	Latvia	141	Niger
101	San Marino	142	Belize

[1] *These are average results for Congo-Brazzaville and Congo-Kinshasa jointly as it is not possible accurately to distinguish between internet references to each individual country.*

143 .... Korea (North)	164 .... Greenland
144 .... Papua New Guinea	165 .... Gambia
145 .... Ethiopia	166 .... Seychelles
146 .... Rwanda	167 .... Tajikistan
147 .... Zambia	168 .... Lesotho
148 .... Kyrgyzstan	169 .... Burundi
149 .... Burma	170 .... Suriname
150 .... Brunei	171 .... Turkmenistan
151 .... Cameroon	172 .... Swaziland
152 .... Cape Verde	173 .... Equatorial Guinea
153 .... Liberia	174 .... Eritrea
154 .... Macau	175 .... Gabon
155 .... Guyana	176 .... Bhutan
156 .... Malawi	177 .... Chad
157 .... Botswana	178 .... Kosovo[1]
158 .... Burkina Faso	179 .... São Tomé & Principe
159 .... Central African Republic	180 .... Antarctica
160 .... Maldives	181 .... Comoros
161 .... Mauritania	182 .... Faroe Islands
162 .... Guinea-Bissau	183 .... Timor-Leste[1]
163 .... Djibouti	184 .... South Sudan[1]

[1] *The very low rankings of Kosovo, South Sudan and Timor-Leste may be explained in part by the fact that all three have only recently become sovereign nations.*

El Salvador and Georgia are not included in this table as it is not possible to measure their rankings. ('El Salvador' means 'The Saviour' in Spanish and references to the country are hidden by the term's religious usage. Georgia is impossible to disentangle from the better-known US state of the same name.)

———————— SOURCES ————————
& FURTHER READING

The information contained in *A World of Curiosities* has been taken from a broad variety of sources. Especially where the primary source is not an academic journal, official organ or contained within a publication of an established news organization of good standing (or similar), I have tried, wherever possible, to obtain secondary corroboration. If this has not been forthcoming, I have generally disregarded the material in the absence of other grounds pointing to its credibility.

With an estimated 15,000 individual references, a conventional bibliography is, for practical and commercial reasons, not a possibility in a book such as this. However, since unsourced information is of little use to anyone wishing to read further, a country by country 'dump' of the great majority of the raw references used in the book can be found at the website www.aworldofcuriosities.com.

Most sources I have used only have relevance to a very narrow factual context. But a few have wider general application, and can often serve as informative entry points for further research. A selection of the most useful internet links includes the following:

GENERAL REFERENCE LINKS

Al-Jazeera (world news archive—non-Western perspective) .... *http://english.aljazeera.net/*

BBC News (world news archive) .... *www.bbc.co.uk/news/world/*

BBC News Country Profiles (background) ...... *http://news.bbc.co.uk/1/hi/country_profiles/default.stm*

CIA World Factbook (statistics) .... *https://www.cia.gov/library/publications/the-world-factbook/*

CNN (world news archive) .... *http://edition.cnn.com/WORLD/*

Economist (world affairs archive) .... *www.economist.com/*

Encyclopaedia Britannica (general encyclopaedia) .... *www.britannica.com/*

Eurobarometer (EU surveys and statistics) .... *http://ec.europa.eu/public_opinion/index_en.htm*

Everyculture (cultural profiles) .... *www.everyculture.com/*

Globalsecurity.org (defence information) .... *www.globalsecurity.org/*

Guardian (the most extensive UK broadsheet world news archive) .... *www.guardian.co.uk/*

IUCN Red List (conservation information on endangered species) .... *www.iucnredlist.org/*

Mongabay (environmental news archive and profiles) .... *www.mongabay.com/*

National Geographic (geography and the natural world) .... *www.nationalgeographic.co.uk/*

New Advent Catholic Encyclopaedia (church history and protocol) .... *www.newadvent.org/cathen/*

New Scientist (science news archive) .... *www.newscientist.com/*

New York Times (world news archive) .... *www.nytimes.com/*

Omniglot (language information) .... *www.omniglot.com/*

Online Etymology Dictionary (etymologies) .... *www.etymonline.com/*

Time Magazine (world affairs archive—material back to the 1940s) .... *www.time.com/time/*

UNESCO Intangible Heritage Convention .... *www.unesco.org/culture/ich/*

UNESCO World Heritage Centre .... *http://whc.unesco.org/*

US Department of State Background Notes (country profiles) .... *http://www.state.gov/*

Washington Post (world news archive).. *www.washingtonpost.com/*

Wikipedia (crowd-sourced encyclopaedia) .... *www.wikipedia.org/*

World Health Organization (health statistics and reports) .... *www.who.int/whosis/en/*

Xinhua (world news—Chinese perspective) *www.xinhuanet.com/english2010/*

———————— IMAGE CREDITS ————————

The images and maps in this book have been derived from sources that the author believes in good faith either to be in the public domain or to be covered by a form of creative commons or GNU licence that allows their reuse (subject to appropriate conditions). While reasonable care has been taken to avoid all other copyrighted material, if you believe that your copyright or other applicable legal right may have been infringed, please contact the author through the publisher.

Copies of all of the non-public-domain source images used in the creation of *A World of Curiosities* may be found at www.aworldofcuriosities.com, where full attribution and licensing information is given for each. Duplicates of all of the derivative images[1] prepared from such non-public-domain originals are also available for download at the same website, subject to the same licensing terms as their antecedents. Where I have felt it might be useful to do so, I have also made copies of the derivative images available for download at Wikimedia Commons (http://commons.wikimedia.org/wiki/Main_Page) under the appropriate creative commons or GNU licence terms.

[1] *Or higher-resolution master versions thereof.*